THE NEW PSYCHOLOGY OF SPORT & EXERCISE

Sara Miller McCune founded SAGE Publishing in 1965 to support the dissemination of usable knowledge and educate a global community. SAGE publishes more than 1000 journals and over 800 new books each year, spanning a wide range of subject areas. Our growing selection of library products includes archives, data, case studies and video. SAGE remains majority owned by our founder and after her lifetime will become owned by a charitable trust that secures the company's continued independence.

Los Angeles | London | New Delhi | Singapore | Washington DC | Melbourne

THE NEW PSYCHOLOGY OF SPORT & EXERCISE

THE SOCIAL IDENTITY APPROACH

S. ALEXANDER HASLAM
KATRIEN FRANSEN
FILIP BOEN

Los Angeles | London | New Delhi
Singapore | Washington DC | Melbourne

Los Angeles | London | New Delhi
Singapore | Washington DC | Melbourne

SAGE Publications Ltd
1 Oliver's Yard
55 City Road
London EC1Y 1SP

SAGE Publications Inc.
2455 Teller Road
Thousand Oaks, California 91320

SAGE Publications India Pvt Ltd
B 1/I 1 Mohan Cooperative Industrial Area
Mathura Road
New Delhi 110 044

SAGE Publications Asia-Pacific Pte Ltd
3 Church Street
#10-04 Samsung Hub
Singapore 049483

Editor: Amy Maher
Editorial assistant: Marc Barnard
Production editor: Imogen Roome
Copyeditor: Sarah Bury
Indexers: Zahra Mirnajafi and Charlotte Pittaway
Marketing manager: Camille Richmond
Cover design: Wendy Scott
Typeset by: C&M Digitals (P) Ltd, Chennai, India
Printed in the UK

Editorial Arrangement, Chapter 1 © S. Alexander Haslam, Katrien Fransen, Filip Boen, 2020
Chapter 2 © S. Alexander Haslam, Katrien Fransen, Filip Boen & Stephen Reicher, 2020
Chapter 3 © Niklas K. Steffens, Katrien Fransen & S. Alexander Haslam, 2020
Chapter 4 © Kim Peters, 2020
Chapter 5 © Matthew J. Slater, Will Thomas & Andrew L. Evans, 2020
Chapter 6 © Katharine H. Greenaway, Sindhuja Sankaran, Svenja A. Wolf & Jardine Mitchell, 2020
Chapter 7 © Jessica Salvatore, Sindhuja Sankaran & DaZané Cole, 2020
Chapter 8 © Pete Coffee, Patti Parker, Ross Murray & Simon Kawycz, 2020
Chapter 9 © Svenja A. Wolf, Amit Goldenberg & Mickaël Campo, 2020
Chapter 10 © Mark Stevens, Tegan Cruwys, Tim Rees, S. Alexander Haslam, Filip Boen & Katrien Fransen, 2020
Chapter 11 © Mark R. Beauchamp & Joseph J. O'Rourke, 2020
Chapter 12 © Mark W. Bruner, Luc J. Martin, M. Blair Evans & Alex J. Benson, 2020
Chapter 13 © Jamie B. Barker, S. Alexander Haslam, Katrien Fransen, Matthew J. Slater, Craig White & Niels Mertens, 2020
Chapter 14 © Chris Hartley, S. Alexander Haslam, Pete Coffee & Tim Rees, 2020
Chapter 15 © Tegan Cruwys, Mark Stevens, Catherine Haslam, S. Alexander Haslam & Lisa Olive, 2020
Chapter 16 © Lisa M. O'Halloran & Catherine Haslam, 2020
Chapter 17 © Filip Boen, Daniel L. Wann, Iouri Bernache-Assollant, S. Alexander Haslam & Katrien Fransen, 2020
Chapter 18 © Clifford Stott, 2020
Chapter 19 © Michael J. Platow & Diana M. Grace, 2020
Chapter 20 © Stephen D. Reicher, Meredith Schertzinger & Fergus Neville, 2020

First published 2020

Library of Congress Control Number: 2020933213

British Library Cataloguing in Publication data

A catalogue record for this book is available from the British Library

ISBN 978-1-5264-8894-7
ISBN 978-1-5264-8893-0 (pbk)

CONTENTS

LIST OF KEY POINTS

LIST OF FIGURES

LIST OF TABLES

CONTRIBUTOR
BIOGRAPHIES

Jamie Barker is a Senior Lecturer in the School of Sport, Exercise and Health Sciences at Loughborough University. His research focuses on applied (sport) psychology and how to develop resilience, well-being and performance in teams using social identity-related strategies.

Mark Beauchamp is a Professor of exercise and health psychology in the School of Kinesiology at the University of British Columbia. His research focuses on the psychology of group processes within exercise and sport settings, especially physical activity behaviour across the age spectrum.

Alex Benson is an Assistant Professor in the Department of Psychology and Director of the Group Experiences Laboratory at Western University in London, Ontario. He is currently investigating how people differ in the roles they strive for and covet within teams and organisations, and leader–follower dynamics.

Iouri Bernache-Assollant is an Associate Professor in social psychology at the University of Bourgogne Franche-Comté. He is particularly interested in how team identification and social context influence the perceptual, affective and behavioural responses of fans and athletes.

Filip Boen is Professor of sport and exercise psychology at the Department of Movement Sciences at KU Leuven. His research focuses on the social-psychological and motivational processes underlying physical activity promotion (especially among the elderly), sport fan behaviour and team-based identities.

Mark Bruner is a Canada Research Chair in Youth Development through Sport and Physical Activity and Professor in the School of Physical and Health Education at Nipissing University in Ontario. His research investigates group dynamics and psychosocial development in youth sport.

Mickaël Campo is an Associate Professor of sport psychology in the Faculty of Sport Sciences at the Université Bourgogne Franche-Comté. His research focuses on the emotions–performance relationship in team sports, especially the effects of identity processes on group-based emotions.

Pete Coffee is a Senior Lecturer in sports psychology at the University of Stirling. He received his PhD from the University of Exeter, UK, and his research focuses on the study of attributions, social identity, and social support in sport and performance contexts.

 DaZané Cole has a dual BA (psychology) and BS (biology) from Sweet Briar College, Virginia, and is pursuing a career in veterinary medicine. She received two summer research fellowships from Sweet Briar's honours programme, the first of which supported her work reported on this chapter.

 Tegan Cruwys is a Senior Research Fellow and Clinical Psychologist at the Australian National University. Her research investigates the role of social relationships in shaping our mental and physical health, particularly in the context of disadvantaged or marginalised groups.

 Andrew Evans is a Lecturer in sport psychology in the School of Health and Society at Salford University. His research focuses on social identities, social identity leadership, Personal-Disclosure Mutual-Sharing, and irrational and rational beliefs.

 Blair Evans is an Assistant Professor in the Kinesiology Department at Penn State University. His research examines how behaviour and well-being are shaped by peer relationships in small groups. He studies groups in varying contexts with a particular focus on athletes with disabilities.

 Katrien Fransen is an Assistant Professor of Performance Psychology at the Department of Movement Sciences at KU Leuven. Her research focuses on how shared leadership benefits team effectiveness and team member well-being, with a particular emphasis on the role of social identity processes.

 Amit Goldenberg is an Assistant Professor at Harvard Business School. His research focuses on understanding the unfolding and regulation of the emotional processes that shape group behaviour. His research integrates behavioural experiments, big-data analysis and computational modelling.

 Diana Grace recently retired from academia. Her areas of research expertise include social development, social influence, tertiary education and Australian Indigenous psychology. She has received numerous awards and recognition for her teaching, research and leadership.

 Katharine Greenaway is a Lecturer and Research Fellow based at the University of Melbourne. Her research focuses on psychological functioning in three main domains: identity processes, human agency and emotion regulation.

Chris Hartley is a Lecturer in sports psychology at the University of Stirling. He practises applied sport and performance psychology across a range of performance pathway and elite sport settings, and his research interests focus on a social identity approach to the study of social support.

Alex Haslam is Professor of Psychology and Australian Laureate Fellow at the University of Queensland. His research focuses on the study of group and social identity processes in social, organisational, health and sport contexts.

Catherine Haslam is Professor of clinical psychology at the University of Queensland. Her research focuses on the study of group and identity processes in clinical and health contexts, particularly in the context of life transitions.

Simon Kawycz is a Lecturer in sport psychology at Liverpool Hope University currently studying for a PhD at the University of Stirling. His research examines social identity, attributions and interpersonal relationships in sport and performance contexts.

Luc Martin is an Associate Professor in the School of Kinesiology and Health Studies, at Queen's University, Canada. His research is in the general area of team dynamics, with a specific focus on topics such as cohesion, social identity, team building and subgroups/cliques in sport and other contexts.

Niels Mertens is a PhD researcher in performance psychology at the Department of Movement Sciences at KU Leuven, Belgium. His research focuses on the identification of high-quality athlete leaders and the development of shared leadership within sport teams.

Jardine Mitchell is an honours graduate based at the University of Melbourne. Her research interests centre on understanding optimal psychological functioning in sports contexts, and she aims to pursue a career as a sports psychologist.

Ross Murray is a PhD student at the University of Stirling. His research is focused on the influence of team dynamics on individual cognitions and behaviours. During his PhD, he examined whether and how team contextual factors structure the way athletes think about their attributions.

Fergus Neville is a Lecturer in organisational studies at the University of St Andrews. His research covers topics such as shared identity, social influence, collective action, intergroup conflict, leadership, intragroup intimacy and crowd experience in sporting and other contexts.

Lisa O'Halloran is a Lecturer in sport psychology at Coventry University. Her research focuses on 'critical moments' and identity development within high-performance sport contexts, particularly professional football.

 Lisa Olive is a Senior Research Fellow and clinical psychologist with expertise in behavioural medicine and performance psychology. She co-leads the Behavioural Medicine Innovation Hub in the Centre for Social and Early Emotional Development (SEED) at Deakin University in Victoria.

 Joseph O'Rourke is a master's student in the School of Kinesiology at the University of British Columbia. His research focuses on social inclusion in sport and mental health settings. He is particularly interested in the experiences and participation of marginalised populations.

 Patti Parker is a PhD student in psychology at the University of Manitoba. Her research is focused on the efficacy of motivation-based interventions to promote adaptive cognitions, emotions and performance in achievement settings.

 Kim Peters is Associate Professor in the Business School at the University of Exeter. Her research focuses on the study of group processes and communication in social, organisational and sporting contexts.

 Michael Platow is a Professor of psychology at the Australian National University. He has published widely on the social-psychology of leadership and social influence; justice, fairness and trust; intergroup relations, including prejudice and discrimination; and education.

 Tim Rees is Professor in Sport at the University of Bournemouth. His research centres on the development of talent and social psychological influences on performance and physical activity, with a particular interest in the contribution of social identity to these dynamic processes.

 Steve Reicher is Bishop Wardlaw Professor of Psychology at the University of St Andrews. His work focuses on the relationship between social identity and collective behaviour, addressing such topics as crowd psychology, intergroup hostility, political rhetoric and leadership.

 Jessica Salvatore is Associate Professor of psychology at Sweet Briar College in Virginia. She studies and teaches about human difference and stigma and their relationship to identity. She is on multiple journal boards and is Associate Editor of the *British Journal of Social Psychology*.

Sindhuja Sankaran is a Postdoctoral Fellow at the Faculty of Psychology, University of Warsaw. Her main research interest is in the field of social cognition, examining cognitive and motivational processes underpining individual and group behaviour, decision making and performance.

 Meredith Schertzinger is completing a PhD in the Schools of Management and Medicine at the University of St Andrews on the consequences of participating in physical activity collectively or alone. She has also published on the struggle for equality in women's professional football.

 Matt Slater is Associate Professor of sport and exercise psychology at Staffordshire University. His research focuses on the psychology of leadership and high-performing teams, as well as the development of psychological programmes to enhance performance and well-being.

 Nik Steffens is a Senior Lecturer and Australian Research Council DECRA Fellow at the University of Queensland. His work focuses on the contribution of identity processes to leadership, followership and health in social, organisational and sport contexts.

 Mark Stevens is a Postdoctoral Research Fellow at the Australian National University. His research focuses on social-psychological influences on physical activity and physical health, with a particular emphasis on the role of social identification and leadership.

 Clifford Stott is a Professor of social psychology and Dean for Research in the Faculty of Natural Sciences at Keele University. His interdisciplinary research uses the social identity approach to understand the social psychological dynamics of police encounters with the public.

 Will Thomas is an Honorary Research Fellow in the School of Psychology at Sussex University. His research focuses on the development of high-performing teams in sport, the military and business using a social identity approach. He puts theory into practice as the CEO of his own company.

 Dan Wann is a Professor of psychology at Murray State University in Kentucky. His research focuses on the psychology of sport fandom, and the causes and consequences of sport team identification. In particular, his work examines fan well-being, coping (e.g., with defeat) and loyalty.

 Craig White is a Wing Commander with the Royal Air Force and a PhD researcher in the School of Sport, Exercise and Health Sciences at Loughborough University. His research focuses on the social identity approach to leadership and the links to resilience and well-being.

Svenja Wolf is an Assistant Professor of sport and performance psychology in the Work and Organisational Psychology group at the University of Amsterdam. Her research focuses on the intersection between group dynamics and emotions, with a particular emphasis on collective emotions.

PREFACE

After having attended a friendly football match between Chelsea FC and Dynamo Moscow to mark the end of World War II, the novelist George Orwell (1945) famously remarked that sport 'is war minus the shooting'. Even if one does not agree entirely with this characterisation (which he based on the fact that it is 'bound up with hatred, jealousy, boastfulness, disregard of all rules, and sadistic pleasure in witnessing violence') you have to concede that he had a point. Stated less controversially, this is that sport is an intense activity that routinely centres on passions that arise in the context of competition between opposing groups. This passion is what motivates us to watch it, to take part in it, to enjoy it. It is also what makes it special.

Yet given the importance of this group-based passion, it might come as a surprise, to the person who comes upon the field of sport and exercise psychology for the first time, that this field pays no special heed to the importance of groups and group life for the mental states and processes of those who watch, run and take part in sport and exercise. Certainly, there is work on group dynamics and group cohesion, but in all this the group is seen as external to the person rather than as having the capacity to be core to their being. As a result, this branch of psychology tends to be focused firmly on the 'I-ness' of the athletes, coaches, administrators and spectators at the centre of the sporting world – their individuality and their sense of themselves *as individuals*. Although there is an immense amount to be learned from such an approach, its core problem – and its huge blind spot – is that it does not allow us to understand the sorts of processes that Orwell observed being played out at Stamford Bridge. After all, as Henri Tajfel (1978) observed, it is not 'I-ness' that makes people go to war but 'we-ness'. Moreover, sport as a whole is shot through with this sense of we-ness – the we-ness that derives from being, and defining oneself, *as a member of a group* (e.g., a team, a club, a profession). Indeed, we find this we-ness at its very heart. So, if we overlook this, then we overlook something that makes sport, well, *sport*.

In very simple terms, this book is an attempt to remove this blind spot. More particularly, it takes 'we-ness' from the periphery of sport and exercise psychologists' consciousness to front and centre of our analytic gaze. Moreover, it is this that makes the psychology we explore 'new'.

Of course, in calling something new, one is always open to the charge that there is nothing new here at all. In one sense this is correct. After all, we are not saying that the psychology of sport and exercise has somehow changed in recent years (i.e., what goes on inside people's heads). Groups and their psychological impact have always been central to these endeavours. This, for example, was something that Aristotle acknowledged over 2,000 years ago when he observed in his *Nicomachean Ethics* that:

In order to feel goodwill for a contestant at an athletic competition, a spectator must sympathetically share his pleasure in the sport and his eagerness for victory. (Pangle, 2002, p. 49)

Our point, then, is simply that psychologists have never before taken especially seriously the task either of understanding what underpins this sympathetic sharing of perspective or of understanding why it is so important for sport and exercise outcomes. This book does. In particular, it does so by focusing on the capacity for psychology to be shaped by *social identity* – a person's sense of themselves as a member of a social group (which can be contrasted with *personal identity*, their sense of themselves as an individual; Turner, 1982).

However, it needs to be said that this focus on social identity is not new either. Since Henri Tajfel and John Turner first wrote on the subject in the 1970s, the theoretical framework they set out has inspired a vast body of research in fields of social, organisational and, more recently, health psychology. As a result, there are dozens of books and around 15,000 publications on the subject (see Postmes & Branscombe, 2010, for a discussion). Strangely, though (and for reasons that are not entirely clear), over most of this period the field of sport and exercise psychology remained largely immune to these influences. This meant that while there were some excellent publications that examined sport psychology through a social identity lens, these remained isolated dots that were rarely joined together into an integrated whole. So while the first paper on social identity and sport was published 30 years ago (Wann & Branscombe, 1990), as Figure P.1 indicates, it is only in the last five or so years that this line of work has really gathered momentum.

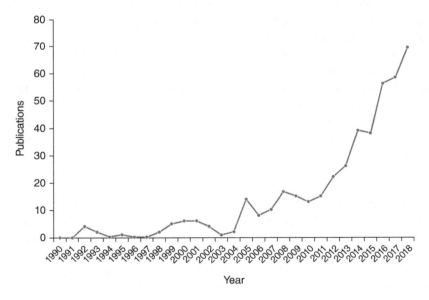

Figure P.1 The exponential rise of research on social identity and sport

Note: Data abstracted from Web of Science based on a search for the terms 'social-ident* and sport*'. It is interesting to note that (a) more than half of all of publications (271/483 = 56%) have appeared since 2015 and (b) more appeared in the first 10 months of 2019 (*n*=50) than had *in total* up to 2006 (*n*=47).

What changed, and what provided the inspiration for this volume, was that over the course of the last decade groups of researchers and practitioners around the world started collaborating on a range of projects that looked to tell the 'bigger story' of social identity and sport. In 2013, this led Pete Coffee to set up the Social IDentity in Exercise and Sport (SIDES) network as a first attempt to create a body that might share and promote the results of these collaborations. This in turn provided the impetus for the three of us to think about trying to bring these researchers together to share their data, their ideas and their visions for the field. The result was the First International Conference on Social Identity and Sport (ICSIS1) held in Leuven, Belgium, in July 2017.

Two things surprised us about this gathering. The first was the amount of interest it generated. We had expected around 20 people to attend but in the event 65 turned up – coming from 15 different countries to listen to 37 presentations (see Figure P.2). The second surprise was the amount of energy and enthusiasm that the conference generated. Rather than being a procession of dry empirical offerings, the presentations – and the discussion they stimulated – were lively, exciting and fresh. And in the wake of this, the proposal for this book was conceived.

Figure P.2 Participants at the first International Conference on Social Identity and Sport (ICSIS1)

Note: Held in Leuven in July 2017, the conference was organised by the three editors of this book and brought together 65 researchers (42 of whom are pictured here) from 15 countries

Going forward, it was decided that ICSIS would be established as a bi-annual conference and that the royalties from this book would support this into the future. True to this, the Second International Conference on Social Identity in Sport (ICSIS2) took place in Stirling, Scotland, in June 2019. Organised by Pete Coffee, Chris Hartley and Nina Verma, this brought together 62 delegates to discuss 35 presentations and proved to be every bit as inspiring as the inaugural event. Not least, this was because ICSIS2 provided an opportunity to showcase the wide range of ideas that form the basis for the chapters below. Plans are now in place for Simon Kawycz and colleagues to host ICSIS3 in Liverpool in 2021, and prospectuses for subsequent meetings are taking shape too.

Ultimately, then, this book is a testament to the spirit of these conferences that bring together, and galvanise, a broad swathe of researchers around the banner of social identity and sport. Our goal in producing the volume was to capture not only the rigour and vigour of these meetings, but also the fun and excitement that they generate – the Wordsworthian sense that 'Bliss [is] it in that dawn to be alive'. The ultimate proof of this, however, is something that can only be gauged by the efforts and enthusiasms that this book inspires in you, the reader. Accordingly, we look forward to hearing – and writing – about these in the future.

ACKNOWLEDGEMENTS

The particulars of the Preface mean that the first people whose input into this volume we need to acknowledge are the many people who contributed to the first two ICSIS conferences and helped to make them such a success. Many of these are authors of the chapters below, but there are also other researchers whom we asked to contribute on the basis of their expertise on specific topics; we would like to thank them too. In particular, we are grateful for the fact that all the contributors to the book worked tirelessly to produce multiple revisions of their chapters with a view to realising our shared ambition for this volume – namely to provide a comprehensive and compelling statement of the social identity approach to sport and exercise psychology.

Alongside this, though, we would like to thank the editorial staff at SAGE for their unfailing encouragement and support over the past three years. From a large and extremely capable team, Becky Taylor (who first commissioned the book) and Amy Maher (who oversaw its long journey to press) deserve to be singled out for their patience, industry and generosity of spirit. We are very grateful too to Imogen Roome for her careful and very professional handling of the proofs, and to Zahra Mirnajafi and Charlotte Pittaway for their painstaking work compiling the indices.

Finally, we would like to thank our partners, families and colleagues for their forbearance and good humour over the extended period of time that it has taken to bring this book together. To paraphrase Kareem Abdul-Jabbar, it is not the person who makes the team, so much as the team that makes the person. We count ourselves very lucky to be playing on yours.

Alex, Katrien, Filip

SECTION 1
INTRODUCTION

1

TOWARDS A NEW PSYCHOLOGY OF SPORT AND EXERCISE

FILIP BOEN
KATRIEN FRANSEN
S. ALEXANDER HASLAM

> I have always believed that exercise is a key not only to physical health but to peace of mind. […] In my letters to my children, I regularly urged them to exercise, to play some fast-moving sport like basketball, soccer or tennis to take their mind off whatever might be bothering them. While I was not always successful with my children, I did manage to influence some of my more sedentary colleagues. Exercise was unusual for African men of my age and generation. After a while even Walter (Sisulu) began to take a few turns around the courtyard in the morning. I know that some of my younger comrades looked at me and said to themselves: 'If that old man can do it, why can't I?' They, too, began to exercise. (Mandela, 1994, p. 584)

The above quote is taken from *Long Road to Freedom* – the autobiography of Nelson Mandela in which, among other things, he writes about the 28 years he was held in detention on Robben Island for being a member of the African National Congress (ANC), at that time a banned organisation that was committed to opposing South Africa's Apartheid regime. It illustrates two important points about physical activity. First, it shows how physical exercise helped the man who would go on to become president remain mentally and physically healthy over the course of his prolonged imprisonment. Long before regular physical activity was being systematically promoted by health services around the world, Mandela recognised its importance not only for his own well-being, but also for the well-being of his 'more sedentary' colleagues.

Second, the quote also speaks to the way in which physical activity is shaped by social group membership. As Mandela points out, at the time, exercise was not a normative behaviour for African men of his age (and despite the increasing evidence and awareness of its benefits, it has not yet become so). At the same time, Mandela notes that he was more successful in convincing his fellow prisoners than his own children. Why would this be the case? Is it because he was more charismatic as a political leader than as a father? Is it because he could directly model his physical activity for his inmates and party members, but not for his children? Either way, it speaks to an interesting dynamic that centres on group membership and social interaction.

After he had been released from prison and become the president of post-Apartheid South Africa, Mandela was the architect of a far more momentous sporting achievement – bringing South Africans together around support for their national rugby team, the Springboks (Carlin, 2008). The Springboks had previously been spurned by the black majority because they were a symbol of white supremacy and Apartheid. So when Mandela decided to publicly present himself as a fan of the Springboks, he was taking a big risk. But the risk paid off when the Springboks unexpectedly qualified for the 1995 Rugby World Cup final. Before that final, the team visited Robben Island and became inspired by the unshaken spirit and conviction that Mandela and his fellow prisoners had shown during their long imprisonment. Moreover, in the final they were able draw on that defiant spirit to overcome the New Zealand All Blacks, the clear favourites, and become world champions. After this David-versus-Goliath victory, black and white South Africans celebrated together on the streets, and Mandela's dream of a united nation was realised, at least in that moment (see also Chapters 2 and 20).

On the one hand, this story is another example of Mandela's unique and legendary capacity to shape the will of others. On the other hand, though, it again shows how individuals' sporting preferences and choices are a reflection of the groups to which these individuals belong. It was only when they saw the national team as an embodiment of a shared identity (as 'us South Africans' rather than 'us white South Africans') that all South Africans came out to support it.

The more general point here, then, is that as with all behaviour, sport and physical activity (in all its forms) is shaped by the complex interplay between individual, social and contextual factors. Interestingly, though, when Stuart Biddle and Nanette Mutrie (2001) reproduced Mandela's quote in the first edition of their ground-breaking textbook *Psychology of Physical Activity*, they used it (and, in particular, the lines 'If that old man can do it, why can't I?') to underline the point that personal feelings of competence and confidence (i.e., a sense of self-efficacy) are central to people's willingness to engage in physical activity. The quote was absent from later editions, but the focus on individual-level explanations of physical activity and sport remained. Indeed, research in sport and exercise psychology has generally tended to see the individual as the primary unit of psychological analysis and the group as an external factor that merely provides a context for the thoughts, emotions and behaviour of individuals.

As we will see in the chapters below, it is clear too that this individualistic perspective has spawned a broad range of empirical and theoretical advances. Yet even though recognition of social and environmental influences on individual psychology has increased over time (e.g., in ecological models of sport psychology; Sallis & Owen, 2002), something is still clearly missing. In particular, there has been a failure to come to terms with the *psychological reality of the group* – the fact that when athletes, fans and commentators talk about 'us' (e.g., 'us Lakers fans', 'us cyclists'), their psychology is not that of the person *as an individual* but the psychology of the person *as a group member*. Importantly, this does not denote just a transformation of perception (so that the person comes to see the world through the lens of a given group membership), but also a transformation of behaviour, so that they now behave, and are capable of behaving, as a group member rather than just as an individual (Turner, 1982). And, as we will also see, this transformation in turn is bound up with a whole range of social influence processes that centre on this internalised sense of group membership – such things as leadership, communication, organisation and teamwork.

In recognition of this gap in the field, recent years have witnessed a dramatic growth of interest in social psychological theories that argue for the distinctive contribution of groups to sport and exercise-related behaviour (Rees, Haslam, Coffee, & Lavallee, 2015; Stevens et al., 2017). Indeed, informed by insights from *social identity theory* (Tajfel & Turner, 1979) and *self-categorization theory* (Turner, Hogg, Oakes, Reicher, & Wetherell, 1987; also referred to as the *social identity approach*; Haslam, 2001), this has given rise to what can be heralded as a *new psychology of sport and exercise*. This places group processes and the psychology that gives rise to them centre stage. More particularly, it argues that group processes are central to most, if not all, aspects of sport and exercise (and many other domains besides). Moreover, these group processes are fundamentally grounded in people's capacity to define themselves in terms of their *social identity* – that is, their sense of themselves *as group members*. Social identity, then, is the psychological force that transforms what would otherwise be just a collection of disparate individuals into a *meaningful group* with a distinct focus, energy and power. It turns lone wolves into a pack, solitary souls into missionary movements, a team of champions into a champion team.

Given how central both groups and group life are to sport, one might expect that social identity theorists would have had a long-standing interest in questions of sport and exercise psychology, and that sport and exercise psychologists would have had a long-standing interest in questions of social identity. However, as we noted in the Preface, the fact is that they haven't. Indeed, we noted there that it is this that makes the psychological analysis that we present in this volume 'new'.

Nevertheless, as we also noted in the Preface, in recent years a large and impressive body of research has quickly built up that has started to bring the study of social identity and sport together and to life (see Figure P.1). Much (perhaps most) of this work has been conducted by contributors to this book. Importantly, though, it has never been systematically integrated into one volume. Neither has it been placed alongside more mainstream empirical work and theory in a text that clarifies, compares and evaluates the different approaches that students, researchers and practitioner scan take to the core topics of sport and exercise psychology.

This, then, is the key gap that the present volume seeks to fill. Its core goal is to flesh out the social identity approach with a view to helping readers understand and appreciate the complex relations between physical activity, exercise and sports on the one hand, and social identity processes and group phenomena on the other. In the process, it seeks to show that this is much more than just a marriage of convenience. That is, it is not simply the case that social identity should be 'of interest' to sport and exercise psychologists, and that sport and exercise should be 'of interest' to social identity theorists. Much more adventurously, we want to show that social identity is an *indispensable* construct for sport and exercise psychology and that sport and exercise is a *particularly powerful* domain in which to test and elaborate social identity theorising.

In the process of setting out on this adventure, this introductory chapter will first provide some conceptual clarifications of the concepts of physical activity, exercise and sport. After this, we provide a brief historical overview of the emergence of sport and exercise psychology as distinct scientific subdisciplines. We then make a more focused case for the importance of a social identity approach to sport and exercise psychology.

PHYSICAL ACTIVITY, EXERCISE AND SPORT: DEFINITION AND CONCEPTUAL CLARIFICATION

Given that there are so many misconceptions about the terms sport, exercise and physical activity, especially in daily life, it is essential that we first provide clear operational definitions of these key terms. In line with most prevailing conceptualisations (Biddle, Mutrie, & Gorely, 2015), we consider physical activity to be an umbrella term that includes all types of movement. More specifically, the well-accepted definition by Carl Caspersen and colleagues sees physical activity as a movement of the body that has three characteristics: (a) it is produced by the skeletal muscles (to distinguish it from more automatically generated movements, such as blinking your eyes); (b) it results in energy expenditure which varies from low to high (to include light forms of movement, such as walking); and (c) it has a positive correlation with physical fitness (which is defined as people's ability to perform physical activity; Casperen, Powell, & Christenson, 1985). In order to lead to positive health outcomes and thus to be considered to be *Health-Enhancing Physical Activity* (often abbreviated as HEPA), energy expenditure is usually required to be well above resting levels, and, where this is the case, it is referred to as 'Moderate-to-Vigorous' Physical Activity (MVPA).

Exercise can be seen as a specific subset of physical activity, as it satisfies all three conditions of the foregoing definition, but requires that activity to have a *strong* positive relationship with physical activity. This reflects the fact that physical activity can only be considered to be exercise when it involves *planned, structured and repetitive bodily movement with the explicit objective of maintaining or improving physical fitness* (e.g., by using the treadmill in the gym). Nevertheless, there is clearly overlap between these concepts, and the distinction between exercise and physical activity is not always clear-cut. For example, if a person deliberately uses a bike instead of a car to go shopping, and with his or her health in mind, are they exercising or only engaging in physical activity?

Sport is a specific subset of physical activity, but it is even more tricky to define. Nevertheless, this is often done by identifying additional characteristics that differentiate sport from physical activity (and sometimes exercise). For example, in one widely accepted definition, Jack Rejeski and Lawrence Brawley (1988) identified seven of these, noting that sport is (a) *rule governed*, (b) *structured*, and (c) *competitive*, and involves (d) *gross motor movement* as well as (e) *strategy*, (f) *skills*, and (g) *chance*. It follows, however, that not all sports are health-enhancing (e.g., darts), and that while there is considerable overlap with the concept of exercise, much depends on the meaning of 'competitive' (e.g., is the competition with another person, with a group or with themselves?). For example, should jogging on your own with the goal of beating your previous best time be considered exercise or sport? It is not always clear either whether the movement that an activity involves is gross enough to qualify as sport. This, for example, is an issue that is often discussed in the context of debates about whether e-sports, fishing or snooker are 'really' sports.

Despite these conceptual ambiguities, the above definitions provide a framework that can be helpful when it comes to distinguishing between the typical manifestations of physical activity, exercise and sport. At the same time, though, the fact that it is possible for people to have different views about the appropriate categorisation for a given activity tells us at least three things. First, that, as with all categorization, in practice there is a strong *subjective* dimension to these definitions and distinctions (Oakes, Haslam, & Turner, 1994). Nevertheless, second, this subjectivity is *structured* such that it is often a reflection of the shared group memberships of perceivers. In particular, those who participate in a given form of exercise or sport are typically much more likely to extol its virtues than those who do not. Cheerleaders, for example, have been keen to have their activity recognised as a sport, while outsiders have tried to deny them this recognition (on moral and philosophical grounds; Johnson & Sailors, 2013). Related to these points, third, there are *higher-order* definitional and conceptual issues that prescriptive attempts to define exercise and sport overlook. In particular, if we reflect on George Orwell's (1945) view (discussed in the Preface) that sport is 'war minus the shooting', it is clear that he was trying to capture something about the nature of sporting competition as intense, engaging and, above all, grounded in collective loyalties and identifications.

One of the key goals of the present volume is to tune in to these collective dimensions of physical activity, exercise and sport. In so doing, we look to explain not only why these dimensions have definitional and conceptual relevance, but also why and how they structure people's actual engagement with the activity in question. And as well as allowing us to explore the 'big picture' issues that Orwell raises (e.g., concerning politics and sport; see Chapters 2 and 20), this allows us to answer much more fundamental questions – such as why people engage in sport and exercise at all.

SPORT AND EXERCISE PSYCHOLOGY: HISTORY AND FUTURE

According to the American Psychological Association (2019), sport and exercise psychology involves 'the scientific study of the psychological factors that are associated with participation and performance in sport, exercise, and other types of physical activity'. In line with this mission, there are two main goals that animate sport psychologists:

> (a) helping athletes use psychological principles to achieve optimal mental health and to improve performance (performance enhancement) and (b) understanding how participation in sport, exercise and physical activity affects an individual's psychological development, health and well-being throughout the lifespan. (American Psychological Association, 2019)

Given their shared historical background and focus, sport and exercise psychology are commonly grouped together as fields of research and practice. Nevertheless, there are some important differences between these two subdisciplines – not least in their underlying concerns – that it is useful to tease out.

Sport psychology

In line with the definition discussed above, sport psychology can be understood as the scientific study of the psychological states and processes that contribute to, and derive from, sporting *performance* and activity. Although one might imagine that this is a relatively new discipline, sport psychology textbooks (e.g., Weinberg & Gould, 2018) commonly observe that some of the first experiments in social psychology – Norman Triplett's (1898) studies of 'Dynamogenic factors in pacemaking and competition' – were actually studies of sport psychology. These were inspired by Triplett's informal observation that cyclists often raced faster when they rode in groups or pairs than when they rode alone. This was something that Triplett confirmed empirically by analysing the results of competitive cycling events (Karau & Williams, 2017). Beyond this, though, he was keen to confirm the finding experimentally – not only to establish causation but also to rule out confounds (such as the fact that when cycling in groups there are mechanical advantages associated with being able to benefit from others' slipstream). For this purpose, he conducted experiments in which he asked children to wind on fishing lines as fast as they could, either alone or in the presence of another child. In line with his hypothesis, Triplett found that the children performed better when they were in the presence of another child, and he suggested that this effect was the result of *social facilitation* – a tendency for the presence of other people (as co-actors or observers) to enhance a person's performance on simple or well-learned tasks (Karau & Williams, 2017).

In more recent years, it has been argued that Triplett, who did not make use of sophisticated statistical methods, overstated this social facilitation effect (Strube, 2005). He also failed to capture its nuances – not least because while the presence of others tends to increase performance on simple tasks, it can also undermine performance on complex or unfamiliar tasks (Karau & Williams, 2017). Moreover, it has been shown that Triplett was not the first to conduct experiments on social facilitation (Stroebe, 2012) and indeed that these were not the first experiments in social psychology (Haines & Vaughan, 1979). Nevertheless, Triplett's research alerts us to the fact that sport psychology has (and has always had) close links with the field of social psychology, and that the two disciplines share a long history – albeit one that is often misunderstood and misrepresented (Smith & Haslam, 2017).

Partly because of this overlap, it was not until 1967 that sport psychology was recognised as a distinct subdiscipline within psychology with the founding of the North American Society for the Psychology of Sport and Physical Activity (NASPSPA). And it was only in 1987 that the American Psychological Association (APA) established a branch devoted specifically to Sport, Exercise and Performance Psychological (APA Division 47). Moreover, despite its grounding in laboratory-based experimentation, most of the early work in sport psychology was applied research in nature (e.g., on coaching) and the field had to wait until 1979 for its first scientific journal – the *Journal of Sport Psychology* – to be established.

Similar trends are also observed outside of North America. Thus, the International Society for Sport Psychology (ISSP) was only established in 1965 and its first scientific journal – the *International Journal of Sport Psychology* – did not appear until 1970. Likewise, in Europe, the European Federation of Sport Psychology (FEPSAC) was founded in 1969, but waited until 2000 to launch its flagship journal *Psychology of Sport and Exercise*. At this point, though, the fact that this journal included the term 'exercise' in its title spoke to the widening focus of sport psychologists. So, while the field had started out being concerned primarily with the performance and well-being of athletes in competitive settings, now it started to explore more general issues of participation in physical activity and health.

Exercise psychology

To understand why exercise psychology emerged as a separate discipline only very recently (much later even than sport psychology) it is necessary to appreciate something of the history of physical activity itself. According to Steven Blair (1988), this unfolded over four broad evolutionary periods. First, in the *pre-agricultural period* (from the dawn of homo sapiens until about 8,000 BC), physical activity was an ever-present feature of life because humans had to hunt and gather to survive. Likewise, in the *agricultural period* (which lasted until the beginning of the 19th century), physical activity was still common but became more focused on strength due to the need to labour in fields. Following this, in the *industrial period* (from around 1800 to 1945), daily physical activity shifted for many people to manual work in factories, but despite the unhealthy working conditions, there was no lack of physical activity. Then finally in the (post-1945) *nuclear period*, technological innovations changed things dramatically and gradually removed the need to be physically active in daily life. From this point to the present day, office work that involves sedentary and physically undemanding activity became increasingly common. Moreover, now people commute to work by car or public transport and, when they get there, they routinely take the lift to reach their office if it is above the ground floor.

In short, this historical overview tells us that for the greater part of human existence (roughly 99.997% of the time that our species has been on the planet), physical activity in different forms was necessary for survival. As a result, humans did not have a choice to be anything other than physically active. Yet in the last 70 or so years this has changed dramatically – so that for most people today physical activity needs to be consciously built into their leisure time or daily activity.

Furthermore, for the first 40 or so years of this nuclear period, researchers gave little thought to the question of what impact physical *in*activity was having on health. Certainly, they generated little hard evidence that it was detrimental to health in any way. Indeed, on the contrary, the reduced need for physical activity was initially welcomed as a blessing for humanity. This is illustrated by an advertisement for Shepard Warner home elevators that appeared in the 1960s (see Figure 1.1). 'Why climb stairs', it asked, 'when you can ride with the finest in home elevators.'

Figure 1.1 A 1960s advertisement for a home lift

It was only in the early 1980s, then, that the realisation started to dawn on researchers that our bodies had evolved to be physically active, and that *hypokinesis* (decreased bodily movement) was a major health risk (e.g., Corbin, 1987). Following this 'discovery' of the health benefits of physical activity, scientists became interested in the new challenge of trying to motivate humans to become sufficiently active in *lethargogenic environments* that were increasingly designed to render physical activity obsolete. In the first instance, this interest came largely from sport psychologists. As a result, journals that had previously focused only on topics of sport psychology (of the form discussed in the previous section) now introduced new sections to address these issues. Moreover, to distinguish between these different lines of research, many of these new sections were titled 'exercise psychology'. Going yet further, several journals changed their name so as to recognise and capture the increasing interest in this new branch of research. This was the case, for example, when in 1988 the *Journal of Sport Psychology* was rebranded the *Journal of Sport and Exercise Psychology*.

It should be noted that the original focus of early exercise psychologists was on promoting vigorous exercise – in particular through activities such as jogging and fitness. This aligned with prevailing norms at that time which suggested that only intensive physical activity would enhance health, such as the work-outs promoted by actress and reborn fitness guru Jane Fonda.

As research in the area advanced, however, it became clear that moderate and even light physical activity might have substantial preventive health effects (e.g., Jakicic et al., 2019). As a result, researchers increasingly focused on promoting 'active living' (e.g., Blair, Dunn, Marcus, Carpenter, & Jaret, 2010) – trying to encourage people to incorporate even small amounts of light activity into their daily routines (e.g., by walking to the grocery store rather than taking the car). This shift, however, meant that the term 'exercise psychology' became somewhat misleading, and so a subset of researchers pleaded for the discipline to be renamed 'physical activity psychology'. This shift in emphasis was seen, for example, in the launch of the *Journal of Physical Activity and Health* in 2004, and in the title of Biddle and Mutrie's ground-breaking textbook *Psychology of Physical Activity: Determinants, Well-being and Interventions* (2001).

These changes in emphasis have also been felt more recently, so that today researchers have come to see the reduction of *sedentary behaviour* (i.e., sitting too long without interruption) as a new and distinct research priority (e.g., Ekblom-Bak, Hellénius, & Ekblom, 2010). However, as with the definitional issues that we broached earlier, there is risk that by focusing on the ever-smaller ways in which the field has been carved up, one loses sight of the common agenda that has animated researchers for the last 40 or so years. In the most basic terms, this centres on the quest to help people *be as physically active as possible* – whether by playing sport, engaging in exercise, doing physical activity or simply getting up off the couch. Moreover, as we will see in the chapters below (e.g., Chapters 12 and 13), by virtue of its status as *a social cognitive theory of human motivation* (e.g., Ellemers, de Gilder, & Haslam, 2004; Haslam, Oakes, Turner, & McGarty, 1996; Tajfel & Turner, 1979), this is an agenda that the social identity approach is peculiarly well positioned to address.

WHY WE NEED A SOCIAL IDENTITY PERSPECTIVE ON SPORT AND EXERCISE PSYCHOLOGY

The previous sections alert us to the fact that the fields of sport and exercise psychology have burgeoned in recent decades. This reflects increasing awareness of the importance of psychology not only for the performance and well-being of athletes (of all forms and at all levels), but also for people's engagement in exercise, and for the business and industry of sport. And whereas once this might have been considered a rather fringe pursuit, today it is clear that it is anything but. So while the sport industry was estimated to be worth a staggering $60.5 billion in 2014, by 2019 this figure was projected to have grown to $73.5 billion (Heitner, 2015).

As they have evolved, the fields of sport and exercise psychology have done a very good job of capturing the ways in which the psychological processes and states of individuals *as individuals* are shaped by, and contribute to, important sport and exercise phenomena. But, as we noted at the start of this chapter, they have done a poor job of engaging with and explaining the ways in which group life, and its distinctive psychology, are implicated in these same phenomena. More particularly (at least for our present purposes), this has meant that up to this point researchers have failed to recognise the capacity for social identity theorising to provide a coherent theoretical framework for getting to grips with the collective dimensions of sport and exercise – dimensions that are not only ever-present but also ever-relevant and ever-potent.

Yet as we noted in the Preface, it would be wrong to suggest that we start with a blank slate. For not only have there been 50 years of social identity research in cognate disciplines to draw on (after Tajfel, Flament, Billig, & Bundy, 1971), but so too in recent years nascent interest in a social identity approach to sport and exercise psychology has rapidly gathered momentum (see Figure P.2). The defining goal of this volume is therefore to build on and focus this momentum through a forensic and far-reaching exploration of the capacity for social identity theorising to shed light on myriad aspects of the world of sport and exercise.

THE STRUCTURE AND CONTENT OF THIS BOOK

As we have seen, this opening chapter of the book has attempted to provide an overview of (conceptual) developments in the field of sport and exercise psychology. These are fields that have traditionally had an individualistic focus (e.g., in their emphasis on the personal identity of athletes and on the cognitions and motivations of individuals as individuals). Nevertheless, we believe that they can be profoundly enriched through attention to the workings of a group-based self defined by a sense of shared social identity.

As a foundation for this claim, the second chapter of this book completes the Introductory section (Section 1) by setting out the theoretical platform for social identity approach. It explains what social identity is, as well as how people come to define themselves in terms of (a particular) social identity and what the implications of this are for their thinking, their emotions and their behaviour. More specifically, it spells out the implications of social identity for key aspects of sport and exercise that we refer to as *the 5Ps*: *participation, performance, psychological and physical health, partisanship* and *politics*. Our analysis also generates hypotheses and principles associated with these different foci that underpin, and go on to inform, the specifics of the various topics that are addressed in the chapters that follow.

Each of the ensuing 18 chapters (Chapters 3 to 20) then goes on to explore a key topic in the field of sport and exercise psychology. Up to Chapter 18, these all have the same structure. Specifically, they start with a critical discussion of prevailing empirical work and theory, and then go on to tease out points of contact with, and divergence from, social identity theorising. Each chapter then articulates an alternative position on the topic suggested by a social identity approach, and reviews some of the key evidence that supports this alternative view. The chapters also all conclude by spelling out some of the broader implications of this approach for issues of theory, research and practice. This structure is designed to ensure that the book as a whole can be used as both a general reader and a textbook, and that it provides readers with a structured framework for understanding and engaging with the sweeping landscape of social identity ideas and research that we traverse.

A key reason for wanting to develop a new psychology of the field is to show how the micro (individual), meso (group) and macro (societal) dimensions of sport and exercise articulate with each other in powerful ways. As US soccer player and Women's Ballon d'Or winner Megan Rapinoe succinctly and eloquently puts it, 'everything is connected' (BBC Sport, 2019). This articulation is conspicuously absent from other forms of contemporary theorising, and yet we believe it holds the key to meaningful advancement of the field. This, then, is the key project that has focused the energies of the book's contributors and is the source of the new insights for theory and practice that they generate. We hope you will find them as exciting and as energising as we do.

2

THE SOCIAL IDENTITY APPROACH TO SPORT AND EXERCISE PSYCHOLOGY

S. ALEXANDER HASLAM
KATRIEN FRANSEN
FILIP BOEN
STEPHEN REICHER

When a fan suggested to Bill Shankly, the manager of Liverpool FC from 1959 to 1974, that football was a matter of life and death, he famously replied, 'No, it's much more important than that' (Corbett, 2009; Kelly, 1995). To get an understanding of what he meant, it is interesting to reflect on some of the details of Shankly's own life. Growing up in a coal mining village in Scotland and spending two years working as a miner himself, he came from a large family that was passionate not only about football but also about community. When he arrived at Liverpool, the team was struggling in the second division and very much a poor relation to the city's big team, Everton. Steadily, though, he built the team up by instilling in his young players a sense that they were privileged to represent the club that bore the name of their city and to play for its fans. His core ethos was that no individual was bigger than the team, but that no individual was smaller than the team either (Bowler, 2013). Shankly's point, then, is that life and death are things that happen to individuals (however great they may be), whereas the great game – and the collective enthusiasm it creates – endures and carries large groups of people on with it.

In these terms, we see that football – like all sport – is never just personal but is also always social. The same is true for its psychology. For while sport is obviously something that individuals take part in, what makes it significant, meaningful and powerful is the fact that they routinely do so not *as individuals* but *as members of social groups*, whether as players in a particular team, as supporters of a particular club, or as followers of a particular sport, and so on. And while this is less self-evidently true of exercise, here too we see that the groups people belong to play an equally significant role in shaping how, where and why they exert themselves. For example, a person's social class will have a bearing on whether they prefer to lift weights or go jogging (Duane, 2014), their gender will determine what gymnastic routines they learn at school, and their nationality will feed into their ability to master American or Australian rules football. To properly understand the psychology of sport and exercise we therefore need a theoretical framework that provides a basis for understanding its group-based dimensions, not only its personal ones. The fundamental reason for this is that, without this collective dimension to its psychology, sport is no sport at all.

The social identity approach seeks to provide just such a framework. At its core, this argues that people's sense of identity – who they think they are, and hence how they behave – is defined not only by their individuality (their personal identity; Turner, 1982) but also by their group membership (their *social identity*; Tajfel 1972). Indeed, in an array of contexts, not least those centring on sport and exercise, it is often the latter that predominates. Thus, as an individual, Bill Shankly might have defined himself in terms of an array of idiosyncratic attributes and tastes, yet in the sporting contexts that made him a household name, it was the fact that he defined himself in terms of particular group memberships (as a player for Preston North End, as manager of Liverpool) that allowed him to make his mark on the world. Indeed, what marked him out as a manager was not only the focus of his social identity, but the strength of his social identification ('But that's where I live!' he once exclaimed to a Belgian hotel clerk who complained that he had merely written 'Anfield' as his address). This observation raises two broad questions that this chapter seeks to answer. First, when and how do people define themselves in terms of a particular sport- and exercise-related group membership (e.g., as a member or fan of a given team)? And, second, what are the consequences of this for their sport- and exercise-related behaviour?

As we will see, answers to these questions draw our attention to five spheres of sports-related activity to which social identity theorising has profound relevance (the 5Ps: Reicher, 2017): *participation* (what sport and exercise activities people engage in), *performance* (how well people do those activities), *psychological and physical health* (how well people feel because of doing those activities), *partisanship* (how people behave as supporters of sport activity) and *politics* (how people acquire and wield power in and through sporting activity). In each of these spheres, an ever-growing body of research also supports key hypotheses concerning the impact of social identity on relevant outcomes. In particular, we will see that the nature and strength of a person's social identity is a significant determinant of each of these aspects of sporting life. At the same time, though, the approach also focuses our attention on the ways in which sporting outcomes are structured by identity-relevant features of *social context* and by identity-based processes of *social influence*. How Liverpool fans behave, for example, depends on who their opponents are, and they are more likely to heed the advice of those they perceive as representing the club than that of those they perceive to be outsiders.

Together these hypotheses speak to the fact that sport is not simply a context for particular forms of social behaviour (e.g., competitive games between groups), but also an arena in which behaviour can be transformed in creative and socially powerful ways. Crunch games, for example, are frequently the stimulus for 'super-human' performance, and big sporting festivals, such as the Olympics, can have a transformational impact on the identity of entire nations (Price & Dayan, 2009). Indeed, in ways that Bill Shankly implicitly understood, we will see that what makes sport so important is its capacity to be a crucible for emergent social identities that are capable of connecting and inspiring people in ways that few other things can.

THE SOCIAL IDENTITY APPROACH

Social identity and social identity theory

In this chapter, and indeed in this book as a whole, our central claim is that social identity theorising provides a new way of thinking about the psychology of sport and exercise. The key reason for this is that it offers a new way of thinking about the construct that is at the heart of all psychology: *the self*. Elsewhere in psychology, and indeed in everyday social interaction, when people talk about 'the self', they are almost always referring to something *singular* about a person. In these terms, to talk about a person's 'self-esteem', 'self-control' or 'self-determination' is to say something about their *personal identity* as a unique individual (Turner, 1982). Yet while this way of thinking about identity dominates psychological theorising, it is clearly the case that our sense of self is not only defined in individual terms. Indeed, the very fact that we can refer to 'we', 'us' and 'our' speaks to the point that the self can also be defined in terms of *attributes and qualities that we share with other people*. Importantly, when we do so, this is not merely a part or figure of speech but reflects the capacity for the self to be defined in terms of *social identity* that is inclusive of other people. In this sense, the Liverpool anthem 'You'll never walk alone' is the anthem of all devout football fans (even those who support Everton; see Viner, 2014, p. 109); for, as a supporter, you do indeed never walk alone.

Social identity, then, reflects the capacity for groups to be internalised into our sense of self ('who we are') so that in a wide array of contexts the way we see the world – and the way we behave within it – are not simply a reflection of our individuality but also of group memberships that we share with other people. When a person plays in a game of football, for example, the sense of self that shapes their perception and behaviour will necessarily be informed by the team they are a member of (e.g., 'us reds'). If it is not, not only are they likely to be very unpopular with their teammates, but more fundamentally they will also struggle to play the game at all (e.g., being unsure about who to pass to, who to expect a pass from, who to listen to, and who to strategise with).

The person who first recognised the significance of this point for human psychology and behaviour was Henri Tajfel (1972). His realisation came from a series of experiments that came to be known as the *minimal group studies* (Tajfel, 1970; Tajfel, Flament, Billig, & Bundy, 1971). In these, schoolboys were assigned to groups that had no prior meaning (e.g., supposedly on the basis of their liking for abstract paintings by Klee or Kandinsky) and had the task of assigning rewards to other members of both their own group (their *ingroup*) and another group (the *outgroup*). What Tajfel and colleagues found was that, even though the groups were designed to be as meaningless as possible, the boys reliably displayed *ingroup favouritism* by giving more points to members of their ingroup than to members of the outgroup.

From the vantage point of established psychological theory, the key point about the minimal groups studies was that there was 'nothing in it' for the boys themselves to behave in this way (because, *as individuals*, they gained nothing; Spears & Otten, 2017). So, instead, what Tajfel came to understand was that ingroup favouritism reflected the fact that the process of acting in terms of their group membership was a way for the boys to make an otherwise meaningless situation *meaningful*. In particular, the process of favouring 'us in the Klee group' over 'them in the Kandinsky group' gave them a *positive and distinctive social* identity.

This motivation, Tajfel suggested, is a fundamental driver of human behaviour. It means that when we define ourselves in terms of a given social identity, we don't just want our ingroup to be different from comparison outgroups: we also want it to be *better*. Apart from anything else, this motivation explains the significance of local sporting derbies, where intergroup comparison, and the invidious consequences of coming off second best, are particularly salient. The point here, then, is that even if you can't be the best team in the world or in your country, you can be the best team in your town – and this is likely to be a key determinant of your self-esteem in a majority of the contexts where you interact with other people (e.g., at work, at school, in local shops).

An obvious point, though, is that while the motivation to achieve positive intergroup distinctiveness can be seen as universal, this does not mean that ingroups always triumph. This is especially true for low-status groups whose position in a given status hierarchy (e.g., a football league) is a direct reflection of this fact. This point was the basis for Tajfel to collaborate with John Turner to develop *social identity theory* (SIT; Tajfel & Turner, 1979). The core insights of this are (a) that *social reality* places constraints on the ways in which group members can achieve a sense of positive social identity and (b) that features of the *perceived social structure* dictate how precisely they deal with this fact. More specifically, as can be seen from Figure 2.1, the theory focuses on the importance of three structural elements: the perceived *permeability* of group boundaries, and the perceived *stability* and *legitimacy* of the ingroup's position in relation to other groups (Tajfel & Turner, 1979; see also Ellemers, 1993; Ellemers & Haslam, 2012).

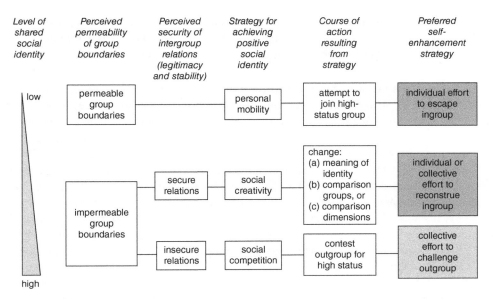

Level of shared social identity	Perceived permeability of group boundaries	Perceived security of intergroup relations (legitimacy and stability)	Strategy for achieving positive social identity	Course of action resulting from strategy	Preferred self-enhancement strategy
low	permeable group boundaries		personal mobility	attempt to join high-status group	individual effort to escape ingroup
	impermeable group boundaries	secure relations	social creativity	change: (a) meaning of identity (b) comparison groups, or (c) comparison dimensions	individual or collective effort to reconstrue ingroup
high		insecure relations	social competition	contest outgroup for high status	collective effort to challenge outgroup

Figure 2.1 Social identity theory's predictions about the impact of perceived social structure on strategies for self-enhancement

In the first instance, if members of low-status groups believe that group boundaries are *permeable*, such that it is possible to leave their group and join a better one, then this is what they will try to do – through a strategy of *individual mobility*. For example, if a football team is relegated at the end of a season, its best players may try to get transferred into a team that stayed up. Yet by the same token, the fact that – in stark contrast to modern players – fans perceive group boundaries to be *im*permeable, makes it far less likely that a supporter of the same team would transfer their allegiances in the same way. If you are a die-hard Everton fan, it is unconscionable that you would consider cheering for Liverpool. Under these conditions, it makes more sense for members of the low-status group to band together and *act collectively* in terms of their shared social identity by trying to improve the conditions of their ingroup as a whole.

If status relations appear to be both stable and legitimate (i.e., *secure*), SIT predicts that members of low-status groups will do this by striving to achieve a sense of positive ingroup distinctiveness through a process of *social creativity* that changes the terms of intergroup comparison in ways that are favourable to the ingroup. As an illustration of this process in action, the sports writer Brian Viner (2014, pp. 108, 110) reflects that as an Everton fan:

> You could say to smug Liverpool fans that supporting Everton showed much more character, was a much greater test of a chap's mettle, than supporting Liverpool. […] I really don't envy Liverpool fans anything […] not even all

the League titles and European Cups, because I still think it's a more special thing to be an Evertonian, and am convinced that Everton is the more characterful club, more viscerally connected with the city.

Likewise, teams that find themselves performing poorly in comparison to others (e.g., on league or medal tables) will be motivated to re-engineer comparison indices in ways that present the ingroup in a better light (e.g., by redefining inclusion criteria or dimensions of comparison; Elsbach & Kramer, 1996). For example, research by Platow, Hunter, Branscombe, and Grace (2014) shows that New Zealanders are more likely than Americans to favour Olympic medal tables that report number of medals *per capita* rather than just the number of medals. Similarly, 'fair play' is more likely to be championed as a virtue by teams that lose than by those that win (Lalonde, 1992; Lalonde, Moghaddam, & Taylor, 1987).

Yet if status relations are impermeable but *in*secure – because they are seen as illegitimate or liable to change – then members of low-status groups are generally keen to engage in direct *social competition* with the high-status outgroup. At the most basic level, all forms of sporting competition are predicated on this possibility (Loland, 2002; Tajfel & Turner, 1979, p. 45). For example, one reason why leagues are differentiated in terms of such things as skill level (e.g., professional vs amateur), age (e.g., seniors vs under 21s) and gender (men vs women) is precisely to preserve the possibility that any team might win. Yet, by the same token, one reason why knock-out trophies (e.g., the FA Cup in English football) are favoured by the players, fans and managers of lower-ranked teams is that they afford opportunities for feats of 'giant-slaying' in ways that leagues do not (Ward, 1989).

The key point here, then, is that social identity-based social competition allows members of groups – especially low-status ones – not only to achieve a positive sense of self, but also to strive to produce significant forms of *social change*, in ways that they would not be able to do otherwise. When status relations are seen as legitimate (as they are in most sporting leagues, for example) this change will often be confined to the domain and dimensions of the competition itself (e.g., so that over the course of Bill Shankly's time as manager Liverpool came to be seen as a superior team to Everton). However, if they are seen as illegitimate, this need not be the case. In particular, it is clear that over time and around the world, sport has been a key vehicle for members of subjugated groups to rally together to challenge and overcome injustice and inequality not only on the field but in the world at large (Field & Kidd, 2013; Numerato, 2018). For example, Jackie Robinson's mobilisation of black baseball players was critical to the advancement of the Civil Rights Movement in 1960s America (Hylton, 1997); the organisation of their own soccer league was a key means through which members of the African National Congress were able to gain traction for the anti-Apartheid cause in 1980s South Africa (Suze, 2013; Tygiel, 1997); and Billie Jean King was a potent flag-bearer for the women's movement in the 1970s (Ware, 2011).

These same creative forces (and associated tensions) are seen today in efforts by Serena Williams to challenge prevailing representations of women and racial minorities in sport (Schultz, 2005; Spencer, 2004). Such events bear testimony to the important role that social identity plays in what Bourdieu (1989, p. 826) portrayed as 'struggles in which what is at stake, *inter alia*, is the monopolistic capacity to impose the legitimate definition of sport practice and of the legitimate functioning of sport activity'. These are struggles that individual-level psychological theories tend to overlook, not least because they have limited means of explaining them. And yet, as we will discuss further below, they are an important part of what social identity theory brings to our appreciation of sport's collective underpinnings and potentiality (see also Chapter 20).

Self-categorization theory

Social identity theory speaks to the importance of social identity for social behaviour in intergroup (i.e., 'us vs them') contexts of a form that is characteristic of sporting contests. Despite this, in its pure form (i.e., as articulated by Tajfel & Turner, 1979, and as represented schematically in Figure 2.1), the theory is rarely explicitly invoked to explain sport and exercise behaviour. In part, this is because it offers no general hypotheses either about *when* people define themselves in terms of a particular social identity (i.e., as members of a specific group), or about the *consequences* of self-definition in these terms. These, however, are central concerns for *self-categorization theory* (SCT; Turner et al., 1987; Turner, Oakes, Haslam, & McGarty, 1994). As a result, this is an extension of social identity theorising that provides the basis for a more general group psychology that is more broadly relevant to the domain of sport (e.g., see Rees et al., 2015; Stevens et al., 2017).

There are three key contributions through which SCT fleshes out and amplifies SIT's original insights that are particularly relevant to the psychology of sport. The first of these is to argue that *social identity is what makes group behaviour possible* (Turner, 1982). More specifically, Turner argued that through a process of *depersonalisation* (or *self-stereotyping*) the self comes to be defined in terms of a category membership that is shared with other ingroup members (as 'we' rather than 'I') and that this is the basis for people both to see themselves, and to act, as group members. Clearly this is a prerequisite for most forms of sporting behaviour. For example, as we intimated above, it is only because a person is able to categorize themselves as 'a red' that they know who to pass to in a game of football, who to cheer for, who to emulate. Moreover, the more they self-stereotype in terms of a given group membership, the more likely they are to take these things on board and the harder they are likely to work to try to do them better.

A second contribution of SCT is to specify more fully how the self-system operates to regulate depersonalisation and thereby make particular social identities psychologically operative or *salient*. Here the theory argues that the salience of a particular social identity (e.g., 'us reds') results from a *context-sensitive (self-)categorization process* which leads people to see themselves as sharing category membership with others to a greater or lesser extent in the situation at hand (Turner, 1985). More specifically, social identity salience is understood to be an interactive product of a person's internal *readiness* to use a particular self-categorization and its perceived *fit* with the external context (Oakes et al., 1994; Oakes, Turner, & Haslam, 1991; see also Heere & James, 2007). The workings of this process are represented schematically in Figure 2.2 (see also Figure 11.2).

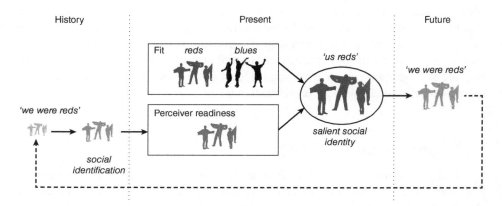

Figure 2.2 A schematic representation of self-categorization theory's analysis of the contribution of perceiver readiness and fit to social identity salience

Note: At a given point in time, a particular social identity (e.g., 'us reds') becomes salient, and hence is a basis for perception and action, to the extent that (a) it makes sense of similarities and differences in the situation at hand (i.e., so that there is high *fit*), and (b) it has been enacted in the past and is ready to be invoked (i.e., so that there is high *perceiver readiness*). The process of enacting the identity (e.g., going to a football match in which you support the reds) also creates a history of *social identification* that contributes to perceiver readiness in the future and thereby increases the likelihood of the social identity becoming salient again.

This analysis serves to highlight two key ideas. First, that a person is more likely to self-categorize in terms of a given social identity (e.g., as an Arsenal supporter) if this group has been a basis for their self-definition in the past (i.e., so that they have a high level of *social identification*; e.g., because they grew up attending Arsenal games with their parents; for a first-hand account of this process, see Hornby, 1992). Second, that a given social identity is more likely to be salient if a given self-categorization makes sense of the similarities and differences that are apparent to a perceiver in the situation in which they find themselves. For example, a person is more likely to define themselves as an Arsenal supporter at a match against Spurs than in a supermarket (where being a Spurs supporter does not normally define meaningful similarities with, and differences from, other shoppers – so long as they are not wearing clothes that display their affiliation with a specific team).

Following up on these ideas, a third contribution of SCT is to spell out the *consequences* of social identity salience. The central idea here is that – as with all categorization (Rosch, 1978) – self-categorization is a basis for *perceived interchangeability*. This means that if, when, and to the extent that a person defines themselves in terms of a given social identity (e.g., 'us blues'), they see themselves as being more connected to and bound up with other members of that social category in ways that they would not be otherwise (Haslam, Oakes, Turner, & McGarty, 1995).

This sense of self-interchangeability that results from depersonalisation has a cascading effect on a wide range of important social behaviours. For example, it is the basis for people to feel connected to other ingroup members (Alnabulsi & Drury, 2014), to trust them (Foddy, Platow, & Yamagishi, 2009), to work with them (Ellemers et al., 2004) and to help them (Levine, Prosser, Evans, & Reicher, 2005). An illustration of the last of these points is provided by the research of Mark Levine and colleagues. This showed that a passer-by whose identity as a Manchester United fan had been made salient was far more likely to stop and help a person who tripped and fell in front of them if that person was wearing a Manchester United shirt rather than a Liverpool one (Levine et al., 2005). However, speaking to the flexibility of the self-categorization processes that are at work here, if the observer's social identity as a football fan in general had been made salient (rather than their identity as a supporter of a specific team), then they were more likely to offer to help the fan of the rival team than someone who appeared not to support any team at all.

Most especially, though, depersonalisation is the basis for *mutual social influence* (Turner, 1991). This means that when people perceive themselves as sharing social identity with others in a given context, they are motivated to strive actively to reach agreement with them and to coordinate their behaviour through activity that promotes their shared identity-relevant interests (a process of *consensualisation*; Haslam, Turner, Oakes, McGarty, & Reynolds, 1998). They do this because under these circumstances they recognise those 'others' as 'self', and hence see them as qualified to inform both their perceptions and their actions. For example, if a female physical education student defines herself primarily as a woman, then her behaviour will be shaped primarily by the views and actions of other members of that ingroup (i.e., other women), because they, unlike members of other groups, are in a position to speak to who she is and what she wants to be; however, if she defines herself as a physical education student, then she will be more open to the influence of other students (both male and female). Indeed, speaking to this point, research by Levine and Reicher (1996) shows that when they are induced to think of themselves as women, female physical education students see a facial scar as more serious than a knee injury (because this is more threatening to their identity *as* women), but that the opposite is true when their social identity as physical education students is made salient (because here a knee injury is more threatening to their identity *as* physical education students).

Importantly too, identity-based influence is also at the heart of *leadership* (Haslam, Reicher, & Platow, 2011; see Chapter 3). This means that the people we are influenced by, and follow, are those who are seen to represent and advance the social identities that are important for us in a given situation. At the most basic level, one consequence of this is that in any game of sport, we are influenced by the leaders of our own team but not by those of an opposing team, and by leaders who 'big us up' rather than run us down (Fransen, Haslam et al., 2015; Fransen, Steffens et al., 2016). But, less obviously, it means that a person's ability to display leadership flows not from their personal qualities in the abstract (e.g., their intelligence or their physical prowess), but rather from their capacity to do *identity entrepreneurship* (Reicher & Hopkins, 2001; Reicher, Haslam, & Hopkins, 2005) such that they are seen as 'one of us' (as representative or *prototypical* of the ingroup) who is 'doing it for us' (advancing ingroup interests) and 'making us matter' (shaping the world in the image of the ingroup; Steffens, Haslam, Reicher et al., 2014). For this reason, problems can arise if leaders are seen to be doing it 'for themselves' or 'for them'. This, for example, is something that José Mourinho discovered during his time at Chelsea and Manchester United where – once he was no longer achieving success for the group – his preferred soubriquet as 'The Special One' proved problematic for his capacity to inspire and motivate his players (e.g., Haslam & Reicher, 2016; Maskor, 2019; see Chapter 3).

In ways that will be elaborated much more fully in the chapters that follow, these various processes are clearly relevant to a wide array of phenomena that are encountered in the realm of sport and exercise. In the remainder of this chapter, though, we focus on clarifying the significance of social identity and self-categorization principles for 'the 5Ps' that lie at the heart of sport and exercise: *participation, performance, psychological and physical health, partisanship* and *politics*.

APPLYING THE SOCIAL IDENTITY APPROACH TO SPORT AND EXERCISE PSYCHOLOGY: THE 5Ps

1. Participation

> The important thing in the Olympic Games is not to win, but to take part.
> (Pierre de Coubertin, cited in Dixon, 1984, p. 210)

A very basic point about sport and exercise is that, beyond one's teenage years, no one *makes* you do it. But even before then, the level of enthusiasm that you show is clearly a matter of choice. The first author, for example, has recollections of being sent as a young schoolboy on a five-mile steeplechase and finding ingenious ways to return, seemingly exhausted, two hours later, having spent most of the time concealed with his friends behind a railway embankment. Yet at the same time, he can recall plenty of other activities (including long runs) that he embraced wholeheartedly. Likewise, most of us will have observed significant variability in our own enthusiasm for a particular sporting activity or event, as well as in the enthusiasm of other people (e.g., our relatives and friends). For example, while the author Nick Hornby ultimately became the most die-hard of all die-hard Arsenal fans, he notes that on his first trip to Highbury in September 1968 'all I really saw … was a bewildering chain of incomprehensible incidents, at the end of which everyone around me stood and shouted. If I did the same it must have been an embarrassing ten seconds after the rest of the crowd' (Hornby, 1992, p. 11).

What determines this variability in enthusiasm? In the case of Hornby, the obvious point is that when he first saw Arsenal play, neither Arsenal nor football had any prior meaning for him. Likewise, when a traveller to Australia first watches a game of Australian rules football, their initial reaction is likely to be one of confusion. Two sets of goal-posts? 18 players a side? No offside? Over time, though, familiarity and engagement with the social identities that underpin any form of sporting activity come to assume a very significant role in the minds and lives of the die-hards who embrace them most strongly – such that in the case of Hornby they become an 'obsession … that survives periodic feelings of indifference, sorrow and very real hatred' (1992, p. 3; Wann & Branscombe, 1990).

Such experiences serve to underline four important points. The first is that coming to understand, appreciate and enjoy sport is an *achievement*. Arguably, there is nothing inherently meaningful in any sport. Nevertheless, it is a testament to humans' capacity to find meaning in things that are inherently meaningless that we can come to find the most arcane activities (golf, tiddlywinks, running on a treadmill) uplifting and exhilarating.

Second, as in the minimal group studies (Tajfel et al., 1971), when we do find meaning, this is generally because, and to the extent that, those activities come to furnish us with a purposive sense of social identity. Being in a golf club, for example, gives you something to do, and something to get excited about, *together with other ingroup members* (Foote, 1951; Neville & Reicher, 2011).

Relatedly, third, the process of taking on a given social identity and coming to identify with a given social group is generally not something a person does on their own. Rather it results from social influence – and, more particularly, *leadership* – typically on the part of other ingroup members (e.g., Hornby's father who took him to his first Arsenal game; the friend who introduces you to golf).

Fourth, at the same time, though, once a given social identity (e.g., as a player in, or fan of, a given team) is taken on board, its expression still varies as a function of social circumstances. In particular, SIT suggests that we are more likely to embrace particular social identities when they provide us with a positive sense of self or at least appear to have the potential to do so. Indeed, this is one reason why a team's success is a significant predictor both of the number of people who attend its matches and of how much they are prepared to pay to do so (Laverie & Arnett, 2000; Liu, 2017; Wicker, Whitehead, Johnson, & Mason, 2017).

A rich and growing body of social identity research bears these various points out. In particular, there is evidence that people are more likely to engage in exercise to the extent that they identify with a group for which exercise is normative (Terry & Hogg, 1996). Along related lines, an impressive body of research by Mark Beauchamp and colleagues shows that people are more likely to engage in exercise when they are able to do so together with other ingroup members (e.g., other women, other people of the same age; Beauchamp, Carron, McCutcheon, & Harper, 2007; Beauchamp, Dunlop, Downey, & Estabrooks, 2012; Dunlop & Beauchamp, 2011a, 2011b; see Chapter 13). And, at the same time, as Mark Stevens and colleagues (2017) note, exercise is more likely to be sustained when it becomes the basis for an emergent sense of social identity (e.g., as seen in the success of programmes such as 'Baby Bootcamp' and 'Swimming for Seniors').

Related to these observations, it is also clear that the *ways* in which people engage in sporting activity are dictated by the *contents* of the social identities that inform their participation. This is seen, among other things, in the examples we provided above of the ways in which gender, class and nationality shape a person's preference for particular forms of exercise and sport (e.g., weight-lifting over running, cricket over baseball).

A more whimsical illustration emerges from the archival research of Sandra Heck (2011), who recounts that the first time the modern pentathlon was included in the Olympic Games (in Stockholm in 1912), the only American competitor was Lieutenant (later General) George S. Patton. Patton might have won a medal but for his performance in one event, pistol shooting. However, he ended up coming fifth because he insisted on using his military pistol rather than the more accurate target pistol used by other competitors. As Heck notes, 'His refusal to use the target pistol can be interpreted as a true loyalty to the army, which was so strong that he even accepted to take disadvantages compared to his opponents [because he wanted to] remain (and advertise) ... more the officer than the athlete' (2011, p. 418).

Other examples of self-handicapping in the interests of a salient social identity are found in the case of the Scottish runner Eric Liddell (immortalised in the film *Chariots of Fire*) who refused to compete in the 100 metres on a Sunday in the 1924 Olympic Games because this conflicted with his religious beliefs, and the Egyptian pentathlete Aya Medany who retired from the sport because it banned the full-body swimsuits which her Muslim faith required her to wear. More generally, it is clear that for sports people who are very religious, their religion often 'spills over' into the way they play and into the way they present themselves to the sporting public (Feezell, 2013). However, the same is true for other identities too, as seen in the black power salutes of American athletes at the 1968 Mexico Olympics (Wiggins, 1992) and black American football players 'taking a knee' in 2018 to protest against institutional racism (Intravia, Piquero, & Piquero, 2018; see Chapter 20).

Stevens and colleagues' work also speaks to the importance of identity-based leadership in these various processes. In particular, their studies of amateur sports teams show that team coaches and captains play a critical role in motivating team members both to play in particular ways and to participate in team activity more generally (Stevens, Rees, & Polman, 2019; Stevens, Rees, Steffens et al., 2019; see also Chapters 10 and 12). More specifically, Stevens et al.'s (2020) longitudinal research shows that leaders' capacity to build, represent and advance a sense of shared identity in the teams they lead serves to build social identification among team members in ways that go on to drive their subsequent participation. In short, as Pierre de Coubertin's identity leadership in garnering support for the idea of the modern Olympic Games shows very clearly (see Weiler, 2004), getting people to believe in sport as a vehicle for the development of a particular sense of 'us' is a prerequisite to getting them to both show up and stump up.

2. Performance

We are the champions. (Queen)

But sport, of course, isn't simply about showing up and knowing which team to play or barrack for. How hard do you try, and how well do you perform? Again, social identity and social identification both have a significant role to play here. Indeed, in line with some of the arguments that we advanced in the previous section, a key point is that members of any group (e.g., players, coaches, supporters) will generally work harder for that group the more they self-categorize in terms of that group membership in any given context.

Although this is a hypothesis that has primarily been examined in other fields (notably organisational psychology; e.g., see Ellemers et al., 2004; Haslam, 2001), multiple strands of sport and exercise research support this claim (see Chapter 5). Some early evidence comes from research by Holt (1987, cited in Brown, 1988). This revisited a classic experimental paradigm devised by Ringelmann at the end of the 19th century and involved agricultural students performing a rope pulling task, akin to a tug-of-war, in groups containing up to eight members (see Kravitz & Martin, 1986). What Ringelmann had found was that, as one would expect, the students exerted more pull the more of them there were in the group. However, as group size increased, the amount of pull exerted by each person decreased – so that in groups of eight, the students exerted just 49% of the pull that they did when they were alone.

This effect is typically attributed to *social loafing*, whereby individuals are found to put less effort into group tasks than they do when performing individually (e.g., Ingham, Levinger, Graves, & Peckham, 1974; Latané, Williams, & Harkins, 1979). Holt, however, replicated Ringelmann's experiment under conditions which heightened social identity salience among the teams of rope-pullers in one of three ways: (a) by allowing prior interaction between them, (b) by asking them to devise a name for their group, or (c) by creating teams who already had a sense of shared social identity (as flatmates). There was no difference in the performance of these three types of group, but in stark contrast to Ringelmann's findings, on average, groups performed 19% *better* than the sum of their efforts as individuals.

In contrast to the pattern of social loafing observed by Ringelmann (and subsequently widely reported in the research literature), this study thus suggests that when they share a sense of salient social identity, athletes will engage in *social labouring*, whereby they work *harder* than they would as individuals. This capacity for shared social identity to fuel improved performance was also confirmed in a more recent study by Matthew Slater and colleagues, which examined performance in a soccer tournament – UEFA Euro 2016 (Slater, Haslam, & Steffens, 2018). These authors explored the relationship between the passion shown by team members during the singing of national anthems (which the researchers took to be a proxy for social identification) and team performance in the tournament's 51 games. Results showed that the teams whose members sang their national anthems with greater passion (as rated by independent judges) went on to concede fewer goals. Furthermore, the impact of this pattern was more marked in the knockout stages of the competition, where greater enthusiasm was associated with a greater likelihood of victory.

In this way it appears that sharing a passion for us is a good platform from which to deliver for us. Once more, though, it is clear that group leaders have an important role to play in this process. This point is confirmed by the experimental research of Fransen and colleagues (Fransen, Haslam et al., 2015; Fransen, Steffens et al., 2016) which explored the ways in which leaders' identity entrepreneurship impacts on team performance. In these studies teams took part in either basketball or soccer practice and were exposed to a leader (an experienced player who was in fact a confederate of the experimenters) who was either positive about the team and its efforts (e.g., commenting enthusiastically 'Great play, team! Keep it up and we will win this contest easily!') or negative ('Your level of performance is really poor... this is hopeless'). In both studies leaders who were more positive about the team cultivated a stronger sense of team identification among players and this in turn led to significantly better performance on critical trials that involved taking free throws or dribbling a football through a series of cones and then shooting into a small goal. Moreover, in the second of these studies, Fransen, Steffens and colleagues (2016) showed that these effects were mediated by *identity leadership*, such that the positive leaders led their teams to perform better in part because they were judged by those team members to be doing a better job of creating, representing, advancing and embedding a shared sense of us (e.g., as assessed by items such as 'Our captain acts as a champion for our team', and 'Our captain creates a sense of cohesion within our team'; Steffens, Haslam, Reicher et al., 2014).

Yet in the cut and thrust of actual sporting performance it is clearly the case that the group dynamics at play are often much more complex than this. In particular, high team identification can lead to *over*-confidence, which compromises performance (Haslam et al., 2006). It can also create pressure to perform in which the fear of living up (or rather down) to negative ingroup stereotypes interferes with the flow that is required to perform at one's best (see Chapter 7).

Moreover, criticism of the ingroup can itself be borne out of a high level of social identification, and an associated desire to eradicate its faults (Packer, 2008). At the same time, though, research by Packer (2014) shows that those who identify highly with a group are inclined to voice criticism in private rather than public in ways that allow its constructive potential to be maximised. Thus, while Alex Ferguson was famous for giving players 'the hairdryer treatment' in the Manchester United dressing room (Lovett, 2017), the effect of this on the team – and its subsequent performance – was very different from that of the dressing downs delivered by José Mourinho to his team in acrimonious press conferences (Westbury, 2018).

The general point here, then, is that those things which promote a sense of shared identification among performers tend to have positive impact on their performance, but that this effect is also moderated by the nature of the group in question and the correspondence between the content of its identity and the task and context at hand. Apart from anything else, this means that there will be sporting and exercise contexts in which shared social identity leads performers to not perform at all. On the one hand, this can be because athletes themselves (or their governing bodies) choose not to perform, as was the case with rugby union and cricket teams who refused to tour South Africa under Apartheid in the 1970s and 1980s (Booth, 2003, 2012). On the other hand, it can be because other groups prevent them from participating. This was the case with the first ever sporting boycott – where the men of Sparta were barred from the 420BC Olympic Games because they had broken the Olympic truce (Goldsmith, 1995). Not forgetting,

Ingrid Curcurru

of course, that prior to the 20th century, all women (and members of many other groups besides) were barred from participating in professional sport, until such time as they had banded together to assert their right to be more than mere spectators (Cahn, 1994).

Figure 2.3   Demonstrators protest against the Springboks tour of England in 1969

Source: PA Images

All these examples serve to reinforce the point that social identity and performance are inextricably linked in so far as most (if not all) sporting and physical activity is predicated on the sense of 'us' (e.g., 'us runners', 'us United fans'), which makes it both meaningful and possible. For this reason, we can see that the operative word in Queen's crowd-pleasing anthem to victory is 'we'. After all, so far as we are aware, there is no song 'I am the champion', and, if there were, it is unlikely anyone would sing it with the same passion as Freddy Mercury.

3. Psychological and physical health

> Sport is a preserver of health. (Hippocrates, cited in Watt, 2003, p. 3)

One of the main justifications for participating in sport and exercise is that, as Hippocrates noted, it is good for your health. As justifications go, this is a pretty good one as there is plenty of solid evidence to support this claim. For example, in a meta-analysis of 148 studies involving over 300,000 participants, Julianne Holt-Lunstad and colleagues found that greater levels of physical activity were a reliable predictor of reduced risk of mortality, such that people who are more physically active are 1.22 times more likely to survive than people who are less physically active (Holt-Lunstad, Smith, & Layton, 2010). This suggests that one important reason why social identity can be a basis for health is that, as we have seen, it is a basis for increased participation in sport and exercise (see also Chapter 10). Indeed, consistent with this point, in a study of nearly 2,000 people recruited from GP surgeries in Scotland, Fabio Sani and colleagues found that the more groups of which people were highly identified members, the more likely they were to engage in healthy behaviour, including (a) smoking less, (b) eating more fruit and vegetables, and (c) taking regular exercise (Sani, Madhok, Norbury, Dugard, & Wakefield, 2015).

There is, however, a more direct way in which social identity impacts on health, and this is by providing a basis for a sense of *social connection*. In this regard, we noted above that the depersonalisation process through which people come to define themselves in terms of social identity is a basis for such connection. As spelled out by SCT, a key reason for this is that shared social identity transforms people who, as individuals, are *apart from the self* (i.e., 'others') into people who, as group members, are *a part of the self* (Turner et al., 1987).

By way of illustration, as individuals, people travelling on the London Underground generally have no sense of connection to each other and, as a result, are inclined to treat each other as strangers – with indifference and disregard. However, if circumstances lead them to see themselves as sharing social identity, then they will see themselves as having much more in common and their psychological orientation to each other will become much more positive (Drury, Cocking, & Reicher, 2009; Novelli, Drury, Reicher, & Stott, 2013). More prosaically, a range of controlled experimental studies – including those that involve minimal groups – show that manipulations which make salient a social identity that is shared with another person (e.g., as Australians, team members, or Klee-likers) serve to make that person appear more similar to the perceiver (Haslam et al., 1995).

Furthermore, as well as changing abstract perceptions of similarity and connectedness, developing a sense of shared social identity also changes our openness and receptivity to others. Not only do we understand others to be more yoked to us when we see them as ingroup members, but once we relate to them in this way, we also embrace them much more enthusiastically. This even extends to the way we react to their body odour, with research by Reicher and colleagues showing that after handling a sweaty football shirt, students run away to wash their hands much more quickly when it is the shirt of a rival university team rather than that of an ingroup (Reicher, Templeton, Neville, Ferrari, & Drury, 2016).

One key reason why social identity (and social identification) tend to have positive implications for health is thus that it serves to counteract – and indeed is inherently antithetical to – a sense of psychological isolation (Cruwys, Haslam, Dingle, Haslam, & Jetten, 2014). But does this really matter? Most people think not. Certainly, when asked, most members of the general public regard the health consequences of social isolation to be far less serious than those associated with such things as poor diet, smoking and lack of exercise (for evidence, see Haslam, McMahon et al., 2018). But they are not. Indeed, the meta-analysis by Holt-Lunstad and colleagues (2010) that we alluded to earlier shows social integration to be a *stronger* predictor of reduced mortality risk than all other health-related behaviours, such that people who are socially connected to others are 1.64 times more likely to survive than those who are not.

In health terms, then, the principal value of sport and exercise may lie in the fact that the social identities they promote (e.g., as member of a football club or a gym) provide a basis for feeling connected to others in ways that stave off the devastating effects of social isolation and loneliness. Indeed, speaking to this point, Catherine Haslam and colleagues cite evidence from researchers at La Trobe University's Centre for Sport and Social Impact which estimated that for every $1 invested in running an Australian rules football club, there is at least a $4.40 return in social value in terms of increased social connectedness, well-being and mental health status (Haslam, Jetten, Cruwys, Dingle, & Haslam, 2018). By way of comparison, the authors note that the return on a $1 investment in Type 2 diabetes reduction is around $1.55 (Luce, Mauskopf, Sloan, Ostermann, & Paramore, 2006).

In line with this logic, research by Tegan Cruwys and colleagues has shown that interventions which seek to address problems associated with social isolation by connecting vulnerable adults to social and sporting groups in the community have a very positive impact on participants' mental health, *provided that* those groups are a basis for social identification (Cruwys, Haslam, Dingle, Jetten et al., 2014). This insight has also been the basis for a successful intervention – GROUPS 4 HEALTH – which successfully tackles social isolation by building meaningful social identities among participants, often by helping them to join groups that centre on sporting and exercise activity (Haslam, Cruwys, Haslam, Dingle, & Chan, 2016; Haslam, Cruwys et al., 2019).

Significantly too, social identities of the form built by these interventions achieve their effects in large part by constructing participants' social and psychological *resources*. In particular, in line with the theoretical logic that we spelled out above, shared social identity is a basis for people (a) to give *support* to others and to receive it in return (Haslam, Reicher, & Levine, 2012), (b) to achieve a sense of personal *control* (Greenaway, Haslam et al., 2015), and (c) to gain a sense of *self-efficacy* and *agency* (Reicher & Haslam, 2006). As we will see in later chapters in this book, the field of sport and exercise proves to be particularly fertile when it comes to demonstrating these relationships – in part, because the social identities at play here are often exceptionally strong (see Chapters 6, 14 and 15).

Consistent with this idea of social identity as a resource, evidence from a large number of studies also supports the argument that the more social identities a person has access to (i.e., the more group memberships they have internalised as part of their self), the better their cognitive, mental and physical health. This is seen, for example, in studies which show that tobogganists recover quicker from physical exertion (Jones & Jetten, 2011) and that golfers are more inclined to persevere in the face of failure (Green, Rees, Peters, Sarkar, & Haslam, 2018) the more they are induced to reflect on having a lot of (rather that only a few) social identities.

At the same time, though, it is also the case that social identity can be a basis for behaviour that is *harmful* for health. In particular, as we have seen, it can be a basis for excluding those who are perceived to be 'outsiders' from participating in sport (e.g., on grounds of gender, class or race). Identification with groups that have or develop toxic norms can also clearly be detrimental both for members of those groups (as seen in examples of drug-taking among cyclists and body builders; Monaghan, Bloor, Dobash, & Dobash, 2000; Chapter 20) and for members of other groups (e.g., supporters of rival football teams; see Chapter 18).

Yet despite these important counter-examples, evidence suggests that shared social identity generally has positive implications for health (Haslam, Jetten et al., 2018). The key reasons for this are that social identities which centre on sport and exercise not only encourage us to do things which keep us fit; they also encourage us to do those things *together with like-minded others*. In this, they are one of the principal sites for the delivery of *social cures* in which the pathway to health is as much social psychological as physiological (Haslam, Jetten et al., 2018; Jetten, Haslam, & Haslam, 2012). Indeed, the truth of Hippocrates' 2,000-year-old dictum can be seen to result precisely from the fact that it is the perfect instantiation of *both* these pathways.

4. Partisanship

> By the Olympic oath I ask for only one thing: loyalty to sport. (Pierre de Coubertin, cited in Killanin & Rodda, 1976, p. 140)

As the oath that he fashioned attests, de Coubertin's aspiration was for the Olympic Games to be an event in which competitors cast aside loyalties to their nation and instead embraced ideals focused on the celebration of athletic excellence – ideals associated with the growth of the 19th-century international sport movement that he championed (Weiler, 2004). Yet while these ideals have continued to be an important focus for Olympic ideology and discourse, it is clear that the success of the Games owes at least as much to their status as a venue for pursuing deep-seated rivalries and even hatreds. This was seen, for example, in 'grudge matches' between the Soviet Union and the USA in the basketball final at the 1972 Munich Games and in the ice hockey final at the 1980 Winter Olympics in Lake Placid. Indeed, as Buckel observes, a general feature of the Games is that 'despite de Coubertin's efforts, politicians view sport and the Olympics as a means of reinforcing national identity and spectators experience a "vicarious identification" with the triumph of a national team' (2008, p. 98).

True, except often there is nothing vicarious about it. Certainly, home crowds will sometimes 'adopt' an athlete or team from another nation to support. However, even here their choice is rarely random, and instead affections often alight on those who have the prospect of beating a rival outgroup (in the same way that Spurs fans often attest to supporting two teams: Spurs and whoever is playing Arsenal). Moreover, the home crowd's primary loyalties will almost always be shown most enthusiastically for those who present their ingroup in the most positive light: Cathy Freeman in the 400 metres at the 2000 Sydney Games, Du Li in the 50 metres rifle shooting at the 2008 Beijing Games, and Mo Farah in the 5000 metres at the 2012 London Games.

The common truth to which these examples speak is that sport is an intensely *partisan* pursuit (see Chapters 17 and 18). This point is brought home forcefully in Albert Hastorf and Hadley Cantril's (1954) classic paper 'They Saw a Game'. This reported on the aftermath of the 1951 end-of-season American football game between Dartmouth and Princeton. The two teams were historic rivals who up to that point had both won all their games – meaning that the match was a title-decider. The first point to note is that, as a result of the significance of this intergroup contest, the match itself was fiercely competitive, exactly as SIT would predict (Heere & James, 2007). Emblematic of this ferocity, the nose of one Princeton player was broken as well as the leg of one Dartmouth player.

After the match, though, the researchers were interested to explore the perceptions of commentators and spectators who had witnessed the violence that came to define the match. What Hastorf and Cantril observed was that these perceptions suggested that the Dartmouth and Princeton spectators had watched two very different games. On the one hand, the *Daily Princetonian* reported that 'Both teams were guilty but the blame must be laid primarily on Dartmouth's doorstep. Princeton, obviously the better team, had no reason to rough up Dartmouth.' The *Dartmouth*, on the other hand, reported that 'The game was rough and did get a bit out of hand in the third quarter. Yet most of the roughing penalties were called against Princeton' (1954, pp. 129–130). Moreover, when spectators were asked how many infractions the two sides had committed, Dartmouth observers reported having seen an average of 4.3 against their team and 4.4 against Princeton, but Princeton students recalled seeing 9.8 against their side and only 4.2 against Dartmouth. On this basis the researchers concluded:

> The data here indicate that there is no such 'thing' as a 'game' existing 'out there' in its own right which people merely 'observe'. The 'game' 'exists' for a person and is experienced by him only in so far as certain happenings have significances in terms of his purpose. (Hastorf & Cantril, 1954, pp. 129–130)

The key point to add is that, as we have noted, this purpose was not *personal* in the sense of being unique to each spectator, but rather was structured by their highly salient social identities and a high degree of identification with their own team.

As an extension to this point, it is apparent that sports supporters are acutely sensitised to the implications of particular events for their collective self-esteem, and, as a result, feel the effects of loss and derogation at the hands of identity-relevant outgroups particularly keenly. In this vein, Branscombe and Wann (1994) showed that Americans' collective self-esteem was particularly diminished when they were shown an ingroup being defeated at the hands of an identity-relevant outgroup (the American boxer Rocky losing to the Russian boxer, Ivan Drago, in a mocked-up scene based on the film *Rocky IV*). This is one reason, for example, why Viner's (2014) account of his experiences as an Everton supporter dwells in detail on the agony of their 3–1 loss to

Liverpool in the 1986 FA Cup final (where he notes that he might have called his memoirs *Bloody Liverpool Ruined My Life*; 2014, p. 7). At the same time, though, these effects are felt even more keenly to the extent that perceivers identify strongly with the ingroup in question.

These dynamics also have deep emotional resonances (see Chapter 9; Campo, Mackie, & Sanchez, 2019). Thus, in a study of supporters of an amateur football club (Northfield Town), Richard Crisp and colleagues found that, after their team had lost a game, low identifiers tended to feel sad more than angry, while high identifiers tended to feel angry more than sad (Crisp, Heuston, Farr, & Turner, 2007). Low identifiers' sadness also fuelled avoidant action tendencies (notably, avoidance and disidentification), while high identifiers' anger also fed into approach action tendencies (notably, a desire for revenge). Beyond this, research by Clifford Stott and others (see Chapter 18) also shows that, under specific circumstances, high identifiers' action tendencies can be a basis for extreme forms of intergroup violence (e.g., Stott, Hutchison, & Drury, 2001; Stott & Reicher, 1998).

Relatedly, third-party observers will often experience, and express, a particular sense of emotional satisfaction – in the form of *schadenfreude* – when they see high-status identity-relevant outgroups lose. This point emerges from a series of studies by Colin Leach and colleagues which examined the reactions of Dutch participants to losses by the German and Italian football teams (Leach, Spears, Branscombe, & Doosje, 2003). Among other things, in ways predicted by SIT, these Dutch participants were more likely to display *schadenfreude* when status relations between groups were perceived to be illegitimate, as here, laughing at the misery of others appeared more justified and perceivers were also more motivated to challenge the status hierarchy.

In this regard, too, it is notable that even though de Coubertin's motivations in shaping the Olympic movement are generally understood to be noble, they were motivated in no small part by a desire to 'get one over' those who championed other forms of sporting activity and event. In particular, although early in his life he had been something of an Anglophile (see Mandell, 2000), he ultimately strove to differentiate the Olympic movement and its internationalist and enlightenment values from those that he associated with sport as it was practised in the British Empire. Thus the well-known quotation at the start of this section actually concludes with de Coubertin reflecting that 'it is the sportsman's spirit that interests me and not respect of that ridiculous English concept that allows only lone millionaires to dedicate themselves to sport without being tied to an out-of-date dogma' (Killanin & Rodda, 1976, p. 140).

Ironically, then, we find evidence of identity-based partisanship in sport even in the aspiration to be non-partisan. Indeed, as Persson and Petersson (2014, p. 197) note, we see that 'although Coubertin insisted that the Olympic Games must stand above politics (e.g., when he argued against a boycott of the 1936 Olympics in Berlin), the Olympic myth is rooted in a very political vision of the world.' This brings us neatly to the last of the '5 Ps' to which the social identity approach brings traction.

5. Politics

Sport is politics through other means. (Goldberg, 2000, p. 63)

It is commonplace for commentators, especially politicians, to opine that politics has no place in sport. This, for example, was the view expressed by Dennis Thatcher in raising objections to the anti-Apartheid boycotts of South Africa that we mentioned earlier. 'We are', he suggested in 1980, 'a free people, … and we have the right to play where we like' (cited in Hain, 1982, p. 232). Interestingly, though, his wife, the Prime Minister Margaret Thatcher, had no such qualms when, only a few months later, she urged British and Commonwealth athletes to boycott the Olympic Games in Moscow. At that point she proclaimed that 'for British athletes to take part in the games in Moscow this summer would be for them to seem to condone an international crime' (Hain, 1982, p. 232). As evidence of similar contradictions, 34 years later, in seeking to stave off the threat of another boycott, this time of the Sochi Winter Olympic Games, the Russian President Vladimir Putin argued that 'politics has no place in sport', while elsewhere making it clear that he saw the success of the Games as an intensely political project that would showcase the strength of the modern Russian state to the world (Persson & Petersson, 2014).

These illustrations serve to underline three important points. The first is that what makes sport political is precisely its capacity to be a vehicle for the mobilisation of group-based power in ways envisaged by SIT. In this respect, Putin follows a long line of national leaders who have recognised the capacity for sport – and, in particular, the Olympic Games – not only to galvanise, enact and project national identity, but also to give life to a particular vision of the *content* of that identity. The most chilling illustration is provided by the Berlin Games of 1936. On the one hand, these were an instantiation of Goebbels' idea that 'German sport has only one task: to strengthen the character of the German people, imbuing it with the fighting spirit and steadfast camaraderie necessary in the struggle for its existence' (cited in Rippon, 2006, p. 17). On the other hand, they were envisioned as a global marketing exercise for the Nazi project, intended to bear testimony to the toughness of the German Volk and the vaunted superiority of Ayrian ideals of racial purity. Indeed, in line with these ambitions, the programme of events was designed to culminate in a crescendo of 'emotional-patriotic impact' (Mandell, 2000, p. 199). At the same time, though, it needs to be recognised that, as identity festivals, sporting events such as the Olympics need not assume this sinister form. The 2000 Games in Sydney, for example, were marketed as 'the friendly games' (Platow, Nolan, & Anderson, 2003), and designed to culminate in a symbolic show of reconciliation by giving rein to the athletic talents of the Aboriginal runner, Cathy Freeman (Hassan, 2018) – although, as Magdalinski (2000) observes, because it failed to speak to the deep-seated concerns of indigenous communities, this reinvention of Australian identity was not unproblematic.

The second point is that precisely because political mobilisation is often a threat to the status quo (in ways predicted by SIT), it is routinely resisted by the groups that it threatens at the same time that it is embraced by those it empowers. Conservatives and progressives, for example, have very different views about American football players' decision to kneel during the national anthem (Dhital, 2019).

The third point is that where it serves as a vehicle for social identity-based mobilisation, sport can be a powerful vehicle for *social change* – again, in very much the way that SIT anticipates (Tajfel & Turner, 1979). Again, though, this can be either regressive or progressive. Thus, on the one hand, it is clear that the 1936 Olympics were an important catalyst for the emergence of a Nazi state – not least in demonstrating the National Socialists' ability to orchestrate and stage immense shows of power, something their critics had previously questioned (Mandell, 2000). Yet, on the other hand, as Nelson Mandela recognised, sport proved to be critical to the reshaping of South Africa in the post-Apartheid era (Mandela, 1994). Not only did this result from the power of the sporting boycotts that we have already discussed, but, more importantly perhaps, it arose from Mandela's own skills as an identity entrepreneur who used sport as a vehicle for uniting blacks and whites around a new sense of common identity (see Chapter 20). Carlin (2008) provides a vivid account of the way in which these dynamics played out:

> During apartheid, the all-white Springboks and their fans had belted out racist fight songs, and blacks would come to Springbok matches to cheer for whatever team was playing against them. Yet Mandela believed that the Springboks could embody – and engage – the new South Africa. And the Springboks themselves embraced the scheme. Soon South African TV would carry images of the team singing 'Nkosi Sikelel' iAfrika,' the long-time anthem of black resistance to apartheid. … South Africans of every color and political stripe found themselves falling for the team. (Cited in Haslam et al., 2011, p. 89)

Thus, as Goldberg (2000, p. 69) notes, 'although sports historically have been used to demonstrate the superiority of one system (or people) over another, [they can equally be] an avenue to demonstrate similarities and bring societies (and people) closer together, preparing the way for eventual public policy changes' (see also Hassan, 2018). The success of the British Football Association's anti-racism programme 'Kick it out' is a case in point, and Levermore (2008) identifies a range of similar programmes that have been at the forefront of efforts to improve public health (e.g., AIDS reduction) and human rights (e.g., the elimination of child labour) around the world.

It is fair to say that, to date, these large-scale social dynamics have been a relatively marginal concern for social identity researchers working in the field of sport and exercise. Nevertheless, we would argue that a particular strength of the social identity approach is its capacity to specify and explain links between micro-psychological processes and macro-social phenomena of this form. Indeed, it was appreciation of these links – and a concern that they were tellingly absent from mainstream psychological theorising – that drove Tajfel and Turner to develop SIT in the first place (see Brown, 2019; Haslam, Reicher, & Reynolds, 2012; Reicher, Haslam, Spears, & Reynolds, 2012). Accordingly, there would appear to be a strong case for using the approach to reinvigorate our appreciation not only of the fact that sport has a political dimension (e.g., in mobilising some social identities rather than others), but also of the specific ways in which this is true.

CONCLUSION

In this chapter we have tried to clarify the broad relevance of social identity and self-categorization processes for key dimensions of the psychology of sport and exercise. Our core argument has been that because sport and exercise are inherently social (i.e., group-based) activities, we need a psychological analysis that engages with and helps to understand its distinctly social features. In particular, we need an analysis that does justice to the fact that because the groups at the heart of sport and exercise – the teams we join, the clubs we support, the activities we pursue – are always more than simply the sum of their individual parts, so too is their psychology. In short, we need a psychology of *we-ness*, not just I-ness.

More specifically, through our exploration of key facets of sporting life about which the social identity approach has particularly distinctive things to say (i.e., the 5Ps), we have seen that social identity research provides support for five central hypotheses:

> H1. Participation in sport and exercise is grounded in social identification with relevant groups (*the participation hypothesis*).

> H2. Sport and exercise performance is shaped by social identification with relevant groups and the norms, values, affordances and goals associated with salient social identities (*the performance hypothesis*).

> H3. Health and well-being are enhanced by identification with groups that have health-enhancing features (*the health hypothesis*).

> H4. People's engagement with, and partisan orientation to, the different groups they encounter in sport and exercise contexts is structured by relevant social identities and associated levels of social identification (*the partisanship hypothesis*).

> H5. Examination of social identity dynamics in sporting contexts provides a basis for understanding and engaging with their inherently *political* nature (*the politics hypothesis*).

Beyond this, though, in the process of exploring these hypotheses we have also shown that there is broad support for three overarching principles:

> P1, P2. Social identities and social identification – and hence the sport and exercise-related behaviours they give rise to – are heavily structured by both (a) social context (*the context principle*) and (b) social influence and, most especially, leadership (*the influence principle*).

P3. Sporting and exercise contexts give rise to emergent forms of social identity that make sport and exercise both captivating and transformational (*the emergence principle*).

Together, these hypotheses and principles speak to collective dimensions of sporting life that other more individualistic approaches tend to overlook or neglect. Among other things, in this they speak to the capacity for a team of champions to be an altogether different entity from a champion team, and – to return to the quote from Bill Shankly with which we started – for a recreational weekend pursuit to assume an importance greater than life and death.

A fundamental point which emerges from all these examples is that the key things that sport and exercise have to offer *psychologically* – the thrills, the agonies, the exhilarations and the torments – are not experienced by everyone. Instead, as writers like Hornby (1992) and Viner (2014) make clear (typically with awareness of the potential for wry humour), they are accessible only to *insiders*. Above all else, then, to explain this fact we need a psychology that gets to grips with the means by which the groups we encounter in the world of sport and exercise *get under our skin* and become internalised into our sense of self. This is what the social identity approach provides. In the process, it shows not only how sport becomes powerful through social identity, but also how social identity becomes powerful through sport. Indeed, it is by virtue of its unique capacity to shed light upon both aspects of this dynamic that sport emerges as a particularly exciting domain in which to explore and expand upon the core tenets of the social identity approach.

Moreover, as we have attempted to show, the research that this body of theorising stimulates seeks to account not only for the mundane facts of sporting participation and the like, but also for the truly transformative feats that sportswomen and men are capable of. This we would argue is what, to date, the field of sport and exercise psychology has lacked, but what it needs in order to do justice to the inspirational nature of its core subject matter. Bill Shankly, Eddy Merckx and Serena Williams would demand no less. Neither would your sporting heroes.

SECTION 2
PERFORMANCE

3
LEADERSHIP

NIKLAS K. STEFFENS
KATRIEN FRANSEN
S. ALEXANDER HASLAM

In each case we see the weekly self-sacrifice of players who are willing to go beyond the point where their bodies are telling them to stop because their leaders – Klopp and Guardiola – have persuaded them to do it, for their own benefit, and in the service of a grand design for which history will remember them. (Hayward, 2019)

In the 2019 *Daily Telegraph* article from which the above quotation was taken, the sports journalist Paul Hayward focused on the outstanding leadership of two of football's most enigmatic managers – Pep Guardiola of Manchester City and Jürgen Klopp of Liverpool. In particular, he focused on the impact that the two managers had on their players – regularly motivating them to play well beyond what they thought their capabilities would allow them to do. Subsequent events proved this analysis right, with both teams going on to write sporting history. Guardiola's team won the English Premier League for the second consecutive year while performing a unique Treble in also winning both the FA Cup and the Carabao Cup. At the same time, while duelling with Manchester City for the league title, Klopp's Liverpool went on to win the UEFA (European) Champions League.

As Hayward observes, the two managers' ability to bring out the best in their players had little to do either with their greatness as individuals or with the unique capabilities of their players. Instead, it was a consequence of these managers' ability to *transform* players' understanding of themselves and their relationship to others so that they realised their actions were contributing to something bigger than themselves – the team – which would be a vehicle for them to achieve something truly exceptional. In other words, extraordinary achievement became possible because the players were encouraged to see the team's interest as their own interest because *the team had been internalised as part of their sense of self*.

Yet while key insights offered by such an analysis might seem plausible, it is notable that these are not commonly articulated within contemporary approaches to leadership. In large part this is because these approaches fail to provide a detailed theoretical analysis of the psychology of the self – or, more particularly, of the ways in which this can be a basis for leadership and social influence as well as group behaviour more generally. As we saw in Chapter 2, these considerations lie at the heart of a social identity approach to leadership. In light of the fact that leadership is widely defined as a leader's ability to motivate group members in ways that encourage them to contribute to shared goals (House, Javidan, & Dorfman, 2001), it is perhaps also surprising that few approaches have sought to understand leadership as a group process itself, or to theorise about its collective underpinnings. One of the key insights of the social identity approach is that leadership is a group process which revolves around the psychology of leaders – and followers – *as group members*.

This chapter starts with a review of influential contemporary approaches to leadership in sport and exercise contexts, focusing on work which has explored processes of transformational leadership, need-supportive leadership and shared leadership. After this, we outline the core tenets of a social identity approach to leadership before identifying key points that emerge from this approach and which contribute to our appreciation of the ways in which leaders are able to channel team members' efforts in pursuit of collective goals. These points all centre on the idea that the creation and mobilisation of a sense of shared social identity is foundational to leaders' efforts to inspire and direct the teams they lead. While this analysis helps us to understand the remarkable achievements of leaders like Guardiola and Klopp, it also has broader relevance to the very wide range of sports and exercise achievements for which leadership is essential.

CURRENT APPROACHES TO LEADERSHIP

Transformational leadership

Like many other approaches to the study and practice of leadership, the notion of *transformational leadership* has its origins in organisational research. Indeed, in light of similarities between sporting activity and key aspects of organisational life (e.g., teamwork; Day, Gordon, & Fink, 2012; and see Chapter 5), organisational insights have been increasingly applied to sport and exercise contexts. In the case of transformational leadership, this construct was originally developed to explain how leaders are able to motivate others so that they perform beyond expectations (Bass, 1985). In developing answers to this question, researchers argued that transformational leaders excel in four key domains (the four Is; Bass & Riggio, 2006; see Figure 3.1). First, they show *inspirational motivation*, in part by defining a desirable mission (e.g., winning the Champions League in Klopp's case). Second, they exert *idealised influence* by modelling desirable behaviour (e.g., high levels of enthusiasm for the team). Third, they provide followers with *intellectual stimulation* (e.g., engaging them in team plans and strategy). Finally, they show *individual consideration* (e.g., by being sensitive to the needs of different players).

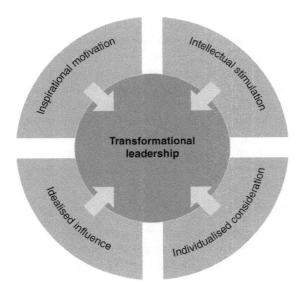

Figure 3.1   The four Is of transformational leadership

Transformational leadership has become an influential theory in the realm of sport and exercise, where it is used to explain the success of a range of leaders whether they be managers, coaches, captains or rank-and-file athletes (Price & Weiss, 2013). In this vein, there is an abundance of research which shows that sport groups and teams function better to the extent that their leaders are perceived to display transformational leadership behaviours (for reviews, see Arthur, Bastardoz, & Eklund, 2017; Hoption, Phelan, & Barling, 2007; Turnnidge, & Côté, 2018). For instance, research shows that when athletes perceive their leaders to be transformational (i.e., to display the four Is described in Figure 3.1), this perception is associated with more favourable outcomes, including greater athlete motivation (e.g., Arthur, Woodman, Ong, Hardy, & Ntoumanis, 2011), improved athlete well-being (e.g., Stenling & Tafvelin, 2014), stronger team cohesion (e.g., Smith, Arthur, Hardy, Callow, & Williams, 2013), and better team performance (e.g., Charbonneau, Barling, & Kelloway, 2001).

One reason why this theory has been so influential is that several standardised questionnaires have been developed to assess leaders' transformational impact (e.g., the Multifactor Leadership Questionnaire and the Differentiated Transformational Leadership Inventory). These are easy to administer in cross-sectional and longitudinal studies, with the aim of assessing the power of perceived transformational leadership to predict specific outcome variables. However, as van Knippenberg and Sitkin (2013) point out, this theoretical framework has some significant conceptual shortcomings which limit its capacity to explain how leadership really works. One key problem is that by assessing transformational behaviours (i.e., behaviours that are perceived to be inspirational and foster positive outcomes) and then using these behaviours as 'input' to explain positive leadership outcomes, the approach confuses the *explanandum* (the thing that needs to be explained) with the *explanans* (the thing that does the explaining). In short, these problems of circularity flow from the fact that researchers typically assess the same thing (the transformational nature of leaders) twice – first as input and then as output. Indeed, by only assessing *perceptions* of transformational leadership behaviour, we learn relatively little about what precisely it is that allows leaders to *be* transformational. For this reason, the challenge of explaining the impact of those various behaviours and processes that serve as the basis of leaders' ability to inspire greater motivation and performance in followers remains largely unresolved.

Need-supportive leadership

Another approach that has gained considerable traction in sport and exercise contexts is *need-supportive leadership* (Amorose & Anderson-Butcher, 2007; Mageau & Vallerand, 2003). In contrast to work on transformational leadership (which did not derive from a coherent existing theoretical framework), need-supportive leadership was developed largely by building on the extensive and coherent body of psychological theorising spelled out in *self-determination theory* (SDT; Deci & Ryan, 1985; see Chapters 6 and 19). Nevertheless, despite differences in their origins, there are some important parallels between transformational and need-supportive leadership. In particular, both theories focus on the importance of leaders being responsive to others' needs (either by showing individual consideration or by displaying various other behaviours that satisfy potential followers' needs). However, need-supportive leadership provides a more fine-grained theoretical specification of what these needs are, of how they can be satisfied, and of the motivational consequences that flow from their satisfaction.

Specifically, based on SDT's proposition that humans have three fundamental needs for *autonomy*, *competence* and *relatedness*, this need-supportive approach argues that leaders (e.g., coaches) are more likely to be able to motivate others to the extent that they engage in behaviour that fulfils these needs for the individuals they are seeking to lead (e.g., members of a given team). Scholars have argued that these need-supportive behaviours can take a range of forms. For example, autonomy-supportive leadership might involve providing team members with choices within given limits while also avoiding controlling behaviours or those that focus on material reward; competence-supportive leadership might involve giving opportunities for team members to show initiative and providing a rationale for various activities as well as supportive feedback; and relatedness-supportive leadership might involve acknowledging team members' feelings and giving them opportunities to socialise (e.g., Mageau, & Vallerand, 2003). SDT argues that by satisfying the needs of others, these behaviours enhance those others' intrinsic motivation and subsequent goal-directed behaviour.

Consistent with SDT, empirical evidence shows that when sport and exercise leaders are perceived to have an interpersonal style that is characterised by need-supportive behaviours, this leads to range of positive outcomes. For example, athletes are found to be more (intrinsically) motivated (e.g., Jõesaar, Hein, & Hagger, 2012), to perform better (e.g., Gillet, Vallerand, Amoura, & Baldes, 2010), and to have improved well-being (e.g., Adie, Duda, & Ntoumanis, 2012). In this vein, it should be noted that formal leaders (e.g., coaches and captains) are not the only people who can satisfy others' needs in this way. Informal leaders within the team (i.e., rank-and-file players) can also satisfy their teammates' needs and, by doing so, succeed in improving their motivation, performance and well-being (Fransen, Boen, Vansteenkiste, Mertens, & Vande Broek, 2018; Mertens, Boen, Vande Broek, Vansteenkiste, & Fransen, 2018).

Yet despite the array of findings that support these ideas, SDT has a number of important limiting assumptions. As noted in Chapters 6 and 19, a key limitation arises from the conceptualisation of self that underlines this theorising. This reflects the fact that the theory limits itself to a fixed notion of the individual or personal self, whereas it is apparent that the self that is at the heart of self-determination changes as a function of social context (e.g., Doosje, Haslam, Spears, Oakes, & Koomen, 1998; Haslam & Turner, 1992). For example, Sarah, who is a caring mother at home, can turn into a die-hard fan when immersed in a football match and cheering for her favourite team (Arsenal, say) on the terraces. At home and when interacting with her children, Sarah may think, feel and behave in line with her social identity as a mother, but surrounded by fellow fans on the terraces she is more likely to think, feel and behave in line with her social identity as a supporter of Arsenal. So, while at home Sarah may be quite restrained, considerate and polite, on the terraces she may be much more outgoing, boisterous and rude (e.g., to the referee and players on the opposing team). Importantly, too, as the quote at the start of this chapter suggests, in many contexts, the self has the capacity to *expand* so that others are included within it. On the terraces, for example, Sarah's fellow fans may be included within her sense of self, so that she thinks of herself, and behaves, not as 'I, Sarah' and 'you, Mary' but as 'us Arsenal fans'.

Following on from these points, a related limitation of SDT is that it proposes that individuals have a specified set and level of needs and that when leaders act in ways that satisfy these needs, positive outcomes inevitably follow. However, as work informed by transformational leadership suggests (but does not fully explain), effective leaders often serve to *transform* the needs of followers. The success of Guardiola and Klopp, for example, arises not so much from the fact that they satisfied followers' needs, as from the fact that they created an appetite for an expanded set of needs. Moreover, again, these were needs that related not to players as individuals (e.g., 'what I, Mo Salah, need') but to players *as team members* ('what we, Liverpool, need'). In this way, then, we see that leaders are not constrained by a pre-existing set of psychological concerns and realities, but instead work *creatively* with others to develop new concerns and realities that centre on new, expansive forms of self and associated needs.

Shared leadership

Another approach that has recently been associated with an upsurge in interest in domains of sport and exercise (and others besides) is *shared leadership*. Like transformational leadership, this approach was originally developed to explain leadership in organisations (Pearce & Conger, 2003). In contrast to hierarchical approaches to leadership, which focus on the formal leader (e.g., the coach or captain), this approach argues that leadership is most effective when it is done not by one individual alone but instead is distributed or shared. In line with this idea, meta-analytic evidence from organisational contexts suggests that teams tend to be more effective both (a) when they have more leaders and (b) when they are *seen* by members to have more leaders (as typically assessed by social network analysis; D'Innocenzo, Mathieu, & Kukenberger, 2016; Wang, Waldman, & Zhang, 2014).

Providing some insight into the extent to which leadership is shared in sport and exercise contexts, research also shows that in the vast majority of (successful) sport teams, athletes typically perceive there to be not just one but multiple leaders (Fransen, Vanbeselaere, De Cuyper, Vande Broek, & Boen, 2014). Furthermore, research shows that across a range of sport contexts, teams that are understood to have shared forms of leadership (e.g., so that multiple athletes in the team are seen as leaders) are seen to function better and also perform better (for a review, see Cotterill & Fransen, 2016).

This approach makes several important contributions to our understanding of team functioning. In line with some of the points made in previous sections, one of its core insights is that leadership is not only performed by those who have roles as formal leaders and upon whom the gaze of analysts (e.g., pundits, fans) typically falls. Instead, this line of research makes it clear that leadership can be displayed by individuals who have no formal leadership role within a team, and that it can be displayed by more than one of them.

Again, though, despite these strengths, the approach has important theoretical shortcomings. One is that even though the approach argues that leadership should be distributed or shared, the core ideas of the theory do not specify what forms or aspects of leadership should be shared nor how much they should be shared (cf. Wang et al., 2014). For example, while it is acknowledged that there is considerable value in having what the Australian hockey coach Ric Charlesworth (2001) refers to as a *leaderful team*, it is clearly the case that this may sometimes be problematic (i.e., such that 'too many cooks spoil the broth'). What are the parameters here, and what is the process that makes the sharing of leadership effective? In answering these questions, it is clear that we need a more detailed theoretical specification both of *why* sharing leadership works more for some groups and teams than for others, and of the mechanisms that account for its impact on team functioning.

One body of theorising that can help to answer questions like these is provided by the social identity approach. Among other things, this addresses questions about when particular levels of shared leadership may be beneficial in teams and why shared forms of leadership are often associated with positive team outcomes. Beyond this, though, and perhaps more importantly, this approach tackles leadership from a very different perspective – one which sees sharedness as something that is foundational to *all* effective leadership. However, this is not primarily about sharedness of role, but instead about sharedness of identity. It is to this approach that we turn next.

A SOCIAL IDENTITY APPROACH TO LEADERSHIP

As discussed in Chapter 2, the social identity approach (SIA) integrates social identity theory (SIT; Tajfel & Turner, 1979) and self-categorization theory (SCT; Turner et al., 1987). A core tenet of both theories is that individuals can perceive themselves and others not only as unique individuals (as 'I' and 'you'; in terms of *personal identity*), but also in terms of shared group membership (as 'we' and 'us'; in terms of *social identity*; Turner, 1982). The SIA further argues that perceiving self and others in terms of shared group membership (e.g., 'us athletes', 'us members of Team X') has qualitatively distinct implications for a person's cognition, emotion and behaviour. Apart from anything else, this means that when individuals share social identity, the groups that define that identity are always more than simply the sum of their individual parts (Asch, 1952; Turner, 1982). Specifically, as we saw in Chapter 2, when people perceive themselves to share group membership with others, this perception then provides the platform for a range of psychological resources (e.g., social support, a sense of control and collective self-efficacy, a sense of meaning and purpose; Haslam, Jetten et al., 2018) and for energising behaviours that are aligned with the values, norms, ideals and goals of the group.

Building on these ideas, shared social identity can be seen to play a role in shaping several important attitudes and behaviours across a range of domains (e.g., social, organisational, and health-related; see Ellemers, 2012; Haslam, 2014; Haslam, Jetten et al., 2018). However, as summarised in previous reviews (e.g., Beauchamp, 2019; Bruner, Dunlop, & Beauchamp, 2014; Rees et al., 2015) and as this book as a whole attests, social identity is also implicated in a wide array of sport and exercise behaviours. Among other things, but of particular relevance to the present chapter, it has been argued to be a basis for processes of *mutual social influence* that are at the heart of leaders' ability to influence others to contribute to shared goals (Haslam et al., 2011; Steffens, Haslam, Reicher et al.,

2014; Turner, 1991; for reviews see Slater, Coffee, Barker, & Evans, 2014; Stevens et al., 2017). This idea is central to this chapter, and it is one that we unpack in more detail in the sections that follow.

Key point 1: Leadership is a group-based social influence process that revolves around a sense of shared social identity between leaders and followers

As outlined above, social identity – a sense of shared 'we-ness' with others – is important not only because it provides access to psychological and social resources, but also because it serves to energise collective behaviour. In particular, this sense of 'we-ness' is important because it directs individuals' behaviour towards particular values and goals (and not others) by underpinning shared beliefs about who 'we' are and where 'we' want to go. At a very basic level, this 'we-ness' is also a basis for mutual influence as people are more likely to see other members as a source of influence (Chrobot-Mason, Gerbasi, & Cullen-Lester, 2016; Fransen, Haslam, Steffens, & Boen, 2020) and to be mobilised to work in the group's interests when they see those others as embodying who and what 'we' are (Slater, Coffee, Barker, Haslam, & Steffens, 2019; see also Chapter 5). This is for the very basic reason that when we define ourselves in terms of particular social identity (e.g., as a member of Team X) we look to those who best embody that identity (e.g., the most *prototypical* members of Team X; Hogg, 2001; Turner & Haslam, 2001) to help us understand what being a member of this team means and entails.

Building on these ideas, the social identity approach argues that leadership is a group-based social influence process that revolves around the process of cultivating, representing and promoting a sense of 'we-ness' with others whose efforts one is seeking to galvanise and direct (Ellemers et al., 2004; Haslam et al., 2011; Hogg, 2001; Platow, Haslam, Reicher, & Steffens, 2015; Steffens, Haslam, Reicher et al., 2014; van Knippenberg, 2011). More specifically, researchers have argued that leaders' capacity to motivate others to work towards the goals of a collective (e.g., a team, a club, a sport discipline, a sport profession, an association) rests on their capacity to create, embody, advance and embed a shared sense of 'us' (Haslam et al., 2011; Steffens, Haslam, Reicher et al., 2014).

As shown in Figure 3.2, this theorising can be summarised in a four-component model of *identity leadership*. This asserts that, to be effective, leaders need:

1. to be *identity entrepreneurs* who create a sense of social shared identity (rather than divide the group) and also clarify what a given group is about and what it stands for (Reicher, Haslam, & Hopkins, 2005; Reicher & Hopkins, 2001).

2. to be *identity prototypes* such that they are seen by those they seek to influence as central (rather than marginal) to the group and as embodying the attributes that define what it means to be a member of the group (Hogg, 2001; Platow & van Knippenberg, 2001).

3. to be *ingroup champions* such that they are seen to promote the interests and goals of the group (rather than their personal interests or the interests of other groups; Haslam & Platow, 2001; van Knippenberg & van Knippenberg, 2005).

4. to be *identity impresarios* who devise structures, activities and events that allow group members to live out their sense of shared social identity (Haslam et al., 2011).

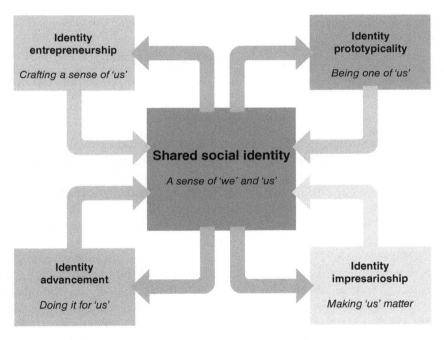

Figure 3.2 The four-component model of (social) identity leadership

One way in which we and others have set about testing the validity and usefulness of this model is by developing an instrument to assess its four components: the *Identity Leadership Inventory* (ILI; Steffens, Haslam, Reicher et al., 2014). This assesses the extent to which a given leader is seen by followers (e.g., other members of their team) to engage in each of these four dimensions of identity leadership. To give a sense of the ILI's content, the short form of this instrument is reproduced in Table 3.1.

Table 3.1 The short form of the Identity Leadership Inventory (ILI-SF)

Component	Item
Identity prototypicality (*'Being one of us'*)	This leader is a model member of [Group X].
Identity advancement (*'Doing it for us'*)	This leader acts as a champion for [Group X].
Identity entrepreneurship (*'Crafting a sense of us'*)	This leader creates a sense of cohesion within [Group X].
Identity impresarioship (*'Making us matter'*)	This leader creates structures that are useful for [Group X] members.

Note: The ILI assesses the four components of identity leadership discussed by Haslam et al. (2011). The long form of this instrument (which has 15 items) can be found at our website. It has been shown to have good psychometric properties and to be a good predictor of leadership outcomes (notably of followers' performance and well-being).

Source: Steffens, Haslam, Reicher et al. (2014). The ILI and ILI-SF are copyright © 2013 by N. K. Steffens, S. A. Haslam, and S. D. Reicher. All rights reserved. Subject to permission from one of the first two authors, the ILI is free to use in academic research and can also be used for commercial purposes for a small fee (which is used to support ongoing research).

Results from multiple studies in a range of organisational contexts show that the ILI has good construct and discriminant validity and that even though, as one might expect, the four components that it assesses are correlated, they are better treated as distinct elements. Furthermore, the inventory has been shown to have good criterion validity in so far as the extent to which a given leader is perceived to engage in identity leadership has predicted a number of important group outcomes – notably greater perceived team support, stronger team identification and higher job satisfaction.

Importantly too, the ILI's construct, discriminant and criterion validity has also been proven in the context of sport. Specifically, in a study of 421 members of a large number of basketball, football, volleyball and handball teams in Belgium, we and other colleagues showed that the perceived identity leadership of leaders was positively associated with team members' team identification, their team confidence and the team's task cohesion (with relevant correlations ranging from $r = .29$ to $r = .52$; Steffens, Haslam, Reicher et al., 2014, Study 4). More recently, the validity and utility of ILI has also been confirmed in a global project conducted by a large team of international researchers led by Rolf van Dick and Jérémy Lemoine (van Dick et al., 2018). This involved translating the ILI into 13 languages and then examining its psychometric properties and predictive power in 20 different countries across all six inhabited continents (all translated versions to date are freely accessible at: https://tinyurl.com/y2jtmkxt). Consistent with findings of previous studies, this provided evidence that the ILI has a high degree of construct validity across countries (with results showing that the underlying theoretical model is reliable and has good fit to the data), and that the four dimensions of identity leadership that it captures are unique and distinct from each other.

Importantly, van Dick and colleagues' study also went beyond previous research in providing evidence of the ILI's incremental criterion validity, showing that the extent to which leaders are perceived to engage in identity leadership is *uniquely* associated with a range of positive group outcomes (notably team identification, trust in the leader, job satisfaction, organisational citizenship and innovative behaviour) above and beyond the effects of transformational leadership, authentic leadership and leader–member exchange (which also serve to satisfy follower needs). Thus while, as noted above, there is some overlap in the operationalisation of the constructs at the core of different leadership theories, it is clear that there are unique benefits that arise from leaders' ability to create, represent and promote a shared sense of 'we' among those they seek to mobilise.

Key point 2: Identity leadership is a basis not only for improved individual and team functioning in sport but also for better health and well-being

While a large body of evidence speaks to the general validity and usefulness of the identity leadership model and the tools that assess it, an emerging body of theorising and evidence shows that identity leadership plays a foundational role in a range of specific sport-related outcomes. Not least, as intimated in Chapter 2, identity leadership is critically implicated in people's willingness to engage in sport and exercise activity in the first place. This is a point that Mark Stevens and colleagues (2018) make on the basis of a study that examined the contribution of identity leadership to the enthusiasm of 583 members of an array of different sport teams and exercise groups. As predicted, this found (a) that group members' perceptions of their leader's identity leadership were positively associated with those members' identification with the group in question and (b) that this identification was in turn associated with participants' greater participation in group activities (notably, their attendance at training or at classes). The finding that identity leadership played an important role in enhancing participation not only in team sport but also in exercise groups was particularly noteworthy. For in most exercise groups (whether these involved circuit training, strength and conditioning, or cycling), participants performed relevant tasks by and for themselves (not in or for a team). Nevertheless, group identity – and a leader's ability to represent and promote this – was still an important means of promoting engagement. Identity leadership, then, is beneficial not only for teams but also for individuals.

Providing further support for the claim that identity leadership is a basis for sport participation, Stevens and colleagues (2020) replicated and extended these findings in a longitudinal study with participants from an assortment of amateur sports teams. Results revealed that team leaders' identity leadership was associated with an increase in members' team identification and increased attendance (even when controlling for initial levels of identification and attendance). Further evidence of the role of identity leadership in fostering engagement in exercise groups comes from a prospective study of 255 members of various exercise groups conducted by Steffens, Slade, Stevens, Haslam, and

Rees (2019). Findings indicated that the perceived identity leadership of group exercise instructors was associated not only with higher attendance by exercisers at subsequent classes, but also with those exercisers' self-reported effort during those classes. As well as this, the results of the study showed that instructors' identity leadership enhanced members' identification with others in their class together with their perceived comfort in the exercise environment and that these two variables were both mediators of increased attendance and effort. In other words, instructors' identity leadership encouraged people to exercise in part because it made them feel more at home in the company of other exercisers and in the potentially off-putting spaces where they were exercising (where it is common to encounter strange noises, smells and people; e.g., Žitnik et al., 2016). Finally, identity leadership was found to predict exercise engagement above and beyond need satisfaction as specified within need-support models (even when controlling for exercisers' satisfaction of their need for autonomy and competence).

Yet in addition to contributing to motivation and performance outcomes and indirectly to health through physical participation in sport and exercise, identity leadership has also been shown to have a direct impact on individuals' health and subjective well-being (for reviews, see Haslam, Steffens, & Peters, 2019; Steffens & Haslam, 2017). In this regard, organisational research shows that when team leaders engage in identity entrepreneurship, this is associated with higher subsequent levels of vitality and engagement among team members as well as reduced burnout (Steffens, Haslam, Kerschreiter, Schuh, & van Dick, 2014; Steffens, Yang, Jetten, Haslam, & Lipponen, 2018). Recent research by Charlotte Edelmann and colleagues also shows that it is not only formal leaders who can provide this identity leadership, but also all other members of a given team. These rank-and-file members, then, have the capacity to nurture members' feelings of identification with the team in ways that promote not only team effectiveness but also well-being (in the form of enhanced work satisfaction and reduced burnout; Edelmann, Boen, & Fransen, 2020). Other research by the second author and colleagues provides further evidence of these same processes in sport contexts (Fransen, Haslam, Steffens, Mallett et al., 2020b). Here players in elite rugby teams were found to be healthier and have higher levels of well-being to the extent that other members of their team were perceived to be providing high-quality identity leadership that served to foster a sense of shared identity in the team.

The research reviewed above suggests that identity leadership makes a real difference to the functioning of teams and the individuals within them (Fransen, Haslam, Steffens, & Boen, 2020). But what can leaders actually *do* to build and strengthen (perceptions of) identity leadership? This is a question that a series of experimental studies led by the second author and colleagues have sought to address in recent years. In the first of these (Fransen, Haslam et al., 2015; see also Fransen, Steffens et al., 2016), participants (who were previously unknown to each other) formed small basketball groups of five players, one of whom was a male confederate. In all groups, the experimenter introduced the confederate as the team leader and underscored the legitimacy of this appointment by noting his older age, his exceptional skills and his superior knowledge of the game. This was done by ensuring the confederate was on average six years older than other players, by indicating he had more experience than them, and by giving him the answers to a basketball quiz that all participants had to complete, so that he appeared more knowledgeable than them. Following this, the teams engaged in what they were led to believe was a national shooting contest that involved their team trying to score as many free shots as possible (in a competition where each player had 10 free throws). The experimental manipulation then involved half of the teams having a leader (the confederate) who expressed high confidence in the team during the competition, and the other half of the teams having a leader who expressed low confidence in the team. Compared to participants who were exposed to a leader who expressed low team confidence, those exposed to a leader who expressed high team confidence not only had greater confidence in the collective ability of their team, but also actually performed better by scoring more free shots. Moreover, statistical analysis showed that the leader's expression of team confidence had this impact on team members in part because this led them to see him as showing more identity leadership. In other words, it was because the up-beat leader helped players feel part of 'us' that he helped them to go on and score more points.

However, expressing confidence in a team is only one of many things that leaders can do to cultivate and promote a sense of shared identity among that team's members. In a study of cyclist groups, Mark Stevens, Tim Rees, Nik Steffens and colleagues (2019) used a more direct manipulation of identity leadership that involved a confederate seeming either to be out for themselves (e.g., as signalled by references to 'I' and 'me') or to be in it for their team (e.g., as flagged by references to 'we and 'us'; after Platow, van Knippenberg, Haslam, van Knippenberg, & Spears, 2006; Steffens & Haslam, 2013). Following this, the researchers looked at how well the group members who were exposed to these different models of leadership performed on a time trial where they were asked to cycle as quickly as possible. As predicted, there were marked differences in the cyclists' objective behaviour as a function of the amount of identity leadership that the leader displayed. Specifically, during the first 60 seconds of the trial, participants who were led by someone who displayed high levels of identity leadership showed higher maximum heart rate variability (an indicator of effort) and higher power output (an indicator of performance) than those who were exposed to a leader who displayed low levels of identity leadership.

In sum, evidence from a growing number of studies across a wide range of contexts (spanning different sports, competition levels and countries) makes it clear that identity leadership has a key role to play in the achievement of key sport and exercise outcomes. In addition to cross-sectional studies, there is also experimental evidence that speaks to the importance of leaders' cultivation and promotion of a sense of 'we' and 'us' for the success of their leadership. The bottom line here is that great leadership is not about leaders convincing us that they are 'the special one' (the fateful soubriquet of Chelsea and Manchester United's former manager José Mourinho; see Haslam & Reicher, 2016; Maskor, 2019); instead, it is about them convincing us that *we* are special. Nevertheless, having set out evidence that supports this theoretical claim, the question this raises is whether, and how, this theory can be used to make a difference *in practice*. What, if anything, can we do to develop would-be leaders' ability to engage in identity leadership? This is the question to which we turn next.

Key point 3: Identity leadership can be enhanced by leadership development programmes that provide would-be leaders with relevant guidance and training

Over the past decade, multiple programmes of research have been conducted with the aim of translating principles of identity leadership into practice. This work is important not only because it addresses the extent to which this approach can help to make a difference in practice, but also because translating theory into practice provides a useful platform for testing and developing that theory. This process of translating theory into practice is also valuable because it helps to bring the distinct building blocks of a theory into focus (since different theories would typically suggest quite different interventions).

Initial translations of identity leadership into practice centred on research that the chapter authors and other colleagues conducted with leaders of allied health teams in a large Australian hospital (Haslam et al., 2017). In the process of taking these leaders through a series of structured steps designed to help them appreciate the value of a social identity approach to leadership and then use its principles to lead their teams more effectively, this led us to develop and test a leadership development programme that we called *5R*. This name comes from the five modules that are included in the programme: (1) Readying, (2) Reflecting, (3) Representing, (4) Realising, and (5) Reporting (see Figure 3.3).

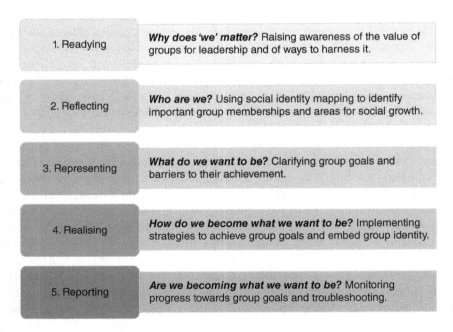

1. Readying	**Why does 'we' matter?** Raising awareness of the value of groups for leadership and of ways to harness it.
2. Reflecting	**Who are we?** Using social identity mapping to identify important group memberships and areas for social growth.
3. Representing	**What do we want to be?** Clarifying group goals and barriers to their achievement.
4. Realising	**How do we become what we want to be?** Implementing strategies to achieve group goals and embed group identity.
5. Reporting	**Are we becoming what we want to be?** Monitoring progress towards group goals and troubleshooting.

Figure 3.3 The five modules of the 5R leadership development programme

The 5R programme has a number of key distinctive features. Most particularly, where traditional approaches to leader training and development tend to focus on leaders in isolation and in contexts removed from their normal sphere of activity, 5R encourages leaders to engage directly with the groups they are seeking to lead. Accordingly, each module takes leaders through a specified set of activities and, after this, leaders then take the teams they have responsibility for through those same activities. This provides participants with practical experience in managing social identities on the ground. At the start of the next module, participants then report back on their experience and feed outcomes forward into the next phase of the programme. In this way, 5R is designed to include and mobilise followers (the team members for whom leaders have responsibility) rather than to exclude them from the leadership process and the broader dynamics of team development and change.

At the start of the programme, participants take part in a *Readying* module, in which they learn about the importance of group and social identity processes for leadership, group behaviour and health, and also engage in activities that illustrate this. Following this, the *Reflecting* module centres on a *social identity mapping* process (Cruwys, Steffens et al., 2016). This involves participants identifying the groups that are important to them in their day-to-day life and to represent the relationship between those groups (see the Appendix for further details, and also Chapter 15). In this, the process provides insight into people's subjective representations of the key identity-based relations that structure their behaviour (Peters, Haslam, Ryan, & Fonseca, 2013). In the *Representing* module participants are introduced to activities that encourage them to work with the groups that have been identified in the previous session and to give their members identity-focused *voice*. In particular, they do this by allowing them to clarify and articulate the nature of the group's identity by uncovering group members' shared values, aspirations and behaviours – and the goals on which these centre. In the *Realising* module, participants then work together to develop strategies that will help achieve these goals and to embed these in both policy and practice. The final *Reporting* module involves participants providing and being given feedback about their progress in tracking towards group goals. This ensures that the ideas, activities and objectives of the programme are embedded in the group's culture, while also providing a platform for subsequent iterations of the process it entails.

Confirming the capacity for 5R to achieve its key objectives, evaluation of the original trial indicated that participation in the programme enhanced participants' ability to engage in identity leadership (there was no effect on their motivation in part because this was already high at the start), as well as their (collective) goal clarity and team identification (Haslam et al., 2017). Importantly, too, there were no effects of participation in 5R on variables that were not targeted by the programme – notably participants' motivation and ability to engage in behaviour that seeks to strengthen their (personal) identity as a superior individual (indeed, their motivation to do so decreased over time). Similar findings have also emerged from subsequent adaptations and trials of the programme in a wide range of leadership contexts (e.g., Gopinathan, 2017; McMillan et al., 2019).

Although the 5R programme has not been run and tested in its entirety with leaders of sport and exercise teams, there are a range of related interventions that have been trialled in this domain. In an early study of this form, Matthew Slater and Jamie Barker (2019) conducted a leadership intervention with the UK Paralympics soccer team, focusing over a two-year period on the core 3Rs spelled out by Haslam, Reicher and Platow (2011): Reflecting, Representing and Realising. In this intervention, the researchers created a senior leadership team (consisting of three key members of the staff and four athletes) who were introduced to core ideas captured within each R and then implemented the programme's activities with the entire team. The researchers administered measures of interest at baseline, at several time points throughout the intervention, and then again at the end of the intervention. To allow for a rigorous assessment as well as to take account of changes within the team over the course of the programme, the intervention was also repeated in the second year. Results showed that, on both occasions, it was conducted participation in the programme that enhanced athletes' identification with the team and their perceptions of staff members' identity leadership. Beyond this, while there was no effect on the extent to which athletes felt mobilised, the intervention also increased the hours of practice that athletes invested away from the team. These results are noteworthy not only because they provide evidence of the capacity for identity leadership to increase the engagement of (elite) athletes (as shown elsewhere, e.g., by Fransen, Steffens et al., 2016; Stevens et al., 2020), but also because they show that programmes which seek to develop identity leadership have positive consequences both for individual team members and for team functioning as a whole.

Taking this work further, Katrien Fransen, Alex Haslam, Nik Steffens and colleagues (2020a) have also developed a sister programme – the *5R shared leadership program* (5R^S) – and examined its utility across several sport contexts. This programme aims to combine insights from social identity theorising with those from shared leadership discussed earlier in this chapter. In particular, it does this by empowering multiple leaders within the team to engage in processes of identity leadership. In this programme, all team members first complete a social network analysis to identify those athletes in the team who are consensually seen as providing the best quality athlete leadership across four key roles: as a task, motivational, social and external leader (Fransen, Vanbeselaere et al., 2014; Fransen, Van Puyenbroeck, 2015). This process ensures these athletes are seen as legitimate leaders within the team and, on this basis, they are then formally assigned to a leader role. These appointed athlete leaders then work together with other members of their team to implement various activities and solicit continuous input over the course of the programme.

In contrast to the 5R programme, 5R^S employs an exercise in the Reflecting phase which challenges participants to reflect on their shared values and norms and to integrate these in an overarching team trademark which then informs their ongoing activities. By way of example, a volleyball team that completed the programme identified their core values as having older and younger players playing together (i.e., without any age differentiation), having each other's back, encouraging each other, being open and accessible, ambitious, understanding, valuing humour, seeing the team as a second home, being confident and having good relations. The team members then brought these values together in the trademark of a *wolf pack*: the idea of being one family, fighting together against common enemies (Fransen, et al., 2020a). In contrast to the focus on general goals in the Representing phase of the original 5R programme, 5R^S also focuses on goals related to each of the four leadership roles: task, motivational, social and external. The respective appointed leader in this role takes responsibility for the process of generating these goals and following up on progress towards them.

Figure 3.4 An elderly walking group participating in the 5R^S Shared Leadership Program

Source: Eddy Van Acker

These various innovations suggest that it is possible to develop identity leadership in ways that enhance team functioning, not only by increasing participants' motivation and commitment but also by improving their health. Nevertheless, in the years ahead, we and others will need to develop and test additional identity leadership interventions to address the manifold challenges of leadership in an array of sport and exercise (and other) contexts. In these it is also going to be particularly important to establish how (and how much) these interventions can contribute to a broad set of outcomes. Based on the evidence that we have to date, our sense is that they have the capacity not only to improve motivation and performance, but also to play a very significant role in helping leaders foster health, well-being and resilience in the groups and teams they aspire to lead.

CONCLUSION

Leadership is a topic that lies at the heart of sport and exercise. In this chapter, we summarised established as well as emerging approaches to this topic and went on to outline ways in which a social identity approach advances on these. This review made it clear that prevailing models of leadership are limited – as a framework for both analysis and action – primarily because they focus on qualities of leaders *as individuals*. In contrast, the social identity approach suggests that, to be effective, leadership needs to embrace the power of the collective that arises from a sense of shared identity that brings people together *as team members* and thereby motivates them to go much further than they can – and *think* they can – when they think and act as lone entities.

In providing a fuller understanding of the self, group and influence processes that are key to effective leadership, we argued that these social identity principles are uniquely positioned to explain how and why leaders are able to motivate and direct others. Supporting these claims, the research that this approach has spawned makes it clear that identity leadership helps not only to drive motivation and performance, but also to deliver other important team and individual outcomes – not least in promoting a sense of belonging, purpose, support and agency in ways that sustain health and well-being. Research also makes it clear that there are a range of behaviours that leaders can engage in to 'do' identity leadership better. This indeed is the basis for a number of promising interventions that seek to develop identity leadership with a view to enhancing individual and team functioning.

Against this background, it is perhaps surprising that so few approaches to leadership home in on a theoretical specification of the ways in which leaders can – and need to – meaningfully engage with a shared sense of 'we-ness'. And even though the social identity approach seeks to do exactly this, it is also the case that there are a range of intellectual and practical challenges that future work still needs to address and resolve. Yet, as with leadership itself – to borrow lines from the quote with which we started – these are challenges that we will be better able to rise to if we are able to unite researchers and practitioners around the grand design that the social identity approach lays out. We hope we can, and that this chapter has helped persuade future leaders of the merits of this collective enterprise.

4
COMMUNICATION

KIM PETERS

> That's the sound of Wimbledon: that hush. ... That hush, when everyone is fully expectant of something brilliant to happen ... that exciting stillness, anticipation; and then this huge roar when it's all developed into something really wonderful. (Whiston, 2011)

In the BBC Radio 4 documentary, *The Sound of Sports*, sound designers reproduce the soundscapes of an array of sports – from Wimbledon and the Boat Race to Olympic show jumping and archery – and describe the lengths to which they go to capture and recreate these sounds. Without these rich and vivid soundscapes, they argue, sport loses its ability to engage people (a claim that is borne out by the fact that almost 1,000 people were employed to record and mix the sounds of the 2012 London Olympics). Much of this sound is produced by athletes *doing* their sport: the thud of a ball, the thwip-thwip of an arrow, the grating of a skater on the ice. But what remains is arguably even more important: the chants of fans, calls of players, shouts of coaches, judgements of umpires, cries of the victorious and analyses of commentators. This *communicative action* is an essential part of what the spectator expects sport to sound like and it is also central to its capacity to excite and absorb them.

Of course, communication is even more important to sport that this. This is because it not only increases spectators' involvement and enjoyment, but actually makes sport as we know it possible. Like any collective endeavour, sport requires that all those who engage in it are able to communicate effectively with one another: coaches and athletes, team members and their teammates, players and the public, sporting bodies and sponsors. This begs the question: if communication is as vital for the success of sports as a social and commercial enterprise, how can those in sports ensure that their communications are effective? This chapter aims to provide some answers to this question by presenting an overview of the major theoretical approaches to communication. In the process, it aims to show that the social identity perspective can provide important practical answers to questions of how to communicate in ways that are likely to foster enjoyment, effort and effectiveness in sport. It starts, though, by presenting an overview of some of the research that can substantiate the claim that communicative action is both prevalent in sport and essential to it.

THE IMPORTANCE OF COMMUNICATION IN SPORT

Sport is generally considered to involve the performance of skilful physical behaviour in a context that has some competitive element (Sport Accord, 2011). While the behaviours that fall within this definition are many and varied (from running and throwing to riding or driving), they are united by the fact that they are not communicative. That is, they are behaviours that are not primarily directed towards the transmission of information from one person to another. That said, some definitions of sport (e.g., Rejeski & Brawley, 1988) make reference to the importance of strategy, and this is clearly communicative. Nevertheless, even when the core behaviours of sport are not themselves communicative, they co-occur with behaviours that are.

North American football provides a particularly vivid example. This game consists of four 15-minute quarters, includes an average of only 11 minutes of play, and lasts around three hours (Biderman, 2010). Even if we exclude the 30–40 minutes of commercial breaks that are permitted during National Football League (NFL) games, the amount of time that is spent in play is extraordinarily small. So what is the most important behaviour in the time that remains? Communication. This includes the breaks and time-outs that are formally set aside for communication between coaches and their teams, and the huddles for players to relay strategic information before each play. It also includes the continual back and forth among players and between players and officials throughout the game. Together, this can explain why the NFL has been described as a 'gabfest' – an activity to which chatter is as central as it is in any other place of work (Pennington, 2018). Although the stop-start nature of NFL games may provide more plentiful opportunities for communication among those on the field than is the case in more continuous sports, there is evidence for the pervasiveness of communication in even these latter settings. For instance, it has been estimated that tennis, table tennis and badminton players spend around 10% of match time, and almost 70% of break time, talking to their teammates (Wegner, Bohnacker, Mempel, Teubel, & Schüler, 2014). Of course, communication is not limited to those who are on the field of play: coaches and spectators on the sidelines are also often to be found communicating with players and match officials (e.g., Mouchet, Harvey, & Light, 2014).

As would be expected on the basis of the sheer prevalence of communication in sport, there is a widely held belief that it matters. For instance, spectators often exhort players to communicate more (LeCouteur & Feo, 2011), and athletes and coaches identify communication as one of the most important determinants of the quality of a team's performance (Webster, Hardy, & Hardy, 2017). There is a belief too that communication can be used competitively, as athletes believe that they can use derogatory 'trash-talk' to put opponents off their game (Kniffin & Palacio, 2018). Fans also appear to believe that they can improve their team's performance through their chants and songs or vilification of match officials or opponents (Armstrong & Young, 1999). In the case of the NFL, this extends to fans' attempts to make so much noise that they make it much more difficult for players on the opposing team to communicate with one another. Indeed, these communicative behaviours on the part of spectators may account for at least some of the home-ground advantage that is enjoyed in many sports (Nevill & Holder, 1999; Thirer & Rampey, 1979).

There is some evidence that communication can affect sporting performance. For instance, athletes have been found to express higher levels of satisfaction with coaches who provide positive, timely and supportive feedback, and lower levels of satisfaction if their coaches are verbally aggressive (e.g., shouting or insulting athletes or engaging in personal verbal attacks; Dwyer & Fischer, 1990; Kassing & Infante, 1999; Sinclair & Vealey, 1989). And in an especially impressive analysis of the impact of communication, Domagoj Lausic and colleagues conducted a detailed study of communication among 10 female college top-division tennis players (Lausic, Tenenbaum, Eccles, Jeong, & Johnson, 2009; see also Lausic, Razon, & Tenenbaum, 2015). These players were randomly paired to form doubles teams and then played a round-robin of matches. During these matches, the communication of players was recorded, and subsequently categorized by content. Importantly, the authors found that although the opportunity to communicate was equivalent for winning and losing teams, there was a wide disparity in the number of messages exchanged. In particular, the members of winning teams were twice as likely to communicate as members of the teams that lost. There was evidence too that winning teams not only differed from losing ones in terms of the amount of communication; they also sent a greater variety of messages, and used twice as many action statements. On this basis, the researchers suggested that winning teams made greater use of communication to build a shared understanding of the state of the game and to develop and update strategy, and that it was this that underpinned their superior performance.

In sum, then, there is evidence that communication is both an inextricable part of how sport is done, and essential to people's ability to do it at all. Without communication, athletes would be less skilful, would struggle to work together, and would be less motivated to succeed. Without communication, it would also not be possible to engage and organise the many groups and stakeholders that play an important role in producing sport in the modern world.

CURRENT APPROACHES TO EFFECTIVE COMMUNICATION

Communication is the substrate of our daily lives. It is one of the main things that we do in social settings, whether at work, at home or at leisure. It is *the* main way in which we pursue our myriad social goals in these settings. This is because communication allows us to directly alter the thoughts of others and consequently their behaviour. To understand how communication achieves this, it is useful to consider what communication exactly is. Communication has been defined as the process whereby one person manipulates another's material environment (e.g., by producing sound waves or changing patterns of light) in a way that leads the second person to form a mental representation (e.g., a belief, attitude or action tendency) that is similar to that intended by the first person (Sperber & Wilson, 1986). In essence, then, it is the process that allows people to *transmit*, and thereby come to *share*, information. In sport, it is used by coaches to improve an athlete's technical proficiency, by players to motivate teammates or convey tactical guidelines, by spectators to encourage their favourite athletes and/or disrupt opponents, and by commentators to enlighten and entertain. It is also used by all the social actors involved in the production of sport (i.e., governments, organisations, unions, community groups, and so on) to formulate goals and coordinate their efforts to achieve them. In other words, without communication, there would be no sport as we know it. However, although communication is ubiquitous and seemingly effortless, it can easily go astray. The core problem is how communicators can ensure that the mental representation that their communicative actions induce in their audience is indeed the one they intend.

Knowing the code: The encoder-decoder model

> I'm always concerned about [sign-stealing] throughout the [baseball] season. So we do a good job of changing sequences and paying attention. ...
> If we feel there's something going on, we change the signs. (Alex Cora, manager of the Boston Red Sox, cited in Sheinin, 2018)

One of the most well-known models of communication is the *encoder-decoder model* (for an overview, see Krauss & Fussell, 1996). According to this model, successful communication requires that an encoder is able to translate his or her mental representation into a code and transmit it along a communication channel to the decoder who is able to perform the reverse translation to reveal the mental representation. This model thus suggests that the secret to successful communication is having a shared code that the encoder and decoder can both draw on. This claim is obviously true: most of us will have experienced first-hand the barrier that unshared languages, dialects, jargon and slang present to effective communication. Indeed, a number of sports take advantage of the fact that codes can be used to communicate information selectively to those 'in the know' while keeping everyone else in the dark.

Particularly notable among these sports are NFL and baseball. In the case of the NFL, one of the most important tasks facing a new recruit is memorising the team's strategic playbook, which can contain hundreds of potential procedures, each paired with a code that a player needs to learn and implement if the play is called in a game. This code allows the coach or quarterback to make a play call on the field (e.g., 'Red right 30 pull trap' or '896 H-shallow F-curl') that the players on their own side will understand, but their opponents will not. Some teams, like the New England Patriots, are recognised as having particularly complex playbooks, and the failure to adequately grasp the associated code has been associated with some players failing to make an effective contribution to the team (see Figure 4.1).

Figure 4.1 Code is commonly used to communicate in sport

Source: Wikipedia commons; Keith Johnston, Pixabay

Code plays an important role in baseball and softball, too. During a game, players and coaches can be seen exchanging sequences of hand gestures that involve touches to their arms, head and apparel. The most important messages are those exchanged between the catcher and the pitcher about the type of pitch that will be thrown. In light of the potential usefulness of this message to the opposing team, it is not surprising that there is a long history of so-called sign-stealing. When successful, this allows the player at second base who is able to monitor the exchanges between the catcher and pitcher to warn the batter about the pitch that they are likely to receive. This is not without controversy though, and in 2018, there were particularly heated accusations around the Red Sox's use of electronic equipment to steal signs (individuals on the side lines used video replay to extract signs and then relayed them to players). To counter the possibility that opponents have cracked their code, teams will sometimes also change their code throughout the season (as described by Alex Cora, the manager of the Red Sox, in the quotation above), although this runs the risk that players may struggle to remember, and thus effectively use, the evolving code.

The importance of a shared code to communication can also be seen in communicators' attempts to take the perspective of their audience and employ a code that they believe is likely to be shared. One classic study speaking to this point was conducted by Susan Fussell and Robert Krauss at Columbia University (Fussell & Krauss, 1989). In this, 17 pairs of friends were brought into the lab and individually asked to provide written descriptions for 30 abstract line drawings in order to help their friend correctly identify each line drawing at a later point in time. One month later, the participants were brought back into the lab, presented with a series of written descriptions, and asked to select the drawing that they thought the description referred to. Unbeknown to them, these descriptions could be of three kinds: (a) ones that they themselves had written for their friend, (b) ones that their friend had written for them, or (c) ones that unknown participants had written for their own friends. The researchers found that participants were most accurate at identifying figures on the basis of their own descriptions (getting almost 90% correct). Interestingly, though, they were slightly better at identifying figures on the basis of the messages that their friend had written with them in mind (60% accurate) than they were at identifying messages that strangers had designed for other people (55%). Fussell and Krauss (1989) argued that these findings show that people (a) try to design messages that they believe will be understood by their audience, and (b) are somewhat successful at doing so.

Further evidence of people's attempts to design messages that are likely to be understood by their audience is provided by the work of Nathanael Fast and colleagues (Fast, Heath, & Wu, 2009). In an initial experiment, participants were asked to read some information about the performance of eight baseball players and then to send an email about this information to a stranger. There were two key manipulations in this study. First, half of the list included players who had received relatively little media attention, but had achieved very high performances over the season; the remaining players had received a great deal of media attention, but had very average seasons. Second, participants either were (or were not) told that the person who they were emailing was a baseball fan. The researchers found that what participants chose to communicate about depended on the fame of the players as well as the expertise of the audience. In particular, when emailing an expert audience, people spent more time communicating about the stellar (but relatively unknown) players than the mediocre (but famous) ones. In contrast, when emailing a non-expert, participants showed exactly the opposite pattern: they spent more time communicating about the famous (mediocre) players than the unfamiliar (stellar) ones. In sum, these findings suggest that communicators try to increase the likelihood that their communication will be successful by transmitting information they anticipate will be meaningful to their audience, and that their audience will therefore be able to engage with.

Inferring communicators' intention: The relevance model

> Of course I sing out 'black bastard', but I don't mean it. It's all part of being at the footy on a Saturday [afternoon]. The media makes too much of [racial taunts]. It's just a way of letting out your feelings. (Male AFL fan, cited in McNamara, 2000, p. 19)

While knowing the code and knowing which code to use is essential for successful communication, there is evidence that it is not always enough. In particular, in many circumstances there is a gap between what is said (and thus what can be extracted from the code) and what is meant. The quote above, provided by a male Australian rules football fan, is a vivid (if unsavoury) example of this phenomenon. For when interviewed about their homophobic or racist chanting (Magrath, 2018; McNamara, 2000), these fans argued that their chants were not meant to convey any actual prejudice. They claimed that these chants were instead meant to communicate their passion for their team and their desire for their team to win. Regardless of how much credence we give these accounts, the point is that in sport, as in life more generally, people do not always say what they mean and they do not always mean what they say.

This raises the obvious question of how recipients of communication are meant to work out what exactly it is that a communicator means. In trying to account for people's abilities to bridge the gap between the literal and intended meaning of a message, Sperber and Wilson's (1997) *relevance theory* argues that correctly decoding the literal meaning of a message is a necessary, but not sufficient, condition for communication. According to this theory, the audience is also required to make an inference about the communicator's intended meaning. Doing this requires that audiences assume that the message is *relevant* given the information they (believe they) share with the communicator, such as knowledge of their previous interactions, recent events, the progress of the conversation to this point, and so on. For example, when FIFA President Sepp Blatter said in a series of television interviews in 2011 that racism is not a problem in football and that most problems can be settled with a handshake, many people called for his resignation because they understood this to be inconsistent with the worldwide drive to acknowledge the seriousness of racism and to do everything possible to root it out. So although Blatter claimed that 'I was misunderstood', his comments were interpreted against the backdrop of anti-racism programmes such as the FIFA's own 'Say No to Racism' campaign, with which they appeared to be inconsistent (BBC, 2011).

Having taken this contextual information into account, people then settle on the inference that maximises the relevance of the message, given this shared knowledge. In the case of Blatter, for example, his comments were given greater weight (and seen as particularly problematic), precisely because they went against the grain of high-profile anti-racism campaigns. This tendency for communicators to make the assumption that each contribution to a conversation is directly relevant to what has been said up to that point explains why non-sequiturs can so effectively derail a discussion. Indeed, the linguistic philosopher Paul Grice has argued that the overarching maxim of conversational logic is to 'be relevant' (Grice, 1975).

The frequency of indirect language in conversation, including that associated with politeness, sarcasm and humour, points to people's capacity to correctly infer that the speaker means something very different – often the direct opposite – of what he or she has said. However, making the correct inference is not always so straightforward. For instance, it is likely that many listening to fans' racist or homophobic chanting will react to the literal meaning of the chants, rather than what fans (e.g., those interviewed by McNamara, 2000, and Magrath, 2018) say they intend. Such failures are also evident in our more quotidian communications – not least, in social media use (something which has often proved to be particularly problematic for prominent sports stars; Holmes, 2011). In line with this point, Justin Kruger and colleagues found that people were rather poor at correctly recognising whether the content of an email was (or was not) sarcastic (Kruger, Epley, Parker, & Ng, 2005). They were, however, more accurate at judging sarcasm when the statement was conveyed verbally, as communicators tended to introduce a range of paravocal cues that signalled their sarcastic intentions. Indeed, it has been suggested that the emergence of emoticons in contemporary electronic forms of communication is due to people's difficulties in effectively using indirect language over these channels. These function as a supplementary code that signals the communicator's social intention and, alongside with a written message, help recipients understand a message's intended meaning (e.g., Thompson & Filik, 2016).

These difficulties of making the correct inference are apparent in many team sporting contexts. One of the most important sources of contextual knowledge that communicators can draw on when inferring another person's intended meaning is an understanding of the objects (e.g., the people and events) that are in that person's visual field. So a person's query of 'What is that?' is more likely to be answered satisfactorily if their audience can see what 'that' is. Doing this is greatly facilitated by a common physical orientation and the establishment of a shared gaze, as this helps speakers to be confident about which object a particular utterance is referring to. However, the highly complex, rapid and dynamic nature of many team sports is an impediment to any common physical orientation and often makes it hard for players to establish a shared gaze. This means that players can sometimes struggle to understand exactly what is meant by their teammates' shouts of 'watch out!' or 'pass!' Consistent with this analysis, LeCouteur and Feo (2011) found that communication during netball matches was frequently unsuccessful. In particular, players' directives to one another were often ambiguous, as they assumed they had a shared orientation and visual awareness when in fact they did not. Unsurprisingly, when this was the case, other players' responses to these messages were often inappropriate because the intended meaning had not been effectively transmitted.

Keeping it simple: The parsimony model

If we were to extract one key practical learning from these classic perspectives on communication, it is probably that those wishing to avoid miscommunications should keep their messages simple. This means developing a shared code, and sticking to it, much as pilots and air traffic controllers do to ensure the efficient and clear transmission of information. At all costs, communicators should avoid sending messages that require the audience to make complex inferences about their intentions. Especially in rapid team sports, teams should therefore work to establish a shared code that can be used during play to pass information efficiently and effectively (Reimer, Park, & Hinsz, 2006).

In line with this *parsimony model*, Eccles and Tran (2012) suggest that there are a number of steps that communicators can take to ensure that their message gets through. These include sending a message multiple times over multiple channels and checking to ensure that the message has been correctly understood. They also suggest that the audience can improve their chances of retaining the integrity of the message that they need to encode by remembering the HEAR acronym: head up, eyes front, attend fully and remain silent.

But is this all there is to it? As we will see in the next section, almost certainly not. For sometimes – especially when communication occurs across the contours of shared social identity – HEARing is not enough to hear, or for one's message to be heard.

A SOCIAL IDENTITY APPROACH TO EFFECTIVE COMMUNICATION

Current perspectives on communication suggest that communicators can, by keeping their messages simple, increase the likelihood that they will be understood. However, it does not take much reflection to realise that this is not the ultimate answer to the question of how to maximise communicative success. This is because it requires effort to develop and memorise a shared code, to build redundancy into the messages we send, and to attend carefully to the messages that others send to us.

As any coach knows, increasing athletes' engagement with their teaching therefore takes more than getting them to keep their heads up and their eyes forward. To increase engagement, it is necessary to engage athletes' minds – they must *want* to learn before they will bother to listen to, and hear, what you have to say. It is also the case that while restricting our communication to simple and literal messages may have the desirable effect of reducing misunderstanding, it will also sharply limit the range of understandings we can hope to create. In our everyday life, we violate conversational directness because, among other things, being polite, telling jokes and using sarcasm and innuendo allow us to pursue a broader range of social goals than is possible through more direct and simple conversational means. Accordingly, to communicate effectively it is useful to consider what can make it more likely that communicators correctly understand one another's intentions, thereby bridging the gap between the literal message and what is actually meant. Here again, the communicator's *motivation* is key.

In line with this point, this section discusses the role that social identity can play in motivating communicators to construct the right messages and process them attentively. In particular, it explores evidence which suggests that when people perceive that they share a social identity – when they think of themselves as 'us' and 'we' – they will be more motivated to be on the same page, and consequently more willing to do the hard conversational work that is required to get there.

According to the social identity perspective (Tajfel & Turner, 1979; Turner, 1982), when people think of themselves in terms of their social identities (i.e., the group memberships that they share with others) rather than their individual identities (i.e., the characteristics and attributes that make them unique and special), this has important consequences for the way in which they relate to those around them. In particular, there is evidence that when people identify more highly with a given social group, they are more motivated to affiliate with other members of that group (i.e., ingroup members) and to coordinate their goal-directed actions with them than they are with members of an outgroup (Haslam, Turner, Oakes, McGarty et al., 1998). People are also more inclined to regard other ingroup members as a reliable source of information about the world

(McGarty, Turner, Oakes, & Haslam, 1993). These observations imply that shared social identity should increase the effectiveness of communication (Postmes, 2003). In support of this point, there is evidence that social identity determines (a) who we communicate with, (b) the quality of the messages that we send, and (c) our ability to extract the intended meaning from those messages. This, indeed, is the basis of three key points that can be divined from a social identity approach to communication in sport, and that the following sections now elaborate in turn.

Key point 1: Social identity mobilises communication

Although communication is ubiquitous in our daily lives, we are not equally likely to interact (and therefore communicate) with everyone in our social world. More particularly, there is evidence that social identities play an important role in shaping the flow of information, such that people are more likely to send messages to other members of their ingroup rather than to members of outgroups. Soccer fans, for example, are more likely to communicate with fellow fans of their team than with fans of the opposing team. In part, of course, this reflects the fact that in the world at large they may know more ingroup members, and have more contact with them. Importantly, though, this pattern has also been replicated in minimal group studies that control for these (and other) variables (Dovidio et al., 1997; after Tajfel et al., 1971; see Chapter 2 for a discussion of this method). In these, participants were more likely to disclose personal information when talking to a fellow ingroup member than to an outgroup member – even though that person was a complete stranger to them. A similar pattern has also been shown in a range of organisational settings, where the strength of a person's identification with their workplace is found to be positively associated with their willingness to provide information about their experiences to their colleagues (Flanagin, Hocevar, & Samahito, 2014) and with the likelihood of their engaging in spontaneous conversation with their fellow team members (Hinds & Mortensen, 2005).

There is also evidence that the existence of a shared social identity can shape communication in a range of sporting contexts. For instance, surveys of sports fans have found that more highly identified fans show different patterns of communication at sporting events than less identified fans. More specifically, in their survey of 407 individuals, Kelly Rocca and Sally Vogl-Bauer (1999) found that the more highly identified fans were, the more likely they were to think that it was appropriate to make verbal remarks towards players and game officials. And in a survey of 89 attendees of a men's basketball game, Daniel Wann and colleagues found that fans who identified more strongly with their team were more likely to report making instrumentally aggressive calls to players – messages that they believed would facilitate their team's performance (Wann, Waddill, Bono, Scheuchner, & Ruga, 2017).

However, social identification does not just affect willingness to communicate with others in sporting contexts; it also shapes one's openness to others' communication. This point emerges from research that Natalie Brown, Michael Devlin, and Andrew Billings (2013) conducted with fans of the mixed-martial arts Ultimate Fighting Championship

(UFC). This found that fans' identification with the UFC was a strong predictor of their consumption of UFC media (e.g., in the news or on the internet). Indeed, high identifiers consumed over three times more media per week than low-identifiers (14.8 hours vs 4.17 hours). In other words, willingness to obtain information from, and about, proponents of a given sport is largely determined by one's identification with the sport and those who represent it.

Such dynamics are borne out in a coaching context too. In particular, Gregory Cranmer and Scott Myers (2015) surveyed 158 former high-school athletes and found that those respondents who considered their coach to be an ingroup member reported having more symmetrical communication with those coaches. Interestingly, too, these same respondents also reported engaging in more cooperative communication with their teammates. This work reinforces the point that shared social identity creates the first necessary condition for successful communication: willingness to communicate.

Key point 2: Shared social identity improves message encoding

As we noted above when discussing the encoder-decoder model, effective communication requires communicators to translate their mental representation into a code that will be understood by their audience. However, getting outside one's own head and stepping into another's is effortful (and only ever imperfectly achieved). This suggests that communicators will be more likely to attempt to construct the right message for an audience (and be successful in their attempt) when they are highly motivated to engage constructively with that audience. A large of body of work in the tradition of *communication accommodation theory* (Giles, Coupland, & Coupland, 1991; Giles, Taylor, & Bourhis, 1973) provides support for this hypothesis. Among other things, this has shown that communicators are more likely to adjust their communication to help an audience understand them when they regard that audience as an ingroup. In particular, this is something they do through *convergence* to the audience's communication style. For example, a person will typically speak more slowly when speaking to a child or to a non-native speaker.

As a corollary, though, if communicators see an audience as an outgroup, then their communication is more likely to show *divergence*. This, indeed, is something that Katie Drager and colleagues have observed in communication between Australian and New Zealand sport fans for whom trans-Tasman sporting rivalry is highly salient (e.g., having agreed with the statement 'In most sports the team I most want to beat is Australia'; Drager, Hay, & Walker, 2010). In particular, when these fans were asked to read aloud a series of statements about Australia, their New Zealand accents became much more pronounced – in ways that clearly signalled their lack of affinity with their rivals.

Further evidence for the importance of a shared social identity for message encoding is provided in a recent experiment by Greenaway, Peters, Haslam, and Bingley (2016). Participants in this were randomly allocated to one of two minimal groups (representing a 'deductive' or 'inductive' processing style) and asked to construct a written version of the diagrammatic instructions that accompany a Lego model. Participants were told that these instructions would subsequently be used by a member of either their own group or the outgroup to construct the model. Although independent raters did not find any objective differences in the instructions that participants wrote to ingroup or outgroup audiences, participants who were highly identified with their group reported putting significantly more effort into writing high-quality instructions for an ingroup audience. These highly identified participants also expected that an ingroup audience would work harder to make sense of their instructions than an outgroup audience. At the same time, participants who did not identify with their assigned group did not report any differences in their effort to create high-quality instructions on the basis of their audience.

Together, this work suggests that shared social identity not only motivates communication (as discussed in the previous section), but also motivates people to engage in more thoughtful encoding – in ways that subsequently increase the likelihood of them getting their message across. Among other things, this is one reason why sports commentary that appears to embrace only a very narrow model of its audience's identity (e.g., as able-bodied, middle-class white males) is frequently challenged by those whom it is seen to exclude (Hinds, 2019; O'Halloran, 2017). It also explains why commentary that is more inclusive ultimately attracts a more diverse audience.

Key point 3: Shared social identity improves message decoding

> To fans of cricket all over the world and to all Australians who are disappointed and angry: I'm sorry. (Steve Smith, 2018, cited in Martin, 2018)

In March 2018, the captain of the Australian cricket team, Steve Smith, broke down in tears as he issued a public apology for his role in the bowler's decision to tamper with the ball during a test match against South Africa. Public apologies are not rare events in the sporting world: from losing teams apologising for letting their supporters down to athletes apologising for personal failings (e.g., drug use, domestic violence) or, as in this example, cheating at their sport. One key concern that audiences have when listening to such apologies is whether to believe the literal meaning of the message: is the apology sincere, or not? In the case of the cyclist Lance Armstrong's memorable apology for cheating and bullying ('I'll spend the rest of my life trying to earn back trust and apologise to people for the rest of my life'), the consensus seems to be 'not'. However, in the case of Steve Smith and the Australian team, interpretations of Smith's sincerity appeared to be shaped by social identity concerns. Thus, while many Australians ultimately responded positively to Smith's apology (the *Sydney Morning Herald* columnist, Peter FitzSimons, wrote 'Mr Smith, you have raised a fine son'), the same could not be said for the South Africans. For instance, an editorial of South Africa's *The Mail & Guardian* (2018) remarked that 'this cricket cheating business is exactly what Australia stands for'.

This example suggests that, as well as determining how messages are encoded, social identity can have an impact on message decoding too – that is, the way a message is interpreted by those who receive it. More specifically, people are more likely to make an effort to decode a message in a thoughtful way and to make favourable inferences about the source's intended meaning to the extent that they share a social identity with that source. For example, we are more likely to believe a player's claim that a bad tackle was an accident if we are a coach or supporter of the same team (e.g., see St John, 2019).

There are a range of studies that back up this claim. For instance, Tim Grice and colleagues surveyed 142 public hospital employees about their perceptions of the quality of information that was provided by their colleagues (Grice, Gallois, Jones, Paulsen, & Callan, 2006). They found that these employees perceived the quality (as well as the amount) of information that they received from other ingroup members to be higher than that of information they received from outgroup members. For this reason, it has been observed that people's perceptions of communication quality are a very good barometer of the level of shared identity within a given group (Haslam, 2001). Indeed, complaints about 'poor communication' often speak to a more fundamental problem with identity-based social relations – and it is typically the case that these need to be improved before efforts to improve communication quality will get any purchase.

There is evidence too that more positive reactions to ingroup messages also result in more successful communication (i.e., communication that results in the desired behaviour). This was something that Katharine Greenaway and colleagues observed in another minimal group study – this time one that presented participants with a set of written instructions for building a Lego model that had supposedly been written either by an ingroup or an outgroup member (Greenaway, Wright, Reynolds, Willingham, & Haslam, 2015). Here the researchers found that participants perceived the instructions to be of significantly higher quality when they believed they had been written by an ingroup member. Moreover, when they believed instructions to have been provided by an ingroup member, participants *actually built* better models – as measured by the number of successfully completed steps and the number of left-over bricks. Similar findings were also reported by Aimée Kane (2010) in a study of the ability of groups to adopt a newcomer's more efficient technique for building origami sailboats. This found that when the newcomer shared a social identity with the group, the group tended to discuss the newcomer's knowledge more thoroughly, and was subsequently more likely adopt their superior technique, than was the case when they did not share identity.

Together then, this evidence suggests that messages are more likely to fall on fertile ground when the audience considers a communicator to be an ingroup (rather than an outgroup) member. This is because a sense of shared identity motivates recipients to decode messages more carefully and in ways that are more likely to give them access to those messages' intended meaning. And so, in the example above, Steve Smith's apology was most likely to achieve its intended effects – eliciting forgiveness and the possibility of future redemption (and employment) – among his fellow Australians, who would be more inclined than the fans of other nationalities to listen to him with a sympathetic (non-cynical) ear. This suggests that the key to effective message interpretation is not so much a shared physical orientation (as suggested by the relevance model), as a shared *psychological* orientation. Certainly, to understand where someone is coming from, it helps if you are looking at the world from the same vantage point, but that vantage point is conferred more by shared identity than by anything else.

CONCLUSION

This chapter has argued that communication, as the main way in which we can directly shape the content of other's minds, and consequently their actions, is essential to sport – as indeed it is to any collective human endeavour. And in light of this, we asked what people in sport can do to increase the likelihood that their communications are able to foster sporting enjoyment, effort and effectiveness. Our review of current approaches to communication points towards the importance of having a clear, shared code and keeping messages as literal as possible. However, while this guidance may help in many circumstances, it is apparent that it works by eliding much of what makes communication so powerful – its ability to support the achievement of a wide range of complicated and subtle social goals.

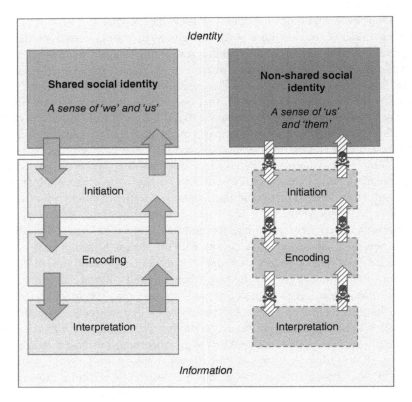

Figure 4.2   A social identity model of communication

Note: The key point that this figure makes is that shared social identity is a basis for the three key components of communication: initiation, encoding and interpretation. At the same time, there is a reciprocal relationship between communication and identity such that these processes of information transfer themselves play a role in building a sense of shared identity.

Drawing on the social identity perspective, we have argued that communication is most likely to succeed when participants want it to, when they want to talk to one another, and are motivated both to encode understandable messages and to work towards understanding the messages that they decode. This motivation, we argued, is underpinned by a sense of shared identity. Indeed, as suggested by Figure 4.2, shared social identity has a bearing on (and is itself shaped by) all three key components of effective communication: initiation, encoding and interpretation.

Accordingly, a key way to ensure that the lines of communication between the many stakeholders in sport are open and of high quality is to build the shared social identity that orients people towards each other and motivates them to get onto the same page. How precisely one can do this is an issue central to the dynamics of leadership and teamwork that are discussed in other chapters in this volume (notably in Chapters 3 and 5). At the same time, it is apparent that structural and contextual factors can also impede these efforts. Yet in this regard, one of the most significant features of sport is that it has the capacity to break down barriers to shared identity (e.g., of religion, nationality and language) and to open up lines of communication in a way that few other things can. Indeed, it is this that can sometimes make sport itself a particularly powerful method of communication.

5

TEAMWORK AND GROUP PERFORMANCE

MATTHEW J. SLATER
WILL THOMAS
ANDREW L. EVANS

You talk about the legacy and what that means. … But I think the other thing that was really important was the *connection between people* – and the greater those connections, the more resilient and the stronger we were, the *better* we were. (Graham Henry, cited in Kerr, 2013, p. 80, emphasis added)

Graham Henry was the much-celebrated former head coach of the New Zealand rugby team – the All Blacks. On the one hand, the All Blacks are an international rugby team like many others. They start test matches with 15 individuals on the pitch and a substitute bench. They have a typical coaching set-up including a head coach, a range of specialist coaches, together with science and medical staff (e.g., physiotherapists, strength and conditioning coaches, psychologists). The population of their country is small – under five million people – which makes them smaller than 126 other countries. So, nothing special. Nevertheless, the All Blacks are the most successful international rugby team ever. Their win rate has hovered at around 80% for decades and under Henry the All Blacks won over 85% of their test matches (88 of 103 to be precise); they have been the number-one rugby team in the world since 2009. By any standards, this is a quite remarkable achievement. For sport psychologists, then, the obvious question is 'How do they do it?'

As can be seen in the quote with which we started, for Henry the answer lies in the connection between the people in and around the team. In this chapter, we explore this notion of connection between people in two halves. In the first half, we analyse how teamwork has been conceptualised in sport and exercise psychology to date and how researchers have examined the relationship between teamwork and performance. In the second half, we draw on social identity and self-categorization theories to map out a novel approach to teamwork and performance in the context of sport.

CURRENT APPROACHES TO TEAMWORK AND GROUP PERFORMANCE

The field of sport and exercise psychology has blossomed through the examination of a range of individual factors that contribute to effective performance: self-efficacy, motivation and anxiety management, to name just three. A primary goal of these endeavours has been to explain how individual-level psychological variables can contribute to sporting achievement. In this, researchers have also achieved a certain amount of success. For example, evidence from a meta-analysis indicates that self-efficacy has a small but positive relationship to performance (Woodman & Hardy, 2003).

In contrast, only a limited amount of theory-based research has been concerned to explore the group-level processes that contribute to sporting performance. Nevertheless, in what follows, we review the small body of literature that has explored key questions about the contribution of group dynamics to excellence in sport. As we will see, this work focuses on three main themes: (a) team cohesion, (b) team confidence and (c) teamwork.

Team cohesion

The study of cohesion in sport was pioneered by Albert Carron together with his colleagues Lawrence Brawley and Neil Widmeyer. Together, they define team cohesion as 'a dynamic process that is reflected in the tendency for a group to stick together and remain united in pursuit of its instrumental objectives and/or for the satisfaction of member affective needs' (Carron, Brawley, & Widmeyer, 1998, p. 213). To characterise this phenomenon, Carron and colleagues developed the *multidimensional conceptual model of cohesion* presented in Figure 5.1 (Carron, Widmeyer, & Brawley, 1985; see also Chapter 11).

This model identifies two types of cognition that group members hold regarding the cohesiveness of their sport team. As Figure 5.1 indicates, these relate to the nature of (a) group integration and (b) individual attraction to the group. Group integration refers to an individual's perceptions about the closeness and similarity within the team as a whole (e.g., reflected in a sense that 'Our team would like to spend time together in the off-season'). Individual attractions to the group refer to an individual's perceptions about their motivations and desire to remain part of the team (e.g., a sense that 'I am going to miss my team members when the season ends'). Furthermore, these perceptions about group integration and individual attraction to the group can be focused on task or social aspects of the group. Task orientation relates to a sense that the team comes together to complete the task or goal in front of them (e.g., winning a specific hockey match). Social orientation relates to a sense that the team come together around non-task or target-irrelevant activities (e.g., going for a meal together). Accordingly, the model defines four key forms of team cohesion: (1) group integration – task; (2) group integration – social; (3) individual attractions to group – task; and (4) individual attractions to group – social.

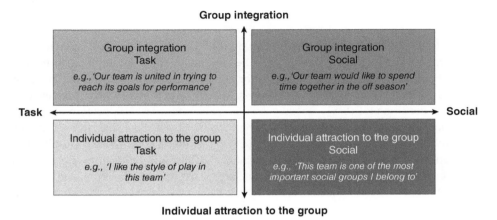

Figure 5.1   The multidimensional conceptual model of cohesion

But how exactly does cohesion – and these specific forms of it – relate to sporting performance? Of the evidence that does exist on group-level processes in sport, this is the question that has probably received the most attention from researchers (Eys, Bruner, & Martin, 2019). For example, although it was conducted almost 20 years ago, a meta-analysis by Carron, Colman, Wheeler and Stevens (2002) identified 46 studies that had examined the cohesion–performance relationship. Moreover, the authors found a significant moderate-to-large relationship between team cohesion and performance (effect size = 0.67). In other words, the more cohesive a sport team is, the more likely they are to perform better.

But, beyond this, there is more to the story, including a range of moderators and varied patterns across the four cohesion constructs. For example, contrary to expectations, Carron and colleagues' meta-analysis also revealed that the relationship between cohesion and performance was stronger for female teams than male teams (effect size = 0.95 vs 0.56). More recently, researchers have examined coaches' perceptions of the cohesion–performance relationship in male and female teams through semi-structured interviews (Eys et al., 2015). Broadly, this revealed both similarities and differences. In particular, the cohesion–performance relationship was generally understood to be important in both male and female teams. Moreover, in line with the arguments of Carron, Colman et al. (2002), there was support for the notion that high levels of cohesion were more important for performance in female than male teams (Eys et al., 2015). Yet, in addition, the coaches believed that social cohesion was more relevant for performance in female teams than male teams. At the same time, the strength of the performance–cohesion relationship (whereby poor performance leads to poor cohesion) was perceived to be greater for male teams; while in contrast the strength of the cohesion–performance relationship (whereby poor cohesion leads to poor performance) was perceived to be greater in female teams. In sum, the coaches understood the relationship between cohesion and performance to be complex and moderated by a range of cultural, personal and interpersonal factors (Eys et al., 2015).

As part of efforts to understand group performance, the examination of cohesion has led to an awareness that cohesion and performance are reciprocally related. That is: (a) cohesion energises a team to achieve task completion and high performance, while (b) task completion and high performance are also likely to boost athletes' perceptions of how cohesive their team is. Indeed, the relationships between task cohesion–performance (0.51), social cohesion–performance (0.60), performance–task cohesion (0.64) and performance–social cohesion (0.72) all show similarly significant and moderate to moderately large effects (Carron, Colman et al., 2002). Despite this, it is pertinent to note that the two performance–cohesion relationships are stronger than the two cohesion–performance relationships. That is, better performance predicts greater task and social cohesion better than greater task and social cohesion predict better performance.

While performance is arguably the ultimate outcome variable in sport in light of the resulting accolades, trophies and prize money, a focus on more process-based variables is also important given the myriad of factors that influence performance outcomes. Collectively, cohesion has been found to be positively related to more controllable group processes, such as cooperation with group norms (Prapavessis & Carron, 1997) and the likelihood of athletes returning to play for the same team in the following season (Spink, Wilson, & Odnokon, 2013). In other words, it appears that athletes who perceive their team to be more cohesive in one season are more likely to still be competing for that team in the following season.

Despite these advances, in a recent review, Eys, Bruner, and Martin (2019, p. 44) observe that 'much is still unknown about cohesion'. Accordingly, there are a range of issues for researchers who are interested in cohesion and performance to resolve. In particular, Eys and Brawley (2018) point the empirical lens towards temporal factors (e.g., pertaining to season-long longitudinal dynamics) and mediational factors (pertaining to underlying mechanisms) that would speak to the processes that explain established relationships – notably those between cohesion and performance. They also note that there is scope for more creative assessment of these constructs and for more work with under-explored populations (e.g., in areas of youth sport; see Chapter 12).

It is also worth noting that Carron and colleagues' (1985) approach to the study of sport cohesion was informed by the work of Mikalachki (1969), who advocated that cohesion should be divided into task and social dimensions. Additionally, Carron and colleagues (1985) pointed to leadership literature proposing that most theories of leadership contain an assessment of task and social dimensions (e.g., after Cartwright & Zander, 1960). As we have seen, the task and social dimensions are clearly important to sport teams. But to restrict our analytic focus to just these two dimensions may do violence to the varied, multiple and dynamic nature of sport team cohesiveness.

Team confidence

Alongside consideration of the importance of individual confidence – an athlete's belief in their own ability – the renowned psychologist Albert Bandura (1997) also introduced an awareness of the importance of *team* confidence. This was something he referred to as *collective efficacy* and which he defined as 'a group's shared belief in its collective capability to organise and execute plans and actions required to produce given levels of attainment' (Bandura, 1997, p. 477). In simple terms, team confidence thus refers to believing in your team. To illustrate, imagine that you are an All Black debutant sitting in the changing rooms a few moments before you go onto the pitch. You scan the changing room, looking around at your teammates, and consider the upcoming competition. To what extent do you believe that together you can collectively achieve the required performance level (e.g., communicating well, expending sufficient effort, displaying necessary skill and executing team plans)?

Team confidence has received less attention than cohesion (Fransen, Mertens, Feltz, & Boen, 2017). Nevertheless, the available evidence points to the beneficial effects of high collective efficacy not only for increased effort (Greenlees, Graydon, & Maynard, 1999) but also for team performance across a range of sports (e.g., Myers, Feltz, & Short, 2004). Alongside these research endeavours, progress has been made in the way that team confidence has been conceptualised. In particular, Katrien Fransen and colleagues (Fransen, Decroos et al., 2015; Fransen, Kleinert et al., 2014) have distinguished between two types of team confidence: (1) collective efficacy (as originally defined by Bandura), and (2) team outcome confidence (see also Fransen et al., 2017). While collective efficacy focuses on athletes' belief in their team's ability to accomplish those things that could lead to success (e.g., playing well), team outcome confidence refers to their belief in the team's ability to actually achieve a given goal (e.g., to win, regardless of how well they play).

Despite understanding the positive benefits of team confidence, it was not until relatively recently that researchers examined the dynamic nature of team confidence. But contemporary in-the-moment research has allowed scholars to answer such questions as 'Does team confidence fluctuate during a competitive match?' In this vein, Fransen, Decroos and colleagues (2015) administered updated collective efficacy and team outcome confidence measures before a match, at half-time and then again when the match had finished. Findings supported the view that team confidence is dynamic and fluctuates during performance. Moreover, collective efficacy (Study 1 and 2) and team outcome confidence (Study 1 only) at half-time were found to be associated with athletes' perceptions of second-half performance. The researchers also found consistent evidence that perceptions of team performance (e.g., in the first half) predicted future perceptions of collective efficacy and team outcome confidence (e.g., at half-time ahead of the second half of play). This suggests that both types of team confidence – collective efficacy and team outcome confidence – are relevant predictors of team functioning and success. They also lead us to reflect on what can be done to strengthen athletes' confidence in their team.

In a similar way to individual confidence, team confidence is derived from a range of sources. Bandura (1997) identified four: (a) performance accomplishments (e.g., such that an All Blacks debutant feels confident in their team because of the All Blacks' winning record), (b) vicarious experiences (e.g., seeing another team beat their next opposition), (c) verbal persuasion (e.g., encouragement from the coaching staff), and (d) physiological and emotional states (e.g., being fit and energised in the run-up to a game). Beyond these, though, more recent evidence suggests that leadership behaviours are important antecedents of team confidence. For example, there is evidence that team confidence can be dampened by autocratic coach behaviours (Hampson & Jowett, 2014).

When leadership is discussed in relation to team sports, it is often coaches who people think of first. Yet in addition to this role that coaches play, researchers have also examined the influence of athlete leadership on team confidence (Fransen, Decroos, Vande Broek, & Boen, 2016; see also Chapter 3). In particular, Fransen and colleagues compared the influence of coaches and athlete leaders and showed that each make a unique contribution to team confidence. Speaking more deeply to this relationship, the results of this research also indicated that when coach and athlete leaders help to increase team confidence, they do this primarily by building athletes' identification with their team (Fransen, Decroos et al., 2016). In other words, both coaches and athlete leaders foster team confidence in the team by helping to create a shared sense of 'us' within their teams.

At the same time, though, Fransen and colleagues note that athlete leaders can have both positive and negative effects on athletes' team confidence (as assessed in terms of both collective efficacy and team outcome confidence; Fransen, Haslam et al., 2015; Fransen, Steffens et al., 2016). Specifically, these researchers found that when athlete leaders expressed high confidence in their team's abilities and chances of winning, this spread throughout the team so that the confidence of other team members also increased, together with their performance. Nevertheless, when athlete leaders expressed a lack of confidence, this had a detrimental impact on their teammates' own confidence and this in turn had a detrimental effect on their performance (Fransen, Haslam et al., 2015).

Teamwork

Despite meta-analytical evidence that teamwork processes are positively related to team performance in organisational settings (e.g., LePine, Piccolo, Jackson, Mathieu, & Saul, 2008), teamwork and its impact have received only limited attention from sport and exercise psychologists. Indeed, it was not until 2014, when Desmond McEwan and Mark Beauchamp proposed a definition and conceptual model of teamwork for sport that the area sprung to life. McEwan and Beauchamp (2014, p. 233) define teamwork as 'a dynamic process involving a collaborative effort by team members to effectively carry out the independent and interdependent behaviours that are required to maximise a team's likelihood of achieving its purposes'. Combining a myriad of independent and interdependent behaviours, one good example of teamwork on the sports field is the scrum in rugby union. In the case of the All Blacks, for example, this has a series of multiple reiterative components which include (a) planning for scrum formation, (b) implementing plans in the context of scrumming against the opposition, (c) individually and collectively reflecting on what went well and what needs to improve, and (d) changing behaviour in the next scrum.

More generally, teamwork can be seen to comprise five overarching components which take the form of discrete *teamwork behaviours*: *preparation* (e.g., team goal setting), *execution* (e.g., effective communication on the field of play), *evaluation* (e.g., monitoring and reviewing various aspects of performance), *adjustment* (e.g., solving a problem such as creating a new set-play for the next opposition), and the *management of team maintenance* (MTM; e.g., effectively managing conflict). Work by other researchers also integrates these components within an overarching framework in which they are understood to be mediators between particular inputs (e.g., the particular game a team is playing) and relevant outcomes (notably performance and psychological states; see McEwan & Beauchamp, 2014; Mathieu et al., 2008; Rousseau, Aubé, & Savoie, 2006). This can be seen clearly in the framework developed by Desmond McEwan and Mark Beauchamp (2014), which is represented schematically in Figure 5.2.

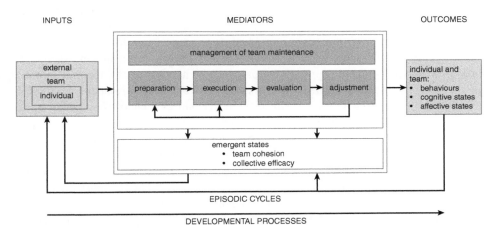

Figure 5.2 Conceptual framework for teamwork and team effectiveness in sport

Note: In this framework distinct teamwork components are understood to mediate the relationship between particular inputs and relevant outputs. This figure is a slightly simplified version of McEwan and Beauchamp's (2014) model which itself builds upon Mathieu et al.'s (2008) Input-Mediator-Outcome framework and Rousseau et al.'s (2006) teamwork behaviours framework.

Source: Based on McEwan & Beauchamp (2014)

Viewing teamwork in this way, McEwan and Beauchamp (2014) position teamwork as a team process (involving observable behaviours such as communication, cooperation and setting team goals), and there are points of contact with research on cohesion and collective efficacy discussed in the sections above. In particular, this is because cohesion and collective efficacy are seen as two emergent states within the mediator section of the teamwork model that are reciprocally linked to teamwork behaviours.

Flowing from this definition and model of teamwork, McEwan and colleagues have also (a) developed a measure of teamwork behaviours (the *multidimensional assessment of team in sport* (MATS); McEwan, Zumbo, Eys, & Beauchamp, 2018); (b) piloted the use of an intervention to boost teamwork behaviours (McEwan & Beauchamp, 2020); and (c) begun to investigate the consequences of teamwork behaviours in sport teams (McEwan, 2020). In the latter, McEwan and Beauchamp (2020) provided feedback to teams based on their response to each dimension on the MATS. Then, each team took part in a tailored intervention to target aspects of teamwork which were sub-optimal (as identified by the MATS). This involved team-building activities such as collective/individual goal setting, the introduction of briefs/debriefs and the creation of key team behaviours. Importantly, those teams who engaged in the intervention went on to display improved teamwork.

Regarding the impact of teamwork on pertinent outcomes, McEwan (2020) provided evidence for positive relationships between perceptions of teamwork and athletes' satisfaction with the team's performance, and these were in part mediated by task cohesion, social cohesion and collective efficacy. In other words, teamwork that creates (task and social) cohesion and team confidence in turn leads to higher satisfaction in sport team performance. In addition, there was a relationship between athletes' ratings of teamwork and their satisfaction with their own individual performance, and this was mediated by their enjoyment of their sport and their commitment to their team. In sum, then, it is apparent that perceptions of teamwork are associated with a range of important sporting outcomes (e.g., satisfaction with individual and team performance) and that this relationship is mediated by key group (e.g., cohesion) and individual-level factors (e.g., enjoyment) that come into play in the context of sport-related teamwork.

In organisational settings, too, it has been suggested that teamwork processes have stronger relationships with team effectiveness in situations that involve high (vs low) task interdependence (e.g., firefighters trying to extinguish a fire versus cleaners trying to tidy a house; LePine et al., 2008). This possibility has not been examined in sport, but Carron, Colman et al.'s (2002) meta-analysis revealed no differences in the cohesion–performance relationship between coactive (e.g., golf) and interactive (e.g., basketball) sports. Nevertheless, this null finding is important for sport and exercise psychology. For it points to the fact that it is an oversimplification to suggest that teamwork is only important in interactive team sports such as ice hockey, basketball, netball, rugby and so on. It is important in coactive sports and fundamentally in individual sports too. Indeed, arguably there is no truly solo sporting endeavour whereby an athlete trains, plans and competes entirely on their own. Rather, across the globe, it is clear that individual athletes routinely train in groups together with other athletes. Further, what are traditionally defined as individual sports, such as tennis or golf, not only have team events (e.g., the Davis Cup in tennis, the Ryder Cup in golf) but also involve athletes participating in an interconnected and interactive social world. For example, at the elite level, athletes typically have large teams and entourages supporting them. And at all levels of sport, including its grassroots, athletes regularly draw on social support from family, friends and staff – and this proves to be vital to their success (see Chapter 14). Teamwork thus transcends all sporting activities, and for this reason efforts to understand its psychology are foundational to sport and exercise science.

A SOCIAL IDENTITY APPROACH TO TEAMWORK AND GROUP PERFORMANCE

The foregoing sections highlight the many different ways in which research on cohesion, team confidence and teamwork have helped researchers and practitioners better understand the complex and dynamic nature of sport teams in performance terms. Yet at the same time, there are important limitations to the insights that this work has provided. In what follows we focus on two of these: (a) the fact that sport teams are about more than just task and social components; and (b) the observation that *social identity* is a critical precursor and mechanism for explaining relationships between teamwork-related dynamics and performance. Indeed, appreciating this latter point paves the way for a social identity approach to teamwork and group performance that has the capacity to revitalise our appreciation of this topic.

Speaking to the first of these points, it is apparent that beyond task and social components of teamwork (Carron et al., 1985) there are other aspects interwoven with being part of a sport team that are important to athletes. These include enjoyment and fun (Slater, Coffee, Barker, Haslam, & Steffens, 2019), innovation and creativity, as well as history and tradition (Slater, Barker, Coffee, & Jones, 2015). As noted in Chapter 2, when individuals perceive themselves to share a social identity with others, their cognitions and behaviours reflect the values, norms and ideals that define the group (Turner, 1999). Yet while task and social components are clearly important dimensions of these values, norms and ideals, these do not fully account for what defines sport teams' social identities across different contexts (e.g., different sports, different standards of competition, different cultures). As Slater (2019, p. 19) outlines in his book *Togetherness: How to Build a Winning Team*:

> Values may reflect particular outcomes – such as being successful – but can also reflect things such as historical values, friendship values, and traditional or creative values. These values are fundamental because – when individuals feel part of a team – they guide their thoughts and behaviour.

This observation points to ways in which insights from the social identity perspective have the capacity to enlarge our appreciation of the multifaceted aspects of identity that underpin and inform teamwork.

Second, current approaches to teamwork and group performance typically fail to address issues of underlying mechanism (a notable exception being research by McEwan, 2020). Reflecting on the cohesion literature, Eys and Brawley (2018) thus observe that we need to know a lot more about what it is that creates, supports and sustains cohesion. And what precisely is it that makes cohesion beneficial for sport team performance? It is here that insights from social identity theorising have the potential to be especially valuable.

At the same time, this body of theorising also helps us to understand how leadership impacts on teamwork (e.g., see Chapter 3). As we have seen, coaches and athlete leaders have a key role to play in promoting athletes' team confidence. But is this role as simple as providing positive messages to boost efficacy and avoiding negative messages so as not to dampen it? The answer is clearly no. For the impact of such communications depends on social identity processes (e.g., see Chapter 4). As Peters notes in that chapter, a key issue is how athletes construe these messages. More particularly, social identity principles point to the fact that the impact of such confidence-building or confidence-diminishing messages varies as a function of the extent to which those who provide them are perceived to be 'one of us' (rather than 'one of them'). This means that encouragement is most likely to have the desired impact when it is provided by ingroup members with whom athletes share a sense of identity-based psychological connection.

Empirical evidence in sport has supported this claim by demonstrating that social identification is a key moderator of the relationship between feedback and performance in ways suggested by Figure 5.3 (e.g., Fransen, Haslam et al., 2015; Fransen, Steffens et al., 2016). It follows too that one key way in which coaches and athlete leaders can shape athletes' collective efficacy and team outcome confidence is by fostering their psychological connection with the team. In line with this point, evidence suggests that leadership that serves to create a collective sense of 'us' plays a key role in boosting team confidence (e.g., see Chapter 3).

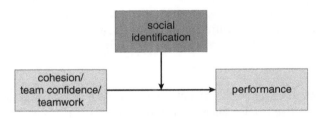

Figure 5.3 Schematic representation of the role of athletes' identification with their sport team in the relationship between cohesion/team confidence, teamwork and performance

Along similar lines, within McEwan and Beauchamp's (2014) teamwork model social identity is understood to be an outcome (on the right of the model in Figure 5.2). Yet social identity is not only an outcome of teamwork; it can also be a precursor to it as well as a mechanism that plays a critical role in underpinning the various relationships that this model specifies in ways suggested by Figure 5.4. As an outcome, social identity may thus arise from effective cooperation, quality communication and a unified team working together in pursuit of its performance targets. But, more than this, social identity is also a platform for both individual outcomes (e.g., commitment; Martin, Balderson, Hawkins, Wilson, & Bruner, 2018) and group outcomes (e.g., team confidence; Fransen, Coffee et al., 2014; Fransen, Kleinert et al., 2014; Fransen, Steffens et al., 2016) that are known to make important contributions to sport performance.

Thus, social identity functions as an antecedent to teamwork behaviours (e.g., communication). So while it is the case that if the players in a team cooperate and communicate well, this will lead them to identify more strongly with the team, it is also the case that if they identify strongly with the team, this will lead them to cooperate and communicate more effectively. Indeed, more strongly, following Turner (1982; see Chapter 2), we can argue that *social identity is what makes teamwork possible* because it is what makes the team a psychological reality.

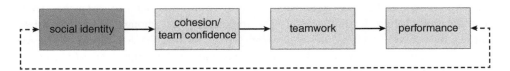

Figure 5.4 Schematic representation of the contribution of social identity to cohesion team confidence, teamwork and performance

In what follows, we build on these points to explore and spell out the added value of a social identity approach to an appreciation of teamwork and group performance in sport. In doing so, we draw on the principles of social identity and self-categorization theories, as well as the growing research evidence which supports them, and powerful stories from the world of elite sport. In this way, we hope to pave the way for future researchers and practitioners to participate in the endeavour both to understand the complexities of teamwork and to develop tools for effective intervention to promote teamwork and high performance.

We do this primarily by reconnecting with *the performance hypothesis* outlined in Chapter 2, which argued that 'sport and exercise performance is shaped by social identification with relevant groups and the norms, values, affordances and goals associated with salient social identities'. This is a hypothesis that aligns closely with the observation of Graham Henry with which we started – namely, that it was the *connection between people* that led the All Blacks to become the best rugby team in the world. More specifically, we would argue that it is the internalisation of a strong sense of shared social identity that underpins the All Blacks' phenomenal teamwork and success – and that of many other sport teams besides. Indeed, as we will see, this is a point that is central to all three of the key points that we derive from a social identity approach to teamwork and group performance.

Key point 1: Athletes are more likely to identify with teams that have positive and distinct social identities, and their identification is a foundation for teamwork and group performance

When individuals define themselves in terms of a particular social identity (e.g., as a team member of the All Blacks or of Manchester United), they want that group to be different from, and better than, other (out)groups (e.g., the Australian Wallabies or Liverpool). In other words, when we see ourselves as belonging to a given team, we want that team to have values that define it as unique and special (e.g., to play the best attacking football in the league, or to be known for developing youth talent). We also strive to outperform relevant outgroups on these dimensions, and to perform better than them more generally. Indeed, this is a key prediction that flows from social identity theory's principle of *positive distinctiveness* (Tajfel & Turner, 1979). Positive distinctiveness feeds into global self-esteem such that being a member of a special and high-performing team makes its members feel good about themselves in ways that also foster their team identification (Rubin & Hewstone, 1998). Importantly too, though, when an athlete defines themselves in terms of social identity (e.g., as 'me the All Black' or 'us All Blacks'), this then drives attributes, qualities, behaviours and emergent states (e.g., cohesion) that are beneficial for teamwork and performance excellence (in ways suggested by Figure 5.4).

In this way, social identity is the foundation of teamwork and high performance (*the performance hypothesis*; Chapter 2). For instance, a team of athletes whose members have internalised a given sport club as part of their sense of self – so that they socially identify with the club – are more likely to feel united with other club members in ways that motivate them to work together to attain the collective target (e.g., to win a match). Arguably, without social identity, some sense of task cohesion can still exist, so that members of a team who do not have a sense of 'us-ness' nevertheless come together to work towards a given goal (although even here, some sense of shared identity – e.g., as a footballer – may still be necessary). In the absence of this, though, the quality of teamwork is likely to be diminished. Do team members give each other social support? Does task-based cohesion alone ensure that they have the well-being of other team members at the forefront of their mind? Will they be focused on creating a legacy for the club so that future generations can thrive and achieve success too? Likely not.

At the elite level, for example, athletes who lack a sense of shared social identity are more likely to focus on their narrowly defined personal interests, such that they come in to 'do their job', but not much more – in the terminology of organisational psychology, displaying little in the way of organisational *citizenship* (see Ellemers et al., 2004; Haslam, Powell, & Turner, 2000). It should be no surprise, then, that this mindset is ultimately likely to harm the team's performance.

There are countless examples of these dynamics at play in professional sport (e.g., football) where athletes leave the club for personal interests following a season where they have shown limited interest in the team. Yet, when athletes define themselves as part of a given team, such that the team is internalised as part of their social identity, then their thoughts and behaviours are qualitatively different (Haslam, 2001; Turner, 1982). Now, their behaviours and appraisals of situations are understood through the lens of 'what is best for the group'. As a consequence, team members will strive with, and for, the team to be successful (Slater & Barker, 2019). For example, they are more likely to display *sports citizenship behaviours*, such as watching other games at the club, providing advice to younger players, acting as a positive role model to others, volunteering to assist the club, and demonstrating that they are part of the overall community of the sport club.

The point here is that they do these things for their social self, and these behaviours serve to advance their collectively defined self-interest by helping to create a team that is both more positive and more special. Thus, both on and off the pitch, it is social identity that stokes the fire of teamwork and group performance.

Importantly, the foregoing analysis is supported by systematic research informed by the social identity approach to sport. At an individual level, Bert De Cuyper and colleagues studied professional cyclists in UCI-ranked teams and found that those cyclists who identified more strongly with their team exerted more effort on behalf of their team (De Cuyper, Boen, Van Beirendonck, Vanbeselaere, & Fransen, 2016). Likewise, Matthew Slater and colleagues (2018) examined whether the mobilisation of effort reported by athletes varied as a function of the identification that they felt with their team's coach (who was also the person asking them to complete a given task). Results indicated that, compared to those who had weak identification, athletes who were highly identified with their coach were willing to dedicate 18.7% more time to the task that he or she asked them to perform (Slater, Turner, Evans, & Jones, 2018).

At a group level, too, researchers have found that social identity with a sport team is positively associated with (a) greater collective efficacy (e.g., Fransen, Coffee et al., 2014; Fransen, Kleinert et al., 2014), (b) higher task and social cohesion (Fransen, Decroos, et al., 2016), and (c) better performance on sport-specific tasks (e.g., Fransen, Haslam, Steffens et al., 2015; Fransen, Steffens et al., 2016), as well as (d) superior competition outcomes (winning or losing in an international tournament; Slater, Haslam, & Steffens, 2018).

One interesting context in which to explore whether there are any links between team identification and group performance is when athletes play for a national team and have the opportunity to signal their identification with that team during the singing of their national anthem. Is it the case that the social identification that they display in this context has any bearing on performance? This was a question that we attempted to investigate in the context of the national anthems sung by footballers before the 51 matches at the UEFA Euro 2016 tournament (Slater et al., 2018). More specifically, this research examined the relationship between the level of passion displayed by each team during their national anthem (as an indication of social identification) and the team's performance in the match that followed. In line with the performance hypothesis discussed above, findings indicated that international teams that sang their anthem with greater passion (displaying greater social identification) went on to concede significantly fewer goals in the upcoming match. In addition, as the tournament progressed into the knockout phase and matches became more important, greater passion was associated with a significantly greater likelihood of victory.

The fact that the passionate rendition of one's national anthem is a determinant of subsequent team performance also points to the psychological impact of the All Blacks' Haka – the Maori dance that the team traditionally performs immediately before the start of all its rugby matches. Indeed, the effects of this can be seen to be two-fold. First, as in Slater et al.'s research, the Haka demonstrates to the All Blacks themselves that 'we all define ourselves as part of this group' and that 'we are unified in our quest of victory'. But at the same time, it also sends the same signal to the opposition, in a way that can clearly be very intimidating (Jackson & Hokowhitu, 2002).

In summary, then, a large and growing body of evidence points to the important and powerful role that sport team identification – and the connections to individuals within teams that it creates – play in driving both teamwork and performance. Specifically, it determines how willing athletes are to exert effort on behalf of their team, how unified they are (in task and social terms), and how much belief they have in one another. These key elements of teamwork then feed into task-specific and overall team performance in ways suggested by established models of the form developed by McEwan and Beauchamp (2014; see Figure 5.2).

Key point 2: Athletes have multiple social identities, and the alignment of these has implications for teamwork and group performance

Groups do not exist as meaningless collections of individuals and every group has the capacity to be internalised as part of a person's sense of self. When this happens (i.e., when individuals identify with a sport team), the success and failure of that team is felt personally (and socially) because the self is implicated in team processes, performance and outcomes. Illustrations of this principle abound in the sporting world. For example, it is seen in sport fan behaviour where a team's victory leads to joy, happiness and connectedness, while defeat leads to sadness, disappointment and disconnection, but these emotional experiences are moderated by fans' identification with the team in question (e.g., Crisp, Heuston, Farr, & Turner, 2007; see Chapter 17). And of course, as we saw in the previous section, it is also seen in athletes themselves. When athletes depersonalise in this way, they strive on behalf of the collective that informs their social identity because their life as part of that collective (e.g., as an All Black) is central to their sense of self. Accordingly, they have everything to gain (and lose) from their team's performances because its successes are their successes – as are its failures.

Yet when different identities come together, things get more complex. For example, in international competitions across sports it is typically the case that athletes from a range of clubs come together to form a national team, to train as a unit, and to compete against other nations. The England football team during the millennium decades of the 1990s and 2000s provides an interesting case study that speaks both to the power of professional footballers' club identities and to the deleterious effects that these can have when players come together to compete for their country. Throughout this period, although the team was consistently ranked in the world's top 10, it appeared to consistently underperform (Williams, 2010). A key point here is that while the England football team of the time was full of individual star players, they serially underperformed as a *team*.

Today, many of these same England players are employed as television pundits to report on football matches. So it was that following one match in 2017, three of the England players who epitomised this era of English football – Rio Ferdinand, Steven Gerrard and Frank Lampard – came to have a frank discussion about the basis for their team's underperformance (BT Sport, 2017). For Ferdinand, the problem was primarily one of conflicting identities. As he put it:

We were nicknamed the golden generation. Expectations were huge for us, as a national team, to go out there and win something. That is probably what held us back, not being able to separate out club ties and international ties.

Ferdinand went on to share a story about his relationship with Frank Lampard. He disclosed how, when he and Lampard played together for West Ham between the ages of 16 and 21, the two were inseparable. They travelled together, they roomed together, they socialised together and enjoyed playing together. Yet following their joint academy development at West Ham, the two players transferred to different clubs – Ferdinand to Manchester United and Lampard to Chelsea. Ferdinand went on to discuss how at this point, the two players stopped talking to one another, yet never fully addressed the fact that they had stopped speaking. Reflecting back on this time, he noted wistfully:

> We didn't hate each other but I didn't want to give him anything that he might take back to Chelsea; I didn't like him any more really because he played for Chelsea; he was getting his hands on a trophy that I wanted.

What this example makes clear is that the players in question felt strong ties with their clubs and that these identities remained salient (i.e., psychologically operative; Oakes et al., 1991) when they came together to train and compete for their country. Yet, as a country, England wanted – and needed – their players to come together to think and behave in terms of their shared English identity. Indeed, it can be argued that this is precisely what happened when England reached the semi-finals of the World Cup in 2018 – where a group of players who were perhaps not so great individually as those of the millennium decades nevertheless came together as part of a team that was seen to over-achieve (at least compared to their predecessors). The basis for this was something that Frank Lampard acknowledged before the tournament got underway when he reflected on the lessons England's manager, Gareth Southgate, had learned from the team's previous bitter experiences:

> Southgate has this issue under control. We didn't hate each other. It was natural, human nature when competing against each other every week. It was an underlying factor but not an excuse. To counteract it, you have to work hard at it. Gareth is definitely aware of it. He's got a good young bunch seemingly more together. (Pratt, 2018)

This analysis is further corroborated by various accounts from players that as they headed away to do international duty for England in the millennium decades, their club managers would often lecture them to be careful to not pick up an injury. For example, Gary Neville and Nicky Butt (former Manchester United players) have commented on the efforts to which Sir Alex Ferguson (the Manchester United manager at the time) would go to protect his players (e.g., Lynch, 2018; McDonnell, 2014). Ferguson was not happy about the media scrutiny his players faced on international duty. He also made it clear that if one of his players picked up an injury, he would be the first to know and the player in question would be sent straight home. Indeed, he sometimes stopped players from going on international duty in the first place, as ensuring they remained fresh and injury-free was imperative for the club's success.

The point here, then, is that during the millennium years English players' club successes and failures appeared to matter more than the successes and failures of their country. Clearly, the players themselves would have wanted to win for both their club *and* their country, but when there was a choice to be made, the club came first. This observation also highlights the need for leaders (e.g., managers and coaches) to actively develop team identities in ways that integrate athletes' identities defined at different levels of abstraction (Haslam, Eggins, & Reynolds, 2003; Peters, Haslam, Ryan, & Fonseca, 2013; see also Chapter 13). This way, star players from different club teams can still come together, and work effectively as part of a national team. At the same time, the challenge of switching between contextually relevant identities that this example foregrounds points to elaborations of social identity theorising that can add substantively to our understanding of the dynamics of cohesion, team confidence and teamwork which go beyond the insights afforded by alternative approaches.

A further real-life illustration of the switching between multiple identities can be observed following televised football matches where head coaches shake hands with their opponents. Many coaches simply shake the hands of the opposition and say 'well-played', but not Pep Guardiola (the current Manchester City head coach). Often Guardiola spends a moment or two talking with an opposition player. Whether that player takes the praise, harsh words or advice given by the coach depends on which social identity is salient for them at that time (i.e., that of their own team or a superordinate one as a footballer). It is certainly the case, though, that if Guardiola were to give the advice during the match itself, when the athlete was giving their all for their team (e.g., Arsenal), they would almost certainly ignore – and possibly resent – it. After the game, the same can still happen, and the player may reply with a polite 'thank you' if their team identity is still salient. Nevertheless, if following the final whistle, the player embraces the identity of 'us footballers', then a different reaction is likely. Now the opposition coach and athlete are part of the same category – part of what is sometimes referred to as the same 'football family'. Where this is the case, the player is going to be much more willing to listen to the coach's feedback and advice. Indeed, they may even actively seek it out.

Key point 3: The content of social identities shapes teamwork and group performance

Social identity content refers to the values, norms and characteristics that define a group (Turner, 1999). Identity contents guide the nature and direction of the group by informing group members about the attitudes, emotions and behaviours that are characteristic of 'us' and which define their sense of self – and telling them what to think, feel and do – when social identity is salient (Turner, 1999; Turner et al., 1987; see Chapter 2). In the context of the London 2012 Olympic Games, Matthew Slater and colleagues (Slater et al., 2015) observed that leaders such as performance directors within Team GB (e.g., British Athletics) regularly provided information about team values in their media communication. For example, in a television interview, one performance director noted that the content of their team's identity centred on being down to earth, paying attention to detail, innovation and exemplifying Britishness:

> They [the athletes] are brilliant role models, they are not multi-million pound athletes that you can't get close to, they're open, they're transparent, they're very engaging and you know, I think we should be proud of the crazy attention to detail that this team will go to in preparation for the Games, for the innovation that we will try and show and when we are really, really under pressure and the guys have got their backs against the wall, they'll come out with that true British spirit and fight.

After the 2012 Olympics, another performance director, Andy Parkinson, spoke to the heritage of British Rowing and their history of performance excellence – and recognised this as a stimulus for motivating rowers of the future (White, 2016):

> We need to add a bit of narrative, let people know the stories of how our amazing rowers made it into those boats. … What we can do is say, 'Look this is a really healthy sport, the values are amazing, the lessons of team work invaluable'. And best of all, the fact is you too could be a medal winner in eight years. So come and try it.

In these two cases it is clear that the leaders in question sought to mobilise group members towards the team's vision of optimal performance by focusing on the unique identity content of their teams (Slater et al., 2015). From a social identity perspective, this content shapes the thoughts, emotions and behaviours of the athletes within those teams so that when an athlete identifies with them, this content drives what they do in ways that direct the nature of performance. And while the majority of teams preparing for and competing at the highest levels of sport (e.g., in the Olympic Games) are seeking performance excellence, the underpinning meanings and values of the teams will be unique (Slater, Evans, & Barker, 2013). Thus, going beyond the task and social components that Carron and colleagues (e.g., Carron, Colman et al., 2002) identify as being important aspects of cohesion, there is a potentially infinite range of identity content(s) that uniquely defines sport teams as cohesive entities in ways that stimulate performance.

Another powerful illustration of the impact of identity contents on athletes' behaviour comes from the 2016 World Series Triathlon final race in Cozumel, Mexico (BBC, 2016). With 700 metres remaining, British athlete Jonny Brownlee was leading the race, over 100 metres ahead of his nearest two rivals – his brother Alistair and Henri Schoeman (a South African). Victory for Jonny Brownlee would give him the World Series title, but with a little over half a kilometre to go he began slowing down, losing control of his legs and struggling to stay on the track (for video, see Guardian Sport, 2016). He had truly 'hit the wall'. Alistair Brownlee and Henri Schoeman soon caught up with Jonny, and at this point Alistair and Henri were going toe-to-toe battling it out for first place. Alistair could have continued to run on and tried to win the race, but he did something different. He stopped and collected his brother Jonny – wrapping his arm around him and jogging with him all the way to the finish line before throwing Jonny over the line before himself for second place (Alistair finished third). The point here is that in the final stages of this race, the key values that were driving Alistair Brownlee's thoughts and behaviours changed. His identity and hence the nature of his behaviour shifted from being focused on his own personal performance to being focused on the performance and well-being of 'us Brownlees' – and as a result his behaviour became caring and supportive. As his identity changed (so that it was informed by a higher level of self-categorization), so then did his identity content. Rather than being ultra-competitive, he became caring, supportive and empathic (see also Chapter 14). The point that this rather dramatic example makes is that athletes' identities often change in response to context and, as they do, so to do the thoughts and feelings that shape the nature of their performance.

Figure 5.5 Alistair Brownlee helps his brother Jonny at the 2016 World Series Triathlon in Cozumel, Mexico

Source: Delly Carr, Associated Press

This observation in turn makes it clear that analysis and appreciation of social identity content provides a framework for understanding the attitudes and behaviours of athletes – and of the way that this changes with context. For instance, if an environment that promotes antagonistic identity content by fostering unhealthy competition between athletes (e.g., because they are vying for starting places or contracts at the end of the season), then this is likely to undermine their propensity for teamwork. In contrast, if an environment promotes supportive and positive identity content (e.g., when athletes work together to promote a charitable cause), then teamwork will be more likely.

At the same time, though, as noted in Chapter 2, there are times when social identity content will compromise performance or lead to no performance at all (e.g., when competing on a Sunday conflicts with an athlete's identity as a Christian). While not being conducive to high performance, these contents may nevertheless have other benefits. In the case of Parkrun, for example, the fact that it encourages non-competitive running helps to encourage a wide range of people to participate in exercise. Likewise, in junior sports, identity content that focuses on enjoyment can stimulate engagement and resilience in a way that a focus on winning at all costs does not (see Chapter 12).

But beyond identity content alone, it also matters whether an understanding of this content is *shared* within members of a given team – that is, whether all members of the team have a shared sense of 'who and what we are'. In particular, it is critical that understandings of identity content are shared by team members and their *leaders*. The importance of this point was underlined by a recent study with 160 athletes from a range of sports, led by Matthew Slater and colleagues (2019). This found that the extent to which identity contents were shared (vs not) between leaders and team members had a significant bearing on leaders' ability to motivate those team members. More specifically, findings indicated that when athletes shared the same understanding of identity content as their coach (e.g., 'we all value friendships'), they were more inclined to invest time on team-relevant tasks than was the case when they did not share that understanding (e.g., because the coach valued friendships but the team valued results). Results of a second study also indicated that shared (vs non-shared) identity content was the basis for increased behavioural effort on the part of team members – as measured by the time they expended on a task. Furthermore, mediational analysis confirmed that this effort in turn led to improved task performance.

In this way, we can see that shared identity content is a critical determinant of athletes' ability ultimately to perform well on a given task. At the same time, it is clear that leaders play a key role in cultivating this sense among team members that 'we all value the same things'. They, then, are best able to motivate team members to reach 'our' goals when their identity entrepreneurship engenders a sense that those members share the same beliefs about what it means to be a member of 'our' group. Just as an orchestra needs to be on the same page to play a symphony, so too the conductor plays a special role in ensuring this is the case.

CONCLUSION

The above review speaks to the fact that social identity processes are foundational to the dynamics of teamwork and group performance. In particular, this is because they are a basis for the sense of psychological *connection between people* to which Sir Graham Henry referred in the quotation with which this chapter stated. So, armed with this analysis, let us conclude by returning to reflect in more depth on Henry's quotation. When people first read this, they might imagine that his reference to the importance of the 'connection between people' points to the dyadic one-to-one connections between players, or between players and the coach. But Henry did not refer to players (or for that matter to coaches). Perhaps this was deliberate. For perhaps Henry was alluding instead to something bigger that was defined at a higher level of abstraction – a sense that the *connection between people* was not a matter of personal bonds between individuals as individuals, but a *depersonalised* connection between individuals *as team members* (Hogg, 1992). Potentially at least, this higher-order sense of self encompasses performance directors, science and medicine staff, and media officers, as well as fans and indeed all New Zealanders. Indeed, one of the things that is significant about the All Blacks is that all these different parties share, and are characterised by, a strong sense of internalised All Black identity.

In this way, the identity of the All Blacks reflects and creates a powerful, broad and enduring interconnected network. It is this – and the associated striving for the positive distinctiveness of all those who share this identity – that then ultimately drives the exceptional levels of teamwork and performance seen in the All Blacks and that has created the legacy of which those who represent and support the team are so proud. As Henry attests, creating and tapping into this special sense of social identity is no easy matter. Yet failure to do so paves the way to collective disappointment of the form that Lampard, Ferdinand and others of England's 'golden generation' experienced. Accordingly, this is a process upon which practitioners and researchers need to focus assiduously – and where their energies are likely to be most productively engaged as they seek to understand and promote teamwork in the future.

6
MOTIVATION

KATHARINE H. GREENAWAY
SINDHUJA SANKARAN
SVENJA A. WOLF
JARDINE MITCHELL

Champions keep playing until they get it right. (Billie Jean King)

Motivation – the ability to initiate and persist in goal pursuit – is foundational to athletic effort and outcome. Comprising a number of behavioural components, including direction and choice, persistence, continuation after a break, and intensity, motivation structures athletes' effort on and off the field (Maehr & Braskamp, 1986). Imagine an athlete who has decided to run a marathon. She understands that without motivation comes no reward. Without determination to improve and inclination to invest effort, no amount of natural talent will produce the desired outcome. As the above quote from tennis legend Billie Jean King attests, to go from budding athlete to expert sportsperson requires commitment to making the most of one's abilities over time, and ongoing resolve in striving to achieve one's goals.

At elite levels, motivation and the effort this engenders shape much in an athlete's life – from physical fitness and training, to diet and sleep patterns, as well as social relationships on and off the field. Even (and perhaps especially) when athletes reach professional levels it is important to maintain motivation, because it helps them to manage anxiety about performance, cope with setbacks and attain peak performance. Indeed, at elite levels of sport, the differences in physical ability between players is so small that psychological factors such as motivation often become a defining factor in predicting success (Mallett & Hanrahan, 2004). For this reason, it is clear that motivation is a topic at the heart of all sporting endeavour.

In this chapter, we explore current theoretical perspectives on motivation that help to clarify what it is and how it operates to deliver peak performance in individual and team sports. We discuss some limitations of these current approaches, and outline a framework for understanding motivation through a social identity lens. The social identity approach, we argue, has the potential to capitalise on knowledge derived from decades of research on motivation and to leverage this into a new perspective with significant theoretical and practical implications for sport science.

CURRENT APPROACHES TO MOTIVATION

Motivation has an extensive history in academic research. Some of the earliest work on this topic was by Clark Hull (1932), who observed that effort invested in accomplishing a goal increases as goal attainment becomes more likely. Although this conclusion was drawn by observing rats running a maze to achieve a food reward – with speed increasing as distance to the food decreased – it is nevertheless useful in seeking to explain goal pursuit in humans (Bonezzi, Brendl, & De Angelis, 2011). Indeed, much of the modern work on motivation has built on this foundation to understand what promotes goal pursuit and achievement. For example, mirroring Hull's rats, consumers have been shown to accelerate coffee purchases as they approach the end of a '10th free' loyalty card (Kivetz, Urminsky, & Zheng, 2006). In the sports context, athletes are often observed to give 'one last push' as they complete a given event (e.g., a race), and this is also often a feature both of others' efforts to motivate them despite their fatigue, and of their own self-talk (McCormick & Hatzigeorgiadis, 2019). This method of motivation can also be seen when a person puts in extra effort as they reach the end of a given exercise routine (e.g., in the last five push-ups of a workout). Given the centrality of motivation to success in most life domains, this topic has fascinated scholars in a range of disciplines in the social sciences, including economics and psychology.

Economic approaches to motivation

Economic approaches conceptualise motivation primarily as a process that incorporates components of reward and punishment. This traditional approach suggests that people should be rewarded when they perform well as this will increase their motivation to continue the behaviour, but that they should be punished when they perform poorly, as this will reduce their motivation to continue the behaviour. Within this 'carrot and stick' framework, money is often considered to be the prototypical reward or incentive with which to motivate performance. This, indeed, is the logic behind paying athletes large sums at elite levels (Berri & Krautmann, 2006; Lazear, 2000; Lazear & Rosen, 1981). For example, Premier League soccer stars earn a £75,000 per-game bonus on top of their almost £400,000 weekly salary.

The traditional economic approach relies on people being rational when it comes to weighing the costs and benefits of engaging in particular actions. This assumption of *perfect rationality* is questionable, however. Not least, this is because (as we will see below) there is plenty of evidence that people's motivation sometimes declines the more they are paid (Deci & Ryan, 1985). As a result, in recent years this traditional economic model has been supplanted by a *bounded rationality* perspective.

Born of research in behavioural economics, the notion of bounded rationality speaks to the fact that people do not always operate in precisely rational ways (Simon, 1955). In particular, it suggests that money will not always motivate people to perform their best. In line with this point, research has shown that far from leading to better performance, salary raises in elite sports actually often do not predict a player's subsequent scoring statistics (White & Sheldon, 2014). In fact, recent research has shown that financial incentives might not motivate athletes to invest any more effort than they would otherwise (Skorski, Thompson, Keegan, Meyer, & Abbiss, 2017). One reason for this is that the prospect of winning large sums of money can increase the pressure on athletes to deliver a certain level of performance and, ironically, undermine their performance by leading them to 'choke'.

It is important to remember that when people 'choke under pressure', they do not simply produce poor performance in absolute terms, but rather suboptimal performance relative to their previous standards (Beilock & Gray, 2007). Moreover, this less-than-optimal performance does not reflect a random fluctuation but instead is a response to a high-pressure situation. In line with this point, choking has been found to occur across many diverse task domains when incentives for optimal performance are at a maximum (Beilock & Carr, 2001; Lewis & Linder, 1997; Masters, 1992). For example, Hickman and Metz (2015) studied choking among athletes by investigating the link between rewards and performance in PGA Tour data from 2004 until 2012. On the basis of their findings, they argue that choking among professional golfers is particularly likely to occur when large rewards put an intense amount of pressure on them in ways that interfere with their performance. To understand these counterintuitive findings, we therefore need to move beyond economics and turn to a field that is able to explain (sometimes aberrant and non-rational) human behaviour: psychology.

Psychological approaches to motivation

To understand why traditional economic approaches do not perfectly capture the nuances of what motivates people, we explore three major theories drawn from classic theorising in psychology. These theories all provide important insight into how to increase goal-based persistence, effort and, ultimately, attainment in sports domains and beyond.

Cognitive theories

One major class of theories of motivation concerns people's thought processes about, and attributions for, their behaviour. One of the earliest theories of this form was Victor Vroom's (1964) *expectancy-value model*. This proposed that good performance is an outcome of people's expectations for success and of the value that they attach to engaging in a particular action. According to this perspective, people will be most likely to engage in (and succeed at) activities that they think they can master and which have high importance for them. By way of example, the model assumes that an athlete who aims to run a marathon will perform better when she is confident that she will perform well and when running that marathon is very important for her (e.g., because she sees it as a tribute to her beloved father who was a marathon runner).

This expectancy-based explanation has also been invoked to explain why many athletes feel they have an advantage when playing at home rather than away (Kent, 2016) – since, on the one hand, they are likely to feel that high performance is more valued when performing in front of a home crowd, while at the same time also having greater expectation of success. The model also helps to explain how performance can be enhanced or compromised when competing in team rather than individual sports since, depending on the context, groups can either enhance or reduce people's expectations of performing well (Hüffmeier, Dietrich, & Hertel, 2013; Osborn, Irwin, Skogsberg, & Feltz, 2012; Samendinger et al., 2017).

The expectancy-based model runs into some difficulty when attempting to explain certain phenomena in sport, such as the 'underdog' phenomenon. By way of example, the 2018 FIFA World Cup saw the Icelandic team perform exceptionally well, while Germany performed poorly. This was unexpected, given that the German team was broadly expected to win while the Icelandic team was not. One explanation for this is that the lack of public expectations placed on the Icelandic team meant that they approached the field with a 'nothing to lose' mentality that allowed them to give – and reach – their best. On the other hand, Germany, the defending champions, were expected to win, and this may have created pressure that undermined performance. Indeed, along these lines, a range of commentators have argued that England's poor performance at World Cups down the years can be attributed to the 'weight of expectations' that accompanied them. Reconciling these findings within the framework of expectancy-value theory, it appears that personal expectations of success may predict greater motivation and performance while expectations from others have the possibility to undermine the same. As we discuss later in this chapter, such a reconciliation requires a social identity lens, which is capable of predicting whose expectations matter for motivation.

Another influential cognitive theory is *social cognitive theory* (Bandura, 1986). As a basic theory of human agency, this argues that thoughts and cognitions are a central substrate of motivation and behaviour. Specifically, a person's sense of *self-efficacy* – their belief that they can complete a given task even in the face of barriers – is understood to be a foundational cognition that underpins good performance (Feltz, Chow, & Hepler, 2008). In a way, self-efficacy can be seen as situationally specific *self-confidence*. It has been shown to impact on the types of activity people choose to engage in, the effort they devote to those tasks, and the level of persistence they show in the face of failure (Moritz, Feltz, Fahrbach, & Mack, 2000), with greater perceived self-efficacy associated with greater motivation. In these terms, self-efficacy can be seen as a basic building block of motivation, such that greater confidence in one's ability to complete a task is a key driver of motivation and self-belief. By way of example, consider Joe Davis, the Derbyshire-born snooker player who won the world championship 14 times between 1926 and 1939. Having every reason to be very confident about his game, it is not hard to imagine that he had a significant advantage over his opponents before any match – particularly a big one. Indeed, on top of his ability, a high sense of personal self-efficacy seems likely to have been a major contributor to his unrivalled feat of never losing in a world championship.

Learned helplessness

In general achievement contexts, success or failure can be evaluated using self or other-referenced criteria (Nicholls, 1989). For instance, an athlete may compare their performance in training (e.g., in a 100-metre race) to their actual performance in a given competition. This would typically be seen as a 'self' criterion, where an athlete (the Jamaican sprinter Merlene Ottey, say) engages in *intrapersonal* (within-person) comparisons. On the other hand, if she judges her success or failure on the basis of whether she has won a 100m race or performed better than her competitor, this is an other-referenced (between-person) criterion. In this way, success and failure in competition can have both *intrapersonal* and *interpersonal* standards of comparison. Moreover, when athletes consistently win or lose, they are likely to develop a particular orientation towards competing, adopting a self-label of being a 'successful' or 'unsuccessful' athlete.

Failure or success can also be framed by different categories of comparison. So if an athlete fails to beat their personal best (as Ottey did at the Jamaican National Senior Trials before selection for the Sydney Olympics in 2000), that athlete may still consider the performance as failure – even though, in absolute terms, they still perform very well. Alternatively, if the athlete is simply unable to reproduce their training performances in competition, this might also be a basis for them to see themselves as a failure. And of course, when an athlete loses a competition it is the *perception* of loss that predicts their sense of failure. This indeed is one reason why coming third (and winning a bronze) can sometimes feel better than coming second (and losing a gold; Medvec, Madey, & Gilovich, 1995).

The importance of such perceptions is underlined by research by the second author and colleagues, which observed the existence of consistent 'successful' versus 'unsuccessful' mindsets among athletes (Sankaran, von Hecker, & Sanchez, 2019; see also Yeager & Dweck, 2012). These were found to be based on an intrapersonal standard of comparison: more specifically, a comparison between performance in training and performance in competition. In this research, track and field athletes from Wales were recruited to explore the difference in relative performance levels of athletes with successful and unsuccessful mindsets. To that end, athletes' performance in various track and field events was measured during their peak training period (i.e., two weeks before a competition) and then compared to the average of their last five most recent competition performances prior to the training period. The results revealed differences in the relative performance levels between the two groups, but only in competitions – such that athletes who had unsuccessful mindsets were unable to perform at their best when under pressure. From this perspective, then, success can be see understood as resulting from successful mindsets, allowing athletes to harness the same amount of motivation and effort in competition as they do to training. And in these terms, unsuccessful athletes are those whose mindsets make them unable to translate their hard work in training onto the field when the outcome really matters.

More broadly, a large psychological literature has been devoted to understanding this 'unsuccessful' mentality, as captured by the classic theory of *learned helplessness*, which often occurs following repeated failure (Abramson, Seligman, & Teasdale, 1978; Maier & Seligman, 1976; Seligman, 1975). In a seminal demonstration of this phenomenon, Seligman and Maier (1967) exposed dogs to inescapable electric shocks, before later exposing them to electric shocks that could be escaped by jumping over a low partition. Dogs that were initially trained in the uncontrollable context (i.e., when they could not escape the electric shocks), eventually stopped trying to avoid the shocks, and later did not take advantage of chances to escape. Yet at the same time that those dogs deprived of control became withdrawn, passive and listless, those that were exposed to *controllable* aversive shocks did not show learned helplessness and were able to escape the shocks when opportunity to do so arose.

The logic behind the theory of learned helplessness suggests that motivation for a behaviour becomes disrupted when people are exposed to uncontrollable events. Here they learn that the outcomes of their actions (e.g., winning or losing a race) are independent of their own actions (e.g., training hard for the race). When people come to see outcomes as uncontrollable, they thus invest less effort in trying to achieve them because they no longer perceive outcomes to be contingent on their actions (Abramson et al., 1978; Alloy, 1982). As a result, failure – particularly repeated failure – undermines subsequent motivation and performance (e.g., Boyd, 1982; Frankel & Snyder, 1978; Hiroto & Selgiman, 1975; Kuhl, 1984).

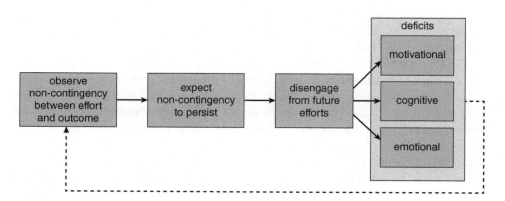

Figure 6.1 The cycle of learned helplessness

This insight has shaped the literature on control deprivation as well as providing a basis for contemporary understanding of human depression (Alloy, Peterson, Abramson, & Seligman, 1984; Brown & Siegel, 1988). As Figure 6.1 suggests, the general pattern of events for learned helplessness to emerge is as follows: first, individuals perceive a non-contingency between effort and outcome; second, they expect the non-contingency will remain in the future; and third, they disengage from future efforts (Abramson et al., 1978). Learning that these outcomes are uncontrollable is said to result in three main deficits: *motivational, cognitive* and *emotional*. On the sports field, these deficits may lead an athlete to invest effort in training but then notice that she is unable to reproduce similar levels of performance in competition. The athlete may then come to believe that she is unable to win in competition and consequently chooses to disengage from training or from the sport entirely.

As an example of this, imagine a situation in which, regardless of the amount of effort that Jim, a pole-vaulter, invests during training, he is unable to perform at an expected level in competition. Under these circumstances, Jim is likely to attribute this failure to internal causes – for example, coming to see himself as lacking the requisite amount of skill to do well in the event. He will then approach future competitions not knowing how he will perform in them (or fearing he will not be able to perform well), and thereby experience uncontrollability. In this way, he is liable to become a victim of learned helplessness. This learned-helplessness loop is also likely to be reinforced by maladaptive thinking patterns (e.g., pessimistic attributions, heightened anxiety, maladaptive perfectionistic standards and a negative mindset; Sankaran, 2018).

Yet while the model of learned helplessness suggests that this process is self-reinforcing (as indicated in Figure 6.1), there is nevertheless some evidence which shows that it is possible to escape. Indeed, Benson and Kennelly (1976) demonstrated the reciprocal process of *learned competence*, whereby a successful outcome paired with awareness of contingency on effort resulted in better performance. Moreover, in some cases, successful outcomes in uncontrollable circumstances can create the *illusion of control* (Matute, 1996), which then helps to overcome learned helplessness. When unchecked, such a process can lead to the development of sports superstitions and magical thinking (Rudski, 2001). Indeed, researchers have noted that many (perhaps most) athletes have a favourite practice or ritual of this form – for example, touching the ground and pointing to the sky, kissing the ground, wearing lucky underwear, or insisting on having the same number on their shirt (Sasvári, Harsányi, Dér, & Szemes, 2019). Superstitious behaviour of this form can be understood as an effort to compensate for the uncontrollability of the situation they find themselves in and as an associated search to regain control. And in line with the learned-competence model, this can have a positive impact on their motivation (and performance) because it helps them feel that what they do matters and will make a difference (Greenaway, Louis, & Hornsey, 2013).

Self-determination theory

One of the most influential and widely studied approaches to motivation in (and beyond) sport is Edward Deci and Richard Ryan's *self-determination theory* (1985, 1987, 2000; see also Chapter 19). This is based on an analysis of psychological needs and regulations in which behaviour is understood to vary on a continuum which reflects the degree to which it is personally chosen, self-initiated and self-directed (Deci & Ryan, 2000). As set out in Figure 6.2, the behavioural regulations associated with different levels of self-determination range from those that involve no self-determination (on the left of the figure) to those that involve full self-determination (on the right).

Figure 6.2 The continuum of self-determination

Source: Adapted from Deci & Ryan (2000)

Amotivation is the lowest form of self-determined motivation and represents a lack of intention to engage in a given behaviour. People who are amotivated often feel incompetent and experience no connection between their behaviour and expected outcomes (in a manner similar to the experience of learned helplessness). An amotivated athlete, for example, might express a complete lack of interest in training or competition – as was the case when the Swedish double Olympic cross-country skiing gold medallist, Johan Olsson, announced his retirement from the sport in 2017. 'I have thought about it a lot and I feel now that I no longer have the motivation', Olson remarked; 'I no longer have the great motivation needed to continue my elite investment and all the sacrifices it entails' (International Ski Federation, 2017).

Moving further up the self-determination continuum, external and introjected regulations represent what Deci and Ryan (1985, 2000) refer to as *controlled motivation*. Athletes whose behaviour is regulated in this way engage in sport not out of personal choice but because they experience pressure to do so. In the case of *external motivation*, this pressure comes from external sources, such that an athlete would aim to achieve rewards such as prize money or trophies, or to avoid punishment or negative evaluation in the eyes of others. In the case of *introjected motivation*, the pressure comes from within, such that an athlete may participate out of guilt or shame or because he or she wishes to be recognised for their achievements. In general, forms of amotivation and controlled motivation are often thought to be less beneficial in improving performance.

Identified and integrated regulations are more highly ranked self-determined motivations (i.e., towards the right-hand end of Figure 6.2). Technically, these are forms of *autonomous motivation* because in both cases behaviour is initiated by choice. However, these forms of motivation are still not at the highest end of the self-determination continuum because the behaviour itself is not necessarily experienced as enjoyable. To be more specific, *identified motivation* (i.e., engaging in a behaviour because it is valued) explains why some athletes will often repeat monotonous drills. Although such behaviour is not experienced as fun, athletes will do the drills if they are convinced they will lead to improvement (which is the main goal in autonomous forms of motivation). When experiencing *integrated motivation*, people will engage in a behaviour because it becomes integrated into their sense of self. This means that behaviour becomes more than just something that is engaged in because it (or its outcome) is valued. So while an athlete with identified motivation may say 'I want to do this to succeed', the athlete with integrated motivation will say 'I want to do this because it's part of who I am.'

The most self-determined form of motivation is intrinsic motivation. This form of motivation is characterised by being interested in and enjoying actions – whether physical activity, exercise or sports – for their own sake. It is considered to be the optimal form of motivation and is associated with greater sports enjoyment, effort, positive attitudes, behavioural intentions to train, and persistence (Vlachopoulos, Karageorghis, & Terry, 2000). Intrinsic motivation has parallels with the motivational state of *flow*, which is characterised by complete immersion in an activity (Csikszentmihalyi, 1975, 1990). When in flow, athletes lose sense of time and self as they become one with the activity in which they are engaging. This state was captured well by the left back of the Arizona Cardinals, Dennis Gardeck, when he was overheard telling his teammates 'I don't play football, I am football' (@CoachRev, 2018).

Self-determination theory has identified a number of factors that facilitate or undermine motivation, and help people transition from low to high levels on the self-determination continuum. In particular, higher levels of self-determination are fostered by conditions that support what are seen to be three basic needs: the need for autonomy, the need for competence and the need for relatedness.

The *need for autonomy* relates to people's *need to feel that they direct their own behaviour.* Satisfaction of one's need for autonomy is linked to better performance as well as better well-being (Wheatley, 2017). However, perceptions of autonomy can be difficult to maintain in contexts with a high degree of interdependence, either between people or other interrelated features of a system (Väänänen & Toivanen, 2018). This can have implications for team-based sports, where individual athletes are sometimes at risk of having autonomy undermined by top-down pressures on their actions or time (e.g., when feeling they must obey the instructions or wishes of coaches, teammates or even fans).

The *need for competence* refers to the *need to feel competent in the task at hand* and to have the opportunity to refine one's skills on that task. Feeling competent is generally considered fundamental to motivation in the sports context, such that unless a person feels reasonably competent, he or she will be unmotivated to participate (Duda, 2005; Reinboth & Duda, 2006). This need has particular links with the concept of learned helplessness, which we described above. For example, a cyclist who does not feel capable of performing well in an upcoming competition may feel incompetent and be at risk of developing learned helplessness. In contrast, if her teammate feels a sense of mastery over her performance in competitions, she is more likely to develop the opposite mentality of learned competence.

The final basic need is the *need for relatedness*, which refers to *a feeling of connectedness to others.* As with other non-sports domains, feelings of relatedness with others in the sport context are key to feeling motivated to engage in a given activity (Deci & Ryan, 2000; Stults-Kolehmainen, Gilson, & Abolt, 2013). For example, a soccer player who feels connected to other members of his team may be motivated to continue training not only to improve his individual mastery of the game, but also because it allows him to spend time with people he likes and cares about.

Notwithstanding its impact and its capacity to speak to a range of sporting phenomena in a language that is descriptively rich, several questions remain about the nature of the processes at the heart of self-determination theory (see also Chapter 19). Most particularly, it is clear that, as with other dominant theories of motivation that we have examined, the self that these relate to is very much a *personal* self – the self as an individual rather than as a group member. So although the idea of a need for relatedness speaks to the possibility of a more social self, this need is 'tacked onto' the person rather than being seen as in any way integrated into their sense of who they are. But just as an activity (such as football) can be integrated into a person's sense of their personal self (so that Dennis Gardeck could say 'I am football'), so too it, and the group they are part of, can be integrated into a sense of *collective self.* This is articulated, for example, in the Queensland Reds' slogan 'We are Queensland'. Moreover, as we will discuss further below, it seems that processes of this form also have the capacity to *transform* the nature of motivation, such that what is extrinsic to an athlete as an individual (e.g., the welfare of a teammate) may become intrinsic to them as a member of a team (Ellemers et al., 2004; Haslam, 2001). It is with a view to precisely such possibilities that we turn to social identity theorising on this topic.

A SOCIAL IDENTITY APPROACH TO MOTIVATION

The classic approaches to motivation we have reviewed thus far help to explain individual motivation and situational constraints on its development and progress. As noted above, most of these theories take as their locus the individual, and aim to understand how to better motivate a person to expend more energy or effort on a given task. What is less explained by these theories, however, is the role of *other people* in guiding motivation. A desire to provide this opens the way for a more *social* model of sport psychology that examines the role of social identity processes in athletes' motivation.

In this context, it is somewhat surprising that social factors have been comparatively ignored in motivation theories, given very early seminal work by Triplett (1898) showing that performance improves when in the presence of others. In his research (which are sometimes considered the first experiments in social psychology; see Chapter 1), Triplett observed that cyclists performed better when racing against other cyclists rather than against the clock. This was a pattern that he was subsequently able to replicate under more controlled conditions in the laboratory (Karau & Williams, 2017). Moreover, in the century since, this *social facilitation* effect has been observed in other athletic contexts and beyond (e.g., in academic and sartorial domains; Hüffmeier, Krumm, Kanthak, & Hertel, 2012; Markus, 1978; Zajonc, 1965). Nevertheless, other research building on this early work observed that, far from always motivating better performance, the presence of other people sometimes reduces motivation. This *social loafing* effect was first observed by Ringelmann (1913, cited in Kravitz & Martin, 1986), who found that men did not pull as hard collectively in a rope-pulling competition as they did when pulling alone. This finding too has since been replicated in a number of settings, including musical and organisational contexts (Karau & Williams, 1993; Latané, Williams, & Harkins, 1979).

The conclusion to be drawn from this celebrated early psychological research is that motivation is shaped by the social context in which people find – or put – themselves. Moreover, the effects of social context can be both good and ill. That is, the presence of other people can both improve and undermine a person's motivation to engage in a range of tasks (e.g., Haslam, 2004).

Unfortunately, the power of this simple observation has been somewhat lost in subsequent work. In what follows, we argue that the social identity approach has much to offer in uncovering the extent and nature of social impacts on motivation and performance. For not only does this perspective make obvious the fact that social context matters; it also provides a theoretical framework for understanding – and making concrete predictions about – when others will enhance, and conversely reduce, motivation.

Key point 1: Social identity is a basis for motivation and needs

As noted in Chapter 2, the social identity approach is composed of two theories: social identity theory (Tajfel & Turner, 1979) and self-categorization theory (Turner, Hogg et al., 1987). One of the core insights of this approach is that groups shape personal psychology through their ability to be internalised into a person's sense of self, as an aspect of their *social identity*. Moreover, it is people's ability to shift from thinking in terms of personal identity (as 'I' and 'me') to thinking in terms of social identity (as 'us' and 'we') that makes group life possible (Turner, 1982). In ways suggested by Figure 6.3, construing oneself in terms of group memberships therefore has a powerful impact on a person's

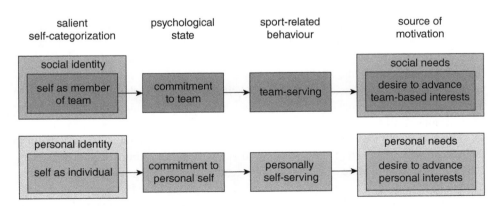

Figure 6.3 The relationship between self-categorization and sporting motivation

psychological state as well as on their interaction with others. These, then, are two factors that are foundational in structuring optimal athletic performance. For example, when acting in terms of personal identity, two people may behave towards each other as strangers and be motivated only by their personal needs. However, if these individuals perceive that they share a social identity, they will see themselves as having more in common, and be more motivated by their shared social needs (Haslam et al., 2000). In this way, social identity furnishes people with a motivational platform for a range of group behaviours that seek to advance the perceived interests of the ingroup to which that identity relates. In particular, it is a basis for cooperation, teamwork and group performance in ways discussed in other chapters in this book (e.g., Chapters 5 and 11).

In this, though, a key message of the social identity literature is that groups structure individual psychology and behaviour only to the degree that they are internalised into a person's sense of self and hence become personally important (Haslam, Jetten et al., 2018). That is, motivation is shaped not by membership in 'any old' group, but rather only by those groups that people define themselves (i.e., self-categorize) as members of and identify with. For example, a person will be much more likely to get up early and travel for three hours in foul weather to watch a football match if they identify (self-categorize) as a supporter of one of the teams that is playing. That said, groups that people do not identify with can have an impact on their behaviour, but the nature of this impact will tend not to be aligned with the interests of the group in question (and sometimes will be diametrically opposed to those interests). For example, if an Everton fan were motivated to watch a match in which Liverpool were playing, it would likely be to cheer on the side of Liverpool's opponents (Viner, 2014).

Perhaps more than in any other domain, these group dynamics are readily apparent in the arena of sport. It is easy, for example, to imagine striving on behalf of one's cherished team, or to beat a despised opponent (De Cuyper et al., 2016). In this context, people are particularly willing to identify with groups that furnish them with a positive sense of self (Ellemers, 1993). Cleary, many sports teams do this, thereby offering a heady opportunity to feel good about oneself (Cialdini et al., 1976; see Chapter 17). Indeed, as noted in Chapter 2, this is also why teams attract more supporters – and more enthusiasm from those supporters – when they are doing well rather than poorly. At the same time too, group identification generally motivates people to put in effort on behalf of a team, and this motivation typically becomes more pronounced the more important it is to make that effort for the group (e.g., if it is playing in a major competition or against a rival team; Slater, Haslam, & Steffens, 2018).

But more than these basic 'us and them' dynamics, shared social identity impacts on the processes that promote, direct and sustain motivation (Ellemers et al., 2004). Not least, it does this by making salient a particular set of group-based needs. In this vein, research has shown that people are more likely to identify with groups that help them to feel autonomous, competent and related to others (Greenaway, Amiot, Louis, & Bentley, 2017). Likewise, in studies of elite Belgian female basketball, volleyball and football players and world-class Norwegian female handball players De Backer and colleagues (2015) found that group identification was enhanced when teams adopted a mastery orientation that prioritised competence building over performance.

In work contexts, too, we find that group identification is more strongly associated with autonomous forms of motivation than with controlled forms of motivation (Greenaway et al., 2019). In the sports context, perceived similarity with other members of an exercise group is also associated with greater enjoyment of sport activities, which is an indicator of intrinsic motivation (Beauchamp, Crawford, & Jackson, 2018; Bennett et al., 2018). This suggests that if athletes can be led to identify with their sport, they will be more likely to engage in the sport out of genuine enjoyment and interest – a motivational state that promotes good performance and encourages persistence – rather than out of duty or an external reward. Indeed, as Figure 6.4 suggests, a key point here is that social identification has the capacity to transform activities that would otherwise be a source of extrinsic motivation (because they are external to the self) into ones that are intrinsically motivating (because they are internal to the self).

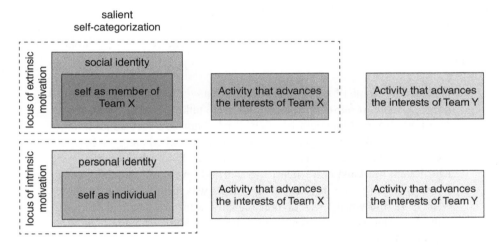

Figure 6.4   Social identity can transform extrinsic sources of motivation into intrinsic ones

Key point 2: Shared social identity is a basis for control and self-efficacy

In addition to meeting basic needs, shared social identity structures self-efficacy, which, as we saw earlier, is a foundational cognition underpinning motivation. Even though people sometimes think of groups as undermining personal control through subjugation of personal desires for the good of the group, research shows that group identification actually promotes feelings of control (Greenaway, Cruwys, Haslam, & Jetten, 2016; Greenaway, Haslam et al., 2015). For example, in an analysis of data from the World Values Survey (encompassing around 62,000 respondents in 47 countries) the first author and her colleagues showed that higher levels of community identification were reliably associated with a heightened sense of personal control (which in turn fed into improved well-being). Although this point has (to our knowledge) yet to be tested in a sporting context, it seems highly likely that the same pattern would be replicated here, such that identification with a team or a sport is a source of control and self-efficacy even in the face of failure. This is seen, for example, in accounts that Hornby (1992) and Viner (2014) provide of their personal experiences as teenagers enduring the slings and arrows of footballing fortune.

This may be for a few reasons. One is that groups themselves are agentic and capable of achieving tasks that are beyond the hope of any one individual to accomplish. When people identify with a group, they internalise attributes of that group into their self-concept (Latrofa, Vaes, Cadinu, & Carnaghi, 2010), and thus may come to see themselves as more agentic. Another reason is that groups offer structure and predictability in a random and chaotic world, and thus help people to feel more in control by helping them understand how to navigate their life experiences (Kay, Gaucher, Napier, Callan, & Laurin, 2008). Indeed, in a BBC World Service documentary, Alan Pringle, a football researcher from the University of Nottingham, made the point that in a world where people's personal fortunes go up and down, identification with a sport team has the capacity to give them a unique sense of personal security and potency:

> Whether it's football, cricket, rugby or whatever, all support gives you hope. In some of our early research we were talking to a lad who was at Mansfield Town. Mansfield is a very small team in a very small mining town in the middle of England that never really reached the great heights. He was saying 'When I was a kid I went to Mansfield; when I was a teenager I went to Mansfield; when I was married I went to Mansfield; when I was divorced I went to Mansfield; when I was married again I went to Mansfield; and when I was divorced again I went to Mansfield', and the only thing that was consistent in his whole life was this team. (*The Why Factor*, 2019)

The latter explanation may be slightly more likely than the former. This is because, as we have seen, group identification is associated with greater personal control even when the group itself has failed and therefore is not currently agentic (Greenaway, Haslam et al., 2015). Thus, even if a sport team loses, to the degree that an athlete feels strongly identified with them, they will feel more in control of their life in general and potentially also feel more control over their sport performance. This process appears to extend to feelings of collective efficacy as well. For example, in experimental studies of basketball and soccer teams, Fransen and colleagues found that group identification was associated with greater feelings of collective efficacy and improved performance (Fransen, Haslam et al., 2015; Fransen, Steffens et al., 2016) . Speaking to the importance of leadership in structuring this phenomenon, these processes were also strengthened when athlete leaders were able to bolster team members' identification with their team.

On top of this, shared social identity also helps people to avoid learned helplessness. Because groups offer a sense of personal control (Greenaway, Cruwys et al., 2016; Greenaway, Haslam et al., 2015), it follows that they can also help people to combat the negative psychological effects of control deprivation. This point has been confirmed in work by Fritsche and colleagues which shows that when people are deprived of control, having them think about a group to which they belong fortifies them psychologically (Fritsche, Jonas, & Fankhänel, 2008; Fritsche et al., 2013). One reason for this may be that the ability to rely on a group takes the pressure off individual performance. As a result, shared identity can be an antidote to the listlessness commonly shown by people who fail repeatedly. Here, then, so long as we have others around us whom we believe can help us achieve our goals – and this is typically people with whom we share social identity – motivation can be preserved.

Finally, too, beyond a sense of self-efficacy, shared social identity also shapes expectancy-related beliefs. As we saw earlier, these are an important precursor for motivation to be kindled. For example, group cohesion is associated with greater expectations of good performance and greater subjective task value – cognitions that are known to increase motivation (Gammage, Carron, & Estabrooks, 2001; Graupensperger et al., 2019; Gu, Solomon, Zhang, & Xiang, 2011; Spink, McLaren, & Ulvick, 2018; Spink, Ulvick, Crozier, & Wilson et al., 2014; Spink, Ulvick, McLaren, Crozier, & Fesser, 2015). Indeed, to the extent that group cohesion structures these cognitions, it is also associated with more positive motivational outcomes, such as training attendance (Burke, Carron, Eys, Ntoumanis, & Estabrooks, 2006; Carron, Hausenblas, & Mack, 1996).

CONCLUSION

Motivation is at the heart of all sporting pursuits, and understanding how to promote, direct and sustain it is critical to ensuring success. Current approaches to motivation have made strides in understanding this process, but, as we have seen, they tended to focus on the individual at the expense of their social context. Yet in the athletic arena, as in all areas of life, our social connections with others structure our psychology and behaviour. And this is particularly true of those that revolve around a sense of shared group membership. In shaping basic needs, cognitions and feelings, shared social identity acts as a fuel for motivation in individual and team sports.

Moreover, as we have also seen, in this it provides the basis for the motivational building blocks that are captured by the classic theories outlined above. In particular, it is a source of the psychological needs specified in self-determination theory, the thought processes specified in cognitive theories, and the control perceptions that ward off learned helplessness. In sum, it is apparent that *groups and the social identities that underpin them provide a strong and distinctive basis for people to achieve the sense of purpose, efficacy and control that are foundational to motivation.* Ironically, then, for what seems at face value to be a relatively personal psychological state, motivation often comes more from without than from within.

NOTE

The work of Katharine Greenaway was supported by an Australian Research Council's Discovery Early Career Researcher Award (DE160100761).

7

COGNITION AND PERFORMANCE

JESSICA SALVATORE
SINDHUJA SANKARAN
DAZANÉ COLE

I really have a point to prove but it can become a mental problem if you think about it too much. There is too much pressure on the track, too much expectation. Each time I am on the track, people expect me to win and beat the world record. (Asafa Powell, former 100 m gold medallist, cited in Broadbent, 2007)

Thoughts are not incidental or trivial accompaniments to sporting performance but active ingredients of it. On several occasions, the Jamaican sprinter Asafa Powell clocked times for the 100 metres below 10 seconds. Nevertheless, he consistently underperformed in high-pressure contexts such as the Olympic Games and World Championships. In the above quote he points to the role of thinking as something that contributed hugely to his underperformance at these critical meetings. As any good coach knows, the coaching toolkit is therefore not just about helping athletes to suppress frustration, to achieve optimal arousal or to work effectively together. For as well as these things, a coaching toolkit also needs to include strategies for effectively managing athletes' cognitions and beliefs – how they approach an event, how they process information about it, what they think about the various challenges they confront, and how they explain their successes and failures.

Figure 7.1 Cognition affects performance

Note: This is a photograph of Jamaican 100m sprinter and former world-record holder, Asafa Powell (on the right), in the process of winning a heat at the Osaka World Championships in 2007. In the final, he was leading at one point but ended up finishing third. Powell later said that he 'panicked' and was 'thinking too much' about the 'high expectations' that people had of him (Broadbent, 2007).

Source: Wikipedia

In short, sport is as much about 'getting your mind right' as it is about getting your body right. As we will see in this chapter, diverse cognitive processes – including expectations, attributions and threat – have a profound bearing on the way athletes perform. In what follows, we will explore these cognitive processes as well as the main theories that have traditionally been used to explain their operation. However, we also go beyond these traditional accounts to explore the ways in which cognition – and hence performance – is shaped by athletes' group memberships, and by the social identities with which these are associated. These social identities, we argue, are aspects of the cognition–performance relationship that have tended to be overlooked by both researchers and practitioners. To address this lacuna, this chapter seeks to show how infusing a social identity analysis can enhance our understanding of the cognition–performance link. It also suggests that exploiting this understanding in practice can help athletes to mobilise cognition to improve (rather than impede) their athletic performance.

As we will see, one of the main limitations of the prevailing research in this field is that it has tended to be unnecessarily *individualistic*. That is, it conceptualises the athlete primarily, and often exclusively, *as an individual* rather than as someone who is *a member of a group*, and whose cognitions – in particular, their expectations, attributions and sense of threat – reflect this. Looking at these same issues through the lens of shared identity, we are therefore able to gain additional insight into the processes that can make performance 'go wrong' (as well as those that can make it 'go right'). After cataloguing these insights, we conclude by considering *why* social identity processes have been relatively overlooked in the literature on cognition and sport performance. The answer, we suggest, has a lot to do with the individualistic model of the person (here, the athlete) that prevails in psychology as a whole. Accordingly, by rethinking this, we argue that sport psychology can have a corrective function not just for the field of sport but for psychology as a whole.

CURRENT APPROACHES TO THE LINK BETWEEN COGNITION AND PERFORMANCE

Standard ways of thinking about the relationship between thought and performance are based in disparate literatures that are not typically in conversation with one another. In what follows, we organise these current approaches into what we refer to as the 'three Ts': traits, tools and threats.

The traits approach

The first way of thinking about cognition is distinct from the other two in that it conceptualises cognition in terms of traits: relatively stable internal tendencies or habits (such as rumination) that are developed, cultivated and become ossified over time. We think of this as broadly comprising not just thinking-related personality traits, but indeed all individual differences that relate to cognition (e.g., a person's attributional style; see also Chapter 8).

One of the traits that has been most widely studied in sporting contexts is *trait anxiety*. This refers to a stable tendency to experience negative emotions such as fear, stress and anxiety across a range of social situations. Measurement scales include items such as 'Before or while I compete in sports, I worry I will not play well' (see Smith, Smoll, & Schutz, 1990). Researchers have identified a negative relationship between trait anxiety and performance across a range of contexts, such that high levels of trait (as well as state) anxiety are found to impair performance (e.g., Baumeister & Showers, 1986; McCarthy, Allen, & Jones, 2013; Murray & Janelle, 2003). However, while anxiety has cognitive components, it is primarily affective (i.e., emotion-based; as discussed in Chapter 9) and, as a result, little research has examined how it feeds directly into thinking and cognition.

The research that has explored this link between traits and cognition affirms that these are important for performance. For example, a large project on the psychological characteristics of high-achieving British athletes confirmed that they typically share the trait of *conscientiousness* (Rees et al., 2016). Athletes who score higher on this trait are more likely to stick to their training programme, to attend all their training sessions, and to give their best not just in competition but also in preparing for it.

Yet while striving towards excellence generally serves athletes well, this can become maladaptive when it takes the form of *perfectionism* (Hill, Mallinson-Howard, & Jowett, 2018). More specifically, athletes' competition performance is typically compromised to the extent that they show signs of *perfectionistic concerns* – that is, concerns about making mistakes, concerns about the discrepancy between their standards and their performance, and concerns about negative evaluation and rejection by others (Stoeber & Otto, 2006). Perfectionist concerns in athletes have also been found to be related to competitive anxiety in ways that adversely affect performance via the anxiety–performance link described above (Flett & Hewitt, 2005). Indeed, this capacity for anxiety to impair performance through its impact on cognition can be seen in the reflections of the Belgian tennis player Filip Dewulf on the unhelpful workings of his mind:

> Making errors was not an option for me and I could get really upset about it. Each point I lost was a personal defeat. Even wonderful actions by my opponent were transformed by my brain into clumsy fumblings by myself. (Dewulf, 2003, p. 71)

While perfectionism and conscientiousness are examples of traits that support the discipline and achievement motivation required for sport performance, other important traits link directly to a person's characteristic 'thinking style'. In particular, a common cause of performance failures in sport is *overthinking*. This was recognised by tennis legend Arthur Ashe when he spoke about 'paralysis by analysis' – the process whereby performance is compromised because attention is diverted to intensive cognitive processing (e.g., overthinking the technical aspects of a stroke instead of tracking the ball trajectory and registering cues from one's opponent; Bergland, 2013).

Similarly, Asafa Powell's reflections on how he 'panicked' and thought about the 'negative consequences of not meeting expectations' (Broadbent, 2007; see Figure 7.1) point to the more general trait of *negative thinking*. In this regard, athletes who are consistently unsuccessful in competitions have also been observed to show higher levels of trait *rumination* than athletes who are consistently successful (Sankaran, von Hecker, & Sanchez, 2019). Trait rumination is defined as having ongoing, repetitive negative thoughts that activate negative memories and schemas (Nolen-Hoeksema & Morrow, 1991; Pyszczynski & Greenberg, 1987). Ruminative thinking can be conceptualised as thinking too much and thinking too negatively (Sankaran et al., 2019), and it is linked with both negative expectations (Carver, Blaney, & Scheier, 1979) and performance difficulties (particularly in the form of *choking*; Hill, Hanton, Matthews, & Fleming, 2010; Nolen-Hoeksema & Morrow, 1991). As Shakespeare put it in *Measure for Measure*, 'Our doubts are traitors, and make us lose the good we oft might win by fearing to attempt' (cited in Charlesworth, 2004, p.18). The truth of this is readily apparent in sport – where it is clear that rumination often has an adverse impact on performance (e.g., Roy et al., 2016; Tahtinen et al., 2020). Here too the consequences of rumination align with those of maladaptive perfectionism (e.g., Blankstein & Dunkley, 2002).

Finally, there is also evidence of a relationship between the *need for cognition* and sports performance (Sankaran et al., 2019). Need for cognition represents an underlying tendency to (need to) think and engage in information processing and reasoning activities (Cacioppo & Petty, 1982). It has been conceptualised as a general trait associated with two tendencies: first, a tendency to extract information from the immediate environment; and second, a tendency to be in a state of 'cognitive vigilance'. So, in the case of elite athletes, the natural tendency to draw information from both the external environment (e.g., about a competitor or the audience) and one's internal state (e.g., related to one's own anxiety or pressure to perform) is likely to be heightened among those who are high in need for cognition. Here too, Sankaran and colleagues (2019) argue that need for cognition can be allied with the notion of 'thinking too much'. As people with a high need for cognition tend to over-process information in ways that ultimately impair performance, this need can be perceived as an indicator of a maladaptive thinking style. Consistent with this, Sankaran and colleagues (2019) in their research, which included 67 elite and semi-elite track and field athletes from Wales and England, found that those who were high (vs low) in rumination and need for cognition had a greater susceptibility to 'choke under pressure' in the context of high-stakes competition. All athletes had been training and competing for a minimum period of three years.

This work on (mal)adaptive information processing styles resonates with an older literature on individual differences in attributional patterns – often referred to as a person's *explanatory style* (see also Chapter 8). A key observation here is that some people are prone to adopt a pessimistic explanatory style in which they engage in excessive self-blaming and catastrophising in response to failure or other negative events. Indeed, this is a key component of a 'persistent cognitive pattern' that Aaron Beck (1964) considered to be characteristic of depression and other psychopathology. So it is perhaps unsurprising that these same thought patterns have negative implications for sporting performance. For example, work by Tim Rees and colleagues has found that gymnasts who blame themselves after a disappointing performance, and believe that one failure will end their career, typically find it harder to perform well (and to continue to perform well) than gymnasts who are able to shrug off a poor performance as 'bad luck' or as the result of circumstances beyond their control (Rees, Ingledew, & Hardy, 2005).

Along these lines, it is fairly well established that the classic pattern of self-serving attributions, in which people explain success with reference to internal factors (e.g., 'I am good') and failure with reference to external factors ('I was unlucky'), proves generally to be adaptive in the domain of sport (as it is elsewhere; Lau & Russell, 1980). What is less clear, however, is whether it is appropriate to see these cognitive patterns as the manifestation of stable traits. Optimistic self-talk, for example, may bolster confidence and performance, but it is also clear that it can be a product of successful performance.

Furthermore, athletes take an active role in interpreting and construing feedback from others. So while we know that performance typically suffers when failure is seen as beyond a person's control and as unlikely to change (Coffee, Rees, & Haslam, 2009), it is also apparent that this pattern is qualified by features of social context. In particular, as Coffee and colleagues discuss in Chapter 8, the attributions that a person makes are affected by the feedback they receive from others and also depend on who those others are (Rees, Salvatore et al., 2013).

In sum, while it is tempting to regard the cognitions that impact athletic (and other) performance as a reflection of stable individual differences (traits), there is little direct evidence to support this analysis. Instead, then, it is more generally the case that the link between cognition and performance is *context-specific*, so that as the context changes so does the nature of the link. We saw this, for example, in the case of Asafa Powell, where the effects of overthinking on performance only manifested themselves in the context of high-stakes competition (see Figure 7.1). As a result, there is more evidence for a modified trait approach in which the perceiver (athlete) plays a less passive role. In this view, the athlete's cognitions are liable to change as a function of such things as context, goals and personal history: Amélie Mauresmo will think different thoughts, in different ways, depending on whether she is playing a major tournament at home (the French Open) or away (Wimbledon), and this difference is a product of her active construal of the personal meaning of her social (French national) identity. Such a position suggests that people's self-concept develops over time – partly as the product of repeated experiences – and then (if adaptive) allows them to deal appropriately with the demands of a specific situation (e.g., a specific athletic competition). In this way, what is commonly understood as personality (the impact of traits) can perhaps better be described as *personal identity* (Turner, 1982). This means, for example, that when a female pole vaulter asks herself, 'Can I get over this bar?', she is asking something about *who she is* as well as something about what she can do. As we will see below, conceptualising cognition in identity-based terms has significant implications for the way we engage with the problems that cognition can create for performance. Not least, this is because while personality is (by definition) hard to change, identity is more fluid and hence more malleable.

The tools approach

A second approach to the link between cognition and performance in sport focuses on skills and practices that athletes can learn to help them overcome challenge and adversity. Once learned, these practices may then be available as a resource for them to use whenever it is appropriate to do so. This approach links cognition to *self-regulation* in conceptualising cognition as something that is actively deployed by a person to help them improve their performance – in much the same way as they might use a piece of equipment like a cricket helmet or baseball glove.

A good example of one such tool is *imagery*. Here a wealth of evidence suggests that if athletes imagine executing a task successfully before they perform it (e.g., a golfer imagining the arc of a putt across a green) or imagine themselves achieving positive outcomes (e.g., the ball ending up in the hole), this will lead to better performance (Beilock, Afremow, Rabe, & Carr, 2001). Likewise, in the midst of a demanding physical challenge, people can be helped to overcome pain by being distracted through a focus on external imagery (Padgett & Hill, 1989). For example, a synchronised swimmer may be able to overcome her physical exhaustion during training sessions if she thinks about the crowd applauding her success at a major event (and the associated fact that, as Sarah Bombell observed, 'the pain of discipline is far less than the pain of regret'; cited in Plasker, 2009, p. 163).

Moreover, the same approach can also help athletes to avoid bad performance, although here the objective is to avoid imagining negative outcomes. So, while a golfer will tend to putt better if she imagines her ball dropping into the hole before she takes a putt, the same will be true if she avoids imagining it sliding past the hole. A problem here, though, is that *over-monitoring* can have ironic effects. For focusing too much attention on a given task (e.g., the explicit monitoring of motor performance) is known to impair performance (Wegner, Ansfield, & Pilloff, 1998). So if our golfer says to herself, 'I must *not* think about slicing the ball', ironically she *is* thinking about slicing it in ways that increase the chances of her ball veering wildly off-course. Indeed, studies with juggling (Smith & Ellsworth, 1981) show that over-monitoring of this form is particularly harmful for well-learned or familiar motor tasks.

Another tool that is widely used to regulate athletic performance is *goal setting* (Locke & Latham, 1990). This involves approaching performance with a pre-set goal in mind, with evidence suggesting that this is likely to be more beneficial if the goal is *specific, challenging* and *realistic* (Weinberg & Butt, 2014). This means, for example, that an elite athlete will typically perform better if their goal is to win at least a bronze medal rather than just to 'do their best' – providing that this does not either stretch them too much or too little. At the same time, too, it is generally beneficial to have a goal that is focused on approaching a desired outcome, such as a successful performance or a win, rather than avoiding an unwanted outcome, such as a loss (Jordet & Hartman, 2008).

Imagery and goal setting are widely used by sporting and exercise coaches to improve athletic performance. Indeed, imagery has been referred to as 'the most powerful mental tool' that athletes can deploy (Taylor, 2012). Moreover, it is clear that the absence of useful thoughts and/or the presence of toxic ones can compromise athletic performance just as surely as inappropriate training, poor diet or illness. Accordingly, developing and learning how to use these cognitive tools is a good investment of time and effort.

Again, though, it is worth asking whether the 'tool' framework is the best way to conceptualise these processes. On the one hand, thinking of imagery and goal setting as tools that athletes can learn over time and then deploy when needed is certainly more empowering than thinking of cognition as the product of dispositional traits that are largely unchangeable. But on the other hand, conceptualising cognitions as tools sets them apart from the person, and fails to recognise that when imagery and goals are most effective, this is because they are aligned with (and become *integrated into*) a person's sense of self (Ellemers et al., 2004). Moreover, this sense of self is often as much social (e.g., about 'our' goals) as personal (about 'my' goals). More generally then, in ways that we elaborate further below, there is value in moving away from an approach which sees cognitions as 'things', to one which sees them as *processes* that centre on the dynamics of a variable self.

The threats approach

A final approach to the cognition–performance relationship focuses on the need for athletes to negotiate features of their environment that present themselves as *threats* to who they are and what they want to do. This approach therefore differs from the trait approach and the tools approach in focusing on matters of social context.

The key point here is that in a wide range of domains humans routinely have *thoughts* about threats that have significant consequences for their performance. In sport, as elsewhere, these threats generally relate to a person's sense of self (including their sense of competence or ability; Fredrickson & Harrison, 2005). Awareness of these threats then creates forms of pressure that can often lead to choking (Baumeister & Showers, 1986).

One form of self-threat that has been a particular focus for research is *stereotype threat*. As originally defined by Claude Steele (1997), this refers to threat that arises when a person becomes aware that their behaviour may confirm a negative stereotype about a group or social category they belong to. In the realm of athletics, for example, a European runner racing against African athletes may experience threat due to an awareness of European athletes' inferiority in long-distance events.

Such threats have been most widely studied in relation to gender, race and age stereotypes. However, they can be based on social categorizations or group memberships of any form. In a football match against Germany, for example, English penalty-takers may experience an analogous threat due to their knowledge of England's poor previous performance in penalty shoot-outs (Alleyne, 2009). The group involved does not even need to be broadly or profoundly stigmatised within society; the group must simply come off badly in a stereotype comparing its performance in some valued domain to that of some other group.

As a corollary, it is also the case that awareness of positive stereotypes about an ingroup can lead to improved performance through a process referred to as *stereotype lift* (Walton & Cohen, 2003). This, for example, might be something that German penalty takers might benefit from. Nevertheless, there is evidence that while positive stereotypes can boost performance, under certain circumstances they too can lead to choking, especially in the presence of an observer (Krendl, Gainsburg, & Ambady, 2012). This is typically explained with reference to an *evaluation apprehension* effect. Imagine, for instance, that the German football team experience a high-pressure situation (such as a crucial penalty shoot-out situation in the next World Cup). One might generally expect the stereotype here to work to their benefit. However, since the stakes are high and the whole world is watching and evaluating them, this increases the possibility that a German penalty-taker will 'choke' under pressure.

But how is such impairment brought about? What is stereotype threat *doing*? Research points to a range of cognitive mechanisms that seem to be at play here, of which three have been seen to be particularly important (Pennington, Heim, Levy, & Larkin, 2016).

First, stereotype threat can prompt *intrusive negative thoughts* about the task itself (Cadinu, Maass, Rosabianca, & Kiesner, 2005), as well as overthinking (Beilock & McConnell, 2004). As discussed above, these can lead to explicit monitoring of one's own behaviour that impairs performance of athletic tasks, particularly if they are well learned or highly familiar ones. Relatedly, thinking about stereotypes can be so distracting that it leaves insufficient resources (of attention and effort) for the athletic task itself (DeCaro, Thomas, Albert, & Beilock, 2011). All such forms of self-consciousness interrupt performance. This reflects the fact that when athletes perform a habitual task well (e.g., driving a golf ball), they are typically in a state of *flow* in which they are not directly aware of what they are doing, but rather doing what comes 'naturally' (Csikszentmihalyi, 1990). Stereotype threat, however, can make them become self-aware in ways that interrupt this flow (Hermann & Vollmeyer, 2016).

Second, stereotype threat can be a source of *demoralisation* that affects performance even in the absence of explicit monitoring or overthinking. In particular, this can have a negative impact on the planning stages of actions that occur prior to the execution of a particular task (Chalabaev, Brisswalter et al., 2013). For example, in the lead-up to a penalty shoot-out, players who are experiencing stereotype threat may be thinking more about the reaction of the crowd in the event that they miss than about where they need to aim the ball. In the longer term, an athlete demoralised by the awareness of stereotypes may also develop *self-handicapping* strategies for protecting themselves from these aversive thoughts, such as failing to engage in sufficient practice. These strategies may also be reinforcing (and therefore hard to break out of) because such self-handicapping provides an alternative explanation for failure that can be (relatively) more tolerable than the idea that there might be some truth to painful stereotypes (Stone, 2002; see also Chapter 8).

Third, stereotype threat can disrupt an athlete's *goals* in ways that lead them to shift their focus from the goals they are striving to achieve (e.g., to run the 100 metres in under 10 seconds) to goals that they are striving to avoid (e.g., repeating mistakes that were made in a previous race). This seemingly small shift in focus can make an important difference in athletic outcomes. For example, French female soccer players completing a ball-dribbling task were found to perform significantly worse when they were exposed to the stereotype that women are worse than men at this task, and this performance impairment was mediated by an increased focus on failure avoidance rather than goal attainment (e.g., a tendency to agree that 'it is important for me to avoid being one of the worst performers on this test' rather than 'it is important for me to perform better than others on this test'; Chalabaev, Sarrazin, Stone, & Cury, 2008, p. 149).

The accumulated effect of all these processes can be quite powerful, leading some researchers to suggest that stereotype threat is at the heart of a range of persistent disparities in sporting achievement, in particular, those associated with both race and gender (Chalabaev, Sarrazin, Fontayne, Boiché, & Clément-Guillotin, 2013). Indeed, given the accumulated impact of these processes, one might well ask how athletes who are members of threatened groups ever manage to succeed (Haslam, Salvatore, Kessler, & Reicher, 2008). Nevertheless, the fact that they *do* sometimes succeed suggests that there is something missing from this analysis. To understand what this might be we need to move beyond an analysis of threat that conceptualises athletes in purely individualistic terms. The key thing, then, is to recognise that the threats athletes face are social and not just personal. That is, they are intimately tied to their group membership, in ways that have profound psychological consequences. By better understanding the collective context in which athletes compete, and the collective self that this implicates, we should therefore be able to better understand not only why they succumb to threats, but also why and how they can overcome them.

Summary

The link between thinking and (athletic) performance is a robust one. Accordingly, it would clearly be a mistake not to take thinking into account when trying to improve one's own or others' athletic performance. At the same time, though, as with many other areas of sport psychology, the role of groups – and associated social identities – in shaping athletes' thought processes tend to be overlooked. The exception to this is in stereotype threat research which underlines the fact that the groups one belongs to have a powerful impact on both cognition and performance. Even here, though, this impact is seen primarily to contribute to performance deficit – with little attention being paid to the potential benefits of shared identity. This leaves open the question of whether shared identity might be mobilised in ways that turn the cognition–performance relationship to an athlete's advantage. This is a question that we can only answer by taking social identity a lot more seriously than sport and exercise psychologists have to date.

A SOCIAL IDENTITY APPROACH TO THE LINK BETWEEN COGNITION AND PERFORMANCE

In an effort to plug the gaps that the foregoing review exposed, in the remainder of this chapter we seek to re-examine the cognition–performance link through the lens of social identity theorising (e.g., as reviewed in Chapter 2). This perspective points us to the potential for social identity-based cognitions to be powerful determinants of a wide range of athletic outcomes. In particular, it suggests that just as social identities can be a source of threat or thinking that undermines performance, so too they can be a source of inspiration that enhances it.

Key point 1: Sport-related cognitions are not random or idiosyncratic but are shaped by social identity-based social influence

Thinking is a social activity, so it would be a mistake to conceptualise thoughts as de-contextualised from social influence. Yet that is precisely what the standard approaches that we outlined above typically do. That is, they treat the thoughts that are associated with traits and tools (and even in some cases threats) as somehow independent of the social ecology in which athletes live. In this context, shared identity is both a constraint and facilitator of thinking. To illustrate this, in this section we focus on the *placebo effect* in sport, as this is a powerful demonstration of the impact of one particular type of thought, namely *expectations*.

The placebo effect occurs when an inert substance is described as an active substance and exerts effects that mimic those of that active substance. For example, an athlete may drink decaffeinated coffee before a training session but believe that they have drunk caffeinated coffee and then feel – and display – extra energy during the session that follows. On the flip side, the *nocebo effect* is the name given to similar *negative* influences, such as the poor coordination displayed when someone who believes they have consumed large amounts of alcohol has actually been drinking non-alcoholic beverages. Both effects have been repeatedly observed in sporting contexts with placebos and nocebos that include anabolic steroids, carbohydrates and caffeine (for a review, see Beedie & Foad, 2009). The two effects are generally understood to arise from *self-fulfilling expectancies* (Kirsch, 1985).

There are many examples of these placebos and nocebos operating in the world of sport. One is provided by *placebo analgesias* that are sometimes used to divert athletes' attention away from pain (e.g., in the form of a sugar pill that is believed to be an aspirin). Work by Luana Colloca and Fabrizio Benedetti (2009) suggests that these are effective because (and to the extent that) people acquire an expectation of a painkilling effect through *social learning*. The fact that this learning is so important is a reflection of the more general fact that humans are social animals who know what to expect in the world at large (in ways that give them a competitive advantage) because they are attuned to information that others provide about that world (Turner, 1991).

Another example can be seen in the realm of athletic nutrition, where the belief that carbohydrate ingestion improves athletic performance created a fad in the 1980s and 1990s for 'carb-loading', with pasta dinners the night before competitions. Consuming carbohydrates certainly has some benefits for performance, but some of the apparent or felt benefits are in fact placebo effects (Clark, Hopkins, Hawley, & Burke, 2000). Accordingly, nowadays athletes typically have a more complex appreciation of the value of carbohydrates, with many seeing them as having more negative than positive effects on the body. This in turn alerts us to the fact that the power of placebos derives from prevailing *social norms* about the benefits of particular substances, norms that are susceptible to change. This means that athletes 30 years ago would consume – and benefit from – large carbohydrate intake in ways that would not be seen (or be beneficial) today. Although (to our knowledge) no experiment has directly tested this proposition, other experimental evidence certainly supports the claim that perceptions and cognitions are heavily structured by social influences, and that these can affect performance for better or worse independently of the inherent properties of a particular stimulus or substance (e.g., see Haslam, Jetten, O'Brien, & Jacobs, 2004; Platow, Voudouris et al., 2007).

Yet social identity theorising does more than simply alert us to the fact that expectations are 'socially tuned'. In particular, it suggests that some people are better able to tune our expectations than others. This means that when it comes to placebo effects, our relationship with the source of information about a given stimulus or substance matters. More particularly, as noted in Chapter 2, people are generally only influenced by messages (e.g., about the nature of a substance and its benefits) to the extent that they identify with their source (i.e., such that they are seen to emanate from an ingroup; Turner, 1991; see also Chapter 4). Indeed, if people are influenced by a message from an outgroup source, it is typically in an unintended way.

These identity-related things, we argue, have a significant bearing on the operation of placebo (and nocebo) effects. By way of example, Major League Baseball player Steve Finley reportedly wore a pouch of minerals around his neck that he was given by a former teammate on a previous team, and he shared the practice with another of his teammates, Darin Erstad (Miller, 2005). This was understood by Finley and Erstad as a source of both strength and healing, and given what we know about placebos, it probably was. Nevertheless, it seems likely that these effects would be less apparent if the minerals were sourced from a stranger or, worse, from a player for the Oakland A's (a long-term rival of one of Finley's teams).

Relatedly, social identity theorising also gives us a way to understand the value of collective sport team rituals (such as the All Blacks' Haka; Bonk, Leprince, Tamminen, & Doron, 2019) and certain sporting superstitions (such as teammates agreeing to grow a 'playoff beard'). These rituals and superstitious behaviours on the part of athletes may seem like magical thinking, yet evidence suggests that they can be effective (Bleak & Frederick, 1998). One reason for this is that they are a form of placebo that is strongly grounded in shared social identity. Indeed, more generally, one might argue that placebo-based expectations (and their very real impacts) are a collective *accomplishment* (Levinovitz, 2015) that flows from the capacity for shared identity to define and create social reality (Haslam, Turner, Oakes, Reynolds, & Doosje, 2002).

These various observations suggest to us that there is considerable value in paying attention to the way in which shared identity drives athletes' cognition and, through this, their performance. Nevertheless, it is revealing that a recent consensus statement from experts across many disciplines, considering the mechanisms that underpin placebo effects in sport, made no reference to groups and collectives as sources of beliefs (Beedie et al., 2018). This points to a more general shortcoming in sport psychology, namely that researchers have talked about sport-related beliefs as if they were independent of collective influences. Indeed, within the field there appears to be a shared normative understanding that when considering the mechanisms that mediate between cognition and performance it is best to think as 'micro' as possible (e.g., by looking to neurobiology and the role of brain structures; Beedie et al., 2018; Zani & Rossi, 1991). We think this is a mistake and that our understanding of the role of cognition in sport will benefit from challenging ourselves to take the social sources of athletes' thoughts a lot more seriously than we have to date. In short, we need to think a lot more 'macro'.

Key point 2: The construal of performance-related feedback is shaped by social identity

Performance-related feedback is a form of communication and, as Peters notes in Chapter 4, all communication is subject to interpretative processes that are informed by social identity. This means that shared identity provides a platform for the interpretation of feedback in ways that feed directly into performance (see also Chapter 8). To illustrate this in practice, in this section we focus on work which looks at how athletes respond to *feedback* from other people – in particular, feedback about the causes of success and failure as well as coaching more generally.

Thinking of feedback through the lens of shared identity encourages us to recognise the importance of the collective context and content that shapes how athletes understand both *what* they are hearing and *why* they are hearing it. For example, if members of the England football team hear themselves referred to dismissively as 'chokers', their reaction will necessarily depend on whether the speaker is an insider (e.g., one of their own coaches) or an outsider (e.g., a hostile journalist).

This dynamic is revealed by a study that Jessica Salvatore conducted with Tim Rees and colleagues, which examined athletes' recovery from downward performance spirals (Rees, Salvatore et al., 2013). This took the form of an experiment in which participants had to throw three rounds of darts, each separated by performance feedback. Importantly, participants were blindfolded, and so could be led to believe that they had failed at the task – being told that they had scored just six out of 30 in the first round and three out of 30 in the second round (performance that was labelled as 'failure'). However, this feedback was also paired with specific claims about why participants had failed and how likely they were to fail again. More specifically, after the first round they were given the discouraging information that their performance was beyond their control and unlikely to improve, but after the second round they were told, more encouragingly, that it was within their control and could change. Crucially, too, this feedback was given by someone who was either an ingroup member (a student at the same university) or an outgroup member (a student at a rival university).

In line with social identity principles (notably the *influence principle* described in Chapter 2), our key prediction was that the source of the feedback would have a significant bearing on whether it was taken on board. This proved to be the case. More particularly, we found that discouraging feedback impaired subsequent performance and that encouraging feedback improved it – but *only* when that feedback came from an ingroup source. Furthermore, participants who reported wanting to prove the outgroup wrong and to prove the ingroup right showed the most notable reversals of their downward performance.

In this way, the study underlines two key points. First, that feedback is more likely to have its intended effects when it is provided by an ingroup (rather than an outgroup) source. Second, that these effects are stronger when they tap into pre-existing group-based motivations. In this case, then, the encouraging feedback was most potent when, as well as being provided by an ingroup member, it also stimulated a sense of intergroup rivalry.

Studies conducted by Sankaran reinforce the point that how we interpret feedback is shaped by social identity (Sankaran, 2012). In all three studies, elite and semi-elite track and field athletes were recruited from sport training institutes in Cardiff, Wales. The athletes were selected based on criteria that they had been training and competing for a minimum period of three years and were under the supervision of a coach. The athletes belonged to the elite/sub-elite sporting category and had all participated in county, national or world championships. Long-distance runners were excluded because they did not engage in high-intensity training before the competition. Athletes with disabilities were also excluded. All training performances were recorded one or two weeks before the actual competition, thereby ensuring that the athletes indeed were in full training. In Study 1, athletes were encouraged to think of themselves as belonging to one of two *groups* – either as athletes who are consistently successful in competitions or as athletes who are consistently unsuccessful. More particularly, those athletes who performed better in training than in competition were labelled as unsuccessful athletes, while those who performed better in competition than in training were labelled as successful athletes. In Study 2 and Study 3, the athletes' coach then provided them with feedback about their performance in a training session. The key question was whether the athletes' responses to feedback (i.e., their subsequent performance) would be affected by the group to which they had been assigned.

In Study 2, after running 100 metres, the coach gave the athletes either positive feedback ('good job; great timing') or negative feedback ('that was a poor performance'). After this, the athletes were asked to run again. The key finding here was that the feedback had most impact on the group for which it was *fitting* (in ways suggested by self-categorization theory; Oakes et al., 1994). Thus, the performance of 'successful' athletes improved after they were given positive feedback (but was unaffected by negative feedback), while the performance of 'unsuccessful' athletes declined after they were given negative feedback (but was unaffected by positive feedback).

In Study 3, the coach provided athletes either with no feedback (just a head nod) or neutral feedback ('run tall, swing your arms'). Here, the performance of 'successful' athletes did not change in either condition, but the performance of those labelled unsuccessful declined in both. Along the lines of the results of the previous study, we reasoned that these patterns reflect athletes' internalisation messages that are relevant to their (social) identity. So while Study 2 showed that athletes who see themselves as successful internalise positive feedback and that athletes who see themselves as unsuccessful internalise negative feedback, these findings suggest that ambiguous information is interpreted through the lens of one's (social) identity. In this case, then, an 'unsuccessful' athlete is more likely than a 'successful' one to interpret neutral feedback in a negative way (e.g., seeing the instruction to 'run tall' as a sign of deficiency). In line with this analysis, researchers have confirmed that athletes who are labelled 'successful' make more optimistic inferences about their performance while those labelled 'unsuccessful' make more pessimistic inferences (Sankaran, 2012).

The key point that these divergent lines of research reinforce is that social identity provides an important lens through which sport-related feedback is interpreted. Rather than feedback having information value on its own, its impact is always structured by perceivers' sense of self and, more particularly, by a sense of oneself as a member of a particular group. As a result, the meaning and impact of feedback varies not only as a function of the perceivers' own group membership, but also as a function of their identity-based relationship with the source of that feedback. Accordingly, while it may be true of feedback that 'if it doesn't challenge you, it doesn't change you' (cited in Tong, 2014), we would add that to produce change, feedback needs to do more than just challenge. It needs to *resonate*. And this is a matter of identity, not just information.

Key point 3: Shared social identity is generally a psychological asset rather than a liability for athletes and can be mobilised as a source of cognitive strength

The literature on stereotype threat that we discussed above speaks to the point that identity – both personal and social – is at the heart of the cognitive dynamics that create performance impairments (and indeed, that create threat itself). Indeed, partly as a reflection of this point, as their ideas evolved, researchers in this area came to reconstrue (and relabel) the phenomenon of stereotype threat as *social identity threat* (e.g., Steele, Spencer, & Aronson, 2002; see also Branscombe, Ellemers, Spears, & Doosje, 1999).

This means, for example, that a white man who does not identify as an athlete is not threatened by the stereotype 'white men can't jump' in the same way that an aspiring varsity player might be (Schmader, Johns, & Forbes, 2008). As noted above, the point then is that these are not merely individual threats. Rather, they intimately tie the individual to the group and reflect the individual's group membership in ways that have psychological consequences both for performance and for well-being (the second and third 'Ps' discussed in Chapter 2).

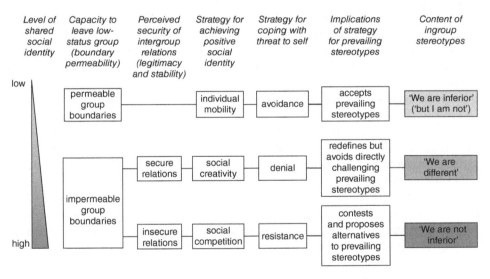

Figure 7.2 Social identity can be a basis for resisting stereotype threat

Note: This figure is a logical extension to Figure 2.1. It points to the fact that while a social identity associated with membership of a low-status group (e.g., women soccer players) can be a threat to a person's self-esteem and a source of stress, it can also be the basis for people to access cognitive alternatives which point to the instability of existing conditions and envision ways in which these unfavourable conditions can be changed (Haslam & Reicher, 2006). These cognitions are then a basis for group members to overcome stereotype threat rather than succumb to it.

Source: Haslam, Salvatore et al. (2008)

Yet while researchers have acknowledged the importance of social identity for the experience of threat, they have not fully reckoned with the capacity for cognition that is grounded in shared social identity to directly buffer athletes from the negative effects of stereotype threat. Thus, as researchers have developed interventions for combatting stereotype threat effects, they have tended to insist that shared identity functions exclusively as a liability (as in the white male basketball player example above). In contrast, we would note that the most promising interventions leverage shared identity as an asset and specifically focus on how people can come to envisage alternative states of the world and of intergroup relations. In ways originally suggested by Tajfel and Turner's (1979) specification of social identity theory, this analysis therefore suggests that while there are conditions under which athletes will 'buy into' negative self-stereotypes, there will also be conditions under which they *resist* them and develop *cognitive alternatives* (Reicher & Haslam, 2012; see Figure 7.2). Critically, though, the development of a sense of *oppositional social identity* (of 'us' against 'them') is critical to this resistance (Haslam & Reicher, 2012; Haslam, Salvatore, Kessler, & Reicher, 2008).

Supporting this analysis, research that the first author conducted with Tim Rees has shown that athletes' performance can improve when they are encouraged to *challenge* the validity of threatening stereotypes (Salvatore & Rees, 2014). More specifically, studies of hundreds of athletes playing different sports and encountering diverse types of threat indicate that athletes are readily amenable to the induction of a *stereotype-sceptical mindset* that protects their performance. One sample involved male soccer players each taking 10 penalty shots after being reminded of the negative national stereotype (that English footballers are bad at penalties) or after being reminded of it and then encouraged to question and challenge it. As predicted, those in the latter condition scored more penalties than those in the threat-only condition. We conceptually replicated this result with female footballers and male and female cricketers, with each group being reminded of a respective relevant stereotype.

This research reminds us that while stereotypes can be a source of threat, their negative effects are not inevitable and can be overcome. In particular, social identity theory gives us reason to believe that changing the way that people think about group relations (and what stereotypes mean in the context of those group relations) can be an effective means of combatting classic underperformance effects. This, for example, was something that the England football manager Gareth Southgate attempted to do prior to the 2018 World Cup by seeking to build positive relations with English journalists in ways that led the players to no longer see them (and their articles) as a source of external threat. Apart from anything else, this meant that the players were no longer hostage to what the journalists wrote:

> 'We've spoken to the players about writing their own stories,' said the manager, Gareth Southgate, after the team beat Colombia in an unprecedentedly victorious (for England) penalty shootout. 'Tonight they showed they don't have to conform to what's gone before. They have created their own history. … We always have to believe in what is possible in life and not be hindered by history or expectations. (Saner, 2018)

More generally, understanding social identity *as an asset* allows us to generate a set of new insights about the relationship between cognition and performance. More specifically, it is apparent that the content of thoughts about *valued groups* does not necessarily need to undermine performance. Thinking about groups can help performance – indeed, the more groups, the more help (Jones & Jetten, 2011). Furthermore, if we fail to acknowledge that people value their groups and that they derive benefits from their connection to those groups (in ways discussed by Cruwys et al. in Chapter 15), then this limits our imagination when it comes to trying to reduce the disruptive effects of certain types of thinking. For example, it is telling that, to date, most recommendations for countering stereotype threat have focused on ways of distancing oneself from the stereotype (e.g., by drawing the individual away from their ingroup) rather than on ways of challenging the stereotype. This means that they are more strategies of avoidance that 'treat the symptom' than strategies of resistance that try to 'treat the disease' (Cole, 2017; see Figure 7.2).

For this reason, we suggest that the way forward involves designing interventions that do not try to deny social identity but rather seek to affirm its value (e.g., in ways suggested by the GROUPS 4 HEALTH programme; Haslam, Cruwys et al., 2016, 2019). Moreover, we need research that systematically compares the effectiveness of such interventions with that of interventions which fail to do so or which actively undermine this link. The general point here is that efforts to clarify how social identity both constrains *and liberates* thinking are important because this seems certain to give us a richer appreciation of its capacity to both impede and facilitate performance. In addition to this, they should allow us to develop a framework for understanding how cognitions can change, and be changed, over time – rather than being set in stone (as trait approaches suggest). As Gareth Southgate's comments attest, this speaks to the capacity for social identity to be a cognitive platform for rewriting history, not just reproducing it.

CONCLUSION

The role of cognition in performance has a double-edged quality: it has the potential to cause great damage, but can also be harnessed towards transformative ends. In this chapter, we have tried to amplify our understanding of why this is the case by showing that thoughts are structured and are given meaning not just by people's individuality, but also by the groups of which they are members and which are a basis for their sense of social identity. Moreover, through their power to structure cognition in this way, these social identities prove to be a source of both under- and over-achievement. Either way, they are game-changers.

These observations, though, beg one final question. If it is so important, why is social identity routinely overlooked when psychologists focus on matters of cognition? One might think that this link would be a no-brainer (especially in the field of sport, where threat and team dynamics abound). Clearly, though, it is not. In part, this is a reflection of the individualistic model of the person that is dominant in North America, where many of the most influential ideas about cognition (and sport psychology) were developed (Pepitone, 1981). Indeed, as we noted above, in line with this metatheoretical bent, for decades the field has seen calls for researchers and thinkers in the field to go more and more micro (e.g., see Zani & Rossi, 1991).

Given this, it should come as no surprise that those working in the field of performance and sport psychology generally fail to conceptualise athletes and their thinking as products of group life and the social sense of self that it engenders. Nevertheless, this chapter is an exhortation to change this state of affairs and for researchers to invest in the task of bringing a properly social model of the human subject to bear on the analysis of cognition in sport. Indeed, doing so would put us in a better position to make advances both on the field of play and in the field of psychology.

8

ATTRIBUTION

PETE COFFEE
PATTI PARKER
ROSS MURRAY
SIMON KAWYCZ

A lot of hard work goes in. … It's a massive team effort. (Rory Best, captain of the Irish Rugby Union team on winning the award of 2018 World Rugby Team of the Year, cited in Hanratty, 2018)

Attributions are explanations about why particular behavioural or performance outcomes occurred, and these explanations enhance our ability to predict and control events in the future. Consider for a moment whether it is even possible to experience sport and not consider attributions for behaviours and performances. How would young athletes develop and improve if they did not evaluate why a performance went well (to repeat that success) or why a performance went poorly (to correct behaviour in the future)? What would sport commentators comment on if they could not debate motives for behaviour and reasons for a team's success or demise?

As pondering such questions makes clear, attributions are front and centre of the experience of sport. Most obviously, attribution processes are extremely relevant in sporting contexts because these typically involve, and require, clear explanations for success and failure. In the above quote from Rory Best, for example, we see that he attributes his team's success to 'a lot of hard work' and 'a massive team effort'. But equally he might have said, 'we were very lucky' or 'they made a lot of mistakes that we were able to capitalise on'. Would this have mattered? And, if so, what would the consequences have been (e.g., for team dynamics, motivation and future performance)?

These are the sorts of questions that the present chapter seeks to address, in exploring the ways in which attributions shape key sporting processes and outcomes. The chapter will review predominant theoretical approaches to attributions in sport and exercise psychology (Rees et al., 2005; Weiner, 1985, 2012, 2018). We will look at approaches to help athletes and exercisers think more positively (through attributional retraining) and consider why there are differences in the way that we explain our own and others' behaviours. The chapter will then move on to discuss how the social identity approach can enrich our understanding of attribution processes in sport and exercise settings.

CURRENT APPROACHES TO ATTRIBUTION RESEARCH

Attribution theory

Bernard Weiner (1985) proposed that human behaviour can be motivated by the way individuals explain the causes of events or behavioural outcomes. Take, for example, the case of a golfer, Cathy, who fails to make the cut in a major tournament. Weiner's (1985, 2012, 2018) attribution theory suggests that the way she explains this outcome to herself will have consequences not only for her well-being, but also for her future behaviour, such as her motivation to come back and try to make the cut in the next tournament. In particular, the theory predicts that she is going to be more motivated to do this if she convinces herself that she adopted the wrong strategy, did not practise enough or was simply unlucky this time, than if she believes her failure is a sign that she just doesn't have what it takes to succeed.

Weiner argued that attributions for negative, important or unexpected events occur quickly, often outside awareness, and that these attributions can significantly impact an individual's subsequent cognitions, emotions and motivated behaviour. In particular, he postulated that attributions (i.e., causal explanations of events) can be classified in terms of three dimensions or properties: *locus of causality*, *stability* and *controllability*.

Locus of causality refers to whether an event (technically, an *explanandum*: a thing to be explained) is perceived to be caused by a factor internal or external to an individual (anchored by an internal or external pole; Weiner, 2014). In our golfing example, attributions to bad luck would be external, while attributions to lack of ability are internal. These would play an important role in determining Cathy's emotional responses to her failure – not least her self-esteem and sense of worth and her willingness to persevere rather than give up.

Stability refers to whether an event is perceived as transient or unchanging. This causal property is critical in determining expectancies of future success (or failure) and is tied to various emotions, including (but not limited to) confidence, anxiety, hopelessness and hope. If Cathy believes her failure to make the cut is a one-off event and something that can change (e.g., if she changes her strategy), she will feel more hopeful and be less likely to give up than if she thinks her performance is unlikely to improve in future.

Finally, the *controllability* dimension refers to whether an event is seen to be caused by factors that are under a person's control or beyond his or her control. This dimension is associated with judgements of responsibility so that the more controllable an outcome is, the more likely an individual is to take responsibility for it. If Cathy attributes her failure to bad luck, then this is clearly beyond her control, and she does not need to feel responsible for it. However, if she sees it as a reflection of her (lack of) effort or selection of a poor strategy, then missing the cut is clearly down to her. In the latter cases, where failure is seen as controllable, this is likely to trigger a specific cluster of emotions in the person who experiences it, including guilt, anger and regret. It may also invite criticism from onlookers (who might be more sympathetic if the outcome was uncontrollable; Weiner, Graham, & Chandler, 1982).

This analysis alerts us to the fact that there are myriad ways in which any particular sporting outcome can be explained. In Cathy's case, for example, failure to make the cut could be explained by her lack of ability (an internal, stable, uncontrollable attribution), by adopting the wrong strategy (internal, unstable, controllable), or by her coach's poor instruction (external, stable, uncontrollable). Here, a sense that it results from lack of ability is likely to produce lowered expectancy of success and feelings of shame and hopelessness since Cathy may view the cause as personal and unchanging. Using a wrong strategy, however, is more likely to increase her expectancy for success and produce feelings of guilt and a sense of responsibility because the cause is seen as something that can change and is within her personal control. By the same token, we can see that Rory Best's attribution of his team's success to 'a lot of hard work' (an internal and controllable attribution) is likely to produce pride and high levels of self-esteem, together with a positive sense of responsibility.

More generally, as Figure 8.1 indicates, Weiner (1985, 2012, 2018) argues that attributions are tied to behaviour change through a temporal sequence in which they first affect cognitions and emotions, and then in turn shape behaviour. A key idea here, then, is that making the 'right' attribution is an important way to produce desired forms of behaviour down the track. In Cathy's case, for example, if she is going to go on to greater things in golf, it will be important for her to see her failure as something more than simply a reflection of her lack of ability.

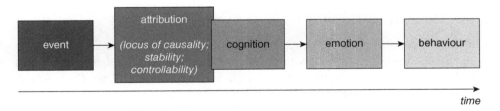

Figure 8.1 Attribution theory

When it comes to efforts to promote positive outcomes in sport, the dominant line of theorising has placed particular emphasis on the importance of the controllability dimension (e.g., Biddle, 1993; Hardy, Jones, & Gould, 1996). In particular, Tim Rees and colleagues (2005) proposed that research in sport and exercise psychology should focus on the main effects of controllability as well as on the way that controllability interacts with *generalisability*. Generalisability relates to stability (as defined in Weiner's theory) and also globality and universality. *Globality* concerns the degree to which the cause of an event is seen as likely to affect a wide (vs a narrow) range of situations; *universality* concerns the degree to which the cause of an event is seen to be common to all people (vs unique to an individual; Rees et al., 2005).

The first author and his colleagues have examined the interactive effects of controllability and generalisability and have provided empirical evidence of the conditions under which controllability is pertinent to future outcomes (e.g., Coffee, Greenlees, & Allen, 2015; Coffee & Rees, 2008a, 2008b, 2009). For example, in the case of our golfer Cathy, if her failure is seen as being due to something that is likely to affect a wide range of situations, then it is important that she has control over these factors and can influence them (Coffee et al., 2015; Coffee & Rees, 2008b). Such attributions might include ineffective practice or using the wrong strategy. Indeed, as these are attributions that will affect a number of new future situations for Cathy, it is crucial that she has control over them. For this is likely to enhance her mental state following failure, by boosting expectations for success and positive emotions, and this should result in improved performance in the future.

But what if Cathy attributes her failure to a different global attribution such as, for example, her lack of ability? In this case, Cathy's attribution will again influence a number of new future situations but ones that she has little to no control over. This is likely to impair her mental state following failure, fuelling negative emotions and reducing expectations for success, and in ways that result in poorer performance in the future. Together, then, the interactive effects of controllability and generalisability suggest that while a sense of control over the causes of failure (and success) is always important, its impact on cognitions, emotions and behaviour is dependent on the generalisability of causes (e.g., whether the cause affects a wide versus a narrow range of situations).

Attributional retraining

Building on the foregoing ideas, attributional retraining is a motivation intervention designed to encourage individuals to develop adaptive (e.g., controllable) rather than maladaptive (e.g., uncontrollable) explanations for poor performance (Perry, Chipperfield, Hladkyj, Pekrun, & Hamm, 2014). For example, the retraining may focus on helping an athlete to understand the ways in which outcomes are controllable and unstable (e.g., a consequence of 'strategy'; adaptive) rather than uncontrollable and stable (e.g., due to 'low ability'; maladaptive). Speaking to the efficacy of this approach, a range of studies point to the capacity for attributional retraining to promote positive cognitive, emotional and motivational outcomes as well as to stimulate improved performance and increased persistence across a range of sporting and educational contexts (Le Foll, Rascle, & Higgins, 2008; Perry et al., 2014; Rascle, Le Foll, Charrier, Higgins, Rees, & Coffee, 2015; Rees et al., 2013).

In sport, recent attributional retraining studies have looked at attributions used for individuals' golf-putting and dart-throwing performance. For example, in a study by Olivier Rascle and colleagues (2015), students were randomly assigned to an adaptive (functional) attributional feedback group, a maladaptive (dysfunctional) attributional feedback group and a no-feedback group. Those in the adaptive attributional condition were told that the causes of their performance on the task (e.g., golf-putting) reflected mostly personally controllable and unstable factors (e.g., their effort or strategy). They were also reminded that they could take personal control over the effort they put into the task and that the intensity of effort might change over time. Students in the maladaptive attributional feedback condition were told that the causes of their performance on the task (dart-throwing) reflected personally uncontrollable and stable factors (e.g., task difficulty). They were told these factors were not something they could control and that they would not change over time. Finally, students in the control condition were given general information about the task (e.g., the distance of the putt, that different skills are required to be a good golfer).

Going back to our original example, let's suppose Cathy was in the adaptive attributional feedback group, and her peer, Jack was in the maladaptive feedback group. The findings of Rascle and colleagues' study suggest that after failing on the golf-putting task, Cathy, who received the adaptive attributional feedback, would be more likely (a) to attribute her performance to controllable causes, (b) to believe she would be more successful in the future, and (c) to persist in practising her putting. Being in the maladaptive feedback condition, Jack on the other hand would be more likely (a) to explain failure in terms of uncontrollable and stable causes, (b) to have lower expectations for future success, and (c) to stop practising his putting. In this way, we see that how Cathy and Jack explain their performance failure is likely to have a big impact both on their expectations of future success and on what they actually do to improve their skills (i.e., through practice) in ways that make success more likely. Aside from research on golf-putting and dart-throwing, research in sport has consistently shown attributional retraining techniques to have similar effects across other domains, including college tennis and basketball at both beginner and recreational levels (Orbach, Singer, & Murphey, 1997; Orbach, Singer, & Price, 1999), and effects on important outcomes, such as objective performance (Rees et al., 2013).

While there is strong evidence for the efficacy of attributional retraining in sport, attribution-based treatment procedures vary considerably. Moreover, they are not as systematic as those that have been implemented in education contexts (e.g., Perry & Hamm, 2017). Education-based attributional retraining treatment protocols typically comprise three phases. Following the delivery of a questionnaire (to collect demographic and baseline data), Phase 1 (*causal search activation*) prompts participants to engage in attributional thinking by considering the causes of failure on some achievement task (e.g., they are asked to think about the last time they did poorly on a course test and the reasons for it). Phase 2 (*attributional induction*) then asks participants to watch a video presentation that encourages them to make internal, controllable attributions and discourages internal, uncontrollable attributions for failure. Often the retraining focuses on only two attributional dimensions (internal and controllable attributions) in order to simplify the content delivery and help students retain the information. Attributional retraining videos have varied in format delivery, and include such things as a conversation between an undergraduate and graduate student, or a PowerPoint presentation in which a narrator explains the benefits of using internal and controllable attributions for poor academic performance (e.g., improved motivation and achievement). Finally, Phase 3 (*consolidation*) involves asking participants to summarise the treatment content and to reflect on its relevance to their own lives (see Haynes, Perry, Stupnisky, & Daniels, 2009). Depending on the study, participants in no-attributional retraining (control group) conditions either do not receive a treatment or are asked to complete a filler task in which they view a presentation of similar length on unrelated course content.

Across a range of educational studies, protocols of this form have been observed to improve students' academic performance (e.g., Parker et al., 2016; Parker, et al., 2018). Indeed, integrating insights from sport and education contexts, researchers have used attributional retraining as part of efforts to improve the academic adjustment of competitive athletes at university. For example, research by the second author and her colleagues (Parker et al., 2016; Parker et al., 2018) found that encouraging competitive student athletes to make adaptive attributions when explaining negative events (e.g., poor performance on a course test) increased their subsequent performance and persistence on academic tasks. These attributional retraining treatments proved to be particularly useful for student-athletes who had perceived themselves to have limited control over their academic course. In an online learning environment, such treatments have also been found to benefit student athletes who are faced with a range of stressors at university. Evidence suggests they do this by enhancing cognitions (e.g., increasing perceived control) which, in line with Weiner's temporal model (see Figure 8.1), then go on to shape emotions and, through this, final grades (Parker et al., 2018).

Attribution biases

Within the attribution literature one prominent research focus since the early 1970s has been on the *biases* that lead perceivers to favour certain forms of explanation over others. In this tradition, one of the patterns that has received most attention is the *actor–observer bias* (Jones & Nisbett, 1972). This relates to the tendency for actors to attribute outcomes – particularly negative ones – more to external (situational) causes than do observers. For example, a male footballer who misses a penalty may blame this on the booing of the crowd or the poor quality of the penalty spot, whereas onlookers might explain it in terms of his inherently poor penalty-taking skills. Likewise, if a basketball team loses an important game, team members might attribute their loss to the poor decisions of the referee, the luck of their opponent or an injury to their own players, while neutral bystanders might simply observe that the team wasn't as good as its opponent.

One potential explanation for this asymmetric pattern of attribution is that actors and observers have access to very different contextual data (Jones & Nisbett, 1972). In line with this point it is clear that the viewpoint or perspective of actors during an action or performance is quite different from that of onlookers. For example, a penalty-taker may see the poor pitch surface, and the basketball team may see that a referee has missed a foul in a way that onlookers cannot. More generally, because actors are looking outward, the situation and environment are more likely to be salient in ways that lead them to make external, situational explanations for behaviour. However, for observers, the actor is more likely to be the focus of attention and hence to be salient in ways that lead them to make more internal, dispositional explanations for behaviour. Again, if we take our golfer Cathy as an example of an actor, she may attribute her missing of a putt to the strong wind blowing in her face. In contrast, observers may see the missed putt simply as evidence of her inability to read the green. Indeed, this failure of observers to take account of the actors' perspective when explaining their behaviour led Ross (1977) to label this the *fundamental attribution error* (see Figure 8.2).

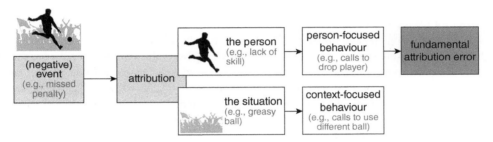

Figure 8.2   The actor–observer effect and the fundamental attribution error

Note: The fundamental attribution error relates to the tendency for observers to explain other people's behaviour with reference to those people's personal characteristics (e.g., lack of skill), rather than situational factors (e.g., challenging circumstances). This can be seen to be a consequence of an actor–observer bias which leads actors to be more sensitive than observers to the situational determinants of behaviour.

Researchers have generally seen the actor–observer asymmetry to be both robust (Jones, 1976) and pervasive (Baron, Byrne, & Branscombe, 2006). Nevertheless, there is evidence that the effect is more nuanced than often supposed, for at least three reasons. First, it plays out differently in the context of intentional (i.e., a specific, deliberate reason for action by an actor, brought about by skill towards some form of outcome) and unintentional behaviours (i.e., a non-deliberate action, brought about by luck that has led to some form of outcome), such that it applies only to unintentional behaviours (Malle,1999). Second, it operates differently in naturalistic settings (i.e., in competition/training environments as opposed to the experimental settings where it has generally been studied; Lewis, 1995). And, third, it is more pronounced for negative events than for positive ones (Malle, Knobe, & Nelson, 2007). Indeed, while athletes may often be reluctant to take personal blame for their failures, they are typically much more willing to take personal credit for their success.

Taking stock of these issues, over the last two decades, Bertram Malle and his colleagues (2007) have developed an alternative approach – *the folk conceptual theory of behaviour explanations*. To understand this, imagine the scenario in which a football player, Lucy, attempts to make a difficult pass up the pitch to a teammate, but is unsuccessful. Within traditional actor–observer bias we might expect Lucy (the player, the actor) to see the failure of the pass to be a consequence of an opposition player getting the better of their teammate (a situational attribution), whereas her coach (Gareth, the observer) may explain the failure as a reflection of Lucy's lack of ability (a dispositional attribution). However, Malle and colleagues argue that explanations of events go further than just situational–dispositional explanations. More specifically, they note that they entail not only internal or external attributions, but also what they refer to as *modes of cause* and *reason explanations*.

Spelling out this point, Malle and colleagues' (2007) theory posits three actor–observer hypotheses. The first pertains to *reason asymmetry*, and implies that actors use more reasons and fewer causal history explanations than observers. In our football scenario, for example, Lucy (the player) is more able to recall the particular reasons for her actions (e.g., why she attempted a difficult pass in light of all the other options open to her), but for Gareth (the coach) these reasons are less observable. Gareth therefore has to rely more on stored knowledge and inferences (*causal history*) about Lucy to explain why she attempted the pass and why she was unsuccessful. As we will discuss further below, this asymmetry is also likely to be affected by, and affect, the relationship between the coach and the athlete – in particular, the extent of their shared social identity (e.g., as members of the same team).

The second hypothesis pertains to *belief asymmetry*. This predicts that actors use relatively more belief reasons and fewer desire reasons than observers. For example, Lucy's decision to attempt the difficult pass is influenced by her knowledge, assessment and the potential outcome of the action at that moment in time. Accordingly, Lucy is more likely to explain her actions with reference to her *belief* that she saw her teammate and her *belief* that she could make the pass and that the pass would lead to a positive outcome for her team. However, for Gareth (the coach), Lucy's beliefs are difficult to infer, and this may lead him to explain her actions with reference more to *desire*-based reasons, such as 'Lucy panicked and wanted to get rid of the ball as quickly as possible to relieve the pressure she was under' (i.e., her *desire* was to protect herself). This type of explanation again has links to the fundamental attribution error highlighted in Figure 8.2.

The final hypothesis pertains to *marker asymmetry*. This asserts that actors are more likely than observers to leave their belief reasons *unmarked* (i.e., to take them as given; Malle, 1999, 2004; Malle et al., 2007). In our example, this means that Lucy (the player) is likely to focus directly on the content of her beliefs (e.g., 'My teammate was in a good position') rather than to say that she 'believed' that her teammate was in a good position. In contrast, Gareth (the coach) is more likely to make reference to Lucy's beliefs; for example, remarking that 'She "believed" that she could get out of trouble by kicking the ball up the pitch.' In this way, observers (e.g., a coach) mark beliefs in order to make sense of aspects of actors' behaviour that they could not otherwise account for.

These three hypotheses anticipate a number of psychological processes which shape the explanations given by both actors and observers. These include how well an observer knows and understands not only the social context of performance, but also the actor (or actors) and how motivated they are to influence the attribution in question. In this context, Malle and colleagues (2007) observed that close (intimate) observers generally portrayed an actor in a more positive light than distant (stranger) observers. Again, this attunes us to insights from the social identity approach in so far as the 'closeness' of observers can be understood to be a proxy for shared social identity, such that close observers see actors as ingroup members and distant observers see actors as outgroup members. Indeed, in what follows, we will expand on this observation to note that social identity processes are a latent feature of most attributional processes in sport (Coffee, 2017).

A SOCIAL IDENTITY APPROACH TO ATTRIBUTION PROCESSES

Chapter 2 drew attention to the five spheres of sports-related activity to which social identity theorising has profound relevance (the 5Ps): *participation* (what sport and exercise activities people engage in), *performance* (how well people do those activities), *psychological and physical health* (how well people feel because of doing those activities), *partisanship* (how people behave as supporters of sport activity) and *politics* (how people acquire and wield power in and through sporting activity). Attribution processes are integral to all five of these spheres of sports-related activity. Furthermore, we argue below that social identity and self-categorization processes are themselves foundational to these attributions. Indeed, the social identity approach suggests that the groups to which people belong can be, and often are, incorporated into their sense of self and, through this, are powerful determinants of all cognitions, including attributions (Turner et al., 1994; see also Chapter 7). In the remainder of this chapter then, we look to explore how social identity-informed attributions determine participation, performance, psychological and physical health, partisanship, and politics.

Consider for a moment the sports and activities you engage in (or do not engage in). What are the reasons (attributions) for your *participation* and how do they affect your emotions and subsequent engagement? And how does your membership of particular social groups affect your reasons for participation? For example, you might say, 'I play football because we – my football team – are really good at it so I'm going to keep playing.' Or you might say, 'I go to exercise classes because we – my CrossFit group – have a lot of fun so I'm going to keep going.' In both these examples, it is clear that attributions of ability and fun are intrinsically informed by group memberships in ways that affect your current and future participation in these activities (see also Chapters 10 and 11).

As a second example, consider how *partisanship* – associated with distinct social identities – affects our explanations of the behaviour of those we observe. Here it is clear, for example, that a Liverpool fan and an Everton fan can watch exactly the same game of football between their two clubs but form very different explanations for the performances they observe (Hastorf & Cantril, 1954). The Liverpool fan might describe the excellent goal that Liverpool scored as a great piece of ingenuity and creativity by a Liverpool striker. An Everton fan, however, might describe exactly the same event as a lucky goal that Liverpool scored due to the deflection of the ball and the obstruction of the goalkeeper's view. Here, then, the social identity-informed partisanship of the fans results in very different explanations for the same observed event.

Yet despite the obvious relevance of social identity processes to attribution processes, at present, they are largely neglected within the attribution literature (not only in sport but also in social psychology more generally; Oakes et al., 1991). In large part, this is because these theories position athletes and observers *as individuals* rather than as members of groups. In what follows, we attempt to correct this oversight by highlighting three key points which emerge from a social identity approach to attributions in sport.

Key point 1: Attributions are shaped by social identities and are made to groups, not just individuals

As we have seen, attribution research in sport typically focuses on athletes' explanations of why they have succeeded or failed. As we have also seen, much of this work has a focus on the individual *as an individual*, so that, for example, self-referent attributions centre on the causes for an athlete's personal performance (e.g., 'what *I* did that made *me* fail'). In other words, the 'self' here is taken to be personal rather than collective. It is clear though, that, like performance itself, this attribution process often has a very significant social dimension. This means that attributions are typically shaped by a range of social factors, not least the people around us. For example, after missing the cut, Cathy's coach might tell her she putted poorly, while her partner might inform her that she wasn't focused enough. This leads to the more general observation that attributions are never made in a vacuum. Instead, they are made in the context of *others'* attributions, and those attributions have an important bearing on our own.

Consistent with this point, a range of attribution experiments have pointed to the profound influence that others can have on performance. In particular, in a range of contexts researchers have effectively manipulated how individuals explain their performance by *providing feedback* of a specified form (e.g., that their failure was due to controllable and unstable factors or else to uncontrollable and stable factors; e.g., Rascle, Le Foll, & Higgins, 2008). Although this feature of experiments is typically taken for granted (and hence is not part of the researchers' theorising) it nevertheless shows how athletes' attributions can be shaped by others in ways that have significant consequences for their performance.

Of course, though, it also matters who provides the performance feedback. For example, when walking off the green after missing the cut in her golf tournament, Cathy might take no notice if a rival tells her she has lost her touch and that it is time for her to retire. However, if that feedback came from her caddie, she would likely take notice. Along these lines, researchers have observed that whether or not one shares social identity with those who provide performance feedback has an important bearing on athletes' perceptions of the feedback and, in turn, on their performance (Rascle et al., 2019; Rees et al., 2013). This means that in applied settings, athletes will often be most influenced by those 'insiders' who are close to them, with whom they share social identity. So while an athlete's own attributions are likely to be sensitive to the attributions made by 'insiders' such as teammates, coaches, family and friends (Rees & Hardy, 2000), the attributions of 'outsiders' (e.g., journalists, rivals) will often be ignored.

Up to this point, our discussion of attributions has focused very much on the personal self (i.e., individuals' explanations for their own individual performance). Clearly, though, athletes also make attributions that are relevant to the collective self (e.g., team members' explanations for their team's performance; Allen, Coffee, & Greenlees, 2012). Indeed, team-referent attributions are commonplace in sport (Gill, Ruder, & Gross, 1982; see the Appendix for a suitable scale from Coffee et al., 2015). It is common, for example, to hear people say things such as 'Arsenal are lucky', 'Germans are good at penalties' and 'referees always favour Manchester United'. Indeed, the quote at the start of this chapter is a good example of one such team-referent attribution – where Rory Best presents the *team's* success as resulting from 'a lot of hard work' and 'a massive team effort'.

In this regard, a key prediction of social identity theorising is that in an array of social contexts – not least sporting ones – individuals internalise group memberships as part of themselves. In particular, individuals who identify highly with a group (high identifiers) are inclined to perceive events from the group perspective, and hence are more likely to make team-referent attributions. Among other things, this means that after a performance, these high identifiers are more likely than low identifiers (or people who identify with other groups) to use the collective pronouns 'we' and 'us' (vs 'I' and 'me') when describing, and making attributions about, their performance.

As one illustration of these points, it is notable that when discussing his game with journalists the professional golfer Jordan Spieth invariably uses the collective pronoun 'we', when referring to himself and other members of his team (e.g., his caddie, coach and trainer; Wacker, 2016). Including his team as part of his self-definition in this way has two distinct consequences. First, it clearly communicates his sense of shared social identity. Second, it means that he is more likely to make team-referent attributions to explain his performance – whether good or bad (e.g., attributing a win to *our* effort, rather than just *my* effort).

Importantly, researchers have noted that the inclination to make team-based attributions tends to have implications for well-being and performance (Allen, Jones, & Sheffield, 2009; Coffee et al., 2015). Identification with a team also increases the likelihood that adaptive team-referent attributions will have a positive impact on future outcomes (Murray, Coffee, Arthur, & Eklund, 2020). For example, if a cricketer, Trevor, identifies highly with his cricket team, he is more likely to see his team's loss as a collective failure (rather than just as his own individual failure), and if his team makes an adaptive team-referent attribution for its loss (e.g., believing it is the result of a poor strategy that they can improve on in future), then he is likely to be more confident in his team's ability to succeed in future. In ways discussed in Chapter 15, these team-based attributions are also likely to enhance his well-being by giving him a greater sense of control, support and agency, as well as a greater sense of *collective* self-efficacy (Haslam, Jetten et al., 2018).

Social identity is also important when examining the effects of intra-team agreement in team-referent attributions. This is something that research by the third author and his colleagues has shown to be associated with positive performance outcomes (Murray, Coffee, Eklund, & Arthur, 2019). Specifically, when team members agreed with fellow team members about the cause of team failure, this then led to a significant improvement in their subsequent performance. This suggests that team performance is enhanced to the extent that team members are on the same attributional page, so to speak. Indeed, even though high levels of agreement and lack of divergent thinking (i.e., disagreement) can be implicated in negative outcomes such as groupthink (Cosier & Schwenk, 1990; Turner, Pratkanis, Probasco, & Leve, 2006), there is generally value in having – and seeking to develop – a shared understanding both of 'why we failed' or 'why we succeeded' (Haslam, 2001).

Indeed, even if team members have different ideas about the cause of a team performance, it seems reasonable to suppose that sharing these ideas will lead to a more comprehensive understanding of the causes behind a team performance. At the same time, though, an environment in which team members make different team-referent attributions also has the potential to create conflict within the group (Mitchell, 2016; Paradis, Carron, & Martin, 2014). For this reason, Tom Postmes and colleagues recommend that teams build norms attached to their social identities that encourage the sharing of information (i.e., disagreement among team members; Postmes, Spears, & Cihangir, 2001). For if teammates feel they can openly discuss their attributions for team failure (and success) without fear of conflict, a more thorough causal search can take place, which will increase the likelihood of team performance improving in future. One reason for this is that the sharing of such information can itself help to build a sense of shared identity in ways that have positive implications for performance and well-being (Postmes, Haslam, & Swaab, 2005; e.g., as discussed in Chapters 5 and 15).

Key point 2: Social identity has an important role to play in attributional retraining

As we have seen, current approaches to attributional retraining have focused on individual-level factors (e.g., 'How can "*I*" control the cause of this outcome?'). However, the social identity approach offers a new perspective on the process of encouraging adaptive thinking (i.e., adaptive attributions) through attributional retraining. In particular, it raises the question of whether treatment protocols might be enhanced by providing individuals with a cognitive platform for accessing group-based resources (e.g., 'How can "*we*" control the cause of this outcome?').

Two studies that speak to the potential of this line of thinking were conducted by Tegan Cruwys and colleagues and examined how social identity might reduce levels of depression by fostering positive attributions (Cruwys, South, Greenaway, & Haslam, 2015). This possibility relates to previous research which shows that depressed people often fail to display the self-serving attributional bias in which credit is taken for personal success and blame is denied for personal failure (e.g.,

Peterson & Seligman, 1984). That is, a depressed person is more likely to attribute negative events to causes like 'I'm just not good enough in everything I do' – something that is about themselves (internal), something that is not going to change (stable), something that influences many areas of their life (global), and something that is unique to them (personal). In their studies, Cruwys and colleagues found that social identity was an important moderator of this trend. More specifically, they found that individuals with stronger social identities – that is, those who had a stronger sense of connection to meaningful groups in their lives (something that the researchers measured in one study and manipulated in another) – were less likely to perceive negative outcomes (e.g., when bad things happen) as internal, stable and global, and, as a result of this, they reported lower levels of depression. Of interest to our suggestion above that collective attributions can provide a cognitive platform for accessing group-based resources, one of the mechanisms that Cruwys and colleagues identified as explaining their findings was a shift in attentional focus among participants with a stronger sense of social identity away from personally self-referent explanations for their behaviour towards explanations that were group-referent. In other words, social identity helped people to see failure as something which wasn't just down to themselves, and as a result helped them stave off depression.

To get a better understanding of this process, we can imagine a situation in which our golfer Cathy is part of a team that did not perform well in their most recent tournament. Social identity research suggests that if Cathy is able to shift away from thinking about this failure in personal terms (e.g., 'How can "*I*" control the cause of the negative outcome?') towards thinking collectively in terms of her team (e.g., 'How can "*we*" control the cause of the negative outcome?'), then this is likely to provide her with access to group-based resources that will facilitate opportunities for adaptive thinking.

The same approach can also be applied to encourage adaptive thinking around personal performance. For example, Cathy might feel that she let the team down due to her poor ability (a maladaptive attribution) and that it was this that led the team to defeat. But encouraging her to draw upon her social identity as a golfer and consider how other golfers might explain a poor performance could help to provide her with access to group-sourced, alternative explanations that are more adaptive. For example, if she has a salient, positive social identity as a golfer, Cathy might be more likely to ask herself, 'How do other golfers explain a poor performance?' This process of critical distancing by looking at the world from the perspective of other ingroup members might also lead Cathy to consider alternative attributions for her poor performance, such as 'poor strategy', or 'inefficient practice' (all adaptive attributions). In sum, then, there are strong grounds for thinking that helping athletes to reflect on events from the perspective of shared social identity (e.g., 'us swimmers', 'us athletes') can provide a cognitive platform for them to access more adaptive attributions for negative events.

It is also possible to apply these ideas directly to attributional retraining interventions in ways that might improve their effectiveness. Above we noted that such interventions typically help participants who tend to make maladaptive attributions to video feedback in which a peer or expert proposes alternative, more adaptive attributions for an event (e.g., seeing poor strategy as the cause of a bad performance outcome; see Perry et al., 2014; Perry & Hamm, 2017). However, the social identity principles discussed above suggest that there are a number of ways that this intervention can be more forensically targeted. First, they suggest that such an intervention is likely to be more effective if participants see themselves as sharing a social identity with the person in the video (i.e., if the peer or expert is seen as an ingroup member; see Haslam, Jetten, O'Brien, & Jacobs, 2004). Second, they suggest that there is value in encouraging participants to make, where possible, team-referent (not just personal) attributions as these will give them more access to group-based resources for explaining and addressing negative outcomes. And third, they suggest that attributional retraining can be more effective if participants are encouraged to understand events from the perspective of other ingroup members, as this will help to facilitate critical distancing that increases their access to alternative, group-sourced adaptive explanations for events.

Key point 3: Social identity shapes observer attributions

According to the social identity approach, to the extent that they define themselves in terms of shared social identity, group members are motivated to think and behave in ways that align them with fellow ingroup members while also differentiating themselves from outgroup members. This means that when they have a high degree of shared social identity, individuals come to see themselves and other ingroup members as functionally interchangeable (Turner, 1982). This in turn affects how they evaluate the actions and behaviour of members both of their ingroup and of other outgroups. In line with this point, a study by Michael Hogg and Elizabeth Hardie (1991) found that highly identified members of an Australian rules football team in Melbourne had significantly more positive evaluations of prototypical group members (i.e., those who were highly representative of the group) than they did of non-prototypical group members (Hogg & Hardie, 1991). Moreover, this prototypicality was in turn a basis for their liking of different players, so that the more players liked other players, the more they embodied the group's identity.

This analysis is also relevant to our understanding of observer attributions and the work of the fourth author of this chapter (Kawycz, Coffee, & Eklund, 2017), where explanations of the behaviour and performance of an actor (e.g., an athlete) are also likely to be structured by perceptions of shared (and non-shared) social identity. In particular, within a sporting context, people are likely to offer positive explanations for the behaviour of athletes the more they see themselves as sharing social identity. This can anecdotally be seen in post-match interviews with players and coaches. For example, when questioned about a poor performance from their team, players and managers typically offer explanations that support their team or teammates, while at the same time attributing defeat to more situational and external factors (e.g., bad referee decisions or the opposition's good fortune).

Research on fan culture provides abundant evidence of ingroup-favouring patterns in explanations of sport-related events or behaviour. As noted earlier, and in line with the fourth author's work (Kawycz & Coffee, 2019), researchers have observed that highly identified fans (observers) are more likely to attribute the success of 'their' athletes/teams (ingroup actors) to internal factors, and the failure of 'their' athletes/teams to external factors (Fink, Parker, Brett, & Higgins, 2009; Madrigal & Chen, 2008). In this sense, a positive 'self-serving' bias is extended to members of the ingroup in the form of a 'team' or 'group-serving' bias. In self-categorization terms, when social identity is salient, the 'team' becomes representative of their 'self'. Typically, then, fans are keen to ensure credit is given to their team for its successes, while also protecting it from blame in the event of failure. Furthermore, as social identity theory suggests, fans will generally strive to compare their team favourably to other teams, such that they root against rival teams and provide negative explanations for their behaviour. As noted in Chapter 2, this is particularly true for highly identified fans who need to recover threatened self-esteem in the face of group failure. These fans are particularly motivated to see 'us' as positively distinct from 'them' – and this applies not just to the way they describe outgroup (and ingroup) behaviour, but also to the way they explain it.

This effect has been observed too when the behaviour of ingroup athletes (actors) is highly problematic or even criminal (Dietz-Uhler & Murrell, 1998). As an example of this, consider the following analysis provided by a fan of Lance Armstrong after the cyclist had been found to have taken performance-enhancing drugs:

> Lance was operating at a very high level alongside competitors who were making the same sacrifices that he was. Take a look at any competitive sport or high-pressure career and there are conflicts of interest. It was against the rules to take performance-enhancing drugs; the fact large numbers of the pro peloton were using at the same time does not excuse Lance's behaviour, but in my eyes it does vindicate him slightly. (Warnakulasuriya, 2017)

Here the fan – a fellow American – clearly shows group-serving bias in seeking to explain Armstrong's actions (see Figure 8.3). More specifically, they seek to diminish the seriousness of the behaviour, presenting it as having resulted from situational (not dispositional) factors. The suggestion that large numbers of other cyclists were taking performance-enhancing drugs also seeks to minimise the need to provide an explanation for the behaviour. This therefore alerts us to a collective dimension to Malle and colleagues' (2007) notions of asymmetry that we discussed above: for when observers identify highly with actors, they too will be motivated to see the world from their perspective and display the same reason, belief and marker asymmetries. In this case, then, the fan's suggestion that there is 'nothing to explain here' mirrors the reason asymmetry that Armstrong himself displayed when pointing to a host of factors that contributed to his behaviour (notably the culture in cycling and the pressure to win; Rodgers, 2013).

Figure 8.3   Group-serving bias among fans

Note: When an athlete – such as Lance Armstrong, pictured here – has been found guilty of illegal or illegitimate sporting behaviour, their supporters will often display group-serving bias in their explanations of the infringement. For example, they may downplay the significance of the behaviour (i.e., attributing it to non-dispositional factors) and/or suggest that it was more a consequence of the environment (i.e., attributing it to situational factors). They will also often display the same reason, belief and marker asymmetries as the athlete themselves.

Source: Wikipedia

Drawing on these examples, future research in this area might do well to consider the way in which attributions are shaped by, and also themselves shape, the coach–athlete relationship. As we noted above, a coach (observer) is typically required to look at why an athlete was successful or unsuccessful and provide explanations for their performance. These explanations have an impact on cognitions towards the athlete, such as attitudes (hard-working, lazy), emotions towards the athlete (happy, angry), and behaviours (kind and engaging, abrupt and disengaging). Furthermore, the explanations that the coach provides can impact both training plans and strategic training decisions in ways that can ultimately help to improve (or not) the athlete's performance. Importantly, though, as Peters notes in Chapter 4, effective communication between the coach and the athlete will be determined by levels of shared social identity *and so too will their attributions*. Indeed, under conditions where athlete and coach share the same social identity, their perspective on social reality – and hence their attributions – will become interchangeable so that, in effect, *the coach is no longer an observer but instead becomes a co-actor*.

In line with ideas presented earlier in this chapter, in this way shared social identity can also help to facilitate effective communication of divergent explanations for behaviour between the coach and the athlete. In particular, this means that criticism or challenge to the athlete's performance is more likely to be seen as constructive and therefore promote growth rather than conflict (Hornsey, Oppes, & Svensson, 2002). For example, if a coach and athlete perceive themselves to share (rather than not share) social identity, then when the coach tells the player that they are not training hard enough and that their technique needs improving, this message is more likely to be received and to lead to increases in motivation and effort (Haslam, 2017). At the same time, in line with ideas presented on the group-serving bias, there is also likely to be a tendency for highly identified coaches to 'protect' their athletes and 'explain away' their poor performance. Here the tendency to focus on situational and non-relevant dispositional attributions for poor performance may lead to a masking of the real causes of poor performance and divert attention away from relevant issues that need to be addressed. Understanding the complex dynamics that are at play here thus provides a rich and important agenda for future research.

CONCLUSION

Attribution processes are fundamental to success. For without attributions, athletes cannot understand why they have succeeded or failed and hence cannot learn from experiences in ways that allow them to avoid future failure. This is true in all spheres of life, not only in sport but also in education, politics, business and social relationships. The goal of this chapter has been to map out the theoretical underpinnings of attribution processes. That said, our review of the models that have dominated this field to date (not only in sport but also in general social psychology) have predominantly focused on attributions *about individuals* made by people who are acting *as individuals*. The role of groups and group processes is thus noticeably absent from these models.

Seeking to correct for this omission, the social identity approach to attributions that we set out in this chapter shows how attention to *group-sourced* and *group-focused* explanations can provide a fuller appreciation of the attribution process. It also provides greater insight into the nature of adaptive explanations for events and behaviours. More specifically, by elaborating three key points that can be derived from this approach, we underscored its relevance to four of the '5Ps' identified in Chapter 2: participation, performance, psychological and physical health, and partisanship.

Yet while it was not explicitly discussed in this chapter, it is clear too that a social identity approach to attributions in sport and exercise contexts also speaks to the fifth P: politics. Not least, this is because identity-based politics is a key determinant of the big-picture issue of *what* we seek to explain in sport. So, among other things, it is social identity that determines whether we focus more on the causes of success in Australian rules football than in snowboarding, or more on the causes of drug-taking in former East Germany or China than in Britain or the United States.

Without a proper appreciation of attribution processes, then, our understanding of sport and exercise psychology is quite limited. Our hope is that this chapter serves to refresh readers' interest in this area and to stimulate a plethora of new research. For while we have explained the relevance of the social identity approach to the study of attributions in sport and exercise, clearly much more remains to be done to develop, test and apply the ideas set out above. In closing, we therefore align ourselves – and hopefully readers – with the attributional discourse of Rory Best in noting that the success of this enterprise is going to require a lot of hard work and a massive team effort.

9

EMOTION AND EMOTION REGULATION

SVENJA A. WOLF
AMIT GOLDENBERG
MICKAËL CAMPO

> While each industry sector has its own distinguishing characteristics, we suggest that the attribute which truly differentiates sport is passion – the passion exhibited by the intense loyalty and emotions [that] the product (the team, the game) generates among participants and fans. (Szymanski & Wolfe, 2016, p.26)

Whether it is the excitement prior to a big game, the dejection after having lost a final, or the anger of being fouled by an opponent, participation in sport and exercise stimulates intense and varied emotional responses. Moreover, these emotional responses extend to all concerned actors – not only athletes (Uphill & Jones, 2007) and coaches (Allan & Côté, 2016), but also spectators (Havard, 2014) and even officials (Friesen, Devonport, & Lane, 2017).

Generally, an emotion describes 'an organised psychophysiological reaction to ongoing relationships with the environment that are of relevance to individuals' goal pursuit' (Lazarus, 2000, p. 230). In sport and exercise, actors experience a range of discrete emotions, which influence their performance and perseverance (Fletcher & Scott, 2010; Neil, Bayston, Hanton, & Wilson, 2013). The joy of winning a competition, the anger at an unfair referee decision, and the anxiety of waiting for a championship game to start are experiences that will be familiar to all readers. On the one hand, emotions facilitate performance and participation. For example, the more excited athletes are about a competition, the more likely they are to keep their focus and ultimately perform well (Stanger, Chettle, Whittle, & Poolton, 2018). Similarly, when long-distance runners' pride is based on their hard work rather than innate superiority (Tracy & Robins, 2007), it positively predicts their training effort and progress (Gilchrist, Sabiston, Conroy, & Atkinson, 2018). Such effects are not restricted to professional athletes. For example, the enjoyment experienced by recreational football players and exercisers has been linked to more positive attitudes towards physical activity as well as greater willingness to engage in it (Frayeh & Lewis, 2017; Garn, Simonton, Dasingert, & Simonton, 2017).

Nevertheless, emotions can also harm performance and participation. For example, basketball players' anger in response to opponents' insults have been found to reduce their performance due to distraction from the game (Ring, Kavussanu, Al-Yaaribi, Tenenbaum, & Stanger, 2019). In research with exercisers, women's experiences of body-related shame were related to reduced physical activity, and students' boredom in physical education classes predicted less class engagement (Garn et al., 2017; Sabiston et al., 2010). So, whether their effects are helpful or harmful, emotions are central to the participation and performance of actors in sport and exercise contexts. To promote optimal engagement, perseverance and performance, it is therefore important to identify and understand both (a) the antecedents and causes of emotions and (b) ways to effectively regulate them.

When trying to provide such understanding, current approaches to emotions in sport and exercise focus on (a) emotion generation, (b) emotions as social phenomena, and (c) emotion regulation. In the first half of this chapter we review each of these approaches in turn. In the second half we then draw on social identity theorising (of the form set out in Chapter 2) to extend these approaches in important ways.

CURRENT APPROACHES TO EMOTIONS AND EMOTION REGULATION IN SPORT AND EXERCISE

Emotion generation

The first consideration with regard to emotions in sport and exercise pertains to how they are generated. One influential framework that is routinely used in sport and exercise to explain how emotions develop is *cognitive-motivational-relational theory* (Lazarus, 1999; Nicholls, Hemmings, & Clough, 2010; Renfrew, Howle, & Eklund, 2017). This posits that emotions result from individuals' *appraisals* of the self-relevant implications of particular events and experiences (Lazarus, 1999; see also Chapter 14). For example, a rower going into a championship race in her home country would likely appraise the situation as highly important and a great opportunity (i.e., high *primary appraisal*; Lazarus, 1999). To the extent that she has practised hard and perceives herself to have strong audience support, she is also likely to perceive there to be positive prospects for her performance (i.e., high *secondary appraisal*; Lazarus, 1999). As a result, she would approach the competition with excitement (Jones, Meijen, McCarthy, & Sheffield, 2009). Generally, actors experience more intense emotions the more relevant a situation is to them, and more pleasant emotions the more they believe that they can cope with the demands of that situation.

Drawing on this approach, research has identified numerous variables that influence appraisal and emotion generation in sport and exercise contexts. For example, athletes' (self-oriented) perfectionism, trait anxiety and mastery-avoidance goals (i.e., striving to avoid performing worse than one wants to) have all been found to positively predict the emergence of guilt and anxiety (Curran & Hill, 2018; Stenling, Hassmén, & Holmström, 2014; Wolf, Eys, & Kleinert, 2014). Similarly, greater anxiety has been shown to result from playing for a high-ranked team, against more skilled opponents and in an away game (Thuot, Kavouras, & Kenefick, 1998; Wolf et al., 2014). On the other hand, stronger task-orientation has been found to predict to greater enjoyment of sport (Bortoli, Bertollo, Comani, & Robazza, 2011). Among exercisers, activity variety has also been linked to more pleasant affect and enjoyment (Hagberg, Lindahl, Nyberg, & Hellénius, 2009; Sylvester et al., 2016).

In all of this research the focus has generally been on the traits and concerns of individual actors. Specifically, the self that is typically implicated in athletes' or exercisers' primary appraisal is the *personal self* (i.e., 'I' and 'me'; Haslam, Jetten et al., 2018; Turner, 1982). However, sport and exercise are highly social contexts, which routinely implicate the *social self* (i.e., 'we' and 'us'; see Chapter 2). As we will see below, this is a blind spot in research on emotion in these contexts and one that a social identity approach can illuminate.

Emotions as social phenomena

Despite the fact that the emotional dimensions of sport are often intensely social, it is only recently that researchers have started to acknowledge this fact. One way in which they have done this is by starting to pay particular attention to so-called *social emotions* – that is, emotions intended primarily to serve social functions and/or experienced exclusively in response to social concerns (Hareli & Parkinson, 2008). Social emotions that have been documented in sport and exercise include long-distance runners' pride in their training progress (Gilchrist et al., 2018), ice hockey goalies' shame in being substituted during a match (Battaglia, Kerr, & Stirling, 2018), exercisers' guilt in response to their lack of physical activity (Castonguay, Sabiston, Kowalski, & Wilson, 2016), envy at another exerciser's physical appearance (Pila, Stamiris, Castonguay, & Sabiston, 2014), and inter-collegiate athletes' jealousy of their teammates (Kamphoff, Gill, & Huddleston, 2005).

Another way in which sport and exercise researchers have started to explore emotions as social phenomena is by investigating social influences on appraisal and emotion development. For example, the presence of friends has been shown to reduce exercisers' anxiety via perceptions of diffused evaluation (i.e., lower primary appraisal) and enhanced security (i.e., higher secondary appraisal; Carron, Estabrooks, Horton, Prapavessis, & Hausenblas, 1999). Conversely, parents' performance-focused achievement goals (i.e., wanting to do better than others) and perceived social responsibility for teammates have been linked with athletes' experiences of greater anxiety (Kaye, Frith, & Vosloo, 2015; Wolf, Harenberg, Tamminen, & Schmitz, 2018). One of the clearest findings in this line of work is that greater team cohesion is associated with a more positive emotional state, in the form of greater excitement and reduced anxiety and jealousy (Eys, Hardy,

Carron, & Beauchamp, 2003; Kamphoff et al., 2005; Prapavessis & Carron, 1996; Wolf et al., 2018; and see Chapter 11).

A third and final way in which researchers have begun to acknowledge the social dimensions of emotions in sport and exercise pertains to investigation of their collective form. *Collective emotions* are understood to involve '[agreement] in affective responding across individuals towards a specific event or object' (von Scheve & Ismer, 2013, p. 406), and athletes from a wide variety of sports have reported experiencing collective emotions (Tamminen, Palmateer et al., 2016). Indeed, it is this intensity of collective emotion that often draws people to sport and which is in many ways its defining attribute. For example, Tom Johnson and colleagues observed that collective pride in winning is a defining feature of the All Blacks rugby team and plays a particular role in motivating the team and defining its members' orientation to a range of team activities (e.g., recruitment, training and promotional ventures; Johnson, Martin, Palmer, Watson, & Ramsey, 2014).

Collective emotions can result from instantaneous emotional congruence among group members in response to shared stimuli (Butler, 2015). These can include exposure to the same experience (e.g., winning a match, feeling cheated by a refereeing decision; Campo, Champely et al., 2019). At the same time, coaches' and peer leaders' emotional expressions play a key role in shaping team members' (collective) emotions (Stebbings, Taylor, & Spray, 2016; Tamminen, Palmateer et al., 2016; van Kleef, Cheshin, Koning, & Wolf, 2019). Collective emotions can also arise from the convergence of teammates' emotional responses over time and hence be an emergent feature of group life (Anderson, Keltner, & John, 2003). For example, statistical analysis has found that cricketers' happiness responses become more consensual over the course of a competition (Totterdell, 2000). Exercisers, too, have been observed to be sensitive to a developing emotional synchrony within their fitness groups (i.e., a sense of all being 'on the same emotional page'; Zumeta, Oriol, Telletxea, Amutio, & Basabe, 2016).

Collective emotions in sport and exercise relate to both task (e.g., collective efficacy, collaboration) and social variables (e.g., unity, communal coping; Tamminen, Palmateer et al 2016; Zumeta et al., 2016). For example, greater team happiness and more positive collective emotions are associated with indicators of improved individual and team performance (Campo, Champely et al., 2019; Totterdell, 2000). Yet while research has started to document these consequences, explaining them has proved more elusive. Again, a key reason for this may be that most researchers approach collective emotions from an individualistic perspective – that is, speaking to the emotions of the individual actor *as an individual*, rather than *as a group member* (i.e., recognising the importance of group-based emotions; Goldenberg, Saguy, & Halperin, 2014). In this, research ignores the distinctly collective dimensions of emotionality in sport (Campo, Mackie, & Sanchez, 2019).

Intrinsic and extrinsic emotion regulation

The third and final consideration with regard to emotions in sport and exercise relates to their *regulation* – that is, the way in which these emotions are controlled and managed (Gross, 1998). As with emotion generation, when it comes to emotion regulation, hitherto sport and exercise psychologists have tended to focus on individual actors. Specifically, their focus has been on *intrinsic emotion regulation* – that is, on actors' efforts to regulate the experience, timeline and expression of their own emotions (Gross, 2015). In this context, athletes have been found (and encouraged) to employ a variety of strategies to manage their emotions. Generally, this regulation has two foci: *antecedents* in the form of cognitions, and physiological or behavioural *responses* (Gross, 2002).

On the one hand, actors such as athletes, coaches or referees are encouraged to manage their emotions using antecedent-focused cognitive strategies, such as self-talk, imagery, or reframing to change their appraisal and attentional focus. For example, prior to a competition, runners have been found to regulate both their performance and emotions by setting themselves specific goals and reflecting on past accomplishments (Stanley, Lane, Beedie, Friesen, & Devonport, 2012). This allows them to feel in control and competent (i.e., high secondary appraisal), which prompts more pleasant emotions (Lazarus, 1999) and, in turn, leads to better performance (Stanley et al., 2012). Similarly, cricketers have been observed to benefit from positive self-talk to regulate emotions induced by opponents' sledging (i.e., attempts to intimidate them or break their concentration; Davis, Davis, Wills, Appleby, & Nieuwenhuys, 2018; see Figure 9.1).

Figure 9.1   Sledging in cricket

Note: Abuse of the opposition, known as sledging, is a feature of a range of sports. However, it is particularly associated with cricket where it is used by the fielding side to intimidate batsmen. Batsmen, for their part, are observed (and encouraged) to engage in a range of cognitive and physiological emotion-regulation strategies to avoid their negative emotional reactions getting the better of them (Davis et al., 2018; Joseph & Cramer, 2011).

Source: Lisa Scott, Pixabay

On the other hand, athletes can regulate their emotions by dealing with the physiological and behavioural response components directly. This can involve such strategies as progressive muscular relaxation, suppression and deep breathing (Jones, 2003). For example, to cope with opponents' sledging, cricketers are sometimes encouraged to use suppression by attempting to conceal their emotions (Davis et al., 2018) or focus on their breathing. As one elite cricketer studied by Samuele Joseph and Duncan Cramer (2011, p. 246) put it:

> I just like [to] try to control my breathing really because obviously if you start getting a bit too pumped you start breathing heavily; just kind of focus on my breathing rather than just breathing kinda thing; just try to slow it down.

The cognitive and physiological emotion regulation strategies that actors in sport and exercise employ can be structured as a function of their temporal development, as outlined in the *process model of emotion regulation* (see Figure 9.2; Gross, 2002; Quoidbach, Mikolajczak, & Gross, 2015). As displayed in Figure 9.2, this model distinguishes between antecedent- and response-focused strategies. First, *antecedent-focused* strategies target the emotion-eliciting situation and its appraisal (cf. Lazarus, 1999). Commensurate behaviours involve selecting situations likely to generate desired (e.g., pleasant) emotions and modifying situations to make helpful emotions more likely. Antecedent-focused emotion regulation also includes cognitive strategies such as focusing attention towards features of the context that support helpful emotions and (re)appraising situations in positive ways. Second, *response-focused* strategies target the emotional response itself. These typically involve behaviours that suppress unwanted (e.g., unpleasant) emotions or modulate the physiological or expressive components of the resultant emotional response (e.g., down-regulating one's heart-rate, changing a frown to a smile).

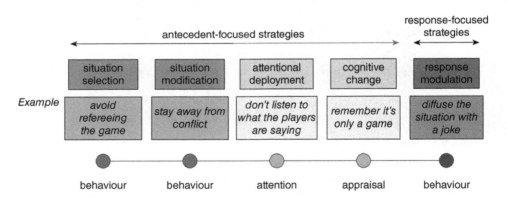

Figure 9.2   The process model of emotion regulation

Note: This model identifies strategies of emotion regulation that can be deployed either to avoid or induce a particular emotional state (i.e., antecedent-focused strategies) or to deal with an unwanted emotional state once it has arisen (i.e., response-focused strategies). The examples here relate to strategies that referees might use to regulate the emotions they experience in the course of a match.

Source: Based on Quoidbach, Mikolajczak, & Gross (2015)

Although (successful) intrinsic emotion regulation is generally associated with improved sporting performance and greater enjoyment (e.g., Tamminen, Gaudreau, McEwen, & Crocker, 2016), antecedent-focused strategies are typically thought to be superior to response-focused ones. Specifically, antecedent-focused strategies address potential problems earlier in the emotion trajectory and hence tie up fewer resources during task execution (Lane, Beedie, Jones, Uphill, & Devonport, 2012). Supporting this claim, referees who dealt with unpleasant emotions primarily by suppressing them (i.e., a response-focused strategy) reported a reduction in their regulatory capacities over the course of a soccer tournament (Friesen et al., 2017). Similarly, tennis players reported that suppressing their anger during a match was associated with worsened performance, and cyclists were slower when they suppressed their emotions rather than expressing them freely (Monaci & Veronesi, 2019; Wagstaff, 2014). Importantly, cyclists' emotion suppression also exhausted them more than freely expressing their emotions (Wagstaff, 2014).

Alongside awakened interest in the social antecedents of emotions in sport and exercise, emotion regulation research, too, has moved towards a more social focus (Friesen, Lane et al., 2013; Zaki & Williams, 2013). As part of this refocusing, athletes have been found to employ intrinsic (i.e., self-focused) emotion regulation strategies not only to manage their own emotions but also to moderate those of their teammates (Tamminen & Crocker, 2013). For example, a team captain may hide her anxiety so she does not worry her teammates prior to an important match. In addition, there is evidence that athletes in a variety of sports (e.g., rugby, ice hockey, volleyball, curling) use both verbal and nonverbal strategies to control or influence the emotions of others. That is, they engage in *extrinsic emotion regulation* (Gross, 2015). Among other strategies, both male rugby and female volleyball players have been found to use humour in the form of banter or jokes to put their teammates in a more positive emotional state (Campo et al., 2017; Palmateer & Tamminen, 2018).

Extrinsic emotion regulation is particularly common among peer leaders and coaches. Often it is part of their role (or 'job' as they would say) to encourage appropriate emotional responses in the other team members in order to facilitate successful performance (Wolf et al., 2018). This may entail calming down an angry teammate after a contested referee call or infusing the team with energy and excitement prior to a match (Friesen, Devonport, Sellars, & Lane, 2013; Wolf et al., 2018). One obvious situation in which coaches work especially hard to regulate their athletes' emotions is in their pre-game and half-time speeches. Indeed, such speeches often constitute the defining scene of many (perhaps most) classic sporting movies (e.g., *Remember the Titans*, *Hoosiers* and *A League of Their Own*). Moreover, research evidence indicates that if such speeches are delivered effectively (e.g., briefly, rationally, and displaying genuine emotions), they can have a positive impact on athletes' emotions and subsequent performance (Breakey, Jones, Cunningham, & Holt, 2009; Evans, Turner, Pickering, & Powditch, 2018; Vargas-Tonsing, 2009).

Successful extrinsic emotion regulation benefits both recipients and instigators (Campo et al., 2017; Tamminen, Gaudreau et al., 2016). Beyond this, though, athletes will sometimes engage in emotion regulation strategies that are beneficial to others but harm themselves (Friesen, Devonport et al., 2013; Tamminen & Crocker, 2013). The most obvious case of this is where players sacrifice their personal hedonic motives (i.e., to feel good) for collective instrumental motives (i.e., to perform well; Tamir, 2016) – for example, by suppressing and hiding their true emotions. An illustration of this was when Brett Favre of the Green Bay Packers played in a critical American football match against the Oakland Raiders the day after his father had died of a heart attack (McGinn, 2018). Such acts of self-sacrifice are hard to understand, however, with reference to personal identities and goals alone. To explain these and other regulatory behaviours properly, we need to invoke a model of self that includes collective parameters. As Chapter 2 anticipated, this is where the social identity approach comes in.

A SOCIAL IDENTITY APPROACH TO EMOTIONS AND EMOTION REGULATION IN SPORT AND EXERCISE

As we have elaborated, emotions are not only highly common in sport and exercise settings; they also influence important outcomes such as performance and participation. Accordingly, their regulation is a central aim of applied sport psychology consulting. Yet, as we have seen, to date, emotion research and its application have tended to approach emotions and emotion regulation largely as individual phenomena. Only recently have they expanded their view to include social factors. In what follows, we elaborate on this social angle and discuss how a social identity approach can enhance our understanding of both emotion development and emotion regulation in sport and exercise. Specifically, we address three key points: (a) that the strength and type of emotions in sport and exercise are shaped by collective (not just individual) concerns, (b) that these emotions link closely to social identity and group membership, and (c) that these social identities and group memberships play a role in determining when and how athletes, exercisers and other actors regulate their emotions.

Key point 1: Actors' social identity determines how and with which emotions they respond to sporting situations and events

Although research is starting to acknowledge the social nature of sport and exercise, a social identity approach (see Chapter 2) to emotion development offers a different understanding (and definition) of precisely what it is that makes emotions social. Specifically, this does not focus on (or even require) the presence and activity of others. Instead, it refers to actors' (e.g., athletes' or exercisers') *self-construal* at a collective rather than just a personal level of abstraction. That is, the self that is implicated in emotion generation is seen to be plural (i.e., 'we' and 'us') rather than just singular (i.e., 'I' and 'me'; Brewer

& Gardner, 1996; J.C. Turner et al., 1987, 1994). In this way, actors' self-concepts extend to include the social categories and collectives to which they perceive themselves to belong. For example, a football fan can be dejected by her team's elimination from a championship tournament even if she had watched the match on TV by herself (and certainly did not actually play in the game). In this instance, she did not appraise the situation on the basis of her personal concerns, but with regard to the concerns of the team with which she identified. In other words, due to social identification, the fan's basis for self-evaluation shifts from the personal to the collective level. This shift is especially visible in the case of fan phenomena such as the tendency to bask in reflected glory (BIRGing; Cialdini et al., 1976; see Chapter 17). Generally, actors are motivated to see and present themselves as capable, good and successful, and this motive extends to the categories and groups with which they identify (Thomas et al., 2017). Thus, fans readily affiliate with successful teams (i.e., bask in their glory), yet they reduce their support for less successful teams (i.e., cut off reflected failure, CORFing; Snyder, Lassegard, & Ford, 1986), because this failure would devalue their collective selves.

Intergroup emotions theory (Mackie, Devos, & Smith, 2000; Mackie & Smith, 2017; Smith, 1993) specifically applies this idea of an extended self-concept to the analysis of emotions (i.e., shifting the focus from narrow personal concerns to broader collective ones). It postulates that actors' identification with a social group (e.g., a football team) and the integration of this group into their psychological self (e.g., by defining oneself as a fan of the team) influences actors' emotional experiences. In line with this, athletes who are members of sport teams report different emotions depending on whether their personal or social identity is salient. For example, a male swimmer interviewed by Katherine Tamminen and colleagues noted that he had mixed emotions as a result of the conflict he experienced between individual and collective goals:

> Last year our team won by like 100 points. So I mean team-wise great, that was good [but] that was one of the worst races of my life. … I kind of just tried to brush off my individual feelings but it's not that easy to do. I was pretty bummed out. I tried to be like 'yay, we won' but I probably would have been happier had I swam fast. (Tamminen, Palmateer et al., 2016, p. 33)

Likewise, as noted in Chapter 2, football fans who identify highly with their team have been found to respond to a team loss with anger (presumably to protect their threatened sense of self), while those who have low team identification react with sadness (presumably being more willing to accept the team's loss because it did not implicate their self so much; Crisp, Heuston, Farr, & Turner, 2007). In the terms of cognitive-motivational-relational theory (Lazarus, 1999), intergroup emotion theory postulates that the shift from individual to collective levels of self also shifts actors' appraisal from personal to group levels (Kuppens, Yzerbyt, Dandache, Fischer, & van der Schalk, 2013; Mackie & Smith, 2017). Thus, actors now appraise situations based on how important they are for the groups to which they belong (i.e., primary appraisal) and on the basis of their capacity as a group to cope with situational demands (see also Chapter 14).

Links to primary appraisal: Feeling on behalf of the group

In the case of primary appraisal (that is, when individuals experience emotions), social identification means that actors no longer respond to situations that impact their personal goals but instead to those that impact the goals of the group or social category to which they perceived themselves as belonging (Goldenberg et al., 2014; Lazarus, 1999). For example, a track and field athlete studied by Tamminen and colleagues observed that:

> Even though I didn't directly participate in [the competition], I was super happy to hear and I was following along and when [my teammates] won I was super proud of them. (Tamminen, Palmateer et al., 2016, p. 32)

These feelings 'on behalf of the [...] team' (Tamminen, Palmateer et al., 2016, p. 32) can be seen as *group-based emotions* (or social identity-based emotions; Campo, Mackie, & Sanchez, 2019; Goldenberg et al., 2014). Other examples of these are found in the football fan who is dejected after her team's loss or the boot-camp instructor who shares his students' pride after they complete a challenging session.

As noted in Chapter 2, it is clearly the case that the capacity to feel these emotions is itself contingent upon social identification. So while you may weep when a team with which you identify strongly loses, a loss experienced by a team in which you have no self-investment is likely to leave you cold. In line with this point, stronger identification is consistently linked with greater emotional reactivity in sport and exercise settings. For example, the more individuals define themselves as exercisers, the more guilt and shame they feel after (imagining) having failed to work out for a while (Flora, Strachan, Brawley, & Spink, 2012). Similarly, individuals who define themselves strongly (instead of weakly) as athletes also experience more negative affect after a knee operation (Brewer et al., 2007). Interestingly, too, if they focus on being an athlete, female sport science students find a knee injury troubling, but if they focus on being women, they are more concerned about a facial injury (Levine & Reicher, 1996). Here, then, it is clear that the group with which one identifies determines the events about which one cares.

As we have hinted at in our own examples, group-based emotions are especially well documented for spectators (see also Chapter 17). For example, fans of college football and basketball teams feel a number of discrete emotions depending on how their favourite team performs (Havard, 2014; Markovits, Shipan, & Victor, 2017). As such, they experience relief and happiness after a team win, anxiety prior to a match against a rival team, and *schadenfreude* (i.e., pleasure at another's misfortune; Smith & van Dijk, 2018) when a rival team loses (especially if the rival team had a higher status; Leach, Spears, Branscombe, & Doosje, 2003). Likewise, envy and disgust have been found to be the primary markers of the pervasive antipathy that fans display towards opposing teams in American college football (Markovits et al., 2017).

Here again, though, the intensity of fans' emotional responses depends on the strength of their social identification. Specifically, greater team identification has been found to predict more intense anger and sadness in response to a team loss (Crisp et al., 2007), more *schadenfreude* in response to a rival loss, and more intense *glücksschmerz* (i.e., displeasure at another's good fortune; Smith & van Dijk, 2018) in response to the recovery of a rival's key player (Hoogland et al., 2015). Indeed, there is evidence that common fan phenomena (in particular, basking in reflected glory, Cialdini et al., 1976; cutting off reflected failure, CORFing, Snyder et al., 1986; glory out of reflected failure, GORFing, Havard, 2014) link closely with group-based emotional responses (e.g., group-based pride, group-based shame, group-based *schadenfreude*) and that these are felt more keenly the more they are grounded in a relevant social identity.

Links to secondary appraisal: Being in control and being supported

Social identification also has an important role to play in determining which emotions individuals experience when it comes to secondary appraisal. In particular, belonging to a group enhances actors' sense of personal control and agency (Greenaway, Haslam et al., 2015) as well as their efficacy and perceptions of competence (Thomas et al., 2017). For example, merely by knowing that she belongs to a team, a volleyball player is likely to feel more in control of, and able to face, the demands of an upcoming match in ways that translate into her feeling more excitement and less anxiety (Jones et al., 2009).

Moreover, being part of a group is bound up with social support (Haslam, Reicher, & Levine, 2012; see also Chapter 14). For example, as discussed in Chapter 2, football fans are more likely to help someone whom they recognise as a fan of the same team than a fan of a rival team (Levine, Prosser, Evans, & Reicher, 2005). Interestingly, though, if fans are encouraged to categorize themselves not as supporters of a particular team but more inclusively as football fans in general, they are then more likely to help fans of another team (but not those who are not football fans; Levine et al., 2005). Perceptions of more social support (e.g., from fellow referees), in turn, make individuals feel more able to cope with situational demands such as a particularly aggressive team (Freeman & Rees, 2009; Rees et al., 2015). Critically, too, it appears that shared emotions play a role in these collective coping processes (Tamminen, Palmateer et al., 2016).

Yet, regardless of situational stakes and coping prospects, a stronger sense of social identity may in itself generate more pleasant emotions. In fact, as can be seen from measures of social identification reproduced in the Appendix an important part of the operationalisation of social identity is *ingroup affect* – that is, pleasant feelings derived from being associated with a particular group (Bruner & Benson, 2018; Cameron, 2004). This ingroup affect is particularly positive if the group with which one associates has high status (e.g., is a successful rather than an unsuccessful football team) because this also enhances actors' self-esteem (Tajfel, 1978; see also Chapter 2). Nevertheless, group membership alone often generates pleasant feelings in part because perceiving oneself as a group member can help satisfy the fundamental need to belong (Baumeister & Leary, 1995; Eys, Bruner, & Martin, 2019; Greenaway, Cruwys et al., 2016). Indeed, one reason why athletes and fans identify with their teams is to gain a sense of belonging and meaning (Thomas et al., 2017) and feeling connected to others typically generates pleasant emotions (Neville & Reicher, 2011).

In this context perceived similarity to others appears to be particularly relevant. For example, as Beauchamp and O'Rourke discuss in Chapter 11, older adults experienced greater group cohesion and more enjoyment, and ultimately attended exercise classes more frequently, if they were grouped with similar rather than dissimilar others (in terms of age, ability and interests; Beauchamp, Crawford, & Jackson, 2018; Bennett et al., 2018). Younger exercisers, too, recalled having felt better and enjoyed their classes more if they saw those classes to have a high degree of entitativity (i.e., a stronger sense of 'one-ness'; Graupensperger et al., 2019).

Key point 2: Social identity as a basis for collective emotions

In addition to helping us understand how and with which emotions actors respond to sporting situations and events, a social identity approach to emotions also provides an explanation of the development of collective emotions in sport and exercise settings. Specifically, individuals' group-based emotions are typically aggregated – and accentuated – in collective emotions, and social identification enhances emotional convergence processes within groups.

Group-based emotions give rise to collective emotions

Very simply, to the extent that members appraise and react to situations on the basis of social identities rather than personal identities, members of the same group should agree in their emotional responses to a given situation or event (von Scheve & Ismer, 2013; see Figure 9.3). Accordingly, to the extent that they are experienced by multiple group members, group-based emotions should generally give rise to collective emotions (Goldenberg et al., 2014). Athletes' reports from a range of sports support this idea in suggesting that a shared social identity and the resultant group-based emotions give rise to emotional consensus within teams (Tamminen, Palmateer et al., 2016). Indeed, this more broadly supports the capacity for social identity to be a basis for group consensualisation (not only in emotions, but also attitudes, beliefs, values, etc.; Haslam et al., 1998).

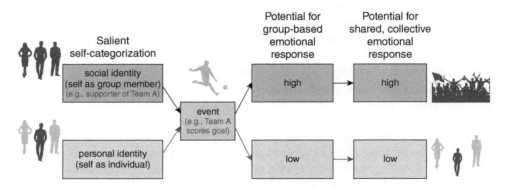

Figure 9.3   Social identity as a basis for collective emotion

Along these lines, we would argue that fans' group-based emotional responses (e.g., to team performance or rival fans; Crisp et al., 2007; Markovits et al., 2017) apply not only to individual actors but to the whole category of (identified) fans, and hence stimulate collective emotions within this group. In line with this point, Spanish and English football fans were found to have distinct emotion profiles in response to events in the 2010 World Cup, which corresponded to their national teams' performance in the competition (Jones, Coffee, Sheffield, Yangüez, & Barker, 2012). Specifically, the Spanish fans (whose team won the competition) experienced much more positive emotions than the English fans (whose team was eliminated in the preliminary phase) and sustained these positive emotions for four days after the end of the tournament. Moreover, the positive emotional responses were not confined to fans who identified highly with the team, presumably because the positive affect associated with winning the World Cup affected the country as a whole (i.e., 'us Spaniards').

Indeed, in addition to stimulating summative group-based emotions, a common social identity often induces a unique and distinctive form of positive collective emotion. Specifically, if members recognise that they are part of the same group and share emotional responses to an event, they are likely to experience *effervescence* (Durkheim, 1995). Effervescence describes an amplified, positive emotional state that results from individuals acting out their group memberships and feeling connected to other group members (Hopkins et al., 2016), along lines portrayed in the quotation from Szymanski and Wolfe (2016) with which we started this chapter. An emotional transformation of this form was documented by Caroline Faure and colleagues among members of the USA triathlon team (Faure, Appleby, & Ray, 2014). More specifically, these athletes experienced group-based pride and excitement upon having been selected to represent their country at the world championships, and these already positive emotions were amplified into a sense of collective effervescence. As one team member observed:

> There's just a specialness of the race. It's almost like it's a once in a lifetime type of feeling. It's almost like the Olympics, even though it's the world championships. It's that similar type of feeling of what you'd think the Olympics would be like. That's why I love it. That's why I love it so much. I can say I'm part of Team USA. There's no other way you can experience that. (Faure et al., 2014, p. 11)

Social identification reinforces ingroup emotional convergence

Indeed, one way in which effervescence appears to arise is via the emotional convergence of group members on a shared emotional state (Anderson et al., 2003) – a process that also depends on actors' social identity. Specifically, because social identification increases members' ingroup focus and valuation (Tajfel, 1978; see also Chapter 2), this also affects their susceptibility to emotional influence from fellow ingroup members. Providing support for this idea, Peter Totterdell found that the more committed professional cricketers were to their teams in terms of identification, involvement and loyalty, the more their own personal happiness was linked to the happiness of their teams while competing in the English County Championship (Totterdell, 2000). And speaking specifically to the notion of effervescence, university students who identified more strongly with their sports and exercise groups, and perceived themselves to be one with the other members, have also been found to experience greater emotional synchrony with their groups (Zumeta et al., 2016).

In a broader context, social identification and shared group membership may also be variables that determine whether actors converge with others' emotions at all. For example, football players expected to feel prouder when they saw other players express pride and more ashamed when they saw others express shame (Furley, Moll, & Memmert, 2015). Importantly, however, these convergence effects only emerged when those who expressed emotion were fellow teammates. When they were opponents, the effects reversed, such that players anticipated feeling more ashamed when observing opponents display pride, and prouder when seeing opponents express shame. In a similar vein, John Drury and Stephen Reicher (2010) note that in sporting crowds, emotions spread quickly through people who support the same team, but not to their opponents and not to those who are policing the game (see Chapter 18). While this may seem obvious, it challenges the traditional view of emotional convergence as automatic 'primitive emotional contagion' (Hatfield, Cacioppo, & Rapson, 1994). Instead, it supports more recent accounts of such processes as socially *bounded*, such that actors allow themselves to 'catch' emotions only from ingroup members (Hess & Fischer, 2013).

Key point 3: Social identity structures emotion regulation

Finally, the social identity approach has important things to say not only about the development of individual and collective emotions, but also about the ways in which actors in sport and exercise contexts regulate their emotions.

A change in self-construal means a change in emotion

Because athletes' (and other sports actors') cognitive appraisal and subsequent emotional responses depend on their (personal vs collective) levels of self-construal, one way in which they can regulate their emotions is by changing their self-construal. This means that while it might be difficult to change group allegiances or leave their teams, actors such as fans and athletes are able to focus more or less on their personal identity and their social identity (Goldenberg, Halperin, van Zomeren, & Gross, 2016; Gross, 2015). For example, to feel happy rather than sad after a meet, the swimmer we quoted earlier might focus on his collective rather than his personal self because his team won while his own performance fell below the standards he had set himself (Tamminen, Palmateer et al., 2016). Likewise, to stay emotionally engaged and excited, a fan can emphasise his national over his club identity if his club has been eliminated from a tournament but another team from his country has not. However, while this might be a useful strategy in theory, principles of normative fit mean that in reality the conditions under which it occurs are limited (Oakes et al., 1994). For example, it takes a lot for Everton fans to align their sympathies with Liverpool supporters and vice versa (but for one of these rare cases, see Figure 14.2 in Chapter 14).

Emotions as descriptors of the group prototype

On a more collective level, emotional responses can also constitute central elements of group prototypes – that is, ideal group-member attributes (Mackie & Smith, 2017; Smith, Seger, & Mackie, 2007; Turner et al., 1987). For example, being (or at least appearing to be) laid back and phlegmatic is one of the attributes that has been said to differentiate English cricketers from their Australian counterparts (Birley, 2013).

These prototypes, in turn, proscribe the expressive and experiential standards to which group-members should adhere in the form of group-specific emotion norms (Hochschild, 1979; Rafaeli & Sutton, 1987). For example, in Australian rules football, players are expected to suppress emotions such as anxiety and fear and this is modelled by team leaders (e.g., coaches; Tibbert, Andersen, & Morris, 2015). This is seen in the case of Joe, a player Stephanie Tibbert and colleagues followed during his rookie season (Tibbert et al., 2015). Joe was plagued by anxiety but encouraged to 'man up' by his coach:

> Look, it's different now. I'm going to try to be a footballer. Coach told me that I might get a senior role for the team if I can start performing well. To do that, I need to be a footballer. I wasn't before, but [the person I was at] home is not who I am now. I am now being a footballer. (Tibbert et al., 2015, p. 72)

The subculture prevalent within the club appeared to value silencing emotion and hiding any vulnerability. Joe learnt that to become a part of this team he had to embrace the subcultural values that being a footballer meant suppressing his anxiety and pretending that it did not affect him, while performing to the expectations of the coach.

Emotion norms not only characterise the context of Australian football. They also distinguish gymnastics (Snyder, 1990) from ice hockey (Friesen, Devonport et al., 2013), and among a number of other sports (Tamminen, Palmateer et al., 2016). As a consequence, emotions also serve as *signals* of social identification and entitativity (Campbell, 1958). Specifically, similar versus different emotional responses indicate who belongs (vs does not belong) to a particular group, the extent to which a given set of individuals actually form a group, and how much a given individual is involved in and identifies with the group. In this way, displaying prototypical emotions can be functional for both teams and their individual members, serving to establish a sense of 'who we are', but also 'who I am as a member of this team'. In line with this point, football fans perceive expressions of congruent emotion as indicators of a shared social identity (Neville & Reicher, 2011) and athletes from different sports see emotions and emotional expression as a means of delineating team boundaries and communicating athletes' commitment to their team (Tamminen, Palmateer et al., 2016; Wolf et al., 2018). As a female volleyball player taking part in research by the first author put it:

> If an exciting game lies ahead and everything is very exciting, I feel very
> influenced by the other team members because I then ... I notice that
> applies to everyone. ... Or you're happy to be able to play together and
> notice that everyone has similar feelings. (Wolf et al., 2018, p. 193)

Intrinsic emotion regulation as emotional conformity

In line with the notion of functionality, group members also tend to have particular
group-based emotional preferences (Porat, Halperin, & Tamir, 2016) in the sense that
they want to conform to the prevalent emotion prototype or norm (Goldenberg et al.,
2020). This is not surprising because more highly identified athletes generally adhere
more strongly to team norms (Benson, Bruner, & Eys, 2017).

When it comes to emotions, actors appear to conform as a result of one or more of
three interrelated motives. First, group members may conform emotionally to uphold
previous commitments (Cialdini, Wosinska, Barrett, Butner, & Gornik-Durose, 1999).
For example, highly identified fans, who are more committed to their team, are less likely
to abandon their team after a bad performance and more willing to tolerate the resulting
experiences of group-based shame than moderately or lowly identified fans (Wann &
Branscombe, 1990). Second, group members may conform to their group's emotion-
related norms to satisfy their need for belonging – that is, to feel that they are part of a
particular group (Porat, Halperin, Mannheim, & Tamir, 2016). As the volleyball player
we cited earlier put it, expressing the same emotion as one's teammates contributes to a
sense of team unity and fit. Third, members may conform emotionally in order to retain
their standing in the group and avoid the social repercussions of not appearing to be a
'team player' (Cialdini & Goldstein, 2004). The latter motive seems to be particularly
prevalent in sport teams. Thus, athletes from a range of sports that Tamminen, Palmateer
and colleagues (2016) interviewed, and the rookie Australian rules footballer that Tibbert
and colleagues (2015) followed, all described adhering to their teams' emotion norms to
gain acceptance within their clubs and avoid the social costs of doing otherwise.

Despite these social benefits, sporting actors' emotional conformity may incur affective
or performance-related costs if the normative emotions generate unpleasant affect and performance impairments, or if they conflict with private, personal identity-based emotions (Porat,
Halperin, Mannheim, & Tamir, 2016; Szczurek, Monin, & Gross, 2012). Along these lines,
Tamminen and colleagues found that athletes experienced a sense of unpleasant dissonance
if they felt obliged to display desired collective emotions but felt differently on the inside:

> Most of the time everyone's just like, follows the trend like 'Oh, wow, that
> was a great game' and everyone displays the emotion that they thought it
> was a great game, but some people might keep it inside like 'Oh man, I had
> an awful game' but you are kind of forced to show an outward emotion I
> would say. (Tamminen, Palmateer et al., 2016, p. 33)

This suppression of undesired emotions can be problematic because it saps athletes' energy
and distracts them from their training and competition preparation (Lane et al., 2012; Smith,

Bundon, & Best, 2016). Setting examples for their teams, peer leaders and coaches in particular are often called upon to engage in this form of *emotional labour* and behave in line with the identity prototypes (Lee, Chelladurai, & Kim, 2015; Tamminen & Crocker, 2013; see Chapter 3). Accordingly, leaders may be at particular risk of experiencing the adverse effects of undesired emotion suppression (Lee & Chelladurai, 2016).

Extrinsic emotion regulation as a benefit for the group

Finally, social identity and emotion norms affect not only actors' intrinsic emotion regulation, but also their extrinsic emotion regulation. Again, athletes with leadership roles are especially likely to work hard to ensure that their team members' emotions align with the prevalent group-prototype or norm (Friesen, Devonport et al., 2013; Wolf et al., 2018). Generally speaking, more identified team members not only provide more social support to their teammates (see Chapter 14), but also are more likely to engage in extrinsic emotion regulation for the benefit of their team (Campo et al., 2017; Campo, Champely et al., 2019). As an example of this, one of the elite French rugby players studied by the third author and colleagues reflected on the way in which his captain [G] had intervened quickly to regulate his exuberance after scoring a try:

> I've scored a try. Watch me jumping [with] joy! I look like a big rabbit! I jumped in every direction. But this seemed to worry G! At that time, he [G] told me 'Stop it now, we haven't won as yet!' He also told me that he didn't want to lose me and that I needed to calm down because the match had not finished. I can tell you that it calms you down immediately! (Campo, Champely et al., 2019, p. 385)

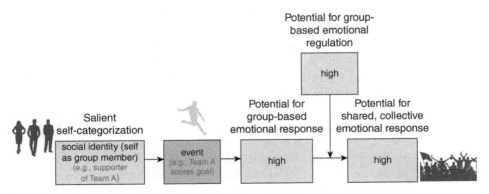

Figure 9.4 Social identity as a basis for extrinsic emotion regulation

Note: This figure points to the role that social identity plays in moderating emotional responses within groups. The more members identify with a team, the more likely they will be to regulate their teammates' emotions. Athletes who are more prototypical of the group's identity (e.g., those in leadership roles) are particularly likely to engage in such regulation.

The key point here is that in the fields of sport and exercise, shared social identity plays a defining role not just in generating collective emotions, but also in managing them in communal ways, in ways suggested by Figure 9.4 (Tamminen, Palmateer et al., 2016).

CONCLUSION

The key goal of this chapter has been to demonstrate how social identity theorising helps us to better understand the individual and collective emotions that are a prominent – and in many ways defining – feature of sport and exercises contexts. Specifically, the social identity approach builds upon appraisal-based theories of emotion development to explain the ubiquitously *social* nature of these emotions. In addition, the social identity approach sheds light on ways in which actors regulate their emotional responses for the benefit either of the individual or of the team. In this, the body of theorising moves beyond a focus on actors' hedonic and performance-related instrumental motives *as individuals* to embrace a constellation of motives that derive from their social identity *as group members* (Tamir, 2016).

Naturally, the relationship between social identity and emotions is circular rather than linear. That is, social identity influences emotion development and regulation, but emotional experience itself influences social identification (Livingstone, Spears, Manstead, Bruder, & Shepherd, 2011). Thus, it is not just the case that social identity provides a basis for collective emotions, but also that these collective emotions loop back to reinforce and consolidate social identity. For example, the experience of collective emotions went on to define the social identity of the English 2003 rugby union world champion team (Morgan, Fletcher, & Sarkar, 2015); and in research by Amanda Frayeh and Beth Lewis (2017), the amount of enjoyment that players experienced as part of recreational soccer teams in turn reinforced their athletic identities.

As well as helping us to better understand emotions, a social identity approach also has a range of tangible implications for emotion management and regulation in practice. First, it speaks to ways in which athletes and exercisers can regulate their emotions by changing the focus and level of their self-construal. Second, it speaks to the ways in which those with leadership roles can shape group-based collective emotions to support group goals. Third, and finally, a social identity approach speaks to the need for sporting organisations and relevant authorities to be sensitive to the way they manage social identities in order to not exacerbate emotional tensions between groups (see also Chapter 18). Like many of the core theoretical insights we developed in this chapter, these implications remain to be fully fleshed out and tested empirically. Nevertheless, by leveraging this theoretical knowledge, we believe that social identity researchers and practitioners will have a key role to play in helping to optimise emotional experiences – and ultimately performance and perseverance – in sport and exercise contexts in the future.

SECTION 3
PARTICIPATION

10

PHYSICAL ACTIVITY

MARK STEVENS
TEGAN CRUWYS
TIM REES
S. ALEXANDER HASLAM
FILIP BOEN
KATRIEN FRANSEN

Sport is a type of physical activity, which is a broader term that encapsulates all bodily movements that result in energy expenditure (Caspersen, Powell, & Christenson, 1985). In line with this definition, exercise – planned, structured and repetitive bodily movements aimed at increasing physical fitness – is also a type of physical activity. So too is incidental physical activity, that which occurs within a person's daily life as part of their regular lifestyle (e.g., walking to the shops). The present chapter will focus on all types of physical activity, including sport, exercise and incidental physical activity.

Physical activity has considerable, wide-ranging and well documented health benefits. In particular, its capacity to reduce individuals' risk of developing non-communicable diseases (e.g., heart disease, type 2 diabetes, colon and breast cancers) has been repeatedly highlighted (e.g., see Lee, 2003; Sattelmair et al., 2011; Sigal, Kenny, Wasserman, Castaneda-Sceppa, & White, 2006). This is particularly important in light of estimates that 9% of all premature mortality can be attributed to physical inactivity (Lee et al., 2012). However, the value of physical activity is not only physiological, with considerable evidence also pointing to its psychological benefits. For example, physical activity has been found to reduce the symptoms and incidence of both anxiety and depression (Dunn, Trivedi, & O'Neal, 2001; Teychenne, Ball, & Salmon, 2008), and to improve self-esteem (Ekeland, Heian, & Hagen, 2005), mood (Kanning & Schlicht, 2010) and cognitive functioning (Lautenschlager et al., 2008).

Based on evidence which has accumulated over many decades, the World Health Organization (2010) recommends that each week adults aged 19–64 should engage in a minimum of either 150 minutes of moderate-intensity aerobic activity, 75 minutes of vigorous-intensity aerobic activity, or a combination of the two. However, despite an ever-increasing awareness of these recommendations and of the benefits of physical activity, rates of participation in physical activity remain a substantial concern. The most recent global statistics indicate that over a quarter of adults (27.5%) worldwide are insufficiently active (Guthold, Stevens, Riley, & Bull, 2018). Even higher rates of insufficient activity (>90%) have been reported based on objective accelerometer data (Tucker, Welk, & Beyler, 2011). These high levels of inactivity have consequences that extend well beyond the negative impact on individuals' health. In particular, physical inactivity also exerts a considerable financial burden on governments in both developed and developing countries (Li, 2014). For example, estimates from the United Kingdom place the cost of inactivity in the region of £7.4 billion per year (Public Health England, 2014), with analyses suggesting that the percentage of total national healthcare costs resulting from inactivity are comparable across high-, middle- and low-income countries (Pratt, Norris, Lobelo, Roux, & Wang, 2014).

Given these statistics, and with the world's population growing, enhancing physical activity participation rates represents a global health priority (Blair, Sallis, Hutber, & Archer, 2012). Indeed, recognising the urgency of this problem, the World Health Organization has set ambitious targets to reduce inactivity by 10% by 2025 and 15% by 2030 (World Health Organization, 2013, 2018). However, despite the efforts of researchers, community organisations and public health agencies, trend data indicate that inactivity rates remain stagnant at best, and may even be increasing, leading to suggestions that these targets are unlikely to be met (Guthold et al., 2018).

Building on recent discussions of the potential for the social identity approach to contribute both (a) to our understanding of physical activity behaviours, and (b) to efforts to promote physical activity (Beauchamp, 2019; Stevens et al., 2017), in this chapter we provide a fresh framework for guiding these efforts. This framework places social factors – and social identification in particular – at the centre of the analysis. First, however, we set the scene for this outline by presenting a short overview of two prevailing theoretical approaches that have dominated the physical activity landscape for the last three decades. Here, while highlighting the strengths of these approaches, we also draw attention to what we consider to be an incomplete analysis within these theories of the impact of social factors on physical activity behaviours.

CURRENT APPROACHES TO UNDERSTANDING AND PROMOTING PHYSICAL ACTIVITY

While early psychological research on physical activity was largely atheoretical, the field took a major step forward in the late 1980s and early 1990s when the first attempts were made to develop and apply theoretical frameworks to understand and promote physical activity. As Rhodes and colleagues (2018) note, theoretical frameworks are essential because (a) they allow for study replication and generalisation, (b) they create a context within which variables under study can be defined and structured, and (c) they lay a foundation for the testing and falsification of hypotheses.

Two approaches in particular have become cornerstones of the physical activity literature – the *theory of planned behaviour* (TPB; Ajzen, 1991) and *self-determination theory* (SDT; Deci & Ryan, 1985). Numerous other theories, including the health action process approach (Schwarzer, 1992), the health belief model (Rosenstock, 1974), self-efficacy theory (Bandura, 1977), and social cognitive theory (Bandura, 1986, 2001) have also been applied in this context. Indeed, in a similar vein, the transtheoretical model (a stage-based model of health behaviour; Prochaska & DiClemente, 1983) and approaches focusing on genetic factors, non-conscious processes, and the role of positive and negative affect have all contributed to the considerable efforts that have been made to (a) understand physical activity behaviours, and (b) promote physical activity. Comprehensive outlines of these approaches, and reviews of the studies that have tested them, can be found elsewhere (e.g., see Beauchamp, Crawford, & Jackson, 2018; Beunen & Thomis, 1999; Marshall & Biddle, 2001; Rebar et al., 2016; Rhodes & Kates, 2015; Rhodes et al., 2018). In this chapter, however, we will focus on what we consider are the two most dominant frameworks in the field: the TPB and SDT.

The theory of planned behaviour

For the last two decades in particular, the theory of planned behaviour (TPB) has been the most widely used theoretical framework in the physical activity domain. A meta-analysis published 15 years ago of exercise-related studies that draw on the TPB (or its preceding version, the theory of reasoned action; Ajzen & Fishbein, 1980) identified 111 studies (Downs & Hausenblas, 2005). More recent estimates suggest that in excess of 200 studies have drawn on the TPB to predict and explain physical activity (Rhodes & Nigg, 2011), with this number likely to have grown substantially in the period since.

The TPB is particularly concerned with predictors of behavioural intentions, which are argued to be the most proximal determinant of behaviours. Specifically, as can be seen from Figure 10.1, the TPB posits three key determinants of behavioural intentions: (a) *attitudes* (e.g., the degree to which a person possesses a favourable perception of physical activity and believes it will lead to desired outcomes), (b) perceived sense of *behavioural control* (e.g., a person's perception of their ability to be physically active and to overcome barriers to physical activity), and (c) *subjective norms* (e.g., a person's perception that doing physical activity is something others think they should do; Ajzen, 1991; see also Hagger & Chatzisarantis, 2014; Hagger, Chatzisarantis, & Biddle, 2002). So, for example, the theory would posit that an older woman would develop positive intentions to go walking on a regular basis (and thus, actually go walking on a regular basis) if she (a) believes that this will help maintain her fitness and ability to continuing playing with her grandchildren, (b) considers herself capable of walking regularly, regardless of unpleasant weather, and (c) believes that her other family members think it is important she stays physically active.

Along these lines, it is worth noting that original conceptualisations of subjective norms in the context of the TPB emphasised the centrality of a person's perceptions of whether important others (e.g., their family, friends or doctor) thought they *should* or *should not* engage in the behaviour in question (i.e., *injunctive* norms; Ajzen, 1991). More recent conceptualisations have, however, recognised the importance of perceptions of whether others *are* or *are not* performing the behaviour in question (i.e., *descriptive* norms; Fishbein & Ajzen, 2011). Indeed, there is evidence that both injunctive and descriptive norms exert an independent influence on behavioural intentions (Rivis & Sheeran, 2003; White, Smith, Terry, Greenslade, & McKimmie, 2009). Despite this, there remains a tendency for injunctive norms alone to be measured in studies that apply the TPB to physical activity behaviours and to other health behaviours (e.g., see Girelli, Hagger, Mallia, & Lucidi, 2016; González, Carmen Neipp López, Marcos, & Rodríguez-Marín, 2012; Hamilton, Kirkpatrick, Rebar, & Hagger, 2017; Hannan, Moffitt, Neumann, & Thomas, 2015; Mistry, Sweet, Latimer-Cheung, & Rhodes, 2015).

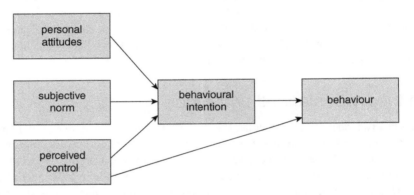

Figure 10.1 Schematic representation of the theory of planned behaviour (TPB)

A considerable body of research supports the TPB's key hypotheses. In particular, this speaks to the proposed relationships between, on the one hand, individuals' subjective norm perceptions, attitudes and perceived sense of behavioural control and, on the other, their behavioural intentions. With regard to physical activity behaviours, this evidence has been drawn from a diverse array of populations, including children (Foley et al., 2008), college and university students (Blanchard et al., 2008), older people (Brenes, Strube, & Storandt, 1998), people receiving cardiac rehabilitation (Blanchard, Courneya, Rodgers, Daub, & Knapik, 2002), and people with chronic health conditions (Galea & Bray, 2006). Moreover, this research has demonstrated the potential for the TPB to explain a relatively high proportion of the variance in individuals' physical activity intentions and behaviours. For example, in a three-wave longitudinal study that tested the predictive validity of the TPB in a sample of 364 school children (aged 9–11), Rhodes, Macdonald and McKay (2006) found that the three predictor variables posited by the TPB explained between 35% and 50% of the variance in physical activity and around

75% of the variance in intentions across their two prediction times. More broadly, a meta-analytic synthesis of studies applying the TPB to physical activity suggests that intention and perceived behavioural control (which has emerged as a more consistent *direct* predictor of behaviour than attitudes and subjective norms) explain approximately 30% of the variance in physical activity, while attitudes, perceived behavioural control and subjective norms explain approximately 40% of the variance in intentions (Hagger et al., 2002).

As this evidence indicates, the TPB has made a valuable contribution to our understanding of physical activity (and health-related behaviours more broadly), and the vast number of studies supporting its propositions is a clear strength of this framework. Nevertheless, the majority of studies that have been informed by the TPB have used correlational or prospective designs (often with a short time interval between data collection points), and findings from these studies have not been equivocal in their support for the theory (e.g., see Bozionelos & Bennett, 1999; Gardner & Hausenblas, 2004). Researchers have argued that those studies which have not supported the TPB have a number of empirical inadequacies (e.g., poorly designed interventions) that may account for their non-significant findings (Ajzen, 2015). Yet others have refuted these claims and, indeed, argued that the TPB is so seriously flawed that it should be 'retired' (Ogden, 2015; Sniehotta, Presseau, & Araújo-Soares, 2014; Trafimow, 2015).

Criticisms of the TPB have tended to focus on (at least) five interrelated concerns. Probably the most common criticism of the TPB relates to what is called the *intention–behaviour gap* – that is, the discrepancy between people's positive *intentions* to engage in healthy behaviours and their actual enactment of those *behaviours* (Rhodes & de Bruijn, 2013b). In this regard, it is notable that many studies which have tested the TPB only measure intentions, which are relatively easy to assess in survey-based research (Baumeister, Vohs, & Funder, 2007; Doliński, 2018), but do not verify the findings by also including an objective measure of behaviour. Moreover, those that do include a measure of behaviour (objective or otherwise) have often found only weak-to-moderate associations between intentions and behaviour (e.g., see Bozionelos & Bennett, 1999; Karvinen et al., 2009; Martin, Oliver, & McCaughtry, 2007). As a result, questions have been raised regarding the predictive validity of the theory (Sniehotta et al., 2014). The intention–behaviour gap has been found to exist for a range of health behaviours, with people falling well short of their lofty intentions to, for example, eat healthily, reduce their smoking and engage in safe sex (e.g., see Mullan, Allom, Brogan, Kothe, & Todd, 2014; Webb & Sheeran, 2006). Evidence also suggests that the gap is particularly large in the case of physical activity behaviours. For example, meta-analyses have shown (a) that medium-sized changes in intention result in trivial changes in behaviour (Rhodes & Dickau, 2012), and (b) that across studies examining the relationship between intentions and behaviour prospectively, approximately half of the total sample fell into the intention–behaviour gap (and may therefore be labelled 'unsuccessful intenders'; Rhodes & de Bruijn, 2013a).

A second criticism of the TPB relates to the measurement of its core predictors. The concept that has received most scrutiny in this regard is perceived behavioural control. Here mixed findings have led to concerns that perceived behavioural control is in fact an amalgamation of several variables (i.e., perceived control, perceived difficulty and perceived confidence; Kraft, Rise, Sutton, & Roysamb, 2011; Trafimow, Sheeran, Conner, & Finlay, 2002), and that the measures typically used to assess perceived behavioural control are in fact better conceptualised as measures of self-efficacy (e.g., see Armitage, 2005; Armitage, Conner, Loach, & Willetts, 1999).

Relatedly, third, there have been concerns that the TPB is not open to empirical falsification (Ogden, 2003), with non-significant findings being attributed to methodological, rather than theoretical, shortcomings.

At the same time, and fourth, the TPB has an exclusive focus on rational, cognitive reasoning. This overlooks evidence that people often make irrational behavioural decisions (e.g., see Frederiks, Stenner, & Hobman, 2015; Williams, Manias, & Walker, 2009) and it leaves little room for other health-behaviour determinants, such as unconscious processes (Sheeran, Gollwitzer, & Bargh, 2013), or those that lie beyond individual control, such as social context. These less deliberate cognitive processes may for example lead a teenager who is walking through a park to join in with a group of his friends who he sees playing football – despite not having previously planned to do so or given extended thought to the pros and cons.

Finally, and perhaps most importantly, efforts to change behaviour via interventions that target elements of the TPB have demonstrated minimal success (Chatzisarantis & Hagger, 2005; Kinmonth et al., 2008; Sniehotta, 2009). For example, using a multifactorial design, Sniehotta (2009) randomly assigned 579 participants to receive a behavioural belief intervention or not, a normative belief intervention or not, and a control belief intervention or not (i.e., to one of six conditions). Despite manipulation checks confirming that these interventions induced positive post-intervention changes in attitudes, subjective norms and perceived behavioural control, the study's results showed that only the control belief intervention exerted a significant effect on objectively assessed attendance (and this effect was very small; $\eta^2 = .007$). Findings such as these have led researchers to raise serious concerns about the suitability of the TPB as a model of behaviour *change* (Sniehotta et al., 2014).

Self-determination theory

At its core, self-determination theory (SDT) proposes that human beings have three fundamental psychological needs – for autonomy, competence and relatedness. *Autonomy* refers to people's need to self-organise experience and behaviour and perceive activity as aligning with their interests, values and goals. In physical activity contexts, fitness professionals such as personal trainers and exercise class instructors have been shown to play a key role in satisfying or frustrating this need, and may do so by offering (or else limiting) exercisers' choice regarding what activities they engage in, acknowledging (ignoring) their feelings and perspectives, and identifying and nurturing (neglecting) their interests (Hancox, Quested, Thøgersen-Ntoumani, & Ntoumanis, 2015; Ntoumanis, Thøgersen-Ntoumani, Quested, & Hancox, 2016).

Competence refers to people's need to feel effective and capable of meeting challenges. This may arise, for example, if they succeed in accomplishing self-relevant physical activity goals (e.g., by achieving daily step count targets or completing a running race). Ensuring goals are individualised and realistic is therefore paramount (e.g., see Silva et al., 2008), as SDT suggests that negative effects are likely to eventuate if goals are not reached and perceptions of competence are diminished as a consequence (Deci & Ryan, 2000).

Finally, *relatedness* refers to people's need to feel connected to, and cared for, by other people. That is, this component of SDT emphasises the importance of people developing connections at an interpersonal (rather than group) level. Applied to physical activity, people's need for relatedness may be fulfilled through the development of positive relationships with other members of exercise programmes or classes (Vlachopoulos, Ntoumanis, & Smith, 2010).

Crucially, SDT is a theory of human motivation: it proposes that the satisfaction of these three needs is crucial to the development of higher quality and more sustainable forms of motivation (i.e., motivations derived from internal choice or personal volition, rather than external pressure or a sense of obligation) to engage in particular behaviours, such as physical activity (Deci & Ryan, 2000; Ntoumanis et al., 2016). These *autonomous* rather than *controlled* forms of motivation are, in turn, proposed to be associated with more adaptive behaviours, such as greater adherence to exercise programmes (see Figure 10.2). Although individual tests of SDT in physical activity contexts have not always provided support for all of the relationships specified in the model (e.g., see Edmunds, Ntoumanis, & Duda, 2006, 2007), the substantial body of research underpinned by the theory generally supports its hypotheses (for reviews, see Ng et al., 2012; Teixeira, Carraça, Markland, Silva, & Ryan, 2012).

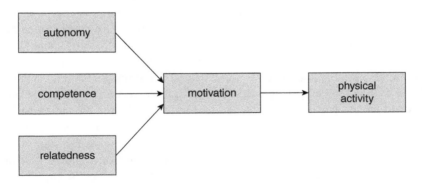

Figure 10.2 Schematic representation of self-determination theory's (SDT) relevance to physical activity

Crucially, too, SDT has demonstrated a capacity to serve as a framework to guide interventions to promote physical activity. For example, Silva and colleagues (2010) conducted a 12-month randomised controlled trial with a community sample of overweight women. Participants received either an SDT-based intervention or were allocated to a control group (and received a general health education programme). The SDT intervention included a suite of strategies that aimed to bolster participants' sense of autonomy, ownership and control over their own behaviours. For example, a 'menu' of options for individuals looking to engage in physical activity was provided, and intervention facilitators were instructed to use neutral language when communicating with participants (i.e., 'may', and 'could' rather than 'should' or 'must'). The study found that participants in the SDT condition reported significantly greater increases in both physical activity levels (i.e., steps per day and minutes of moderate plus vigorous exercise) and percentage weight loss than those in the control group.

Yet while such findings indicate that the specific strategies employed by Silva and colleagues are likely to be useful, there remain some concerns about the theory. For example, while the theory proposes that motivation lies on a continuum from completely autonomous (i.e., intrinsic) motivation to highly controlled (i.e., extrinsic) forms of motivation, it is seemingly possible to be at the same time both intrinsically and extrinsically motivated to engage in a given activity. For example, a person might attend an exercise class both because they enjoy it (intrinsic motivation) and out of a sense of obligation to stay fit, healthy and active (extrinsic motivation).

Beyond this, we highlight one further point that is pertinent to SDT, the TPB and all of the prevailing theoretical approaches to understanding physical activity that we mentioned earlier in this chapter (notably the health action process approach, the health belief model, self-efficacy theory and social cognitive theory). We note that these theories do make some reference to social factors. For example, SDT highlights the importance of feeling connected to other people (via the construct of relatedness), while the TPB specifies the salient role of other people in determining behaviour, including the potential for those to whom we feel stronger connections to have greater influence (via the construct of subjective norms). However, these theories maintain an assumption that our thoughts, attitudes and, crucially, behaviours are determined by our sense of self *as individuals*. Indeed, in direct contrast to the social identity approach, SDT assumes the existence of a single 'true self', with innate needs for autonomy, competence and personal (rather than group-based) relatedness (Deci & Ryan, 2000). This theory – like the others that we have mentioned – thus overlooks the capacity for individuals to possess *multiple selves* that correspond to the identities they possess as members of various *social groups* (Haslam & Turner, 1992; Turner et al., 1994), and, crucially, for these identities to play a fundamental role in determining behaviour. In this way, they also fail to recognise the capacity for social context to lead to *change* in the self or its needs – a key strength of the social identity approach.

Summary of existing approaches

Although the above review outlines both our own and others' criticisms of previous work, our goal was not to dismiss these theories' insights, nor to call for researchers to abandon the theories altogether (as others have done; e.g., see Ogden, 2015; Sniehotta et al., 2014). Rather, we seek to pinpoint some of the key limitations of this work and to elucidate the gaps in understanding that we believe our new social identity model can begin to fill. Certainly, given both the small overall effect sizes (Conn, Valentine, & Cooper, 2002; Harris, Kuramoto, Schulzer, & Retallack, 2009) and the considerable heterogeneity in effect size strength often reported in meta-analyses of physical activity interventions (Conn, Hafdahl, Cooper, Brown, & Lusk, 2009), we do not believe it is in any way contentious to state that there is still a long way to go in the quest to discover the most effective ways of promoting sustained physical activity behaviour change.

In line with this conclusion, a recent meta-analysis of theory-based interventions (broadly defined) that have been tested through randomised controlled trials concluded that, compared to control groups, these interventions have had a significantly more positive impact on the physical activity behaviour of participants (Gourlan et al., 2015). However, the size of this impact was small to medium (Cohen's $d = 0.31$) and this points to the fact that existing approaches are a long way short of providing a comprehensive solution to applied challenges in this field (e.g., see Rhodes et al., 2018). So while noting the promise of recent efforts to move beyond prevailing theoretical approaches (e.g., through the development of integrated models of behaviour change; Hagger & Chatzisarantis, 2014), we think there is value in a fresh approach which concentrates on clarifying the key routes through which *social* factors shape physical activity behaviours.

A SOCIAL IDENTITY APPROACH TO UNDERSTANDING AND PROMOTING PHYSICAL ACTIVITY

The social identity approach encompasses a range of principles that can be fruitfully applied to understanding and promoting physical activity (e.g., see Beauchamp, 2019; Stevens et al., 2017). Of the five hypotheses outlined in Chapter 2, the hypothesis which is most relevant to this domain is the participation hypothesis, which asserts that participation in sport and exercise is grounded in social identification with relevant groups. In this chapter, though, we are interested in presenting a simple and unified model that provides a more focused framework for understanding the social and social-psychological determinants of physical activity (and physical activity behaviour change). Part of the appeal of the TPB and SDT models is their simple and compelling forms (e.g., as represented schematically in Figures 10.1 and 10.2), as well as the ease with which the constructs of interest can be measured. Our new model, the *situated identity enactment* (SIE) model (Cruwys, Platow, Rieger, Byrne, & Haslam, 2016; see Figure 10.3), also seeks to provide a simple framework and readily operationalised constructs, but is based on a social identity framework that seeks to detail the key social variables involved in health behaviour, as well as the primary routes through which these variables affect health behaviour.

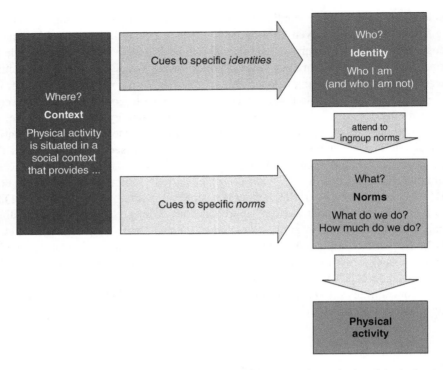

Figure 10.3 The situated identity enactment (SIE) model of physical activity behaviours

Source: Adapted from Cruwys, Platow et al. (2016)

Earlier social identity models of health behaviour often focused exclusively on characterising (and predicting) behaviour as an interaction between social identification and descriptive or injunctive ingroup norms (e.g., see Louis, Davies, Smith, & Terry, 2007; Neighbors et al., 2010; Smith, Terry, & Hogg, 2006). This notion – that the presence, and strength, of shared social identification has a salient impact on the strength of the norm–behaviour relationship – is certainly one of the key predictions made by the social identity approach. However, it is by no means the only prediction made by the SIE model. In particular, this is because the SIE model also specifies the way in which, alongside *social identity* and *social norms* (a term that refers to the standards against which the appropriateness of a certain behaviour is assessed, and that encapsulates both descriptive and injunctive norms; Ball, Jeffery, Abbott, McNaughton, & Crawford, 2010), *social context* is also an important determinant of health behaviour. Crucially, too, the model is also concerned with clarifying how these three factors *interact* (in more intricate ways than have previously been interrogated) to determine behaviour. Specifically, the SIE model states that to best understand a person's engagement with physical activity (i.e., what they do and how much), one needs (a) to take heed of the social norms associated with relevant social identities, and (b) to appreciate that whichever social norms and social identities become relevant is best understood by examining the specific social context in which behaviour takes place.

For example, to predict whether Joanne will attend football practice, one first needs to understand which social groups are salient for her in the hours leading up to football practice. The social context plays a key role here. For instance, if Joanne is at work, her professional identity (e.g., as a physiotherapist) is more likely to be salient than if she is at home (where her identity as a mother is more likely to be salient). Once we know which social identity is salient for Joanne, we can interrogate what the physical activity-relevant social norms are – and are perceived by Joanne to be – for the group to which this identity relates. For example, in this case, the norms of physiotherapy may be seen as highly supportive of physical activity, while those of motherhood may be less so. On this basis, the SIE model would lead us to expect that Joanne's attendance at football practice is better predicted by the context in which she finds herself (e.g., at work vs home) than by her *intention* to attend, as measured at some unspecified time previously.

The SIE model was developed primarily with the goal of shedding light on another set of health behaviours, specifically those related to disordered eating (Cruwys, Platow et al., 2016). Below, though, we apply this model to the physical activity context and draw on the extant literature to evaluate its capacity to both explain and consolidate existing empirical studies relating to key processes through which social factors influence physical activity behaviours.

Key point 1: Physical activity is shaped by social norms

The SIE model proposes that the first, and most proximal, social-psychological determinant of physical activity is *social norms*. This is in line with a large volume of research, from various health domains, demonstrating the relationship between norms and behaviour. For example, a recent review of 69 experimental studies showed that social norms are a robust and powerful predictor of eating behaviours (i.e., both what people eat and how much; Cruwys, Bevelander, & Hermans, 2015).

In the physical activity domain, research focusing on the impact of social modelling provides key evidence for the norm–behaviour relationship. Early research in this area highlighted the impact of families and demonstrated an aggregation effect such that the activity levels of family members were highly correlated (Freedson & Evenson, 1991; Sallis, Patterson, Buono, Atkins, & Nader, 1988). Indeed, longitudinal evidence over the course of a year from the Framingham Children's Study showed that young children were almost six times more likely to be active when both their parents were active rather than sedentary (Moore et al., 1991).

More recently, research has also pointed to a particularly strong link in the activity levels of peers for both children and adolescents. For example, there is consistent evidence that physical activity levels among boys and girls are correlated with the physical activity levels of their friends (Duncan, Duncan, Strycker, & Chaumeton, 2007; Keresztes, Piko, Pluhar, & Page, 2008; King, Tergerson, &

Wilson, 2008). In this vein, longitudinal research by de la Haye and colleagues (2011) found that adolescents both (a) tend to befriend peers who do similar amounts of physical activity, and (b) subsequently model their friends' physical activity behaviours. Indeed, there is even evidence that modelling can help children learn physical activity behaviours and gain confidence undertaking them (Weiss, McCullagh, Smith, & Berlant, 1998).

Perhaps most importantly, research has also pointed to the potential value of modelling-based interventions that seek to *change* social norms. 'Fit 'n' Fun Dudes' is an example of one such intervention. This programme uses fictional characters, which are presented as 'cool' physically active children, to encourage participants to increase their activity levels (Horne, Hardman, Lowe, & Rowlands, 2009). Specifically, participating children listen and are given the lyrics to a song that encourages them to join in being physically active. They also receive a personalised letter with the same message, and are given supporting booklets and pedometers. Trials have documented significant increases in step counts from baseline both during the intervention and at 12- and 14-week follow-ups (Hardman, Horne, & Lowe, 2009; Hardman, Horne, & Lowe, 2011; Horne et al., 2009), while significant differences relative to a control group have also been demonstrated (Hardman et al., 2009; Horne et al., 2009).

Interestingly, and further speaking to the apparent value of attempts to harness the power of normative influence, results of the trial conducted by Hardman et al. (2011) pointed to more sustained increases in physical activity among participants who were in a peer-modelling *only* condition, rather than in a peer-modelling plus rewards condition (where children received small rewards for achieving personalised step targets). That is, once the rewards were removed after the intervention, physical activity levels returned to baseline levels among participants in the peer-modelling plus rewards condition, but continued to increase in the peer-modelling only condition. These findings suggest (a) that the rewards may, in fact, have undermined the long-term effectiveness of the norm-based intervention by fostering extrinsic (rather than intrinsic) motivation (i.e., in ways suggested by SDT), and (b) that, in this case at least, the group- rather than individual-level component of the intervention had greater impact.

Yet while this evidence is compelling, tests of the norm–behaviour relationship have not always shown such large effects. Indeed, meta-analytic evidence has even suggested that 'subjective norms' are generally a weak predictor of behavioural intentions (let alone actual behaviours) in studies based on the TPB (Armitage & Conner, 2001). We argue that, in part, this is due to the failure of the TPB (and research more broadly) to recognise the importance of the *source* of these norms (see also Reynolds, Subasic, & Tindall, 2014). In the following section, we provide evidence that speaks to this critique and, in particular, to our second key point: that people's physical activity behaviours are not shaped by just *any* norms, nor even by those which are dictated by people who we generally consider 'important to us' (i.e., of the form that widely used TPB measures attend to; see Armitage, 2005). Rather, that people's physical activity behaviours are primarily shaped by the norms of the social groups to which they belong and with which they identify strongly.

Key point 2: Shared social identity determines which physical activity norms we attend to

A growing body of work suggests that, when it comes to social influences on physical activity (e.g., norms), the *source* of the influence matters. For example, early meta-analytic evidence pointed to the particularly potent impact of family, friends and others whose views and opinions might typically be considered important (e.g., doctors, work colleagues) on individuals' engagement in structured exercise (Carron, Hausenblas, & Mack, 1996). Moving beyond this, the more specific hypothesis of the SIE model is that *shared salient social identity* is a critical determinant of the capacity for a norm to be perceived as self-relevant and, hence, to exert an influence on behaviour (Turner, 1991). For instance, an Australian may be well aware of a normative sporting culture associated with their national identity, but the norms of this would only be expected to influence their behaviour if, and to the extent that, they psychologically identify as an Australian.

Explicit evidence for the hypothesis that shared identity moderates the relationship between norms and physical activity behaviours remains sparse. However, a recent body of work points to a tendency for people to adhere to group physical activity norms to a greater extent when they identify strongly as a member of the group in question. For example, in a study conducted in the context of Parkrun (a collection of over 1,500 weekly 5km running events around the world), Stevens, Rees and Polman (2019) found that the strength of participants' identification as a 'parkrunner' was positively associated with their objectively assessed Parkrun participation (specifically the number of parkruns that they completed over a six-month period).

Studies have also observed positive relationships between the strength of individuals' identification as members of other groups to which they belong (e.g., their sport team or their exercise group) and their participation in these groups' activities (e.g., Stevens et al., 2018, 2020). These effects are seemingly underpinned (to some extent at least) by individuals' desire to align personal behaviours with those of representative (or *prototypical*) in-group members (Turner et al., 1987), with the caveat that regular participation will be normative in many, but not all, physical activity groups. Indeed, in a two-time-point study involving a sample of sports team competitors recruited from 27 different sports (Stevens et al., 2020), cross-lagged analyses indicated that, although the relationship between group identification and participation may be reciprocal, identification was a stronger predictor of regular participation than regular participation was of identification.

As noted in Chapter 2, a social identity lens can be used to predict not only how *much* physical activity a person does, but also what *type* of activity they do (or do most often). For example, understanding how strongly someone identifies as a member of (a) their tennis club and (b) their snooker club allows us to make predictions about how much tennis and snooker they will play. This time investment in turn is likely to have other important implications, not least because the health benefits of these two activities are likely to be very different.

Interestingly, too, Stevens and colleagues (2018, 2020) provided evidence for the role that physical activity leaders (coaches, captains, exercise group leaders) often play in fostering group members' identification, and hence their participation. These findings complement a growing body of work that speaks to the benefits of targeting both social identities and social norms in efforts to *promote* physical activity. In particular, a body of research has provided support for a key proposition of self-categorization theory, namely (a) that people feel more connected to others with whom they share membership in one or more social categories (e.g., on the basis of gender or age), and (b) that this in turn guides behavioural engagement (Abrams & Hogg, 1990). Of particular note, a recent randomised controlled trial provided strong evidence for the potential benefits of attending to older people's age-related identities (Beauchamp, Ruissen et al., 2018). In this, 627 participants completed a programme of group-based exercise classes (lasting 50–60 minutes) three times a week in groups composed of people who were either (a) of similar age and the same gender, (b) of similar age and mixed gender, or (c) of mixed age and mixed gender. The researchers subsequently found that participants in the similar-age/same-gender and similar-age/mixed-gender groups showed greater adherence to exercise regimes over 12- and 24-week periods than participants in the mixed-age/mixed-gender group, with the largest effects shown in the similar-age/mixed-gender group. Interestingly, these effects were observed despite the researchers not explicitly making age (as a social category) salient (e.g., by encouraging people to enrol in 'exercise classes for older people').

Recent evidence from 'Football Fans In Training' (FFIT) programmes provides further indications of the potential value of attending to social identities in efforts to promote physical activity. First trialled in Scottish professional football clubs (Hunt, Gray et al., 2014; Hunt, Wyke et al., 2014), this initiative has now been tested in football clubs across Europe (Wyke et al., 2019), and is being used in an array of sports, including ice hockey (Gill et al., 2016; Petrella et al., 2017), Australian rules football (Quested et al., 2018), and rugby (Maddison et al., 2019). Seeking to work with rather than against cultural ideals of masculinity, it targets male fans of specific clubs or teams, and involves a 12-week weight-loss programme (with both physical activity and diet components) run at the stadium of the club or the team that participants support. Randomised controlled trials have yielded very promising results, including showing significant improvements at 12-month follow-up on measures of weight loss, sedentary time, step counts and indicators of psychological health, such as self-esteem (Hunt, Wyke et al., 2014; Wyke et al., 2019). Importantly, too, participants in intervention groups have generally out-performed those in control conditions (who are placed on a waiting list). Although professional sport settings are used for Fans In Training programmes because these are considered a powerful 'hook' through which to engage men in weight-loss programmes (Quested et al., 2018), adherence to the programmes may equally be attributed, we believe, to the common social identity that participants share as fans of the same team, and the interaction that is assured between ingroup members.

Yet despite this evidence for the benefits of attending to identities as part of efforts to *increase* physical activity, there is also potential for identities, and the norms associated with them, to act as *barriers* to participation. For example, a review of socio-cultural barriers to women's physical activity participation identified childcare and household work as key factors that stop women reaching recommended physical activity levels (Abbasi, 2014). Indeed, research indicates that, in some societies, norms dictating that women should be the primary caretakers of the home are so deeply rooted that it is considered inappropriate and even selfish for women to engage in recreational activities of any form (Parra-Medina & Messias, 2011). There is also evidence of similar norm-related barriers among more specific groups. For example, concerns regarding performing free bodily movements and wearing culturally unsuitable clothes that expose parts of the body (particularly in front of men) have been identified as barriers to Asian and Somalian womens' participation in exercise (Devlin et al., 2012; Lawton, Ahmad, Hanna, Douglas, & Hallowell, 2006).

Although the studies summarised above indicate that both norms and identities interact to shape physical activity behaviours, this interaction hypothesis has yet to be fully tested, with norms often assumed rather than measured or manipulated. For example, in the studies by Stevens and colleagues, group identification was directly assessed but group norms relating to physical activity participation were not (Stevens et al., 2018; Stevens, Rees & Polman, 2019). Nevertheless, research by Terry and Hogg (1996) speaks more directly to this interaction effect. These researchers found that university students' perceptions of their friends' and peers' exercise-related norms influenced these participants' own exercise intentions only among those who identified strongly with this reference group. However, the focus on intentions – rather than actual behaviours – means that Terry and Hogg's (1996) findings should be interpreted with caution (along the lines of our discussion of the intention–behaviour gap above).

A clearer indication of the benefits of attending to both norms *and* identities, and, crucially, of the potential to reap benefits by challenging the norms associated with particular identities, is provided by the recent 'This Girl Can' campaign. Originating in the United Kingdom (but subsequently adopted elsewhere), this campaign was designed to address the fear of judgement that acts as a barrier to females' participation in physical activity. The campaign used girls and women of all ages and backgrounds to communicate slogans such as 'I kick balls, deal with it' and 'Sweating like a pig, feeling like a fox' (see Kemp, 2016). In line with social identity principles, these messages can be seen to have served two primary purposes: (a) to capitalise on girls' and womens' gender-based identity, and (b) to redefine the norms associated with this identity in order to create a perception that exercising, and not worrying what one looks like when exercising, is both acceptable and common for girls and women. Further enhanced by resources that help girls and women to find the right way to get active for them (see This Girl Can, 2018; Figure 10.4), this campaign has been credited with increasing participation rates among girls and women of all ages and backgrounds, and helping to close the physical activity gender gap (Sport England, 2016) – a rare degree of success for a health promotional campaign (see Brown et al., 2012).

Figure 10.4 'This Girl Can' campaign

Source: Sport England

In light of the success of this campaign, and the growing body of research indicating that identities and norms interact to influence physical activity behaviours, there is now good evidence to suggest that explicitly targeting (i.e., seeking to change or manipulate) the physical activity norms that people associate with particular identities may represent a fruitful intervention strategy. However, while there is consistent evidence for an interaction between norms and identity in the context of other health-related behaviours (e.g., see Louis et al., 2007; Neighbors et al., 2010; Smith et al., 2006), there remains a clear need for research to test this hypothesis in the physical activity domain. That is, experimental and intervention-based research is needed to show how norms and identities interact to shape not only individuals' physical activity intentions (cf., Terry & Hogg, 1996) but, more importantly, both their actual participation in physical activity (e.g., assessed via daily or weekly step counts) and their behaviours when undertaking this activity (e.g., their effort and engagement levels).

Key point 3: Social context provides cues to specific identities and thus determines which identities become salient in driving physical activity

A third proposition of the SIE model is that social context is an important determinant of physical activity. Social context can include a whole raft of factors related to the environment in which physical activity does – or does not – take place. The SIE model proposes that there are two particular pathways through which context is important in determining physical activity. The first of these (discussed in this section) is that social context influences which social identities are likely to be cognitively salient for a person and which thereby influence their behaviours.

In this regard, as we noted in Chapter 2 (see Figure 2.2), self-categorization theory (Turner et al., 1987) points to two aspects of the social context that determine which identities become salient for an individual. The first of these is *comparative fit*. This relates to the perceived similarities and differences between sets of individuals (or things associated with them; e.g., attitudes and behaviours) in a given situation (Doosje et al., 1998). By way of example, imagine a typical gym environment that is divided into separate areas for weight training and cardiovascular exercise (e.g., treadmills, rowing machines). If all the women in the gym are using the cardiovascular machines, while all the men are using the weights, *gender* is likely to be a salient social identity and serve as an organising category that 'helps' people (e.g., a person entering the gym) to understand and respond in what they might consider an appropriate way (i.e., by engaging in the type of activity that appears gender-normative). On the other hand, if all the younger people in the gym were lifting weights while all the older people were engaged in pilates, then *age* would be more likely to become a salient social identity.

The second aspect of context that determines which social identity becomes salient is *normative fit*. This relates to the point that a particular social identity is more likely to become salient in contexts where there is congruence between, on the one hand, the attributes and behaviours of members of the social category and, on the other hand, the attributes and behaviours that are considered normative for members of that social category (Oakes et al., 1991). So, in our gym example, if it were the women lifting weights and the men on the cardiovascular equipment, gender would be *less* likely to become a salient social category, because this does not map as clearly onto gender-based social norms for exercise (i.e., expectations about what it is acceptable and common for men and women to do).

Evidence from physical activity settings that speaks directly to these points is sparse. However, research in the broader health domain provides suggestive evidence and a clue to the way in which these processes might play out in physical activity contexts. In particular, Tarrant and Butler (2011) examined the impact of making particular social identities salient on individuals' intentions to engage in health-related behaviours. Specifically, in the first of their two studies, they recruited a sample of British university students. They told half the students that the purpose of the study was to understand *students'* attitudes towards health, and the other half that the purpose of the study was to understand *British people's* attitudes towards health – a manipulation of identity salience that was further reinforced via a questionnaire. The students then indicated the extent to which they perceived these two social identities to be associated with (a) drinking alcohol within safe limits, and (b) reducing salt intake. As expected, the students indicated that they perceived these two healthy behaviours to be more congruent with the identity 'British' than that of 'university student'. After this, participants indicated their own intentions to perform these healthy behaviours. Results showed that those in the British identity condition reported greater intention to reduce both alcohol consumption and salt intake than those in the university-student identity condition. In this way, the findings point to the fact that cues which make particular identities salient – which people in turn associate with specific (e.g., healthy or unhealthy) norms – play an important role in shaping their behaviour. Furthermore, they suggest that providing cues to identities that have positive (e.g., health-enhancing) normative content may be a fruitful strategy for intervention.

Unfortunately, in physical activity settings, this approach is not routinely adopted. In fact, particular groups in society (e.g., older people, people from low socio-economic status backgrounds) are often identified as 'problem groups' who require special consideration and are deemed befitting of focused attempts to increase activity levels (e.g., see Armitage & Arden, 2010; King, 2001). While the classification of these groups as needing attention to improve their physical activity is well-founded – statistics indicate that these groups are among the least active in society (e.g., see Sport England, 2018) – our contention is that, in line with Tarrant and Butler's (2011) findings, labelling them as such is not helpful. This is because doing so makes it more likely that people will subsequently seek to live out the norms associated with those identities (Oyserman, Fryberg, & Yoder, 2007), in this case increasing the likelihood that they will remain inactive. A better approach could be to make other identities salient that have more positive normative connotations for physical activity. For instance, making racial identities salient may be beneficial in some cases – for example, as part of attempts to encourage participation in sports with proportionally high participation rates among black people (e.g., basketball; Turner, Perrin, Coyne-Beasley, Peterson, & Skinner, 2015). Indeed, along these lines, and speaking to the potential for identity salience to influence behaviours in physical activity contexts, recent research found that a group of experienced female basketball players whose black identity had been made salient performed better on a free-throw task than a separate group of players whose gender identity had been made salient (Howard & Borgella, 2018).

Key point 4: Social context provides cues to specific physical activity norms and thus determines their relevance (or not) in a particular situation

The SIE model also specifies a second pathway through which context is important. Specifically, social context directly influences the salience of particular social norms, often by providing cues to these norms. In this way, we argue that context provides cues that inform both the *amount* and *type* of physical activity that people do.

One example of how these processes play out to influence physical activity levels is provided by the growing body of evidence that points to the impact of the built environment on physical activity. In particular, there is robust evidence for a positive relationship between the walkability of neighbourhoods (e.g., assessed considering the use of land and the number of residential units and intersections per square kilometre) and physical activity in adults (e.g., walking for active transportation, walking for leisure, accelerometer measured moderate-to-vigorous physical activity; Hajna et al., 2015; Owen et al., 2007; Sallis et al., 2009; Sundquist et al., 2011). Similarly, reviews of physical activity correlates have consistently identified the proximity of, and access to, facilities (e.g., sports centres, parks, playgrounds) as factors that contribute to physical activity levels, particularly among children and adolescents (Davison & Lawson, 2006; Mitchell, Clark, & Gilliland, 2016; Sallis, Prochaska, & Taylor, 2000).

A clear illustration of the way in which context shapes the types of activity in which people participate is provided by evidence that people are much more likely to use a bicycle if they live in a town, city or country (a) where cycling for transport is normative, (b) where there is a large network of cycle lanes, and (c) where people perceive cycling to be safe (de Geus, De Bourdeaudhuij, Jannes, & Meeusen, 2008; Fraser & Lock, 2011). Indeed, in line with these findings, it is also no surprise that at the Winter Olympic Games, medals are typically shared among countries which have areas covered by ice and snow for large parts of the year (see Calfas, 2018). In such countries, contextual cues will reinforce the perception that participating in winter sports is normative from a young age (leading to more regular participation and the greater likelihood of skill mastery). These cues (such as adverts for skiing lessons) are, however, far less likely to be present in countries that have warmer climates (e.g., Australia).

Of course, this evidence may be interpreted in ways that do not rely on normative influence – for instance, by positing a direct relationship between accessibility and availability of facilities, on the one hand, and physical activity, on the other. We argue, though, that seeking to explain participation trends through consideration of environmental and geographic factors *alone* fails to recognise (a) that people are active agents who make choices about what activities they engage in, and (b) that they make these choices in socially structured contexts, rather than social vacuums. That is, just because it snows regularly in the town where someone lives does not guarantee that they will take up skiing. Instead, the regular snow acts as a cue to norms about how the people who live in this town, and with whom they identify, behave (e.g., making salient that most of the town residents know how to ski), which in turn drives their motivation to live up to those norms (e.g., by learning to ski). This observation leads us to urge researchers and practitioners to consider more closely the social-psychological mechanisms (in particular, the norms) that underpin contextual influences on physical activity behaviours when they are seeking to understand and moderate those behaviours.

CONCLUSION

In the first part of this chapter we outlined the widespread problem of high, and largely stagnant, physical inactivity rates. We then turned our attention to two theoretical approaches – the theory of planned behaviour (TPB) and self-determination theory (SDT) – that have, over the past three decades, become dominant guiding frameworks for researchers seeking to understand physical activity behaviours and devise interventions to promote physical activity. While charting the partial success of these approaches and outlining the substantial contributions that they have made to the physical activity literature, we also noted their limitations, together with the benefits that may be derived from a new model that places social factors at the heart of its analysis.

In the second part of the chapter we outlined a situated identity enactment (SIE) model that does exactly this, and presented evidence that supports its key propositions. This model asserts that social norms, social identities and social context are all powerful determinants of physical activity, and it articulates how these three social factors interact to shape the behaviours that underpin physical activity. Crucially, the SIE model proposes that a social identity model of physical activity behaviour is not solely reducible to an identity x norm interaction, but that social context provides vital cues both to particular identities and to particular norms, and thus also plays a key role in determining individuals' behaviour. Throughout our discussion, we have noted opportunities to enhance physical activity interventions by attending to the SIE model's key hypotheses, and seen the success of efforts (deliberate or otherwise) that have begun to do this (e.g., through campaigns and initiatives such as Fit 'n' Fun Dudes, This Girl Can and Fans In Training). It is our strong conviction that if we are to achieve the ambitious physical activity targets that have been set for communities around the world (World Health Organization, 2013, 2018), then continuing to capitalise on opportunities to harness social norms, social identities and social context for positive behaviour change, in the way that this model outlines, has a major role to play.

11

GROUP-BASED PHYSICAL ACTIVITY PARTICIPATION

MARK R. BEAUCHAMP
JOSEPH J. O'ROURKE

Groups constitute an ever-present feature of everyday life. As humans draw their first breath and enter the world, they immediately live and typically develop within family groups. As they progress through childhood, they form friendship networks and become members of school classes. As they enter the world of work, they become members of groups that vary from the ordinary (e.g., committees, project teams) to the exclusive and specialised (submarine crews, surgical teams, military platoons). And then in their leisure time they become members of groups such as musical bands, social clubs, sport teams and exercise classes (to name but a few). Indeed, as Dorwin Cartwright and Alvin Zander noted in their seminal text *Group Dynamics*, 'Whether one wishes to understand or to improve human behaviour, it is necessary to know a great deal about the nature of groups' (1960, p. 4).

Groups are generally considered to represent 'two or more individuals who are connected by and within relationships' (Forsyth, 2014, p. 4). Their members typically have a shared awareness of their group membership (i.e., consider themselves to be a group and have a similar understanding of its nature and purpose), and display some degree of behavioural interdependence. The present chapter centres on one particular type of group: the *physical activity group*. The focus of such groups is typically to support the health-promoting behaviours of its members. Although sport teams represent a particular type of physical activity group, they are not the focus of attention in this chapter.

While the types of physical activity groups that we discuss in this chapter share several common features with sport teams (e.g., perceptions of shared membership), members of most physical activity groups (i.e., groups concerned with promoting physical fitness through exercise) tend to be particularly concerned with personal health and lifestyle outcomes (e.g., weight loss or fitness). In contrast, as discussed in Chapter 1, sport teams tend to be more concerned with achieving collective outcomes (e.g., collective performance) and typically engage in highly structured conjoint functioning (e.g., operationalising a team strategy; Beauchamp, 2019). So while the psychological processes subsumed within sport teams (particularly those related to team *performance*) were discussed in Chapters 4 and 5, this chapter is primarily concerned with physical activity *participation* through groups.

So why focus on physical activity participation and, in particular, physical activity conducted in groups? Participation in regular physical activity, irrespective of whether this is done individually or in groups, is associated with an extensive range of benefits. These include improvements in cognitive and physical function across the life span (Mandolesi et al., 2018) as well as helping in the prevention and treatment of multiple chronic diseases (Pedersen & Saltin, 2015; Warburton, Nicol, & Bredin, 2006). Ostensibly, being physically active on one's own should be a much simpler endeavour than being active with others in groups, as it demands fewer resources (in particular, it does not require the recruitment and coordination of other people). However, what is now evident from a series of important meta-analytic reviews is that when people engage in physical activity in group-based settings, they are much more likely to *sustain* their participation (Burke, Carron, Eys, Ntoumanis, & Estabrooks, 2006; Carron, Hausenblas, & Mack, 1996; Dishman & Buckworth, 1996). As we will see below, one reason for this is that groups are able to harness various psychological resources that can make the experience of physical activity psychologically *appealing*.

As with the other chapters in this book, we begin with a synopsis of the prevailing frameworks and approaches that have been applied to this topic, and proceed to explain how the social identity approach (Haslam, Jetten et al., 2018; Turner et al., 1987, 1994) can provide unique and novel insights that are not captured by those perspectives (albeit that there are important complementarities between those perspectives and the analysis we develop).

PREVAILING APPROACHES TO STUDYING GROUP-BASED PHYSICAL ACTIVITY PARTICIPATION

Two of the most widely used approaches to explain group processes in physical activity settings correspond to separate frameworks developed by Albert Carron and his colleagues. These frameworks provide an analysis of (a) the multidimensional conceptualisation of *cohesion* (Carron, Widmeyer, & Brawley, 1985; Brawley, Carron, & Widmeyer, 1987), and (b) ways to develop cohesion in order to promote physical activity adherence behaviours (Carron & Spink, 1993). The former can be considered a 'conceptual model' of the cohesion construct itself, whereas the latter can be considered an 'implementation model'. In addition to these two frameworks (which for the sake of parsimony will hereafter be referred to as the *Carron approach*), a third model that has received considerable attention within the physical activity domain is the *group-mediated cognitive behavioural* (GMCB) framework developed by Larry Brawley and his colleagues (Brawley, Flora, Locke, & Gierc, 2014; Brawley, Rejeski, & Lutes, 2000). In the sections below we provide a synopsis of (a) the conceptual underpinnings of these frameworks, (b) the empirical work that has tested their key tenets, and (c) the applied and intervention work that they have inspired.

The 'Carron approach' to group cohesion

The study of group cohesion has a rich history within both the social and organisational psychology literatures (Dion, 2000). In their early writing on the topic, Cartwright and Zander (1960) contended that cohesion is foundational to the underlying dynamics that exist within groups and that without some degree of cohesion any given group will not exist. Cohesion, then, is the glue that binds group members together – and without this glue there is no group.

Carron and his colleagues defined group cohesion as 'a dynamic process which is reflected in the tendency for a group to stick together and remain united in the pursuit of its instrumental objectives and/or for the satisfaction of member affective needs' (Carron, Brawley, & Widmeyer, 1998, p. 213). On the basis of this definition, they considered cohesion to be a multidimensional construct that includes both task as well as social dimensions (Carron, Widmeyer, & Brawley, 1985). Task cohesion reflects the extent to which members are united around goal-oriented activities and task pursuits (e.g., planning a route in preparation for a hiking trip). In contrast, social cohesion reflects the extent to which members are united around their social, or non-goal-directed, activities (e.g., socialising off the court). In addition to this distinction between task and social dimensions, Carron and colleagues (1985) also considered cohesion to reflect both (a) individual perceptions of how much members are attracted to the group's task and social activities, and (b) group-level perceptions of unity (i.e., group members' perceptions of how united the group as whole is in relation to task and social concerns). This analysis resulted in the two-factor framework presented in Figure 5.1.

This conceptual framework was subsequently operationalised in both sport and exercise settings with a view to understanding the relationships between cohesion and a range of achievement-focused outcomes, such as team performance, as well as participatory outcomes, such as exercise adherence behaviour within different types of physical activity groups. For example, the *Group Environment Questionnaire* (GEQ; Brawley et al., 1987; Carron et al., 1985; Carron, Brawley, & Widmeyer, 1998) has been widely used to study cohesion in sport. Among other things, the research that it has inspired has found that higher levels of task and social cohesion tend to be associated with better performance-related outcomes (Carron, Colman et al., 2002; Filho, Dobersek, Gershgoren, Becker, & Tenenbaum, 2014).

The Carron 'conceptual model' of group cohesion has also been used extensively in physical activity participatory settings. In particular, a large number of studies that have used Estabrooks and Carron's (2000) *Physical Activity Group Environment Questionnaire* (PAGEQ) show that here too greater cohesion is associated with superior outcomes. More specifically, in line with the glue metaphor, there is evidence that the more cohesive groups are, the more their members are inclined to 'stick' with them and feel 'bonded' to their members. For example, a meta-analysis by Carron, Hausenblas and Mack (1996) that sought to examine the social correlates of exercise behaviour found that higher levels of cohesion were related to higher levels of exercise adherence. The effects were larger for task cohesion (Hedges' $g = .61$) than for social cohesion ($g = .25$), although it should be noted that the number of studies that contributed to those analyses was small.

Nevertheless, in the two decades since this meta-analysis was published, other studies have provided support for a relationship between group cohesion and physical activity participation (for a recent review, see Eys & Brawley, 2018). As one recent example, in the Walk Your Heart to Health (WYHH) study, Betty Izumi and colleagues (2015) examined the relationship between leader behaviours, group cohesion and participation in a walking group programme. In this they found that leaders' community-based health-promotion behaviours (e.g., developing social relationships with members of their walking groups) helped to increase participation in the programme. They also found that participation was positively predicted by social cohesion (but not task cohesion). Moreover, social cohesion mediated the relationship between leader behaviours and walking group participation. That is, the more community-based leader behaviours were displayed, the more social cohesion was reported and this then fed into increased participation in the programme. This suggests that when exercise leaders work to develop a sense of unity around a group's social activities, this encourages group members to join in those activities and to continue to do so.

Cohesion, though, is a dynamic group construct that changes over time (Dunlop, Falk, & Beauchamp, 2013). In recognition of this, recent research has sought to examine both within- and between-person correlates of cohesion within physical activity groups (Maher, Gottschall, & Conroy 2015). In particular, Jaclyn Maher and colleagues collected data from participants after every exercise class in a 30-week programme, and examined the intra-individual and inter-individual relations between cohesion and intrinsic satisfaction. They found that perceptions of task and social cohesion varied from one class to another, and that these class-to-class changes in cohesion (in particular with regard to group members' attraction to the group's tasks) were positively associated with their enjoyment of those classes. In other words, the more members of a particular class perceived that class to be cohesive, the more they enjoyed it. Indeed, from a micro-temporal assessment perspective (Dunton, 2018), these findings point to the importance of looking at how a person's bonds to a group fluctuate over time, as it is clear that this fluctuation has significant effects on their psychology and behaviour.

In light of the consistent finding that group cohesion is associated with higher levels of participant retention and adherence behaviours, several researchers have sought to develop group-based physical activity interventions that target group cohesion as the 'mechanism of change'. Along these lines, in their 'implementation framework', Carron and Spink (1993) proposed a causal model of factors that are implicated in the development of group cohesion that could subsequently be targeted through intervention (see Figure 11.1). In this model, group cohesion is understood to be the product of three factors: group structure, group environment and group processes. According to Carron and Spink (1993): (a) *group structure* is represented by variables that include norms and role-related constructs (e.g., position, role clarity, role acceptance); (b) *group environment* is reflected in conceptions of distinctiveness from other groups; and (c) *group processes* are those that centre on personal sacrifices, intra-group interaction (e.g., cooperation) and communication.

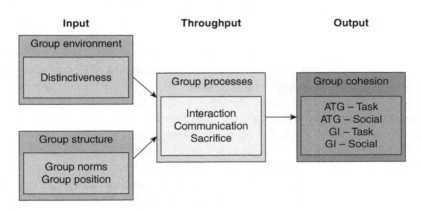

Figure 11.1 Carron and Spink's conceptual framework for cohesion development

Source: Carron & Spink (1993)

In articulating the conceptual bases for their model, Carron and Spink (1993) cited Tajfel and Turner's (1979) seminal work and so it is perhaps not surprising that this model has important points of contact with social identity and self-categorization theories (e.g., as discussed Chapter 2). In particular, these researchers followed Tajfel and Turner (1979) in noting that when people become members of physical activity groups, this initiates a process of social categorization that results in them developing a sense of 'we' that then feeds into a sense of cohesiveness.

Those aspects of the Carron and Spink (1993) model that share particular commonalities with the social identity approach correspond to the roles played by 'group environment' and 'group structure'. For example, Carron and Spink emphasise the importance of developing a sense of group distinctiveness which they suggest can be achieved by developing a group name and distinctive clothing (e.g., group T-shirts), and making distinctive slogans or signs for the class. Although they promote distinctiveness as a means of differentiating members of the focal group from *other* groups, they suggested that this also enables members to develop a sense of 'we' or 'us'. In this sense, their operationalisation of distinctiveness points to *meta-contrast* processes in which the salience of intergroup difference helps to consolidate intragroup similarity (as per self-categorization theory; Haslam, Oakes, Turner, & McGarty, 1995; Turner, 1985; Turner et al., 1987; see Chapter 2).

As well as highlighting the role of distinctiveness, Carron and Spink also underscored the importance of the developing group norms related to exercise behaviour – for example, those which (a) encourage group members to become fitness friends, (b) establish shared goals (e.g., to lose weight together), and (c) promote a strong work ethic. The importance of developing exercise-supportive group norms has subsequently received considerable attention in the health psychology literature (see Dempsey, McAlaney, & Bewick, 2018) and, of direct relevance to this chapter, has been highlighted as a particularly potent construct when it comes to promoting physical activity participation (Kim, Dunn, Rellinger, Robertson-Wilson, & Eys, 2019; Wally & Cameron, 2017; see also Chapter 10).

As Figure 11.1 suggests, the core foci of the Carron and Spink (1993) model involve the contribution of the group environment (e.g., distinctiveness) and structural variables (e.g., roles, norms) in supporting group cohesion. Along similar lines, a complementary body of work informed by social identity principles has highlighted the relationship between social identification among group members and group cohesion (Hogg, 1993). *Social identification* relates to the degree to which a particular group membership is internalised into a person's sense of self (see Chapter 2). Hogg suggested that when members' sense of self is intertwined with the groups of which they are a part (i.e., as a result of social identification) they are more likely to experience a strong psychological bond to the other members of those groups (i.e., in the form of group cohesion). Nevertheless, for all its strengths, what the Carron approach lacks (but the social identity approach offers) is an analysis of psychological process that explains exactly *how* and *why* people closely identify with certain groups but not with others. This is a point we will return to later in the chapter.

What *is* evident from the applied research that has sought to develop group cohesion within exercise settings is that when physical activity interventions are developed that aim to promote group cohesion, this generally results in increased participation in physical activity (e.g., Bruner & Spink, 2010, 2011; Estabrooks et al., 2011; Spink & Carron, 1993). As one example of a programme that was both widely implemented and very effective, Paul Estabrooks and his colleagues developed a group-based walking intervention, Walk Kansas, in which participants had the collective goal of walking the 423-mile distance across Kansas over the course of an eight-week period in teams composed of friends, family members or co-workers (Estabrooks, Bradshaw, Dzewaltowski, & Smith-Ray, 2008). Participants were able to exercise on their own in order to maximise flexibility, minimise barriers to participation, and provide the basis for independent exercise after the programme had ended. Nevertheless, they were clustered into teams of six, engaged in cooperative group goal setting, and reported their individual contributions (i.e., miles walked) to a team captain. The researchers also made use of several strategies highlighted in Carron and Spink's (1993) implementation model to foster a sense of distinctiveness (e.g., having unique self-determined team names, Walk Kansas T-shirts) and ongoing interactions (e.g., promoting occasional group 'get-togethers').

The study generated several noteworthy findings (Estabrooks et al., 2008). First, participants (in particular, those who were inactive or insufficiently active prior to involvement in the programme) displayed significant improvements in physical activity over the course of the eight-week programme, with physical activity levels at the six-month follow-up assessment also superior to those at baseline. For example, at the end of the eight-week programme, participants who had previously been inactive reported engaging in around three more hours of moderate physical activity per week than they had before the programme. At the six-month assessment, they were still engaging in more than two hours of activity per week than at baseline. Furthermore, from a programme scalability perspective, it is notable that in the first year of the programme 5,911 individuals participated, yet by the fifth year of the programme 20,160 people had participated.

Examples of other group-based physical activity interventions that have used the Carron and Spink (1993) implementation model to promote health-enhancing physical activity include a parent-mediated paediatric weight-reduction programme for over-weight and obese youth (Reilly et al., 2018), an exercise promotion initiative among Canadian youth as part of an 'exercise club' (Bruner & Spink, 2010, 2011), and a programme designed to promote both healthy diets and physical activity among African American and Hispanic women in the United States (Lee et al., 2011). In sum, research across a range of contexts and across diverse populations highlights the capacity for interventions that focus on bolstering group cohesion to promote increased group-based physical activity.

The group-mediated cognitive behavioural (GMCB) model

For the most part, physical activity research that has used the Carron approach to pro-mote group cohesion (especially the Carron & Spink intervention framework) has sought to optimise adherence to, and participation in, group-based exercise classes (although there are exceptions; e.g., the Estabrooks et al. study described above). A separate but complementary body of work pioneered by Larry Brawley and his col-leagues (Brawley et al., 2014; Brawley et al., 2000) has sought to harness the power of groups to develop the self-regulatory skills necessary to pursue independent physical activity behaviour away from group settings. In part, this work was a response to criticism of group-based programmes, which noted that adherence can easily dissipate once a group dissolves (King, Rejeski, & Buchner, 1998). To counter this possibility, Brawley and colleagues developed a model that drew on the capacity for groups to retain people within the initial intervention, while also equipping them with the necessary resources to become independent, self-directing exercisers. In essence, this model positions the group as a central mechanism (i.e., the mediator) that drives individual behaviour change and maintenance.

Although the focus of the target behaviour is different within the GMCB approach from that typically applied with the Carron and Spink (1993) approach (i.e., focusing on physical activity *outside* rather that within the group), both models propose that group cohesion is an explanatory variable responsible for individual behaviour change. Specifically, shortly after group formation, the GMCB model focuses on the importance of establishing a sense of group cohesion and identity which subsequently provides the foundation for participants to bolster their self-efficacy beliefs (i.e., beliefs that they can perform the target behaviour; Bandura, 1997) and to learn various self-regulatory strategies articulated within social cognitive theory (Bandura, 1986, 1997; see Chapter 6). These strategies include goal setting, self-monitoring, providing and receiving supportive feedback, self-efficacy enhancement, barrier management, and relapse prevention (Brawley et al., 2014).

A key feature of the GMCB model is its emphasis on strategies that promote a sense of intra-group identity and distinctiveness from other groups (e.g., through the use of group names, group signs and group T-shirts). These shared identities are posited to then become a foundation for participants to discuss, work on and practise the cognitive behavioural skills targeted within the initial (i.e., 'educational') phase. As Brawley et al. (2014, p. 188) note:

> Group discussions about self-regulatory skills that are required for self-managing physical activity focus on highlighting the commonalities between members and objectives they share. For example, one commonality among cardiac rehabilitation patients is their concern about future heart incidents.

After the initial (educational) phase of the GMCB approach, the next phase involves helping participants to 'transition' from their dependency on the group towards self-managed physical activity participation. On the basis of a 'self-management plan' developed during the education phase, participants are encouraged to enact their self-regulation skills to maintain independent physical activity levels, with limited support from intervention facilitators. After this transition phase, which typically lasts around three weeks, the third and final phase then involves participants engaging in independent physical activity without support from programme facilitators.

As with the Carron approach, the GMCB model has been used to promote physical activity participation in a variety of settings and with a range of clinical and non-clinical populations. For example, in one recent study this included the treatment of prostate cancer patients undergoing androgenic deprivation therapy, which included exercise participation as a key component of the intervention (Focht et al., 2018). To name just a few, other examples include the promotion of physical activity among (a) new mothers (Cramp & Brawley, 2009), (b) obese children (Wilson et al., 2012), and (c) older adults involved in cardiac rehabilitation (Focht, Brawley, Rejeski, & Ambrosius, 2004).

And speaking to the viability and efficacy of such programmes, Brawley et al. (2014) reported that effect sizes from GMCB interventions to promote physical activity adherence ranged from $d = .36$ to .86.

While the GMCB framework was not explicitly informed by social identity theorising, as with the Carron approach described above, it is complementary and shares a number of features with it – most obviously, an emphasis on developing a sense of shared identity and on building social identification. As recently highlighted by Beauchamp (2019), it would therefore seem to be worthwhile to look more closely at the degree to which groups embedded within GMCB interventions actually develop a sense of social identification (as this is typically not assessed within GMCB studies), and to see whether this is responsible for downstream effects on physical activity participation.

A SOCIAL IDENTITY APPROACH TO UNDERSTANDING AND PROMOTING PHYSICAL ACTIVITY IN GROUPS

Balanced against the contributions of work that has utilised either the Carron approach or the GMCB framework, in recent years a growing body of research has drawn directly on social identity theorising to understand and promote physical activity participation. For the sake of brevity (and given that the core tenets of the social identity approach are discussed in some detail in Chapter 2), in what follows we provide a brief summary of the conceptual principles that underpin this work, before going on to provide a more detailed overview of the observational, qualitative and experimental empirical evidence that points to the theoretical and practical utility of the social identity approach in this domain.

Psychologically speaking, one of the defining features of groups is that a group exists when it is *psychologically real* for its members – that is, when those people see and define themselves as group members (i.e., as 'we' and 'us' rather than just as 'I' and 'me'; Brown, 1988; Turner, 1982). In this regard, a group is conceptually different from a collection of people who exist in the same physical space as one another, but who nevertheless may not consider themselves to be a group. Passengers on a train, for example, typically do not see themselves as a group unless something happens to give them a sense of shared fate and purpose (Drury, 2012).

So how is this conceptualisation relevant to physical activity groups? Consider the following thought experiment. When Amy goes to her local community fitness centre and takes part in a one-off fitness class (on a drop-in basis), would she perceive herself to be a member of a fitness group? And how might her perceptions differ from those of Bob, who takes part in a regularly scheduled tight-knit class three times per week over the course of several months?

To answer this question, we turn to research on two constructs: entitativity and social identification. In the context of understanding group processes, Donald Campbell defined *entitativity* as a state in which a group is seen to be an entity and to have 'a real existence' (1958, p. 17). In the context of physical activity settings, this has also been referred to as 'groupness' or 'groupiness' (Evans et al., 2019a, 2019b; Spink, Wilson, & Priebe, 2010). In this sense, entitativity operates as an ancillary basis for social identification, whereby people first develop conceptions of the extent to which a group of people display 'group-like' properties (i.e., groupiness), and social identification subsequently reflects the extent to which they then psychologically align themselves with that group.

With regard to the importance of these two constructs for the issues we explore in this chapter, research suggests that when people are members of an exercise group, they are more likely both to exert effort and to enjoy what they do, the stronger their sense of the groups' entitativity and the stronger their social identification with the group (Evans et al., 2019a, 2019b; Graupensperger et al., 2019; Stevens, Rees, Steffens et al., 2019). In other words, in line with the participation hypothesis discussed in Chapter 2, such research suggests that the perception that one is part of a meaningful group (rather than simply one individual person in a collection of individuals) provides a foundation for engagement with the group and its activities. In the next section we build on this observation to explore how insights derived from self-categorization theory can provide an important basis both for understanding the determinants of health-enhancing participatory behaviours in physical activity settings and for effective intervention.

Key point 1: Social identity fit shapes people's preferences for, and engagement in, physical activity groups

In the context of understanding the aetiology of physical activity participation within group settings, an emerging body of evidence points to the predictive utility of social identification within relevant groups. Providing a window into this process, Mark Stevens and his colleagues conducted a series of informative studies which found that when people identify highly with the physical activity groups of which they are members (e.g., agreeing with statements such as 'Being part of this group is an important part of how I see myself'), they were more likely to continue attending and participating with those groups (Stevens et al., 2018, 2020; Stevens, Rees, & Polman, 2019; see Chapter 10). These studies provide evidence that when a person's sense of self is bound up with the physical activity groups that they initially join, this sense of identity-based social connection provides the psychological glue that maintains their involvement.

At the same time, such research also points to the *processes* that lead people to identify strongly with physical activity groups. In particular, and in line with some of the theoretical tenets of self-categorization theory (e.g., Turner et al., 1987; Turner et al., 1994), it appears that this can emerge from (a) factors inherent to the group itself, as well as from (b) the actions of individual social agents such as group leaders. In this regard, one process that is central to people's identification with physical activity groups is *comparative fit*. As specified by Oakes and colleagues (1994), this relates to the principle of meta-contrast, whereby a group typically becomes more meaningful for its members (in ways that increase both social identity salience and social identification) the more it is differentiated from comparison outgroups (see Figure 11.2).

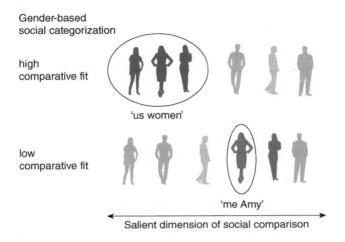

Figure 11.2 Self-categorization theory's principle of comparative fit

Note: Following the meta-contrast principle (Turner, 1985), in the top half of the figure Amy is likely to define herself in terms of a social identity as a woman (and to identify with other women) because here the differences between her and other women are smaller than the differences between her and men. However, in the bottom half of the figure she is less likely to define herself in terms of a social identity as a woman because here the differences between her and other women are no smaller than the differences between her and men.

The significance of the comparative fit principle for members of physical activity groups is demonstrated in a study in which the first author and colleagues surveyed adults in the north of England (Beauchamp, Carron, McCutcheon, & Harper, 2007). In this, adults from 30 to 91 years of age were asked about their interest in exercising in groups composed of younger, middle-aged and older adults. The results revealed a positive preference among respondents for exercising in groups with others around the same age, and a general dislike of exercising with others who were dissimilar to themselves in age. In line with the meta-contrast principle, it thus appears that age is an important dimension of social comparison for would-be members of exercise groups, which feeds into their identification with others in exercise settings.

So does the fact that people identify more with exercise groups when their members are of a similar age translate into actual participation? This all-important question was addressed in a study of new mothers in post-natal exercise classes that the first author and colleagues conducted to examine the impact of perceptions of intra-group similarity defined on a range of dimensions (including values, attitudes and beliefs; Beauchamp, Dunlop, Downey, & Estabrooks, 2012). This study found that perceptions of greater intra-group age-similarity within different classes were associated with greater attendance across multiple exercise programmes. That is, the more the new mothers perceived the members of the post-natal classes to be of the same age as themselves, the more likely they were to participate. Along related lines, William Dunlop and the first author of this chapter collaborated on a study that addressed a similar question using archival data from physical activity classes (Dunlop & Beauchamp, 2012). Again, they found that after controlling for participants' age, age-related similarity within groups was associated with more sustained programme attendance.

Beyond age-related similarity, other work has sought to examine preferences for intra-group gender similarity. In a study that examined exercise preferences in groups, Dunlop and Beauchamp (2011b) found that, among adults, both men and women reported a stronger preference for exercising in same-gender versus mixed-gender groups, with the effects particularly pronounced among overweight or obese people. Clearly, though, this issue of participating in same- versus mixed-gender groups is pertinent to people across the life course, from young children to older adults. In the case of children, a common context for delivering physical activity is school physical education classes. Yet across the globe there is considerable variability in how such classes are delivered – with some schools delivering programmes to separate male and female classes, and others having integrated classes.

In the context of diminished participation in physical activity that typically exists among adolescent girls, Russell Pate and colleagues were keen to explore the impact of these practices on rates of participation (Pate et al., 2005; Saunders et al., 2012). To this end, they evaluated a gender-segregated physical education programme entitled *Lifestyle Education for Activity Program* (LEAP) in the United States that focused exclusively on high-school girls. In this programme, girls displayed higher levels of participation in vigorous physical activity than girls in control schools. As the lead investigator reported in a follow-up interview at the time, these findings can be attributed to the fact that 'Some girls are self-conscious being physically active in a gender-integrated group, and there is a tendency for girls to get marginalised and drift to the sidelines rather than participate actively' (Gehring, 2005). Interestingly, these insights suggest that although in recent years many schools have moved away from separating classes on the basis of gender, because this is seen to promote greater inclusion (which most would consider to be a laudable objective), this may have the unintended and paradoxical effect of decreasing participation, especially among girls.

Complementing these findings, among adults, examples abound of programmes that are specifically developed to align with preferences for same-gender contexts. In particular, Dunlop and Beauchamp (2013) conducted a qualitative study of a highly effective programme in Canada – having 45% of participants regularly active in the programme for 10 years or longer, and approximately 70% active for at least five years. Critically, the programme was provided for older adult men and the class instructors were also older adult men. In explaining their sustained involvement in the programme, participants highlighted the social connectedness among participants as well as the supportive leadership provided by the older adult instructors as major attributes and attractions. Again, these findings accord with the meta-contrast principle (Turner, 1985) in so far as participants for whom gender and age were salient dimensions of social comparison clearly articulated a preference for exercising in same-age and same-gender physical activity groups – finding them both more meaningful and more engaging.

In relation to the principles set out in Carron and Spink's (1993) implementation framework for cohesion development (see Figure 11.1), the foregoing analysis shows how the principles of fit specified within self-categorization theory provide theoretical insight into the group environment and group structure factors that provide the 'input' within this model. That is, the extent to which people identify strongly with a meaningful group acts as a foundation for subsequent group cohesion whereby group members feel psychologically and behaviourally bound to one another. It should be noted that would-be exercisers *also* look to particular social agents of change to help them make sense of the world and to understand their place in it. And in this regard, those who set up and lead exercise groups (i.e., exercise leaders) play a critical role both in making groups psychologically meaningful for their members, and in increasing members' identification with those groups. Evidence also suggests that exercise leaders are more likely to be able to do this if they embody the norms, values and beliefs of the group (i.e., if they are seen as prototypical group members; Haslam, Reicher, & Platow, 2011), and convey norms for action that are in line with those of the group. In other words, the processes that have been shown to be critical to people's participation in exercise groups (notably, entitativity and social identification) are themselves responsive to the *identity leadership* of those who create and manage those groups (Haslam et al., 2011; see Chapter 3). This is an element that is distinctly absent from existing models of exercise participation (e.g., as reviewed in the first half of this chapter), but it is one that those who seek to promote exercise are ill-advised to neglect.

Key point 2: Group-based interventions that explicitly or implicitly target salient group identities can promote physical activity participation

One of the major strengths of the social identity approach, and self-categorization theory in particular, is that it provides a blueprint for guiding interventions and initiatives that can mobilise health behaviour change (e.g., Haslam, Cruwys et al., 2016, 2019). In the context of this chapter, such efforts involve supporting people's engagement in health-enhancing physical activity. Furthermore, given that delivery of these interventions occurs via groups (with the group acting as the vehicle for individual behaviour change), these interventions lend themselves well to being taken to scale and delivered widely (Reis et al., 2016).

In this section we provide an overview of three very different physical activity interventions and initiatives that have either been explicitly underpinned by the social identity approach, or could be described as 'aligning' with a social identity perspective (while not explicitly described by the researchers as having a social identity framing). The research designs that were utilised to evaluate these initiatives varied from the use of a 'true-experimental' design (including the use of a control condition) through to pre-post experimental designs (without a control group) and qualitative methods. Although causal conclusions cannot be inferred from the latter types of design, they are included here because they provide unique insights into the potential for programmes guided by the social identity approach to promote physical activity in the community at large.

These initiatives are also presented with a view to stimulating further research and application that promotes group-based physical activity in a diverse range of settings and populations.

The GOAL trial

The GrOup-based physical Activity for oLder adults (GOAL) trial was a three-arm parallel randomised controlled trial (Beauchamp et al., 2015) that was underpinned by the tenets of self-categorization theory and sought to promote physical activity behaviours among community-dwelling older adults (all aged 65 or older). In this study, older adults were randomly assigned to one of three exercise group conditions. These included (a) exercising with older adults of the same gender (SASG: similar age, same gender condition), (b) exercising with older adults in mixed-gender classes (SAMG: similar age, mixed gender condition), or (c) exercising in exercise classes made up of men and women from across the adult age spectrum (MAMG: mixed age, mixed gender; the control condition). The first two conditions were underpinned by the tenets of self-categorization theory (Turner, 1978, 1985; Turner et al., 1987; Turner et al., 1994) in that classes were limited to older adults (on the basis of evidence reviewed in the previous section which suggests that older adults prefer to exercise with similar-aged others; Beauchamp et al., 2007). The SASG condition used same-gender classes to ascertain whether gender-similarity was a salient categorization variable, when compared to mixed-gender groups (i.e., SAMG condition). In the two experimental conditions (SASG, SAMG) the researchers also used several strategies to strengthen a sense of social connectivity among participants. These included the provision of programme T-shirts, as well as the provision of opportunities for participants to interact with each other over coffee and light refreshments after classes had ended. In this sense, both of the intervention conditions made age-based identity salient (i.e., as 'us older adults'), with the SASG condition also making a gender-based identity salient (i.e., as 'us older men' or 'us older women').

Over the course of the 24-week trial, the results revealed that participants in the two intervention conditions (SASG, SAMG) were significantly more likely to adhere to the programme than those in the control condition (MAMG; Beauchamp, Ruissen et al., 2018). Specifically, while those in the control condition attended an average of 24.3 classes, those in the two intervention conditions attended many more (SAMG = 33.8 classes; SASG = 30.7 classes). Although the researchers had expected that those in the SASG condition might show more adherence than those in the SAMG condition, there was no significant difference in programme adherence between the two groups. Nevertheless, that fact that both intervention conditions displayed improved adherence confirms that offering exercise classes for older adults that are delimited in terms of age can help them sustain their participation. Interestingly, too, when a sub-sample of participants were interviewed about their experiences of the programme, several noted that the social connections derived from interacting with other class members (during and outside the class) helped buffer them against the social isolation they were experiencing in their day-to-day lives and enhanced their overall sense of well-being (Bennett et al., 2018). In line with the health hypothesis discussed in Chapter 2 (see also Chapter 15), this illustrates more generally the 'socially curative' property of meaningful group memberships – and for the capacity of exercise groups to be one particularly potent form that these can take.

Abreast In A Boat: Dragon boating and breast cancer recovery

In the mid-1990s a pioneering sport medicine doctor in British Columbia (Canada), Don McKenzie, pursued a research question within his clinical research programme that challenged the prevailing view at the time (see Kent, 1996). It was thought that if breast cancer survivors engaged in physical activity this would result in lymphoedema, an unsightly enlargement of the upper extremity that is accompanied by a dangerous array of physical and psychological side effects (McKenzie, 1998). His study began with 24 breast cancer survivors (the original *Abreast In A Boat*), whom he enrolled in a six-month dragon boat paddling programme. Dragon boating is a strenuous, repetitive upper body activity that has been shown to produce improvement in both the musculoskeletal and cardiovascular systems (see Figure 11.3).

Figure 11.3   Participants in Abreast In A Boat

Note: Abreast In A Boat is a dragon boating exercise programme for breast cancer survivors. It involves an unusual mode of exercise and a special population, and fosters social identification where women feel that they are all *in the same boat as each other* – both literally and metaphorically.

Source: Dean Salloch

The results of the initial pilot study indicated that physical exercise actually proved to be highly beneficial for these women. Most strikingly, none of them subsequently developed lymphoedema (Matthews & Smith, 1996; McKenzie, 1998). Subsequent studies have reported comparable results (Lane, Jespersen, & McKenzie 2005; McNeely, Campbell, Courneya, & Mackey, 2009), with the programme also deriving notable improvements in health-related quality of life among breast cancer survivors (Ray & Verhoef, 2013). Furthermore, from a knowledge-translation perspective (taking scientific evidence and translating this for the greater good of society), it is notable that engaging in regular physical activity is now considered a 'standard of care' for cancer survivors. Furthermore, what began as a small-scale research project in Vancouver morphed over time into a global movement, with the Abreast In A Boat outreach programme (https://abreastinaboat.com) and the International Breast Cancer Paddlers Commission (www.ibcpc.com).

From a self-categorization theory perspective, qualitative research that has explored the efficacy of the Abreast In A Boat programme speaks to the importance of participants' feeling that they are part of a meaningful group with which they identify strongly. Thus, women's accounts of their positive experiences of the programme consistently focus on the development of camaraderie and feelings of togetherness (Harris, 2012, p. 1). As the women themselves put it:

> We are a living symbol of hope and a vivid demonstration that there is life after diagnosis. Through the strenuous demands of dragon boat paddling we have learned that we can push the limits of our physical endurance and have fun doing it. (abreastinaboat.com)

In sum, by making salient breast cancer survivors' identities as healthy, active and strong women, the Abreast In A Boat programme helps them develop strong bonds with other survivors and embark on a meaningful journey together. This is a journey from which they derive not only improvements in quality of life but also physiological benefits. The sense that, as cancer survivors, they are 'all in the same boat' (Harris, 2012, p. 1) is therefore a powerful metaphor for the multitude of health-enhancing resources that flow from shared social identity.

Run to Quit

Run to Quit is a Canadian initiative that promotes physical activity in groups, as well as smoking cessation. It represents a partnership between the Running Room Canada, the Canadian Cancer Society and a research group led by Guy Faulkner (Faulkner, Hsin, & Zeglen, 2013; Priebe, Atkinson, & Faulkner, 2016). The programme involves a psycho-educational component that makes use of evidence-informed behaviour-change techniques for smoking cessation (e.g., goal setting, self-monitoring), and supports participants' smoking cessation efforts (e.g., through online counselling). The physical activity component involves a 10-week learn-to-run programme that is delivered in running groups. The hypothesised benefits of this centre on increased physical activity and reduced smoking, and these are theorised to be tied to the group's capacity to foster behavioural change partly through changes in participants' running-related and smoking-related identities (Priebe et al., 2016; see also Tarrant et al., 2020).

Testing its capacity to deliver on this promise, the Run to Quit programme was evaluated via an initial pilot study (Faulkner et al., 2013) and, more recently, in running clinics across 21 locations in Canada using a pre-post design (Priebe, Atkinson, & Faulkner, 2017). Results of the latter study indicated that, by the end of the programme, 33.3% of participants who completed the programme achieved five-week continuous abstinence from smoking; 50.8% reported seven-day abstinence; and 90.8% reported a reduction in smoking. In addition, breath-assessed carbon monoxide (CO) levels were measured as an objective indicator of smoking behaviour (assessed with a Smokerlyzer®), and these significantly decreased by the end of the programme. Participants also reported significant increases in running frequency (times/week) and improvements in physical and mental health from baseline to the end of the programme. At a six-month follow-up, using best-practice intention-to-treat analytic procedures, 19.6% of participants reported not smoking and 20.8% were still running regularly. In a separate qualitative evaluation of the programme, participants emphasised the shared purpose and togetherness that emerged in groups as a factor that underpinned their efforts both to stop smoking and to engage in regular running activity (Glowacki, O'Neill, Priebe, & Faulkner, 2018). As one female participant, who was a non-smoker by the end of the study, put it:

> The big thing for me was the group … especially combining the group with the run – I desire to learn to get back to running too, so when you put the group and the running together, that was great. (Glowacki et al., 2018, p. 4)

In appraising the efficacy of Run to Quit, Priebe and colleagues (2017) noted that the programme led to significant improvements in physical activity and commendable levels of smoking cessation among those who completed it. However, the programme also had high rates of attrition. Accordingly, the authors observed that Run to Quit needs further refinement in order to reduce the number of people who drop out. This indeed is another reminder that leadership (and in particular, identity leadership) is required to encourage people to identify with physical activity groups, and that this is likely to be especially important when group goals are demanding.

CONCLUSION

The social identity approach provides a parsimonious and practical framework not only for understanding physical activity participation in a diverse range of contexts and populations, but also for fostering physical activity through intervention. In the first part of the chapter we discussed prevailing approaches that have been used to study group processes within physical activity settings, all of which share some common elements with the social identity approach. We also explained some of the key self-categorization processes through which people develop identities with their groups and affiliative ties to their fellow group members. In particular, we highlighted the importance of physical activity groups being psychologically meaningful for their members in ways that encourage those members to identify with them. We also noted that these processes are not given, but are actively negotiated by group members and are hence reliant on identity leadership that cultivates their sense of the group's meaningfulness and fosters their identification with it. These various processes are represented schematically in Figure 11.4.

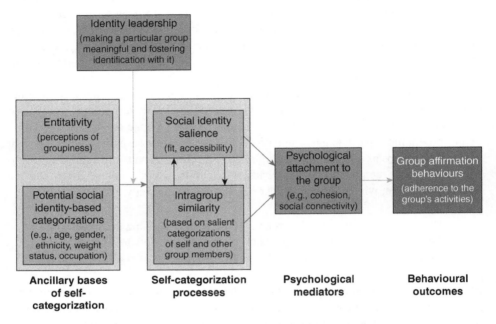

Figure 11.4 Self-categorization processes and adherence behaviour within exercise groups

Source: Adapted from Beauchamp (2019)

The remainder of the chapter represented an overview of recent empirical evidence that has put these ideas to the test (either directly or indirectly) and, in the process, provided important insights into how self-categorization processes shape people's preferences for, and engagement in, health-enhancing physical activity. Here we singled out a number of initiatives that provide powerful illustrations of the way in which the social identity approach can be used to inform effective interventions.

With this latter point in mind, our hope is that this chapter provides a stimulus for researchers and practitioners to devise and test a range of new physical activity interventions in the future. For instance, there has been considerable interest recently in exercising within 'virtual groups', whereby people can exercise from their own home but be socially connected to others within virtual groups using social media. As just one example, in the last couple of years 'Peloton' has become a fast-growing exercise initiative in which people can cycle (on a stationary bike) in a virtual class as well as follow and support each other (giving virtual high-fives), and even engage in video chats while cycling together in real time (Ruiz, 2019). In line with the foregoing discussion of a range of recent group-based exercise initiatives, investigating virtual group activities of this form represents another intriguing setting in which to explore the importance of social identity processes for participatory behaviours.

In the years ahead, we anticipate that demand for such programmes will only increase. This therefore alerts us to the huge opportunity that exists for the development and delivery of bespoke initiatives that promote health and well-being by cultivating shared social identity in a range of target populations. As well as holding considerable promise for the refinement and application of the social identity and self-categorization principles that we have outlined above, this agenda also provides opportunities to meet the needs of marginalised and hard-to-reach populations that are increasingly left behind by the mainstream physical fitness industry.

12
YOUTH DEVELOPMENT

MARK W. BRUNER
LUC J. MARTIN
M. BLAIR EVANS
ALEX J. BENSON

Sydney is a 10-year-old girl involved in her first year of competitive youth soccer. She is a member of a developmental team that provides her with an opportunity to engage in regular physical activity, enables her to work on her technical and motor skills, and serves as an outlet to create connections with friends and develop social skills. Sydney loves being a member of this team, and particularly enjoys the fact that they have a unique cheer, matching uniforms and team tracksuits. Through her involvement in this sport programme, Sydney will acquire physical and psychosocial competencies, while developing healthy self-perceptions that will enable her to engage in life-long participation.

This introductory story highlights the fact that sport is an activity rich with potential for physical, psychological and social growth (Eime, Young, Harvey, Charity, & Paywee, 2013; Figure 12.1). Interestingly, though, despite rhetoric that traditionally speaks to the benefits derived from involvement in youth sport, it is apparent that participation alone does not guarantee these positive outcomes (Côté & Fraser-Thomas, 2016). Simply 'doing sport' is not enough to unlock its power as a developmental agent. For this reason, a growing body of literature has sought to explore the factors that promote these desired outcomes – outcomes that are commonly conceptualised as the '3Ps': *participation, performance* and *personal development* (Côté & Hancock, 2016). Ideal sport programmes will serve as a setting to: *participate* in health-enhancing physical activity as well as the youth's community, foster sport-specific and general skills required for *performance*, and/or *develop* the youth's social skills and self-beliefs.

Figure 12.1 Youth sport facilitates psychological and social development

Source: Pixabay

At surface level, one could imagine that sport programmes striving to improve performance through skill acquisition and personal development might conflict with those that promote life-long participation. However, sport researchers are increasingly demonstrating that these goals are not mutually exclusive (e.g., Harwood & Johnston, 2016). Indeed, when sport programmes emphasise and embrace positive youth development, youth participants have the opportunity to experience the 3Ps simultaneously (e.g., Côté, Turnnidge, & Evans, 2014; Holt, 2016).

Although a plethora of edited texts, chapters and empirical reviews support the idea that youth sport can contribute to development of the 3Ps (e.g., Côté & Fraser-Thomas, 2016; Holt, 2016; Holt et al. 2017), the current chapter will situate developmental sport literature within the broader scope of identity. Specifically, the chapter will draw attention to several outcomes for which social identity theorising has profound relevance: participation, performance and psychological health. This focus on identity in the context of youth development is important, considering that sport experiences are replete with group memberships that may satisfy innate human needs to belong (e.g., Baumeister & Leary, 1995), while providing youth with a distinct sense of *social identity*. Indeed, in line with Tajfel's (1972, p. 292) definition of social identity as 'an individual's knowledge that he [or she] belongs to certain social groups together with some emotional and value significance to him [or her] of this group membership', evidence also suggests that the social identities that are fostered through group life are the source of a range of adaptive behaviours. These centre on connections with other group members, cognitions about the importance and value of the group, and affective responses such as happiness and enjoyment (e.g., Bruner, Boardley, & Côté, 2014; Cameron, 2004; Turner, 1982). With this perspective, sport can make a positive contribution to young athletes' social and psychological development to the extent that youth gain opportunities to develop and enact social identity.

This chapter aims to bring these various lines of research together through an appreciation of sport as a context for social identity to shape youth development. In particular, it does so by introducing a dual-process model that highlights two pathways through which the enactment of social identity in sport contributes to that development. Before outlining this model, however, the chapter starts by providing an overview of the developmental literature specific to sport. After outlining our model, we close the chapter by reflecting on ways in which researchers and practitioners can draw on social identity principles to advance youth development through sport. A key message is that sport is a crucible for learning about, and gaining experience with, social identity, and for this reason is also a crucible for adaptive behaviours that are integral to healthy development more generally.

CURRENT APPROACHES TO YOUTH DEVELOPMENT THROUGH SPORT

Researchers interested in exploring youth experiences in sport have typically relied on frameworks from developmental psychology. Traditionally, researchers and practitioners in youth development focused on reducing youngsters' problems and risky behaviours (Benson, 2003). In recent years, scholars have evolved towards a *positive youth development* (PYD) approach that emphasises a strength-based orientation and focuses on building youth strengths to promote positive, successful and healthy development (Lerner et al., 2005).

The following section outlines three distinct yet closely related PYD approaches that have had a considerable impact on the field of youth development in sport. These take different perspectives on the question of what 'good' youth development experiences entail by focusing on (a) developmental outcomes (e.g., increased confidence), (b) life skills (e.g., use of goal setting), or (c) the integration of these elements within specific social and physical environments.

Developmental outcomes

There are two dominant conceptualisations originating in developmental psychology that prevail in the area of sport. The first focuses on *developmental assets* and follows from Benson's (1997) identification of 40 internal and external assets (or 'building blocks') that young people can acquire through participation in sport and which promote both healthy development and civic engagement. As suggested by Figure 12.2, *internal assets* centre on the personal skills, values, competencies and commitment that arise from young people developing healthy values, social competencies and a positive identity (Search Institute, 2018). In contrast, *external assets* centre on the support, opportunities and relationships that young people acquire from their families, schools and communities. Both types of asset can be seen as building blocks that enhance the likelihood of an individual developing in a positive, productive and healthy way (Leffert et al., 1998; Scales & Leffert, 1999). Importantly, too, whereas PYD can be facilitated by a broad range of organised extracurricular activities (e.g., Fredricks & Eccles, 2008), sport has been identified as a particularly fertile context in which to acquire developmental assets (Fraser-Thomas, Côté, & Deakin, 2005).

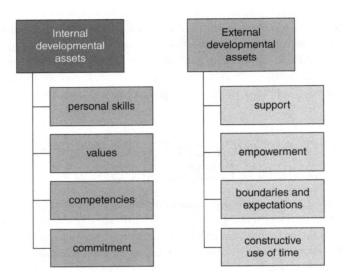

Figure 12.2 The developmental assets framework

The second influential developmental-outcomes approach is the '5Cs' framework developed by Lerner and colleagues (2005). A key tenet of this is that PYD occurs through mutual interactions between individuals and their social context that promote *competence, confidence, connection, character* and *caring/compassion* (i.e., the 5Cs; see Figure 12.3). Returning to the opening story, Sydney has an opportunity to develop many of the 5Cs through the competitive soccer experience, gaining technical and motor skills (competence), meeting new friends (connection), and learning about optimal ways to treat opponents (character). Advocates of this approach argue that participating in well-designed sporting programmes can help youth to develop the 5Cs (Carnegie Council on Adolescent Development, 1989; Lerner, 1995, 2000). Acquiring the 5Cs is also hypothesised to lead to enhanced civic engagement (with self, family, school, community and society) and this *contribution* is referred to as the '6th C' (Lerner, Fisher, & Weinberg, 2000; Lerner et al., 2005).

Although this model has been very influential in the area of youth sport, it has been adapted when applied in sport-specific measures and theory. As an example, Côté and colleagues (2010) proposed a collapsed '4Cs' model that integrates the outcomes of caring and character due to the overlap in these constructs. The revised 4Cs model has been used as a framework for understanding the unique benefits obtained from participation in sport, especially when it comes to understanding how development is shaped by both social interaction (e.g., with peers; Vierimaa, Bruner, & Côté, 2018) and social influence (e.g., through effective coaching; Côté & Gilbert, 2009).

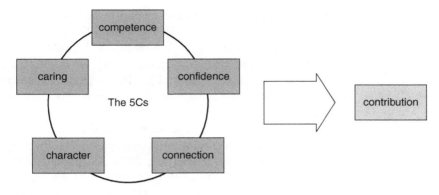

Figure 12.3 The 5Cs framework

Life skills

Researchers consistently point to youth sport as an ideal context for teaching and transmitting life skills across different domains, such as home, school and community (e.g., Danish, Petitpas, & Hale, 1993). In this context, life skills can be defined as 'those internal personal assets, characteristics, and skills such as goal setting, emotional control, self-esteem, and hard work ethic that can be facilitated or developed in sport and are transferred for use in non-sport settings' (Gould & Carson, 2008, p. 60). Initial research inspired by this perspective involved longitudinally tracking and comparing the life skills and developmental experiences of young people who had participated in a range of extracurricular activities, including sport. Like Erik Erikson (1963) and Miranda Youniss and James Yates (1997), we believe that voluntary participation in discretionary activities stimulates assessment of one's talents, values and interests in the social structure. To the extent that more rigidly structured arenas of participation, such as school and work, provide less freedom to explore and express identity options than discretionary activities, adolescents should find more personal development opportunities (including experiences related to reflection and exploration) in youth activities than in academic settings. In support of this suggestion, Hanson and colleagues found that adolescents were more likely to say that the youth development activities (particularly faith-based, service-related and sports) 'got me thinking about who I am' or '... doing new things' than academic classes did, and that those experiences differed, depending on the type of activity (Hansen, Larson, & Dworkin, 2003). Also, activities provide a forum in which to express and refine one's identity (Barber, Stone, Hunt, & Eccles, 2005; Eccles & Barber, 1999). We refer to this aspect of activities as attainment value – the value of an activity to demonstrate to oneself and to others that one is the kind of person one most hopes to be. A key hypothesis here is that the skills that help young people succeed in sport will also prove useful in other aspects of their lives.

Turnnidge, Côté and Hancock (2014) summarised the life skills literature and identified that the burden of evidence demonstrates that sport does provide excellent opportunities for young people to learn a range of transferable life skills that subsequently help them to function adaptively in a range of challenging environments. Nevertheless, there is a lack of consensus about precisely *how* developmental outcomes transfer to the world beyond sport (e.g., school, work). Turnnidge et al. (2014) commented on how many life skills researchers take an *explicit approach*, arguing that sport programmes create – and should be designed to create – an environment in which transferable developmental skills are directly taught to participants alongside sport skills. As an example, the First Tee programme is a national system of youth programmes delivering golf experiences through after-school, community centre and golf course programmes. Curriculum and lesson plans for coaches and pro-gramme leaders integrate golf training with overt discussion of life skills and core values, whereby coaches integrate lessons about managing emotions, appreciating diversity and other life skills (Weiss, Stuntz, Bhalla, Bolter, & Price, 2013). Programme evaluation research has reported the efficacy of the First Tee Program to teach youth life skills in comparison with other activities (Study 1) and longitudinally (Study 2; Weiss, Bolter, & Kipp, 2016). Turnnidge al. (2014) also identified an *implicit approach*, which recommends that sports programmes teach sport-specific skills with no deliberate effort made to make these transferable to other domains. Although there is no evidence that directly contrasts implicit versus explicit approaches, both hold potential. Especially when youth programmes are delivered in at-risk settings, an explicit focus on life skills may be required. Nevertheless, there is strong evidence that well-developed sport programmes also deliver life skill development, so life skills do not have to be taught explicitly.

Integrative approaches

Recognising the merits of both developmental and life skills approaches, in recent years a number of integrative PYD approaches have been proposed, each of which focuses on the ways in which the social and physical environments of youth sport can promote – and be designed to promote – positive developmental outcomes and experiences. Much of this research builds on Bronfenbrenner's (1977, 1999) *ecological systems theory*, which highlights the ways in which development is facilitated by the two-way interactions between individuals and their environment. In particular, this has guided research on the capacity for athletes' development to be shaped by the social environment in which they pursue sport (e.g., Fraser-Thomas et al., 2005; Gould & Carson, 2008; Petitpas, Cornelius, Van Raalte, & Jones, 2005).

Here, two sport-specific PYD models have been particularly influential. First, Côté and colleagues introduced the *personal assets framework* for sport (PAF). This points to the importance of three dynamic elements of sport participation: (1) personal engagement in activities (e.g., do youth have an opportunity to sample multiple sports?), (2) high-quality relationships (e.g., do youth experience close and positive relationships within sport?), and (3) appropriate settings (e.g., are youth from a community with the resources to deliver safe and developmentally oriented sport?) (Côté et al., 2014). The model points to the way in which the dynamic interaction between social and physical environments in the context of the specific sporting activities can promote personal asset development (the 4Cs) and ultimately the 3Ps that we discussed in the Introduction (*participation, performance* and *personal development*). The framework also has limitations. While effectively integrating observations about ideal sport contexts, the PAF does not specify testable propositions about how components interact. With particular relevance for social identification, just as the PAF emphasises the value of personal relationships, it does not disentangle the collective *group-based* aspects of development which would appear to be a central facet of sporting activity (e.g., as discussed in Chapter 2).

Seeking to provide greater insight, Holt and colleagues proposed another integrative model based on a systematic review of qualitative PYD research (Holt, 2016; Holt et al., 2017). This has commonalities with a number other models (e.g., Gould & Carson, 2008; Petitpas et al., 2005) in seeking to explain how PYD is integratively shaped not only by personal relations and organisational factors, but also by the social climate of relationships with others in sport (in particular, peers, parents and adults/coaches).

Homing in on the importance of the social environment, Cairney and colleagues (2018) extended this model to underline the importance of the motivational climate that prevails in sporting contexts. Focused around a goal of being able to measure the subjective quality of sport experiences perceived by youth, they developed a measurement model that disentangles perceptions of the quality of relationships with different members of sport settings and assesses how each links to sport motivation (see Figure 12.4). While this approach provides context regarding which relationships are most critical and the ways that they link to motivation, it again does not unpack the motivational process linking the group environment to behaviour and development. In a sense, these elements are still 'grafted on' to the psychological analysis it provides rather than being seen as in any way core to the development process.

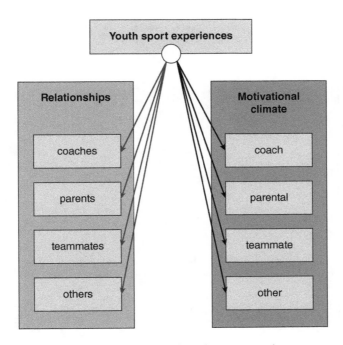

Figure 12.4   The structure of Cairney et al.'s (2018) sport experiences measure for children and youth

Table 12.1 Summary of benefits derived from participation in youth sport as identified by different models

Model/approach	Reference	Confidence and self-esteem	Competence	Positive identity	Connectedness	Sense of purpose	Contribution to community	Positive social influences	Character*
Internal and external assets	Benson (1997)	✓	✓		✓		✓		✓
4/5Cs	Côté et al. (2010); Lerner et al. (2005)	✓	✓	✓	✓				✓
Life skills approach	Gould & Carson (2008)	✓	✓	✓		✓			✓
Personal assets framework	Côté et al. (2014)	✓	✓	✓	✓				✓
Positive youth development through sport	Holt et al. (2017)	✓	✓					✓	
Sport experiences for children and youth	Cairney et al. (2018)	✓	✓		✓			✓	
NRC/IoM: Appropriate youth settings	Fraser-Thomas et al. (2005)	✓	✓	✓			✓	✓	✓
Youth experiences in sport	MacDonald et al. (2012)	✓	✓	✓	✓		✓	✓	✓

Notes: This table is a descriptive attempt and may not depict the entirety of each approach.

NRC/IoM = National Research Council and Institute of Medicine.

*Character development can be positive or negative depending on behaviours endorsed by the group.

The models of youth development reviewed above provide detailed descriptive accounts both of the benefits that can flow from young people's participation in sport (e.g., the 4Cs) and of the social and physical environments that can help to promote these developmental outcomes. These benefits are summarised in Table 12.1, and from this it can be seen that there is a lot of common ground when it comes to documenting the benefits for the development of participation in youth sport.

Yet while these models speak generally to the value of group life for healthy development, they rarely see this as bound up with young people's psychology in ways suggested by social identity research. Much less do they integrate insights from social identity theorising into the explanatory and practical frameworks they set out. In particular, this means that their conceptualisation of the sense of self and identity that is developed though sporting activity centres on a self that is defined in terms of personal identity (the self as 'I' and 'me') rather than social identity (the self as 'we' and 'us'; Tajfel & Turner, 1979; Turner, 1982).

A SOCIAL IDENTITY APPROACH TO YOUTH DEVELOPMENT

In the remainder of this chapter, we address this lacuna and point to ways in which social identity theorising can provide a framework for researchers and practitioners to better understand and integrate the psychological processes that drive (or else undermine) youth development through sport. In particular, based on the theoretical and empirical evidence that supports the social identity approach (SIA; e.g., as set out in Chapter 2), we introduce the dual process *social identity–affiliation and influence model* (SI–AIM) as a framework for this integration.

Key point 1: Social identity is at the heart of youth development through sport

The SI–AIM is based on the idea that social identity amplifies the impact of youth sport experiences and developmental outcomes via two distinct pathways. These are represented schematically in Figure 12.5.

First, the *social affiliation pathway* highlights the proximal psychosocial benefits that young people derive from their social ties and belongingness to a peer group. In particular, it reflects the fact that when a young person integrates a positive and stable group into their self-concept as part of their social identity, such as a sense of themselves as a member of a specific sports team, this has the capacity to increase their confidence, feelings of connectedness and sense of self-worth.

To describe the benefits of social identification in this context, we point to the six cognitive, affective and social interaction processes identified as motivations that underpin identity construction by Vignoles and colleagues (for an overview, see Vignoles,

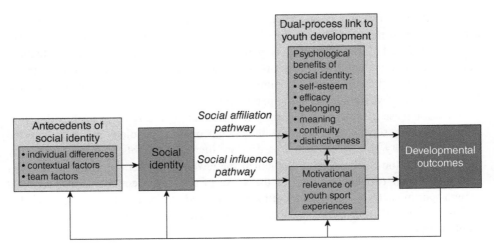

Figure 12.5 The social identity–affiliation and influence model (SI–AIM)

Regalia, Manzi, Golledge, & Schabini, 2006). First, the *self-esteem* motive refers to 'the motivation to maintain and enhance a positive conception of oneself' (Gecas, 1982, p. 20; Tajfel & Turner, 1979). Second, the *continuity* motive refers to the motivation to maintain a sense of continuity in one's sense of self across time and situation (Breakwell, 1986; Sani, 2010; see also Chapter 16). Third, the *distinctiveness* motive relates to a drive to differentiate oneself from others (Vignoles, Chryssochoou, & Breakwell, 2000). Fourth, the *belonging* motive refers to the fundamental human need to form and maintain social relationships (Baumeister & Leary, 1995). Fifth, the *efficacy* motive is oriented towards maintaining and enhancing feelings of competence and control (Breakwell, 1993). And finally, sixth, the *meaning* motive refers to the need to find significance or purpose in one's own existence (Baumeister & Leary, 1995). Importantly, social identity research suggests that the acquisition of meaningful social identities can satisfy all six motives and hence that social identity is a basis for people to gain a sense of self-esteem, continuity, distinctiveness, belonging, efficacy and meaning (Vignoles et al., 2006). This presumption has largely been supported through empirical studies, including 'social cure' research, which is informed by a social identity approach to health (Haslam, Jetten et al., 2018; Jetten et al., 2012: see Chapter 15).

These motives come to life when placed into the example of Sydney the soccer player. By identifying with her soccer team, which is recognisable in her school and community, Sydney may derive a sense of *self-esteem* – and especially *efficacy* when she or her team does good things. Sydney would also gain *belongingness* by knowing she is a valued member of her group – balanced with *distinctiveness* as she recognises her unique role and position in her group as 'different'. She gains *continuity* when she is recognised as a soccer team member in other settings, and stays with her club across seasons. Lastly, belonging to a group where she shares goals with teammates towards higher-order objectives could provide *meaning*.

In addition to the direct consequences of affiliation, the influence of social identification is also contingent on the behaviours and values that predominate within the particular group that a young person belongs to. Here, SI–AIM's *social influence pathway* points to the role that sport-related social identities play in amplifying the influences of others within a young person's social environment. This pathway accounts for research documenting how social identity renders individuals more sensitive and responsive to the positive (and negative) behaviours they observe within their team. The importance of this moderation pathway is confirmed by empirical work which shows that when social identity is salient, depersonalisation occurs, such that a 'person's feelings and actions are guided more by group prototypes and norms than personal factors' (Terry & Hogg, 1996, p. 791). Here, social identity motivates group members to align their behaviour with perceived ingroup norms in ways that are apparent in both exercise and sport contexts (e.g., Spink, Crozier, & Robinson, 2013; Terry & Hogg, 1996; see Chapters 10 and 11). In contrast with the typically positive role of the affiliation pathway, the social influence pathway also points to the potential for social identity to motivate individuals to engage in undesirable or risky behaviours with their peers (e.g., adhering to antisocial norms; Benson, Bruner, & Eys, 2017; Goldman, Giles, & Hogg, 2014). For example, if bullying, substance abuse or racism becomes normative within a group, then those who identify with the group are more likely to engage in these behaviours (Ojala & Nesdale, 2004).

Key point 2: Developing strong social identities through sport has a range of distinctive developmental consequences

Using SI–AIM as a guiding framework, it is possible to reflect on the ways in which its two pathways help us to make sense of the developmental outcomes associated with youth sport that are documented in the research literature discussed in the first half of this chapter. First, it is clear that processes associated with the social affiliation pathway are receiving growing attention in sport. In particular, young athletes who identify strongly with a sport team report a number of both individual and team benefits. For example, work conducted by Murrell and Gaertner (1992) found that young athletes who were in victorious American football teams tended to rate this social identity more positively and to focus less on differences between the team's subunits (e.g., offensive vs defensive players). This is indicative of a more general tendency for social identification to promote group cohesion and a sense of 'togetherness' (Bruner, Boardley, & Côté, 2014; De Backer et al., 2011; see Chapter 5).

Recent work in sport has also drawn on Cameron's (2004) multidimensional conceptualisation of social identity to explore how different aspects of identification with a youth sport team contribute to particular developmental benefits. More specifically, and following Tajfel's (1972) original theorising, Cameron argues that there are three key dimensions to a person's identification with a given group: *ingroup ties* (a sense of belonging and connectedness to the group), *cognitive centrality* (a sense that the group is important), and *ingroup affect* (positive feelings about the group). Research with youth athletes in a number of different sports, including soccer, basketball, hockey, volleyball and baseball, suggests that all three of these dimensions are linked to positive outcomes for team members in the form of increased commitment, improved personal and social skills, greater initiative, enhanced effort, and a stronger sense of self-worth (Bruner, Balish et al., 2017; Martin et al., 2017a).

In addition to these benefits, social identity is also associated with moral behaviour (Rees et al., 2015). Although the relationship between social identity and moral behaviour in sport is complex (as it is in the world more generally; Ellemers, 2018), research by the first author and colleagues suggests that a heightened sense of ingroup ties, cognitive centrality and ingroup affect are all generally associated with more helping and supportive *prosocial* behaviour towards teammates (Bruner, Boardley, & Côté, 2014; Bruner, Broadley et al., 2018). At the same time, though, young athletes with stronger cognitive centrality were also more likely to enact harmful *antisocial* behaviour towards opponents, such as trying to injure an opponent. Athletes with strong social identities may even extend these antisocial acts towards non-normative teammates who appeared to be 'letting the side down' by poor performance or lack of effort (Bruner et al., 2018).

To further shed light on the complexities of the relationship between identity and moral behaviour, we conducted a series of qualitative studies using narrative and stimulated recall methodologies (Bruner, Boardley, Allen et al., 2017; Bruner, Boardley, Forrest et al., 2017). The two studies were completed with samples of male and female competitive youth ice-hockey players. In the first narrative study, interviews were conducted with youth possessing different roles on the team (e.g., verbal cheerleader, social captain). The second stimulated recall study involved the youth athletes commenting on video clips of teammates acting prosocially and antisocially towards each other in practice. These studies pointed to a reciprocal relationship between social identity and moral behaviour such that the social identities that young athletes developed through team membership both shaped and were shaped by their moral behaviour towards teammates and others. If, for example, a team developed a strong family-oriented environment with a norm to be supportive of all team members, players tended to be more supportive of each other, and in turn possessed stronger social identities (Bruner, Boardley, Allen et al., 2017; see also Chapter 14).

When it comes to social influence, an emerging body of research also suggests that a strong sense of shared social identity within a team can amplify the extent to which social behaviours observed within that team also 'spill over' into youth athletes' personal behaviour. For example, a study of university-aged athletes found that female athletes reported more antisocial behaviours towards opponents when they felt these acts were normative on their team, but this association was strongest among athletes with strong social identities (Benson, Bruner, & Eys, 2017). In other words, the more that young athletes identified with a group that had antisocial norms, the more those athletes endorsed those norms as a general way of behaving in their lives. Researchers similarly tested the role of social identity by examining the extent that athletes conformed to normative feedback about one's team, through a protocol that manipulated normative feedback to make it seem like their teammates highly endorsed risky behaviours. When athletes were led to believe that their sport team was willing to engage in risky alcohol use or condone playing while experiencing concussion symptoms, as examples, athletes with stronger social identities were more likely to shift their self-reported behaviour towards the responses of their group (i.e., become more risky; Graupensperger, Benson, & Evans, 2018).

Together, these findings speak to the potential for social identification to foster negative, not just positive, behaviour in the context of youth sport. As a consequence, they also underline the importance of coaches and others who have leadership roles taking steps to monitor the content of social identity and to cultivate identities whose content promotes positive norms and a positive social environment both within and beyond the team (see also Chapter 3). Indeed, the tenets of the SI–AIM orient those who work in the area of youth sport towards the goal of ensuring that young athletes' social identities are linked to positive normative behaviours. In this regard, a key function of SI–AIM is to highlight the interrelationship between social identity-building strategies and efforts to shape the behaviour of individual athletes. This is relevant both (a) to typical sport-based PYD programmes, where a goal is to develop personal assets such as character (e.g., see Petitpas, Cornelius, & Van Raalte, 2007), and (b) to prevention-focused youth development interventions that happen to be delivered within sport (e.g., those which seek to reduce substance use, poor mental health and antisocial behaviour; Greenberg et al., 2003). Speaking to the power of such programmes to change problematic behaviour by targeting the development of positive sport-based social identity, research with teams of female adolescent athletes has shown that positive social norms among teammates and coaches can be powerful mechanisms for positive behaviour change (Ranby et al., 2009).

In addition to amplifying cognitive and behavioural outcomes, social identity has also been found to moderate the relationship between motivation and psychological distress in youth athletes (Vella et al., 2020). More specifically, research with young athletes in a range of sports (soccer, basketball, Australia rules football) observed that to the extent that they identified with their team, players felt more motivated and reported fewer anxiety and depressive symptoms. In part, this was because highly identified athletes reported having a stronger sense of self-determination (in ways suggested in Chapter 6). At lower levels of social identification, however, there was no significant relationship between self-determined motivation and psychological distress or well-being. In line with the general thrust of social cure research (see Chapter 15), this suggests that the mental health benefits associated with participation in organised sports are likely to be reduced if athletes do not identify with the teams or sports that they join.

Key point 3: Sport research may help us understand how to foster social identities

Given the distinct pathways through which social identity can contribute to positive youth development, it is worth reflecting on a range of antecedents that contribute to the development of social identity in the context youth sport. As Figure 12.5 suggests, these include an array of individual differences, team factors and contextual factors. Individual differences include the personal histories and demographic background of participants (e.g., their age, gender and ethnicity) and the *a priori* value of the group to them (e.g., Neel, Kenrick, White, & Neuberg, 2016; Oakes et al., 1994). Team factors relate to the group structure, dynamics and emergent states of the sport team (e.g., those that lead to it being seen as a higher-status or more meaningful entity; see also Chapter 11). Contextual factors include elements of the social environment, such as the competitive level at which a team plays, as well as its relationship and compatibility with other groups.

In line with self-categorization theory's analysis of social identity salience (e.g., Oakes et al., 1994; see Figure 2.2), these factors also interact in complex ways. For example, as discussed in Chapter 2, a young girl's inclination to play tennis is likely to be shaped not only by the skills she has developed in the past (e.g., hand–eye coordination), but also by the existence and status of a school tennis team. Even the value of a school team identity is likely to depend on the country in which she lives and the type of school that she attends.

To date, the literature examining potential antecedents of social identity in sport is sparse. Nevertheless, different strands of research point to the importance of comparative and normative fit for social identity salience (e.g., in ways suggested by Oakes et al., 1994; see Chapter 2). The importance of comparative fit is underlined by research which shows that the degree to which members perceive themselves to be a group (Martin et al., 2017b) and the extent that the outcome of activities requires collaboration among members (Bruner, Eys, Evans, & Wilson, 2015) are both positive predictors of social identity in youth athletes. The importance of normative fit is demonstrated by research in which young athletes kept daily diaries of their interactions with their teammates. As one might expect, athletes identified more strongly with their team to the extent that they reported having more prosocial (vs antisocial) interactions (Benson & Bruner, 2018).

Beyond this, one other important factor that has been shown to predict emergent social identity is *leadership*. On the one hand, this means that young athletes are more likely to identify with a given team to the extent that they have a high-status position within that team (e.g., as its captain). In line with this, research by the second author and colleagues found that in a sample of high-school athletes, those who had leadership roles felt more positive about their group and more connected with teammates compared to team members in non-leadership roles (Martin et al., 2017b). On the other hand, though, leadership itself also plays a key role in cultivating a sense of shared identity within a given team (Haslam, Reicher, & Platow, 2011). This was revealed in a study of young volleyball and handball players, as Maarten De Backer and colleagues (2011) found that athletes were more likely to identify with their team if their coaches were perceived to work hard to satisfy team members' social needs and to promote social justice within the team. Additionally, other research shows that group members who perceive that coaches and teammates are high-quality leaders also report stronger social identification with their sports teams (Fransen, Decroos et al., 2016). This aligns too with more general evidence of the way in which identity leadership contributes to athletes' identification with sport and exercise groups in ways that increase both attendance and exertion (see Chapters 10 and 11).

Consistent with this point, foundational work (e.g., Danish et al., 1993) noted that a central goal of youth development programmes was to foster identification within groups. Indeed, Petitpas and colleagues observed that youth development programmes in sport typically share the goal of fostering a sense of identity and purpose (Petitpas et al., 2005). This is true, for example, of First Tee and Play It Smart programmes, which focus on encouraging young golfers and coaches to identify with the programme in question and then using this as a platform for broader social and intellectual development.

Relatedly, another point that is worth making here is that youth sport is commonly understood as a context for young people to learn about, and acquire, leadership skills. We agree, but in line with the broader themes of this book we would note that leadership itself is a social identity process that involves creating, representing, advancing and embedding a sense of shared identity within a group (Haslam et al., 2011; Steffens, Haslam, Reicher et al., 2014; see also Chapter 3).

CONCLUSION

Sport is recognised as a powerful activity through which to foster the psychosocial development of young people. However, despite the well-established benefits derived from sport involvement, participation rates decline during adolescence, and young people also often report having negative sport-related experiences. Accordingly, an extensive body of literature has sought to explain the nature of youth development through sport, drawing on a range of theoretical approaches to set out a number of influential models of athlete development. These models have a lot in common, and all touch on issues of social identity – not the least in recognising that sport brings young people together in groups and helps them to learn about, and live out, fulfilling group lives. Nevertheless, all existing athlete developmental models fail to see anything particularly salient about social identity, and hence do not draw on social identity theorising as a platform for either theory or practice.

To address this shortcoming, this chapter built on this body of research by introducing the social identity–affiliation and influence model (SI–AIM). This model focuses on social identification as a critical component of a positive sport experience and argues that the experience of social identification in sports contexts provides a platform for the range of benefits identified in existing models. Yet, although we mapped an emerging body of literature that supports this model, it is also clear that there is much more that can – and should – be done to translate social identity insights into practical recommendations to facilitate future youth development through sport. In many ways, then, this chapter aims to be more like a coach's inspiring pre-game speech before an important game than the game itself. We hope that the chapter, and notably the introduction of the SI–AIM, provides researchers and practitioners who are working in the field of youth sport with an exciting new perspective and renewed sense of purpose in striving towards the optimal development of athletes in sport.

13
TEAM IDENTITY DEVELOPMENT

JAMIE B. BARKER
S. ALEXANDER HASLAM
KATRIEN FRANSEN
MATTHEW J. SLATER
CRAIG WHITE
NIELS MERTENS

The New Zealand All Blacks rugby union team are often considered to be the most successful and connected team in the world. Much has been written about how their distinct values and culture behaviours are aligned with togetherness and camaraderie. In particular, one of the fascinations of the All Blacks is their strong sense of shared identity, typified by their performance culture and the famous Haka. Indeed, a key factor in the All Blacks' success has been the development of a new Haka ritual, 'Kapa o Pango' (meaning 'team in black'). Such rituals reflect, remind and reinforce a belief system that reignites team members' collective identity and purpose. Moreover, building a great team requires individuals to enjoy a deep sense of trust in one another and to be up to the challenge of high performance (Kerr, 2013). In this regard, teamwork, togetherness and cohesion are all common adjectives used in relation to team sports to illustrate how a group of individuals are united in their pursuit of sporting excellence. At the same time, these terms are often used to distinguish good teams from bad teams. Getting a group of individuals to understand, communicate, commit and ultimately perform effectively together is seen not only as the panacea for most organisations in business, health and military domains, but also a topic of intrigue and fascination for anyone concerned in team sports.

It is not surprising, then, that sport psychologists have long been interested in understanding what makes a successful team, how best to bring teams out of slumps, and how best to maintain team performance. Accordingly, as Chapter 5 in this book noted, a large and varied body of research has focused on the concept of *team cohesion* as a focus for interventions that seek to bring about positive group change in sporting teams. Against this backdrop, a vast amount of money has also been spent by organisations on trying to develop effective team-building activities.

As we will see, however, these various efforts have had mixed results. In large part, the problem with standard approaches to team development is that there is a mismatch between *recognition* of the importance of shared identity for team functioning and *analysis* that is focused on the psychology of team members *as individuals*. To break this impasse, in recent years researchers have looked to social identity theorising to provide a better understanding of the nuances and intricacies of working with sport teams. As discussed in Chapter 2 (see also Turner, 1982), what is different about this theoretical framework is that it acknowledges *the psychological reality of the group* and focuses on the psychology of team members *as team members*.

A real-world example of such an approach is the method Eoin Morgan and Joe Root, the team captains of the England cricket team that won the World Cup in 2019, used to build a new team ethos (Hoult, 2019). Morgan and Root had realised the importance of a simple team culture that players from different nationalities can buy into, and how values on the cricket field can be mirrored off it. They started building a team philosophy, using the team logo as a simple visual reminder: 'See the crown on top of three lions. That crown represents the team. A vessel owned by no single individual and to be passed on to the next generation. Treasure it for it can be easily broken.' Morgan and Root went one step further by linking the three lions to a clear set of team values: one for courage, one for unity and one for respect. Morgan empha-sised that it is not about only your own – or the team's – performance. It is about representing your country; it is about how you respond to being role models and the values you portray as a team. The ideology displayed by these team captains did not only strengthen their own leadership, but an interview with Morgan (Hoult, 2019) also revealed how it empowered the entire team: 'It has established a lot of leaders within the group and it makes this summer more exciting.' Moreover, former England captain and former director of cricket Andrew Strauss observed how this culture bolstered the team's confidence:

> Teams that win World Cups in any sport deep down believe they can win it. Very occasionally you get a team that has a great run and shocks every-one, including themselves, but by and large it is the big teams who know they can win it, who think they are the best, who come through. These guys know they can win the World Cup. I don't think any England team has known that before. Yes, they have hoped, but they have not known it like this team.

It is this social identity work that we focus on in this chapter. First, we outline the background literature relating to contemporary approaches to enhancing the shared identity of groups with a focus on team cohesion through traditional team-building. Second, we explain how social identity theorising can help us to understand team functioning. In particular, we zero in on the challenges of creating and strengthening a team's feeling of 'we' and 'us' through a focus on (a) the role of coaches in shaping team identity; (b) the importance of self-disclosure and the sharing of personal stories; and (c) the added value of athletes who occupy formal and informal leadership roles in teams.

CONTEMPORARY APPROACHES TO TEAM IDENTITY DEVELOPMENT

Team cohesion

When aiming to improve the feeling of unity in sport teams, researchers have previously tended to see *team cohesion* as the key variable to tackle. As Slater and colleagues noted in Chapter 5, in the context of team sports, cohesion has been defined as 'a dynamic process which is reflected in the tendency for a group to stick together and remain united in the pursuit of its instrumental objectives, and/or for the satisfaction of member affective needs' (Carron, Brawley, & Widmeyer, 1998; p. 213; see also Chapter 11). As this definition suggests, cohesion has two main forms: *task cohesion* (i.e., uniting to reach a common goal) and *social cohesion* (i.e., uniting to enjoy the relationships within the group; Carron, Widmeyer, & Brawley, 1985; see Figure 5.1). To illustrate this, it is possible that some sport teams may be united in pursuit of a common goal but have little interest in socialising with one another outside sport.

As earlier chapters noted, both forms of cohesion have been found to be important contributors to the performance and success of sport teams (Carron, Bray, & Eys, 2002; Carron, Colman et al. 2002; Eys, Burke, Carron, & Dennis, 2010; Loughead & Hardy, 2006). Given this, sport psychologists and team managers have typically been interested in developing team-building techniques that effectively and consistently engender greater team cohesion (e.g., Crace & Hardy, 1997). This quest has led to the identification of four key factors that play a role in the emergence of cohesive teams (Carron & Eys, 2012): (a) environmental factors (e.g., team size); (b) personal factors (e.g., satisfaction with the group); (c) leadership factors (e.g., leadership style); and (d) team factors (e.g., role clarity). As we saw in earlier chapters, by identifying the precursors of team cohesion, the extant sport team cohesion literature provides a solid theoretical foundation for understanding this construct and a clear framework for practitioner intervention. Nevertheless, the nuances of this process and the precise mechanisms through which cohesion both emerges and has impact are poorly specified in the work that has explored this construct (e.g., Eys, Bruner, & Martin, 2019). So while cohesion is recognised as a significant asset, it is unclear precisely how it can be cultivated and harnessed in pursuit of team excellence.

Team-building

To date, the primary focus for efforts to improve team cohesion has been what are commonly referred to as *team-building* interventions. Typically, team-building has been seen as a strategy of team enhancement and improvement that has both task and social functions (Carron & Eys, 2012). Team-building interventions have been found to promote a number of precursors to team cohesion, including group confidence, communication and role understanding. Nevertheless, cohesion itself is generally seen as the core focus for any team-building programme (Bruner, Eys, Beauchamp, & Côté, 2013). And in sport, such programmes have typically taken one of two forms: (a) coach-led interventions or (b) social activities and events.

The first form of intervention is predicated on the view that coaches are, and need to be, the driving force for the development of team cohesion (e.g., Bruner & Spink, 2011). In this vein, coach-led team-building interventions have included programmes that seek to develop shared goals, accept individual differences, share personal information, establish a similar attitude across team members, promote communication, and develop an effective motivational climate (e.g., Carron, 1980; Dunn & Holt, 2004; Eys et al., 2010; Hodge, Henry, & Smith, 2014; Martin, Carron, & Burke, 2009; Prapavessis & Carron, 1997; Ryska, Yin, Cooley, & Ginn, 1999; Turman, 2003). As an example of a coach-led approach, the programme developed for the All Blacks by their coaches Graham Henry and Wayne Smith prior to winning the Rugby World Cup in 2011 focused on developing a shared motivational climate that emphasised collaboration and consensus over hierarchy and autocracy (Hodge et al., 2014). In a study with a more comprehensive experimental design that included both coach-led and activity-based components, Prapavessis, Carron, and Spink (1996) randomly assigned First Division Australian soccer coaches to a team-building treatment, placebo or control condition. Coaches in the treatment condition were taught specific team-building strategies that focused on three techniques to use with their teams during the pre-season and the first six weeks of the season: (a) improving team structure (e.g., providing role clarity and leadership and ensuring conformity to standards); (b) improving the team environment (e.g., promoting a sense of togetherness as well as team distinctiveness); and (c) improving team processes (e.g., focusing on making sacrifices, setting goals and encouraging cooperation). Coaches in the placebo condition were provided with soccer-specific information (e.g., about nutrition and strength training). Counter to the researchers' hypotheses, measures of cohesion that were administered pre-intervention, pre-season and eight weeks into the season revealed no differences between the three conditions.

A second form of team-building intervention focuses on developing cohesion through engagement in social activity of some form. An example of this is provided by the work of Robin Martin and Keith Davids (1995) which studied the impact of participation in a five-day army training course on a team of 22 professional British soccer players. The course included athletic activities (e.g., swimming and hockey), non-athletic activities (such as anti-tank training, i.e., learning to accurately fire on moving targets), and orienteering. Although the study did not include a control group, overall, the course was found to have a positive impact on players' well-being and social cohesion. Likewise, David Rainey and Gerald Schweickert (1988) examined the impact of participation in a 10-day spring training trip on a team of 22 college basketball players who roomed together, ate together and travelled to venues in three vans. The study found that, relative to players who stayed behind, those who went on the road trip did not experience a decline in social cohesion, suggesting that spending time together as a team can help to foster (or at least not erode) social cohesion. However, the authors note that the trip itself did not foster high cohesion. Moreover, because data were collected only one week after the trip had ended, it is unclear whether the meagre benefits that were observed were maintained for any length of time.

Other team-building interventions have focused on promoting team cohesion through meetings and workshop activities where programmes often target lots of different aspects (e.g., workshops on coping, stressors and leadership) simultaneously, meaning that it is difficult to assess the actual contribution of each aspect to overall intervention effectiveness. For example, Karen Cogan and Tent Petrie (1995) conducted a season-long, multidimensional intervention with female collegiate gymnasts. This involved the team receiving 45 hours of activities that included communication and leadership classes, team meeting sessions, completion of the Myers–Briggs personality inventory, as well as a six-hour anxiety-management workshop (focusing on stress management, relaxation and visualisation). Within-group analyses indicated that the programme led to increased social cohesion at the end of the pre-season when most of these activities took place. However, these improvements tailed off after the initial part of the competitive season. Like most of the other studies reviewed in this section, the study thus provided precious little hard evidence that traditional team-building activities help to build cohesiveness in sport teams.

The limitations of team-building interventions

While it is generally assumed that team-building interventions will enhance cohesion in teams, the studies discussed in the previous section are indicative of the fact that this is not straightforwardly the case. Indeed, results from meta-analyses that have tested this proposition report equivocal findings – with team-building in sport teams having only a small effect on social cohesion and no reliable effect on task cohesion (Beauchamp, McEwan, & Waldhauser, 2017; see Figure 13.1). Moreover, research in this domain has been observed to have a range of methodological shortcomings that help to explain these equivocal findings (Bloom & Stevens, 2002; Brawley & Paskevich, 1997; Carron & Spink, 1993; Prapavessis et al., 1996; Stevens & Bloom, 2003; Voight & Callaghan, 2001). As we have seen, these include a failure both to include appropriate control groups and to assess the enduring impact of interventions.

Figure 13.1 Examples of team-building programmes

Note: Although team-building programmes aim to build the team's cohesion, a meta-analysis by Beauchamp and colleagues (2017) indicates that these programmes rarely live up to expectations, having only a small effect on social cohesion and no effect on task cohesion.

Source: Pxhere, Flickr

Another further shortcoming is that team-building interventions are often facilitated (and assessed) by coaching staff. These staff frequently lack the skill set and/or the experience to deliver the interventions in question effectively. Also, their ability to assess programmes' efficacy is limited and often subject to different forms of bias. For example, evaluation of the motivational climate intervention described by Hodge and colleagues (2014) is contaminated by hindsight bias associated with the All Blacks' World Cup success. So, while it is certainly tempting to attribute this success to the programme implemented by Henry and Smith (and many have done so), in the absence of properly controlled research, there are no strong grounds for such an inference.

Moving away from coach-led interventions, alternative approaches thus engage specialist staff – most commonly sport psychologists (working independently or alongside team coaches). An example of this is the season-long team-building intervention that Julie Senécal and colleagues (2008) implemented among a team of 86 female high-school basketball players in Canada. This involved distinct phases of activity that centred on the process of defining, setting, reinforcing and evaluating shared team goals. Specific sessions were devoted to each of the phases to enable the effective delivery of the goal-setting programme and were delivered together by the team coach and a sport psychologist. Eight teams of basketball players took part in the study and were randomly assigned to either the experimental (goal-setting) condition or to a control group.

Speaking to the potential value of such an approach, there was evidence that the teams which participated in the goal-setting programme were more cohesive than those that did not. Nevertheless, the study itself provides little insight into the reasons for the intervention's impact. What precisely is it about group goal setting or the involvement of sport psychologists that helps to create team cohesion? And what effects does this have for team functioning more generally?

Despite the importance placed on traditional team-building strategies, there is a lack of clear evidence to support their effectiveness as a means of building cohesion in sport teams (Beauchamp et al., 2017; Pain & Harwood, 2009). Moreover, the strategies documented in the literature typically fail to extend beyond a general focus on athlete/coach group psychoeducation in the context of generic a theoretical team-building activity, and they are characterised by a lack of systematic theoretical underpinning (Beauchamp et al., 2017; Eys et al., 2010; Martin et al., 2009). On top of this, efforts to examine issues of psychological process and programme efficacy are plagued by a plethora of methodological issues, including over-reliance on cherry-picked data from small-scale, short-term interventions (Barker, Mellalieu, McCarthy, Jones, & Moran, 2013; Bloom & Stevens, 2002; Bloom, Stevens, & Wickwire, 2003).

It is against this backdrop that we turn to the social identity approach. Specifically, in the remainder of this chapter we build on ideas that have been explored in a number of the foregoing chapters to explore how this approach can provide a systematic and evidence-based framework for better understanding and facilitating the development of team cohesiveness. A core point here is that a good way to do this is by zeroing in on the dynamics of emergent *team identity* and the internalised sense of 'we' and 'us' at its heart.

A SOCIAL IDENTITY APPROACH TO TEAM IDENTITY DEVELOPMENT

> I flashed back to 1989 when I took over as head coach and had talked to Michael [Jordan] about how I wanted him to share the spotlight with his teammates so the team could grow and flourish. In those days, he was a gifted young athlete with enormous confidence in his own abilities who had to be cajoled into making sacrifices for the team. Now he was an older, wiser player who understood that it wasn't brilliant individual performances that made great teams, but the energy that's unleashed when players put their egos aside and work toward a common goal. ... Good teams become great ones when the members trust each other enough to surrender the 'me' for the 'we'. (Phil Jackson, cited in Jackson & Delehanty, 1995, p. 21)

In this quotation, Phil Jackson, the former head coach of the Chicago Bulls (with whom he won six NBA championships), underlines the need for players to prioritise shared social identity if a team is to be successful. As he puts it, they need to surrender the 'me' for the 'we'. Yet while team cohesion might increase when players act in this way, the principles that Jackson is referring to here go well beyond cohesion alone and are much more fundamental to team functioning. In particular, this is because they speak to the importance of team identity for team functioning in ways that can be best understood through the lens of social identity theorising (e.g., of the form set out in Chapter 2).

At its core, this body of theory asserts that people can define themselves in terms of both personal identity (as unique individuals) and social identity (as members of groups who share goals, values and interests; Turner, 1982; Turner et al., 1987). This suggests that how people behave is determined not only by their sense of themselves as individuals (i.e., as 'me' and 'you'), but also, and often more importantly, by their sense of themselves as group members (as 'we' and 'us'). And, as Phil Jackson suggests, in the context of team sports it is often *shared team identification* that turns good teams into great ones.

Importantly, although the concepts of team identification and team cohesion might appear similar, they are not the same (De Backer et al., 2011). In particular, whereas cohesion refers to a (potentially superficial) tendency for a group to stick together and to a characteristic of a group that can be appraised from the outside, team identification refers to the process by which a person *internalises* a particular group into a *depersonalised* sense of self (Turner, 1982). This leads them to see the world *from the perspective of that group*, so that they subsequently see its norms, values and goals (i.e., the *content* of a given identity; Turner, 1999) as a guide for cognition and action (rather than their personal norms, values and goals).

Importantly, too, this identification reflects a psychological state that can only be appraised from the vantage point of the perceiver. It also has a range of important consequences – notably in creating a motivation for those who share social identity to *align* their attitudes and behaviours in ways that give rise to group cohesiveness and provide a platform for various forms of social organisation (e.g., teamwork; Haslam, 2004; see also Chapter 5). So whereas team identification is generally a basis for cohesion, cohesion is not necessarily a basis for team identification (Hogg, 1992). And this in particular is one of the key ideas upon which the self-categorization theory – part of the bigger social identity approach – builds. That is, we like the groups we join, rather than joining the groups we like (Turner et al., 1987). This also suggests that rather than focusing on the development of cohesion, researchers and practitioners primarily need to focus on cultivating a sense of shared identity.

Key point 1: Leaders are key drivers of a sense of shared team identity

So how exactly can a sense of shared team identity be developed? Research in the social identity tradition (e.g., as reviewed in Chapter 3) points to the role that *leaders* play in fostering members' identification with a team and how, by doing so, they also promote team cohesion. In particular, this is because, *as prototypical group members*, leaders play a critical role not only in defining the meaning of any given group for other team members, but also – more fundamentally – in helping the group to exist as a psychological entity for those who are in it (Haslam, Reicher, & Platow, 2011; Turner & Haslam, 2001).

In this, then, leaders can be understood as *identity entrepreneurs* who play a central role in both creating and defining a sense of 'us' (Reicher, Haslam, & Hopkins, 2005). A real-world example of this identity entrepreneurship can be observed in the world of rugby union. Here, for teams in the northern hemisphere, the yearly Six Nations tourna-ment involves teams from England, Ireland, Scotland, Wales, France and Italy (Bruner, Dunlop, & Beauchamp, 2014; Harris, 2010), but every four years, 'home nations' players from the first four of these countries come together to represent the British and Irish Lions and compete against the three strongest rugby-playing nations from the southern hemisphere: Australia, South Africa and New Zealand. As John Harris notes:

> There are obvious challenges in melding players and coaches from four different nations and forging a collective identity. Men who were some-times fierce opponents and national rivals in a hard, physical game had to come together some months later to be teammates and touring companions on the other side of the world. These men not only come from different nations, but also from a range of very different social classes and diverse backgrounds. The latter has perhaps been something that has been over-looked in previous academic discussions of the Lions given the focus on the various national identities central to this wider collective. (Harris, 2017, p. 206)

So how should these various identities be managed? This is a dilemma faced by every British and Irish Lions coach, as they have to blend four countries into one (Palmer, 2013). Former Wales flanker Martyn Williams, a Lion in 2001, 2005 and 2009, explains the difficulty in binding 37 players into a cohesive whole ready to compete:

> Meeting up is like your first day at secondary school. You've got your group of mates from primary school – or in this case, the guys you play with for your country – so you tend to stick together. You have to break down all the barriers as quickly as possible. If you are going to be a suc-cessful team, you have to get to know each other off the field. It is up to the senior boys who have been on a Lions tour before to set the tone. On my first tour it was the likes of Keith Wood, Lawrence Dallaglio and Martin Johnson who reinforced the point straightaway – 'Forget your nationality, you're all Lions now'. (Palmer, 2013)

This issue of managing various identities within a team was recognised by Warren Gatland, the head coach of the Lions team in the tour in Australia in 2013, as key for his leadership. To address it, he sought to strengthen the higher-order social identity among the players by strengthening their professional identity as rugby players and emphasising that 'as Lions, we're in this together', while simultaneously downplaying the player's different national and associated class identities (Bruner, Dunlop, & Beau-champ, 2014). Indeed, he focused on working to ensure that, rather than undermining a sense of shared superordinate identity (in ways that appear to have happened on previous Lions tours), national identities actually bolstered the identity associated with the Lions 'brand' (Harris, 2017).

In this, Gatland's approach aligned with strategies recommended by Samuel Gaertner and John Dovidio's *common ingroup identity model* (Gaertner & Dovidio, 2005; Gaertner, Rust, Dovidio, Bachman, & Anastasio, 1994). Bolstered by their sense of shared identity, the team won their first test series victory in 16 years, providing an example of how team unity (of the Lions) could have impacted in the team's success. As Harris (2017) notes, it might also have helped that unlike his predecessor (the former All Blacks coach Graham Henry), Gatland had gone to great lengths to understand the culture and tradition of the Lions – so that despite also being a New Zealander, he was seen as more of an 'insider'.

Clearly, though, as with the models of team-building that we critiqued in the first half of this chapter, evidence of those factors that fuelled the Lions' success is only anecdotal. Nevertheless, rigorous programmes of researchers provide more robust evidence to substantiate these claims. In one of these, Maarten De Backer and colleagues (2011) showed that coaches of elite handball teams had a critical role to play in determining athletes' identification with their team. In particular, to the extent that coaches were perceived by players to support their needs and treat them fairly (i.e., with procedural justice) this increased those players' feeling of 'we' and 'us' in ways that fed into both the task and the social cohesion in the team (see also Chapter 19).

Programmatic work by the third author and colleagues has also observed that identity entrepreneurship is not restricted to coaches but is also displayed by other leaders in a team, and that this plays an important role in strengthening team identification (Fransen, Decroos et al., 2016; Fransen, Haslam, Steffens & Boen, 2020; Fransen, Steffens et al., 2016). For example, a study conducted with 343 players of team sports found that the leadership quality of both coaches and athlete leaders was predictive of a team's task and social cohesion. Critically, though, for our present purposes, both pathways were mediated by athletes' identification with their team (in ways suggested by Figure 13.2; Fransen, Decroos et al., 2016).

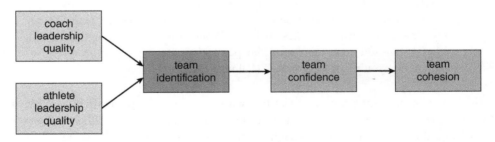

Figure 13.2 Team identification mediates the relationship between leadership and team cohesion

Note: Research by the third author and colleagues with over 300 players of team sport in Belgium showed that the impact of leaders on team cohesion (as judged by other members of their teams) was largely explained by the role that those leaders played in building team members' identification with their team.

Source: Fransen, Decroos et al. (2016)

Yet as we intimated above – in sharp contrast to the construct of team cohesion – to date social identification has received only very limited attention in sports contexts. Nevertheless, having been shown to be a critical underpinning of team cohesion, it makes sense to suggest that team-building interventions would be more effective if they treated team identification as the focal construct rather than the more distal behavioural outcome of team cohesion. This is an observation that we pursue further in the next section.

Key point 2: Team identity can be developed by sharing personal stories and information

The England football team bowed out of the 2014 World Cup in Brazil without a win to their name. In response to this disappointment, then England captain, Wayne Rooney, introduced player-only meetings with the vision of bringing individual star players together as a unified team (BBC Sport, 2014). The sessions involved players sharing stories with one another and focusing on how the team could improve. A key reflection Rooney disclosed following the introduction of the team meetings pointed directly to how some of the quieter players, perhaps those who did not typically find their voice in and around the team, came to the fore and contributed for the team. If this act of player-led sharing is good enough for Wayne Rooney et al., perhaps it is too for other sport teams aiming to develop a shared team identity.

Indeed, this very notion, which has been scientifically termed *personal-disclosure mutual-sharing* (PDMS), has attracted growing attention within the sport psychology literature in recent years (Dunn & Holt, 2004; Holt & Dunn, 2006). PDMS is derived from the approach often seen in support groups (e.g., bereavement, alcoholics) where individuals take turns to disclose personal information about a particular theme or topic. In sport, PDMS is a team-building activity that involves athletes and team members communicating their values, beliefs, attitudes and personal motives with the rest of the team in a safe, supportive and collegiate environment. In particular, mutual-sharing refers to the idea that all team members tell a previously unknown story – about their personal experiences and aspirations – to others in their team. And it is this combined experience of sharing personal stories, and the fact all team members do the same, that creates shared perceptions and meanings among team members (Ostroff, Kinicki, & Tamkins, 2003; Windsor, Barker, & McCarthy, 2011).

Athletes' engagement in PDMS can increase athletes' identification with their sport team by helping the group to develop shared norms, meaning and values. The capacity for PDMS to do this is suggested by a large body of research in the social identity tradition, which has found that self-disclosure among group members helps to build a sense of shared identity (e.g., Turner, Hewstone, & Voci, 2007) and that shared identity also encourages self-disclosure (e.g., Dovidio et al., 1997). Indeed, because shared identity is generally a basis for sharing private information (Greenaway, Wright et al., 2015) people tend to *infer* that they share identity once they find themselves engaging in self-disclosure (Chapter 3). Moreover, the process of self-disclosure can help team members develop good relationships with their teammate (i.e., in-group ties, which is one of the three core dimensions of social identity; Bruner, Dunlop, & Beauchamp, 2014) by providing a platform for strong psychological connection and a sense of belonging. Discovering new information about teammates that would typically remain unknown also encourages empathy based on shared understanding and common experiences of problems and issues (Dryden, 2006; Hardy & Crace, 1997; Olarte, 2003; Orlick, 1990; Yukelson, 2010).

In their work with this procedure, sport researchers have developed two main types of PDMS: relationship-oriented (e.g., Dunn & Holt, 2004) and mastery-oriented (Barker, Evans, Coffee, Slater, & McCarthy, 2014). *Relationship-oriented personal-disclosure mutual-sharing* (rPDMS) is the more popular of these two interventions and targets the development of relationships and bonds between the different members of a given team. These are grounded in, and help to develop, their sense of shared identity – not least because self-disclosure always occurs, and stays, within the boundaries of the team (in ways that increase group entitativity and comparative fit; see Chapters 2 and 11 as well as Figure 11.2). This can be seen from the following excerpts, which give a sense of the instructions typically used to introduce the activity:

> Describe a personal story/situation that will help your teammates understand yourself more. Detail a personal story that you would want everyone to know about, one that would make them want to be in the same team as you and want to play alongside you. Your story can be related to any event that took place in your personal life or in your sporting life. Your story should illustrate something that defines your character, your motives, and your desires. (Barker et al., 2014)

Mastery-oriented personal-disclosure mutual-sharing (mPDMS) requires individuals to reflect upon their strengths and recall their best performance ever in their sport. For example, in some of our own research we asked participants to 'Describe your best performance/s ever in a game of cricket' and then to respond to the question 'What made it your best performance?' (Barker et al., 2014). Typically, athletes share a detailed and emotional story about their pre-, in- and post-match thoughts, feelings and behaviours. The positive effect of this confidence-building athlete reflection can be seen in the athletes' faces, body language and enthusiasm with which they present, which in turn creates an immediately positive team atmosphere. As with rPDMS, this procedure can help to foster psychological connections between team members in ways that foster team identification. In addition, though, the performance focus of mPDMS provides an opportunity for teams to develop identity content (especially values and goals) centred on high performance.

Speaking to the value of PDMS, studies that the first and fourth authors conducted with colleagues in the context of elite youth sport have confirmed that it has a positive impact on a number of social identity-related outcomes (Barker et al., 2014; Evans, Slater, Turner, & Barker, 2013). The first of these was led by Andrew Evans and examined the effects of rPDMS on the social identification of soccer academy athletes as well as two relevant aspects of social identity content (Evans et al., 2013; see also Slater, Coffee,

Barker, Haslam, & Steffens, 2019): friendship-related and results-related social identity content. The former related to shared values, norms and ideals that centred on the friendships and close relationships within the team; the latter related to shared values, norms and ideals that were relevant to the team's performance outcomes. The researchers collected data at four time points and found that rPDMS contributed to a short-term increase in friendship-related social identity content and a sustained increase in results-related social identity content. In addition, the procedure also led to an increase in social identification that was sustained over time. Together, then, these results suggest that this relationship-focused form of PDMS can be a powerful tool for developing a team identity centred on identity content that values both friendships and performance.

Building on these encouraging findings, a second study explored how different types of PDMS might be used to increase social identification and endorsement of these same two types of social identity content (i.e., friendships and results; Barker et al., 2014). In this, elite academy cricketers completed two PDMS sessions during a pre-season tour: in the first, they took part in rPDMS; in the second, they engaged in mPDMS. As hypothesised, quantitative data indicated that after the first rPDMS session, participants' social identification increased together with their friendship-related social identity content. Then, after the second mPDMS session, their social identification remained high but now their friendship-related social identity content increased.

Together, then, these studies provide convincing evidence that PDMS can help to build a sense of shared team identity, as well as forms of associated social identity content that support both social connection and team performance. Moreover, findings from the studies also suggest that different types of PDMS (i.e., relationship vs mastery-oriented) help to bring about changes in identity content that are aligned with programme content. In other words, in a manner consistent with self-categorization theory's principle of normative fit (Oakes et al., 1994; see also Chapter 2), the identity-based changes that are observed post-PDMS reflect the content of the information that athletes share with their teammates.

This in turn suggests that PDMS can be a valuable method for developing team identity and that it does so in ways that help to ensure that that identity is sensitive to a team's unique values and context. By way of example, rPDMS may be a useful way of bringing a team together the night before an important cup match, when match preparation has been completed and there is a danger of becoming overly focused on performance (in ways discussed in Chapter 7).

At the same time, though, rPDMS may also be helpful when sport teams are under-performing. Speaking to this point, Evans and colleagues (2013) noted that the soccer team they studied had lost its first three matches of the season and that this was a significant identity threat for the players – in ways also discussed in Chapter 8. Nevertheless, the authors observed that in this context rPDMS was a catalyst for the players to increase their endorsement of friendship-related social identity content. As one athlete put it following a PDMS session: 'We are not winning on the pitch, but we have strong relationships, and this is keeping the team together.' However, as the season progressed, performance improved and the players' endorsement of friendship identity content reduced to baseline levels, at which point they (and their social identity) became primarily results-focused again.

Despite these promising results, it is clearly the case that research into the impact of PDMS on team identity (and, through this, on team cohesion and team performance) is in its infancy. Going forward, there is thus a clear need for further research in this area. Among other things, this should explore ways in which the technique could be adapted to support more diverse identity contents (e.g., Slater, 2019; Slater et al., 2019) as well as distinctive team identities. There is also scope for more fine-grained research to examine how features of social context (e.g., the arrival and departure of team members; familiarity with the self-disclosure process) moderate the impact of the procedure on team identification. That said, the research that has already been conducted goes beyond the greater part of traditional team-building research (as discussed in the first half of this chapter) in isolating social identification as a potent mechanism for the development of team cohesion. Indeed, our research suggests that this is not 'just another' relevant variable, but the key psychological building block upon which successful teams are forged.

Key point 3: Shared leadership can help to develop shared social identity

PDMS, of course, is not the only way of developing team identity. Indeed, as we noted above, in the normal course of events, the leaders of a team play a key role in this process. Recognising this, our third key point focuses on a leadership development programme that tries to improve the leadership skills of leaders. The programme is designed to benefit those in both formal and informal leader roles, and its focus is on providing *shared leadership* that helps to develop the shared identity of the team (along lines discussed in Chapter 3; see also Charlesworth, 2001; Fransen et al., 2020a).

The concept of shared leadership relates to the previously noted idea that leadership can emanate from both coaches and athletes within a team (Fransen, Decroos et al., 2016; Fransen, Haslam, Steffens, & Boen, 2020; Fransen, Steffens et al., 2016). Supporting this claim, in recent years sport leadership research has indicated that high-quality athlete leaders make a significant contribution to the development of their team's social identity (e.g., as suggested by Figure 13.2). This in turn has inspired researchers to include these athlete leaders as an important focus for interventions that seek to enhance team leadership. In line with this trend, Katrien Fransen, Alex Haslam, Nik Steffens, Niels Mertens and colleagues (2020) built upon the 5R leadership development programme described in Chapter 3 (e.g., see Figure 3.3) by combining it with a procedure designed to promote shared leadership within sports teams. Referred to as the *5R Shared Leadership Program* (5R[S]), this programme aims to imbue team leaders with the skills of *identity leadership* so that they are better able to create, represent, advance and embed the shared social identity of the teams that they lead.

In order to do this, the 5R[S] Program involves two key processes. The first involves identifying legitimate team members to appoint as leaders (i.e., with the aim of implementing a structure of shared leadership). The second takes them through a series of activities designed to hone the identity leadership skills of the appointed leaders.

To identify legitimate leaders within the team, 5R^S employs a technique called *shared leadership mapping* (SLM). This technique harnesses team members' perceptions of the leadership shown by their teammates to create a map of the subjective leadership network within a given team. More specifically, this mapping process involves all team members rating the leadership quality of every other team member on a scale from 0 (*very poor leadership*) to 10 (*very good leadership*). Compared to 'great man' approaches (i.e., those that look only at the formal leader; e.g., see John, 2019) or dyadic approaches (i.e., those that look only at the bidirectional relationship between leader and follower), social network analysis makes the entire group a focus for analysis. Those team members who appear most central in the resultant network (being perceived as the best leaders) are then appointed to a leadership role. Moreover, because SLM builds upon the perceptions of team members, it ensures that the leaders who are selected for leadership roles have a broad support base in their team.

Importantly, too, this mapping process does not identify team members to take on generic leadership roles, but rather identifies their perceived suitability for four distinct leadership roles that the third author and colleagues have identified and validated in multiple studies (after Fransen, Vanbeselaere et al., 2014; Fransen, Van Puyenbroeck et al., 2015). Two of these are on-field leadership roles and two are off-field roles. The on-field roles include the *task leader* (who provides technical and tactical instructions) and the *motivational leader* (who is the main motivator on the field); the two off-field roles include the *social leader* (who promotes good relations and a positive atmosphere in the team) and the *external leader* (who represents the team to groups and agencies outside the team, including the club board, media and fans).

Previous research suggests that teams which have leaders in these four leadership roles have a stronger sense of social identity than those which only have a single leader (Cotterill & Fransen, 2016; Fransen, Vanbeselaere et al., 2014). Accordingly, 5R^S uses the SLM method to identify and appoint the athletes who are consensually perceived as the best leaders in each of the four roles (see Figure 13.3).

After appointing leaders to these four roles, 5R^S builds on the previously established 5R model in order to develop those leaders' leadership skills. However, 5R^S incorporates several changes to 5R (as described in Chapter 3) that make the programme particularly useful in the sport team context. In what follows we will discuss each of these distinctive features.

Most important is the implementation of the shared leadership structure using the process outlined above, especially as these athlete leaders are the team members who lead the brainstorm sessions during the core phases of the programme (Representing and Realising; see Figure 3.3). The 'bottom-up' approach in which every team member is engaged in the process of establishing goals remains a key feature of the 5R^S Program. However, by assigning the appointed athlete leaders to manage this process and ensure good follow-up, the leaders themselves learn the skills associated with managing team identity. Furthermore, in contrast to the standard 5R programme, team goals are established not for the team in general, but for four specific leadership roles. Through this process, teams thus identify task-related goals (e.g., improving the tactical communication on the field), motivation-related goals (e.g., encouraging teammates

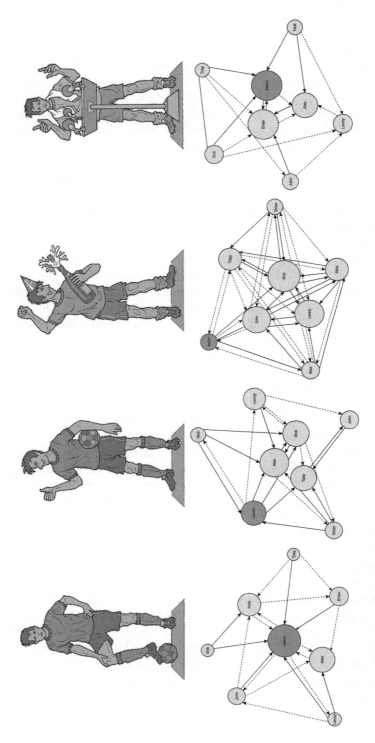

Figure 13.3 Shared leadership mapping

Note: Developed by the third author and colleagues, Shared leadership mapping (SLM) allows researchers and practitioners (e.g., coaches, sport psychologists) to identify the key leaders within the team who are consensually perceived as the best leaders in both on-field roles (as task and motivational leaders) and off-field roles (as social and external leaders). In each of the above networks the coach is highlighted in yellow.

Source: Katrien Fransen

during difficult games), social-related goals (e.g., integrating new team members), and external-related goals (e.g., building a positive relationship with sponsors and officials). The importance of these differentiated leadership roles and goals is highlighted by the head coach of a volleyball team that was one of the first to complete the 5R^S Program:

> It is definitely an added value to work with other functions besides task leadership. You cannot be good in everything. If players focus on too many things simultaneously, their leadership weakens and their contribution to the team diminishes. (Fransen et al., 2020a)

A final difference between 5R^S and 5R is that in the Reflecting phase the social identity mapping exercise is replaced by a *trademark exercise*. Although the mapping exercise is very useful for organisations and teams with formalised sub-entities (e.g., organisations with regional subdivisions), it is often the case that sport teams do not contain formally structured subgroups. Moreover, there is a risk that if they do, these subgroups may have (or develop) different goals from those of the group as a whole (Martin, Evans, & Spink, 2016). So, to obviate the risk of strengthening intragroup boundaries, the trademark exercise focuses on the team as a whole.

More specifically, the trademark exercise involves team members reflecting together on the nature of their shared identity and then representing this in terms of an overarching team trademark. More specifically, athletes are first asked to contrast the core values of their own team with those of teams they are not part of and from which they want to differentiate themselves. They then work to integrate these values within an overarching trademark, to which the team can be held accountable.

The two-fold aim of 5R^S is (a) to implement a structure of shared leadership and (b) to give leaders the experience, skills and confidence to work with their teammates to cultivate and consolidate their team's shared social identity. The value of this process is indicated by the qualitative feedback from members of the volleyball team investigated by Fransen et al. (2020a):

> Our 'we'-feeling has increased since. Often players would refer to this identity during competitive games. I was also able to refer to it at moments when this was necessary, it was a reference point to say; we are in this together, let's go for it. [Head coach]

Moreover, the specific value of the trademark process is seen in another player's observation that:

> Our trademark became integrated in the team by naming our WhatsApp group Wolf Pack. Also, our team yell, which we yelled after every time-out during the game, turned into the captain yelling: 'Wolf!...', followed by the team members responding: 'Pack, whoo whoo whoo!' [Team member 3]

However, as we noted earlier in the chapter, while there is certainly merit in small-scale studies that explore the viability of interventions designed to build team identity, it is necessary to move beyond these in order to substantiate claims about their value. With this in mind, the sixth author recently led a programme of research to experimentally test the effectiveness of 5R^S among Belgian basketball teams which were playing at the national level (Mertens et al., 2020). Eight teams ($N = 96$) were recruited for the study and were randomly divided into two groups: the intervention (treatment) group, which received the 5R Shared Leadership Program, and a control group, which did not receive the intervention. The teams were then tracked throughout the second half of the competitive season. The results of this study provided experimental evidence of the effectiveness of the 5R^S Program. More specifically, relative to the control condition, participation in 5R^S led to increases in leaders' ability to create and advance a shared sense of 'us' as rated by other members of their teams. Teams that had participated in 5R^S also reported having a stronger sense of shared social identity at the programme's conclusion (Mertens et al., 2020).

These results point to the capacity for 5R^S not only to create shared leadership structures, but also to promote identity leadership and team identity development. Nevertheless, further research is clearly needed to explore the programme's generalisability across contexts – both within and beyond sport. For example, there is some evidence that organisational teams can benefit from the implementation of a structure of shared leadership (D'Innocenzo, Mathieu, & Kukenberger, 2016; Nicolaides et al., 2014), and that recreational sporting groups can use 5R^S to harness the health benefits associated with the development of shared social identity (Burton et al., 2018; Holt-Lunstad, Smith, & Layton, 2010; see also Chapter 15).

CONCLUSION

The leaders who work most effectively, it seems to me, *never say 'I.'* And that's not because they have trained themselves not to say 'I.' They don't think 'I.' *They think 'we'; they think 'team.'* They understand their job to make the team function. They accept responsibility and don't sidestep it, but *'we' gets the credit.* This is what creates trust, what enables you to get the task done. (Drucker, 1992, p. 14, emphasis added, cited in Haslam, Reicher, & Platow, 2011)

This chapter started by providing an overview of contemporary approaches to team-building within the sport psychology literature – most of which focus on interventions to increase team cohesion. We noted, though, that evidence of the efficacy of these interventions is limited and that the existing evidence is generally of low quality. An even more fundamental issue is that there are grounds for thinking that the focus on team cohesiveness is misplaced, and that researchers and practitioners might be better advised to direct their energies towards the task of building a sense of shared identity within teams. In the second half of the chapter we turned our attention to a number of programmes that have done exactly this.

Inspired by the broader social identity literature (e.g., as discussed in other chapters in this volume), this alternative line of work suggests that there are multiple ways to develop team identity and, moreover, that there are multiple benefits that flow from programmes that help teams to do this – for example, by focusing on processes of information sharing (as in PDMS) and leadership (as in 5R^S). Accordingly, there appear to be sound theoretical and empirical grounds for shifting the focus of those who work in this area from the question of whether (from the outside) a team appears to be tightly knit, to the question of whether (from the inside) its members see themselves not as a collections of 'I's but as a unitary 'we'. This is critical because, as the above quotation from Peter Drucker suggests, getting people to 'think team' is central to getting them to 'behave team'. Or, to put this another way, *unless players can think as a team, they cannot play as a team*. This realisation makes the challenge of developing team identity a first-order priority in the domain of team sport. As well as explaining why this is the case, our hope is that this chapter gives readers a sense of constructive ways in which this challenge can be effectively tackled.

SECTION 4
PHYSICAL AND PSYCHOLOGICAL HEALTH

14

SOCIAL SUPPORT

CHRIS HARTLEY
S. ALEXANDER HASLAM
PETE COFFEE
TIM REES

Flick through any autobiography of a celebrated athlete and you will find that one of its key themes is social support. Certainly, there will be discussions of training and tactics, distress and disappointment, guts and glory. But the backdrop to all this is likely to be the support the athlete received from key individuals and groups along the way. The mother who drove them to training every day in the middle of winter, the coach who instilled a sense of self-discipline and pride, the backroom team who always had a kind word when things hadn't gone quite to plan. This is beautifully exemplified by a legendary yet bitter-sweet moment from the 1992 Barcelona Olympics, where hot-favourite sprinter Derek Redmond from the United Kingdom tore his hamstring during the 400 metres semi-final. His father, Jim, jumped the balustrades and pushed past event officials to help his son cross the line and finish the race.

> We hobbled over the finishing line with our arms round each other, just me and my dad, the man I'm really close to, who's supported my athletics career since I was seven years old. (Bos, 2017)

Accounts such as this are also often filled with heroic examples of athletes going 'above and beyond' to provide support to others in their team – even to the extent of making personal sacrifices for the 'greater good'. Consider the 2012 Tour de France, when Chris Froome gave up his opportunity to secure personal victory, instead opting to help his teammate Bradley Wiggins secure the coveted *maillot jaune*. Clearly, the role of socially supportive others, across both sport and life more generally, cannot be understated. For this reason, social support plays a key role in optimal functioning across a range of performance contexts – not only in sport, but also in the workplace, at school or at home (Fletcher & Sarkar, 2012; Freeman & Rees, 2009; Sarkar & Fletcher, 2014). Indeed, work by the third author and his colleagues highlighted how supportive families, coaches and networks are key to the development of super-elite athletes (Rees et al., 2016).

Social support may refer to the existence of socially supportive *relationships*, but may also include people's helping and supportive *actions*, and/or an exchange of *resources* with the goal of enhancing positive outcomes for the recipient (e.g., Hobfoll, 1988; Sarason, Sarason, & Pierce, 1990; Shumaker & Brownell, 1984). In the case of Derek Redmond, we see all three of these things at work: he had a supportive relationship with his father, his father went out of the way to do things to help him, and this involved the provision (and receipt) of tangible resources – in this case, literally, a shoulder to lean on. As we will discuss more below, these resources can also take a range of other forms: emotional, esteem-focused and informational.

Social support has been associated with a range of positive outcomes, not only for performance but also for health and well-being. The latter include reduced stress (Clawson, Borrelli, McQuaid, & Dunsiger, 2016; Cohen, Underwood, & Gottlieb, 2000), reduced risk for cancer (Pinquart & Duberstein, 2010) and reduced risk of mortality (Barth, Schneider, & von Kanel, 2010). Indeed, although this point is routinely over-looked (Haslam, McMahon et al., 2018), meta-analytic evidence suggests that *lack* of social support can be at least as bad for a person's health as smoking, obesity and physical inactivity (Berkman & Syme, 1979; Holt-Lunstad, Smith, & Layton, 2010).

Within sport, the benefits of being socially integrated and having socially supportive others have also been well documented. For example, social support has been linked with better performance (Freeman & Rees, 2008, 2009; Gould, Greenleaf, Chung, & Guinan, 2002; Rees & Freeman, 2009, 2010), positive stress appraisals (Freeman & Rees, 2009), improved flow (Bakker, Oerlemans, Demerouti, Slot, & Ali, 2011), more beneficial responses to injury (Mitchell, Evans, Rees, & Hardy, 2014; Rees, Mitchell, Evans, & Hardy, 2010) and greater self-confidence (Holt & Hoar, 2006; Rees & Freeman, 2007), as well as with lower risk of both injury (Carson & Polman, 2012) and burnout (DeFreese & Smith, 2013, 2014; Freeman, Coffee, & Rees, 2011; Hartley & Coffee, 2019a; Lu et al., 2016).

However, is it always the case that social support has beneficial effects in sport? Consider, for example, the hypothetical scenario where a coach or parent provides a young athlete with social support in the form of tactical feedback about '*what went wrong*' during the first set of a disastrous tennis match. Depending on the content and timing of this (otherwise well-intentioned) advice, it is not hard to see that this will not *always* 'work' because it is experienced as stressful rather than supportive. Rather, then, than giving the young tennis player tactical foci to prioritise during the second set, such a message might be interpreted as criticism. It may even instil a sense of negative expectation and pressure to succeed during the second set, leading the young player to resent the so-called 'support' and reject it altogether. In line with this point, there is evidence that, in a range of contexts, social support can have negative effects on athletes – not least *increasing* both burnout and dropout (Sheridan, Coffee, & Lavallee, 2014). This observation begs an obvious question: What is it that makes social support effective? This is the key question that this chapter attempts to answer.

As we will see, the answer to this question is complex. Despite the fact that social support is often thought to be a simple matter ('you either get it or you don't'), it is a nuanced construct and understanding it presents many challenges. In an attempt to navigate our way through these, this chapter begins by introducing the construct of social support and discussing its associations with sport-related outcomes. We then provide an overview of four approaches to the study of social support that are particularly influential in sport psychology today. As well as outlining the key theoretical tenets of these approaches and the evidence that supports them, we also identify their shortcomings. These centre on the fact that contemporary approaches to the study of social support in sport focus almost exclusively on athletes' *personal* experiences and understandings. In this, they relate to questions of the form 'Am I threatened?' and 'What support do I have?'

Such questions are important but we argue that, by its very nature, social support is never entirely personal. Instead, it is a *group* process that routinely raises questions of the form 'Are *we* threatened?' and 'What support do *we* have?' As will become apparent, the dynamics of social support are thus always conditioned by the group memberships – and associated social identities – that bear upon and inform this process. For instance, would one expect the support provided by a fan of a rival team to be as effective as the support provided by a fellow fan of your own team? In this regard, the very same supportive act can sometimes prove beneficial but sometimes prove disastrous. Seeking to make sense of this enigma, the second half of the chapter presents a social identity approach to social support in sport. Among other things, this draws attention to the way in which shared social identity (or a lack of it) conditions athletes' perceptions of both the availability and the utility of support. Understanding this, we conclude, provides a new agenda for both research and practice.

CURRENT APPROACHES TO UNDERSTANDING SOCIAL SUPPORT IN SPORT

One of the challenges associated with studying social support in sport is the diverse ways in which it has been defined and measured. In the wider social psychology literature, social support has been conceptualised as (a) demonstrating that a person is loved and cared for, (b) the subjective judgement of support availability, (c) the mere existence of supportive relationships, or (d) simply an exchange of resources (e.g., Hobfoll, 1988; Sarason, Pierce, & Sarason, 1990; Shumaker & Brownell, 1984). Nevertheless, contemporary conceptualisations of social support generally consider it to be composed of three major subconstructs (Lakey, 2010). First, social support can be conceptualised as a form of *social integration* that refers to the number and types of social ties and relationships within an athlete's social support network. Second, social support can be thought of as *perceived support* that derives from a subjective judgement that support is available and can be accessed if needed. Third, social support can be seen as *received support* (also sometimes referred to as enacted support), referring to the specific helping and supportive actions provided by individuals within an athlete's social support network (Rees, 2016).

To illustrate the difference between these subconstructs, consider the number of social ties in a high-profile athlete's support network. This network might comprise 30 or more teammates, coaches, trainers, physiologists, nutritionists and psychologists. In addition, the athlete likely has a number of family members (partners, parents, children) who accompany them some or all of the time. Further to this, they may have thousands of fans and followers who travel to watch them perform or who support them on social media. All of these social ties that an athlete may have available to them would be indicative of social integration. Realistically, however, the athlete may only perceive support to be available – and actually receive support – from a select few of these social ties. For instance, the athlete could rely heavily on support from one coach, one parent and their physiotherapist (e.g., Abgarov, Jeffrey-Tosoni, Baker, & Fraser-Thomas, 2012; Kristiansen & Roberts, 2010; Nicholson, Hoye, & Gallant, 2011; Sanders & Winter, 2016). Indeed, this highlights that the degree to which an athlete is socially integrated may not be indicative of how much support they perceive to be available or actually receive (nor how effective that support will be; Rueger, Malecki, Pyun, Aycock, & Coyle, 2016).

The latter points speak to the fact that social support can be conceptualised and assessed in a range of different ways (Cohen, Underwood, & Gottlieb, 2000; Holt & Hoar, 2006). One important distinction in this regard is between support that is *perceived* to be available if needed and support that is actually *received* (Freeman, Coffee, Moll, Rees, & Sammy, 2014; Gottlieb & Bergen, 2010; Wills & Shinar, 2000). The importance of this distinction can be illustrated by the example of rock climbing. When climbing, a climber can typically find viable routes to the top of a wall in relative safety because a belayer is holding the other end of the rope. At the same time, though, the climber typically also knows that, if needed, the belayer is available to give support (e.g., advice) about viable routes to the top of the wall. So while received support centres on *manifest* supportive actions, perceived support centres on the mind and *psychological state* of the athlete (Sarason et al., 1990). Although a person's ongoing experiences of receiving support are likely to contribute to their sense that social support is available (Uchino, 2009), these things are not the same. Moreover, as we discuss below, it is often perceptions of support that are stronger predictors of outcomes than received support, and perceptions of support availability may be misaligned with the actual provision and receipt of support (e.g., DeFreese & Smith, 2013; Hartley & Coffee, 2019a; Haslam, Jetten et al., 2018).

As we intimated earlier in the chapter, perceived and received support are typically further broken down into four specific forms of socially supportive behaviour: emotional, esteem, informational and tangible (Rees & Hardy, 2000). *Emotional* support refers to acts that convey a sense of being loved and cared for (e.g., parents emphasising that whatever the outcome of a game, they will always be there for their child); *esteem* support refers to attempts at bolstering a sense of competence and ability (e.g., parents making it clear that they believe their child is capable and talented); *informational* support refers to guidance and instruction (e.g., parents suggesting that their child use a particular strategy to combat anxiety); and *tangible* support refers to material forms of instrumental assistance (e.g., parents driving their child to the game). While the precise wording of these differ across domains (e.g., of organisational, health and sport psychology), on the basis of interviews with high-level sport performers about the nature of their supportive experiences, Rees and Hardy (2000) argued that these four forms of support are all very relevant to sport.

Clearly, though, these different types of social support are not necessarily mutually exclusive. A coach, for example, can provide both esteem and informational support to athletes by discussing both how and when they previously executed a sport-related skill correctly. Accordingly, the four dimensions of support are highly intercorrelated. However, given their unique characteristics, the different types of support will often each have unique relationships with particular outcome variables (e.g., burnout and self-confidence; Freeman et al., 2011; Freeman et al., 2014).

While dominant approaches to studying social support in sport are influenced by social, motivational, developmental and cognitive theorising (Sheridan et al., 2014), most approaches are aligned with theories of *stress and coping* (e.g., Lazarus, 1999; Lazarus & Folkman, 1984). Not least, this is because sport participation routinely involves exposure to a range of *stressors* (i.e., things which pose a threat to the self; Fletcher, Hanton, & Mellalieu, 2006; Sarkar & Fletcher, 2014), and social support is recognised as having the potential to protect athletes from their deleterious impact (e.g., burnout; DeFreese & Smith, 2014; Gustafsson, DeFreese, & Madigan, 2017; Hartley & Coffee, 2019a). In what follows we provide an overview of the four main theoretical approaches to studying social support in sport, with the latter three aligned with this stress and coping process (see Figure 14.1).

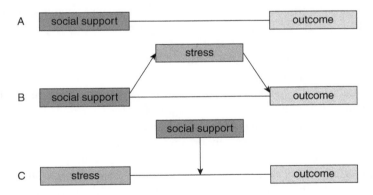

Figure 14.1 Schematic representations of dominant approaches to social support in sport

Note: The main-effects model (A), the stress-prevention model (B), and the stress-buffering model (C) provide different frameworks for understanding the impact of social support on the experience of stress and sport-related outcomes.

The main-effects model

As the top panel (A) in Figure 14.1 suggests, the *main-effects model* suggests that social support has direct benefits for sport-related outcomes independently of other factors, such as stress (Cohen et al., 2000; Cohen & Wills, 1985). In particular, this is because support is theorised to be directly associated with outcomes such as enhanced levels of self-esteem, purpose, control and mastery (Cohen et al., 2000; Thoits, 2011).

However, while the model's simplicity contributes to its intuitive appeal, the evidence that has tested it tells a more complex story. This is seen in evidence that perceived support is more beneficial than received support for golf performance, self-confidence, flow states and burnout (Bakker et al., 2011; DeFreese & Smith, 2014; Freeman & Rees, 2008, 2010; Hartley & Coffee, 2019a). Moreover, although received support has been associated with many of the same positive outcomes (Mitchell et al., 2014; Rees & Freeman, 2007; Rees, Hardy, & Freeman, 2007), it is not always beneficial (Abgarov et al., 2012; Knight & Holt, 2014; Lakey & Orehek, 2011; Uchino, 2009).

So why would receiving social support be less beneficial than simply knowing (or believing) it is available? There are a number of reasons. The first is that when it is actually given, social support can prove to be suboptimal. Informational support (such as advice), for example, can be poor or wrong. Second, people may have unrealistic or poorly calibrated expectations about the effectiveness of received support (Rees & Freeman, 2010; Sarason & Sarason, 1986; Uchino, 2009). Third, acts of support may be viewed as negative or controlling by recipients, and thus result in negative outcomes (Nadler & Jeffrey, 1986; Udry, Gould, Bridges, & Tuffey, 1997). For example, if you were a Little League baseball player you might find that being singled out to receive technical instruction from your coach in front of the whole team is embarrassing and stressful and leaves you feeling humiliated and resentful.

There are also theoretical grounds for expecting differences in the relationship between particular forms of social support and sport-related outcomes. Consider, for example, the support that an aspiring golfer might receive from a parent. Unless the parent is a golf expert, it is likely that any technical instruction (i.e., informational support) they provide will be suboptimal. However, their words of encouragement (i.e., esteem support) may have a more favourable effect. In line with this point, when investigating the main effects of social support on burnout, researchers have found discrepancies in the presence and magnitude of associations between different forms of support and dimensions of burnout. For example, research has demonstrated that all dimensions of perceived support may play an important role in protecting athletes from a reduced sense of accomplishment, while only perceived informational support may protect them from exhaustion (Freeman et al., 2011; Hartley & Coffee, 2019a). Such patterns again underscore the need for researchers to adopt multivariate conceptualisations and methods of assessment when investigating the effects of social support. More generally, while there is some support for the main-effects model (speaking to the fact that it is, on average, a good thing to perceive support to be available if needed), it is also clear that it fails to account for the fact that support can sometimes prove to be unhelpful or even harmful (e.g., Schwarzer & Leppin, 1991).

Accordingly, the model's core prediction – that athletes will benefit from high levels of social support regardless of any other variable of interest – is not always upheld, as it is not always the case that social support has beneficial effects. Indeed, while it tends to be true that perceived support is consistently associated with beneficial outcomes, the relationship between received support and outcomes is quite inconsistent. For instance, a coach may provide technically sound, appropriate and well-timed informational support that has no effect. At the same time, a teammate may provide support that looks on the surface to be unhelpful – team-deprecating humour perhaps – but this can have resound-ingly positive effects.

The remaining theoretical approaches to the study of social support in sport are more closely aligned to the stress and coping literature (Cox, 1978; Lazarus, 1999), and explic-itly linked with Lazarus and Folkman's (1984) *transactional model* of stress and stress appraisal. This model argues that responses to stress are determined in large part by individuals' cognitive response to stressors (see also Chapter 9). Specifically, *primary appraisal* centres on judgements of whether a stressor is threatening to the self in some way, whereas *secondary appraisal* centres on judgements of whether or not one has the resources to cope effectively with any threat. Social support is theorised to impact on these appraisal processes by affecting a person's sense of the social resources they have available to deal with the stressor. The perceived availability of these resources then sub-sequently influences their emotional, cognitive and behavioural responses to that stressor and promotes more favourable stress appraisals and more positive coping solutions.

The stress-prevention model

In sport it is clearly the case that athletes are frequently exposed to stressors which can be seen as posing a threat to the self. For example, these may take the form of concerns about injury, fitness, current form or the demand to perform (Freeman & Rees, 2010; Hartley & Coffee, 2019a). The *stress-prevention model* argues that social support can help athletes to minimise any potentially negative impact of such stressors. In particular, perceiving support to be available when needed (e.g., when a stressor is first encoun-tered) may help an athlete appraise the stressor as non-threatening. Similarly, if a stressor has been appraised as threatening, received support may help an athlete cope when sub-sequent stress starts to impact on relevant outcomes (notably health and performance; Bianco & Eklund, 2001; Cohen et al., 2000).

The model offers a partial insight into how social support can protect against stressors, suggesting that this helps to minimise the stress experienced by an individual, thereby resulting in better outcomes than would result if no social support were available (see Figure 14.1 B). For example, if the stressor took the form of abuse from an opponent in a football match, then social support might help a footballer (a) to make sense of the abuse (e.g., encouraging them to see it as problematic or not), (b) to respond to the abuser (e.g., by confronting them), or (c) to take the matter further (e.g., by striving to stamp out abuse in their sport).

The stress-prevention model has received some support in sport. For example, Raedeke and Smith (2004) found that satisfaction with support was associated with reduction in stress, which in turn helped to protect athletes against burnout. Furthermore, Rees and Freeman (2009) found that perceived support was positively associated with enhanced perceptions of situational control, which was in turn positively associated with challenge appraisals and negatively associated with threat appraisals. Perceived support has also been identified as a key factor in the promotion of resilience in Olympic athletes, for example, by promoting positive adaptations to setbacks (Fletcher & Sarkar, 2012). Such evidence supports the model's core assertion that social support can lead to a reduction in stress. Nevertheless, the model fails to account for evidence that the effectiveness of social support depends on the level of stress that an individual is experiencing and the nature of the stressor they are confronting. In particular, when a person is under a lot of pressure, some forms of social support can sometimes exacerbate rather than ameliorate their stress (Grolnick, 2002). Esteem support, for example, can backfire if it makes athletes over-confident or fearful of letting their supporters down (Thomas, Lane, & Kingston, 2011).

The stress-buffering model

Speaking to evidence that the effect of support is contingent on an athlete's level of stress, the *stress-buffering model* is one of the most influential models in sport (see Figure 14.1 C; Cohen et al., 2000). It argues that social support will have minimal impact on outcomes under conditions of low stress (because here it is not needed) but that it will be more predictive of beneficial outcomes under conditions of high stress. For example, when an athlete is experiencing high levels of stress, high levels of support can protect them from performing poorly. And, conversely, high levels of stress are likely to lead to poorer performance if the athlete has low levels of support.

The stress-buffering model is also aligned with the transactional model of stress and stress appraisal (Lazarus & Folkman, 1984). Specifically, after a person is exposed to stressors which pose a threat to the self, it suggests that both perceived and received support play a role in shaping the impact of that threat. More specifically, both types of support can enhance perceived or received coping resources during secondary stress appraisal, thereby reducing (i.e., 'buffering') the negative effect of stress on sport-related outcomes (Cohen et al., 2000; Cohen & Wills, 1985). At the same time, however, perceived and received support are theorised to exert unique stress-buffering effects (Bianco & Eklund, 2001; Cohen et al., 2000; Rees & Hardy, 2004). Indeed, qualitative and quantitative research has found that both received and perceived support *can* reduce the negative impact of stress on sport-related outcomes such as self-confidence and performance (Freeman & Rees, 2008; Kristiansen & Roberts, 2010; Rees & Freeman, 2007). However, when considered simultaneously, there is mixed evidence for these claims, and it is unclear whether one form of support exerts stronger stress-buffering effects than the other (e.g., Hartley & Coffee, 2019a; Rees et al., 2007).

Overall, then, the stress-buffering approach is valuable both in helping us to understand when social support is likely to be beneficial (i.e., under high levels of stress) and in pointing to the importance of cognitive appraisal for this process. However, evidence for the model is mixed, both in sport and in the wider psychological literature (for reviews, see Cohen & Wills, 1985; Lakey & Cronin, 2008; Rueger et al., 2016). The picture is further complicated by evidence that different dimensions of support are associated with different forms of coping behaviour (Cohen & Wills, 1985; Freeman et al., 2011; Hartley & Coffee, 2019a; Lu et al., 2016). Furthermore, as we will see, the stress-buffering model also fails to account for other factors that appear to play a significant role in determining whether social support is beneficial – notably the social context in which it is provided and the source from which it emerges.

The optimal-matching approach

The *optimal-matching hypothesis* builds on the stress-buffering model by specifying what forms of social support help people to cope with specific stressors (Cutrona & Russell, 1990). As Table 14.1 indicates, this approach suggests that social support is most effective when it comes in a form that helps people deal with the specific nature of the threat posed by a given stressor (see Table 14.1).

Table 14.1 The optimal-matching hypothesis

	Controllability of stressor	Type of support	Type of coping
Optimally matched	Uncontrollable	Emotional + esteem	Emotion-focused
	Controllable	Informational + tangible	Problem-focused
Poorly matched	Uncontrollable	Informational + tangible	Problem-focused
	Controllable	Emotional + esteem	Emotion-focused

This approach characterises stressors as varying in terms of their controllability as well as their desirability, duration and domain. Social support is then expected to be more effective the more compatible it is with these variables. For example, Cutrona and Russell (1990) argue that uncontrollable stressors (e.g., a deselection or a last-minute hamstring injury) typically require forms of social support that enable *emotion-focused* forms of coping. In this instance, then, emotional and esteem support would be more appropriate – and hence more useful – than informational or tangible support. In contrast, controllable stressors (e.g., a flight cancellation or a tyre puncture) typically require forms of support that promote *problem-focused* forms of coping. Here, then, informational and tangible forms of social support would be more appropriate, as they provide viable ways of managing the stressor (e.g., rescheduling the flight or repairing the tyre so that these events disrupt performance as little as possible).

Yet while the optimal-matching model is intuitively appealing and theoretically 'clean', the hypothesis again only receives mixed empirical support, either in sporting domains (Arnold, Edwards, & Rees, 2018; Rees & Hardy, 2004) or beyond (where it has generally been studied; Burleson, 2003; Burleson & MacGeorge, 2002). For example, Ian Mitchell and colleagues (2014) found that when dimensions of social support were matched to specific stressors (e.g., injury), stress-buffering effects were observed for perceived but not received support. Other researchers have also failed to observe main- or stress-buffering effects of optimally matched support on either performance (Rees et al., 2007) or on responses to injury (Rees et al., 2010). For example, research led by Paul Freeman and colleagues (2009), who delivered a well-matched social support intervention during a round of golf, demonstrated that this led to significant improvement in the score for only one of the three high-level golfers who took part in the study.

As with preceding models, this model also fails to conceptualise or account for the influence of other factors that play a significant role in determining whether social support is effective. For instance, irrespective of whether dimensions of social support are optimally matched to the demands of a particular stressor, the social context may dictate whether or not those types of supportive behaviour are warranted (or even resented). The effectiveness of optimally matched social support may also partially depend on provider characteristics. Consider again the example of the golf parent. Here the receipt and impact of optimally matched forms of social support (e.g., for coping with controllable golf-related stressors) may ultimately depend on the parent's golfing expertise. One reason for this is that social contextual factors (e.g., to do with the source and the audience) affect the *meaning* of support and hence play a key role in shaping its impact (Burleson & MacGeorge, 2002; Haslam, Reicher, & Levine, 2012; Viswesvaran, Sanchez, & Fisher, 1999). Accordingly, if we are to understand the dynamics of what makes social support effective, a theoeretical framework is needed which not only makes predictions about when and how social support will be effective, but also conceptualises and accounts for the influence of relevant social contextual factors – notably those which pertain to the *group-based relationship* between providers and recipients of support.

A SOCIAL IDENTITY APPROACH TO SOCIAL SUPPORT IN SPORT

By drawing on the stress appraisal and coping literature (e.g., Lazarus & Folkman, 1984), the main and stress-buffering approaches have sought to understand how different types of social support behaviours contribute to primary and secondary stress appraisals, and how these impact upon sport-related outcomes. However, a weakness of these approaches is that their hypotheses are rather rigid. In particular, they are insensitive to social contextual factors that determine when, how and why social support is beneficial (Thoits, 2011). Relatedly, they are all limited by the fact that they construe stress and the experience of social support in purely *personal* terms (Folkman & Moskowitz, 2004). In particular, most research focuses exclusively on the recipient's perspective and experience of support *as an individual*. However, it is clear that *social support occurs between recipients and providers*, and that *the perceived availability or actual exchange of any social support resources is necessarily conditioned by the nature of their shared group membership*. For example, however optimal it might be, one would not expect support provided by a member of a rival team to have the same meaning or impact as support provided by a trusted teammate.

This speaks to the fact that athletes are never merely 'passive recipients' of support. Importantly, they have support-related preferences, and will often choose how they wish to seek and use support. Importantly, too, these preferences are often grounded in group memberships and associated social identities. For example, research with indigenous Australian Football League players found that they saw other players from similar cultural backgrounds to be their most important source of support (Nicholson et al., 2011). Likewise, in a study where participants learned to play a new game, their willingness to ask for support from teammates was influenced by group norms concerning the perceived appropriateness of this behaviour (Butler, McKimmie, & Haslam, 2018). This meant that players were much more likely to ask for and use support if their teammates did so too. In this regard, it is also clear that group memberships place constraints on who is perceived to be eligible for support (Cruickshank & Collins, 2013; DeFreese & Smith, 2013; Fletcher & Wagstaff, 2009; Freeman & Rees, 2010). More generally, we suggest that the experience of social support in sport is bound up with the dynamics of group life (Rees et al., 2015), and needs to be understood in *social* (i.e., group-based) terms, not just in personal terms.

Another weakness of prevailing approaches to social support is that they fail to explain the capacity for social support to sometimes be the *source* of stress and harm. Most readers will be able to recall situations where others' well-intentioned attempts to provide support have backfired and made things worse. Along these lines, as we noted above, the Little League baseball player receiving corrective technical instruction from the coach in front of his teammates may experience this as embarrassing, punitive or as an attempt to assert dominance. More generally, this suggests that there is a need for a theoretical framework that captures the potential for identity-related processes to *transform* the experience of both support and stress (Haslam & Reicher, 2006).

In line with these arguments, in what follows we flesh out a social identity approach to the study of social support in sport. This builds on prevailing approaches in a number of ways. First, by seeing support as a synergistic exchange between provider and recipient (Hayward, Knight, & Mellalieu, 2017), the approach recognises the importance of the *identity-based relational perspectives* of all those involved in a social support exchange (i.e., not only recipients but also providers, onlookers and other stakeholders; Coussens, Rees, & Freeman, 2015). Second, it provides a framework to explain the influence of the *social environment* that speaks to the importance of salient social identities and their associated content (e.g., support-related norms) for the meaning and experience of support (Butler et al., 2018; Rees et al., 2015). Third, the approach provides a framework that explains the *transformative potential* of support, whereby it can be *both* profoundly debilitating and supremely empowering (Haslam & Reicher, 2006).

The importance of social identity for social support was actually reinforced by the foundational research in this theoretical tradition: the minimal group studies (Tajfel, 1970; Tajfel et al., 1971; see also Chapter 2). Although these studies focused primarily on acts of discrimination and intergroup competition, they also highlighted the point that social categorization has implications for supportive behaviour. Specifically, they showed that even when groups are inherently meaningless, people reliably display favouritism towards members of their ingroup through the assignment of monetary rewards (while strategically withholding points from an outgroup; Tajfel, 1978; Turner, 1975). Thus, although the studies' findings are typically framed as providing a window onto the capacity for social identity to engender discrimination, they can equally – and in many ways more fundamentally – be seen to show how social identity provides a psychological platform for the provision (or withholding) of social support (in this case, tangible support).

Of course, the impact of social identity on social support provision is something that can readily be seen in the world of sport. Consider the 2016 World Triathlon Series in Cozumel, Mexico, where, as Slater and colleagues noted in Chapter 5, within sight of the finish line, Alastair Brownlee of Great Britain gave up his chance to win the final race of the season, instead choosing to help his struggling brother Jonny across the line. Why would an individual who has trained hard to ensure that he has the best chance of winning a competition willingly set aside his own opportunity to do so in order to support a competitor? One answer is that no athlete is ever just 'an individual'. Instead, the social identity approach alerts us to the fact that in a range of social contexts – including sporting ones – how people think, feel and behave is defined by their group membership (i.e., their social identity as members of the same family, club or team; Tajfel, 1972; Turner, 1982).

As discussed in Chapter 2, when this is the case, this serves to transform behaviour so that it is guided by the perspective, interests and needs of the ingroup ('us') rather than those of the personal self ('me'). This also means that when social identity is salient, the dynamics of giving, receiving and utilising social support are also structured by group membership and associated social identity-based relationships between relevant actors (i.e., support providers, recipients, onlookers and other stakeholders). Indeed, as we see clearly in the case of the Brownlee brothers, here acts of personal sacrifice can become acts of collective (and personal) victory. In the sections below we tease out these arguments to shed more light on the complex dynamics of social support in sport.

Key point 1: Shared social identity makes social support possible

In line with the key tenets of self-categorization theory (Turner et al., 1987; Turner et al., 1994), the foregoing analysis provides a basis for understanding how an emergent sense of shared social identity (a sense of 'we-ness') can (re)shape the nature of the relationship between providers and recipients of social support. An underlying point here is that, however people define themselves, they are generally motivated to have – or, more particularly, to *achieve* – a sense of the self as a positive and distinct entity (Tajfel & Turner, 1979). This means, for example, that if a female runner defines herself as an individual, then she will want to see herself as different from, and better than, other athletes – for example, by trying to win a race in which she is competing against other runners. However, we noted above that there are a great many contexts where people engage in self-stereotyping (depersonalisation; Turner, 1982) such that their sense of self is defined by shared group membership (as 'we' and 'us', rather than 'I' and 'me'). Where this is the case, the motivation for positive distinctiveness should now manifest itself as a desire to see the ingroup as different from, and better than, comparison outgroups – for example, by winning a tournament in which our team is competing against other teams. In this context, one of the key points to note about social support is that it is a form of behaviour that is broadly oriented towards this collective goal. That is, it is a manifestation of the aspiration to enhance the interests of a shared social identity.

This is a basic point that has a number of significant implications. The *first* is that, when social identity is salient, people should generally be inclined to support those who are members of an ingroup more than those who are members of outgroups. This, of course, is a basic feature of most sporting encounters where fans, coaches, physiotherapists and sponsors generally support 'us' (whoever 'us' happens to be) rather than 'them'. This is what was found in the stripped-down conditions of the minimal group studies (Tajfel et al., 1971), but, as discussed in Chapter 2, it was also found in studies by Mark Levine and colleagues (2005) which looked at football fans' willingness to help a person who had fallen down in front of them and (seemingly) hurt himself. It was also observed in a study by Michael Platow and colleagues, which found that fans of Australian rules football gave much more money to a charitable cause when it appeared to be supported by someone who was a fan of their team rather than of a rival team or no team at all (Platow et al., 1999).

The *second* implication is that social identity also provides a basis for *expectations of support availability* (i.e., perceived support; Haslam et al., 1998). More specifically, in a situation where people define themselves in terms of a particular group membership (e.g., as 'us reds'), they typically look to fellow ingroup members to help them out (e.g., by giving them useful advice or assisting them if they are in difficulty). As a corollary, though, people generally do not perceive support to be available from outgroup members. And this means that if they *do* get support from an outgroup source, it will often be treated with suspicion because the motivations that drive it are hard to understand. This in turn is a key reason why, as we noted earlier in the chapter, perceptions of support availability (e.g., as measured by the The Team-referent Availability of Social Support Questionnaire, TASS-Q, reproduced in the Appendix) are often misaligned with the actual provision and receipt of support.

Third, and related to the preceding point, it is also the case that when people provide support to outgroup members, the quality of received support will often be inferior to the support provided to ingroup members. For example, the football fans in Platow and colleagues' study (1999) gave significantly less money to charitable causes that appeared to be supported by outgroup members. Likewise, research by René Bekkers (2005) found that parents were far less likely to volunteer to support community sporting activities once their children were no longer involved in them. When it comes to sport, the actual provision of support (e.g., charity) thus often begins – and ends – at home.

Following on from this, a *fourth* point is that support from outgroups will often prove to be suboptimal relative to the support provided by ingroups, partly because it is unexpected and hard to make sense of. In particular, it is unlikely to have the positive effects on well-being and performance that the main-effects model suggests, and this is one key reason why support for this model is generally weak (Haslam, Reicher & Levine, 2012).

Putting these things together, the more general point is that social support is always an *achievement* that is largely *made possible* by a sense of shared identity between those who are party to it. As an example of this point, consider the tendency for powerlifters to slap each other prior to executing a heavy lift. For those who self-stereotype as a powerlifter, this form of esteem support is likely to be interpreted favourably and to help them feel confident and perform well. However, outside the context of this shared identity, the same experience is unlikely to be seen as so supportive and hence unlikely to help a person perform better. Indeed, it may be quite intimidating in ways that actually impair performance. The same is true of the gruelling training regimes that coaches design with a view to helping athletes develop skill and stamina. For the athletes who identify with those coaches and their programmes, these are typically experienced as supportive and necessary. But anyone else would likely experience them as cruel and unusual punishment.

Yet, as noted in Chapter 2, a further key consideration here is that the self-stereotyping process is *context-sensitive*. This means that the social identities that define a person's sense of social identity are not fixed (Oakes et al., 1994). For example, the participants in Levine and colleagues' (2005; Slater et al., 2013) research could self-categorize – and could be led to self-categorize – as supporters of a particular football team at one level of abstraction but also define themselves as football supporters at a higher, more inclusive, level of abstraction. This in turn has implications for who people offer social support to as well as who they receive it from. So the passer-by whose identity as a Manchester United fan had been made salient by the experimenters was far more likely to stop and help the person who tripped and fell in front of them when that person was wearing a Manchester United shirt rather than a Liverpool one. However, the Manchester United and Liverpool fans received the same amount of help (and more than the person who was in a plain T-shirt) if the passer-by's social identity as a football fan had been made salient.

This points to the fact that merely 'having' a shared social identity is not enough for support to be received and to be effective; instead, that identity must be psychologically *salient* in order for it to be harnessed as a useful resource. At the same time, too, it speaks to the capacity for social identity to be redefined in more inclusive ways that allow previously eschewed and unsupported outgroups to be welcomed inside the tent of a more inclusive sense of 'us'. When an opponent is seriously injured, for example, intergroup rivalry will often give way to shared humanity. Thus, when Colin Charvis – the Welsh rugby player – was knocked out during a 2003 test match between New Zealand and Wales in Hamilton, the All Blacks player Tana Umaga left his position to roll Charvis into the recovery position and remove his gum shield.

On a larger scale it was this same recategorization process that allowed Everton fans to reach out in solidarity to their Merseyside rivals after the 1989 Hillsborough disaster in which 96 Liverpool fans died following a horrific crush in the stands. At the time, conservative politicians and some sections of the press blamed Liverpool fans for the crush, but it was subsequently shown to have been caused by negligent policing. As the Everton manager David Moyes wrote in his programme notes after Liverpool fans had been absolved of responsibility for the disaster in 2012:

As part of the football family, I, and everybody at Everton, stand alongside the families who for so long have challenged the authorities over what has now been proved a travesty. I am not only a football manager, I'm a football supporter and a father, and I applaud the families who continued to fight for the ones they loved. (Luckhurst, 2012)

Figure 14.2 Liverpool and Everton fans stand side by side at a Goodison Park memorial service at St. George's Hall, Liverpool for victims of the 1989 Hillsborough disaster

Source: Liverpool Echo

Key point 2: The experience of stress and social support is structured by self-categorization

So how exactly do groups come to agree about the forms of social support they want? As already discussed, social identity theory proposes that when people define themselves as group members, they seek to define themselves and their ingroup positively. Accordingly, it follows that group members' understanding of the value of support will be determined by their sense of the capacity for that support to promote the interests of their ingroup – for example, in helping to deal with a group-specific problem or with a challenge of historical relevance to the group.

By way of example, research conducted by the first and fourth authors of this chapter with a regional Rugby Academy in Scotland observed that transport challenges were an ongoing stressor for both players and support staff (in ways that were not true for urban branches of the same Academy; Hartley & Coffee, 2019b). As a result, members of this group placed a particular value on social support that helped them to tackle these transport challenges. Rather than simply being matched in terms of its abstract content (in ways suggested by the optimal-matching approach; Cutrona & Russell, 1990), support thus needs to match ingroup expectations and needs.

This example also speaks to the fact that in contexts where an athlete's sense of self is defined by their group membership, stress appraisal will be shaped by the circumstances of their ingroup, not just by those that they face as individuals. In ways suggested by Figure 14.3, this is true for both primary appraisal (where the question is not so much 'Is this stressful for me?' as 'Is this stressful for us?') and secondary stress appraisal (where the question is not so much 'Can I cope?' as 'Can we cope?'; Campo et al., 2018; Gallagher, Meaney, & Muldoon, 2014; Haslam, 2004; Haslam, Reicher, & Levine, 2012; Rees et al., 2015).

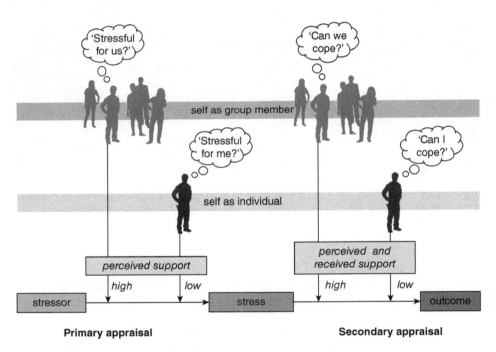

Figure 14.3 The role of social identity in primary and secondary stress appraisal

Note: This figure makes the point that whether a person self-categorizes as a group member (vs as an individual) is likely to influence their primary stress appraisal by affecting how they interpret stressors, and their secondary stress appraisal by affecting their perceptions of the resources they have available to cope with stressors.

This observation suggests that the stress-buffering process (and the terms of the transactional model more generally) will be moderated not only by a perceiver's salient self-categorization, but also by the resources that a salient ingroup is able to provide. For example, observing a poor performance by a football team is likely only to be stressful for those who identify with that team (Burnett, 2002; Davis & End, 2010; Wann et al., 1999; Wann, Culver et al., 2005). Indeed, those who support a rival team are likely to find the poor performance *de*stressing rather than distressing (see Chapter 17). Similarly, a person's sense of their ability to cope with the stress that the team's poor performance causes is likely to be greater to the extent that they get support from fellow ingroup members. So while they may be consoled by the commiseration and encouragement of a fellow fan, the same words on the lips of the fan of a rival team may leave them cold or even more depressed. In the context of coaching, too, while the support of trusted team members may increase a person's sense of mastery and competence, that of outsiders is more likely to be experienced as intrusive, controlling and as undermining an athlete's sense of autonomy and competence (Bolger & Amarel, 2007; Bolger, Zuckerman, & Kessler, 2000).

Evidence that supports this hypothesis emerges from experimental research by the second author and colleagues showing that when they confronted a challenging test, students were only reassured by feedback that the test would be not be stressful if that feedback was provided by an ingroup member (i.e., a fellow student, Haslam et al., 2004). In health settings, too, social identification with support providers is a critical component of the *therapeutic alliance* and as such is generally associated with favourable mental health and well-being-related outcomes (Cruwys, Haslam, Dingle, Haslam, & Jetten, 2014; Cruwys, Haslam, Dingle, Jetten et al., 2014; see also Chapter 15). Similar patterns are also seen in the domain of sport. In particular, a series of experiments by Rees and colleagues (2013) found that encouraging performance feedback in a dart-throwing task helped to improve future performance when it was delivered by an ingroup member (i.e., a student at the same university) but not when it was delivered by an outgroup member (i.e., a student at a rival university).

And speaking to the capacity for social identity to 'get under the skin', research by Jan Häusser and colleagues showed that students' physiological responses to a threatening stressor were attenuated by supportive feedback from others only when the students were induced to self-categorize in a way that defined those others as ingroup members (Häusser, Kattenstroth, van Dick, & Mojzisch, 2012). Critically, this meant that when participants were encouraged to self-categorize as individuals, support proved unhelpful. This speaks to the observation that sport athletes' stubborn determination to 'go it alone' can often work against them. This, for example, is something that the American golfer Brandi Jackson recognised in her own early career where:

> I was afraid to ask for help and I didn't utilise some very valuable people and resources who were available to me during that time. There is a healthy level of stubbornness among athletes that keeps them determined to get better and overcome setbacks, but there is also an unhealthy level of stubbornness that prevents them from being coachable and willing to try new things in order to work on the weaker areas of the game. (Jackson, 2019)

Again, then, we see that whether or not support functions *as support* depends very much on the identity-based relationship between support providers and recipients. Among other things, this means that people often recoil from seeking out support (especially from outgroups) because they believe that it will not be helpful or will come at too great a cost to themselves or their ingroup. As a supporter of the Cork hurling team eloquently put it on a fan website: 'Cork are Cork. They don't need or want anyone's support except their own' (The Free Kick, 2013).

Key point 3: Social identities can constrain access to social support

We have already noted several times that one of social identity theory's core insights is that people are generally motivated to define themselves and relevant ingroups positively. Clearly, though, they do not always succeed in this endeavour – not least because they are often constrained by social and structural realities that limit opportunities for self-enhancement (Tajfel & Turner, 1979). As one very simple illustration of this point, research by Nik Steffens and colleagues found that footballers who play outside their country of birth need to score 32% more goals in a season to win a 'player of the season' award than players who are locally born (Steffens, Crimston et al., 2019). Such data speak to the non-trivial fact that access to support (in this case esteem support) is structured by group membership – so that it is harder to obtain for members of some groups than it is for members of other groups. This indeed is the central theme in ongoing debate about racism, sexism and other forms of discrimination in sport (e.g., based on class, sexuality and religion; Hardin, Genovese, & Yu, 2009; Krane & Barber, 2003).

At the same time, it would be a mistake to assume that shared social identities always lead to favourable support-related outcomes. Indeed, despite a considerable amount of support often being available (e.g., in the form of holistic programmes that provide them with education, career development experience and proactive mental health awareness; Lavallee, 2005, 2019), there are many cases where athletes report feeling inadequately supported within their own teams and sports. So, what's the issue? One problem is that the receipt of support can sometimes be seen to be inconsistent with ingroup norms. For example, athletes in groups that embrace masculine norms (e.g., of 'toughness') may experience barriers to seeking out social support that attends to their emotional or physical needs. Among other things, such norms have been found to be a barrier to male athletes seeking out mental health support (Moreland, Coxe, & Yang, 2018) as well as treatment for concussion (Kroshus, Kubzansky, Goldman, & Austin, 2014).

More generally, the way people engage with social support behaviours depends on how they define the self. Specifically, to the extent that a person defines themselves as a member of a given group, then the defining features of that group (i.e., its identity *content* – e.g., the values, norms and ideals that characterise the meaning of that group; Cerulo, 1995) will shape their understanding of social support (and much else besides). This means that what support is expected to look like – and hence what *counts* as support – may be very different for a group of French rugby players, say, and a junior softball team.

As research by the first and fourth author suggests, this process influences athletes' responses to multiple facets of support, including (a) its design (e.g., their acceptance of what it is trying to achieve), (b) its provision (e.g., their satisfaction with the way it is delivered), and (c) its receipt (e.g., their interpretation of its impact; Hartley & Coffee, 2019b). Groups, differ, for example, in what they want the support to achieve, whom they want the support to be provided by, and how gratitude should be demonstrated for receiving such support. In other words, when they identify with a given group, athletes' membership of that group will shape their sense of what social support behaviours are *normal* (Butler et al., 2018). As research by Tamara Butler (2016) shows, this can facilitate engagement with support when that support is seen to affirm ingroup identity, but lead to disengagement if support is seen to conflict with the prescriptions of ingroup identity.

Along these same lines, research suggests that *identity threat* can drive athletes' concerns that engaging with atypical forms of social support (e.g., mental health support) will threaten a core characteristic of the ingroup (e.g., athletic 'toughness') and therefore be embarrassing or attract social disapproval from other ingroup members (Tarrant & Campbell, 2007; see also Chapter 7). To the extent that this is the case, it is likely to aggravate individuals' stress responses. Moreover, by appearing to signal an inability to cope with, or conform to, group norms, support-seeking can compromise a person's sense of self-esteem (Fisher, Nadler, & Whitcher-Alagna, 1982) because it threatens their standing within the group (e.g., leading them to fear deselection; Nadler, 2002; Nadler & Halabi, 2006). For example, research in medical settings has observed that trainee doctors are often unwilling to seek help because the possibility of engaging with professional support units evokes identity-threatening stigma in being seen to be incompatible with the ingroup characteristic of 'performing at work despite stress or illness' (Wainwright, Fox, Breffni, Taylor, & O'Connor, 2017). Likewise, in the context of sport, many athletes shun support – both on and off the field – for fear of how they will appear to their teammates. As the Ohio State football player Jarrod Barnes observed when reflecting on his own unwillingness to get help with his academic studies:

> It goes back to fear of failure. In class, you don't want to seem dumb if you don't know the answer so you don't answer and don't participate. … I was afraid to ask for help because I didn't know if the professor would view me differently. I didn't engage with my peers because I was afraid of looking stupid. (Chenoweth, 2016)

CONCLUSION

A key message of this chapter is that the dynamics of what makes social support effective are heavily conditioned by the social identities that inform this process in ways specified by both social identity and self-categorization theories. Apart from anything else, this fact helps explain why support for the mainstream approaches to social support that we reviewed in the first half of this chapter is often very mixed. For while social support certainly has the capacity to ameliorate stress, whether or not it does so depends critically on the identity-based relationship between support providers and recipients. As we saw in the second half of the chapter, this means that support really only 'works' when it is provided by a person or group with whom a person sees themselves as sharing social identity. If this is not the case, then support will often be unhelpful and may even prove counterproductive. At the same time, though, we saw that even when it is provided by an ingroup source, support can still be ineffective if it is seen as inconsistent with ingroup norms or as threatening to a person's standing within the group. All this means that the dynamics of support are both complex and nuanced – so that where it *is* effective, support needs to be recognised as a supreme collaborative achievement rather than as something to be taken for granted.

Yet while the social identity approach offers a comprehensive framework for rethinking the psychology of social support in sport, it remains the case that many of the key points we have outlined remain to be properly tested in this domain. Moreover, although key support providers within the sport environment clearly value support, most evince a rather unsophisticated orientation to this process (Knights & Ruddock-Hudson, 2016). Many thus adopt a 'support is support is support' approach, where we have suggested that what the field needs is an approach that is altogether more sensitive to the ways in which precisely the same support can be both supportive and unsupportive depending on social contextual factors that structure the identities of those who are party to it.

One very basic practical conclusion that this leads us to is that those who are interested in providing effective support to athletes need to attend closely to the identity-based perspectives that key stakeholders bring to this process – not only athletes themselves but also friends and family, support staff and professional bodies. In line with this point, in some of our own research we have found that attention of this form is beneficial because it helps to build a sense of shared identity that improves the perceived credibility and trustworthiness of the support that is on offer and provides a platform both for shared understanding and for shared endeavour (Hartley & Coffee, 2019b). In short, helping athletes to better understand 'who we are' is a good basis for them being able to understand 'how we can help'.

15

MENTAL HEALTH AND RESILIENCE

TEGAN CRUWYS
MARK STEVENS
CATHERINE HASLAM
S. ALEXANDER HASLAM
LISA OLIVE

If asked to give examples of the health problems athletes face, the first examples that come to mind are probably pulled muscles, torn ligaments and broken bones. Depression, anxiety and other mental health conditions may be somewhat less obvious. Indeed, these may seem like conditions that should not be a concern for individuals who are often lavishly paid and commonly portrayed as 'superhuman' (McPherson, O'Donnell, McGillivray, & Misener, 2016). But are athletes (elite or otherwise) really immune from mental health conditions such as these, which, at a population level, are a major cause – in most countries, the *leading* cause – of disability (Ferrari et al., 2014; Vos et al., 2015)?

There is now overwhelming evidence that the answer to this question is no. Evidence suggests that poor mental health is as common (if not more common) among athletes as it is among the general population (Gouttebarge et al., 2019; Rice et al., 2016). Not least, this is because athletes face a range of sport-specific stressors and threats to their mental health that the general population typically do not (as also discussed in Chapter 14). For instance, research indicates that sport *burnout* – characterised by feelings of emotional and physical exhaustion, a reduced sense of accomplishment, and sport devaluation (Isoard-Gautheur et al., 2018; Raedeke & Smith, 2001) – affects up to 9% of athletes (Gustafsson, Kenttä, Hassmén, & Lundqvist, 2007). Research has also identified a number of distinct risk factors for burnout in sport, including (a) high expectations, (b) exposure to criticism, (c) too much practice, (d) not enough recovery, (e) perfectionism, and (f) the pursuit of exceptionally high goals (Appleton, Hall, & Hill, 2009; Gustafsson, Hassmén, Kenttä, & Johansson, 2008; Lemyre, Hall, & Roberts, 2008).

Of perhaps even greater concern is evidence that there are high rates of clinical mental health conditions in athlete populations. For instance, in a sample of 224 elite Australian athletes, Amelia Gulliver and colleagues (2015) found that 15% experienced social anxiety, 23% had eating disorders and 27% met the criteria for depression at the time of the survey. These rates are comparable to or slightly higher than the Australian population more generally. Other data also converge on these estimates, for example, indicating that more than one in five college athletes are depressed (Wolanin, Gross, & Hong, 2015; Wolanin, Hong, Marks, Panchoo, & Gross, 2016). A recent meta-analysis indicated that these high rates of mental health conditions affect athletes not only during their sporting careers, but that elevated risk also persists into sporting retirement (Gouttebarge et al., 2019).

At the same time, though, over the last decade, an increasing number of high-profile elite athletes have sought to combat the culture of silence around mental health in sport and the stigma it imbues. For example, the most decorated Olympian of all time, Michael Phelps, and double Olympic gold medallists Kelly Holmes and Victoria Pendleton have all spoken openly about their depression diagnoses, with each describing how they have considered taking their own lives on multiple occasions (see Bergman, 2019; Holmes, 2005; Matthews, 2018; Figure 15.1). Reflecting on his condition, Phelps noted that his problems surfaced shortly after the high of winning eight gold medals at the 2008 Olympic games:

> After '08, mentally, I was over. I didn't want to do it anymore. But I also knew I couldn't stop. So I forced myself to do something that I really didn't want to do, which was continue swimming. That whole four-year period, I would miss at least two workouts a week. Why? Didn't want to go. Didn't feel like going. Screw it. I'm going to sleep in. I'm going to skip Friday and go for a long weekend. (Layden, 2015)

Holmes' mental health problems, on the other hand, started after a series of injuries had put her athletic career in jeopardy:

> I thought: Why me? I'm so committed, so dedicated, why me? I just looked in the mirror and hated myself. I wanted the floor to open up, I wanted to jump in that space, I wanted it to close and I didn't want to go back out. I was in such a bad way. Then I started cutting myself. (Hattenstone, 2019)

One of the first athletes to describe their struggles with mental health was the former England cricketer Marcus Trescothick (see Figure 15.1). Soon after playing a key role in England's historic 2005 win in the test cricket series against Australia (the Ashes), Trescothick returned home early from England's 2006 tour of India with depression symptoms so severe that he had become barely able to function, let alone play cricket for his country. This is a story he tells with admirable candour in his autobiography, *Coming Back To Me* (Trescothick, 2008). In fact, the book starts by putting his mental health front and centre stage:

In the good times, the times before the long days and longer nights when depressive illness turned stretches of my life into a slow death, I had occasionally caught a glimpse of the perfect end to my career as an England cricketer; at The Oval, pausing on my way back to the dressing room to acknowledge the applause celebrating the Test century with which I had just secured our latest Ashes victory. That was what I saw in my sunlit daydreams. That was how it was supposed to happen.

The reality? Hunched-up, sobbing, distraught, slumped in a corner of Dixon's electrical store at Heathrow's Terminal 3 unable to board the 9pm Virgin Airways Flight VS400 to Dubai ... hanging on for the pain and terror with which I had become so familiar during the previous two years to subside and let me breathe. (Trescothick, 2008, pp. 1–2)

Despite these harrowing episodes, in many ways Trescothick's story is a positive one. For while depression ultimately cut his international career short, and he acknowledges that he will have to manage it for the rest of his life, he received professional help and was able to resume his career at English county level – free from the stress of long periods away from home on international tours that had been a key trigger for his condition.

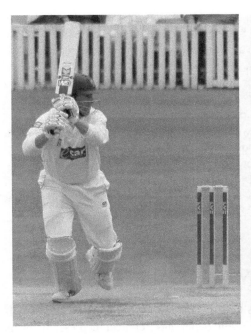 

Figure 15.1 Marcus Trescothick and Kelly Holmes

Source: Wikimedia Commons

The media coverage of these (and other) cases has helped to bring the issue of mental health in sport into the public eye, and has encouraged many sport governing bodies, clubs and coaches to provide support for their athletes. Moreover, the burgeoning interest in elite athlete mental health has culminated in the release of a comprehensive International Olympic Committee (IOC) expert consensus statement on mental health (Reardon et al., 2019).

Nevertheless, much progress remains to be made. Not least, this is because athletes are still less likely than the general population to seek support for mental health (Castaldelli-Maia et al., 2019). This is due to a combination of factors, including a lack of understanding about mental health, a perception that help-seeking is a sign of weakness, and, in particular, a fear of being exposed to mental health stigma. Performance undoubtedly also remains the primary consideration for stakeholders, with athletes' mental health typically a secondary consideration, if it is considered at all (Bauman, 2016). This reflects the fact that sport – particularly elite sport – is big business, with enormous sums of money rewarding not just 'winners' over 'losers', but also those who finish one place higher in a league, or who progress one round further in a tournament. For instance, in 2019 the English Football League Championship playoff final – a single game which decides which of two teams get promoted to the English Premier League for the following season – was estimated to be worth £170 million to the winning club (Ogden, 2019). With stakes as high as this, it is perhaps unsurprising that governing bodies, clubs and coaches have a single-minded focus on performance.

However, this focus overlooks the ways in which athlete well-being and performance often go hand in hand (Fransen, Haslam, Steffens et al., 2020). In particular, evidence indicates (a) that athletes typically perform at a higher level when they are in better mental health (May, Veach, Reed, & Griffey, 1985; Schinke, Stambulova, Si, & Moore, 2018), and (b) that interventions can confer concurrent gains for both mental health *and* performance (Donohue et al., 2015; Gross et al., 2018).

In line with these findings, in this chapter we contend that the provision of better support for athletes' mental health and well-being is critical for two reasons. First, because this is an ethical imperative in its own right. And, second, because it has downstream benefits for athletes' performance. Here we provide an overview of existing approaches to mental health in sport, and pinpoint their key strengths and limitations. We then outline a fresh *social identity perspective* on the factors and processes that impact mental health in sport.

WHAT DO WE MEAN BY MENTAL HEALTH?

Mental health – and indeed all health – is best understood not in terms of discrete illnesses or categories (e.g., such that a person either has 'clinical depression' or is 'normal'), but rather as a continuum, which at any given time each of us falls somewhere along (e.g., see Corey, 2002; Lamers, Westerhof, Bohlmeijer, ten Klooster, & Keyes, 2011). On the one hand, at the positive end of this continuum, one finds people who are free from disease and disorder, and who demonstrate high levels of well-being, functioning and flourishing. On the other hand, at the negative end of the continuum, one finds people who meet criteria for disorders of various forms, those who have a poor quality of life, and those with functional limitations. Crucially, one's position on the continuum is far from fixed. We can move fluidly along it in both directions, with our position at any one point in time determined by *both* individual risk factors (e.g., family history, emotional coping strategies) and various life events and stressors (e.g., missing out on selection for a competition).

This *continuum model of mental health* is consistent with the World Health Organization's (2014) conceptualisation of health as 'a state of complete physical, mental and social well-being and not merely the absence of disease or infirmity'. It is also consistent with a growing body of empirical research which has demonstrated that most psychological phenomena – including mental health symptoms – are normally distributed in the population without any natural 'cut-off points' where people can be logically divided into distinct categories (Haslam, Holland, & Kuppens, 2012). Accordingly, in line with the continuum model, in recent times there has been a growing emphasis on (a) *risk factors* (e.g., insomnia, worry) that cut across diagnostic categories in mental health research (giving rise to what is referred to as *horizontal epidemiology*; Blas, Sommerfeld, & Kurup, 2011; Cieza et al., 2015; Cieza & Bickenbach, 2019; Dolsen, Asarnow, & Harvey, 2014; McEvoy, Watson, Watkins, & Nathan, 2013), and (b) *transdiagnostic interventions* that treat a wide range of mental health problems (e.g., the unified protocol in cognitive behaviour therapy; Wilamowska et al., 2010).

An additional term that is often used in the context of mental health is *resilience*. Both within and outside sport, this has typically been used to refer to the way that people *respond* to stressors. Individuals who are able to endure a greater number or intensity of stressors and remain well (and, particularly in sport, who continue to *perform* well) are considered resilient (Fletcher & Sarkar, 2012; Luthar, Cicchetti, & Becker, 2000). For instance, research outside sport has examined resilience in the context of stressors such as the death of a parent (Greeff & Human, 2004), sexual abuse (Bogar & Hulse-Killacky, 2006) and terrorism (Bonanno, Galea, Bucciarelli, & Vlahov, 2007). Within sport, resilience research has focused on stressors such as injuries, performance slumps, life events and career transitions (e.g., see Fletcher & Sarkar, 2012; Galli & Vealey, 2008). However, this conceptualisation of resilience – and indeed the concept more broadly – has notable limitations, some of which we now describe (for previous discussions, see DeVerteuil & Golubchikov, 2016; Luthar et al., 2000).

First, this model of resilience requires that a negative event or stressor must occur in order for a person to be resilient. That is, it assumes a person can only be resilient *against* the harmful effects of an adverse event of some form. By extension, this also means that only people who have endured similar life events and stressors can be readily compared in terms of their resilience. Second, this definition implies that the best outcome in the face of adversity is *no change*. Yet this underestimates people's capacity to *thrive* in adversity (Bonanno, 2008), and is not in line with a growing body of research which shows that a significant proportion of people who have experienced trauma report *post-traumatic growth* – the perception that the experience of trauma has led to some kind of improvement (in one's self or social relationships, or in life more generally; e.g., see Lelorain, Bonnaud-Antignac, & Florin, 2010; Muldoon et al., 2020; Shakespeare-Finch, Smith, Gow, Embelton, & Baird, 2003; Tedeschi & Calhoun, 2004). Third, a resilience-oriented framework could be construed as shifting responsibility for poor mental health *away* from stressors and events (and the systems and organisations in which they are embedded), and instead placing it on individuals (Oliver, 2017). This is reflected in the emergence of 'resilience training', which often focuses on providing individuals with the tools or skills to help them withstand stressors (e.g., see Fletcher & Sarkar, 2016; Grant, Curtayne, & Burton, 2009; Pidgeon, Ford, & Klaassen, 2014). However, resilience training programmes that overlook broader structural and organisational factors can be considered 'incomplete interventions' (Taylor, 2019, p. 10).

Acknowledging these critiques, in this chapter we focus predominantly on the broader concept of mental health, yet note that the evidence we review, and the propositions that we make, also have specific relevance for boosting resilience. As indicated above, our primary focus here is on what can be done to enhance mental health and resilience in a sports context (and particularly in an elite sports context where stressors can be especially challenging). In line with what has come to be known as *the social cure approach* (after Jetten et al., 2012), a key message of the chapter is that paying attention to the quality of athletes' *group lives*, and working to ensure that these are as meaningful and positive as possible, is critical to achieving this goal.

CURRENT APPROACHES TO MENTAL HEALTH IN SPORT

Individual-vulnerability models

Traditional approaches to mental health in sport have tended to focus on mental *ill*-health. More specifically, a common approach in sport (as well as in many organisational contexts) has been to view people who exhibit signs of extreme stress or mental illness as aberrant exceptions to the assumed norm and that they require targeted intervention (Kelly, Jorm, & Wright, 2007; Saxena, Thornicroft, Knapp, & Whiteford, 2007). In sport, this perspective has created a culture in which athletes have often been unwilling to seek psychological help for fear of losing playing time, their starting role or even their contract (Bauman, 2016). In support of this point, a recent review indicated that stigma remains the biggest barrier to athletes seeking mental health treatment (Castaldelli-Maia et al., 2019).

However, with growing appreciation of the issue of mental health in sport, it is becoming more common for athletes to receive appropriate support and less common for them to face discrimination. Indeed, today explicit efforts are being made to improve understanding of mental health among coaches, support staff and administrators, and to increase their confidence to engage with and provide support to athletes who they suspect are struggling (e.g., see Sebbens, Hassmén, Crisp, & Wensley, 2016). Often, the support that athletes ultimately receive involves referral for treatment of some kind, with the costs of this covered by their club, their sport's governing body or (particularly in organisational contexts) their employer (e.g., see Moesch et al., 2018).

This *identify-and-refer model* is probably the dominant approach to mental health in sport and organisational contexts. It is embodied in the rise of employee assistance programmes, whereby employers subcontract external parties to offer counselling support to their employees (Cooper, Dewe, & O'Driscoll, 2003). Along similar lines, the role of sport and exercise psychologists has transformed in recent times so that in addition to their traditional performance-focused role, they are now responsible for ensuring that athletes receive appropriate mental health support and, in some countries, for directly treating athletes' mental ill-health (Moesch et al., 2018; Weir, 2018).

The identify-and-refer model of mental health has several strengths. Perhaps most importantly, it vastly increases the likelihood that people who are struggling will receive appropriate support from a qualified health professional. It also involves the employer or club taking some responsibility (e.g., financial and moral) for supporting their athletes. However, the model also has a number of notable limitations.

First, it assumes that the drivers of mental health (or ill-health) are contained within individuals and thus, by extension, that providing treatment to those individuals will resolve the presenting problem. This overlooks the contribution to mental ill-health made by numerous factors that are *outside the individual* (e.g., external pressures, toxic team environments and poor leadership; Montano, Reeske, Franke, & Hüffmeier, 2017; Noblet & Gifford, 2002; Sinokki et al., 2009). Crucially, the model also overlooks the potential to promote good health by attending to these factors.

Second, the identity-and-refer model requires that people in need of support are *accurately identified*. This can never be guaranteed, and is a particular problem in sport where responsibility for identifying individuals that need support often falls to people who have no mental health qualifications (e.g., coaches, teammates and support staff; Moesch et al., 2018; Sebbens et al., 2016). For instance, many services and programmes that have been put in place by sport governing bodies and trade unions rely on athletes (a) realising that the services and programmes exist, (b) understanding and acknowledging that they have a problem, and (c) contacting the support services directly (e.g., see Professional Cricketers' Association, 2019; the Professional Football Association, 2019). In practice, this means that access to support is often delayed or only provided to people whose mental health has significantly deteriorated.

Third, while it would be negligent to ignore symptoms of mental ill-health, the treatment-focused approach is typically much more *expensive* than a model which prioritises early intervention or prevention (e.g., see Lynch et al., 2005; O'Connell, Boat, & Warner, 2009; Smit et al., 2006). For instance, in a non-sport context, Filip Smit and colleagues (2006) found that a minimal-contact psychotherapy intervention both (a) reduced the risk of sub-threshold depression patients developing full depressive disorder from 18% to 12% over the course of a year, and (b) had a 70% probability of being more cost-effective than care-as-usual alone. Such findings suggest that the most (cost-) effective way to promote mental health is to provide support to people before problems arise.

Fourth, this model does not align with the widely accepted *continuum model of mental health* that we discussed above. For rather than recognising that people's mental health can fall anywhere along a continuum from excellent to poor, the model creates an arbitrary distinction between those with good and bad mental health (i.e., those who need support and those who do not).

Fifth and finally, although this approach to managing mental health has been widely implemented in sport over the course of the last decade, there is *little evidence that it has led to a reduction* in mental ill-health over this same time period (Schinke et al., 2018). In fact, on the contrary, in recent years the Professional Football Association has reported substantial annual *increases* in the number of footballers approaching them with mental health issues (Bower, 2018). However, relevant data are thin on the ground, and so it is not clear whether (or to what extent) reduced stigma and greater trust in available support pathways have contributed to this trend. Nevertheless, there is little evidence that the identify-and-refer model is fully meeting athletes' needs.

Social determinants models

A further problem with the identify-and-refer model is that the most robust predictors of mental health in the population are *not* the kinds of warning signs that a coach might notice in a struggling team member. So while a player's personality or their lack of coping skills might be recognised as 'red flags', these are not the main predictors of mental ill-health. Instead, the strongest predictors are demographic factors: the wealth of the country and neighbourhood a person lives in, and their gender, ethnicity and stage of life (Blas et al., 2011; Marmot, 2005; Vigo, Thornicroft, & Atun, 2016). Accordingly, an alternative framework – one that is much more common in public health research than in sport – focuses on these social determinants of poor mental health which manifest at the level of culture, context and the environment. These factors can both increase the risk of mental health problems or play a protective role.

At its heart, this *social determinants approach* focuses on how life circumstances beyond individual control lead to unequal access to resources, and how this in turn leads to unequal health outcomes. This framework further acknowledges that various forms of disadvantage are not unrelated, but instead tend to cluster together. For example, people who are raised in poverty are also more likely to be members of a minority ethnic group, to have a parent with a disability, and to attend a school without a counsellor (Cruwys, Berry et al., 2013; Duncan & Corner, 2012). These different risk factors intersect in complex ways and, while each increases the risk of mental ill-health on its own, when more than one is present at the same time the attendant risks can multiply. This is true not only for common forms of mental ill-health (depression and anxiety), but also for severe and chronic mental illness. For example, rates of psychosis onset are higher among recent migrants and in poor, densely populated urban centres (Morgan & Hutchinson, 2010).

In the sporting context specifically, a social determinants approach orients our attention towards each person's 'load' of risk factors. Many of these originate not in the immediate team context, but instead in athletes' life histories. This means that each athlete is not on a 'level playing field' when it comes to the likely impact of additional stressors related to sport, such as an intensive training schedule, conflict with teammates, or a disappointing performance at an international meeting.

One strength of the social determinants approach is that it orients assessment and intervention practices towards the social and contextual factors in peoples' lives that affect mental health. However, this approach also has a number of limitations. First, it prioritises broader structural and social forces, without placing particular emphasis on the importance of local social groups (e.g., clubs or teams). This is problematic because, as we will see, local cultural and normative factors are at least as important as distal factors when it comes to understanding mental health in sport. Second, a framework is needed that allows for dynamic interaction between these multiple levels of analysis. Just as people are shaped by groups, so too they also have the capacity to engage or disengage from groups and, more particularly, to *shape* groups and their norms. There is value, then, in seeking out an alternative to deterministic approaches, which see mental health and resilience as either all about the individual or all about the social context. This 'middle way' is one that is charted by the social identity approach.

A SOCIAL IDENTITY APPROACH TO MENTAL HEALTH IN SPORT

Acknowledging both the strengths and limitations of existing approaches, in the sections that follow we outline a social identity approach to mental health in sport. Specifically, we draw on a large body of social cure research (conducted in both sporting and non-sporting contexts) to spell out the various ways in which social identities and social identification can play a key role in both *protecting* and *improving* individuals' mental health and resilience in sports contexts. Of the five hypotheses outlined in Chapter 2, the health hypothesis – that health and well-being are enhanced by identification with groups that have health-enhancing features – is thus most relevant to our discussion. However, while we address this hypothesis directly in relation to *mental* health, we also make a number of broader assertions that we structure around three key points.

Key point 1: Sport-related social identities are psychological resources that support mental health and provide a basis for a 'social cure'

Over the last decade in particular, a considerable body of evidence has accumulated that speaks to the mental health benefits of group memberships and, more specifically, of the social identities that people develop as members of groups (for a comprehensive review of social cure research, see Haslam, Jetten et al., 2018). More specifically, across contexts that include choirs (Dingle, Brander, Ballantyne, & Baker, 2013), care homes (Haslam et al., 2014) and creative writing groups (Williams, Dingle, Jetten, & Rowan, 2019), research has pointed to the capacity for social identities (a) to *protect* people against threats to their mental health, and (b) to *alleviate* mental health problems. This is true for both positive and negative indicators of mental health across the continuum discussed above: including self-esteem (Jetten et al., 2015), life satisfaction (Haslam, Jetten et al., 2018) and depression (Cruwys, Dingle et al., 2013).

Social cure research has also shown that these benefits generalise to a wide range of populations, including those who are socially disadvantaged or vulnerable. For example, in a sample of 52 adults from a disadvantaged community, the first author and colleagues found that joining a recreational social group – most commonly a casual soccer team – led to significant reductions in depression over a three-month period (Cruwys, Haslam, Dingle, Jetten et al., 2014). Crucially, this reduction was far stronger among participants who developed a strong sense of identification as a member of their new group, and meant that over a three-month period those who identified strongly with their new group experienced a reduction in their depression symptoms from the clinical to the non-clinical range.

There is also evidence (from both sporting and non-sporting contexts) that positive emotions and well-being are outcomes of *shared* identity. For instance, across three studies that were conducted in the context of different crowd events (football matches, a student demonstration and a rock concert), Fergus Neville and Stephen Reicher (2011) provided qualitative and quantitative evidence that perceiving oneself to share a social identity (e.g., as a Dundee United football fan) with people around you at a crowd event (e.g., a Dundee United match) promotes a sense of connection with those people that, in turn, leads to more positive and more intense emotional experiences (see also Chapter 9).

Although the vast majority of research that has examined the relationship between social identity and mental health has been conducted outside sport, sport was in fact one of the *first* contexts in which this phenomenon was examined. Across multiple studies, Daniel Wann and his colleagues showed that people who identify strongly with their local sports teams experienced several psychological health benefits, including greater self-esteem and vigour, as well as reduced depression and loneliness (e.g., see Branscombe & Wann, 1991; Wann, 2006a, 2006b; Wann, Inman, Ensor, Gates, & Caldwell, 1999; Wann & Pierce, 2005; see also Chapter 17). For instance, Wann (2006b) found a positive relationship between the strength of university students' identification as fans of their university basketball team and their subsequent well-being as assessed by measures of personal and collective self-esteem, loneliness and perceived stress.

In a similar vein, research has pointed to the potential for social identification to act as a buffer to protect mental health and reduce burnout in the context of stressful situations. For example, a five-phase longitudinal study that followed two theatre production teams from audition to post-performance found that people who identified more strongly with the production team felt less burnt out during the most demanding phases of production (Haslam, Jetten, & Waghorn, 2009). Along similar lines, recent cross-sectional and longitudinal research by Nik Steffens and colleagues found that organisational leaders can reduce experiences of burnout by *building* a shared sense of identification among employees through acts of *identity entrepreneurship* (Steffens, Haslam, Kerschreiter et al., 2014; Steffens, Haslam, Reicher et al., 2014; Steffens, Yang, Jetten, Haslam, & Lipponen, 2018; see Chapter 3). Recent research by Katrien Fransen and colleagues also provides evidence of similar social cure processes at work in a sporting context. Working with 120 elite Australian footballers, this study found that if team leaders were perceived by team members to facilitate a sense of shared team identification, this was associated with those team members feeling less burnt out and experiencing improved well-being (Fransen, Haslam, Steffens et al., 2020).

These findings bring us to the question of *why* social identities are protective for mental health. In this regard, there is now considerable evidence that speaks to the various ways in which social identities act as key psychological *resources* upon which people can draw when they need to (for an overview see Jetten, Haslam, Haslam, Dingle, & Jones, 2014). For instance, in line with the findings described above, one key resource that social identities provide people with access to is *social support*. In particular, research has indicated that the social support that people derive from their sporting identities is protective against burnout. Indicative of this, across two studies, the third author and colleagues found that social support mediated relationships between social identification and (a) stress, (b) life satisfaction and (c) job satisfaction among participants exposed to high levels of strain (i.e., people recovering from heart surgery, bomb disposal officers and bar staff; Haslam, O'Brien, Jetten, Vormedal, & Penna, 2005). Likewise, in sporting contexts, the social support that college athletes report receiving from their coach and that they perceive to be available from their teammates have both been found to serve as crucial buffers against the development of burnout (DeFreese & Smith, 2013; Lu et al., 2016). Together, then, these findings indicate that one important reason why greater identification with groups enhances psychological well-being is that it leads people to feel more supported (see also Chapter 14).

However, social support is only one resource provided by social identities that is protective of mental health. Social identities can also act as resources in other ways, including in circumstances where people are unable to directly access the *tangible* resources (such as social support) that social identities provide. Of particular note in this regard is experimental research which has shown that athletes' resilience can be enhanced by simply making multiple social identities salient. Specifically, across two studies, Jodie Green and colleagues (2018) found that people who had previously been asked to reflect on at least one important group membership were more likely to persist in practising a golf-putting task after negative feedback than people who did not reflect on any group memberships.

Along similar lines, Janelle Jones and Jolanda Jetten (2011, Study 1) found that the more groups an athlete belonged to the faster their physiological recovery after taking part in a novel sporting task (a bobsleigh, luge or skeleton run). Moreover, in an experiment that manipulated students' salient social identities, those who were asked to reflect on a greater number of group memberships (Study 2) were found to have greater resilience to pain (as indicated by the time they held their hands in a bucket of ice water). These findings speak to the capacity for social identities to promote resilience in the face of specific stressors. More broadly, they suggest that the capacity to draw on important group memberships in the face of stressors and threats to one's mental health is, at the very least, a useful defensive weapon in an athlete's armoury.

Away from elite sport, these findings provide a potential explanation for the well-established mental health benefits of engaging in physical activity for people from all walks of life (e.g., see Lee & Russell, 2003; Saxena, Van Ommeren, Tang, & Armstrong, 2005). That is, we contend that one important reason why sport participation is particularly beneficial for mental health (e.g., in comparison to other kinds of physical activity, such as active travel or housework) is that it typically provides people with access to at least one meaningful group membership (i.e., as a member of the team or club). Indeed, when research and practitioners think about sporting groups, they often focus on the (mental) health benefits of *the sport*. However, we suggest that it is equally important to focus on the (mental) health benefits of *the group* (Gleibs, Haslam, Haslam, & Jones, 2011). For in and of itself, the group is an important health-supporting psychological resource upon which they can draw – especially in the face of stressors that might otherwise compromise both well-being and resilience (Asztalos et al., 2008).

Key point 2: Multiple, compatible identities protect mental health in sport

Much of the research outlined above also speaks to our second key point, namely, that when it comes to mental health, it is generally better to have a lot of social identities than to have only a few, but better to have a few than to have none. This proposition builds directly on our preceding argument that identities represent vital health-enhancing resources for athletes because having access to *multiple* identities increases the *number* and *range* of resources upon which they can draw.

It is also for this reason that athletes who possess a strong athletic identity are at particular risk of *poor* mental health. Although this finding might at first be seen to contradict the evidence reviewed in the previous section, on closer interrogation this is not the case. This is because athletic identity captures the extent to which a person's athletic role defines who they are, often to the *exclusion* of other roles or identities (Brewer, Van Raalte, & Linder, 1993). This can be seen in the most widely used measure of this construct, the Athletic Identity Measurement Scale (Brewer et al., 1993; reproduced in the Appendix), which includes items such as 'I spend more time thinking about sport than anything else' and 'Sport is the most important part of my life'. Given the dominance of the athletic role and the reduction of non-sporting identities that a strong athletic identity often entails and demands (i.e., what is often refered to as *identity foreclosure*; see Adler & Adler, 1991; Beamon, 2012; Brewer et al., 1993; see also Chapter 16), it is no surprise that this has been linked to higher levels of burnout (e.g., see Black & Smith, 2007; Goodger, Gorely, Lavallee, & Harwood, 2007; Martin & Horn, 2013).

In line with this point, research suggests that when people place all their social eggs in one social identity basket (and thus severely limit the resources upon which they can draw) and then experience a threat to that identity (e.g., because they become either temporarily or permanently unable to engage in sport due to injury, illness or retirement), this places them at greater risk of depression and anxiety (e.g., see Giannone, Haney, Kealy, & Ogrodniczuk, 2017; Sanders & Stevinson, 2017; Sparkes, Batey, & Brown, 2005; see also Chapter 16). There are aspects of these dynamics, for example, that one can see in the cases of Michael Phelps, Kelly Holmes and Marcus Trescothick – which we discussed above. All were heavily invested in their social identities as athletes, cut off from other groups, and hence vulnerable to different forms of identity threat.

As a corollary, there is now considerable evidence that speaks to the mental health benefits of possessing multiple social identities. For instance, across eight studies, Jolanda Jetten and colleagues (2015) provided cross-sectional and longitudinal evidence that belonging to multiple important groups boosts self-esteem among children, adults and retirees. Along similar lines, a series of three studies by Katharine Greenaway, Tegan Cruwys and colleagues (2016) provided experimental evidence that *gaining* identities can help alleviate symptoms of depression. Indeed, in one study, these researchers found that simply asking people to write about an occasion when they had either gained or lost an important identity had a significant impact on their mental health. Specifically, results showed that compared to participants in a control condition, those in an 'identity gain' condition reported greater satisfaction of fundamental psychological needs (for belonging, control, meaning and esteem) and, as a result, *reduced* depression. By contrast, participants in an 'identity loss' condition reported lower satisfaction of psychological needs and, as a result, *greater* depression.

In line with these findings, a recent programme of research has also pointed to numerous mental health benefits (e.g., greater life satisfaction, better quality of life and reduced depression) associated with possessing and maintaining multiple group memberships during and after major life transitions (Haslam, Lam et al., 2018; Lam et al., 2018; Seymour-Smith, Cruwys, Haslam, & Brodribb, 2017). The processes at play here are articulated in the *Social Identity Model of Identity Change* (SIMIC; Haslam, Steffens, & Peters, 2019), which recognises that life transitions, such as changing jobs or embarking on retirement, represent a particular threat to health as a consequence of the substantial *social identity changes* that they entail (see Figure 15.2; also Chapter 16).

By way of example, an elite athlete retiring from sport might experience the loss or weakening of a professional identity (e.g., as a netballer), as well as the loss or weakening of an identity as a member of a team-based friendship group. On the other hand, though, retirement could also lead (or allow) an athlete to gain new identities (e.g., as a retired athlete or as a member of a social group that they did not have time to join while playing sport professionally). SIMIC's core assertion is that the capacity to effectively manage social identity changes such as these is critical for people's mental health and well-being in the context of life transitions. Specifically, the model points to the importance of (a) *maintaining* existing identities, (b) *gaining* new ones, and (c) ensuring that maintained and new identities are *compatible*.

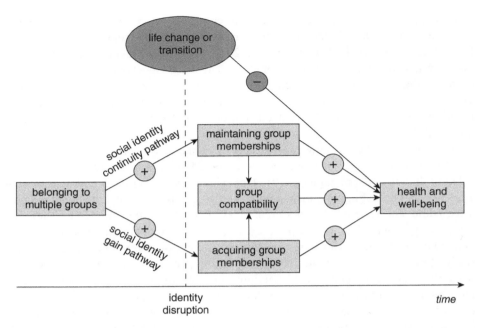

Figure 15.2 The social identity model of identity change (SIMIC)

Source: Haslam, Jetten, Cruwys, Dingle, & Haslam (2018)

This compatibility hypothesis addresses a caveat that applies more widely in relation to the benefits of possessing multiple social identities – namely, that possessing multiple identities can *drain* one's psychological resources if those identities are incompatible (see Brook, Garcia, & Fleming, 2008). Unfortunately, for a retiring athlete, achieving compatibility between new and existing identities is not always straightforward. For example, after several years of living the disciplined lifestyle that is needed for the majority of professional athletes to perform at their best, many may wish to relax the restrictions that they had previously placed on themselves when they retire, such as going to bed early as part of a regimented sleep routine. Although no longer engaging in this behaviour may be congruent with the content of their new identity as a retired athlete, it would likely not align with the norms that exist within groups of their former teammates – groups that they may still wish to be part of and to socialise with. Yet at the same time, the opposite can also be true: if the values of one's previous lifestyle are maintained (e.g., avoiding late nights), this might make it difficult to develop close bonds with new non-sporting groups.

In line with SIMIC's assertions, research has demonstrated that new identities which are incompatible with existing ones can compromise well-being (Iyer, Jetten, Tsivrikos, Postmes, & Haslam, 2009). Indeed, there is now considerable support for SIMIC's three key hypotheses in the context of various life transitions, including beginning university (Praharso, Tear, & Cruwys, 2016), becoming a parent (Seymour-Smith et al., 2017), recovering from acquired brain injury (Haslam, Holme et al., 2008; Jones et al., 2012), and workforce retirement (Haslam, Steffens, Branscombe et al., 2019). As the preceding example demonstrates, these hypotheses are clearly relevant to the transitions that athletes face during and after their careers (e.g., entering elite programmes, transferring between clubs, retiring). However, they remain largely untested in athlete samples. That said, initial support for SIMIC in sporting contexts comes from a study led by the fourth author with retired athletes from Western countries (including Belgium, Germany, Australia; $N=158$) and China ($N=183$) who had engaged in a range of sports at a professional level (e.g., basketball, cricket, track and field, rowing, hockey; Haslam et al., 2020). Up to 55% of Chinese and 43% of Western athletes experienced identity loss in retirement and this had a negative impact on their mental health and life satisfaction. However, those athletes who had belonged to more social groups *before* retirement reported better outcomes. Moreover, this study found that social identities accounted for 76% and 58% of the variance in life satisfaction, and 46% and 61% of the variance in depression, for Western and Chinese samples respectively. Neverthless, as O'Halloran and Haslam note in Chapter 16, more research of this nature is sorely needed to strengthen the foundation – and improve the efficacy – of programmes and interventions that seek to support athletes during these transitions.

Indeed, even without the benefit of such research, there is a clear opportunity to apply the insights afforded by SIMIC, and the social identity approach more broadly, to help improve programmes that aim to support athletes through career transitions, and their careers more generally. Existing programmes, such as the International Olympic Committee's 'Athlete365 Career+' (the Adecco Group, 2019), typically focus on directing athletes towards education, finding a new career after retiring from sport, and developing life skills. These goals are clearly important; and similar programmes, such as the Australian Football League's 'MAX360', which aims to support athletes' holistic development (as people, not footballers) from the outset of their careers (see AFL Players Association, 2014), represent further steps in the right direction. Yet these programmes essentially target the 'symptoms' of social identity change, not the underlying problem. To address this, we suggest that such programmes could be strengthened by including elements that (a) educate athletes about the importance of possessing and maintaining social group memberships for their health and well-being, and (b) furnish them with the skills to maintain existing group memberships and develop new ones (particularly in the context of transitions such as moving clubs or retiring).

One procedure that has proven value in this regard is *social identity mapping* (Cruwys, Steffens et al., 2016). As explained in Figure 15.3, this provides a visual representation of a person's social group memberships and network at a particular point in time. The process can also be used to track changes to group memberships and networks over time (e.g., around periods of significant life change, such as entering an elite athlete programme or when retiring). Importantly, this can then provide a basis for targeted efforts to improve the person's group network in ways that support mental health and resilience.

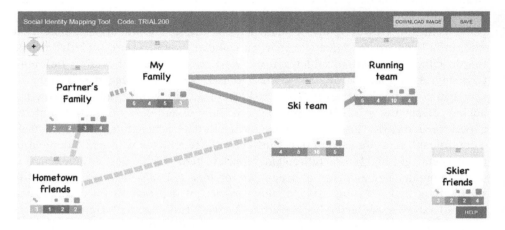

Figure 15.3   Social identity mapping

Note: Social identity maps capture the nature of a person's social identity network at a particular point in time. They can be completed in hardcopy (Cruwys, Steffens et al., 2016) or using an online tool (Bentley et al., 2020). Here the size of a box represents the importance of a group; groups that are similar are placed close together; and the lines between two groups indicate their compatibility. This map is based on one produced by a member of an elite Nordic Ski team studied by Jordan Cascagnette and colleagues (2019).

Source: Adapted from Cascagnette, Benson, Cruwys, Haslam, & Bruner (2019)

The value of programmes that include social identity mapping as a core component has been demonstrated in a range of non-athlete samples. In particular, GROUPS 4 HEALTH – a five-module intervention programme that focuses on processes of sourcing, scaffolding and sustaining meaningful group memberships – has been shown to have positive effects on multiple indicators of mental health. Specifically, it has been found (a) to reduce depression, social anxiety, stress and loneliness, and (b) to improve social connectedness and life satisfaction among students and community members struggling with moderate-to-severe psychological distress (Haslam, Cruwys et al., 2016, 2019). We contend that those who are interested in the mental health and well-being of athletes (e.g., sport governing bodies, clubs and coaches) would do well to take heed of such findings. For they suggest that there is considerable – as yet untapped – capacity to promote mental health by helping athletes to develop and maintain social identity resources. Indeed, not only should this help to make them more resilient, but also it should help them to thrive in the face of the various challenges that sporting life routinely entails.

Key point 3: Social identities are a powerful source of influence in sport, and this can help or hinder health

The preceding two sections have focused primarily on the health-related benefits of possessing multiple social identities that are meaningful and shared. In this section, we focus more closely on the *content* of social identities. Specifically, we examine the ways in which different features of groups – in particular their norms, culture and environment – can impact the mental health and well-being of their members. To this end, we discuss evidence that speaks to the ways in which group memberships can not only promote mental health, but also, in some instances, prove detrimental to it. Understanding and attending to the processes that underpin these diverging effects will, we believe, be vital for future efforts to provide more effective support for athletes' mental health.

One of the principal reasons that groups can have both positive and negative effects on health is that they represent a powerful source of *social influence* (Turner, 1991). For instance, considerable evidence points to the impact of group *norms* on group members' personal behaviours, especially for those who possess a strong social identity as a member of a given group (for reviews, see Reynolds, Subasic, & Tindall, 2014; also Chapter 10). In particular, a body of research has shown that people's engagement in health-related behaviours – for example, their eating behaviour, alcohol consumption and engagement in physical activity – are heavily determined by the norms of the groups to which they belong and with which they identify strongly (e.g., Liu, Thomas, & Higgs, 2019; Neighbors et al., 2010; Terry & Hogg, 1996).

Far less research has examined the role that norms play in the context of mental (as opposed to physical) health. A notable exception was a study by Tegan Cruwys and Sathiavaani Gunaseelan (2016). Among 250 people with clinical depression, this study observed that people who identified more with other depressed people reported poorer well-being. Crucially, this relationship was moderated by the perceived norms of depressed people, such that identifying strongly as a depressed person facilitated convergence towards group norms centring on depressogenic thoughts and behaviours.

Along similar lines, research has also shown that the capacity to transition from defining oneself in terms of a social identity with negative normative health connotations to a social identity that has positive normative health connotations plays a central role in supporting health improvements. Specifically, in a sample of 132 adults recruited upon entry to a drug and alcohol therapeutic community, Genevieve Dingle and colleagues (2015) found that *identity change* – such that participants shifted from a substance-using identity to a recovery identity – accounted for 34% of the variance in the amount of alcohol that they consumed, for 41% of the variance in the frequency with which they consumed alcohol, and for 49% of the variance in their life satisfaction at six-month follow-up (see also Dingle et al., 2019, for an extension of these findings to commitment to sobriety).

These findings highlight the contrasting ways in which social identities can impact health and speak to the important point that not *all* social identities are health-enhancing. Indeed, further research has pointed to more fine-grained nuances, with

evidence showing that a single group membership can have diverging effects on different facets and indicators of health. For example, in a sample of young adults
participating in a two-week summer school, Jennifer Howell and colleagues (2014)
found that those who were most central in this emerging social group (assessed via
social network analysis) had the best mental health (e.g., reporting the greatest levels
of happiness). Yet at the same time, these people also (a) engaged in less healthy
behaviour (in the form of heavy drinking), and (b) experienced poorer physical
health (reporting more physical ill-health symptoms such as coughs, sore throats and
stomach aches). Similar findings have also been observed among athletes, with Jin
Zhou and colleagues finding that, although the strength of university sports team
members' identification with their team was associated with greater well-being, it
was also associated with greater alcohol consumption (Zhou, Heim, & Levy, 2016;
see also Graupensperger, Benson, & Evans, 2018).

The key point for athletes and sport leadership, then, is that while belonging to
social groups is crucial for athletes' mental health and well-being, sporting and non-
sporting identities can impact athletes' health in both positive and negative ways.
Indeed, when it comes to athletes' sporting identities specifically, this assertion is further supported by a body of research which shows that the prevailing 'motivational
climate' within teams can have significant effects on their members' well-being (e.g.,
see Alvarez, Balaguer, Castillo, & Duda, 2012; Ntoumanis, Taylor, & Thøgersen-
Ntoumani, 2012; Reinboth & Duda, 2004). In particular, this research has often
focused on the perceived climate created by the team's coach, and demonstrated that
there are mental health and well-being benefits (e.g., greater self-esteem and vitality)
associated with a *task-involving climate* in which team members perceive that: each
player has an important role; cooperative learning is encouraged; and effort and
improvement are emphasised. On the other hand, though, this research has also shown
that when coaches create an ego-involving climate in which members perceive there is
intra-team member rivalry, mistakes are punished and praise is reserved only for the
most talented athletes, this is associated with indicators of negative mental health and
well-being (e.g., exhaustion and burnout).

In line with points made in several other chapters in this volume (e.g., Chapters 3,
11 and 13), this research highlights the important role that group *leaders* can play in
promoting (or else suppressing) group members' mental health and well-being.
However, while these findings are informative, a social identity analysis of leadership
moves beyond a 'one size fits all' model (e.g., one that assumes that creating an identical, supposedly optimal, climate will be equally effective for all teams). Specifically,
it argues that leaders will be most effective when they understand the distinctive social
identity of the group they are seeking to lead and then act in ways that represent,
advance and embed that identity (Haslam, Reicher, & Platow, 2011; Steffens, Haslam,
Reicher et al., 2014; see Chapters 3 and 13).

The recent case of Bury Football Club is an extreme example of the negative
health consequences that can unfold when leaders pay no attention to the identity and
climate of the group they are leading. In 2019, Bury was expelled from the English

Football League after being a member for 125 years. This occurred despite relative success on the pitch (indeed, the club had won promotion in the previous season). The ultimate cause appeared to be 'toxic and ignorant ownership of the club', which left the club in irreversible financial difficulty (see Halliday, 2019a). This was summed up by the club owner's admission that he 'didn't even know there was a football club called Bury' (see Haigh, 2019). The effect of this was felt not only by the club's staff, but also by its fans, for whom the club's demise spelled the loss of a key group membership and associated social connections and networks. The seriousness of this was indicated by the fact that, in the wake of the news, a number of Bury fans reported seeking mental health support to deal with this loss (Halliday, 2019b). Once again, then, this example highlights the ways in which sports group memberships are inextricably linked to mental well-being. Moreover, it demonstrates that the behaviours of those responsible for the fate and culture of those groups can have substantial implications for the mental health of all those affiliated with them.

CONCLUSION

In the first part of this chapter we introduced the topic of mental health in sport, and provided evidence that speaks to the widespread prevalence of mental ill-health among athletes, including among those who have reached the pinnacle of their sport. We then provided a brief overview of prevailing approaches to mental health in sport. While noting the strengths of these models – and the progress that their application to sports settings has heralded (e.g., in terms of increasing the likelihood that athletes who are struggling will receive some support) – we also noted their limitations. This led us to reflect on the benefits that might be derived from a new approach that recognises the many important ways in which social groups and associated social identities shape athletes' mental health and well-being.

In the second part of this chapter, we therefore drew on social identity principles to flesh out a new approach to mental health in sport. Drawing on theoretical propositions and supporting evidence from a broad body of 'social cure' research, we outlined some of the key ways in which social groups (a) *impact* athletes' mental health, and (b) might be more effectively harnessed in attempts to *improve* athletes' mental health. Our intention here was to provide an analysis that would be useful for athletes, as well as coaches, support staff, governing bodies and other key stakeholders who are interested in supporting athletes' mental health and well-being. In particular, our analysis encourages these parties to take heed of evidence (a) that social groups represent key resources for athletes; (b) that belonging to multiple social groups is beneficial because it increases the number and range of resources upon which athletes can draw; (c) that a singular focus on one's role as an athlete can increase vulnerability to mental ill-health; and (d) that the content of athletes' social identities can shape their mental health in both positive and negative ways. Moving forward, it is vital that sporting stakeholders accept responsibility for the mental health of the athletes in their care. That is, rather than outsourcing responsibility either to athletes themselves or to the broader health system, they must pursue better ways to support athletes throughout their sporting careers. It is our strong conviction that the social identity approach has a key role to play as a guiding framework for such efforts. Primarily, this is because it enriches our understanding of the challenges to mental health that athletes face, and provides a more targeted framework for the production of interventions designed to address these challenges and create mentally healthy and resilient athletic communities.

16
CAREER TRANSITIONS

LISA M. O'HALLORAN
CATHERINE HASLAM

Because I had to retire through injury, it felt as though I had been robbed of my rights and the dreams that I was hoping to achieve. Once I realised that 'I am now not a rugby player any more', there was a really tough period. It's such a destructive experience on a personal level – everything is affected by it. That experience of feeling valued and adored. Suddenly you're not as good; you're not in the limelight. (Ollie Phillips, World Sevens Player of the Year in 2009)

The first time I retired I was 27 after the London Olympics. I thought '[...] this is the best thing I'll ever do'. I moved back home to Kenya. When I arrived, there was this realisation that you're on your own. I felt lost. It was like I had fallen off a cliff. It took me six months to find my feet, but I was still looking for that identity. (Crista Cullen, Winner of hockey bronze medal at 2012 Olympics)

These striking quotations are taken from a 2018 *State of Sport* report conducted by the BBC to explore the impact of retirement on professional sportspeople. The report centred on the findings of a survey of 800 retired athletes and one of its headline findings was that, since retiring, around half of the respondents had had concerns about their mental or emotional well-being. The report flagged this as a pressing challenge for professional bodies that have responsibility for managing players' careers – an issue that has been echoed by athletes around the world (see Four Corners, 2017; Insight, 2017).

Retirement represents one of the most important transitions that an athlete will have to face – namely, that associated with getting out of their sport. Nevertheless, there are also other transitions involved in getting into sport – developing mastery, entering sporting academies, making it to selection – alongside any associated relocations. As the above quotations attest, transitions have major implications for identity as they all involve negotiating *identity change*. More particularly, all involve the prospect of significant *identity gain* but also, ultimately, *identity loss*. Research to date in this field has focused largely on the contribution that the strength of a person's *athletic identity* makes to how well an athlete negotiates these career transitions. This has been defined as 'the extent to which an individual identifies with the athletic role' (Brewer, Van Raalte, & Linder, 1993, p. 237; see also Lantz & Schroeder, 1999, p. 547). Notable here is an experience that is common among young athletes progressing towards a professional career in sport, namely that of *identity foreclosure*, characterised by early personal commitment to an athletic role with little exploration of alternatives (Marcia, 1966). It is not hard to understand why clubs and teams might encourage the development of an exclusive athletic identity and see other identities as 'surplus to requirements' or 'an unwanted distraction'. In line with this, there is evidence that athletic identity can be a driver of high performance. At the same time, though, having an exclusive athletic identity can make it hard for athletes to adjust successfully to some career transitions. And as the reflections of Ollie Phillips and Crista Cullen suggest, it can be especially problematic in the context of retirement.

To date, most of the research that has attempted to understand these different outcomes has focused on processes of individual psychology (i.e., those associated with intrapsychic dynamics or personality). As a result, group processes have not been a major consideration within established theorising in this area. Nevertheless, as we will see, these group processes have a key role to play in such transitions. Indeed, this is a point which is highlighted by various strands of social identity research that we will focus on in the second half of this chapter. These suggest that an athlete's group memberships – not only as a member as of a particular team or profession, but also (potentially) as a member of non-sport-related groups – have a key role to play in all phases of career transition: from the building and strengthening of athletic identity to the negotiation of its loss and the acquisition of alternative identities.

In order to make the case for a social identity approach to both the analysis as well as the management of career transitions in sport, this chapter starts by outlining Erik Erikson's (1963) theory of personality development, which has informed the conceptualisation of athletic identity and subsequent theoretical perspectives on career transitions. We then outline a social identity perspective on these issues, explaining how social identities shape the development of personal (athletic) identity and the process of adjusting to the loss of that identity. Throughout the chapter we use the example of English Premier League Academy football to contextualise both the phenomena and the theories of career transition in sport. Importantly, this provides a concrete example of what contributes to undermining transitions with a view to making recommendations about how they might be better managed.

CURRENT APPROACHES TO CAREER TRANSITIONS IN SPORT

Personality and identity development models

The study of identity development can be traced back to Sigmund Freud's early writings on the psychosexual bases of personality at the beginning of the 20th century (Schwartz, 2001). Erikson extended Freud's work by highlighting the role of social relationships and interaction (and not just biological factors) in identity development and growth (Shaffer & Kipp, 2010). In doing so, Erikson was the first to consider personality formation from a psychosocial perspective (Erikson, 1959; Kroger, 2004).

Erikson suggested that an individual's personality develops in eight successive stages across the life span (Brown, 1961; Schultz & Schultz, 2005). Each stage embodies a unique psychosocial challenge or 'crisis' for the individual, in which a cluster of biological, psychological and social forces come into play (Erikson, 1959; Fleming, 2004; Haber, 2006; Kail & Cavanaugh, 2007; Sneed, Schwartz, & Cross, 2006). Erikson argued that crisis resolution must be achieved in order for the individual to move on successfully to the next stage of development (Erikson, 1950, 1959). In this he also stressed that failure to achieve resolution during any of the eight stages may disrupt the later development of a healthy personality (Erikson, 1950, 1959; Fleming, 2004).

Of central importance to this work – and to our concerns in this chapter – is Erikson's fifth stage: *identity versus identity diffusion*. This stage is assumed to occur between the ages of 12 and 18 years. In order to achieve resolution, and further strengthen identity, it is argued that during this stage an individual must find optimal forms of identity achievement and avoid the threat of role confusion (Erikson, 1950). As such, the aim of this stage is for an individual to consolidate their chosen values and beliefs into their sense of identity as they strive towards 'ego synthesis' (Boa, 2004; Erikson, 1959; Marcia, 1980). It is important to note that this does not involve an individual simply 'learning' who they are (Erikson, 1950). Rather, in order to strengthen personal identity, an individual should actively explore different societal roles, attitudes, ideologies and occupations (Erikson, 1959; Fleming, 2004). This is necessary to allow the individual to make provisional commitments to life plans that will ultimately provide them with a sense of belonging in society (Marcia, 1980).

Building on these ideas, James Marcia (1966) introduced the *identity status model* to explain how such resolution might be achieved (Schwartz et al., 2013). This drew on data from the Identity Status Interview (ISI), which classified individuals into one of four identity statuses depending on how far their identity resolution had progressed (Kroger & Marcia, 2011; see Figure 16.1).

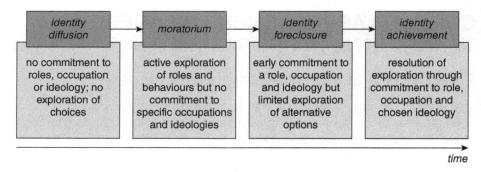

Figure 16.1 Marcia's four identity statuses

The first status of *identity diffusion* is characterised by an absence of commitment to any roles, occupation and ideology, and involves little to no exploration or evaluation of alternative choices in these areas. Moving beyond this, *moratorium* is a state in which an individual is still actively exploring alternative roles and behaviours but has yet to make a decision to commit to specific occupations and ideologies. After this, *identity foreclosure* occurs when an individual has made an early commitment to a role, occupation and ideology without considering other options. Finally, *identity achievement* arises when an individual has actively explored different roles before committing to a preferred role, occupation and chosen ideology (Kroger & Marcia, 2011; Marcia, 1966; Marcia et al., 1993; Meeus, 2011; Mikulincer & Shaver, 2007; Waterman, 1988). Where an individual is unable to successfully reach identity achievement despite continued attempts to do so, there is 'aggravated confusion' (Erikson, 1968) and less potential for crisis resolution (Côté & Levine, 1987).

Although Marcia's model provides an important elaboration of Erikson's work, it has also been criticised for being outdated and for not reflecting modern experience that involves young people extending their exploration period well into their 20s (e.g., while at university, trying out various different job roles or travelling). Nevertheless, it is argued that there are contexts in which the age range specified by Erikson and Marcia's theorising is still applicable, not least in the domain of sport participation (O'Halloran, 2019). In particular, Erikson's (1950, 1959) fifth stage coincides with the specialising years (ages 13–15) and the investment years (ages 16+) that are specified within Côté's (1999) *developmental model of sport participation* (DMSP; O'Halloran, 2019).

Marcia's notion of identity achievement is of particular relevance to specific identities developed by those who excel in sport. These athletes typically dedicate thousands of hours to practising their chosen pursuit throughout the specialising and investment years (Côté, 1999; Ericsson et al., 1993). This dedication contributes to strengthening and embedding their athletic identity, often at the expense of other identities. For example, in the process of becoming an elite gymnast, a young woman may have to set aside other identities (e.g., those associated with studying, friendship, recreation and relationships).

If the committee had their way, and it is one of their recommendations that is the first time a player would concentrate on the All Ireland Championships -see Irish Times 2009

In line with this point, evidence shows that international soccer and hockey players, world-class triathletes, and gymnasts typically spend over 10,000 hours engaging in focused practice during their childhood and adolescent years – significantly more time than their less-successful peers (Baker, Côté, & Deakin, 2005; Helsen, Hodges, Van Winckel, & Starkes, 2000; Helsen, Starkes, & Hodges, 1998; Law et al., 2007). Such engagement is strongly encouraged to develop talent, as illustrated by the Elite Player Performance Plan (EPPP) that the Premier League introduced in 2011 in an attempt to address the lack of 'home-grown' talent playing first-team football. Under the EPPP, Category 1 Academy coaching hours increased from 2,500 hours to 8,500 hours between the ages of U9 and U18. According to the EPPP, U9 is the beginning of the first stage in formal Academy football training known as the Foundation Phase. During their U16–U18 years, players enter the final stage known as the Professional Development Phase. Typically, by U18, the player will be offered a professional contract at a club or will be 'released'. While invested hours alone do not guarantee expertise (see Aggerholm, 2015), the structure of the EPPP programme highlights the time and effort that is invested by young athletes into their sport in the process of developing their talent. Given this, it is not surprising that such programmes lead participants to develop a strong – and sometimes exclusive – athlete identity.

Athlete identity and career models

As noted above, one of the downsides of a single-minded focus on identity achievement is that elite young athletes may lack opportunities or incentives to meaningfully explore other roles and identities (Brewer et al., 1993). As such, they are at heightened risk of *foreclosing* their identity during their adolescent years (Brewer et al., 2000; Marcia, 1966). Within the sport psychology literature, this exclusive focus and high identification with the sporting role is reflected in the strength of a person's 'athletic identity' (Brewer et al., 1993; Visek et al., 2008).

Research suggests that there are positive and negative consequences of having strong and exclusive identification with the athletic role (Williams, 2007). On the one hand, research has found that a strong athletic identity has a positive impact on life satisfaction and overall psychological well-being, as well as on performance, participation and long-term adherence to training regimes. Athletic identity is also associated with high levels of self-confidence and social benefits, such as an expanded social network (Horton & Mack, 2000; Lamont-Mills & Christensen, 2006; Settles et al., 2002; Sparkes, 1998; Wiechman & Williams, 1997; Williams, 2007).

On the other hand, when it is strong and exclusive, athletic identity also comes with costs (Lamont-Mills & Christensen, 2006; Park et al., 2013; Williams, 2007; see Figure 16.2). For instance, retired athletes with a strong athletic identity are more susceptible to a range of mental health problems, including feelings of loss, depression and hopelessness, than those with a weaker and less excusive athletic identity (Carless & Douglas, 2009; Douglas & Carless, 2006; Lavallee & Robinson, 2007). A strong athletic identity can also result too in more negative psychological responses to events such as poor performance, injury and deselection (Brewer et al., 1993; Brown & Potrac, 2009; O'Halloran, 2019). This has also been found to lead to emotional disturbances and inadequate coping when dealing with various career setbacks or challenging events (Brown & Potrac, 2009; Rongen et al., 2015). It is for these various reasons that athletic identity is so central to understanding career transitions in sport.

Figure 16.2 The double-edged sword of athlete identity

Note: Research points to the fact that there are distinct advantages to developing an identity as an athlete – on performance, participation and long-term adherence to one's training regime as well as on self-confidence (e.g., Williams, 2007). Yet at the same time, there can be significant downsides if this identity excludes all others as a result of *identity foreclosure*. These are likely to come to the fore when an athlete retires or experiences events within their career which are perceived as threatening to their role as an athlete (e.g., long-term injury, deselection).

Source: Thomas Wolter, Pixabay

Those who take on an 'athletic career' choose deliberately to be involved in sport over a number of years with the aim of achieving their full potential in their chosen field of professional performance (Alfermann & Stambulova, 2007). Developmental models initially understood this as a process of talent development that took the form of a journey through a succession of stages beginning in childhood, moving to adolescence, and then into early adulthood (see Bloom, 1985; Côté, 1999). However, the career development literature has evolved so that more recently it focuses on psychosocial development that involves changes in domains such as emotion and cognition as well as relationships and social support. This shift has arisen, in part, from recognition of the increasing demands that are placed on young athletes today. These include expectations to achieve and cope with external stressors – for example, those associated with media intrusion and organisational practices, financial implications of performance outcomes, and lifestyle choices and social constraints associated with intense training schedules (Mellalieu et al., 2009; Pummell, 2008).

Yet as well as failing to offer an integrated analysis of the range of personal and developmental processes we have discussed, an overarching limitation of all the models of athletic identity that we have considered thus far is that their conceptualisation of identity is profoundly individualistic. Here, then, questions of identity focus on the psychology of *me* and *I*, never (or only very rarely) on the psychology of *we* and *us*. Although this individualistic focus has provided important insights into the career span and lived experience of athletes, we would argue that these are shaped not only by athletic identity but also by the wider social contexts in which athletes develop, express and sometimes lose, their sense of self. These contexts are ones in which a *social* sense of self (for example, as derived from membership of sporting clubs, teams and organisations) looms large. As noted in Chapter 2, there is therefore clearly space for researchers to embrace a more holistic concept of identity, which also attends to these social dimensions of self – an athlete's *social identity*. Indeed, in what follows, we suggest that by addressing the wider social context into which players' personal *and* social identities are intersubjectively woven, it is possible to develop a much richer understanding of the psychology of career transitions.

A SOCIAL IDENTITY APPROACH TO CAREER TRANSITIONS IN SPORT

While the above approaches focus their analysis on matters of personal identity, this is not the only form of identity that plays out in the sporting arena. As Chapter 2 and work by Rees, Haslam and colleagues (2015) highlight, an athlete's sense of belonging with their team, with their club and with their wider profession can all influence player behaviour, skill development, performance, access to support and appraisal of stress (including that associated with career transitions – points that are also reinforced in Chapters 7, 10 and 15 of this book). Indeed, as we will argue, in career transitions, loss of team and club identity can be as significant, psychologically, as loss of personal athletic identity, and it can be even more important in the transition to retirement.

This point is suggested by the reflections of the Australian field hockey player, Simon Orchard, on the sense of loss that he experienced upon retiring from Australian hockey:

> Nothing can replace … the joy that sport (and in particular hockey with Freo) brings to my life. A sense of belonging, a family environment, a brotherhood of mates … and a home away from home. (Orchard, 2017b)

In Orchard's case – as in most of those discussed in the BBC (2018) *State of Sport* report – it was clear that his sense of belonging and connectedness with teammates, and local Fremantle hockey club, had a critical role to play in transition to a life after elite sport. This, however, has been largely ignored in previous models of career transition. To address this gap in the field, in the remainder of this chapter we therefore explore the various ways in which social identities and social identification shape athletes' career transitions. Here we focus in particular on how social identities can be harnessed to support players' development of expertise and performance over the course of their careers, and on how they can also function in protective ways to counteract any negative consequences that arise from the inevitable loss of their role as athletes. As this discussion makes clear, as things stand, data to support our key points is limited. However, by raising them, we hope to define an important agenda for future research efforts.

Key point 1: Career transitions involve social identity change

Social identity theorising recognises that the self is not only composed of those attributes and traits that are unique to an individual (i.e., the sense of *I*; e.g., 'me Simon'), but also defined by the social groups to which we belong (e.g., '*us* Australians', 'us Freo players'). Fundamental to this approach is the idea that, when groups are internalised as part of a person's sense of self, they provide the platform for distinctive forms of experience and behaviour. For example, when Simon Orchard defined himself as a member of a particular team (e.g., '*us* Kookaburras'), this then provided a basis for him to share with his teammates an experience of joy in response to particular group-relevant events (e.g., qualifying for the World Cup in 2018) but also to share despair in relation to others (e.g., losing to the Netherlands in the semi-final shootout). However, these same events would have held no particular significance (and may have no significance at all) for outsiders who have different group-based interests (e.g., because they are in a different team or do not follow hockey).

But, like athletic identity, social identification is a double-edged sword. This means that it is beneficial in some contexts but costly in others. On the one hand, strong group identification provides people with access to a range of psychological *resources* (Jetten et al., 2015) that, among other things, fuel motivation and performance, as well as a sense of control and agency (e.g., as noted in Chapter 6). Yet the downside of this is that when people lose important group memberships (e.g., as a result of retirement), this not only tends to diminish their sense of self, but also reduces their access to those resources, often at precisely the point when they need them most (Haslam, Steffens, Branscombe et al., 2019). It follows, too, that managing these resources can be critical when it comes to adusting to the life changes that career transitions bring.

One model that speaks to these dynamics is the *social identity model of identity change* (SIMIC; Haslam, Holme et al., 2008; Jetten et al., 2009; see also Chapter 15). This model integrates and extends the above theorising to explain how social group memberships and associated social identities shape people's responses to life transitions – not only in sport but in the world at large. As represented schematically in Figure 15.2, one of SIMIC's core ideas is that all life changes bring with them uncertainty and an associated threat to well-being. This is true irrespective of whether they are positive (e.g., joining an elite programme) or negative (e.g., retiring due to injury or deselection). However, the model also highlights a number of key group processes that can help people to effectively manage these threats.

SIMIC argues that one key factor which protects people who are going through life transitions is belonging to *multiple social groups*. The key reason for this is that the more important group memberships one has, the more resources one can draw on to cope with a given life change (Jetten et al., 2009). More particularly, this protection is understood to be provided through two pathways. The first is a *social identity continuity* pathway. Here, having multiple groups increases the likelihood that, in the context of disruption to a person's established group memberships (and associated social identities), at least some of their old networks are maintained and remain intact in the face of life change. The logic is that of not having all one's eggs (in this case, social identities) in one basket.

In the context of life transition, though, it is clearly the case that people often lose old identities because the change they are going through requires them to give up particular group memberships. This is where a second *social identity gain pathway* comes into play. Here, to help ameliorate any negative effects of this loss, and provide a basis for self-redefinition, SIMIC points to the importance of developing new valued group memberships and associated *new social identities*. Multiple group memberships contribute to this by acting as a scaffold and experiential platform through which new groups can be joined. For example, a runner who has to give up competitive running is more likely to find new avenues for self-expression and development when a number of other groups that they belong to (e.g., colleagues, friends, family) can open these avenues up for them. A case study is provided by the life of Roger Bannister, the Oxford University medical student who was the first person to run a four-minute mile and who, after he gave up athletics, went on to a successful career as both a neurosurgeon and a sport administrator (Saunders, 2018).

Importantly, though, for these new groups to provide a positive basis for support and growth, they must be *compatible* with the other groups in a person's life (Iyer et al., 2009). This is because relationships are likely to be strained when new and old identities are at odds with each other, or when tensions between past and present identities undermine the capacity for either to be a positive resource (Jetten et al., 2014). For example, if an elite athlete becomes a sports commentator when they retire, this may create tension if it takes them away from their family (whose members had been hoping to spend more time with them).

At the same time, SIMIC suggests that a person is more likely to adjust successfully to life change if incompatibilities can be resolved by bringing a person's post-change social identities into alignment. This is something that athletes can often achieve through the forging of new careers which draw upon their skills and experiences but remould these around a new social identity (e.g., as a coach or as a journalist). As Gearing (1999, pp. 56–57) notes in the case of professional footballers:

> Once they have succeeded in refashioning their former identities as professional footballers into a 'post-football identity', their memories and reminders of the past can be a positive factor as they age – whether these occur through the recollection of fans, the occasional magazine article or commemorative programme, or through narrative exchanges about past games with other former players.

There is now a large body of evidence that supports SIMIC's core tenets in relation to a wide range of life changes, including transitioning to university study (Iyer et al., 2009; Kwok, Haslam, Haslam, & Cruwys, 2019), becoming a parent (Seymour-Smith et al., 2017), recovering from stroke (Haslam, Holme et al., 2008), moving into residential care (Gleibs et al., 2011; Haslam, Haslam et al., 2014), and, most recently, in retirement from the workforce (Haslam, Lam et al., 2018; Haslam, Steffens, Branscombe et al., 2019). And while SIMIC has yet to be tested in the context of sporting career transitions, there are a number of clear predictions that the model makes to guide future research in this area. In relation to the foregoing discussion, two of these predictions are particularly important.

Prediction 1: Exclusive social identification (e.g., with a particular team or sport) is likely to reduce well-being in the context of career transitions

SIMIC emphasises the value of belonging to multiple groups prior to life change, as this is the basis from which a person accesses the psychological resources associated with social identity maintenance and social identity gain. Often, though, professional bodies and coaches encourage athletes to do precisely the opposite in the interests of developing their talent and boosting their performance. For example, as we saw earlier, this is the logic that underpins the EPPP's policy of ensuring that young footballers devote many thousands of hours to training in their formative years. Certainly, strong and exclusive identification with one's team may have positive ramifications for performance on the field (although, as Jodie Green and colleagues note, even this will not always be the case; Green et al., 2018). However, even where this is true, exclusive social identifications are likely to have negative consequences off the field, where a lack of positive group memberships to fall back on and occupy one's time can be a source of fatigue, boredom and even delinquency (e.g., in the form of substance misuse, gambling or criminal behaviour; Best et al., 2016; Sani et al., 2015). In contrast, having access to a range of alternative social identities (e.g., with one's family, community and other interest groups) is likely to have positive consequences both on and off the field.

It is also the case that exclusive social identification (e.g., with a particular team) is likely to be particularly problematic in the context of retirement – especially if it is unplanned (e.g., when it results from injury or deselection). This point emerges from interview-based research by Brian Gearing (1999), in which retired professional footballers were asked how they coped with the challenges of establishing a new identity after they had given up the game. Here it was common for players to highlight the challenges created by the strong cultural values and behavioural norms of professional football, as these created a 'gravitational pull' from which they struggled to break free to forge a new life after the game. Accordingly, where a player's sense of self-worth is derived solely from their social identity as a player in a particular team or sport, the loss of that identity through retirement can leave them socially barren and devoid of the social and psychological resources that they needed to cope with this major life change.

Prediction 2: Strong social identification (e.g., with a particular team or sport) can support adjustment in retirement if it is integrated as an aspect of an athlete's broader network of social identities

Losing one's personal athletic identity through retirement from sport is inevitable, and, as noted earlier, this often exacts a heavy toll on mental health, health behaviour and adjustment. It is here, though, that *social* identification (e.g., with one's team, club or sport) may serve an important protective function – providing it is part of a wider network of social identities associated with multiple group memberships. In this context, social identification has the potential to enable a retired player to live out their sporting identity by facilitating connections to other people with whom they identify (e.g., other players, fans) even though they themselves can no longer play. Indeed, this process of living out the joys (and sometimes the heartbreaks) of the game is similar to that experienced by team supporters more generally (e.g., in ways suggested in Chapter 17).

Social identification makes connections of this form possible because it is a process through which the others are embraced as contributors to a person's sense of self – as a result of depersonalisation in which the group (and not the personal self) is the salient basis for self-categorization (Turner, 1982). However, there is a caveat to this in line with our first prediction about multiple group membership above – namely, that these effects of social identification are more likely to be positive to the extent that they are not exclusive. Again, this is because the connections forged by social identification are likely to be more sustainable to the extent that they are distributed across a network of group-based ties rather than concentrated on a single group node.

Although we have highlighted only these two predictions, there are numerous others that can be derived from SIMIC, relating to concepts of social identity continuity, social identity gain and social identity compatibility. Although these predictions are consistent with a range of qualitative observations in this area (e.g., those of Gearing, 1999) it is also the case that, as things stand, there is at this time little or no quantitative evidence to support them in the sport psychology literature. Nevertheless, social identity theorising and its instantiation in SIMIC paves the way for a new way of thinking about career transitions in sport and, through this, to new directions for intervention (Haslam et al., 2020).

Key point 2: Social identification has an important but complex role to play in career development

As we noted in the first half of this chapter, to date much of the identity work on career transitions has focused on a sportsperson's personal identity and role as an athlete. This identity predicts motivation, commitment and success when playing sport (Brewer et al., 1993; Horton & Mack, 2000). However, we noted too that it has also been found to compromise athletes' adjustment to particular transitions – for example, moving from youth to senior level or from team to team, or changing from an active role as an athlete into retirement. In certain instances, this has also been found to lead to emotional disturbance that affects an athlete's capacity to develop meaningful identities outside sport

(Brown et al., 2018; Cosh et al., 2015; Gulliver et al., 2015; Stambulova et al., 2009). Nevertheless, little attention has been paid to players' wider social identities in the context of this change (e.g., their identity as a member of a particular team or club), despite the huge resources (e.g., time, effort, money) that are invested in building these identities over the course of an athlete's career (e.g., Chapters 5 and 13).

Again, one illustration of this investment is the English Premier League's EPPP strategy which, as we noted earlier, is used to guide English football players through the sport's professional Academies (Nesti et al., 2012; Nesti & Sulley, 2015; Premier League, 2011; Roe & Parker, 2016). The stated intention of this development is to give each player the greatest opportunity to achieve their full potential. This involves providing players with multiple levels of support (but primarily increased coaching hours) with the aim of developing talented players who can go on to secure professional contracts and seek out a career in the game. The most elite clubs in English football are granted access to U12–18 players on weekdays during 'core coaching hours' (between 9 am and 5 pm) with the understanding that tutoring will take place at the Academy so that they do not fall behind in their education. In practice, though, the majority of young players disassociate themselves from the education process at this point, and connect more strongly with the Academy and their clubs as they commit to football as a profession (Parker, 2000). Indeed, an ethnographic study by Christopher Cushion and Robyn Jones (2012) of young players being inducted into one elite team ['Albion'] found that Academy coaches work hard with players to construct a particular (and often exclusive) football identity in this context, which is primarily focused on the internalisation of the values and perspective of their club. As they observe:

> Constant messages, from how and where to dress, eat, train, play and behave, given to the players at Albion reinforced conformity through constraining ritual. Hence, the training sessions and games, and their continual reproduction, were an affirmation of the existing regime and, therefore, a containment of choice. (Cushion & Jones, 2012, p. 286)

Indeed, in the interests of supporting the development of team identity, coaching staff within a professional football Academy go to considerable lengths to encourage obedience, collective loyalty and conformity among players (Cushion & Jones, 2012; Parker, 1996).

As other chapters in this book attest, there is considerable value in developing team identification of this form – given its capacity to enhance player motivation and performance, and to contribute to the development of the expertise and skill that players need to transition into professional contracts (e.g., see Chapter 6). Additionally, this has the potential to benefit team cohesiveness and functioning (e.g., see Chapter 5). Relatedly, evidence also shows that such identification can improve the self-esteem of group members (Phua, 2012) and increase their social integration (Wann & Weaver, 2009) as well as promote psychological health by increasing extraversion and reducing alienation (Branscombe & Wann, 1991; Wann & Weaver, 2009).

But what are the consequences of building a strong and exclusive team identity at the point where a player can no longer continue in the sport that defines them? Like loss of the personal athletic self, it seems plausible that loss of team identity might also serve to compromise athletes' mental health and well-being. And, again (as noted in Key Point 1 in this chapter), this is particularly likely to be the case when that identity is exclusive. At the same time, though, unlike personal identity, social identity might provide a basis for athletes to resist and overcome some of the downsides of sport retirement. Not least, this is because the social identity (e.g., of the team or sport) with which a player is connected can live on in ways that an athlete's personal athletic identity cannot.

This possibility is manifest through the capacity for former players to maintain links with their clubs and sports through ambassador work, punditry, coaching and management roles, all of which provide a basis for social identity continuity in ways argued in SIMIC. And even where such roles are not available, such continuity can also come from the maintained sense of connection to the team and sport with which one identifies (as also reported in the case for fans; e.g., Wann & Branscombe, 1993; see Chapter 17).

So, coming back to the idea of depersonalisation, when a retired player self-categorizes as part of a team or as a player of a particular sport, they can still live out the joys of winning (and the pain of losing) through other athletes, despite not being in a position to play themselves. To the extent that this is the case, if it is appropriately nurtured and managed, it seems likely that sport or team-related social identification can continue to serve a protective function for retired players. Nevertheless, at this stage, this remains largely a theoretical point, as the capacity for social identification to function as an effective resource in retirement – or in the context of any other career transition – has yet to be empirically tested and proven.

CONCLUSION

I was at the top of my game – England captain, first choice, 63 caps, I knew what I was and what I was doing. I felt like I was at the top of my mountain. Then suddenly it feels as if you're not needed on the top of that mountain and you plummet to the bottom. You don't know where you're going or how to look up. Your whole being is almost taken away from you. I started sobbing [after England won the 2014 World Cup]; I was happy that some of my best mates were out on the pitch, but I was absolutely devastated and gutted that this hadn't happened four years earlier. (Catherine Spencer, England rugby captain in 2012, cited in BBC, 2018)

All of a sudden, a huge chunk of your identity, purpose and sense of belonging is removed. A life that took not moments, not days, not weeks, but years of effort and devotion is gone, with nothing but a set of 'guidelines' and a good-luck email left to help you overcome the slippery slopes of 'the transition'. (Simon Orchard, Australian [field] hockey player, cited in Orchard, 2017a)

As we have emphasised throughout this chapter, identity is fundamental to career transitions in sport. This is true all the way from a person's early development as an athlete to their retirement. Where researchers have reflected on these matters, their focus to date has been largely on understanding the role of personal athletic identity in these transitions – notably, how a person comes to see themselves as an athlete, what the implications of this are, and what happens when they lose that identity.

This research is important, but, as we have seen, it has largely overlooked the role that social identity processes play in career transitions in sport. These relate to the various groups that athletes join and leave over the course of their career and to the sense of identity they derive from these: derived from their club, their team and their profession. As we have seen, these social identities are not only bound up with personal identity, so that what it means for a person to be an athlete cannot be separated from the various groups they are in; but they also exert a particular influence of people's experience of career transitions. In particular, this is because such things as injury, deselection and retirement generally involve loss of highly valued social identities and, in the absence of any alternative identities to fall back on or to acquire, this can be devastating. In the words of Catherine Spencer above, it can be like plummeting down a mountain.

Accordingly, not only does attention to matters of social identity have the capacity to support the development of a more holistic understanding of career transitions in sport; as we suggested in the second half of this chapter, it also provides a new perspective from which to work with athletes to better mitigate the negative impact of within-career events which threaten and undermine a person's sense of social identity. Going forward, the key goal for researchers and practitioners is therefore to translate the knowledge we have gained about these identity dynamics into practical interventions that support more successful adaptation to retirement and other career transitions. In providing a solid foundation for this activity, the social identity approach we have outlined moves us a step closer to this important goal.

SECTION 5

PARTISANSHIP

17

FAN BEHAVIOUR AND LOYALTY

FILIP BOEN
DANIEL L. WANN
IOURI BERNACHE-ASSOLLANT
S. ALEXANDER HASLAM
KATRIEN FRANSEN

One thing I know for sure about being a fan is this: it is not a vicarious pleasure, despite all the appearances to the contrary, and those who say they would rather do than watch are missing the point. Football is a context where watching *becomes* doing. ... The joy we feel ... is not a celebration of others' good fortune, but a celebration of our own; and when there is a disastrous defeat the sorrow that engulfs us is, in effect, self-pity, and anyone who wishes to understand how football is consumed must realise this above all things. (Hornby, 1992, pp. 186–187)

Why do sport fans, and in particular fans who support a sport team, often behave so strangely? We are sure that many readers, especially those who do not feel much affinity to sport, are at times astounded by the extent to which fans sympathise with their favourite team. Those readers might pity the fans for depending upon the performance of athletes with whom they have no personal relationship, and at times even look down on them for displaying such intense emotions, ranging from ecstasy to downright depression. The readers might behave like the popular cartoon character Obelix, the fat friend of Asterix the Gaul, who, when he encounters non-Gallic cultures and customs, exclaims: 'These Romans are crazy!' or 'These Britons are crazy!'

Sport fans do indeed do remarkable, seemingly 'crazy' things. For example, during the 2018 Football World Cup, Belgium (the country of the first author of this chapter) experienced a collective frenzy when the national team, the Red Devils, qualified for the semi-finals. Even though the most popular political party at that moment was striving for an independent Flanders – a process which would effectively split the country in two – hundreds of thousands of Flemish citizens gathered in streets and squares around gigantic television screens to share their joy and sadness when Hazard and Kompany were playing for a united Belgium. Suddenly, countless houses displayed flags with the Belgian colours instead of the Flemish lion, and the mirrors of cars were dressed with tricoloured devil's ears, at least until the moment Belgium was eliminated. Similar phenomena were observed in other countries that performed well in the same competition, as seen in England, where complete strangers exchanged the greeting 'It's coming home!' as their national team progressed in their efforts to bring the cup back where it 'belonged'.

Yet the most extreme forms of fan behaviour are typically seen not among the fans of national teams, but among those of club or college teams. For some, this connectedness with their team is something they take to the grave. This, for example, explains why the fans of a number of soccer teams across the world have the opportunity to be buried in a coffin in the colours of their favourite team (e.g., Fluminense and Flamengo in Brazil, FC Reading in England, Schalke 04 and Borussia Dortmund in Germany). Similar services are also now available in the United States for a range of collegiate and professional baseball and American football teams.

On the basis of extreme behaviours such as this, many people see sport fans as a poorly developed human sub-species, characterised by a dangerous form of irrationality (see also Chapter 18). Indeed, as Marsh (1977, p. 256) notes, many newspaper readers are routinely told that 'Soccer fans [are] *worse* than animals.' In this chapter, we follow Marsh in challenging this prejudicial view of sport fans and their actions. We will argue instead that the passionate behaviour of sport fans can be attributed largely to the *meaning* that their identities as sports fans assume in a particular social environment, rather than to their personalities.

In this sense, sport fans constitute very interesting 'guinea pigs' to help us better understand the importance of social context, and of internalised group norms, for human behaviour. In this context, we also make the point that various forms of fan behaviour do not fundamentally differ from group behaviours that occur in other contexts. The same underlying laws apply, and moreover these can largely be seen as the manifestation of social identity processes (e.g., as discussed in Chapter 2). For this reason, we agree with the American journalist Eric Simons (2013, p. 312), who concluded his book on *The Secret Lives of Sports Fans* by noting that 'We sport fans are glorious expressions of all the wondrous quirks and oddities in human nature.' Indeed, in line with this sentiment, we suggest that fandom serves as a vivid illustration of how important and ingrained group behaviour is for humans – and that rather than being base or dysfunctional, this is actually a manifestation of our inherent sociality.

THE INTENSITY OF GROUP BEHAVIOUR IN SPORT CONTEXTS

In what follows, we argue that compared to group behaviour in other contexts (e.g., in organisations, politics or pop culture), group behaviour becomes more easily intensified in sport contexts due to three specific structural characteristics of sporting competitions: (a) the zero-sum nature of events (i.e., so that outcomes involve either winning or losing), (b) the frequency, intensity and clarity of performance feedback (i.e., so that everyone knows who has won and who has lost), and (c) the enormous level of attention that sport receives in society (e.g., in the media, in culture and in everyday conversation).

First, the zero-sum nature of sporting competitions means that in sport there is by definition a winner and a loser, and that they are publicly known. Although you can occasionally draw a game, ultimately there can only be one champion. In contrast, in other spheres of human activity, it is often possible for everyone to win. In many political systems, for example, multiple parties can win an election and form a coalition. And in business, many organisations can succeed and do so to the benefit, rather than the detriment, of others. Indeed, it has been argued that human progress has been driven by the transition from zero-sum interactions, such as war, to non-zero-sum interactions, such as trade (Wright, 2000). In sports, however, such non-zero-sum situations are unwanted because they go against the 'spirit' of competition, as captured by the sporting adage that 'A tie is like kissing your sister' (Gozzi, 1990, p. 291).

Indeed, a telling example of what happens when a sporting contest becomes non-zero-sum is the so-called 'Disgrace of Gijón'. This refers to the 1982 World Cup soccer match in which West Germany and Austria had to play against each other in the final game of the first round. The other teams in their group, Chile and Algeria, had already played their final game against each other the day before. Consequently, Germany and Austria knew before starting their game that if Germany were to win by one goal, both Germany and Austria would qualify for the next round at the expense of Algeria. Even if you have never heard of this game, you can probably imagine what happened. And so it was: after an early German goal, both teams refused to attack anymore and shamelessly passed the ball around the midfield for around 70 minutes without any intention of scoring. Neutral spectators felt betrayed, started to whistle and eventually waved white handkerchiefs in protest. But this had no impact on the teams' game plan. Although the Algerians subsequently filed a complaint, FIFA (the football governing body) could not sanction the German and Austrian teams. After all, they had not broken any rule, but simply shown a lack of sportsmanship and fair-play. Indeed, Germany and Austria were themselves both trapped by a non-zero-sum reward structure that meant both teams could 'win' so long as the score remained 1–0. Needless to say, though, because it was such a debacle, FIFA decreed that in future tournaments the final games of the qualifying round would be played at the same time. The lesson of Gijón was thus that just as nature abhors a vacuum, so sport abhors a non-zero-sum reward structure.

The second unique structural characteristic of sports is that participants and their fans receive immediate and very clear feedback about the status of their team: the winner is the team with the highest score (or the fastest time, etc.), and the best teams are those that win most frequently. Sometimes intense discussions take place about how (un)deserved a certain victory is, and about whether the (video-) referee has made a mistake, but ultimately it is crystal clear to anyone which team has gained the most points and is therefore the winner. Yet in other walks of life it often much more difficult to identify the winner. For example, the political sphere is one where the winner depends very much on who you listen to and which paper you read. Moreover, all parties can interpret a political event in their own favour – as seen when supporters of both sides claim victory after televised election debates. Only when there are elections do political parties receive immediate and clear feedback in the ways that sports teams do. However, elections take place infrequently (just imagine if there were an election each week). In effect, then, this means that athletes and fans have to live with permanent 'election fever' as, over the course of a season, they receive unambiguous zero-sum feedback about their status at least once per week (and sometimes almost daily). The emotional and behavioural consequences of feedback on group status are direct, intense and ongoing. In a way that is not really true for any other group, elation and deflation are the staple diet of athletes and sport fans.

As a final structural characteristic, in most societies and cultures, people have a seemingly insatiable desire for sports news, rendering comparisons between players and teams permanently salient. As a result, sport fans are continuously bombarded with information about the status of their favourite athletes and teams. Indeed, it is astonishing how much exposure sport receives in the media and how much it is a part of both culture and everyday conversation (Lowes, 1999). What is more, this exposure is not reserved for extraordinary feats, but frequently relates to mundane and rather prosaic details of sporting life, such that it is sometimes referred to as the toy department of news media (Rowe, 2007). It is hard to imagine a world in which music or fashion (or science and education) would receive the same amount of attention.

The consequence of the three abovementioned structural characteristics of sport competitions is that sport fandom constitutes an engaging gateway to better understand human behaviour, and group behaviour in particular. In line with this point, in what follows, we will focus on social identity-related motivations that underpin and direct the behaviour of sport fans. In particular, we focus on fans' striving to belong to a group with a high status, their internalisation of both healthy and unhealth behaviours as group norms, and their desire for ingroup continuity. Through the lens of these motivations, our core purpose will be to show how the social identity framework helps to explain the fourth P of sport and exercise discussed in Chapter 2: *partisanship* (how people behave as supporters of sport activity). But first we will briefly explore the other approaches that researchers have developed to capture the mysteries and intrigues of fandom.

CURRENT APPROACHES TO SPORT FANDOM

Marketing approaches

A large number of researchers have examined fandom from a marketing perspective. In particular, they have tried to identify and formulate marketing principles that could be used to bind fans as customers to their team, and hence to influence their consumption patterns. For example, a multitude of studies have focused: (a) on the ways in which sponsors should connect their brand to the team (Biscaia, Correia, Rosado, Ross, &

Maroco, 2013; Chien, Kelly, & Weeks, 2016; Parganas, Papadimitriou, Anagnostopoulos, & Theodoropoulos, 2017); (b) on whether and how teams themselves should be positioned as a brand (Abosag, Roper, & Hind, 2012; Watkins, 2014); and (c) on how spectators, including fans, can be segmented and categorized as a function of their spending and supporting behaviours (McDonald, Leckie, Karg, Zubcevic-Basic, & Lock, 2016; Shapiro, Ridinger, & Trail, 2013; Solberg & Mehus, 2014). Although links have been made with social identity concepts such as team identification (e.g., Ballouli, Reese, & Brown, 2017), these marketing studies tend to focus on very specific economic outcomes. With some exceptions (e.g., Lock & Heere, 2017), they do not offer a comprehensive understanding of why die-hard fans often engage in extreme consumption behaviours, such as travelling thousands of miles a year to support their team.

Sociological approaches

Sociological perspectives on sport fandom tend to focus on political issues such as (a) the construction of national identity in international competitions (e.g., Barrer, 2007; Fielding, 2017; Holmes & Storey, 2011; McCarthy, 2007; Ziesche, 2018), (b) the under- or over-representation of minority groups such as females (e.g., Hoeber & Kerwin, 2013; Toffoletti, 2014), (c) the participation of people from particular class (Thrane, 2001) or ethnic backgrounds (Coackley & Donnelley, 2003), or (d) on the violent extremes of partisanship, in particular hooliganism (e.g., Rookwood & Pearson, 2012; Sekot, 2009).

One famous quasi-anthropological account of hooliganism is provided by the work of American journalist Bill Buford who spent eight years befriending football hooligans in England, in particular of supporters of Manchester United. The resulting book, *Among the Thugs* (Buford, 1990), provides a fascinating and detailed first-hand account of the culture of hooliganism in English soccer. However, as noted by many critics (e.g., Sigal, 1992), while Buford provided vivid descriptions of the fans' behaviour (e.g., during a number of riots), his explanations for that behaviour were rather reductionistic (e.g., suggesting that hooligans see riots as fun due to the endorphin production that these events stimulate). That said, he noted that rioting can make hooligans feel connected to their community and, as a result, sometimes lead them to act in 'noble' ways, thereby being a stimulus for extreme behaviour that can be constructive as well as destructive. However, as with other sociological accounts, such as Elias and Dunnings' (1986) *catharsis theory*, which characterised hooliganism as the manifestation of participants' desire to escape mundane reality, Buford's attention to the group-based determinants and consequences of hooliganism was very limited.

In addition, even though violence constitutes an important problem in some sports (in particular, soccer; Spaaij & Anderson, 2010), this is often overstated. Indeed, as Marsh (1977) notes, there is evidence that football fans are actually *less* violent when they attend football games than they are in other contexts. Moreover, only a very small minority of sport fans can accurately be categorized as hooligans –

that is, as spectators who deliberately go to a sports game in order to fight with others (Wann, Melnick, Russell, & Pease, 2001). Hooligans, then, should be clearly distinguished from fans who merely get involved in violence as a result of emerging group dynamics (Stott, Adang, Livingstone, & Schreiber, 2007). Indeed, as Stott explains in Chapter 18, a social identity analysis can help us to understand why it is that ordinary fans sometimes get caught up in behaviour that, as unique individuals, they would eschew. However, given the complexity of the phenomenon of hooliganism and the dynamics of sport-related riots (and their unrepresentativeness of fandom in general), in the present chapter we will focus on behaviours that are more typical of fan behaviour.

Personality and demographic approaches

Many psychological studies on fandom have tried to construct, or at least help to develop, a personality and/or demographic profile of sport fans (for a review, see Wann & James, 2019). Nevertheless, this research has generally failed to uncover many significant or meaningful relations between fan behaviour and personality characteristics. For example, studies suggest that fandom is associated neither with introversion–extraversion (Schurr, Wittig, Ruble, & Ellen, 1998), nor with impulsivity, openness, agreeableness and conscientiousness (Appelbaum et al., 2012), nor with optimism (Wann, Pierce et al., 2003) or trait aggression (Wann, Shelton, Smith, & Walker, 2002).

By contrast, and not surprisingly, sport fandom has been found to be positively related to demographic characteristics such as being male, being old or being a sport participant yourself (James, Delia, & Wann, 2020). It should also be noted that in addition to a number of methodological shortcomings (e.g., a focus on North American sport cultures, an inconsistent definition of fandom and the absence of a clear theoretical rationale), a personality approach to sport fandom, generally fails to take account of the momentary social context in which fandom is expressed, regardless of the individual features that might or might not dispose fans to specific actions. A key point here, then, is that sport fans do not behave and interact with others in a social or historical vacuum that is void of any sense of rivalry or solidarity with specific teams. On the contrary, when it comes to understanding fan behaviour, historical and social context is (almost) everything. And this is where a social identity perspective provides an essential contribution to our understanding of that behaviour.

A SOCIAL IDENTITY APPROACH TO SPORT FANDOM

In line with the quote by Nick Hornby that we used to open this chapter, a social identity perspective on sport fandom makes the point that fans do not merely 'support' a team because they like and sympathise with it, in the same way as preferring one thing over another (e.g., a type of food, a colour, a brand of beer). Rather, sport fans, and in particular *die-hard* fans, support their team because *they actually feel that they are part of the team*. Or to put it more succinctly, fans feel that they too *are the team*, and that the particular team on the field has the honour and duty to represent 'their' team. In other words, for them, the team has been internalised as a part of their self. As Brian Viner (2006) notes in his book *Ali, Pelé, Lillee and Me*, this also explains why, as a schoolboy, he knew (and 40 years later can still remember) which of his classmates was a fellow Everton supporter but not know (or remember) their first names.

For outsiders it can sometimes be hard to understand this intensity of engagement, and the sense of light and dark that it gives rise to. Why is it, for example, that a particular player can be cheered so enthusiastically by fans when playing for their own team one season, and then jeered so viciously the following season if they transfer to another team? From a social identity perspective, though, such contrasting behaviours are perfectly understandable, given that wearing a different shirt transforms the same player from an ingroup member to an outgroup member. Moreover, the depth of feeling that is witnessed here clearly goes beyond the ingroup favouritism that results from the 'mere categorization' effect observed in the minimal group studies that were discussed in Chapter 2 (Tajfel et al., 1971). Here, then, a player who defects to another team will be subjected to abuse because – and to the extent that – he is perceived as having betrayed the identity of the team ('us'). This is especially the case for players who once were prototypical team leaders but then move to play for the team's main rival, thereby sacrificing to their personal interests what they mean for the group's identity.

A striking example of this dynamic was seen in January 2015, when the Belgian international football player Steven Defour returned to the stadium of Standard Liège, the club for which he had been the central midfielder from 2006 and 2011, and which he had led to two long-awaited championship titles. However, after a failed international adventure, Defour did not return in the red shirt of the home team (as many had expected), but in the purple shirt of Anderlecht, Standard's greatest rivals. To 'welcome' him home, the fans of Standard unravelled an enormous tifo (i.e., a flag held up by supporters), the size of a complete grandstand, displaying a masked figure with a sword in one hand and the head of Defour in the other, accompanied with the words 'RED OR DEAD' (see Figure 17.1). The Belgian soccer world was shocked by this display of callousness. However, the game was allowed to start without warnings, and despite the general disgust expressed in the media, the club received only a modest fine of 5000 euro (and an agreement that tifos would be checked and approved by the club before all future games). It appears that the treatment meted out to him by the fans had the desired effect, as he lost his temper during the game and was sent off with a red card after two unnecessary infringements (e.g., deliberately kicking a ball into the crowd), much to the delight of the jeering Standard fans, who saw their team win the game against 10 opponents.

Figure 17.1 Standard Liège fans 'welcome' Steven Defour back to their ground

Source: Yorick Jansens/AFP/Getty Images

How can we understand the relative tolerance of the Belgian footballing authorities for this appalling act of partisanship? Before answering this question, we would make two observations. First, that attempting to understand such behaviour does not imply that it should be condoned or forgiven. Explaining a social psychological phenomenon is not the same as excusing it. Second, it is important to note that only a limited number of defectors are treated in the same way as Defour.

A social identity analysis of this phenomenon might start from the observation that Defour had not only been the captain of Standard, but with his passion and intensive playing style, had come to symbolise the hot-tempered atmosphere of Liège (which is not accidently called 'the Fervent City'). In many interviews, he had proclaimed that his personality and play fitted well with Standard – much more than with the more technical, academic and elite culture of Anderlecht. For this reason, Defour was perceived by Standard fans as having a leadership role by virtue of the fact that he was both 'one of us' (i.e., an ingroup prototype) and 'doing it for us' (an ingroup champion; Haslam, Reicher, & Platow, 2011). So while other renegades could be excused to some extent for following the big money and were seen as outgroup members the moment they put on a purple shirt, Defour could not be forgiven for choosing to move to Anderlecht because he had represented the social identity of Standard so well. For this reason, he was seen as peculiarly disloyal and traitorous to Standard's identity, and his act of perceived treason negated the successes for which he had previously been responsible – even though these had taken Standard back to the very top of Belgian football. Indeed, it was precisely because he was once so loved as an exemplary ingroup member that he became reviled once he appeared to spurn that ingroup.

Yet while the treatment meted out to Defour was extreme, it is far from exceptional. Indeed, a very similar pattern was observed when the US basketball player LeBron James decided to join the Miami Heat, after having played the first seven seasons of his professional basketball career for the Cleveland Cavaliers (where he was a two-time

NBA Most Valuable Player and a six-time NBA All-Star). James announced his decision on a 75-minute live show on ESPN, in which he stated (Abbot, 2010):

> This is very tough … in this fall I'm going to take my talents to South Beach and join the Miami Heat. I feel like it is going to give me the best opportunity to win and to win for multiple years, and not only just to win in the regular season or just to win five games in a row or three games in a row I want to be able to win championships. And I feel like I can compete down there.

Soon after James's decision was made public, the website of the Cavaliers criticised his decision as 'selfish', 'callous', 'heartless' and 'cowardly betrayal'. The business magazine *Forbes* went on to identify James as one of the world's most disliked athletes (van Riper, 2012).

To conclude, we believe that hostile reactions to renegade players can be understood as an expression of outrage that reflects the fact that symbolic leaders are seen to have betrayed and damaged the core identity of a valued ingroup. As we have seen, famous examples in sport all involve prototypical leaders who have brought their team success, but then leave that team, not just for a better or better-paying one, but for one that is a hated rival. In social identity terms, then, this is a potent double-whammy. For not only does it leave 'us' weaker, but it makes 'them' stronger. And for die-hard fans this can be very hard to stomach.

The case of 'renegade' players serves as just one illustration of the added value that a social identity perspective can bring to an understanding of fandom in sports. In the sections below, we will focus on three key points about fandom that are inspired by research in this tradition that further underline the usefulness of this approach. These points do not constitute an exhaustive list, but rather are representative of the way in which social identity principles can help to explain the seemingly 'crazy' behaviours that sport fans display – in particular, the often-intense loyalty referred to in the title of this chapter. More specifically, we will look at loyalty as a strategy in response to game outcomes (Key point 1), at the consequences of loyalty in terms of physical and psychological health (Key point 2), and finally at loyalty as an issue of identity continuity in the wake of structural changes such as a new stadium name or a merger (Key point 3).

Key point 1: The more fans identify with their team, the more their behaviour is affected by the team's status

Sport fans tend to underestimate the extent to which experiences of success and failure shape the expression of their fandom. Robert Cialdini et al. (1976) were among the first researchers to demonstrate this point and reveal the strategic nature of sport fans' allegiances. They conducted a number of elegant field studies which cleverly demonstrated people's tendency to emphasise their association with sport teams that were successful (rather than unsuccessful). Cialdini and his co-workers labelled this inclination to overtly display one's connection to successful groups *basking in reflected glory* (or BIRGing). he mirror image of this is the tendency to avoid or hide our association with a negatively evaluated group, a phenomenon referred to as *cutting off reflected failure* (or CORFing) (Snyder, Lassegard, & Ford, 1986).

In their first field study, Cialdini and colleagues (1976) observed students on Mondays at seven universities across the United States. Their observations revealed that on the Mondays following a victory of the local football team, a relatively higher proportion of students wore apparel displaying the logo or name of their university than on the Mondays following a defeat or a draw. A second field study showed that when students were asked to describe a victory of the university team, they used the pronoun 'we' significantly more to designate their team than when they were asked to describe a defeat. A third study indicated that this tendency to engage in BIRGing was more pronounced when the students' public image had been threatened first. More specifically, when the students had been given a difficult general knowledge test on which they performed poorly, they were more likely to refer to their victorious university team as 'we' than when they had been given an easier one on which they did well. In other words, students tended to compensate for a low-status personal identity by emphasising their connection with a high-status group.

On the basis of these results, Cialdini and colleagues concluded that people strive to be associated with a positively evaluated source (in this case a winning football team), because they assume that this positive evaluation will be transferred to themselves by perceivers – a process which can be understood to reflect the perceived interchangeability that results from shared self-categorization (Turner, 1982). More generally, this principle of 'success by association' is routinely employed by marketing strategies that seek to link famous people to particular products. The logic here is that customers will buy these products in the belief that some of the star's appeal will brush off on them when they do. Indeed, this is one reason why many successful athletes earn more money from advertising than they do from the direct income they receive from playing sport.

It should be emphasised that although BIRGing and CORFing were discovered, and have been widely replicated, in the context of sport (Bernache-Assollant, Lacassagne, & Braddock II, 2007; End, Dietz-Uhler, Harrick, & Jacquemotte, 2002; Jensen et al., 2016), these behavioural tendencies reflect fundamental social-psychological processes that also play out in other group contexts. For reasons we outlined in the introduction, these patterns will often be more pronounced in the domain of sport, but it is not difficult to expose similar behaviour in other contexts.

As an illustration of this point, Boen, Vanbeselaere, Pandelaere and colleagues (2002) conducted a field study to test whether BIRGing would also emerge in a political context (something other researchers had doubted; e.g., Sigelman, 1986). Two days before the general elections in Flanders, 10 observers unobtrusively registered 482 addresses of private houses that displayed at least one poster or one easily removable lawn sign that supported one of the parties in the election. The day after the elections, these observers then checked whether those same houses were still displaying their poster(s) or lawn sign(s) – a behaviour analogous to wearing merchandise that proclaims one's favourite sport team. The results revealed a strong positive linear relationship between the performance of the political parties (relative to the previous election) and the percentage of houses that continued to display their support for that party: the better the election result, the more likely it was that party supporters continued to signal their support. A follow-up study indicated that the BIRGing of the most successful political party lasted for more than one week. The same pattern of findings was also replicated one year later in a communal election (Boen & Vanbeselaere, 2002).

BIRGing can thus be used strategically by sport fans and members of other groups to raise their status in the eyes of others. But it can also constitute a strategy to heighten our self-esteem (i.e., our private sense of our own self-worth). In line with this point, Boen, Vanbeselaere and Feys (2002) showed that the tendency for people to associate with successful teams is not restricted to public behaviours, but also applies to private behaviours. More specifically, they investigated how often fans of 16 Belgian and 18 Dutch soccer teams surfed to the websites of their team, a behaviour that is not directly visible to others. The researchers observed that significantly more unique fans visited the website after their team had just won a game rather than lost one. Interestingly, this effect was not moderated by pre-game expectations, nor by the size of the victory or loss. In other words, fans' interest in their team did not depend on the newsworthiness of a given result; all that mattered was whether their team had won. These results suggest that fans tend to avoid engaging with the loss of their team not only to protect their public image (as Cialdini and colleagues' original impression management analysis would suggest), but also to protect their self-image. This accords with a social identity analysis which argues that – at least for high identifiers – identity-related behaviour is driven not just by strategic concerns, but additionally by a sense that the team is *part of the self*. In these terms, as discussed in Chapter 2, when their team wins, fans win – and this therefore shapes both what they do in public and what they do in private.

It is also the case, though, that a social identity approach would lead one to expect that fans' behaviour would depend on their identification with their club (e.g., as measured by the Sport Spectator Identification Scale; see James, Delia, & Wann, 2020; Wann & Branscombe, 1993). This is indeed the case: those who identify highly (die-hard fans) react very differently to victory and defeat from those with lower identification (fair-weather fans). In particular, research consistently finds that die-hard fans maintain their association with an unsuccessful team much longer than do fair-weather fans (e.g., Kwon, Trail, & Lee, 2008; Spinda, 2011). In other words, where low identifiers are inclined to desert their team once it starts to perform poorly, high identifiers make a virtue of sticking with it through thick and thin.

Speaking to this point, Koenigstorfer, Groeppel-Klein and Schmitt (2010) conducted a longitudinal study of die-hard fans of soccer clubs in the German Bundesliga that were relegated to a lower division. Their findings indicated that levels of (self-reported) BIRGing and CORFing did not change for these highly identified fans after relegation, and were not different from highly identified fans of teams who had not been relegated. Interestingly, the fans' self-connection with the team even increased after relegation. In line with a social identity analysis, the authors concluded that this was because fandom for these die-hard fans is about expressing identity and an associated attitude to life, in ways that require them to stand by it, not only in the good times but also in the bad.

Reinforcing this point, in a sample of French physical education students, identification with the French national rugby team proved to be a reliable determinant of fan loyalty in the face of defeat (Bernache-Assollant, Laurin, Bouchet, Bodet, & Lacassagne, 2010). More specifically, after the students had watched a video of the French team's defeat, the high identifiers did not distance themselves from their team (e.g., by CORFing), but instead engaged in a strategy of *blasting* that involved derogating their opponents and their fans (Cialdini & Richardson, 1980). This strategy of social completion on the part of high identifiers can also be understood from the perspective of social identity theory (Tajfel & Turner, 1979) by realising that die-hard fans are likely to see group boundaries as impermeable. For after years of proclaiming their loyalty to their team, supporting another team is simply not an option for them in the way that it might be for low identifiers, who can deal with threats to their self-esteem by transferring their support to a team that is more successful (i.e., a strategy of personal mobility; as discussed in Chapter 2).

Interestingly too, in a subsequent study, Bernache-Assollant, Chantal, Bouchet and Lacassagne (2016) asked French participants to watch another video – this time one that featured the French national rugby team beating South Africa. Here, BIRGing mediated the relationship between participants' team identification and their sense of national belonging, so that the more participants identified with the French rugby team, the more they were willing to engage in BIRGing (e.g., wearing French team jerseys), and this in turn increased their sense of national belonging. These results suggest that highly identified spectators need to share the victory of their team as a way to increase identification, at least at the national level.

Key point 2: Fandom can affect health and well-being – for better or worse

A stereotypical view of sport fans might lead one to imagine that their 'passive' hobby would be related to a range of unhealthy behaviours, such smoking and drinking. However, at least among American college students, research has found no relationship between sport fandom and either tobacco use (Wann, 1998b) or alcohol consumption (Wann, 1998a). Likewise, in the context of Welsh rugby, Simon Moore and his colleagues found no relationship between the health-related eating behaviour of fans and their team's performance in a given game (Moore, Shepherd, Eden, & Sivarajasingam, 2007).

Nevertheless, there is some evidence that fandom can sometimes be the cause of unhealthy eating. More specifically, Cornil and Chandon (2013) hypothesised that American football fans would consume more unhealthy food after their favourite team had lost a game. They argued that the defeat would impact the food-intake of the fans, in that the negative emotions experienced because of the defeat would disturb their self-regulatory skills. In line with this hypothesis, they found that on Mondays following a

Sunday National Football League (NFL) game, saturated-fat and food-calorie intake increased significantly in cities whose teams had lost the day before, while this intake decreased in cities with winning teams and remained stable in comparable cities without an NFL team or cities with an NFL team that did not play. Interestingly, and in line with a social identity approach, these effects were more pronounced in cities with the most committed fans, who might have the strongest craving for comfort food in the wake of defeat. Similar results also emerged from a second study that assessed the actual or intended food consumption of French soccer fans who had previously been asked to write about or watch highlights of matches that their teams had either won or lost. Again, fans' motivation to consume unhealthy – but comforting – junk food increased after seeing, or just thinking about, their team being defeated.

These results point to the negative consequences of fan identification for health. However, the authors also propose a potential remedy for these negative effects of team failure on eating behaviours. For in a follow-up study in the same paper, some fans were given the opportunity to spontaneously self-affirm. More specifically, fans in the self-affirmation condition had to rank a list of values in order of personal importance, and write a few sentences about why their top-ranked value was important to them, while fans in the control condition had to list the main features of a chair. The findings revealed that the unhealthy eating consequences disappeared in the self-affirmation condition. In other words, by focusing on the positive characteristics of their personal identity, the behavioural consequences of a (temporarily) negative social identity could be counteracted, which is in line with the *social identity approach* (SIA).

The above-mentioned findings seem to suggest that fans are at risk of engaging in unhealthy behaviour when their team is not performing well. However, the social identity of fans can also be used to promote healthy behaviours, providing that their club makes an effort to present these healthy behaviours as normative for the ingroup. Illustrative support for this point is provided by Football Fans In Training (FFIT), a men-only weight management programme delivered to groups of men at professional soccer clubs. This programme (which has also been developed for supporters of other sports and was discussed in Chapter 10) encourages men who are ardent fans of different soccer clubs across Europe to lose weight by participating in fitness regimes in the facilities of their favourite club. The programme motivates men who might otherwise be reluctant to take part in such initiatives to do so because this allows them to have physical and symbolic proximity to an entity with which they identified highly (Hunt, Gray et al., 2014). Speaking to the power of this identification-based dynamic, the 12-week intervention led participants to lose significantly more weight over a one-year period than those in a control condition, namely 4.94 kg in favour of the intervention, which is also clinically relevant (Hunt, Wyke et al., 2014).

Although Hunt and her colleagues do not explicitly refer to social identity processes, it is clear that their work is broadly in line with 'social cure' research, which is informed by a social identity approach to health (Haslam, Jetten et al., 2018; Jetten et al., 2012). More specifically, it is clear that Football Fans In Training seeks to enhance health by providing group members with opportunities to live out a valued group membership through health-enhancing normative behaviour that they perform together with fellow ingroup members. It should also be noted that fans exercise together near their team's stadium and in the official outfit of their club, thereby fostering the internalisation of new behavioural norms that have been endorsed by official representatives of their club. In all this, then, fans' team identification proves to be a potent resource for healthy behaviour change (in ways also discussed by Tarrant, Haslam, Carter, Calitri, & Haslam, 2020).

Research by Wann and colleagues also helps to flesh out the socially curative potential of sport fandom. In particular, an online survey of 1,400 avid sport fans showed not only that sport fandom was extremely important to the respondents and intensified their affective reactions to sporting events, but also that it was perceived to be a highly social activity that had very few negative consequences for their interpersonal relations (Wann, Friedman, McHale, & Jaffe, 2003).

Inspired by these findings, Wann (2006a) developed the *team identification–social psychological health model*, to explain the positive relationship between identification with a local sport team and social psychological health (see Figure 17.2). This argues that team identification facilitates well-being by increasing the social connections among fans. In ways that social identity and self-categorization theories would predict, this relationship was also moderated by threats to social identity and efforts to cope with those threats. Predictions derived from this model have been confirmed among both college students (Wann, Hackathorn, & Sherman, 2017; Wann, Waddill, Polk, & Weaver, 2011) and older sport fans (Wann, Rogers, Dooley, & Foley, 2011)

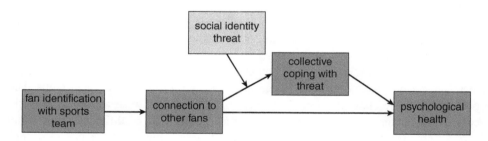

Figure 17.2   The team identification–social psychological health model

We would point out that social identity processes come into play in determining whether sport fans will provide or receive help in an emergency situation. As demonstrated in the first study of the classic paper by Levine and colleagues (see also Chapter 2), fans are more likely to help someone in need (e.g., who has fallen during jogging and is shouting in pain), when this person is wearing a shirt of their own favourite team than when wearing a shirt of a rival team or a plain shirt (Levine, Prosser, Evans, & Reicher, 2005). Importantly, in a follow-up study these authors showed that this form of ingroup favouritism could be counteracted when the more inclusive social category of football fans had been made salient. In that case, help was extended to joggers wearing a shirt of the rival team, but not to joggers wearing a plain shirt.

For this reason, we would argue that future research should focus more directly on ways in which social cure interventions might be applied more systematically to fandom with a view to improving the health of the large number of people who are sport fans. As an example of such an intervention, in November 2016 the Belgian soccer club KAA Gent broadcasted clips during half-time in the team's home fixtures. In these clips, the club's coach and one of its players openly discussed how they coped with failures in their life and encouraged fans to talk with others about their mental problems instead of hiding them. More generally, such initiatives speak to the huge potential for sport-based identity leadership to harness social identification and social connection in the interest of promoting health in society at large.

Key point 3: Fans typically find social identity change troubling

Even if there are sound economic reasons to change the name of a club or a stadium, or to redesign a logo or a team shirt, marketers are often surprised by the level of resistance to change that sport fans display. Their surprise stems from a failure to understand how important and pervasive the social identity of sport fans can be and how, for fans, their sport is much more than a game. For example, in a survey of English football fans, respondents tended to agree with the statement that their preferred football team's home stadium was their home too (Charleston, 2009).

As a consequence, if a club leaves its home ground for a new stadium or the stadium is renamed, this can be very disturbing for fans. As an illustration of this point, in his book *Home From Home*, journalist and West Ham fan Brian Williams describes how in 2016 his life as a supporter was turned upside down by West Ham's move from the legendary Upton Park (the Boleyn Ground) (capacity: 35,000) to the Olympic Stadium (capacity: 60,000) (Williams, 2017). Although the move was said to be necessary for the club 'to reach the next level', the consequences for die-hard fans were profound. For example, fans had to abandon their lifelong match-day rituals in the lively residential area where Upton Park was located and journey to the isolated Olympic Park where only corporate catering was available. For this and other reasons, the gigantic but soulless new stadium (which was originally built to host athletic events during the 2012 London Olympic Games) failed to feel like a new home.

Riffing on this experience, Williams complains that football has become a managerial exercise in brand marketing that ignores the historical dimensions of the deeply ingrained social identities that are bound up with being a fan of a sport club. In a similar vein, Josh Boyd (2000) argues that the latter-day practice of giving corporate names to stadiums does violence to the public memory of what are, in identity terms, sacred sites (see also Nauright & Schimmel, 2005; Woisetschläger, Haselhoff, & Backhaus, 2014). A telling example is the Westfalenstadion of the very popular German football club Borussia Dortmund. Facing serious financial problems in the beginning of this century, an insurance company offered the club enough money to change the name to Signal Iduna Park from 2005 until 2021.

Despite the financial salvation by the insurance company, the fans still refer to the stadium as Westfalenstadion and refuse to use the official name.

In line with this argument, John Reysen and colleagues showed that fans perceive such changes to constitute a serious threat to their team's distinctive identity and that this in turn can elicit feelings of anger, particularly among those who are highly identified (Reysen, Snider, & Branscombe, 2012). Likewise, a study by John Schultz and John Scheffer (2018) argues that the removal or replacement of a team's long-standing mascot can represent a significant social identity threat for those same highly identified fans. These various lines of evidence suggest that what clubs package as reform, fans can often experience as heresy – striking at the heart of an identity they hold dear and that defines their core sense of selfhood.

This point is even more true when the primary identity of a team itself undergoes change. For this reason, fans often perceive mergers between sport clubs as a very profound form of social identity threat. Nevertheless, over the course of the last few decades, a large number of clubs have merged – largely out of economic necessity. For example, of the 24 Belgian professional soccer clubs that played in the two highest leagues in the 2018–2019 season, 12 (i.e., 50%) have been involved in a merger. Likewise, when the Australian Rugby League merged with the Australian Super League in 1998, the need to cut the competition down from 20 teams to 14 led to the creation of three newly merged entities. In these, as in most other such cases, the newly merged club was typically presented as a melding of the two (sometimes three) pre-merger clubs, with names, colours and traditions reconfigured in a new kaleidoscopic combination.

As a social identity approach would lead us to expect, and in line with work on organisational mergers (Terry, 2003; van Leeuwen & van Knippenberg, 2003), such events can have a seismic impact on fans – again, especially the high identifiers. Accordingly, in a survey of the fans of two Belgian soccer clubs that were about to merge, the first author and colleagues found that the more fans identified with their club, the more likely they were to resent and oppose the merger (Boen, Vanbeselaere, & Swinnen, 2005).

Nevertheless, Boen and colleagues found that high identifiers were ultimately still more likely than low identifiers to become fans of the new club, so long as their team's pre-merger identity was *perceived to be* sufficiently represented in the newly merged club. Likewise, in a study of the fans and players of a Belgian first-division basketball club that had merged the previous season, identification with the pre-merger club emerged as the strongest predictor of identification with the newly merged club (Boen, Vanbeselaere, Pandelaere, Schutters, & Rowe, 2008). Here again, though, for the fans, the perceived continuity of their pre-merger ingroup in the newly merged entity was a significant predictor of their identification with this new entity. Thus, the more they saw the merged club as a continuation of their team's previous identity, the more they identified with it.

In all these examples it is again apparent that the social identity approach provides us with a useful framework for understanding sports fans' reactions to the challenges of sporting life. Beyond this, though, we see that it also provides practical insights that can help sport administrators negotiate those challenges more successfully than they might otherwise. As we have seen, this is important not only for the financial health of their sport, but also for the mental health of their fans.

CONCLUSION

In this chapter we have not tried to offer an exhaustive review of all the research that has been conducted on sport fandom to date from a social identity perspective. Rather, by focusing on three illustrative key points, our aim has been to show that the social identity approach provides an essential addition to analyses of sport fan behaviour put forward by researchers from other (sub)disciplines (e.g., marketeers, sociologists, personality psychologists) and from other theoretical perspectives. Our sense is that the theoretical framework that underpins this approach (e.g., as set out in Chapter 2) provides a wealth of new insights into fan-related phenomena that augment and enrich the field in important ways and help to flesh out our appreciation of the fascinating world of sport fandom.

Because it exemplifies many of the key points we have made, we close this chapter by continuing the quote from Nick Hornby with which we started. The last sentence, in particular, captures the essence of a social identity perspective on fandom:

> The players are merely our representatives, chosen by the manager rather than elected by us, but our representatives nonetheless, and sometimes if you look hard you can see the little poles that join them together, and the handles at the side that enable us to move them. I am part of the club, just as the club is part of me. (Hornby, 1992)

18

CROWD BEHAVIOUR AND HOOLIGANISM

CLIFFORD STOTT

In May 1990 at Maksimir Stadium in Zagreb rioting developed between fans of the Croatian team Dinamo Zagreb and the Serbian team Red Star Belgrade. The riot fore-shadowed the subsequent war of independence and happened just weeks after elections in which the parties favouring Croatian independence had won the majority of votes. As the rioting was taking place, one of the Dinamo players, Zvonimir Boban, former Deputy Secretary General of FIFA, assaulted a police officer, whom he believed was mistreating a Dinamo supporter. Boban was subsequently proclaimed a national hero of Croatia for this act and is said to have stated after the incident that he 'was a public face prepared to risk his life, career, and everything that fame could have brought, all because of one ideal, one cause: the Croatian cause' (Baxter, 2018). Another key participant in the riot was Željko Ražnatović, who was then leader of the Red Star Ultras, the fan movement of Red Star Belgrade. Ražnatović, better known as Arkan, went on to form the notorious para-military group *Arkan Tigers*, which was responsible for many of the genocidal atrocities of the subsequent war in the former Yugoslavia. As noted in Chapter 2, Bill Shankly famously opined that football was more important than life and death. It is self-evident from this above example that, however extreme one might consider Shankly's statement to be, football partisanship sometimes directly entails these very things.

Football is by far the most popular spectator sport in the world. Nevertheless, the partisanship of the football crowd is notorious not just for its passion, but for its propen-sity for collective violence, or what is more commonly referred to as football 'hooliganism'. One of the most high-profile and significant incidents of hooliganism ever witnessed in Europe was the Heysel Stadium disaster in 1985, where 39 people were killed, most of whom were fans of the Italian club Juventus. Their deaths were the result of crushing that occurred as a wall collapsed under crowd pressures that were created as fans sought to move away from rioting between Liverpool and Juventus fans within the stadium. The disaster was regarded by the popular press and football authorities at the time as having been the direct result of English 'hooligans' provoking the confrontation. Regardless of the veracity of this assertion, English football clubs were subsequently banned from international competitions for five years and hooliganism was cemented as the *English disease*.

Beyond this, though, the Heysel disaster also set in motion an array of international policy responses. These created the context for a great deal of academic theorisation, but equally served to frame some other fundamentally important issues. The first was to cement the idea that these high-profile incidents of football hooliganism were crowd events, or more accurately were patterns of collective action and intergroup interaction that developed in the context of crowds. The second was to embed the idea of hooliganism as a way of describing these processes. As a description, though, we can see that this is extremely imprecise – covering everything from individual drunken boisterousness to mass disaster.

Pushing aside the problematic nature of the terminology, this chapter will explore the issue of collective partisanship in sport through a focus on the issue of football-related collective conflict or hooliganism. The chapter begins by exploring two of the most influential early theoretical approaches to hooliganism with a view to exploring (a) how these have framed our understanding of the issue and (b) the ways in which this conceptualisation has impacted upon contemporary understanding and policy. Here we will see that concepts of a socially structured self, group behaviour and intergroup dynamics were actually quite central to early theoretical understanding of hooliganism, but that these formative explanations became mired in false assumptions that collective conflict, like that witnessed at Heysel and in Zagreb, could be understood simply as a process in which so-called hooligans acted out a relatively fixed form of working-class masculinity. Moving on from this, the chapter will then explore how the social identity approach redefines hooliganism as crowd action and, in the process, not only redefines our understanding of the topic but also helps to tackle the problems it can create by reshaping the ways football is policed. The chapter concludes by underscoring the ways in which social identity is central to an enriched understanding of the interrelationship between partisanship and collective conflict.

CURRENT APPROACHES TO CROWD BEHAVIOUR AND HOOLIGANISM

Symbolic interactionism and the rules of disorder

Academic theorisation on football hooliganism kicked off in the 1970s and 1980s amid rising public and political concern about the phenomenon in the UK. Comprehensive reviews of this literature are provided elsewhere (e.g., Frosdick & Marsh, 2007), but this section focuses on what is one of the most influential works in the field: Peter Marsh, Elizabeth Rosser and Rom Harré's (1978) monograph *The Rules of Disorder*. This ground-breaking text set out to challenge hegemonic media discourses about the mindless, meaningless and pathological nature of hooliganism. The book provides a detailed empirical study of the behaviour and phenomenology of fans who stood regularly on the home terrace, or London Road End, of Oxford United FC (a club that Marsh was Director of at the time). A key conclusion of the authors' research was that the crowd that populated the terrace was not chaotic and mindless, but instead organised and structured.

This structure had three key dimensions. First, the fans identified with distinct groups, that they labelled the *Newbies*, *Rowdies* as well as the older and more powerful *Town Boys*. Second, the groups had a social hierarchy that individuals could progress through over time. Third, and most central to the researchers' thesis, they argued that these groups were a platform for working-class youth to engage in ritualised aggression, in the form of football hooliganism, in ways that gave meaning to hooligans' otherwise disempowered lives and through which they could gain status and self-esteem.

Figure 18.1   Oxford United's Manor Ground in the 1970s

Note: The ground was the site of Peter Marsh and colleagues' (1978) ground-breaking ethnogenic study of football fans' behaviour *The Rules of Disorder*. This suggested that the deviant behaviour of different groups of fans was a collective performance structured by a shared set of normative rules that they had learned and internalised.

Source: Steve Daniels, Geograph

This analysis of hooliganism was based on some key post-war sociological theories and assumptions. In particular, from a functionalist and social determinist perspective the researchers drew upon the work of Talcott Parsons (1962) to argue that to understand hooliganism one has to consider the role of the school as a social context in which children take on board the values necessary for adult life within the larger industrial social order. Yet while the structural power relations of the classroom were important, Marsh and colleagues asserted that the 'social structure of the society of the classroom seems to us as well adapted to be the nursery of crime as it is of good behaviour' (1978, p. 3). For them, then, it was not so much the classroom as the autonomous power relationships of the playground that were important, because it was here that identities of youth sub-cultures of deviancy were developed through an emergent 'world of ritual and formal genesis of a respected self' (1978, p. 3). In this way, hooliganism was understood not only as a phenomenon that arose from a deviant subculture within the structural context and institutions of the industrial working class, but also as a manifestation of the collective self as it operated within the structures and dynamics of institutionalised power.

Marsh and colleagues also recognised the importance of social representations, particularly with regard to the role of media discourses about hooliganism. Utilising Stanley Cohen's (1972) concept of the moral panic, they asserted that hooliganism was to some extent linguistically constructed by powerful groups as a form of modern 'folk devil'. In this sense, hooliganism was seen to be a rhetorical construct that served a sociological function, acting as an example of that which is proscribed, thus allowing powerful political actors to entrepreneurially position themselves as a solution to the 'crisis of public order' (see Reicher, Hopkins, & Condor, 1997). In this respect, Marsh and colleagues' work was part of a wider body of Marxist cultural theory (e.g., see Hall, Critcher, Jefferson, Clarke, & Roberts, 1978), which aimed to challenge the media hegemony of moral condemnation. In this case, it did so by proposing an alternative theoretical account of what was happening on the football terraces, 'an account based not on the second-hand rhetoric of myth-creating media men but on our faith in people's ability to render their own social action intelligible and meaningful' (Marsh et al., 1978, p. 10).

Marsh and colleagues did not limit their ideas of social construction merely to discourse. They also drew on Howard Becker's (1963) *labelling theory*, in which 'deviance' was understood not as an intrinsic quality of a given act, but to be the consequence of that act being categorized and acted upon by powerful others (the mass media, courts, police, etc.). In addition, they drew upon the work of Melvin Pollner (1974) to add social psychological flesh to the sociological possibilities implied by Becker of an alternative and parallel 'insider' view. As they saw it, the fact that a 'deviant' act is constructed, defined and sanctioned provided – at least from the perspective of subordinated groups – a material opportunity for agency and empowerment. As suggested by Jock Young (1971), in this way, hooligans were understood as groups from disempowered communities otherwise denied full participation in the mainstream economic social order. As such, they actively embraced 'deviancy' to provoke 'meaningful and societal reactions' which, as an otherwise subordinated group, 'better generates meaning for itself in a world where societal reactions deny them the full status of persons' (Marsh et al., 1978, p. 12). In a context of structural and ideological disempowerment, hooliganism on the football terraces, like delinquency in the playground before it, was thus seen as a context in which subordinated groups could generate identity, symbolic subculture, status hierarchies, power and autonomy.

Another interesting feature of these researchers' theoretical and empirical approach is that it was heavily influenced by Rom Harré's other work focusing on the micro-sociological construction of the self, or *ethogenics* (Harré, 1977). Ethogenics aims to understand the processes by which individuals attach meaning to their actions and form their identities from the structure of 'rules' and cultural resources that surround them. Accordingly, Marsh and colleagues' empirical approach focused heavily upon the phenomenology of those involved in hooliganism. Indeed, in these terms, they argued that a person's social life can be understood as a 'performance' that exists along two dimensions. First, this performance involves *actions* (i.e., social behaviour), and second it involves *accounts* in which these actions are interpreted, criticised and justified. The researchers argued that these performances of group action are only possible because individuals possess a stock of social knowledge that can be revealed both in actions and in accounts of them. As such, they proposed that their 'work is aimed primarily at discovering the context and organisation of social knowledge and belief an individual member has to have to be able to perform reasonably adequately the social life of his [sic] group' (Marsh et al., 1978, p. 15).

In this way, it can be seen that Marsh and colleagues were intimately interested in the content of football fans' identities (although they did not frame their work in these terms). Moreover, their approach saw hooliganism as group behaviour and argued that acting as a group member required access to a set of 'rules'. Importantly, too, they went on to define the 'rule' as a metaphor to describe 'something held (although often tacitly) by all members of a group or community as representations of legitimacy and acceptability. Implicit in the holding of such rules are notions of ought and should' (Marsh et al., 1978, p. 16). They also contended that these 'rules' are cognitive in so far as they play a role in the way situations are defined (what they call 'rules of interpretation'). These contextually bounded interpretative rules, or socially shared guides for action, were understood to feed a set of prescriptive rules that 'enable [group] members to choose between possible modes of conduct available to them and to maintain a sense of propriety and social legitimacy' (1978, p. 16). Moreover, they argued that these rules are open to change as a result of group-based action, which 'can subsequently lead to changing definitions of the situation which in turn will alter the directions of conduct' and propose that there will be 'a very high degree of consensus concerning the rule ... among members of the group or sub-culture in which the rule applies' (1978, p. 16).

It is also the case that for Marsh and colleagues (1978) the collective conflicts which constituted hooliganism were not merely the products of forms of fixed 'rules' or identities. Instead, the distal and proximal intergroup processes that impacted on football fans were seen to play a key role in 'deviancy amplification' (Young, 1971, p. 52; also Wilkins, 1964; see Figure 18.2). By this means, the researchers understood hooliganism to involve a feedback loop in which societal reactions to hooliganism in turn produce increasing deviancy. In particular, they contend that the agencies of law and order, and other 'outsiders' who sustain the hegemonic ideology, constitute 'controllers'. Both the controllers and the deviant group construct theories in order to explain and account for the actions and reactions of the other. Both controllers and deviants then test and advance their theories through the interactions, conflicts and incidents in and around football matches. In these terms, hooliganism is understood not only to be a product of social structural relationships, but also to be a dynamic intergroup phenomenon that sits within a social psychological process of interaction and dynamic power relations. These relations are played out primarily in the context of crowd events in which 'the hypotheses of the controllers about football fans, and of the football fans about the mentality of the controllers, will determine the direction and intensity of the amplification process' (Marsh et al., 1978, p. 12).

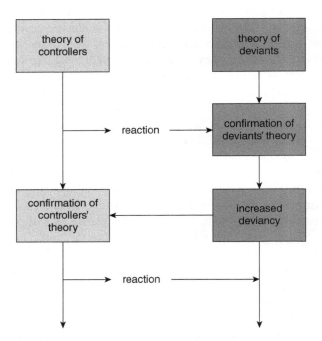

Figure 18.2 An illustration of the deviancy amplification process

Note: The theory of 'deviancy amplification' describes an intergroup process in which the perspectives and actions of controllers create a social context that provokes and exacerbates 'deviancy' among subordinated groups.

Source: Based on Young (1971, p. 52)

It should be clear from this summary that Marsh and his colleagues saw the phenomenon of hooliganism as meaningful for those involved. It is also clear that they understood such meanings to be group-based, contextually defined, and the basis for collective action. In this sense, their theoretical account clearly resonates with some of the core concepts of the social identity perspective (e.g., as outlined in Chapter 2; Turner et al., 1987).

Unfortunately, though, this theoretical position was more a rationale for their study than a conclusion of it. This meant that, while the data they presented supported their model, the researchers constructed and deployed theory primarily to justify their decision to observe and talk to those involved in football-related violence. This was quite a methodological leap at a time when (as today) non-experimental methods were typically given short shrift, but it was disappointing that the researchers ultimately fell back on a rather clumsy and psychologically reductionist form of evolutionary theory to make sense of their findings. This involved asserting that much of the 'violence' of hooliganism was inevitable because it was ritualised 'aggro' that served the function of dissipating men's underlying tendency to be aggressive. In this it was seen to satisfy a fundamental drive for male bonding, which in turn served the useful, if somewhat ironic, function of helping to maintain the social order. Yet this was an analysis for which the researchers had little or no evidence, and it rather undermined the much-needed nuance which their meticulous field research brought to the topic.

Figurational sociology and the working-class hooligan

Marsh and colleagues' (1978) conclusion that football hooliganism is largely symbolic working-class 'aggro' has had a major impact on popular understandings of football crowd violence (e.g., see the BBC documentary, *This is Millwall*; *Panorama*, 1977). However, the influence of their work on policy was more limited. Moreover, over time, the more nuanced aspects of the researchers' social psychological theory got somewhat lost. Not least, this was because their analysis gave way to a second major theoretical contribution to the field. In this, Eric Dunning and his colleagues drew upon two bodies of theoretical and empirical work to try to explain the broad patterns of football hooliganism evident in the city of Leicester over the course of the 20th century. In particular, they were keen to dispute the idea, prevalent at that time, that football hooliganism was a relatively new phenomenon. On the contrary, they argued that in fact collective disorder had always been associated with the sport.

Importantly, Dunning and his team were based in the Sociology Department at the University of Leicester. This was a department that one of the most influential sociologists in the history of the field, Norbert Elias, had played a key role in establishing. Elias's intellectual influence was fundamental to Dunning and colleagues' approach. Indeed, the 'Leicester School's' key contribution (Dunning, Murphy, & Williams, 1988) combined Elias's *figurational sociology* and concept of 'civilising processes' with a classic study of street gangs in the slums of Chicago (Suttles, 1968).

More specifically, through their analysis of historical data concerning the behaviour of football fans in Leicester, the researchers were able to observe two key patterns. First, that the overall levels of collective disorder in the context of football had ebbed and flowed over the course of the 20th century. Second, that those who became involved in football hooliganism tended to have the same lower working-class socio-economic background. The researchers went on to explain a broad decline in football hooliganism as evidence of a 'civilising' processes whereby 'growing affluence and increasing "incorporation" may have had "civilising" effects on the majority of working-class people' (Dunning et al., 1988, p. 227). However, the continued presence of hooliganism in and around football was understood to be a consequence of there being residual pockets of working-class people who had failed to be touched by these processes – 'what is today the less incorporated and relatively impoverished "rougher" working-class minority, the social segment from which the football hooligans are principally recruited' (1988, p. 227).

Using the work of Gerald Suttles (1968) as their starting point, the researchers went on to provide a theory of why and how these communities adhere to 'macho tendencies' (Dunning et al., 1988, p. 229). As they put it, 'such aggressive tendencies do not derive simply from the manner in which "rougher" working-class communities are integrated into the wider society. They also come from, and are reinforced by, specific features of lower working-class communities' (1988, p. 230). For Dunning and his colleagues, these 'features' were essentially patterns of cultural socialisation that revolved around what Suttles (1968), in his classic study of Chicago slums, had called 'ordered segmentation'. Specifically, gender separation, poor parenting and economic deprivation were argued to have led to young men in these communities to be socialised into all-male street gangs in which violence was the primary currency of status. As such, males from the 'rough' working class developed particularly aggressive styles of masculinity, as well as a desire to fight in the service of the reputation of their locality. In this way, hooliganism was explained as arising from the convergence of the 'rough' working class onto the terraces in football grounds. This was a convergence that the researchers attributed:

> to an 'advertising' of the game as a context where fights and 'exciting' incidents regularly take place, a process which had the unintended consequence of making football attractive to 'rougher' working-class males who gain status and enjoyment from involvement in such affairs. (Dunning et al., 1988, p. 234)

While it is sociological in origin, Dunning and colleagues' theoretical approach is akin to what are often referred to in crowd psychology as *convergence theories* (see Reicher, 1987; Stott & Drury, 2016). These have at their heart the idea that there are specific individuals and groups who have relatively fixed identities which leave them predisposed to violence and confrontation, although in this case the tendency among hooligans is seen to be socially determined by structural and cultural processes. For a variety of reasons, it is then assumed that these 'rough' working-class hooligans congregate in football crowds and use them as a platform to live out these tendencies in the form of hooliganism (although what this actually entails is never fully explained).

This theoretical approach has the attraction not only of accounting for the general patterns of football hooliganism over time, but also of being simple and according with the earlier conclusions of Marsh and colleagues (1978). Nevertheless, it is limited by an inability to explain either why specific incidents of hooliganism occur, when and where they do or why they take a particular social and normative form. Why is it, for example, that hooliganism is more common at some football matches (e.g., local derbies) than at others, and why does it vary – in both form and intensity – across specific subgroups (e.g., the 'Newbies', 'Rowdies' and 'Town Boys' studied by Marsh et al., 1978)? Why too is it not always confined to working-class men (Free & Hughson, 2003)?

The inability to explain variability of this form contributed to the demise of the figurational theory of football hooliganism in the wake of substantive critiques (e.g., see Free & Hughson, 2003; Giulianotti, Bonney, & Hepworth,1994). Again, though, as with Marsh and colleagues' earlier work, this research played an important role in shaping contemporary popular understandings of the causal dynamics and nature of football hooliganism. Unlike Marsh and colleagues' work, however, it was also important because Dunning and colleagues' ideas developed alongside, and fed into, the formulation of specific laws, policies and practices by authorities (both in the UK and internationally) that sought to get to grips with what was becoming an increasingly high-profile social issue. The Leicester School was particularly influential in this regard, not least because they were funded for several years by the Football Trust, a government-funded body established in 1975 to improve the safety of sport stadiums in the United Kingdom. Their hooligan analysis presupposes that violence is simply the product of the presence of those predisposed to confrontation. Moreover, it implies that in order to control the problem it is necessary to take a security approach involving surveillance, criminal intelligence, coercion, prosecution and banning. This perspective meshes well with the views of many of those in government and in the security agencies who have responsibility for addressing the challenges that hooliganism represents and creates. And, partly as a result of this, it remains the dominant approach to football policing around the world today (Tsoukala, 2009).

A SOCIAL IDENTITY APPROACH TO HOOLIGANISM

A feature of major historical examples of football hooliganism is that they are invariantly crowd events (e.g., the 1985 Heysel Stadium disaster). Thus, what requires explanation is not hooliganism *per se*; instead, we need to account for the emergence of specific patterns of collective or crowd action. In line with points that were made in Chapter 2, the social identity approach explains collective action within crowds in terms of a shift in the focus of self-definition among participants – away from their idiosyncrasies towards their *shared group-based attributes*. Correspondingly, as suggested by the performance hypothesis outline in that chapter, it argues that those who share this social identity will tend to adhere to the norms, values and beliefs of that social category as it relates to the specific situation.

Importantly, too, shared identity also determines who and what can become influential or prototypical within the crowd and also shapes and limits what people can and will do within it (Reicher, 1987). Social identities have this impact because they determine what behaviour is appropriate or legitimate and affect dynamics of power governing the ability of crowd members to act. From this perspective, then, the patterns of collective conflict observed within football crowds (i.e., hooliganism) are less about the violent predisposition of fans (i.e., hooligans) than about the form and content of shared identities and the ways in which their form and content are shaped and reshaped by the surrounding social context (e.g., Stott, Adang, Livingstone, & Schreiber, 2007, 2008).

Key point 1: Rather than being 'senseless', hooliganism is shaped by intergroup dynamics

Towards the end of the sanction period imposed on English clubs in the wake of the Heysel Stadium disaster, the English national team, who were still allowed to compete at an international level, qualified for the 1990 World Cup finals in Italy. Given the now-notorious and very salient reputation of England fans, the tournament was organised in such a way that England would play their opening three fixtures on the island of Sardinia, a 14-hour ferry journey away from the Italian mainland. Prior to the tournament, the Italian police and significant components of the local population on the island expressed the view that England fans were dangerous and therefore required significant levels of coercive control if their perceived tendency towards confrontation was to be curtailed. For example, approximately 7,000 Italian police were sent to the island to manage the few thousand England fans expected to travel. Several local media outlets had also been busy constructing a detailed narrative of the threats they assumed that English fans would uniformly pose. As one Italian newspaper headline trumpeted, the English were the 'Violent Tribe' and, as a consequence, 'an emergency plan' had been launched in Sardinia to deal with these invading 'Attilas' from the north (*L'Espresso*, 17 May 1990).

Perhaps unsurprisingly, large numbers of England fans arriving on the island experienced significant hostility from locals and police. For example, following England's opening fixture against Egypt, a large crowd of England fans gathered near the city's main railway station. Given a lack of accommodation in the city, the majority of England fans who had attended the match were staying in holiday resorts on other parts of the island. However, the match had been played in the late evening, so by the time England fans arrived back in the city centre the last scheduled trains and buses had left. With no public transport available, hundreds of England fans had little choice but to gather as a crowd outside the railway station. Initially, the situation was calm but as they waited for the authorities to organise some form of transport, a small group of locals walked into the crowd and began swinging heavy metal chains. After the crowd surged to escape the violence, several England fans reacted aggressively towards the protagonists, resulting in the entire crowd of England fans being baton-charged by police. The following day British newspaper headlines once again attributed the disorder to rampaging English hooligans.

These forms of intergroup interaction between locals, police and England fans were indicative of a general pattern that went on for several days in numerous parts of the island. This was important because as the police *imposed* their definition of England fans as hostile, they created a social context that shaped the form and content of England fan identity over time – in ways represented schematically in Figure 18.3. Initially, England fans had largely seen themselves as opposed to confrontation and perceived those who were seeking to be confrontational as anti-normative. Over time, though, collective experiences of the illegitimacy of intergroup relations with police – experienced as the arbitrary application of unwarranted and indiscriminate police coercion – changed what it meant to be an England fan. This intergroup process in turn fed an increasing sense of the normative legitimacy of confrontation among those who identified as England fans. In particular, it increased the perceived legitimacy of confrontation with the police and culminated in a major riot just prior to England's second match on the island against the Netherlands.

Just prior to the match, around 6,000 England supporters gathered outside the railway station and began to march together towards the stadium. Observational and interview data suggests that the majority of those involved had no prior intention of engaging in confrontation and saw their collective action of marching towards the stadium as both normative and legitimate. But, fearing disorder, the police used their batons to disperse the crowd. Given the recent history of interaction, those in the crowd experienced police intervention as another unwarranted attack. However, during prior encounters fans had been relatively disempowered against the police. In the context of this crowd, those historical power relationships were momentarily reversed. As a consequence, several England fans confronted the police during this initial intervention. Faced with hostility, police fired tear gas and mounted further baton charges into the crowd, such that even those actively seeking to avoid confrontation were targeted by police. As one female fan observed:

> We were innocent bystanders walking along to the match at the back of the crowd. Tear gas was thrown so we ran and got caught in the crowd. The police came, and we tried to get out, we couldn't, we got batoned further and further into it. We tried to pick a person off the floor who was hit with a baton, but a policeman broke his rifle butt over my back. My skin is broken, and I am really badly bruised. (Stott & Pearson, 2007, p. 80)

After a short period of time the crowd was contained, corralled and escorted to the stadium.

For several weeks prior to the tournament the British authorities and media had been arguing that a conspiracy existed between English and Dutch hooligans to create disorder. So, perhaps unsurprisingly, following the riot, the UK Minister for Sport issued a press release that described it as 'an orchestrated incident ... that was a sickening reflection that a mindless minority of thugs could bring English football into international disrepute'. He was also 'grateful to the police for their swift, tough, and decisive action, which diffused this situation and prevented other incidents'.

In contrast, from a social identity perspective, it is possible to understand the riot as crowd action in which police coercion had actually played a causal role – in ways that are represented schematically in Figure 18.3. Both before and during the incident, the relatively indiscriminate use of force by police towards England fans had shaped and reshaped the identities driving collective action. Their attempt to police hooliganism had 'amplified' the problem, such that more and more fans were drawn into a social context where what it meant to be an England fan was defined in terms of being anti-police, a form of identity that both legitimised and enabled confrontation towards them when power relationships were momentarily reversed within the context of the crowd. Indeed, as the rioting developed, it can be seen that this behaviour was normative and patterned in so far as only the police were subjected to collective attacks (Stott & Reicher, 1998).

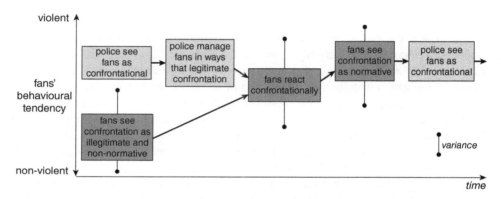

Figure 18.3 A schematic representation of the intergroup dynamics that shaped the behaviour of England fans at the 1990 World Cup

Note: Initially, England fans were generally opposed to confrontation and perceived those who were seeking to be confrontational as anti-normative. However, Stott and Reicher (1998) argue that, over time, collective experiences of the treatment by the police changed what it meant to be an England fan in ways that led fans to behave more violently.

Key point 2: Indiscriminate treatment by authorities can create a sense of shared social identity that leads otherwise non-violent fans to support violence

A further opportunity to examine and nuance a theoretical understanding of the intimate relationship between hooliganism, social identity and intergroup dynamics came when both England and Scotland qualified for the 1998 World Cup Finals in France. Here England were drawn to play their opening match against Tunisia in the southern city of Marseilles. Throughout three days surrounding this fixture there were a series of collective confrontations between England fans, local youths and police. The most serious and large-scale of these was a riot that took place during the match in a public viewing area that had been set up on the city's beach. Hundreds of England fans came to be involved in active confrontation, several England fans were stabbed, riot police fired several volleys of tear gas to disperse the crowd from the area, and dozens of England fans were arrested and some subsequently imprisoned. As at previous World Cups, the British media and police authorities attributed its cause to the presence of hooligan fans. Along with such explanations came compelling calls for the government to create new laws that would prevent known hooligans from travelling aboard, even in the absence of a criminal offence. Such laws were subsequently enacted but, once again, research informed by social identity principles suggested a very different array of causal dynamics (Stott, Hutchison, & Drury, 2001).

As the tournament began, England fans started to gather in bars in and around the Old Port area of the city to drink and behave raucously in ways that are often normative for football fans (Pearson, 2015). During these early stages, some two days before the match itself, there appear to have been several hostile interactions between some England fans and locals, most likely racist provocations and insults initiated by relatively small contingents of England fans. However, as other England fans continued to arrive in significant numbers, perhaps as a result of the earlier provocations, local youths began 'unprovoked' attacks on crowds of England fans across the Old Port area. These attacks were at times extremely violent, involving the use of weapons such as knives and baseball bats. During these confrontations, it was evident that despite being present in significant numbers, the police did little if anything to intervene or, if they did, they targeted England fans rather than those initiating the confrontations.

It was in this intergroup context that collective violence began to escalate. Our data suggested that the relatively indiscriminate hostility by local youths and police created a form of 'common fate' for England fans. This social context led them, regardless of prior disposition, to both gather together for self-protection and to construct a collective identity defined in terms of illegitimate outgroup action. In effect, the proximal intergroup context functioned to manifest a form of identity for England fans within which conflict against outgroups was perceived as legitimate and hence normative, as well as rendering those prepared to confront hostile outgroups as prototypical and hence influential ingroup members. Against the idea that this hostility was the manifestation of any predisposition on the part of fans, it is worth noting too that according to police data, of the hundreds of England fans arrested in Marseilles, around 95% of them were not previously known to the police and, as such, had no recorded history of prior involvement in football-related disorder. Instead, then, what we see again is that individuals' support for violence was largely the outcome of emergent intergroup dynamics in which violence (rather than non-violence) became normative for the ingroup.

Key point 3: Authorities can act in ways that lead potentially violent fans to protect peaceful norms

While there are many differences in English and Scottish football culture, in the 1970s and 1980s both groups had a historical reputation for football hooliganism. However, in the years leading up to the '98 World Cup in France, Scotland fans had begun to reshape their notoriety by shunning collective confrontation in favour of a form of 'carnivalesque', boisterous and drunken revelry (Giulianotti, 1991; Giulianotti et al., 1994;

see also Pearson, 2015; Figure 18.4). With their now-positive reputation preceding them, police and locals were apparently much more welcoming to Scottish fans when Scotland played their opening fixture in Bordeaux. Nevertheless, it was evident from observational data in that city that, despite their reputational differences, the heavy drinking and boisterous behavioural norms of the Scots were not that dissimilar to the collective behaviours displayed by England fans prior to their interactions with hostile outgroups (Stott, Hutchison, & Drury, 2001). What appeared to be different was the way in which those carnivalesque actions were interpreted and reacted to by the local police and population. In effect, the same collective behaviours were labelled by powerful 'controllers' as malign hooliganism in one context but as benign boisterousness in the other.

Figure 18.4   Scottish football fans at the 1998 World Cup in France

Note: In contrast to England fans, Scottish fans cultivated a reputation for being 'carnivalesque' (Stott et al., 2001). This meant that, although much of their behaviour was very similar to that of the England fans at the same tournament, it did not provoke a hostile response from locals or police.

Source: *Daily Record*

The Scottish fans' experiences of being allowed to collectively express their identity without provoking a hostile response from locals or police appears to have led to a perception among them of intergroup legitimacy. This perception of the proximal intergroup context was paralleled by displays of a strong 'self-regulation' culture; in effect, the Scottish supporters started 'self-policing'. Thus, it was not that Scottish fans did not have fans that fitted a profile of a hooligan or that no one engaged in acts that could be interpreted as hooliganism, or even that there were not fans present among the Scots who behaved violently. Rather it was that if such acts did occur, other Scotland fans would tend to actively intervene to prevent any further escalation and to isolate and marginalise those transgressing otherwise-peaceful ingroup norms. As one Scottish supporter described it, concerning another who had acted violently towards a local as they were playing football:

> The guy with the Tunisian top got the ball and ... the Scottish guy stuck his fuckin' head on him. Next thing there was about twenty, thirty guys with kilts on booting fuck out of the Scottish guy. Nobody wanted to know him, just thought he was a complete wanker. (Stott et al., 2001, p. 372)

It was also apparent that this form of norm enforcement was, at least in part, strategic. Fans understood that if they could maintain a positive reputation from one venue to another, they would not invite the kind of sanctions surrounding England fans, such as bars shutting early or hostile policing. In this way, by 'self-policing' they would be free to indulge in their transgressive drunken revelry without being attacked or arrested. However, as a caveat, it should be noted that when Scotland fans *did* experience contexts of intergroup illegitimacy, they too displayed evidence of similar shifts towards seeing conflict as both legitimate and normative for their category as a whole.

Through this and our earlier study, it was also evident that the major incidents of hooliganism among English fans could be understood quite powerfully in terms of a social identity approach to crowd behaviour (see also Drury & Reicher, 2000; Reicher, 1996b; Stott & Drury, 2000). What is also evident is that the dynamics of identity in the context of these crowds were not merely cognitive but genuinely social psychological – such that the form and content of fans' behaviour can be seen to be the result of group-level social action and interaction. Here, as with Marsh and colleagues' (1978) concept of 'rules' and 'deviancy amplification', the perspective and actions of one group (e.g., the police) serves to create the context for the other (e.g., fans). The identity-based reaction of the latter then forms the social context for the former in an ongoing social and psychological process of escalation.

This social identity perspective represents a radical departure from the hooligan accounts of the figurational approach. Moreover, it also makes it clear that if one wants to avoid incidents of intergroup hostility and violence, then this is not merely a question of restricting the movement of those suspected of being hooligans. It necessarily involves examining and changing the ways in which football fans are policed.

Key point 4: Authorities can police crowds in ways that limit displays of hooliganism

The first opportunity to achieve translating the above social identity theorising into practice was provided by the policing operation surrounding fans attending the UEFA European Football Championships in Portugal, Euro 2004. At this tournament, the country's main police force, the *Polícia de Segurança Pública* (PSP), decided to innovate and develop a novel 'low-profile' policing model. Critically, this was informed by the identity-based theoretical approach to crowds described above, which had been developed into a model of good practice (Stott & Pearson, 2007).

In the world of policing football there is a well-established, internationally adopted framework for categorizing football fixtures in terms of the level of risk they are judged to pose to public order. This form of event–risk classification is primarily an organisational matter for the police, in that in the planning phase it serves as the means for commanders to justify decisions and unlock processes required to mobilise large numbers (sometimes hundreds) of police officers that they see as necessary to manage the perceived potential for partisan confrontation between hostile groups of fans. For example, fixtures between the Netherlands and Germany have a long history of violent confrontation between fans. During Euro 2004, it was that fixture that secured the highest risk classification for the tournament. These categorizations are often determined on the basis of criminal intelligence concerning the number of hooligans, officially referred to as 'risk fans', that it is assumed will be present. In addition, the judgement that a match is high risk also flows into models of policing which assume that public order can be maintained through deterrence-based instrumental compliance and strategic incapacitation (Gilham, 2011). In these contexts, police tend to adopt a reliance on surveillance to 'spot' risk fans. They then use highly visible displays of riot police and vehicles to demonstrate their capability to use force and seek to corral and contain opposing fans into specific but different locations.

As we have seen, from a social identity perspective, risk to public order is less a matter of the presence or absence of 'risk fans' than it is about social identities and group-level meanings and how these relate to the patterns of intergroup and intragroup interaction that unfold in a given context. Indeed, from this perspective, criminal intelligence and deterrence-based approaches to policing can actually be counter-productive because they tend to ignore these social identity dynamics and can create intergroup relationships between police and fans that are perceived as illegitimate and ultimately increase the likelihood of public disorder (Drury, Stott, & Farsides, 2003; Hoggett & Stott, 2010; Stott & Reicher, 1998). As we have discussed, this in turn can underpin the emergence of forms of social identity within the crowd that empower confrontation and undermine the capacity for crowd self-regulation. Thus, an event that may have been classified by police as low risk can become problematic because the social identity dynamics of the crowd function to amplify behavioural norms consistent with hooliganism (e.g., in ways suggested by Figure 18.2). As we have also seen, these processes can emerge regardless of prior individual or collective intent.

The social identity approach therefore encourages the police to move away from fixed categorizations of events towards an understanding that at any given event there is always a *continuum of risk* ranging from high to low, which is capable of change as the event unfolds. In turn, it proposes that movement up and down this dynamic risk continuum is often governed by the perceived legitimacy of police use of force. If police actions are seen by those in the crowd as proportionate to or in balance with the circumstances, then fans will tend to self-regulate and disorder will be minimised if not completely avoided. However, where this balance between risk and police action is not achieved, self-regulation will decrease and the normative conditions necessary for collective conflict will emerge (Stott & Pearson, 2007).

This model of dynamic risk and balanced tactical profile was adopted by the European Council in 2006 (Council of the European Union, 2006). This adoption was a direct result of the fact that at Euro 2004 the PSP utilised it to create a policy on the police use of force for the tournament (Stott & Pearson, 2007; see Figure 18.5). This policy revolved around a model of information-led tactical intervention into crowds that operated at four levels. In light of Key point 2 above, a primary goal of this policy was to achieve an approach to the use of force that would, wherever possible, avoid indiscriminate coercive action against crowds as a whole, if only small sections of that crowd were actually involved in threatening disorder. Level 1 focused on officers in normal uniform working in pairs. Their function was concentrated on moving through crowds, interacting with and talking to fans, working to build friendly interactions and facilitate positive behaviour. Where these tactics identified emerging tensions in a crowd, if they could not be resolved at Level 1, officers could be reinforced by a Level 2 intervention, which would be a larger squad of police, still in ordinary uniform, who would seek to resolve the problem without using force. If tensions escalated further, these officers could then put on protective helmets and draw batons, which would escalate it to a Level 3 intervention. If that approach failed to deal with the tensions, then the riot units in full protective equipment and armed with batons, dogs, tear gas and a water cannon would provide a Level 4 capability. These Level 4 units would be close by but kept deliberately out of sight unless it was judged that the level of observable risk justified their deployment. This concept, which was subsequently adopted by police in Sweden and Denmark (see Stott, Havelund, & Williams, 2019), subsequently came to be referred to as the *graded tactical approach*.

Figure 18.5   English football fans and police at the 2004 European Football Championships in Portugal

Source: Stott et al. (2007)

In order to evaluate this theory-led approach, throughout the Euro 2004 tournament both qualitative and quantitative data were gathered using both ethnographic and structured observations (Stott et al., 2007, 2008). In this way, researchers were able to monitor and measure police deployment and the subsequent behavioural norms of fans during a large sample of match days in all match cities under the jurisdiction of the PSP. These observational accounts were then supplemented by phenomenological analyses of interview and survey data collected from supporters, which were used to explore the evolving content of their social identities and their perceived relationships to the surrounding social contexts.

The key findings were that the policing model was successfully implemented across match cities. Fans tended to perceive such policing as legitimate and this in turn helped to maintain a form of unified football fan identity whose norms revolved around collective revelry and positive intergroup relationships. While there were fans present who were known hooligans, they actively avoided disorder and even became actively involved in important moments of collective of self-regulation when tensions did develop. Over the tournament as a whole there were no major riots in match cities and those incidents of collective disorder that did take place happened in areas under the jurisdiction of Portugal's other major police force, who did not adopt the theory-led graded tactical approach (Schreiber & Stott, 2015; Stott et al., 2007, 2008; Stott & Pearson, 2007).

CONCLUSION

This chapter sought to use the issue of football hooliganism to explore the dynamics of partisanship. It began by drawing on an incident that characterised the political nature of football partisanship and the relationships between crowds, context and identities, and by stressing how this must be considered when seeking to understand the phenomenon. Recognising, but pushing aside, the problematic nature of the concept, the chapter moved on to explore two of the seminal theoretical and empirical contributions to the study of football hooliganism. The first of these painted a complex sociological and social psychological picture of the processes through which one could begin to see hooliganism as a form of subcultural deviancy that provided identity and gave meaning to otherwise disempowered groups. The chapter sought to demonstrate how this seminal theoretical approach mirrored, in very different conceptual language, some of the social psychological processes articulated in more powerful and parsimonious terms by the social identity approach. What Marsh and colleagues (1978) conceptualised as 'rules' were in effect social identities embedded within proximal and distal relationships of status and power. Importantly, they too saw that the 'rules' that drove the group behaviours that constituted hooliganism could be constructed, shaped and amplified through the actions and perspectives of the authorities. The chapter then briefly explored the more influential 'figurational' account of Erik Dunning and his colleagues. While their figurational sociology certainly acted as a key foundation to the field now referred to as the sociology of sport (Curry, 2019), the convergence account of hooliganism that it implied was limited in its capacity to explain the form and specificity of collective disorder.

The chapter then moved on to discuss the social identity approach to hooliganism. Two high-profile riots, which had acted at that time as the basis for media representation, popular understanding and governmental responses to hooliganism, were analysed as crowd actions. In turn, this created an opportunity for an ethnographic focus on their underlying social identity and intergroup dynamics. The data and analysis that were made possible through this empirical and theoretical approach resonated with a wider body of work on crowd psychology (e.g., Drury & Reicher, 2000; Reicher, 1984, 1987, 1996b; Stott & Drury, 2000), which exposed how these incidents of collective conflict emerged through complex historical intergroup processes. Here it was evident that the form and content of the social identity of fans was shaped and reshaped by a context that was imposed upon them, most notably by specific forms of policing. Dynamics of power and (il)legitimacy appeared to be central to this identity and were driven as much by the expectations and actions of the authorities as they were by the pre-existing disposition of fans (see also Drury, Stott, & Farsides, 2003; Stott & Reicher, 1998). Equally, it was also possible to understand how a sense of intergroup legitimacy among Scottish fans led to forms of 'norm enforcement' that helped de-escalate tensions.

Once conceptualised in this way, it was then possible to begin a programme of work deliberately designed to shape police practices. As and where this was achieved, it was evident that this led to an improved capacity to manage social identity and intergroup processes in ways that led to the threat of hooliganism being reduced if not completely removed (Stott et al., 2007, 2008). Central to this latter programme of work has been a framework of 'participant action research', which seeks to drive a social identity-informed approach into policing football at an international level. This programme of work is ongoing in the UK and elsewhere in Europe and has led to further important changes in the way hooliganism is understood and managed (Brechbühl, Schumacher Dimech, & Seiler, 2017; Stott, Havelund, & Williams, 2019; Stott, Hoggett, & Pearson, 2011; Stott, Khan, Madsen, & Havelund, 2020; Stott, Pearson, & West, 2019; Stott, West, & Radburn, 2018).

Considered together, this body of research serves to underscore two key conclusions. First, that there is value in understanding hooliganism as dynamic, identity-based collective action. To draw upon the action research motto of Kurt Lewin (1952, p. 169), we see that there is 'nothing so practical as a good theory' (see also Haslam, 2014; McCain, 2016). Here, not only does an identity-based approach help us to advance academic theory, but it also contributes to the co-production of knowledge in ways that empower effective human-rights-focused ways of preventing hooliganism. This sees partisan fans not just as part of the problem to be repressed, but also as part of the solution to be empowered (Stott & Gorringe, 2013).

Second, this work additionally points to something fundamental about the nature of social identity. As we saw in Chapter 2, social identity theory (Tajfel & Turner, 1979) and self-categorization theory (Turner et al., 1987; Turner et al., 1994) focus predominantly upon the psychological processes through which the social context can be internalised via a shared sense of collective self. Yet the study of partisanship in football shows how this sense of self and the collective actions it enables are shaped not merely by cognitive processes, but also by the ways in which groups act and interact over time. Moreover, while the perceived (il)legitimacy and 'stability' of these intergroup interactions is central to emergent social behaviour (Tajfel & Turner, 1979; see also Ellemers, 1993; Ellemers & Haslam, 2012), so too are the dynamics of power. On the one hand, powerful groups have a capacity to impose their worldview, thereby creating the social context for others. On the other hand, particularly in the proximal context of the crowd, the perceived *stability* of otherwise embedded social structural relationships of power appear open to change, even if only momentarily. In this sense, as we saw from events in the Maksimir Stadium in Zagreb at the beginning of this chapter, football crowds are places of social change. They are also places that demonstrate that identity itself is as much sociological as psychological.

SECTION 6

POLITICS

19

COMPARING THE SOCIAL IDENTITY APPROACH WITH SELF-DETERMINATION THEORY

MICHAEL J. PLATOW
DIANA M. GRACE

In this chapter, we examine two theoretical approaches to human behaviour that are relevant to sport psychology – *self-determination theory* (SDT) and *the social identity approach* (SIA; composed of social identity theory (SIT) and self-categorization theory, SCT). Our intent is not to demonstrate the superiority of one approach over the other. Rather, we wish to explore the theories *as theories*, and examine their potential compatibility and points of divergence, particularly with respect to their applicability to sport and exercise. We investigate whether the two can be potentially integrated at specific levels of analysis or whether they are fundamentally incompatible.

The question that the reader may be asking, of course, is why we have chosen to make this comparison at all. The relevance of the SIA in the context of this edited volume is clear. However, in championing this relatively new approach within the domain of sport psychology, it behoves us to consider the work that has come before us and the theoretical frameworks that have guided that work. It is for this reason that we have chosen to focus on SDT, given the substantial body of work that has applied this theory to domains of sport and exercise. Indeed, when conducting a literature search prior to writing this chapter, we identified over 200 papers containing both the words 'self-determination' and one of 'sport', 'athlete' or 'coach' in the title alone (not counting the many other sport- and exercise-related papers that have drawn on SDT as a theoretical framework without mentioning it in the title). In this book as a whole, then, we cannot ignore this substantial body of work, nor pretend that this work has not been conducted.

At the same time, in comparing the two theories, we were mindful that the sheer weight of evidence will necessarily be on the side of SDT, if only because of the relatively nascent foothold of the SIA within the sport literature. Indeed, comparing theories simply by counting the number of studies that provide support for one or the other, or by assessing the amount of variance accounted for by one theory or another, would ultimately be of little value. Instead, we take this opportunity to investigate relevant issues at a deeper level by interrogating the two theories' fundamental assumptions in a way that should help researchers and practitioners choose one over the other as a guiding framework for their future work. To foreshadow our conclusions, we believe that the relative compatibility of the two theories depends both on researchers' and practitioners' own level of analysis, and on their theoretical and applied goals. Simply put, the compatibility (or lack of it) depends on the problem one is trying to solve.

SELF-DETERMINATION THEORY: A THEORY OF SELF-CONCEPT AND MOTIVATION

Self-determination theory has been used to frame and guide a broad array of research within sport psychology, including, *inter alia*, analyses of the motivation of both individual athletes (e.g., Mallett & Hanrahan, 2004) and sport teams (Mertens et al., 2018), the coaching of athletes (e.g., Adie, Duda, & Ntoumanis, 2012; Reynders et al., 2019), and the behaviour of fans (e.g., Funk, Beaton, & Alexandris, 2012). The popularity of SDT for the analysis of sport and sporting behaviours arises because, at its core, it is a theory of self and human motivation. It provides a basis for understanding how and why people strive to achieve, even under contexts of adversity, hardship and failure. These are precisely the contexts in which sport attitudes and behaviours are often manifest. Indeed, achievement in sport often requires a dedication that mirrors the asceticism of monks in requiring athletes to forsake comfortable and pain-free lives in pursuit of a potentially unobtainable goal. For the fans who sit on the sidelines and remain comfortable on their couches, the physical endurance is often completely absent – but nevertheless, as observed in Chapter 17 , the psychological question remains as to why those of us who prefer the comfort of our lounges continue to support our teams even when they perform poorly.

For SDT, the answer to this question can be found in an understanding of people's motivations and their abilities to satisfy specific basic needs. One of the three fundamental needs assumed by SDT is that of *autonomy*, behaving with a 'feeling of volition' (Ryan & Deci, 2000, p. 74). In sport, this need for autonomy refers to athletes' needs to feel in control over their life and actions. This need can be satisfied when athletes are positively engaged in their training and personal development plans (Ntoumanis & Mallett, 2014). According to SDT, autonomy is the 'central force' in the ontology of both individuals and societies (Deci & Ryan, 2012, p. 85). For this reason, the pursuit of the satisfaction of this need is seen to be a central motivation driving people's behaviours.

Building upon this assumption of a need for autonomy, the most favourable outcomes of individuals' endeavours are often observed to emerge from actions that are most *self-determined* (Deci & Ryan, 2012; Ryan & Deci, 2000). These are actions that are understood to be derived from internal motivations that people engage in only because of personal interest or enjoyment, and because the actions are inherently satisfying to the individual actor. They are behaviours the actor has chosen out of free will, without influence or persuasion from others, independently of the demands of the physical or social context. Although it is stated simply here, this is a non-trivial motivational analysis when we consider individuals' choice of activities, and their behaviours in contexts that appear to be – at least temporally – intrinsically *un*satisfying. Take, for example, the case of a long-distance runner who has the aim of winning a major race (see Figure 19.1). She will have to spend many hours engaging in a range of gruelling training activities, some of which are unlikely to be very rewarding on their own. Yet however unpleasant it is, she consciously undertakes the training because it is part of her plan to make it to the top. It is in explaining such adherence that SDT's appeal is apparent.

Figure 19.1 Self-determination

Source: Mabel Amber, Pixabay

In addition to the need for autonomy, SDT proposes two further fundamental needs, the volitional pursuit of which can further contribute to overall self-determination in individuals' actions. These are the needs for *competence* and *relatedness* (Deci & Ryan, 2012). Simply put, individuals need to feel competent and effective in what they do (e.g., developing and achieving the skills needed to be a scratch golfer); and they have the desire to feel accepted and meaningfully connected with others (i.e., to feel part of the basketball team and not isolated from it; Baumeister & Leary, 1995; Deci & Ryan, 2000; Sherif & Cantril, 1947). Collectively, the satisfaction (or non-satisfaction) of these three fundamentally assumed needs is understood to determine individuals' motivational orientations towards various pursuits.

As Figure 6.2 suggests, between these two extremes are various degrees of external and internal motivation. For example, *external regulation* is a specific type of external motivation resulting from a desire to secure a reward or to avoid punishment, as might be seen in a volleyball player – Kim – who undertakes additional strength training only to win praise or avoid criticism from her coach. Another type of external motivation is *introjected regulation*, which results from an internalised, pressuring voice, where behaviour is guided by a sense of guilt, worry or shame. An example might be Kim undertaking strength training because she would feel ashamed not to be putting in additional effort. *Identified regulation* occurs when the strength resulting from the training is seen as a worthwhile pursuit in itself (i.e., this does not involve enjoying the training for itself, only the result of that training), while *integrated regulation* involves taking up strength training because engaging in a range of training methods is part of what makes Kim 'who she is'. Only when a goal becomes fully psychologically integrated and consistent with other needs is its pursuit argued to be internal. However, even this is not necessarily fully self-determined, as the origin of the motivation (e.g., seeking accolades for achieving a particular goal) will often stem from outside the individual.

For any goal in any context, people can vary along this continuum, being less or more self-determined in their pursuit of activities. In this way, motivation is understood to be neither binary nor uniform, either within or between individuals. This dimensional variability in turn allows for the variety of individual behaviours, pursuits and sources of life satisfaction that we see across the spectrum of human activity.

Applied to the domain of sport psychology, it is easy to see the predictive value of this motivational analysis. In particular, this is because higher levels of self-determination are associated with (a) increased effort, persistence, concentration, positive affect and willingness to engage in a difficult physical task (e.g., Standage, Duda, & Ntoumanis, 2005, 2006), (b) increased persistence in sport activities (e.g., Calvo, Cervelló, Jiménez, Iglesias, & Murcia, 2010), (c) increased emotional well-being (Smith, Ntoumanis, Duda, & Vansteenkiste, 2011), (d) decreased burnout among elite athletes (Lonsdale & Hodge, 2011), and (e) decreased levels of past and intended future use of performance-enhancing drugs (Barkoukis, Lazuras, Tsorbatzoudis, & Rodafinos, 2011). In sum, then, the positive consequences of self-determined engagement in sport and athletic activities appear to be powerful and compelling. So, in the case of Kim, the more her motivation is near the self-determination end of the continuum, the more likely it is that she will continue the additional strength training.

SOCIAL IDENTITY AND SELF-CATEGORIZATION THEORIES

In contrast to SDT, social identity and self-categorization theories may, at first glance, appear to be unlikely candidates to apply to sporting and exercise domains. As noted in Chapter 2, these are theories of group process whose historical origins lie in the analysis of intergroup conflict, prejudice, discrimination and stereotyping. So, while group processes clearly play key roles in many sports, simply equating group processes in general with sport and exercise is oversimplified, if not simply wrong – if only because many sports, of course, are not team-based. However, like SDT, social identity and self-categorization theories are ultimately theories of the self, with each outlining cognitive and motivational processes associated with the psychological self-representation and the maintenance of positive self-views.

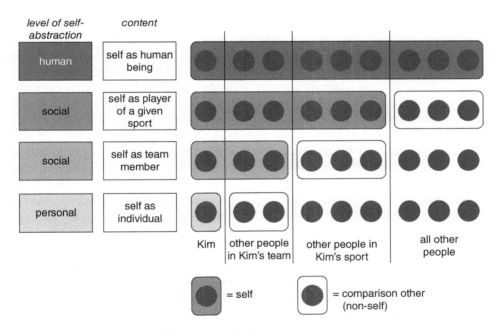

Figure 19.2 Hierarchies of self-categorization

Note: The darkly shaded regions indicate those others who are included in a person's (in this case Kim's) definition of self at different levels of abstraction. Thus, self-definition becomes more inclusive at higher levels of abstraction. The lightly shaded regions indicate others who are compared with self at different levels of abstraction. These are the people who are part of the self at the next highest level of abstraction. Intermediate social identities could exist between those presented here (e.g., self as member of a national team, self as sportsperson).

Source: Adapted from Haslam (2004)

Outlined most explicitly in self-categorization theory, cognitive representations of the self are assumed to take the form of self-categorizations (Turner et al., 1987). These are dynamic, context-dependent self-representations that involve seeing the self as the same or identical to some other class of stimuli, typically other people (e.g., allowing people in some instances to say, 'we athletes', with the implication that there are shared, common features among them). As Figure 19.2 suggests, these self-categorizations are assumed to vary along a hierarchy of inclusiveness. At the most inclusive level, the person is self-categorized with all other humans; at the most exclusive level they are self-categorized with no one else (i.e., categorizing themselves in terms of *personal identity*, where self is seen as a unique individual; Turner, 1982). Between these two extremes are all other ingroup–outgroup categorizations (i.e., social identities), such as those that involve representing the self as a player of a particular sport or as a member of a particular sports team.

Of the many assumptions outlined within the SIA, three are particularly relevant to the current analysis. First, the self-concept is assumed to be dynamic and context-sensitive. That is, the approach eschews the assumption of a *necessarily* stable and 'true' self. Rather, any currently salient self-representation is understood as 'true', such that it is psychologically valid in that particular context (Turner et al., 1987, 1994). Nevertheless, while valid, not all self-representations are *valued*. For example, membership in particular groups (e.g., as an Indigenous person) may be stigmatised in ways that make that identity difficult in some circumstances or with some people, and yet it does not make that identity any less meaningful. Moreover, one's Indigenous identity may (and should) become less relevant (though in no sense less real) in the sporting context when one's identity as, say, a footballer is at the fore. It is not until attention is drawn to that Indigenous identity – as it was very negatively in the case of Adam Goodes, an Australian football player who received racial taunts by crowd members – that it becomes the salient identity (Augoustinos, Callaghan, & Platow, 2019). In this case, the result of constant emphasis on one identity (Aboriginal) rather than on what should have been the relevant identity (football player) led to Goodes' retirement from football, despite his young age and his profound talent.

This highlights the second critical assumption of the SIA: people can and do vary in their degree of identification with any salient self-category (e.g., Ellemers, Spears, & Doosje, 1999). In other words, people vary in the degree to which they believe any salient self-category is important for their contextual self-definition. So, while some people may embrace a social identity through thick or thin (e.g., as die-hard sport fans do), others may seek to change their social identities as they might change their clothes in response to fashion trends (as fair-weather sport fans do; Wann & Branscombe, 1990; see Chapter 17).

Finally, social identity theory makes the simple motivational assumption that people would prefer to have a positive self-concept than a negative one (Tajfel & Turner, 1986). And given that this self-concept can be either personal or social, people are assumed to pursue both personal and social identity enhancement when they can. It is here, with variability in the levels of social identification and dynamic self-categorizations, that the social identity approach has been most clearly integrated into analyses of sport psychology (e.g., in ways discussed in Chapter 2). For example, it leads us to predict that among sport fans, those who are highly identified with a given team are more likely to engage in prosocial behaviour towards others (e.g., giving money to a charity) if those others support the same team (rather than an opposing team; Platow et al., 1999). Similarly, higher levels of social identification with a sport team predict higher levels of psychological well-being when that team does well (as shown by Branscombe & Wann, 1991; see Chapter 17), but they also creatively reconceive what successful performance is when that team performs less well (e.g., Platow, Hunter, Branscombe, & Grace, 2014). Finally, the SIA predicts that athletes who have higher levels of social identification with a given sporting activity will be more likely to engage in this activity (e.g., as shown by Stevens, Rees, & Polman, 2019; see Chapter 10).

COMPARING APPROACHES

As noted at the start of this chapter, it is precisely because both SDT and the SIA can be – and have been – employed in the analysis of sport and exercise psychology that it is worthwhile examining them side-by-side. Accordingly, it is to this comparison that we now turn. We do this by focusing on three different levels of analysis: empirical, conceptual and theoretical.

Empirical complementarity

One of the most direct ways to compare SDT and the SIA is simply to identify ways in which they can usefully be both incorporated in specific empirical analyses of human behaviour, including sport and exercise. Each approach has its own rich empirical tradition, including scales used to measure the key concepts of self-determination and social identification (e.g., see the Appendix). We can therefore ask if employing the specific tools (e.g., the specific scales) that have been developed within each theoretical approach will allow us to build more useful empirical models to understand and explain particular behaviours. Perhaps, empirically, these two theoretical approaches can be complementary, with each explaining attitudes and behaviours at different psychological stages or even at the same stage but to different degrees. This is precisely what has been done by a joint Canadian and Australian research team.

In one study, Katharine Greenaway and her colleagues sampled Australian university students early in these students' university careers, and again six weeks later. Following SDT, the researchers measured: levels of students' need satisfaction (e.g., 'How free and choiceful do you feel in this university group?' as a measure of autonomy satisfaction); their levels of social identification with their university (following SIA, e.g., 'I have a lot in common with other students at my university'); and various outcome variables, such as personal well-being and academic satisfaction (Greenaway, Amiot, Louis, & Bentley, 2017). Using structural equation modelling, the researchers showed that a positive change in students' need satisfaction was a positive predictor of positive changes in students' social identification with their university. In simple terms, the more students' self-determination needs were satisfied in the context of their university life, the more they identified with their university. Moreover, the greater the increase in students' social identification with university, the greater was the improvement in their personal well-being and their academic satisfaction. This is an extremely valuable study if only because it demonstrates how measurement tools from both SDT and the SIA can be integrated into a single empirical programme. Indeed, here, one set of processes (i.e., SDT processes) appear empirically to be the antecedents of the other. In this case, then, the theoretical approaches are empirically complementary.

In a more direct analysis of the two approaches within a sport context, Catherine Amiot and colleagues measured the consequences for well-being and self-actualisation of sport fans' derogatory behaviours directed towards an outgroup sport team (and fans) (Amiot, Sansfaçon, & Louis, 2013). In the context of Canadian hockey rivalries, the authors wondered what the psychological consequences would be of insulting and making fun of one's opponents. This sporting context provided a valuable test of key aspects of SDT, as it assumes that negative behaviours (in this case, derogatory behaviour towards others) stem from thwarted need satisfaction (cf., Deci & Ryan, 2012). The SIA, on the other hand, predicts that negative intergroup behaviour can simply be a way of enhancing one's sense of positive ingroup identity via positive differentiation between 'us' and 'them' (Tajfel & Turner, 1986). In line with both theories, what the researchers found was that derogatory intergroup behaviour *that was relatively self-determined* led to relatively high levels of psychological well-being, self-actualisation and positive social identification. Here again, we observe an empirical relationship between self-determination and social identity processes such that people experienced the most favourable self-concept when ingroup favouritism was self-determined.

In a third example of how SDT and the social identity approach can be empirically complementary, a study conducted in Australia by Emma Thomas and colleagues expanded upon the self-determination concept by changing the assessment of self-determination so that it referred to the plural ('Australians') rather than the singular ('I'; Thomas, Amiot, Louis, & Goddard, 2017, Study 2). This subtle alteration to the standard assessment procedure meant that participants' self was still implicated in their responses, but that response items now measured a sense of *collective* self-determination (e.g., asking respondents whether they engaged in a behaviour 'because Australians care' rather than 'because I care'). In a political help-giving context (where participants were asked about their motivations for giving aid to Nepal), the researchers found that participants' higher levels of social identification with a group representative were associated with higher levels of collective self-determination. On this basis, the authors concluded that collective self-determination represented the degree to which the group and its authorities 'allow group members to act autonomously, and in ways consistent with the expression of core group values' (Thomas et al., 2017, p. 674). In other words, this analysis showed how an empirical self-determination analysis of human motivation could reasonably be broadened to include a self, conceptualised at more abstract levels (see Figure 19.2).

Finally, a recently published study by a team of Belgian researchers provides an interesting empirical contrast to this study by Thomas and colleagues (2017). Whereas that previous study identified the empirical feasibility of collective self-determination, the Belgian study by Bart Reynders and colleagues (2019) found that coaches' implementation of SDT principles (e.g., seeking to satisfy athletes' need for autonomy) yielded enhanced benefits for athletes *primarily in individual sports* (e.g., swimming, athletics, tennis) rather than those in team sports (e.g., volleyball, soccer, rugby). This suggests that the focus on individual psychology within SDT may be more conducive to success in individual pursuits, while the more group-oriented focus of the SIA may lend itself to success in collective, team pursuits.

In different ways, these four studies provide evidence of the empirical complementarity of SDT and the SIA. Here the evidence suggests that the two theories can sit side-by-side, each explaining different aspects of behaviour and/or different stages in the behaviour chain. From this empirical work, it would thus appear that there is not necessarily a need for researchers and practitioners to choose one theory over the other as both have their own independent empirical support. Moreover, the processes outlined by each can be observed to operate simultaneously in a single empirical context. Indeed, as the four studies we have discussed show, using both allows researchers to examine more complicated models, assess multiple psychological processes, and reliably account for greater variability in key empirical outcomes. This means that practitioners, including sport psychologists, can reasonably employ the evidence garnered from these empirical analyses to answer a wider range of applied questions than they can by using either theory on its own. This point is confirmed by other empirical work that also examines processes associated with each theory (e.g., Coatsworth & Conroy, 2009; Neys, Jansz, & Tan, 2014; Vlachopoulos, Kaperoni, & Moustaka, 2011). Nevertheless, it remains the case that studies which seek to integrate these two approaches are rare (especially in sport and exercise contexts). Accordingly, the lack of integrated research highlights opportunities for further empirical investigation in the future.

Conceptual commonalities

At a conceptual level, there are important commonalities between SDT and the SIA. In particular, each approach employs concepts that have broad similarities to concepts employed in the other approach. In this way, the two theories may not simply be complementary at an empirical level, but may instead be understood as addressing the same social and psychological processes, albeit representing these using slightly different language.

The importance of social relations

Consider, for example, the importance of social relations in each theoretical perspective. As noted above, SDT assumes that humans have a basic need for relatedness. As Deci and Ryan (2012, p. 87) observe, people 'need to experience relatedness to other people and groups' (although within SDT this has primarily been operationalised as interpersonal relatedness).

Indeed, this assumption that people have a basic need to belong has a long history in psychology, dating back at least to the work of Muzafer Sherif and Hadley Cantril (1947).

Empirically, attempts to thwart this need for relatedness via interpersonal ostracism have been shown to increase negative affect, such that people feel bad when they are socially excluded by other individuals (Legate, DeHaan, Weinstein, & Ryan, 2013). This effect has been demonstrated extensively in the context of an online game called Cyberball, in which a virtual ball is initially passed between a participant and two 'other people' (who are represented virtually). After a period of time, the other two people pass it only between themselves, thereby excluding the participant (Hartgerink, Van Beest, Wicherts, & Williams, 2015). When they are ostracised in this manner, cyberball players reliably report a lower sense of belonging, lower self-esteem, a lower sense of meaning in life and greater anger.

In contrast to the work in this experimental paradigm, charitable giving has been shown to result from attempts to fulfil a need for relatedness by providing participants with social support (Pavey, Greitemeyer, & Sparks, 2011). More relevant to the domain of sport psychology, Martyn Standage and colleagues (2005) found that increased support for relatedness among physical education students (as well as support for other assumed needs specified by SDT) enhanced those students' need satisfaction (including related-ness need satisfaction) and that this, in turn, enhanced their subjective well-being and preference for challenging physical education tasks. Here, then, participants who agreed that their physical education teacher encouraged them to work together felt closer to others and, in turn, were more willing to engage in challenging exercise.

This assumption of a need for relatedness highlights the importance of developing associations and identifications with others, in much the same way as the social identity approach presupposes. Indeed, recent empirical work informed by social identity principles has shown that group members' expressions of ingroup favouritism enhance their sense of belonging (Hunter et al., 2017). In this way, beyond their empirical complementarities, the two theories share some critical *conceptual* similarities. These similarities, however, are not perfect. Critically, the SIA does *not* propose a *need* for relatedness or a *need* to belong (Platow, Hunter, Haslam, & Reicher, 2015). Nevertheless, the idea that people readily associate themselves with social categories (i.e., ingroups) that include others *is* a basic assumption of the approach – although it is argued that this assumption arises simply from the *psychological reality of groups* rather than from an abstract individual need (Oakes et al., 1994).

There are additional ways in which we can observe conceptual commonalities between the two theoretical approaches. In the domain of social relations, for example, a key feature of applications of SDT (including in sport and clinical psychology) pertains to others' ability to guide people in ways that help them to act in accordance with their core values (i.e., to be more autonomous and self-determined). Empirical support for this idea comes from research by Anthony Amorose and Dawn Anderson-Butcher (2007) which showed that perceived autonomy support from coaches led players to have an enhanced motivational orientation towards a relevant sporting activity. Moreover, this relationship between perceived autonomy support and motivational orientation was mediated by a sense of need satisfaction (see also Reynders et al., 2019). In other words, players were more motivated when coaches helped them to feel that their decisions were their own (rather than being orders from the coach) because this gave them a sense of self-determination (rather than a sense of being controlled).

In other research, coaches' autonomy-supportive behaviours have been shown to be directly and positively predicted by their level of empathic concern for athletes. Critically, too, work by Doris Matosic and colleagues (2017) shows that empathic concern is directly, and negatively, predicted by coaches' narcissism levels. This suggests that the success of coaches results from them focusing on *others* rather than on themselves.

Undoubtedly, coaches guide, direct, encourage and support players. In this way, coaches are leaders who ultimately influence players' behaviours, be it positively or negatively. In terms of our current analysis, the influence and leadership processes of successful coaches can be seen to follow processes outlined in the SIA (e.g., Haslam, Reicher, & Platow, 2011). As discussed in Chapters 2 and 3, the social identity analysis of leadership assumes that influence – including the influence of coaches – is made possible only through a sense of shared social identity between leaders and those they are attempting to influence (Platow, Haslam, Reicher, & Steffens, 2015). In this way, for example, the success of coaches' autonomy support may well be made possible only because it is predicated on (and helps to reinforce) a sense of 'us' between them and their players. As the great American basketball coach Bobby Knight put it, 'To be as good as it can be, a team has to buy into what you as the coach are doing. They have to feel you're a part of them and they're a part of you' (Knight & Hammel, 2002, p. 314). Accordingly, this sense of 'us' will often be something that coaches seek to cultivate through identity entrepreneurship.

Likewise, as Platow, Haslam, Reicher, Grace, and Cruwys (2020) observe, respect can be a powerful way to create a shared social identity, and the autonomy support that coaches provide can be one of many ways of expressing respect towards their players. In other words, through their provision of autonomy support, coaches may actually be building a sense of shared social identity with players, and it is this that ultimately allows them to have greater influence over those players' motivations, attitudes and behaviours.

The importance of autonomy

As noted from the outset, SDT assumes a basic human need for autonomy. Indeed, according to Deci and Ryan (2012, p. 86), 'Knowing whether people's motivation is … autonomous is … important for making predictions about the quality of people's engagement, performance, and well-being.' If there is one central principle to SDT, this might well be it.

There is no doubt that the empirical support for this assumption is strong. This is evidenced by a cross-cultural meta-analysis of 36 independent samples, conducted by Shi Yu and colleagues (2018), that found a positive and strong relationship between autonomy and subjective well-being ($r = .46$). It is not surprising, therefore, that the sheer empirical force of this relationship should lead to the autonomy concept being incorporated into other conceptual analyses.

This is precisely what John Turner (2005) did in developing an analysis of social power based on self-categorization theory. Although autonomy played no role in Turner's original explication of SCT (e.g., Turner et al., 1987), he unabashedly relied on this concept in his attempt to differentiate 'coercion' from 'influence'. For Turner, coercion strongly limits individuals' and group members' autonomy and, as with Deci and Ryan (2012), it is seen to have very negative consequences. Thus, for Turner, 'freedom from coercion becomes ... important, and whatever advances one's freedom is redefined positively...' (Turner et al., 1987, p.13). In this way 'the general rule is where possible to disguise coercion as legitimate authority and minimise the threat to the target's perceived freedom' (p. 16). Turner further relied on SDT principles when he explains that 'the coercion of a target tends to increase social distance ... induce private rejection of the influence attempt and *engender resistance and reactance* [with] the goal of rejecting control and restoring freedom' (p. 16, emphasis added). In so far as it emphasises the importance of autonomy, this analysis of power is wholly consistent with SDT's core assumptions.

To summarise this section on conceptual commonalities, there is clear overlap in the concepts employed by SDT and the SIA. Both approaches provide a basis for individuality *and sociality*, and both view autonomy as an important human motivation. This commonality provides further reason to consider the two theoretical perspectives as potentially complementary. For not only can we observe the operation of principles from both perspectives in single empirical analyses, but also the conceptual commonalities provide a basis for identifying a more inclusive, overarching framework for understanding human motivations, attitudes and behaviours.

Theoretical chasm

The previous two sections highlight opportunities for empirical and conceptual integration between SDT and the SIA. In this final section, however, we make the claim that the two perspectives are, in fact, theoretically *incompatible*. This incompatibility is revealed through a deeper interrogation of fundamental assumptions within each approach. In the end, as we outline below, each approach makes opposing and irreconcilable assumptions about the self in its explanations of human motivation, attitudes and behaviour. Specifically, two of these assumptions pertain to the *nature of the self-concept* itself and the *genesis of human needs*.

The individualistic 'true self' versus the dynamic individual and collective self

Self-determination theory, like many psychological theories of the self (e.g., Gaertner, Sedikides, Vevea, & Iuzzini, 2002), assumes there is such a thing as a core, true self. This is fundamental to SDT's analysis of intrinsic and extrinsic motivations. Only attitudes and behaviours that emerge genuinely from within the individual are understood to be expressions of truly intrinsic motivations. Motivation is considered intrinsic only when the individual is freed from constraints imposed by the material and social context:

'Intrinsically motivated behaviours are those that are freely engaged out of interest without the necessity of separable consequences' (Deci & Ryan, 2000, p. 233). Thus, it is through expression of the true self's preferences that people are ultimately most self-determined. Moreover, despite seeking social relations with others, this true self remains highly individualistic. So while individuals can develop *relatively* internal motivations via the internalisation of goals and preferences of others (see Figure 6.2), intrinsic motivations emerge only from each individual in his or her uniqueness.

In contrast, the social identity approach – and SCT in particular – rejects any notion of a core, 'true self'. As noted above, in this theory, the self is understood to be dynamic and context-dependent (Onorato & Turner, 2004). As Turner et al. (1987, p. 46) observe explicitly, 'It is fundamental to our assumption that ... the personal self reflects only one level of abstraction of self-categorization, of which more inclusive levels are just as valid and in some conditions more important.' In this way, 'Personal self-categorizations are not regarded ... as having any privileged status in defining the self. They do not represent the "true" individual self which in some way invests the other levels with their significance.' The self is both individually and collectively represented, and no representation is any more psychologically valid and true than any other. This means that people can and will act in accordance with the norms and values of a salient self-category (as defined at a particular level of abstraction) and, when they do, these actions will be 'self-determined' at that level of self-representation (see also Kachanoff, Wohl, Koestner, & Taylor, 2020). We note, however, that this theoretical analysis does not directly invoke the concept of self-determination. Consider, for example, the motivation of a highly competitive athlete helping a collapsed opponent across the finish line (e.g., the case of Johnny Brownlee; see Chapter 5). One explanation for this behaviour is that the opponent is really an ingroup member at a higher level of self-abstraction – as both competitors are athletes (i.e., they share a common group membership) with the norms and values of fair play and integrity. From an SIA perspective, simply because the helping behaviour reflects a more abstract sense of self and integration of collective norms into that self-representation, this behaviour is *no less* of a true reflection of self than running past the collapsed competitor to achieve personal victory.

Interestingly, SDT does not actually offer an analysis of how the self is construed beyond the fundamental assumption that, *inter alia*, individuals have 'innate psychological needs' (Ryan & Deci, 2000, p. 68) and are 'liberally endowed with intrinsic motivational tendencies' (p. 70). In contrast, SCT explicitly outlines the social and psychological processes through which the self-concept is constructed and represented within each individual. In particular, it draws on principles of cognitive psychology, which explain how people form cognitive representations of stimuli in their world (McGarty, 1999; Oakes et al., 1994; Turner et al., 1987). In this way, one might imagine that the processes outlined by SCT could reasonably serve as antecedents for the self that is implicated in SDT. Unfortunately, though, this simple integration is not theoretically possible, due primarily to the incompatibility of metatheoretical assumptions concerning the core/true and individual self on the one hand, and the dynamic and collective self on the other.

Innate needs versus socially constructed needs

As we have already noted, SDT assumes three innate psychological needs: competence, relatedness and autonomy (Deci & Ryan, 2012; Ryan & Deci, 2000; see also Figure 10.2). Researchers working within the SIA, however, have shied away from explicit claims about the nature of human needs. Although clear motivational constructs have been identified, including self-esteem (Abrams & Hogg, 1988), uncertainty reduction (Hogg, 2000) and meaning making (McGarty, 1999), their status as needs, let alone *innate* needs, remains unclear. Thus, as noted above, despite being a theory of social behaviour, the SIA does not assume a *need* to belong and/or a *need* for relatedness (Platow, Hunter et al., 2015).

This absence of fundamentally assumed needs, though, does not mean that social identity theorists eschew the concept of needs altogether (Greenaway, Cruwys et al., 2016). As with SDT, needs are tied directly to the self, but because the SIA assumes a dynamic self, needs are also dynamic (Haslam et al., 2000). Of course, people can have individual needs – needs that are tied to their personal self-categorizations. But they can also have social needs; these would be needs explicitly tied to their social self-categorizations. Critically, however, because the SIA rejects the view of the personal self as somehow the 'true' self, social needs are seen to be just as valid and fundamental as personal needs. Moreover, because the self is actively constructed within a specific context, these valid and fundamental needs can also be (re)constructed by context. What a sportswoman needs when she is acting as an individual (e.g., competence in the form of personal success, and relatedness in the form of personal recognition by others) is therefore no more fundamental or important than what she needs when she is acting as a member of a particular team (e.g., competence in the form of *collective* success and relatedness in the form of *collective* recognition). In this way, the approach avoids any recourse to innateness.

On the basis of such arguments, the SIA recognises the psychological validity of socially constructed needs – seeing these as true needs associated with a particular psychologically valid self-concept. They *are* internal because they emerge from people's salient self-concepts, albeit self-concepts that are construed to include other ingroup members and determined, at least in part, by the broader social context (Turner et al., 1994). In contrast, SDT would consider any social needs to be a form of external motivation. This is seen when Deci and Ryan (2012, p. 88, emphasis added) observe that 'socially transmitted motivation and regulations can become fully internalised and form the basis for autonomous or self-determined *extrinsically* motivated behaviour.' An example of this is when people engage in sport and exercise activities because they have internalised the social-normative understanding that these are fundamentally beneficial for their physical and psychological health. For these people, then, this type of integrated regulation would still fail to represent full and proper self-determination.

This interrogation of the two theories' needs-based assumptions again points to ways in which they are ultimately irreconcilable. This means that one of the theories would have to abandon its view of the nature of human needs for any rapprochement between the two to be possible. However, such abandonment would alter one or other theory to such an extent that it would become, in effect, a completely new theory (or, possibly, simply a restatement of the other). And this is unlikely to please anyone.

An empirical rapprochement?

Before we end this section of our analysis, we consider one final attempt at an empirical rapprochement between the two theories. This is, of course, how we began our analysis: by recognising that SDT and the SIA could be (and in fact are) empirically complementary. For this, we consider one of our own studies (Grace, David, & Ryan, 2008). As the study was *not* originally designed to examine SDT principles, we are aware that the data remain open to critique from that perspective. Nevertheless, the study helps to illustrate the issue of whether or not rapprochement is possible.

The study is particularly relevant because it employs a free-choice paradigm not dissimilar to that used in early studies of intrinsic motivation among children (e.g., Lepper & Greene, 1975; Ross, 1975). Free-choice paradigms are useful when assessing predictions derived from SDT, as the very structure of these is intended to remove all external reward incentives. In the study, children ($\approx$ 4 years and 2 months old) first completed a task (sorting pictures and answering questions) that made psychologically salient either their social identity as a child (as opposed to an adult) or their social identity as a boy or girl. They went on to watch a video of a same-sex adult and opposite-sex child play with toys (e.g., choosing a red Mickey Mouse hat and putting it on backwards). The children were then provided with exactly the same toys as in the video, and were invited to play (in any way they wished) with whatever toys they wanted. No external incentives were provided.

The results were very clear: in free play, children engaged in behaviours of the same salient self-category models as themselves (i.e., either as a child or as a boy/girl). From a social identity perspective, we can see that the children in this study had free choice and hence their behaviour reflected an internal motivation – so there is no reason to consider their behaviour as anything other than self-determined. From the perspective of SDT, however, these findings may be, at best, seen as only 'somewhat internal' in that the behaviour emerged from what Ryan and Deci refer to as 'regulation through identification' (2000, p. 72); hence, the children's behaviour is unlikely to be interpreted as fully self-determined due to the influence of external factors. Herein lies the critical question: how can behaviour (in a free-choice context) be considered intrinsically motivated when there has been an external influence on that behaviour? Social identity theorists answer by arguing that it is precisely when the self is defined in group-based terms that group motivation is no longer extrinsic but instead *becomes intrinsic* (Ellemers et al., 2004; Haslam et al., 2000; see also Figure 6.4). In the end, wherever one sits on this debate, it is clear that the Grace et al. (2008) study exposes important differences between the two theoretical analyses in their fundamental assumptions concerning (a) the nature of the self (as stable vs dynamic, as individual vs both individual and collective) and (b) the psychological validity and motivational force of that self in any given context.

CONCLUSION: THE WAY FORWARD FOR SPORT AND EXERCISE PSYCHOLOGY

In this chapter, we have examined some key features of the social identity approach and self-determination theory. Given the prominent role of SDT in the field of sport and exercise psychology, we saw this as imperative for the goals of this volume. Setting about this task, we noted first that there is some clear evidence of empirical complementarity. Researchers have unquestionably accounted for a greater amount of variance when seeking to explain key outcomes by including measures associated with concepts derived from both theories. This means that sport psychologists can build more comprehensive empirical models in both laboratory and applied contexts by using standard measures developed within the two empirical traditions. For example, by examining the process of social identity-based leadership, one might see how athletes and coaches work together to develop goals that are subjectively experienced as highly self-determined by members of their teams. This high sense of self-determination could then, in turn, be shown to build social identity among team members in ways that positively affect their performance and well-being outcomes.

Second, we observed clear evidence of conceptual commonality between the two theoretical approaches. Both theories, for example, address issues of affiliation with others. The self-categorization analysis of power also strongly assumes a need (or at least a striving) for autonomy. However, further conceptual clarity is essential if an attempt to reconcile differences between the two theoretical approaches is sought. For example, because, as we noted, there is no 'need to belong' within the social identity approach, the precise status of needs is a useful focus for future conceptual work in this domain (e.g., as noted by Greenaway, Cruwys et al., 2016; see also Chapter 6).

Yet, despite their respective strengths, we believe that the two theories are, at core, incompatible. Indeed, as we saw, the examination of basic assumptions underlying the two theories exposes them as fundamentally different. We therefore caution both researchers and practitioners to be clear about what each theory does and does not assume. At the same time, because the social identity approach is relatively new to the field of sport and exercise psychology, we recognise the need for more social identity research to allow fuller and more detailed comparisons and evaluations between the SIA and SDT. This is especially important given the current preponderance of SDT research in this area. Here, then, a key function of this chapter – and of the current volume as a whole – should be to help clarify precisely what it is that a social identity analysis adds to the study of sport and exercise psychology.

We end with a final caution that, in choosing one theoretical approach over another, one must not be swayed simply by the *amount* of research in each domain. By this criterion, all theoretical and empirical efforts would stagnate, and progress would become increasingly hard to make. Ultimately, of course, choosing an approach will depend on the goals of the researcher or practitioner. For example, one may simply have a problem-solving goal, reasonably following Laudan's principle that, 'A theory should solve a maximal number of empirical problems while generating a minimal number of anomalies'

(Laudan, 1996, p. 80). Yet even this requires researchers to clarify the assumptions that underpin these goals and the precise problem that they seek to solve (e.g., concerning the conceptualisation of the relationship between the individual and the group), as this provides the basis for choosing one set of assumptions (and one theory) over another.

In this regard, a function of this chapter has been to bring the assumptions that underpin SDT and the SIA into sharper relief, in ways that allow them to be interrogated more forensically in future research. We hope that our analysis encourages researchers and practitioners to engage more closely with the important issues of psychological theory that the two approaches raise – in particular, those relating to the nature of the self. In turn, we hope that this will help readers to select a theory for their own purposes on a more informed basis with: better knowledge of its parameters, its assumptions and its scope; greater appreciation of the questions it can and cannot answer; and, most importantly, a clearer sense that data collection will not resolve the important conceptual differences between the two theories.

Above all else, however, we hope this chapter makes it clear that when it comes to explaining well-being, motivation and performance in sport, there are distinct theoretical paths between which one needs to choose. Moreover, the fact that the path laid out by self-determination theory is better trodden than that defined by the social identity approach does not necessarily make it the right one to follow. After all, as the American football coach Jerry Rice observed, success is often about doing what others don't, so that tomorrow you can do what they can't.

20

THE POLITICAL PSYCHOLOGY OF SPORT

STEPHEN D. REICHER
MEREDITH SCHERTZINGER
FERGUS NEVILLE

The preceding chapters in this book have looked at the many ways in which social identity impacts sport. Among other things, they show that it shapes participation, motivates performance and underpins the behaviour of supporters. In this chapter we turn this focus around and ask whether and how sport shapes social identity. And, in so doing, we ask a bigger question: Does sport impact the wider nature of our societies? More specifically, does sport help to define the identities we live by, the nature of the social groups we join and encounter, and the relationships within and between these social groups?

These are big questions that are difficult to answer definitively. And it is important to stress from the start that we won't be providing simple or definitive answers. For while there are many claims as to how sport has impacted society, there is little in the way of systematic analysis. For this reason, this chapter will be less a summary of existing psychological literature than a review of historical and contemporary examples that will be used to set an agenda for future research, more specifically for a political psychology of sport.

Accordingly, we begin by exploring a number of the more striking instances that seemingly attest to the power of sport to shape social identities, and we then use these to structure a set of questions relating to the ways in which sport can define social relations in society.

DOES SPORT IMPACT SOCIETY?

The Olympic Games seem a good place to start, being one of the largest global sporting events. As noted in Chapter 2, the modern Olympic movement was created explicitly as a means of changing relations between society and replacing conflict with harmony. The website of the Olympic movement accordingly quotes its founding father, Baron de Coubertin as saying:

> Wars break out because nations misunderstand each other. We shall not have peace until the prejudices that now separate the different races are outlived. To attain this end, what better means is there than to bring the youth of all countries periodically together for amicable trials of muscular strength and agility? (International Olympic Committee, 2019)

But de Coubertin was not naïve. He recognised that, even if the Olympic movement sought to use sport for peace, others had very different ends in mind: 'Athletics can bring into play both the noblest and the basest passions', he noted, 'they can be used to strengthen peace or to prepare for war' (International Olympic Committee, 2019). And, over time, it is perhaps the nationalist rather than the internationalist dimensions of sport which have acquired most prominence (e.g., see Orwell, 1945, as discussed in Chapter 1). That is, much attention has been paid to the ways in which sport is used to redefine nations and to help them reassert themselves against others – and rather less to how sport can unite nations and help them overcome differences.

In the case of the Olympics, the 1936 Games in Berlin are the most notorious of all. In his book on *The Nazi Olympics*, Richard Mandell cites Hans Grass as arguing that 'athletes should be seen not as sportsmen, but rather as political troops who treat the sporting contests only as their particular branch of the great struggle as a whole' (Mandell, 2000, p. 292). However, such a sentiment is far from unique to 1936, to Germany, or to the Olympics. Almost everywhere one looks, sportspeople are treated as soldiers of a particular stripe – or, in countries without military forces, as a substitute force. Thus, it has been said of Costa Rica (which has had no army since 1948 and utilises what would be military spending on education and healthcare) that 'We have no soldiers, only Soccer Players' (Sandoval-Garcia, 2008, p. 215, capitals in original). Equally, wherever one goes in the world, one will find claims that specific sporting events have impacted the history of the nation. So let us look at these more closely.

Sport and social relations within the nation

Sometimes these claims about the impact of sport concern intragroup relations. Most powerfully, it has indeed been suggested that sport can help in the creation of nations – or at least to create cohesion out of fragmented groups. For instance, the victory of India over England in the 1948 Olympic hockey final – against their former colonial masters and played in London – is often credited with bringing the country together after the centrifugal forces of partition in 1947. Thus, before the final, Jawaharlal Nehru, the first prime minister of India, emphasised the importance of the team for the state of the nation. As Balbir Singh Sr, one of the team's forwards, recounts: 'He told me that it was important that we kept winning on the world stage. "Tell all your teammates", he said, "India needs this badly"' (Raghunandan, 2018).

A more recent example involves the fan base of the Northern Irish football team. Their supporters have traditionally been regarded as hardline Loyalists who excluded members of the Republican community. This resulted in several high-profile incidents of fan sectarianism, including during a match against the Republic of Ireland in 1993, and the jeering of the Northern Irish player Neil Lennon in 2001 after he signed for Celtic (a Scottish club with a large Irish Nationalist following). Lennon retired from international football in 2001 following death threats apparently from the Loyalist Volunteer Force. As a counterforce to these tensions, the 'Football For All' campaign within Northern Ireland created the 'Green and White Army' to function as an amalgamation of fan groups from different cultural backgrounds (Bell, Somerville, & Hargie, 2019). Indeed, this effort at bringing the fanbase – and country – together was recognised by UEFA in 2006 when they gave Northern Irish fans the Brussels International Supporters Award (since renamed the European Football Supporters Award) for their attempts to rid matches of sectarianism.

However, as noted in Chapters 1 and 2, probably the most striking demonstration of the capacity for sport to unite a country comes from South Africa. At the 1995 Rugby World Cup final in Johannesburg, the recently freed president, Nelson Mandela, appeared to the crowd wearing a Springbok jersey and cap, a gesture which helped secure the participation of whites – and, more specifically, Afrikaners, in the South African 'Rainbow Nation'. In his book *Playing the Enemy*, John Carlin quotes the South African player Morné du Plessis, as saying:

> This crowd of white people, of Afrikaners, as one man, as one nation, they were chanting 'Nel-son! Nel-son! Nel-son' … I don't think I'll ever experience a moment like that again. It was a moment of magic, a moment of wonder. It was the moment I realised that there really was a chance this country could work. (Carlin, 2008, pp. 221–222)

Equally, though, sport can also divide a nation – or at least, it can confirm the exclusion of certain groups from the national community. In this respect, there is a tragic circularity to the history of rugby union in South Africa. For if, in 1995, it helped overcome the racial exclusions of apartheid, in 1903 it helped form a white nation. After the Boer war had divided Dutch from British colonists, the 1903 tour by a British rugby team helped bring them back together again. To quote Zachary Bigalke: 'As a cultural representative of the nascent state, the national rugby team entrenched the exclusion of black and coloured individuals in the formation of this new national identity' (2019, p. 154).

In a similar vein, sport has served both to exclude and to include women in the public sphere and various national communities. Following the 1979 Islamic Revolution in Iran, women were banned from entering football stadiums, reflecting the gender inequality within the nation more broadly. This total ban remained in effect until 2019 when Sahar Khodayari, an Iranian woman who was passionate about football, self-immolated on 2 September 2019, following her arrest for attempting to attend a match (Wamsley, 2019). Following pressure from FIFA and both domestic and international outrage at the incident, women were finally permitted to attend the 2022 World Cup qualifying match between Iran and Cambodia on 10 October 2019 (Mansoor, 2019). The stadium was empty beyond the packed women's section, and other women were denied entry despite the extra space within the stadium (Malekian, 2019). Although the women were only allotted 3,500 seats in a large stadium, had to park in a separate location, go through a separate gate, and sit in an isolated section, it was still seen as a major moment for gender equality with Iran. Whether these restrictions remain in place for future matches, and what the impact of Khodayari's death and subsequent policy change will be on the empowerment of Iranian women, remain to be seen.

However, the intragroup impact of sport is not limited to relations between different parties within the nation; it can also help determine who gets to lead the nation. Sporting victory, it is sometimes argued, boosts incumbents who can bask in reflected glory. Sporting failure, though, is sometimes said to lead incumbents to lose. In the midst of the 1970 general election campaign, England went down to a 3–2 defeat to West Germany. According to the then Labour Minister for Sport, Denis Howell, this was integral to his party's defeat: 'The moment goalkeeper Bonetti made his third and final hash of it on the Sunday, everything simultaneously began to go wrong for Labour for the following Thursday' (Keating, 2010).

Sport and relations between nations

But claims about the impact of sport on politics often concern intergroup (not just intra-group) relations. In some cases, this is limited to perceptions and feelings. Thus, it has been argued that the victory of the Netherlands over Germany in the semi-finals of the 1988 European football championship – and more specifically, the image of Ronald Koeman apparently wiping his backside on a German shirt in celebration – was interpreted as a symbolic reversal of occupation during World War II (during which the Germans had, among other things, confiscated all Dutch bicycles). Kuper (2011) thus describes how:

> Nine million people, 60% of the population, celebrated on the streets. It was the largest public gathering since the Liberation. 'It feels as though we've won the war at last' said a former Resistance fighter on TV. … In the Leidseplein square in Amsterdam, people threw bicycles (their own?) into the air and shouted, 'Hurray, we've got our bikes back!'

In other cases, it is argued that the change in power relations in sport had led to actual conflict, because dominant groups feel threatened by a resurgent underdog. As an example, it has been suggested that the 5–4 victory of Czechoslovakia over the Soviet Union in the

1968 Olympic ice hockey final was a catalyst for the Soviet invasion of Czechoslovakia later that year. Thus, the Czechoslovakian player Jan Havel recounts:

> The tanks rolled in in '68 … because the nation was united behind hockey and behind beating the Russians and the Soviets got scared. … Hockey served as a proxy battlefield. As Russian tanks overran Czechoslovakia, '5–4' graffiti appeared everywhere, offering a reminder of the outcome of the Olympic match. (Scheiner, 2018)

As Stott notes in Chapter 18, a similar dynamic has been proposed as one factor leading up to the 'Homeland War' between Croatia and Serbia of 1991. On 13 May 1990, the Croatian football team of Dinamo Zagreb played a Yugoslav First League game at home against the Serbian team of Red Star Belgrade. During the encounter, Serbian police attacked the Dinamo fans. Dinamo players, notably the captain Zvonimir Boban, responded by attacking the police. This is said to have given the Croatians confidence in fighting back, and a memorial outside the Dinamo ground today commemorates: 'All the Dinamo fans for whom the war started on May 13, 1990 and ended with them laying down their lives on the altar of the Croatian homeland' (Milekic, 1996).

But if sport can empower people to assert their nationhood, it is claimed that it can also disempower them and undermine national self-assertion. For example, Scotland went to the 1978 Football World Cup with high hopes. Their humiliating defeat and elimination in the first round have been linked to the vote against Scottish devolution in 1979. As Andrew Marr puts it: 'The "We were rubbish" hangover certainly contributed to the outcome' (cited in the Scottish Football Blog, 2010).

A somewhat different dynamic linking sport to international relations has more to do with conceptions of legitimacy than the sense of empowerment. One example of this involves another actual war – the famous 'football war' between Honduras and El Salvador in 1969 that followed a highly fraught set of qualifiers for the 1970 World Cup between the two nations. On the day of the decisive third play-off game in Mexico City, El Salvador broke off diplomatic relations claiming that some 12,000 Salvadorians had been forced to flee Honduras following the previous game. Three weeks later they launched an air attack on Honduras.

Another example involves a trade war (or, more accurately, the threat of a trade war). This is the famous cricketing 'bodyline controversy' of 1933, in which Australians were outraged at the tactics of English bowlers aiming for the bodies of the opposing batsmen. Mindful of its broader political significance, the Australian cricketing authorities cabled a message to the English on 18 January 1933 saying that:

> Bodyline bowling assumed such proportions as to menace best interests of game, making protection of body by batsmen the main consideration. Causing intensely bitter feelings between players, as well as injury. In our opinion is unsportsmanlike. Unless stopped at once [it is] likely to upset friendly relations between Australia and England. (Frith, 2002, p. 22)

Indeed, the accusation of being 'unsportsmanlike' was seen as so extreme that there were fears it would disrupt diplomatic and trade relations between the two countries. Things were only settled when the Australian prime minister, Joseph Lyons, persuaded his cricketing board to back down. They wrote another cable which, while still objecting strongly to bodyline bowling, stated: 'We do not regard the sportsmanship of your team as being in question' (Green, 1989, p. 154).

Some recent research has examined the framing of intergroup relations through sport in more systematic ways. Prior to the 2014 Football World Cup, a YouGov global survey of fans worldwide noted a correlation between a country's least favourite participating team and the current political tension between the two countries (Aisch, Leonhardt, & Qauealy, 2014). Moreover, a subsequent study found similar results when examining Jewish-Israeli attitudes towards the German national team (Samuel-Azran, Galily, Karniel, & Lavie-Dinur, 2016). In line with this, the media are well known for framing sporting fixtures in terms of international rivalries in ways that thereby help to reproduce such rivalries. John Vincent and colleauges (2010), for example, showed how both English and German media outlets described a football match between the two nations as a continuation of their World War II rivalry.

But this is not inevitable. Sport does not invariably reproduce international conflicts; it can also critique and challenge them. As Kausik Bandyopadhyay (2008) argues, while Pakistan and India are locked in a long-standing international dispute, the Indian cricket team's 2004 tour of Pakistan was marked by goodwill and friendship as fans and cricket boards of both nations were able to come together in their love of the sport. Similarly, an in-depth quantitative and qualitative analysis of football fans from 18 European countries concluded that despite cultural and political differences, the supporters all ultimately speak the 'language of football' (Parks, 2008). This is reminiscent of what is perhaps the most famous incident of sport's capacity to overcome intergroup rivalry. On Christmas day 1914 at the start of World War I, for several hours on the western front, German and British soldiers stopped fighting to play football between the two lines of trenches in No Man's Land (Hughes, 2014). While the incident was not unique and indeed can be seen as just one example of a 'live and let live' ethos between the opposing armies (Ashworth, 2004), it has acquired iconic status. Indeed, the moment was recently recognised with a memorial in which Prince William commented at the ceremony, 'Football has the power to bring people together and break down barriers' (Hughes, 2014).

In sum, there are many examples which suggest that de Coubertin was right in suggesting that athletics (and sport more generally) can be a force for harmony and a force for conflict: that it can both strengthen peace and lead to war. Again, though, it should be noted that, in either case, the examples we have marshalled are suggestive rather than definitive, and there is little conclusive evidence that it was sport that had the consequences claimed for it. Accordingly, there is a pressing need for more systematic studies that might support strong causal claims. Nevertheless, at a minimum, there is a prima facie case that the answer to the question posed in this section is in the affirmative: yes, sport *does* impact society.

The examples we have provided here have also done a little more. We have begun to suggest some of the ways in which this impact occurs (i.e., by informing relations within the nation as well as relations between nations). We have also begun to describe some of the different processes through which these impacts are achieved. It is now time to look rather more closely at precisely how sport impacts society.

HOW DOES SPORT IMPACT SOCIETY? ✗

In order to understand the impact of sport on relations within and between nations it is useful to start by considering the nature of nationhood. Here we draw on the work of Benedict Anderson on the nation as an *imagined community* (Anderson, 1991). This notion reflects the fact that it is not possible for every member of a given country to be physically co-present at any point in time. For this reason, the idea of a national community can only be an imaginative construct rather than something that is directly experienced or perceived. What, then, allows us to have such a sense of nationhood? Anderson puts it down to a series of conditions; for our purposes, the critical one has to do with the role of the media and, more specifically, the way that, in consuming the news, we have a sense of others across the country attending to the same news in the same way.

One might expect this to be particularly true when the news concerns those things that in themselves can be seen as 'national', and nothing fits this better than the fate of national sporting teams. For reasons discussed in Chapter 2, we would expect all those who see themselves as nationals to react in the same way to their country's triumphs and failures. As an Olympic gold medal is won, or a World Cup-winning goal is scored, we cheer and at the same time imagine people the length and breadth of the land cheering like us. And, as a result, we have a sense of being part of the national community.

But, in so far as these sportspeople are representative in a symbolic as well as a formal sense – that is, in so far as they are *the imagined community made manifest* – we can also use their triumphs and failures to tell us something about ourselves. More specifically, we can evaluate the nation's place and standing in the world from the performance of the people and teams that represent them. More generally, sport constitutes a key arena in which we form representations both of ourselves and of others.

Once again, the Olympic Games are a prime example of this. Olympic opening ceremonies are particularly rich resources for examining how a nation wishes to be seen, the elements which it seeks to highlight in the national story, the voices which are heard, and also the groups which are rendered invisible and silent (Billings & Angelini, 2007; Hogan, 2003). In this way, such events can be seen as feats of *identity impresarioship* in which hierarchies of class, gender and race which run through the broader society are reproduced and reinforced (Haslam, Reicher, & Platow, 2011; see also Chapter 3).

But, of course, relatively few people actually attend Olympic events. Rather, the nation watches them on TV or reads about them in their newspapers. Hence, the impact of these events is mediated through the media. And, unsurprisingly, media coverage is heavily slanted towards the outlet's country of origin (Angelini, MacArthur, Smith, &

Billings, 2017). Furthermore, as a result of this ingroup favouritism, the Olympics have been shown to increase viewers' nationalism and patriotism (Billings, Brown, & Brown, 2013; Billings, Brown, & Brown-Devlin, 2015; Seate, Ma, Iles, McCloskey, & Parry-Giles, 2017) and this may explain why, more generally, international sporting events typically serve to increase national pride within the host country (Leng, Kuo, Baysa-Pee, Grain, & Tay, 2015).

Equally, media coverage of the Olympics shapes the way we represent other nations, with this coverage frequently reflecting international rivalries and existing stereotypes. The impact is particularly acute in the case of host countries which receive global coverage that is far from restricted to their sporting accomplishments. Thus, a longitudinal study of a German sample by Christiana Schallhorn (2020) showed how their views of Brazil changed through its hosting of the 2014 FIFA World Cup and the 2016 Olympic Games. More particularly, the country came to be seen as poorer, crisis-ridden and riddled with crime. Yet for all that, Germans became more desirous of visiting Brazil (for reasons that are not entirely clear, but which may reside in Brazil still being understood as 'exotic' and because Germany won the tournament).

In sum, then, there is strong evidence that the Olympics in particular, and sport in general, play a part in the way we represent our own nation and others. This is clearly of considerable importance. But it still underrepresents the ways in which sport impacts society in two important ways.

On the one hand, the impact is not just on the way that we represent the nation. It also affects the way that we represent other key social categories through which the social world is organised – notably 'race' and gender. For these categories too, like that of the nation, can be thought of as 'imagined communities' which can never be assembled together at one time in one place. And for these, sport plays a major part both in allowing us to imagine a common category and in shaping the way in which we imagine it. The one big difference, though, is that we don't have teams defined primarily in terms of these categories (e.g., it is rare to have a 'black team' and even though there are plenty of women's teams which are characterised as such, they are usually also characterised in terms of nation or club rather than gender alone). Accordingly, individual athletes often play a far larger part in helping define – and, more importantly, *re*define – the place of groups in the world (Kaufman & Wolff, 2010).

In this regard, no sportsperson has had more impact than Muhammad Ali. Recall Ali's famous declaration that 'I ain't got no quarrel with them VietCong.' Mike Maquesee comments that 'Ultimately it became the "I" of all those who felt they had no quarrel with the VietCong – and all those who felt they did have a quarrel with America' (Marqusee, 1999, p. 209). In other words, Ali came to embody a whole movement – one which brought together the black community, students and wider anti-Vietnam War campaigns.

With the advent of social media, the ability of individual athletes to represent broader categories has grown considerably (Hayat, Galily, & Samuel-Azran, 2019). For example, the basketball player LeBron James has a large social media presence through which he is able to speak out on topics such as 'Black Lives Matter' – the US movement formed in response to police violence and racism against African Americans. In this way, he draws attention to a community and also creates a community for discussion (Coombs &

Cassilo, 2017). But along with that capacity to influence comes an increasing obligation to speak out. Accordingly, the US women's national footballer Alex Morgan commented:

> I had a dream of being a professional soccer player, and I never knew it entailed … standing up for things I believe in, standing up for gender equality. But now I don't know a world where I just play soccer. It goes hand in hand. (Goodman, 2019)

On the other hand, whether we are talking about nation, race, gender or any other category, the impact of sport on social categories is not reducible simply to a matter of representation. Indeed, there are multiple ways in which sport affects category formation. To start with, particularly in repressive contexts, sporting events provide a space where groups can legitimately come together without being repressed, gain a sense of solidarity and empowerment, and express and consolidate their identities. For instance, at the World Cup qualifier between Hong Kong and Iran on 10 September 2019, Hong Kong fans refused to sing the National Anthem of the People's Republic of China and instead sang the Hong Kong anthem 'Glory to Hong Kong'. Many more examples of this can be given: for instance, the resistance that Spartak Moscow fans showed to the Soviet regime (Edelman, 2009), the resistance that Catalonian fans of FC Barcelona showed to Franco (Burns, 2011), and the resistance towards Britain shown by players of Gaelic sports. Indeed, the Gaelic Athletic Association was set up in 1884 specifically as 'a means of consolidating our Irish identity' (Gaelic Athletic Association, 2019, p. 4).

Next, sport can provide members who are prepared to work, and even fight, for the group, with access to social structures which scaffold the ongoing existence of the group. If, as argued above, the behaviour of football supporters and players was instrumental in fomenting the 'Homeland War' of 1991 in the former Yugoslavia, they also provided many of the shock troops in that conflict. Not least, this was because members of the official army had been schooled in loyalty to Yugoslavia. Hence nationalist leaders in Croatia and Serbia doubted their reliability in taking action against the other. Thus, Vladan Lukic, the former president of the football club Red Star Belgrade, praised those fans who were fighting as combat troops and asserted that: 'Many of our loyal supporters from the North End of the Marakana stadium [Red Star's home ground] are in the most obvious ways writing the finest pages of the history of Serbia' (Foer, 2011, pp. 21–22).

Sport can also provide the organisation and the leadership which subsequently enables the emergence and empowerment of groups in society. The role of the 'Island Rugby Board' (IRB) on Robben Island – ostensibly simply organising a league for rugby in South Africa's primary site for political prisoners – played a key role in the development of the African National Congress (Mandela, 1994). Thus, it has been argued that 'The detailed operations of the IRB … suggested that these activities were part of a process to build a new polity and a nascent parliament within prison' and that the IRB was 'a nascent post-apartheid prototype' (Snyders, 2019, p. 148).

Finally, sport can provide a distraction, demobilising particular groups as well as mobilising others. For instance, in Italy in 1948, following the shooting of the Communist leader Palmiro Togliatti, riots broke out, a general strike was called, and there were fears of an armed uprising. The Italian president, Alcide de Gasperi, famously phoned Gino Bartali, the Italian cyclist, and implored him to do what he could to win stages in the Tour de France that was currently under way. The next day, in one of the most famed exploits in the history of the Tour, Bartali broke away and won Stage 13 by a massive six minutes and eighteen seconds. There was huge rejoicing back in Italy: 'Instead of protesting and fighting, people ... started cheering and toasting each other. Gino's victory changed their mood completely.' Indeed, as Giorgina Rietti, an Italian Jew who had vivid memories of his success, recalls: 'Italians who thought they were going to hurt each other ended up drinking together' (McConnon & McConnon, 2012, p. 225). Sport therefore has the ability to bring people together, establish leadership, empower and mobilise people in both constructive and destructive directions.

Having looked at the various ways in which sport can impact social identity and social relations in society, let us now turn to the various aspects of social identity upon which sport impacts and hence the various dimensions along which social action and social relations are shaped and reshaped. Here we can make a distinction between impacts upon (a) the boundaries of identity (who belongs in the group), (b) the sense of intimacy and cohesion between members of the group, (c) the content of the group identity (the norms, beliefs, and values which shape what 'we' should do), (d) the status and power relations *between* groups (i.e., intergroup relations), (e) the status and power relations *within* groups (i.e., intragroup relations), and (f) the prototypes of the group (who represents 'us' and hence is qualified to lead us?). In the following section we consider each of these six dimensions in turn.

WHAT DIMENSIONS OF SOCIAL IDENTITY ARE SHAPED BY SPORT?

Group boundaries

Concerning the capacity for sport to help define the boundaries of a social category, we have already seen examples from South Africa where rugby was used at different times in order to help create an exclusive 'white' nation and then, later, an inclusive 'rainbow nation' (further examples are provided in Chapters 13 and 14). Its power in this regard was emphasised by Nelson Mandela himself when he observed:

> Sport has the power to change the world. It has the power to inspire. It has the power to unite people that little else does. It speaks to youth in a language they can understand. Sport can create hope where there was only despair. It is more powerful than governments in breaking down racial barriers. It laughs in the face of all types of discrimination. (Mandela, 2000)

Certainly, Mandela's words inspired Siya Kolisi, who in 2019 became the first black South African to lead his country to a World Cup win. And Kolisi in turn used his victory speech to inspire further progress in his troubled homeland: 'We love you South Africa and we can achieve anything if we work together as one' (Elbra, 2019).

Group cohesion

But sport does not just serve to define who is included in the group. It can also serve to create and strengthen social bonds between group members. In exactly the way that Anderson (1991) describes, it is through imagining other members of the group experiencing media reports of an event in the same way as ourselves and at the same time, that we get a sense of nationhood and hence of connection to other members of the group. As we have already suggested, this will be particularly acute when the event in question is seen as national, and to the extent that it is meaningful for a national ingroup. And what could be more national and more meaningful than one's country playing in the World Cup final of its national sport?

To capitalise on this fact, in a recent study, the third and first authors collaborated with a large team of social identity researchers from multiple countries to study a sample of ordinary New Zealanders before and after their team – the All Blacks – played in the 2015 Rugby World Cup Final (Neville et al., 2019). After the game (which the All Blacks won), social relations – even between strangers – were transformed. People reported talking to people they had never met before to celebrate the victory, knowing that fellow nationals, even if complete strangers, would be aware of the result and share their own pleasure in it. Not only that; our survey data showed that their sense of physical and mental well-being was also enhanced (in ways suggested in Chapter 15). This positive transformation of social relations through shared identification was exemplified by the following comments from three people who participated in our diary study. First, shared identity led to a sense of intimacy with strangers: 'Nobody was a stranger anymore and everyone celebrated together.' Second, this intimacy endured beyond the match itself in ways that served to improve the quality of routine interactions: 'My neighbour started a conversation even though she doesn't usually say more than a hello to me when we've waited for the bus on other days.' Third, these interactions with strangers were characterised by intensity and positivity: 'Everyone is just so elated. Every interaction is positive and heightened.'

A related phenomenon was recorded during the Football World Cup in 2006 in research by Norbert Kerstings (2007). Although Germany lost in the semi-finals, the experience of hosting the tournament and going deep into the competition reportedly eased tension between Germans and German immigrants, as they united together as German football fans. Whereas much of our evidence is suggestive and anecdotal, in these two studies we have systematic longitudinal evidence that attests to the power of sport to contribute to the formation of social identities which we love and live by.

Content of group identity

Another key claim is that sport is critical to defining ingroup norms, what we are, and the values that define us. There is, for instance, a large literature on the role of organised sport during the Victorian era in inculcating the values of 'muscular Christianity' which made English schoolboys suitable subjects for running the Empire. For instance J. E. C. Welldon, the Headmaster of Dulwich College, asserted: 'If there is in the British race, as I think there is, a special aptitude for "taking up the white man's burden" *[sic]* … it may be ascribed, above all other causes, to the spirit of organised games' (cited in James, 1995, p. 207). Likewise, Cyril Norwood, another prominent Victorian headmaster, explained: 'You are not learning to win Olympic championships on the Marlborough playing fields. You are learning to serve' (cited in Mangan, 2013, p. 97).

During the 20th century in the United States, sport was used as a way to socialise immigrant children, by teaching honour, obedience and patriotism (Gorn & Goldstein, 1993). Furthermore, recent studies have shown that group dynamics in sport participation can influence positive youth development in areas that include personal and social skills, goal setting and initiative (Bruner, Balish et al., 2017; see Figure 12.1). And so, it is that as a result of the countless hours and extreme dedication to sport that they display, university-level and professional athletes can come to define themselves in terms of their physical prowess and skill. This in turn leads to great difficulty when an athlete experiences injury or termination of their career because, as O'Halloran and Haslam observe in Chapter 16, these injured athletes don't know how to define themselves beyond sport and in terms other than those of an athlete identity (e.g., in terms of physical prowess; Willard & Lavallee, 2016; Wylleman, Alfermann, & Lavallee, 2004).

But if sport has this power to define us, then the question of which sports are played and by whom becomes an issue of great ideological concern and of moral policing. On the one hand, ensuring that the 'right people' play the 'right sports' is a way of maintaining stereotypes and ensuring that everyone keeps to their allotted place in society. So, to be more concrete, traditional ideas of men being active subjects and women being passive objects is enshrined in the way that masculine sports prioritise physicality and women's sports value grace. At the same time, when women start playing men's sports (e.g., rugby) and vice versa (e.g., when men play netball) this can be viewed as absurd or monstrous – as an inversion of the 'natural order' of things (Antonowicz, Jakubowska, & Kossakowski, 2020; Davies & Deckert, 2020; MacArthur, Angelini, Billings, & Smith, 2017; Neville, 2019; Quayle et al., 2019). The same is true when black people play 'white' sports (e.g., lacrosse) and vice versa (e.g., basketball; Haslerig, Vue, & Grummert, 2020; Parry, Cleland, & Kavanagh, 2019). As an example, Michael Gennaro documents elite concerns about the popularity of table tennis among Nigerian boys in the post-independence period because the game was seen as quintessentially feminine (involving no contact, indoor play in a domestic sphere, and a lot of sitting around and 'gossiping'; Gennaro, 2019, p. 23). He quotes one commentator saying: 'I was really disgusted at seeing healthy young boys playing ping-pong' (2019, p. 14).

Intergroup relations

The issue of defining the nature of the ingroup is inextricably bound up with the way we understand intergroup relationships. This is especially the case in the domain of sport, as this is about power and about victory, both literally and metaphorically. Hence, in defining the ingroup as potent, one also challenges its subordination by an outgroup. We have already seen how success in football has been claimed as a key factor in Catalan opposition to the central Spanish state, giving people confidence in their struggle for independence. In line with this, Burns (2011) points to the specific role of Barcelona Football Club. He observes:

> [The] Spanish League championship always meant something more than a mere trophy. It became a matter of identity. … Beating its main rival, Real Madrid, meant a victory of democracy over a politically centralised and culturally repressed Spain. (Burns, 2011, p. 348)

Such empowerment through sport is certainly not limited to national groups. If anything, it has played a greater party in the politics of race and gender. In the case of race, there are many accounts of the significance of Joe Louis' boxing victory over the German Max Schmeling on 22 June 1938. This match was represented as a fight between a black man and a representative of white supremacism, and the response to Louis' win among members of the black community was summarised by the veteran civil rights activist Andrew Young: 'that was Freedom-day' (Marqusee, 1999, p. 26). But the impact was not limited to the US. In South Africa, Cody Perkins (2019) reports similar responses among the oppressed majority there. As one respondent, who was a child at the time, recalled: 'Daddy could hardly contain himself as he told us how the Brown bomber smashed the "great Aryan" into defeat in just 124 seconds of the first round' (Perkins, 2019, p. 97).

South African blacks likewise felt empowered by the accomplishments of Jesse Owens at the 1936 Olympics, and particularly his victory over the South African (white) champion. The *South African Sun* newspaper (whose readership was primarily black) described this unambiguously in terms of race relations: 'Grimbeek, the best sprinter for the Union, was drawn next to Owens in the second round of the 100 metres and was left standing by the "Black Flash" at 20 metres' (Perkins, 2019, p. 96).

Intragroup relations

But, of course, race, gender and nation are not separate categories. They intersect in many ways, and one of the core social questions of our time is the place of groups defined by this intersectionality in the nation. And here again, there are good reasons to suppose that sport has a crucial role to play. Speaking to the position of black people in the USA, we can look back to a number of iconic moments: the Black Power salute by Tommie Smith and John Carlos on the Olympic rostrum in Mexico in 1968 (Smith & Steele, 2007); Kareem Abdul-Jabbar's boycott of the same Olympics (Abdul-Jabbar, 2017) because he did not want to confer glory on a country which so oppressed black people; and Muhammad Ali's already cited refusal to serve in Vietnam (Marqusee, 1999).

But in recent years, no event has had more impact than NFL quarterback Colin Kaepernick's decision to kneel rather than stand through the playing of the US National

Anthem. While some observers argued his action disrespected the nation and its armed forces, Kaepernick explained that his gesture was designed to highlight the pervasive nature of race inequality and police brutality within the USA. While Kaepernick is now unable to find a team willing to employ him, he has become a prominent civil rights campaigner, and also the face of a Nike advertising campaign with the tagline 'Believe in something. Even if it means sacrificing everything' (Montez de Oca & Suh, 2020).

Going from race to gender, very similar arguments apply. Nowadays, men and women are allowed to participate in the same sports and events. Nevertheless, many observers have noted that sport remains a bastion of gender inequality (e.g., when it comes to pay, media attention and fandom; Alsarve & Tjønndal, 2020; Tjønndal, 2019; Velija & Hughes, 2019; Williams & Hall, 2018). But, precisely because of this, sport has also been a domain in which gender inequality has been contested. For example, the 1973 victory of Billie Jean King over Bobby Riggs in a challenge match that was billed as a 'battle of the sexes' has been seen as a key moment in second-wave feminism. To quote Susan Ware: 'What she proved that night in a courageous performance of physical prowess and nerves of steel was that women did not choke, women were not frail and weak, women could face pressure and take it – live, on national television, with no second takes' (Ware, 2011, p. 2). Indeed, King claimed that, decades later, she was approached by strangers who explained to her how that match had changed their lives by allowing them to seek education, participate in sport, or even leave damaging relationships (Ware, 2011). Tennis legends Venus and Serena Williams continued King's fight, and were instrumental in male and female tennis players receiving equal prize money for the first time at Wimbledon in 2007 (Golden, 2018).

Equally, sport has been used to address women's position within the nation and there is no better example of that than the US women's national football (soccer) team. Controversially, the 2015 Women's World Cup, the pinnacle of women's football, was played in Canada on artificial turf rather than grass. This was seen as a health hazard and an insult (Schertzinger, 2015). The US striker Sydney Leroux stressed that this was less an issue of safety than of equality: 'The men would never play a World Cup on [Astro] Turf, so why should the women?' (Pilkington, 2014).

The resultant debate went much further than safety and respect. It became a touchstone for wider debates about gender inequality in US society. Abby Wambach, the most decorated football player in US history, explained during the 2016 ESPY (Excellence in Sport Performance Yearly) awards that while fellow Icon Award members Peyton Manning and Kobe Bryant walked away from their sports with financial stability and freedom, the vast majority of female professional athletes do not experience this freedom. Although Wambach worked just as hard, day in and day out, as any male athlete, she would be required to work far harder following the end of her career to make a living (Goodman, 2019).

By the time of the next Women's World Cup in 2019 in France, hard words had solidified into action. The team filed a class action gender-discrimination lawsuit against the US Soccer Federation (the USSF) and, following their victory in the final on 7 July, fans in the stadium in Paris chanted 'Equal Pay! Equal Pay!' (Das, 2019). At the time, members of the American women's team were paid just 38 cents to every male dollar despite being considerably more successful and bringing in considerably more money. For example, in 2015, following their World Cup victory that year, they brought in $1.9 million more in revenue. For the fiscal years 2016–18 the figure was $900,000 (Kelly, 2019). As we write, the women's team are still in dispute with the USSF, which claims that men and women's football represent two functionally distinct organisations beyond the factor of sex (Bachman, 2019; Das, 2019).

The issues raised by the team are not limited to pay, however. Several players, most prominently Megan Rapinoe (Best FIFA Women's Player, 2019; see Figure 20.1), used the limelight to challenge gender injustice more broadly, highlighting movements such as #MeToo and Time's Up, which deal with issues of sexual harassment and sexual assault (Goodman, 2019). Moreover, she did not limit her advocacy to gender issues, but also highlighted the LBGTQ cause and Black Lives Matter. As Rapinoe herself has put it, in this way she is 'using the platform of soccer for good and for leaving the game in a better place, and hopefully the world in a better place' (cited by Longman, 2019).

Figure 20.1 Megan Rapinoe

Source: Jamie Smed, Wikimedia Commons

Leadership

It is a very short step from addressing how sport affects the general position of different parties within the group, to discussing its impact on who gets to lead the group. In line with this point, there are many illustrations of how sport has been used to legitimate positions of authority and leadership. For example, during the 1970s the military regime in Ghana set up an elite sport club called SS74 as a means of demonstrating that soldiers were both part of the people and representative of the best values of the people – and hence worthy of leading the people. More specifically:

> [The purpose of SS74] was to illuminate the positives of the Ghanaian military by portraying excellent military virtues, such as discipline, dedication and loyalty to the nation. … Moreover, the military model club was supposed to close the gap between civilians and the military by showing its civilian counterparts that soldiers were not aliens, but humans who earn achievements through hard work. (Agyekum, 2019, p. 78)

As well as establishing subgroups as leadership material, sport is often used by individuals to show how they fit national prototypes, especially masculine prototypes that emphasise agency, energy and power. No one is more adept at this than Russian president Vladimir Putin, who among other things plays an annual hockey match in which he invariably outshines everyone else. In the 2019 game, for instance, which Putin's team won 14–7, he himself scored at least eight goals, although the official Kremlin release claimed 10 for the president. And lest it be thought that this is purely a Russian phenomenon, the too-good-to-be-true exploits of Kim Jong-un and Donald Trump on the golf course can be seen to serve a similar function (Girard, 2011; Reilly, 2019).

But sport isn't only used to establish leadership; it can be used to contest leadership. Throughout the Soviet Union, for instance, certain football teams were controlled by factions of the state and used to establish their prestige, while, conversely, support for other teams was a means of opposing the state. We have already mentioned Spartak Moscow, which had a particularly famous rivalry with Dynamo Moscow (the team of the secret police). On the cover to his book on the history on the club, Robert Edelman (2009) argues that 'To cheer for Spartak was a small and safe way of saying "no" to the fears and absurdities of high Stalinism.'

CONCLUSION

In the 139th of his famous *Pensées*, the philosopher Blaise Pascal bemoaned the fact that human beings are so frivolous that 'though full of a thousand reasons for weariness, the least thing, such as playing billiards or hitting a ball, is sufficient enough to amuse him' (1958, p. 41). While phrased more eloquently than most, this is a rather common observation. For all the passions it arouses, sport is ultimately ephemeral and insignificant. After all, it's only a game.

The aim of this chapter has been to contest this commonplace. Far from being a distraction from the things that really matter in society – inequality, discrimination and war, on the one hand; cohesion, solidarity and community, on the other – sport plays an important part in the making (and unmaking) of all of these.

Or rather, there is an arguable case for the role of sport in the making both of groups and of the relations between groups that constitute our society. This is because, as we made clear at the start, and as we have reminded readers throughout, most of the evidence we have presented is suggestive at best. With the exception of a few systematic studies that establish clear causal links between sport and social outcomes (e.g., concerning the impact of New Zealand's rugby union World Cup victory on subsequent cohesion among New Zealanders; Neville et al., 2019), the bulk of what evidence we have presented is either circumstantial or anecdotal.

So, yes, it may be possible to find black voices who expressed delight at the victory of Joe Louis over Max Schmeling, but how widespread was this and can one really claim that he, Jesse Owens and others were a significant component of the struggle for black equality in the USA? Whatever may have been claimed of it, based on secondary accounts, can we really conclude that Billie Jean King's victory over Bobby Riggs actually contributed to second-wave feminism? Did sport actually legitimate the military's hold on leadership in Ghana? More generally, how can we equate what people may have been trying to achieve through sport with what was actually achieved? Megan Rapinoe certainly tries to make a difference, but does she succeed? Does any sportsman or -woman, any sports commentator, any sporting impresario?

To put it slightly differently, much of the evidence we have presented in this chapter has served to generate hypotheses rather than test them. We do not see this necessarily as a weakness. As Blumer (1969) has argued, it may be true that hypothesis testing has been fetishised in recent times as the sole significant dimension of the research process. But in fact, along with hypothesis generation and hypothesis validation it is only one part of the research process, while all parts are interdependent and of equal importance.

Our eyes, then, are primarily on the future rather than the past. We have sought to lay out an agenda for research yet to be done. And, in line with the structure of this chapter, this agenda has three components.

The first component involves establishing clear evidence that sport does indeed influence social relations and political outcomes. For instance, beyond the reminiscences of politicians, can we demonstrate that sporting successes and failures impact the outcome of elections? Do sporting victories empower subordinate groups to challenge dominant groups? Such provocative suggestions deserve better data than we have today.

The second component has to do with elucidating the processes by which sport impacts society. In a book on social identity and sport, we have, not surprisingly, concentrated on the formation and definition of those social categories which define who we are, our relations to others, and our place in the world. Can we show that watching sport together impacts, say, the strength and salience of national identity? Can we show that what happens in sport impacts the substantive content we ascribe to our nationhood?

And finally, the third component of our agenda involves clarifying all the various aspects of our social identity that may be shaped by sport. Along the lines we have outlined, there is much to explore in terms of how sport affects group boundaries and group cohesion, ingroup stereotypes, inter- and intragroup relations, and even leadership of the group.

This is a challenging agenda. It is always difficult to demonstrate how psychological processes relate to macro-social outcomes. But the prize is worth the effort. Some faltering steps have already been taken along this path. Hopefully, by the time of the second edition of this book there will be considerably more to say and perhaps we will be able to put even more scientific heft behind the observation of Bill Shankly – with which Chapter 2 started – that football (and, we would add, sport more generally) is not a matter of life and death. It's much more important than that.

APPENDIX
MEASURES OF SOCIAL IDENTIFICATION, SOCIAL IDENTITY, AND SOCIAL IDENTITY PROCESS

This appendix provides details of a range of measures that have been developed to assess and explore social identity-related phenomena and processes in sport and exercise contexts. In this, it has a similar function to appendices provided in other texts that apply social identity and self-categorization principles to applied contexts (e.g., organisations, Haslam, 2001, pp. 271–279; and healthcare, Haslam, Jetten, Cruwys, Dingle, & Haslam, 2018, pp. 346–379; Jetten, Haslam, & Haslam, 2012, pp. 345–367). There are two key reasons why such measures were collated in those volumes, and why we have done so again in this one. First, to provide readers with a sense of how the key constructs that are discussed in the chapters above are typically assessed. Second, to provide a practical resource that readers might find useful in their own work.

The measures are organised into three sections. The first section presents measures of *social identification* that capture the degree to which people identify with a particular sport-related group. The second section presents measures of *social identity* that capture the nature of the groups that define people's sense of self in sporting contexts. The third section presents measures of various *social identity processes* that are studied in sport and exercise contexts (e.g., leadership, group-based attribution, social support).

As is true in other domains, if you are going to use these measures yourself it will often be necessary to adapt a measure to suit the particular sport or exercise context in which you are interested, or to address the particular issues that are being explored in a given piece of research. In most cases adapting a scale will be straightforward and simply involve changing the referent in each item (e.g., specifying the team that a respondent is a fan of). However, in some cases this process will be more complex and its implications (e.g., for the measure's validity) will need to be thought through carefully.

Exactly which measure a practitioner or researcher chooses to use will depend on factors such as the setting (e.g., laboratory or field), the time available for measures to be completed, the response format (e.g., pencil-and-paper or line), and the number and capacity of respondents. In particular, such considerations will have a bearing on whether one uses longer or shorter scales, and ones that are more general or specific to a particular context or issue. And of course these choices will also depend on the purposes for which data from a given measure are going to be used.

SOCIAL IDENTIFICATION MEASURES

Social identification

This scale was developed by Tom Postmes and colleagues (2013; see Reference note below) following earlier work by Bertjan Doosje, Naomi Ellemers and Russell Spears (1995) that assessed Dutch students' identification with the category 'psychology student'. The items are widely used by social and organisational psychologists (e.g., see Haslam, 2001), and the scale can be used to measure social identification with a wide range of groups. The items can easily be adapted for use in sport and exercise settings by substituting the name of a relevant team or group. As in all other cases below (unless otherwise noted) participants typically respond on seven-point scales and these have end-points labelled 'do not agree at all' (1) and 'agree completely' (7).

Different dimensions of identification can also be assessed using other more elaborate measures (e.g., the 14-item measure developed by Leach et al., 2008). However, if one requires a shorter scale, Postmes and colleagues (2013) noted that the first item of the scale ('I identify with [relevant group]') can itself be used as a single-item measure of social identification that it is both reliable and valid. These researchers also found that it was highly correlated with the four-item scale (r = .84).

1. I identify with [members of Group X].*

2. I see myself as a [member of Group X].

3. I am pleased to be a [member of Group X].

4. I feel strong ties with [members of Group X].

    Scale used in original publication:

    completely disagree 1 2 3 4 5 6 7 completely agree †

Note: * Item used for one-item version of the scale (Postmes et al., 2013).

† It is possible to use a different number of scale points (e.g., 5, 9 or 11) but be aware that this will affect one's ability to make comparisons between studies.

Reference: Postmes, T., Haslam, S. A., & Jans, L. (2013). A single-item measure of social identification: Reliability, validity and utility. *British Journal of Social Psychology*, *52*, 597–617.

Social Identity Questionnaire for Sport (SIQS)

This scale was developed by Mark Bruner and Alex Benson (2018; see below) based on earlier work which conceptualised social identification not as a global construct, but rather as multidimensional. Along the lines of previous work by Mark Bruner and colleagues (2014) and James Cameron (2004), this conceptualisation sees identification as involving (a) ingroup ties (i.e., perceptions of similarity, bonding and belongingness with other group members), (b) cognitive centrality (i.e., the importance of being a group member), and (c) ingroup affect (i.e., the positive feelings associated with group membership). Based on these definitions, two of the dimensions are cognitive in nature (ingroup ties, cognitive centrality), whereas ingroup affect pertains to emotion. The findings from the study support the SIQS as a psychometrically sound measure of social identity in sport that can be used to model social identity either along three specific dimensions or as a global construct.

The following questions are designed to reflect how you feel about being a part of your team. Please circle a number from 1 (strongly disagree) to 7 (strongly agree) to indicate your agreement with each of the statements.

1. I feel strong ties to other members of this team.

2. I find it easy to form a bond with other members in this team.

3. I feel a sense of being 'connected' with other members in this team.

4. Overall, being a member of this team has a lot to do with how I feel about myself.

5. In general, being a member of this team is an important part of my self-image.

6. The fact that I am a member of this team often enters my mind.

7. In general, I am glad to be a member of this team.

8. I feel good about being a member of this team.

9. Generally, I feel good when I think about myself as a member of this team.

Note: Scores for the three dimensions of social identification are obtained by averaging responses to different sets of items: *ingroup ties* = 1, 2, 3; *cognitive centrality* = 4, 5, 6; *ingroup affect* = 7, 8, 9.

Reference: Bruner, M. W., & Benson, A. J. (2018). Evaluating the psychometric properties of the Social Identity Questionnaire for Sport (SIQS). *Psychology of Sport and Exercise, 35*, 181–188.

Sport fan identification

This measure is a revised version of a scale previously developed by Daniel Wann and Nyla Branscombe (1993) to assess sport fans' identification with their team. A problem with the earlier version of the scale was that it failed to differentiate between fans who had low identification with a team and those who did not identify at all. To get around this problem, Jeffrey James and Elizabeth Delia teamed up with Wann to create this revised scale that included an initial question that differentiates between these two very different states of identification.

Do you identify yourself as a fan of the [team name], even if just a little bit?

Please circle the appropriate answer.*

Yes——No

Please think about [team name] as you answer questions A–G. Please circle the appropriate number on the scale next to each question.

A. How important to you is it that [team name] win?

a little important 1 2 3 4 5 6 7 8 very important

B. How strongly do you see yourself as a fan of [team name]?

slightly a fan 1 2 3 4 5 6 7 8 very much a fan

C. How strongly do your friends see you as a fan of [team name]?

slightly a fan 1 2 3 4 5 6 7 8 very much a fan

D. During the season, how closely do you follow [team name] via any of the following: in person or on television, on the radio, on television news or a newspaper, or the internet?

a little 1 2 3 4 5 6 7 8 very frequently

E. How important is being a fan of [team name] to you?

a little important 1 2 3 4 5 6 7 8 very important

F. How much do you dislike [team name]'s greatest rivals?

dislike a little 1 2 3 4 5 6 7 8 dislike very much

G. How often do you display [team name]'s name or insignia at your place of work, where you live, or on your clothing?

occasionally 1 2 3 4 5 6 7 8 always

Note: * An individual answering 'no' would be directed to skip the scale questions.

Reference: James, J. D., Delia, E. B., & Wann, D. L. (2020). 'No' is not 'low': Improving the assessment of sport team identification. *Sport Marketing Quarterly*, *28*, 34–45.

Crowd identification

John Drury (2012) measured crowd identification retrospectively using a two-item scale that he had previously developed with colleagues (Drury et al., 2009). Working with Hani Alnabulsi, he then extended this to create the five-item scale below and used this to assess shared identity among pilgrims attending the Hajj (Alnabulsi & Drury, 2014; see below).

1. I felt that I was part [of the crowd].

2. I felt at one with the people around me [in the crowd].

3. I felt a sense of togetherness with others [in the crowd].*

4. I felt unity with others [in the crowd].*

5. I felt strong ties with other people [in the crowd].

    Scale used in original publication:

    disagree strongly 1 2 3 4 5 6 7 agree strongly

Note: * Items used for two-item version of the scale (Drury et al., 2009).

Reference: Alnabulsi, H., & Drury, J. (2014). Social identification moderates the effect of crowd density on safety at the Hajj. *Proceedings of the National Academy of Sciences*, *111*, 9091–9096.

SOCIAL IDENTITY MEASURES

Athletic identity

As discussed by O'Halloran and Haslam in Chapter 15, athletic identity is defined as 'the extent to which an individual identifies with the athletic role' (Brewer, Van Raalte, & Linder, 1993, p.237). This is a construct that Britton Brewer and colleagues (1993) first sought to measure with the 10-item *Athletic Identity Measurement Scale* (AIMS). However, subsequent research suggested that the scale's validity was improved by omitting three items, and this led to the creation of the abbreviated version of the scale reproduced below (Brewer & Cornelius, 2001; see below). Rather than measuring one unified construct, the scale may be better understood as capturing three distinct dimensions of athletic identity: *social identity*, *exclusivity* and *negative affectivity* (Hale, James, & Stambulova, 1999; Visek, Hurst, Maxwell, & Watson, 2008). The validity of this scale has subsequently been confirmed in a range of other studies which speak to its capacity to predict a range of both positive and negative sporting outcomes – including commitment to one's sport and difficulty adjusting to retirement. At the same time, some researchers have criticised the AIMS for failing to include positive affectivity as an aspect of athletic identity, arguing that positive (not just negative) experiences make an important contribution to athletes' motivation and well-being (Cieslak, 2004).

1. I consider myself an athlete.

2. I have many goals related to sport.

3. Most of my friends are athletes.

4. Sport is the most important part of my life.

5. I spend more time thinking about sport than anything else.

6. I feel bad about myself when I do poorly in sport.

7. I would be very depressed if I were injured and could not compete in sport.

> Scale used in original publication:
>
> strongly disagree 1 2 3 4 5 6 7 strongly agree

―――――――

Note: Scores for the three dimensions of athletic identity are obtained by averaging responses to different sets of items: *social identity* = 1, 2, 3; *exclusivity* = 4, 5; *negative affectivity* = 6, 7.

Reference: Brewer, B. W., & Cornelius, A. E. (2001). Norms and factorial invariance of the Athletic Identity Measurement Scale. *Academic Athletic Journal*, *15*, 103–113.

Exercise identity

Developed by Dean Anderson and Charles Cychosz (1994; see below) this scale is used to measure the degree to which a person defines themselves as someone who engages in exercise. The scale was initially developed to assess the exercise identity in college students – where it was shown to have high reliability and to predict participation in exercise. These patterns have subsequently been replicated in a range of other populations where exercise identity has also been found to predict commitment to exercise (Anderson, Cychosz, & Franke, 1998) and enjoyment of exercise (Wininger & Pargman, 2003).

1. I consider myself an exerciser.

2. When I describe myself to others, I usually include my involvement in exercise.

3. I have numerous goals related to exercising.

4. Physical exercise is a central factor to my self-concept.

5. I need to exercise to feel good about myself.

6. Others see me as someone who exercises regularly.

7. For me, being an exerciser means more than just exercising.

8. I would feel a real loss if I were forced to give up exercising.

9. Exercising is something I think about often.

    Scale used in original publication:

    strongly disagree 1 2 3 4 5 6 7 8 9 strongly agree

Reference: Anderson, D. F., & Cychosz, C. M. (1994). Development of an exercise identity scale. *Perceptual and Motor Skills*, *78*, 747–751.

Multiple identities

This measure is used to assess the extent to which people perceive themselves to belong to multiple social groups and is a central element of what are referred to as the Exeter Identity Transition Scales (EXITS; e.g., Haslam et al., 2008; see below; Jetten et al., 2015). It can be used to index multiple forms of group belonging in the present (i.e., as a Time 1 measure; Iyer et al., 2009) or retrospectively to assess group belonging at some point in the past (e.g., Haslam et al., 2008). Both scales have good internal reliability.

1. I belong[ed] to lots of different groups.*†

2. I join[ed] in the activities of lots of different groups.†

3. I am [was] friendly with people in lots of different groups.*†

4. I have [had] strong ties with lots of different groups.

Scale used in original publication:

do not agree at all 1 2 3 4 5 6 7 8 9 agree completely

_____

Note: * Items used for two-item version of the scale (Jetten et al., 2010).

† Items used as basis for three-item version of the scale (Jetten et al., 2015).

Reference: Haslam, C., Holme, A., Haslam, S. A., Iyer, A., Jetten, J., & Williams, W. H. (2008). Maintaining group memberships: Social identity continuity predicts well-being after stroke. *Neuropsychological Rehabilitation*, *18*, 671–691.

Multiple group listing

Catherine Haslam and colleagues (2008) developed a multiple-identity scale to capture changes in group membership in the course of a life transition. It first requires participants to write down the names of groups that are (or were) important to them, up to a maximum number (e.g., six). They are then asked to reflect on these groups and to indicate (a) how important this group is (or was) to them, and (b) the compatibility of this group to the other groups to which they belong. This measure provides a rich source of data that can be used to examine the influence of (a) the number of group memberships, (b) the type of group memberships that respondents list, and (c) the types of group memberships that are compatible with other identities. It can also be adapted to measure other aspects of group life (e.g., the amount of support that various groups provide). The measure is intended to assess the groups that respondents belonged to *before* a life-changing event (e.g., retirement) and then again to assess the groups that respondents belong to currently, *after* the life-changing event. However, the measure can also be used to capture multiple group membership at a single time point.

This questionnaire refers to the types of groups that you [used to belong to] [and] [now belong to]. These groups could take any form and be either formal or informal – for example, they could be leisure or social groups (e.g., book group or gardening club), community groups (e.g., church group), sporting groups (e.g., rugby club), work groups (e.g., sales team), professional groups (e.g., trade union), or any others you can think of.

Please list in the first column up to six groups* that you belong[ed] to [before/after] [the life-changing event]. Then indicate for each of these groups in the second and third column how important this group [was/is] for you and how well it [fitted/fits] with your other groups.

Group memberships [before/after] [the life-changing event]	How important [was/is] this group to you [before/after] [the life-changing event]?	How well [did/does] this group fit with your other groups [before/after] [the life-changing event]
1.	not at all 1 2 3 4 5 6 7 very	not a lot 1 2 3 4 5 6 7 a great deal
2.	not at all 1 2 3 4 5 6 7 very	not a lot 1 2 3 4 5 6 7 a great deal
3.	not at all 1 2 3 4 5 6 7 very	not a lot 1 2 3 4 5 6 7 a great deal
4.	not at all 1 2 3 4 5 6 7 very	not a lot 1 2 3 4 5 6 7 a great deal
5.	not at all 1 2 3 4 5 6 7 very	not a lot 1 2 3 4 5 6 7 a great deal
6.	not at all 1 2 3 4 5 6 7 very	not a lot 1 2 3 4 5 6 7 a great deal

Note: * Be aware that the maximum number may create a frame of reference that has other implications. In particular, Young, Brown, and Hutchins (2017) note that the higher this number is, the more likely it is to make respondents feel that their social lives are deficient.

† Number of important groups calculated as the number of groups multiplied by their mean rated importance.

Reference: Haslam, C., Holme, A., Haslam, S. A., Iyer, A., Jetten, J., & Williams, W. H. (2008). Maintaining group memberships: Social identity continuity predicts well-being after stroke. *Neuropsychological Rehabilitation*, *18*, 671–691.

Social identity continuity

This measure was first used in research by Catherine Haslam and colleagues (2008) to assess the degree to which stroke survivors were able to maintain their pre-stroke social group memberships. The scale is another component of the Exeter Identity Transition Scales (EXITS).

1. After [life transition] I still belong to the same groups I was a member of before [life transition].

2. After [life transition] I still join in the same group activities as before [life transition].

3. After [life transition] I am friendly with people in the same groups as I was before [life transition].

4. After [life transition] I continue to have strong ties with the same groups as before [life transition].

Scale used in original publication:

do not agree at all 1 2 3 4 5 6 7 8 9 agree completely

Reference: Haslam, C., Holme, A., Haslam, S. A., Iyer, A., Jetten, J., & Williams, W. H. (2008). Maintaining group memberships: Social identity continuity predicts well-being after stroke. *Neuropsychological Rehabilitation, 18*, 671–691.

Social identity mapping

The nature of a person's social identity can also be established using *social identity mapping* (Cruwys et al., 2016; see also Best et al., 2014; Haslam, Best, Dingle, Mackenzie, & Beckwith, 2017). This engages participants in the process of simultaneously representing a number of key social identity constructs in a way that allows for their systematic comparison and assessment. In its basic form, mapping involves participants constructing a visual map that (a) identifies the groups to which they subjectively belong as well as their psychological importance, (b) describes theoretically relevant aspects of these group memberships (e.g., the degree to which a group membership is positive), and (c) represents the similarity and compatibility of these groups to each other. By this means, the procedure serves to create a visual representation of a person's social world that captures key features of relevant social identities and their interrelationship.

Importantly, the visual nature of the process means that, unlike standard rating scale measures, the map not only gives researchers, but also participants themselves, insight into important social identity constructs. This makes it particularly useful in intervention contexts where insight of this form is beneficial – as it is in the context of career transitions (see O'Halloran & Haslam, Chapter 15) and in Groups 4 Health (Haslam et al., 2016, 2019).

The instructions below are for the paper-and-pencil version of the mapping procedure, but an online version is also available (Bentley et al., 2020). An advantage of the online version is that the complex data that can be garnered from the process are collected automatically (rather than having to be hand-entered). Note too that the procedure can be customised so that the information collected in Stage 2 is adapted to the particular issues that are being addressed by the researcher or practitioner.

Stage 1: Identifying your groups

Please think about all the groups that you belong to. These groups can take any form, for example, they could be broad opinion-based or demographic groups (e.g., feminist; Australian), leisure or social groups (e.g., book group or gardening group), community groups (e.g., church group), sporting groups (e.g., rugby or tennis club), work groups (e.g., sales team), professional groups (e.g., trade union), or any others you can think of.

To start the process of social identity mapping, write down the names of each of these groups on separate Post-it notes. Remember that the size of the Post-it note matters, so write down the name of each *very important* group on a large Post-it note, write down the names of each *moderately important* group on separate medium sized Post-it notes, and the name of each *less important* group on separate small Post-it notes.

Stage 2: Thinking about your groups

1. How typical (or representative) are you of your social groups?

Indicate how typical you are of each of the groups identified in your map using a scale from 1 to 10 (where 1 = not at all typical, 10 = very typical). Write this rating in the top left corner of each Post-it note.

2. How many days in a month do you engage with each group?

If you engage with this group every day, the number would be 30. If it is every week, then the number would be 4. Write this number in the top right corner of the Post-it for each of your groups.

3. How much support do you get from each group?

Rate how much support you get from each group on a scale from 1 (no support at all) to 10 (a very high level of support). Write this rating in the bottom right corner of the Post-it note for each of your groups.

4. How positive do you feel about being a member of each group?

Rate how positive you feel about being part of each group on a scale from 1 (not very positive at all) to 10 (very positive). Write your rating in the bottom left-hand corner of each Post-it note.

Stage 3: Mapping your groups in relation to each other

1. How different are your groups from each other?

We know that some groups are very similar to each other because they like or do similar things, but others are very different from each other. Here, we would like you to show how similar and different your groups are to each other. Do this by placing your Post-it notes close together if they are similar, and further apart if they are different. So, if two groups are very similar to each other, place them close to each other on your map, but, if two groups are very different from each other (e.g., they do different things, have different members, or it feels different being a part of each), place them far away from each other.

2. How easy or difficult is it to be a member of your groups at the same time?

Because we typically belong to a number of groups, it can be hard at times trying to juggle them. In your social identity map, we would like you to use different lines to show how easy or hard it is to be part of different groups at the same time. For example, if you belong to a chess club it might be very easy to also be a member of your family, but not that easy to also be a member of your rugby club.

Show the ease or difficulty of being part of multiple groups at the same time by using different types of lines. If two groups are very easy to belong to simultaneously then join them with a straight line.

_____

If two groups are moderately easy to belong to simultaneously, join them with a wavy line

If two groups are hard to belong to simultaneously, join them with a jagged line.

_____

Reference: Cruwys, T., Steffens, N. K., Haslam, S. A., Haslam, C., Jetten, J., & Dingle, G. A. (2016). Social Identity Mapping: A procedure for visual representation and assessment of subjective multiple group memberships. *British Journal of Social Psychology*, 55, 613–642.

Personal identity strength

This scale was developed by Jolanda Jetten and colleagues (2010; see below) to assess the extent to which people have a clear understanding of who they are as individuals. The items were adapted from a self-clarity scale that had originally been developed by Jennifer Campbell and colleagues (1996), and a personal identity strength scale devised by Gamze Baray and colleagues (2009).

1. I know what I like and what I don't like.

2. I know what my morals are.

3. I have strong beliefs.

4. I know what I want from life.

5. I am aware of the roles and responsibilities I have in my life.

   Scale used in original publication:

   do not agree at all 1 2 3 4 5 6 7 agree completely

_____

Reference: Jetten, J., Haslam, C., Pugliese, C., Tonks, J. & Haslam, S. A. (2010). Declining autobiographical memory and the loss of identity: Effects on well-being. *Journal of Clinical and Experimental Neuropsychology, 32*, 408–416.

SOCIAL IDENTITY PROCESS MEASURES

Identity Leadership Inventory (ILI)

This scale was developed by Niklas Steffens and colleagues (2014; see below) to capture the four aspects of leadership originally discussed by Haslam, Reicher and Platow (2011; see Figure 3.3). On the basis of previous research that has explored leadership from a social identity perspective, these dimensions relate to a leader's perceived ability to represent the group (*identity prototypicality*), to champion the group (*identity advancement*), to create a group's identity (*identity entrepreneurship*) and to embed the group's identity in lived reality (*identity impresarioship*). As discussed in Chapter 3 above, Steffens and colleagues conducted a range of studies that confirmed the scale's construct validity, discriminant validity and criterion validity, including one with members of basketball, soccer, volleyball and handball teams in Belgium which showed that the perceived identity leadership of leaders was a good predictor of both team members' team identification and team confidence, and the team's task cohesion (Steffens et al., 2014; Study 4). The validity of the instrument was subsequently confirmed in research conducted in 25 countries/regions as part of the *ILI-Global project* (van Dick et el., 2018). As a result of this, the ILI is now available in 21 languages (these can be accessed online at www.goethe-university-frankfurt.de/73247942/Surveys_in_all_languages).

1. This leader embodies what [the group] stands for.

2. This leader is representative of members of [the group].

3. This leader is a model member of [the group].*

4. This leader exemplifies what it means to be a member of [the group].

5. This leader promotes the interests of members of [the group].

6. This leader acts as a champion for [the group].*

7. This leader stands up for [the group].

8. When this leader acts, he or she has [the group's] interests at heart.

9. This leader makes people feel as if they are part of the same group.

10. This leader creates a sense of cohesion within [the group].*

11. This leader develops an understanding of what it means to be a member of [the group].

12. This leader shapes members' perceptions of [the group's] values and ideals.

13. This leader devises activities that bring [the group] together.

14. This leader arranges events that help [the group] function effectively.

15. This leader creates structures that are useful for [group members].*

Note: * Items used in the short form of the measure (ILI-SF).

Scores for the four dimensions of identity leadership are obtained by averaging responses to different sets of items: identity prototypicality = 1, 2, 3, 4; identity advancement = 5, 6, 7, 8; identity entrepreneurship = 9, 10, 11, 12; identity impresarioship = 13, 14, 15.

Reference: Steffens, N. K., Haslam, S. A., Reicher, S. D., Platow, M. J., Fransen, K., Yang, J., ... & Boen, F. (2014). Leadership as social identity management: Introducing the Identity Leadership Inventory (ILI) to assess and validate a four-dimensional model. The Leadership Quarterly, 25, 1001–1024.

Team-Referent Attributions Measure in Sport (TRAMS)

This scale was developed by Pete Coffee and colleagues (2015; see below) to assess four aspects of team-related attributions in sport: controllability, stability, globality and universality. The capacity of the tool to capture these aspects of attributions has been confirmed for members of soccer, rugby, cricket, basketball and hockey teams that were both successful and unsuccessful. As discussed by Coffee and colleagues in Chapter 8 above, studies that have validated the measure found that when the causes of team defeat were perceived to generalise across situations, controllability predicted subsequent collective efficacy. Following team victory, stable attributions were also positively associated with a subsequent sense of collective efficacy.

In the space below, write the single most important reason for how your team performed.

The most important reason was _____

Think about the reason you have written above. In general, to what extent is your reason something that ...

1. your team could control in the future

2. remains stable across time

3. relates to a number of different situations your team encounters

4. in the future, your team could exert control over

5. is a common cause of performance for other teams

6. you feel remains constant over time

7. affects a wide variety of outcomes for your team

8. is a cause of performance that other teams relate to

9. stays consistent across time

10. in the future your team could change at will

11. influences the outcomes of new situations your team will face

12. can be used to explain the performances of other teams

13. your team could regulate in the future

14. influences all situations your team encounters

15. is a cause of performance for other teams as well

Scale used in original publication:

not at all 1 2 3 4 5 completely

Note: Scores for the four dimensions of team-referent attributions are obtained by averaging responses to different sets of items: *controllability* = 1, 4, 10, 13; *stability* = 2, 6, 9; *globality* = 3, 7, 11, 14; *universality* = 5, 8, 12, 15.

Reference: Coffee, P., Greenlees, I., & Allen, M. S. (2015). The TRAMS: The Team-Referent Attributions Measure in Sport. *Psychology of Sport and Exercise, 16,* 150–159.

The TASS-Q: The Team-referent Availability of Social Support Questionnaire

This scale was developed by Pete Coffee and colleagues to assess the four forms of team-based social support commonly observed in sport: *emotional support, esteem support, informational support,* and *tangible support* (Coffee, Freeman, & Allen, 2017; see below and also Chapter 14). The content and criterion validity of the scale has been confirmed in a number of studies with athletes involved in various team sports (primarily rugby, hockey and cricket). As discussed by Hartley and colleagues in Chapter 14, these validation studies have also found that team-based esteem support is a positive predictor of collective efficacy, and that team-based emotional support is a positive predictor of team cohesion (Coffee et al., 2017).

Below is a list of items referring to the types of help and support a team may have available to them. Please indicate to what extent your team has these types of support available.

If needed, to what extent would someone ...

1. provide your team with comfort and security

2. reinforce the positives

3. help your team with travel to training and matches

4. enhance your collective-esteem

5. give your team constructive criticism

6. help with tasks to leave your team free to concentrate

7. give your team tactical advice

8. always be there for your team

9. instill your team with the confidence to deal with pressure

10. do things for your team at competitions/matches

11. care for your team

12. boost your team's sense of competence

13. give your team advice about performing in competitive situations

14. show concern for your team

15. give your team advice when the team is performing poorly

16. help your team organise and plan competitions/matches

Scale used in original publication:

not at all 0 1 2 3 4 extremely

Note: Scores for the four dimensions of team-referent support are obtained by averaging responses to different sets of items: *emotional support* = 1, 8, 11, 14; *esteem support* = 2, 4, 9, 12; *informational support* = 5, 7, 13, 15; *tangible support* = 3, 6, 10, 16.

Reference: Coffee, P., Freeman, P., & Allen, M. S. (2017). The TASS-Q: The Team-referent Availability of Social Support Questionnaire. *Psychology of Sport and Exercise*, *33*, 55–65.

REFERENCES

@Coach Rev (2018, April 30). If you tell @DGardeck he can't do something, you better believe he'll do it. Once heard him tell his teammates 'I don't play football, I am football.' [Twitter post]. Retrieved from: https://twitter.com/glennrevell/status/990619683723374592 (Accessed August 12, 2019).

Abbasi, I. N. (2014). Socio-cultural barriers to attaining recommended levels of physical activity among females: A review of literature. *Quest, 66,* 448–467.

Abbot, H. (Producer). (2010). LeBron James' decision: The transcript. *ESPN.* Retrieved from: www.espn.com/blog/truehoop/post/_/id/17853/lebron-james-decision-the-transcript (Accessed November 2, 2019).

Abdul-Jabbar, K. (2017). *Coach Wooden and me: Our 50-year friendship on and off the court.* London: Hachette UK.

Abgarov, A., Jeffrey-Tosoni, S., Baker, J., & Fraser-Thomas, J. L. (2012). Understanding social support throughout the injury process among interuniversity swimmers. *Journal of Intercollegiate Sport, 5,* 213–229.

Abosag, I., Roper, S., & Hind, D. (2012). Examining the relationship between brand emotion and brand extension among supporters of professional football clubs. *European Journal of Marketing, 46,* 1233–1251.

Abrams, D., & Hogg, M. A. (1988). Comments on the motivational status of self-esteem in social identity and intergroup discrimination. *European Journal of Social Psychology, 18,* 317–334.

Abrams, D., & Hogg, M. A. (1990). Social identification, self-categorization and social influence. *European Review of Social Psychology, 1,* 195–228.

Abramson, L. Y., Seligman, M. E. P., & Teasdale, J. D. (1978). Learned helplessness in humans: Critique and reformulation. *Journal of Abnormal Psychology, 87,* 49–74.

The Adecco Group (2019). Athlete365 Career+. Retrieved from: www.olympic.org/athlete365/career/ (Accessed October 21, 2019).

Adie, J. W., Duda, J. L., & Ntoumanis, N. (2012). Perceived coach-autonomy support, basic need satisfaction and the well- and ill-being of elite youth soccer players: A longitudinal investigation. *Psychology of Sport and Exercise, 13,* 51–59.

Adler, P. A., & Adler, P. (1991). *Backboards and blackboards: College athletes and role engulfment.* New York: Columbia University Press.

AFL Players Association (2014). What is MAX360? Retrieved from: www.aflplayers.com.au/article/what-is-max360/ (Accessed April 20, 2020).

Aggerholm, K. (2015). *Talent development, existential philosophy and sport: On becoming an elite athlete.* New York: Routledge.

Agyekum, H. A. (2019). 'The best of the best': The politicization of sports under Ghana's Supreme Military Council. In M. Gennaro & S. Aderinto (Eds.), *Sports in African history, politics, and identity formation* (pp. 73–88). London: Routledge.

Aisch, G., Leonhardt, D., & Qauealy, K. (2014). World Cup opinions in 19 countries: Likes, dislikes, predictions. *New York Times* (June 10). Retrieved from: www.nytimes.com/2014/06/11/upshot/world-cup-opinions-in-19-countries-likes-dislikes-predictions.html (Accessed December 5, 2019).

Ajzen, I. (1991). The theory of planned behavior. *Organizational Behavior and Human Decision Processes, 50,* 179–211.

Ajzen, I. (2015). The theory of planned behaviour is alive and well, and not ready to retire: A commentary on Sniehotta, Presseau, and Araújo-Soares. *Health Psychology Review, 9*, 131–137.

Ajzen, I., & Fishbein, M. (1980). *Understanding attitudes and predicting social behavior.* Englewood Cliffs, NJ: Prentice-Hall.

Alfermann, D., & Stambulova, N. B. (2007). Career transitions and career termination. In G. Tenenbaum & R. C. Eklund (Eds.), *Handbook of sport psychology* (pp. 712–733). Hoboken, NJ: John Wiley & Sons.

Allan, V., & Côté, J. (2016). A cross-sectional analysis of coaches' observed emotion-behavior profiles and adolescent athletes' self-reported developmental outcomes. *Journal of Applied Sport Psychology, 28*, 321–337.

Allen, M. S., Coffee, P., & Greenlees, I. (2012). A theoretical framework and research agenda for studying team attributions in sport. *International Review of Sport and Exercise Psychology, 5*, 121–144.

Allen, M. S., Jones, M. V., & Sheffield, D. (2009). Attribution, emotion, and collective efficacy in sports teams. *Group Dynamics: Theory, Research, and Practice, 13*, 205–217.

Alleyne, R. (2009). The reason why England players choke at penalties. *The Telegraph* (September 24). Retrieved from: www.telegraph.co.uk/news/science/6224129/The-reason-why-England-players-choke-at-penalties.html (Accessed November 23, 2019).

Alloy, L. B. (1982). The role of perceptions and attributions for response-outcome noncontingency in learned helplessness: A commentary and discussion. *Journal of Personality, 50*, 443–479.

Alloy, L. B., Peterson, C., Abramson, L. Y., & Seligman, M. E. P. (1984). Attributional style and the generality of learned helplessness. *Journal of Personality and Social Psychology, 46*, 681–687.

Alnabulsi, H., & Drury, J. (2014). Social identification moderates the effect of crowd density on safety at the Hajj. *Proceedings of the National Academy of Sciences, 111*, 9091–9096.

Alsarve, D., & Tjønndal, A. (2020). 'The Nordic female fighter': Exploring women's participation in mixed martial arts in Norway and Sweden. *International Review for the Sociology of Sport, 55*, 471–489.

Alvarez, M. S., Balaguer, I., Castillo, I., & Duda, J. L. (2012). The coach-created motivational climate, young athletes' well-being, and intentions to continue participation. *Journal of Clinical Sport Psychology, 6*, 166–179.

American Psychological Association (2019). What is sport and exercise psychology? Retrieved from: www.apadivisions.org/division-47/about/resources/what-is (Accessed December17, 2019).

Amiot, C. E., Sansfaçon, S., & Louis, W. R. (2013). Uncovering hockey fans' motivations behind their derogatory behaviors and how these motives predict psychological well-being and quality of social identity. *Psychology of Sport and Exercise, 14*, 379–388.

Amorose, A. J., & Anderson-Butcher, D. (2007). Autonomy-supportive coaching and self-determined motivation in high school and college athletes: A test of self-determination theory. *Psychology of Sport and Exercise, 8*, 654–670.

Anderson, B. (1991). *Imagined communities: Reflections on the origins and spread of nationalism* (6th ed.). London: Verso.

Anderson, C., Keltner, D., & John, O. P. (2003). Emotional convergence between people over time. *Journal of Personality & Social Psychology, 84*, 1054–1068.

Anderson, D. F., Cychosz, C. M., & Franke, W. D. (1998). Association of exercise identity with measures of exercise commitment. *Journal of Sport Behavior, 21*, 233–241.

Angelini, J. R., MacArthur, P. J., Smith, L. R., & Billings, A. C. (2017). Nationalism in the United States and Canadian primetime broadcast coverage of the 2014 Winter Olympics. *International Review for the Sociology of Sport, 52*, 779–800.

Antonowicz, D., Jakubowska, H., & Kossakowski, R. (2020). Marginalised, patronised and instrumentalised: Polish female fans in the ultras' narratives. *International Review for the Sociology of Sport, 55*, 60–76.

Appelbaum, L. G., Cain, M. S., Darling, E. F., Stanton, S. J., Nguyen, M. T., & Mitroff, S. R. (2012). What is the identity of a sports spectator? *Personality and Individual Differences, 52*, 422–427.

Appleton, P. R., Hall, H. K., & Hill, A. P. (2009). Relations between multidimensional perfectionism and burnout in junior-elite male athletes. *Psychology of Sport and Exercise, 10*, 457–465.

Aristotle (340BC/2000). *Nicomachean ethics.* (R. Crisp trans). Cambridge: Cambridge University Press.

Armitage, C. J. (2005). Can the theory of planned behavior predict the maintenance of physical activity? *Health Psychology, 24*, 235–245.

Armitage, C. J., & Arden, M. A. (2010). A volitional help sheet to increase physical activity in people with low socioeconomic status: A randomised exploratory trial. *Psychology & Health, 25*, 1129–1145.

Armitage, C. J., & Conner, M. (2001). Efficacy of the theory of planned behaviour: A meta-analytic review. *British Journal of Social Psychology, 40*, 471–500.

Armitage, C. J., Conner, M., Loach, J., & Willetts, D. (1999). Different perceptions of control: Applying an extended theory of planned behavior to legal and illegal drug use. *Basic and Applied Social Psychology, 21*, 301–316.

Armstrong, G., & Young, M. (1999). Fanatical football chants: Creating and controlling the carnival. *Culture, Sport, Society, 2*, 173–211.

Arnold, R., Edwards, T., & Rees, T. (2018). Organizational stressors, social support, and implications for subjective performance in high-level sport. *Psychology of Sport and Exercise, 39*, 204–212.

Arthur, C. A., Bastardoz, N., & Eklund, R. C. (2017). Transformational leadership in sport: Current status and future directions. *Current Opinion in Psychology, 16*, 78–83.

Arthur, C. A., Woodman, T., Ong, C. W., Hardy, L., & Ntoumanis, N. (2011). The role of athlete narcissism in moderating the relationship between coaches' transformational leader behaviors and athlete motivation. *Journal of Sport and Exercise Psychology, 33*, 3–19.

Asch, S. E. (1952). *Social psychology.* Englewood Cliffs, NJ: Prentice-Hall.

Ashworth, T. (2004). *Trench warfare 1914–18: The live and let live system.* London: Pan Books.

Asztalos, M., Wijndaele, K., De Bourdeaudhuij, I., Philippaerts, R., Matton, L., Duvigneaud, N., … Cardon, G. (2008). Specific associations between types of physical activity and components of mental health. *Journal of Science and Medicine in Sport, 12*, 468–474.

Augoustinos, M., Callaghan, P., & Platow, M. J. (2019). 'Labelling people racists is almost as hurtful as racism itself': Negotiating prejudice in the 'cut and thrust' of everyday life. Unpublished manuscript, University of Adelaide.

Bachman, R. (2019). U.S. women's soccer team ends mediation talks without agreement: The two-day talks between the players and the U.S. Soccer Federation were an effort to settle a gender-discrimination lawsuit. *Wall Street Journal* (December 10). Retrieved from: www.wsj.com/articles/u-s-womens-soccer-team-ends-mediation-talks-without-agreement-11565824496 (Accessed December 5, 2019).

Baker, J., Côté J., & Deakin, J. (2005). Expertise in ultra-endurance triathletes early sport involvement, training structure, and the theory of deliberate practice. *Journal of Applied Sport Psychology, 17*, 64–78.

Bakker, A. B., Oerlemans, W., Demerouti, E., Slot, B. B., & Ali, D. M. (2011). Flow and performance: A study among talented Dutch soccer players. *Psychology of Sport and Exercise, 12*, 442–450.

Ball, K., Jeffery, R. W., Abbott, G., McNaughton, S. A., & Crawford, D. (2010). Is healthy behavior contagious: Associations of social norms with physical activity and healthy eating. *International Journal of Behavioral Nutrition and Physical Activity, 7*, 86.

Ballouli, K., Reese, J., & Brown, B. (2017). Effects of mood states and team identification on pricing in the secondary ticket market. *Sport Business and Management: An International Journal, 7*, 276–292.

Bandura, A. (1977). Self-efficacy: Toward a unifying theory of behavioral change. *Psychological Review*, *84*, 191–215.

Bandura, A. (1986). *Social foundations of thought and action: A social cognitive theory*. Engelwood Cliffs, NJ: Prentice-Hall.

Bandura, A. (1997). *Self-efficacy: The exercise of control*. New York: Freeman.

Bandura, A. (2001). Social cognitive theory: An agentic perspective. *Annual Review of Psychology*, *52*, 1–26.

Bandyopadhyay, K. (2008). Feel good, goodwill and India's friendship tour of Pakistan. *International Journal of the History of Sport*, *25*, 1654–1670.

Barber, B., Stone, M. R., Hunt, J. E., & Eccles, J. S. (2005). Benefits of activity participation: The roles of identity affirmation and peer group norm sharing. In J. L. Mahoney, R. W. Karson, & J. S. Eccles (Eds.), *Organized activities as contexts of development: Extracurricular activities, after-school and community programs* (pp. 185–210). Mahwah, NJ: Lawrence Erlbaum.

Barker, J. B., Evans, A. L., Coffee, P., Slater, M. J., & McCarthy, P. J. (2014). Consulting on tour: A dual-phase personal-disclosure mutual-sharing intervention and group functioning in elite youth cricket. *The Sport Psychologist*, *28*, 186–197.

Barker, J. B., Mellalieu, S. D., McCarthy, P. J., Jones, M. V., & Moran, A. (2013). A review of single case research in sport psychology 1997–2012: Research trends and future directions. *Journal of Applied Sport Psychology*, *25*, 4–32.

Barkoukis, V., Lazuras, L., Tsorbatzoudis, H., & Rodafinos, A. (2011). Motivational and sportspersonship profiles of elite athletes in relation to doping behaviour. *Psychology of Sport and Exercise*, *12*, 205–212.

Baron, R. A., Byrne, D., & Branscombe, N. R. (2006). *Social psychology* (11th ed.). Boston, MA: Pearson.

Barrer, P. (2007). 'Satan is God!': Re-imagining contemporary Slovak national identity through sport. *Sport in Society*, *10*, 223–238.

Barth, J., Schneider, S., & von Kanel, R. (2010). Lack of social support in the etiology and the prognosis of coronary heart disease: A systematic review and meta-analysis. *Psychosomatic Medicine*, *72*, 229–238.

Bass, B. M. (1985). *Leadership and performance beyond expectations*. New York: Free Press.

Bass, B. M., & Riggio, R. E. (2006). *Transformational leadership* (2nd ed.). Mahwah, NJ: Erlbaum.

Battaglia, A., Kerr, G., & Stirling, A. (2018). An outcast from the team: Exploring youth ice hockey goalies' benching experiences. *Psychology of Sport and Exercise*, *38*, 39–46.

Bauman, N. J. (2016). The stigma of mental health in athletes: Are mental toughness and mental health seen as contradictory in elite sport? *British Journal of Sports Medicine*, *50*, 135–136.

Baumeister, R. F., & Leary, M. R. (1995). The need to belong: Desire for interpersonal attachments as a fundamental human motivation. *Psychological Bulletin*, *117*, 497–529.

Baumeister, R. F., & Showers, C. J. (1986). A review of paradoxical performance effects: Choking under pressure in sports and mental tests. *European Journal of Social Psychology*, *16*, 361–383.

Baumeister, R. F., Vohs, K. D., & Funder, D. C. (2007). Psychology as the science of self-reports and finger movements: Whatever happened to actual behavior? *Perspectives on Psychological Science*, *2*, 396–403.

Baxter, K. (2018). Soccer has been part of Croatia's identity even before there was a Croatia. *Los Angeles Times* (June 12). Retrieved from: www.latimes.com/sports/soccer/la-sp-world-cup-france-croatia-20180712-story.html (Accessed November 23, 2019).

BBC (2011). Sepp Blatter says on-pitch racism can be resolved with handshake. Retrieved from: www.bbc.com/sport/football/15757165 (Accessed July 30, 2019).

BBC (2016). Jonny Brownlee: Alistair helps brother over finish line in dramatic World Series finale. Retrieved from: www.bbc.com/sport/triathlon/37402716 (Accessed November 2, 2019).

BBC (2018). *State of Sport*. Retrieved from: www.bbc.com/sport/42871491 (Accessed August 30, 2019).

BBC Sport (2014). England: Wayne Rooney calls player meetings to help team gel. Retrived from: www.bbc.co.uk/sport/football/29138379 (Accessed April 20, 2020).

BBC Sport (2019). Megan Rapinoe: Ballon d'Or winner on Donald Trump, arrogance and equal pay. *Women's football* (December 16). Retrieved from: www.bbc.com/sport/football/50622330 (Accessed December 17, 2019).

Beamon, K. (2012). 'I'm a Baller': Athletic identity foreclosure among African-American former student-athletes. *Journal of African American Studies, 16*, 195–208.

Beauchamp, M. R. (2019). Promoting exercise adherence through groups: A self-categorization theory perspective. *Exercise and Sport Sciences Reviews, 47*, 54–61.

Beauchamp, M. R., Carron, A. V., McCutcheon, S., & Harper, O. (2007). Older adults' preferences for exercising alone versus in groups: Considering contextual congruence. *Annals of Behavioral Medicine, 33*, 200–206.

Beauchamp, M. R., Crawford, K. L., & Jackson, B. (2018). Social cognitive theory and physical activity: Mechanisms of behavior change, critique, and legacy. *Psychology of Sport and Exercise, 42*, 110–117.

Beauchamp, M. R., Dunlop, W. L., Downey, S. M., & Estabrooks, P. A. (2012). First impressions count: Perceptions of surface-level and deep-level similarity within postnatal exercise classes and implications for program adherence. *Journal of Health Psychology, 17*, 68–76.

Beauchamp, M. R., Harden, S. M., Wolf, S. A., Rhodes, R. E., Liu, Y., Dunlop, W. L., ... Estabrooks, P. A. (2015). GrOup based physical Activity for oLder adults (GOAL) randomized controlled trial: Study protocol. *BMC Public Health, 15*, 592.

Beauchamp, M. R., McEwan, D., & Waldhauser, K. J. (2017). Team building: Conceptual, methodological, and applied considerations. *Current Opinion in Psychology, 16*, 114–117.

Beauchamp, M. R., Ruissen, G. R., Dunlop, W. L., Estabrooks, P. A., Harden, S. M., Wolf, S. A., ... Rhodes, R. E. (2018). Group-based physical activity for older adults (GOAL) randomized controlled trial: Exercise adherence outcomes. *Health Psychology, 37*, 451–461.

Beck, A. T. (1964). Thinking and depression: II. Theory and therapy. *Archives of General Psychiatry, 10*, 561–571.

Beedie, C. J., Benedetti, F., Barbiani, D., Camerone, E., Cohen, E., Coleman, D., ... Harvey, S. (2018). Consensus statement on placebo effects in sports and exercise: The need for conceptual clarity, methodological rigour, and the elucidation of neurobiological mechanisms. *European Journal of Sport Science, 18*, 1383–1398.

Becker, H. S. (1963). *The outsiders*. New York: Free Press.

Beedie, C. J., & Foad, A. J. (2009). The placebo effect in sports performance. *Sports Medicine, 39*, 313–329.

Beilock, S. L., Afremow, J. A., Rabe, A. L., & Carr, T. H. (2001). 'Don't miss!' The debilitating effects of suppressive imagery on golf putting performance. *Journal of Sport and Exercise Psychology, 23*, 200–221.

Beilock, S. L., & Carr, T. H. (2001). On the fragility of skilled performance: What governs choking under pressure? *Journal of Experimental Psychology: General, 130*, 701–725.

Beilock, S. L., & Gray, R. (2007). Why do athletes choke under pressure? In G. Tenenbaum & R. C. Eklund (Eds.), *Handbook of sport psychology*. Hoboken, NJ: Wiley.

Beilock, S. L., & McConnell, A. R. (2004). Stereotype threat and sport: Can athletic performance be threatened? *Journal of Sport and Exercise Psychology, 26*, 597–609.

Bekkers, R. H. F. P. (2005). *Charity begins at home: How socialization experiences influence giving and volunteering*. Paper presented at the 34th Arnova Annual Conference, Washington, DC, November 17–20.

Bell, J., Somerville, I., & Hargie, O. (2019). The structuration of a sporting social system? Northern Ireland fans, Football for All and the creation of the Green and White Army. *International Review for the Sociology of Sport* (Online publication; doi: 10.1177/1012690219862917).

Bennett, E. V., Hurd Clarke, L., Wolf, S. A., Dunlop, W. L., Harden, S. M., Liu, Y., ... Beauchamp, M. R. (2018). Older adults' experiences of group-based physical activity: A qualitative study from the 'GOAL' randomized controlled trial. *Psychology of Sport and Exercise*, *39*, 184–192.

Benson, A. J., & Bruner, M. W. (2018). How teammate behaviours relate to athlete affect, cognition, and behaviours: A daily diary approach within youth sport. *Psychology of Sport and Exercise*, *34*, 119–127.

Benson, A. J., Bruner, M. W., & Eys, M. A. (2017). A social identity approach to understanding the conditions associated with antisocial behaviours among teammates in female teams. *Sport, Exercise, and Performance Psychology*, *6*, 129–142.

Benson, J. S., & Kennelly, K. J. (1976). Learned helplessness: The result of uncontrollable reinforcements or uncontrollable aversive stimuli? *Journal of Personality and Social Psychology*, *34*, 138–145.

Benson, P. L. (1997). *All kids are our kids: What communities must do to raise caring and responsible children and adolescents*. San Francisco, CA: Jossey-Bass.

Benson, P. L. (2003). Developmental assets and asset-building community: Conceptual and empirical foundations. In R. M. Lerner & P. L. Benson (Eds.), *Developmental assets and asset building communities: Implications for research, policy, and practice* (pp. 19–43). Norwell, MA: Kluwer.

Bentley, S. V., Greenaway, K. H., Haslam, S. A., Cruwys, T., Steffens, N. K., Haslam, C., & Cull, B. (2020). Social identity mapping online. *Journal of Personality and Social Psychology*, *118*, 213–241.

Bergland, C. (2013). The neurobiology of grace under pressure: 8 habits that stimulate your vagus nerve and keep you calm, cool, and collected. Retrieved from: http://makingsenseoftrauma.com/wp-content/uploads/2016/02/neurobiology-of-grace-under-pressure.pdf (Accessed April 15, 2020).

Bergman, S. (2019). Cycling champion Victoria Pendleton reveals she planned to take her own life: 'I don't want to see tomorrow'. Retrieved from: www.independent.co.uk/life-style/victoria-pendleton-mental-health-depression-suicide-cycling-everest-a8741826.html (Accessed April 20, 2020).

Berkman, L. F., & Syme, S. L. (1979). Social networks, host resistance, and mortality: A nine-year follow-up study of Alameda County residents. *American Journal of Epidemiology*, *109*, 186–204.

Bernache-Assollant, I., Chantal, Y., Bouchet, P., & Lacassagne, M. F. (2016). Understanding the consequences of victory among sport spectators: The mediating role of BIRGing. *European Journal of Sport Science*, *16*, 719–725.

Bernache-Assollant, I., Lacassagne, M. F., & Braddock, J. H. (2007). Basking in reflected glory and blasting – Differences in identity-management strategies between two groups of highly identified soccer fans. *Journal of Language and Social Psychology*, *26*, 381–388.

Bernache-Assollant, I., Laurin, R., Bouchet, P., Bodet, G., & Lacassagne, M. F. (2010). Refining the relationship between ingroup identification and identity management strategies in the sport context: The moderating role of gender and the mediating role of negative mood. *Group Processes & Intergroup Relations*, *13*, 639–652.

Berri, D. J., & Krautmann, A. C. (2006). Shirking on the court: Testing for the incentive effects of guaranteed pay. *Economic Inquiry*, *44*, 536–546.

Best, D., Beckwith, M., Haslam, C., Haslam, S. A., Jetten, J., Mawson, E., & Lubman, D. I. (2016). Overcoming alcohol and other drug addiction as a process of social identity transition: The Social Identity Model Of Recovery (SIMOR). *Addiction Research and Theory*, *24*, 111–123.

Beunen, G., & Thomis, M. (1999). Genetic determinants of sports participation and daily physical activity. *International Journal of Obesity*, *23*, S55–S63.

Bianco, T., & Eklund, R. C. (2001). Conceptual considerations for social support research in sport and exercise settings: The case of sports injury. *Journal of Sport and Exercise Psychology*, *23*, 85–107.

Biddle, S. J. H. (1993) Attribution research and sport psychology. In R. N. Murphey & L. K. Tennant (Eds.), *Handbook of research on sport psychology* (pp. 437–464). New York: Macmillan.

Biddle, S. J. H., & Mutrie, N. (2001). *Psychology of physical activity: Determinants, well-being and interventions* (1st ed.). London: Routledge.

Biddle, S. J. H., Mutrie, N., & Gorely, T. (2015). *Psychology of physical activity: Determinants, well-being and interventions* (3rd ed.). London: Routledge.

Biderman, D. (2010). 11 minutes of action. *The Wall Street Journal* (January 15). Retrieved from: www.wsj.com/articles/SB10001424052748704281204575002852055561406 (Accessed July 31, 2019).

Bigalke, Z. R. (2019). The birth of the Springboks: How early international rugby matches unified white cultural identity in South Africa. In M. Gennaro & S. Aderinto (Eds.), *Sports in African history, politics, and identity formation* (pp. 152–166). London: Routledge.

Billings, A. C., & Angelini, J. R. (2007). Packaging the games for viewer consumption: Gender, ethnicity, and nationality in NBC's coverage of the 2004 summer Olympics. *Communication Quarterly*, *55*, 95–111.

Billings, A. C., Brown, K. A., & Brown, N. A. (2013). 5,535 hours of impact: Effects of Olympic media on nationalism attitudes. *Journal of Broadcasting and Electronic Media*, *57*, 579–595.

Billings, A. C., Brown, K. A., & Brown-Devlin, N. (2015). Sports draped in the American flag: Impact of the 2014 Winter Olympic telecast on nationalized attitudes. *Mass Communication and Society*, *18*, 377–398.

Birley, D. (2013). *A social history of English cricket*. London: Aurum Press.

Biscaia, R., Correia, A., Rosado, A. F., Ross, S. D., & Maroco, J. (2013). Sport sponsorship: The relationship between team loyalty, sponsorship awareness, attitude toward the sponsor, and purchase intentions. *Journal of Sport Management*, *27*, 288–302.

Black, J. M., & Smith, A. L. (2007). An examination of Coakley's perspective on identity, control, and burnout among adolescent athletes. *International Journal of Sport Psychology*, *38*, 417–436.

Blair, S. N. (1988). Exercise within a healthy lifestyle. In R. K. Dishman (Ed.), *Exercise adherence: Its impact on public health* (pp. 75–89). Champaign, IL: Human Kinetics.

Blair, S. N., Dunn, A. L., Marcus, B. H., Carpenter, R. A., & Jaret, P. (2010). *Active living every day*. Champaign, IL: Human Kinetics.

Blair, S. N., Sallis, R. E., Hutber, A., & Archer, E. (2012). Exercise therapy: The public health message. *Scandinavian Journal of Medicine & Science in Sports*, *22*(4), e24–e28.

Blanchard, C. M., Courneya, K. S., Rodgers, W. M., Daub, B., & Knapik, G. (2002). Determinants of exercise intention and behavior during and after phase 2 cardiac rehabilitation: An application of the theory of planned behavior. *Rehabilitation Psychology*, *47*, 308–323.

Blanchard, C. M., Fisher, J., Sparling, P., Nehl, E., Rhodes, R. E., Courneya, K. S., & Baker, F. (2008). Understanding physical activity behavior in African American and Caucasian college students: An application of the theory of planned behavior. *Journal of American College Health*, *56*, 341–346.

Blankstein, K. R., & Dunkley, D. M. (2002). Evaluative concerns, self-critical, and personal standards perfectionism: A structural equation modeling strategy. In G. L. Flett & P. L. Hewitt (Eds.), *Perfectionism: Theory, research, and treatment* (p. 285–315). Washington, DC: American Psychological Association.

Blas, E., Sommerfeld, J., & Kurup, A. S. (2011). *Social determinants approaches to health: From concept to practice*. Geneva: World Health Organization.

Bleak, J. L., & Frederick, C. M. (1998). Superstitious behavior in sport: Levels of effectiveness and determinants of use in three collegiate sports. *Journal of Sport Behavior*, *21*, 1–15.

Bloom, B. S. (1985). *Developing talent in young people*. New York: Ballantine.

Bloom, G. A., & Stevens, D. E. (2002). A team-building mental skills training program with an intercollegiate equestrian team. *Athletic Insight*, *4*(1). Retrieved from: http://citeseerx.ist.psu.edu/viewdoc/download?doi=10.1.1.622.1162&rep=rep1&type=pdf (Accessed April 20, 2020).

Bloom, G. A., Stevens, D. E., & Wickwire, T. L. (2003). Expert coaches' perceptions of team building. *Journal of Applied Sport Psychology*, *15*, 129–143.

Blumer, H. (1969). *Symbolic interactionism*. Englewood Cliffs, NJ: Prentice-Hall.

Boa, K. (2004). *Augustine to Freud: What theologians and psychologist tell us about human nature and why it matters*. Nashville, TN: B & H Publishing Group.

Boen, F., & Vanbeselaere, N. (2002). The impact of election outcome on the display of political posters: A field study during communal elections in Flanders. *Political Psychology*, *23*, 385–391.

Boen, F., Vanbeselaere, N., & Feys, J. (2002). Behavioral consequences of fluctuating group success: An Internet study of soccer-team fans. *Journal of Social Psychology*, *142*, 769–781.

Boen, F., Vanbeselaere, N., Pandelaere, M., Dewitte, S., Duriez, B., Snauwaert, B., … Van Avermaet, E. (2002). Politics and basking-in-reflected-glory: A field study in Flanders. *Basic and Applied Social Psychology*, *24*, 205–214.

Boen, F., Vanbeselaere, N., Pandelaere, M., Schutters, K., & Rowe, P. (2008). When your team is not really your team anymore: Identification with a merged basketball club. *Journal of Applied Sport Psychology*, *20*, 165–183.

Boen, F., Vanbeselaere, N., & Swinnen, H. (2005). Predicting fan support in a merger between soccer teams: A social-psychological perspective. *International Journal of Sport Psychology*, *36*, 65–85.

Bogar, C. B., & Hulse-Killacky, D. (2006). Resiliency determinants and resiliency processes among female adult survivors of childhood sexual abuse. *Journal of Counseling & Development*, *84*, 318–327.

Bolger, N., & Amarel, D. (2007). Effects of social support visibility on adjustment to stress: Experimental evidence. *Journal of Personality and Social Psychology*, *92*, 458–475.

Bolger, N., Zuckerman, A., & Kessler, R. C. (2000). Invisible support and adjustment to stress. *Journal of Personality and Social Psychology*, *79*, 953–961.

Bonanno, G. A. (2008). Loss, trauma, and human resilience: Have we underestimated the human capacity to thrive after extremely aversive events? *Psychological Trauma: Theory, Research, Practice, and Policy*, *59*, 20–28.

Bonanno, G. A., Galea, S., Bucciarelli, A., & Vlahov, D. (2007). What predicts psychological resilience after disaster? The role of demographics, resources, and life stress. *Journal of Consulting and Clinical Psychology*, *75*, 671–682.

Bonezzi, A., Brendl, C. M., & De Angelis, M. (2011). Stuck in the middle: The psychophysics of goal pursuit. *Psychological Science*, *22*, 607–612.

Bonk, D., Leprince, C., Tamminen, K. A., & Doron, J. (2019). Collective rituals in team sports: Implications for team resilience and communal coping. *Movement & Sport Sciences*, *105*, 27–36.

Booth, D. (2003). Hitting apartheid for six? The politics of the South African sports boycott. *Journal of Contemporary History*, *38*, 477–493.

Booth, D. (2012). *The race game: Sport and politics in South Africa*. London: Routledge.

Bortoli, L., Bertollo, M., Comani, S., & Robazza, C. (2011). Competence, achievement goals, motivational climate, and pleasant psychobiosocial states in youth sport. *Journal of Sports Sciences*, *29*, 171–180.

Bos, C. (2017). Derek Redmond: The day that changed my life. *Awesome stories*. Retrieved from: www.awesomestories.com/asset/view/Derek-Redmond-The-Day-that-Changed-My-Life (Accessed October 6, 2019).

Bourdieu, P. (1989). Sport and social class. *Social Science Information, 17*, 819–840.

Bower, A. (2018). Footballers seeking mental health help in record numbers – but it's good news. *The Guardian* (October 9). Retrieved from: www.theguardian.com/football/2018/oct/09/football-mental-health-record-numbers-pfa.

Bowler, D. (2013). *Shanks: The authorised biography of Bill Shankly*. London: Hachette.

Boyd, J. (2000). Selling home: Corporate stadium names and the destruction of commemoration. *Journal of Applied Communication Research, 28*, 330–346.

Boyd, T. L. (1982). Learned helplessness in humans: A frustration-produced response pattern. *Journal of Personality and Social Psychology, 42*, 738–752.

Bozionelos, G., & Bennett, P. (1999). The theory of planned behaviour as predictor of exercise: The moderating influence of beliefs and personality variables. *Journal of Health Psychology, 4*, 517–529.

Branscombe, N. R., Ellemers, N., Spears, R., & Doosje, B. (1999). The context and content of social identity threat. In N. Ellemers, R. Spears, & B. Doosje (Eds.), *Social identity: Context, commitment, content* (pp. 35–58). Oxford: Blackwell.

Branscombe, N. R., & Wann, D. L. (1991). The positive social and self concept consequences of sports team identification. *Journal of Sport & Social Issues, 15*, 115–127.

Branscombe, N. R., & Wann, D. L. (1994). Collective self-esteem consequences of outgroup derogation when a valued social identity is on trial. *European Journal of Social Psychology, 24*, 641–657.

Brawley, L. R., Carron, A. V., & Widmeyer, W. N. (1987). Assessing the cohesion of teams: Validity of the group environment questionnaire. *Journal of Sport Psychology, 9*, 275–294.

Brawley, L. R., Flora, P. K., Locke, S. R., & Gierc, M. S. H. (2014). Efficacy of the group-mediated cognitive behavioural intervention: A decade of physical activity research. In M. R. Beauchamp & M. A. Eys (Eds.), *Group dynamics in exercise and sport psychology* (2nd ed., pp. 183–202). New York: Routledge.

Brawley, L. R., & Paskevich, D. M. (1997). Conducting team building research in the context of sport and exercise. *Journal of Applied Sport Psychology, 9*, 11–40.

Brawley, L. R., Rejeski, W. J., & Lutes, L. (2000). A group-mediated cognitive-behavioral intervention for increasing adherence to physical activity in older adults. *Journal of Applied Biobehavioral Research, 5*, 47–65.

Breakey, C., Jones, M., Cunningham, C.-T., & Holt, N. F. (2009). Female athletes' perceptions of a coach's speeches. *International Journal of Sports Science & Coaching, 4*, 489–504.

Breakwell, G. M. (1986). *Coping with threatened identities*. London: Methuen.

Breakwell, G. M. (1993). Social representations and social identity. *Papers on Social Representations, 2*, 198–217.

Brechbühl, A., Schumacher Dimech, A., & Seiler, R. (2017). Policing football fans in Switzerland: A case study involving fans, stadium security employees, and police officers. *Policing* (Online publication; doi: 10.1093/police/pax086/4642978).

Brenes, G. A., Strube, M. J., & Storandt, M. (1998). An application of the theory of planned behavior to exercise among older adults. *Journal of Applied Social Psychology, 28*, 2274–2290.

Brewer, B. W., Boin, P. D., & Petitpas, A. J. (1993). Dimensions of athletic identity. Paper presented at the annual meeting of the American Psychological Association, Toronto, Ontario, Canada.

Brewer, B. W., Cornelius, A. E., Sklar, J. H., Van Raalte, J. L., Tennen, H., Armeli, S., ... Brickner, J. C. (2007). Pain and negative mood during rehabilitation after anterior cruciate ligament reconstruction: A daily process analysis. *Scandinavian Journal of Medicine & Science in Sports, 17*, 520–529.

Brewer, B. W., Van Raalte, J. L., & Linder, D. E. (1993). Athletic identity: Hercules' muscles or Achilles heel? *International Journal of Sport Psychology*, *24*, 237–254.

Brewer, B. W., Van Raalte, J. L., & Petitpas, A. J. (2000). Self-identity issues in sport career transitions. In D. Lavallee & P. Wylleman (Eds.), *Career transitions in sport: International perspectives* (pp. 29–43). Morgantown, WV: Fitness International Technology.

Brewer, M. B., and Gardner, W. (1996). Who is this 'We'? Levels of collective identity and self representations. *Journal of Personality and Social Psychology*, *71*, 83–93.

Broadbent, R. (2007). Asafa Powell hopes that mind games will not find him out in future. *The Sunday Times* (September 24). Retrieved from: www.thetimes.co.uk/article/asafa-powell-hopes-that-mind-games-will-not-find-him-out-in-future-vmkfsxxn6kn (Accessed November 25, 2019).

Bronfenbrenner, U. (1977). Toward an experimental ecology of human development. *American Psychologist*, *32*, 513–531.

Bronfenbrenner, U. (1999). Environments in developmental perspective: Theoretical and operational models. In S. L. Friedman & T. D. Wachs (Eds.), *Measuring environment across the life span: Emerging methods and concepts* (pp. 3–28). Washington, DC: American Psychological Association.

Brook, A. T., Garcia, J., & Fleming, M. A. (2008). The effects of multiple identities on psychological well-being. *Personality and Social Psychology Bulletin*, *34*, 1588–1600.

Brown, D. R., Soares, J., Epping, J. M., Lankford, T. J., Wallace, J. S., Hopkins, D., … Orleans, C. T. (2012). Stand-alone mass media campaigns to increase physical activity: A community guide updated review. *American Journal of Preventive Medicine*, *43*, 551–561.

Brown, G., & Potrac, P. (2009). 'You've not made the grade, son': De-selection and identity disruption in elite level youth football. *Soccer & Society*, *10*, 143–159.

Brown, J. A. C. (1961). *Freud and the post-Freudians*. Harmondsworth, UK: Penguin Books.

Brown, J. D., & Siegel, J. M. (1988). Attributions for negative life events and depression: The role of perceived control. *Journal of Personality and Social Psychology*, *54*, 316–322.

Brown, N. A., Devlin, M. B., & Billings, A. C. (2013). Fan identification gone extreme: Sports communication variables between fans and sport in the Ultimate Fighting Championship. *International Journal of Sport Communication*, *6*, 19–32.

Brown, R. J. (1988). *Group processes: Dynamics within and between groups*. Oxford: Blackwell.

Brown, R. J. (2019). *Henri Tajfel: Explorer of identity and difference*. Abingdon, UK: Routledge.

Bruner, M. W., Balish, S., Forrest, C., Brown, S., Webber, K., Gray, E., McGuckin, M., Keats, M., Rehman, L., & Shields, C. (2017). Ties that bond: Youth sport as a vehicle for social identity and positive youth development. *Research Quarterly for Exercise and Sport*, *88*, 209–214.

Bruner, M. W., & Benson, A. J. (2018). Evaluating the psychometric properties of the Social Identity Questionnaire for Sport (SIQS). *Psychology of Sport and Exercise*, *35*, 181–188.

Bruner, M. W., Boardley, I. D., Allen, V., Forrest, C., Root, Z., & Côté, J. (2017). Understanding social identity and intrateam moral behaviour in competitive youth ice hockey: A narrative perspective. *The Sport Psychologist*, *31*, 173–186.

Bruner, M. W., Boardley, I. D., Benson, A. J., Wilson, K. S., Root, Z., Turnnidge, J., Sutcliffe, J., & Côté, J. (2018). Disentangling the relations between social identity and prosocial and antisocial behaviour in competitive youth sport. *Journal of Youth and Adolescence*, *47*, 1113–1127.

Bruner, M. W., Boardley, I. D., & Côté, J. (2014). Social identity and prosocial and antisocial behaviour in youth sport. *Psychology of Sport and Exercise*, *15*, 56–64.

Bruner, M. W., Boardley, I. D., Forrest, C., Buckham, S., Root, Z., Allen, V., & Côté, J. (2017). Examining social identity and intrateam moral behaviours in competitive youth ice hockey using stimulated recall. *Journal of Sport Sciences, 35*, 1963–1974.

Bruner, M. W., Dunlop, W. L., & Beauchamp, M. R. (2014). A social identity perspective on group processes in sport and exercise. In M. R. Beauchamp & M. A. Eys (Eds.), *Group dynamics in exercise and sport psychology* (2nd ed., pp. 38–52). New York: Routledge.

Bruner, M. W., Eys, M. A., Beauchamp, M. R., & Côté, J. (2013). Examining the origins of team building in sport: A citation network and genealogical approach. *Group Dynamics: Theory, Research, and Practice, 17*, 30–42.

Bruner, M. W., Eys, M. A., Evans, M. B., & Wilson, K. S. (2015). Interdependence and social identity in youth sport teams. *Journal of Applied Sport Psychology, 27*, 351–358.

Bruner, M. W., & Spink, K. S. (2010). Evaluating a team building intervention in a youth exercise setting. *Group Dynamics: Theory, Research, and Practice, 14*, 304–317.

Bruner, M. W., & Spink, K. S. (2011). Effects of team building on exercise adherence and group task satisfaction in a youth activity setting. *Group Dynamics: Theory, Research, and Practice, 15*, 161–172.

BT Sport (2017). Why did England's 'golden generation' fail? Lampard, Gerrard and Rio reveal all. Retrieved from: www.youtube.com/watch?v=kRdbUfcBPZw (Accessed April 12, 2019).

Buckel, B. A. (2008). Nationalism, mass politics, and sport: Cold war case studies at seven degrees. PhD dissertation, Naval Postgraduate School, Monterey, California.

Buford, B. (1990). *Among the thugs: The experience, and the seduction, of crowd violence.* London: Secker & Warburg.

Burke, S. M., Carron, A. V., Eys, M. A., Ntoumanis, N., & Estabrooks, P. A. (2006). Group versus individual approach? A meta-analysis of the effectiveness of interventions to promote physical activity. *Sport & Exercise Psychology Review, 2*, 19–35.

Burleson, B. R. (2003). Emotional support skill. In J. O. Greene & B. R. Burleson (Eds.), *Handbook of communication and social interaction skills* (pp. 551–594). Mahwah, NJ: Erlbaum.

Burleson, B. R., & MacGeorge, E. L. (2002). Supportive communication. In M. L. Knapp & J. A. Daly (Eds.), *Handbook of interpersonal communication* (pp. 374–424). Thousand Oaks, CA: Sage.

Burnett, C. (2002). The 'black cat' of South African soccer and the Chiefs–Pirates conflict. In E. Dunning, P. Murphy, I. Waddington, & A. E. Astrinakis (Eds.), *Fighting fans: Football hooliganism as a world phenomenon* (pp. 174–189). Dublin: University College Dublin.

Burns, J. (2011). *Barça: A people's passion.* London: A&C Black.

Burton, E., Farrier, K., Hill, K. D., Codde, J., Airey, P., & Hill, A.-M. (2018). Effectiveness of peers in delivering programs or motivating older people to increase their participation in physical activity: Systematic review and meta-analysis. *Journal of Sports Sciences, 36*, 666–678.

Butler, E. A. (2015). Interpersonal affect dynamics: It takes two (and time) to tango. *Emotion Review, 7*, 336–341.

Butler, T. L. (2016). Investigating and overcoming barriers to seeking intragroup support. Unpublished PhD thesis, University of Queensland.

Butler, T. L., McKimmie, B. M., & Haslam, S. A. (2018). The approach–avoidance dilemma at the heart of group-based support: Evidence that group identification increases willingness to seek support at the same time that identity-based support threat reduces it. *European Journal of Social Psychology, 49*, 31–46.

Cacioppo, J. T., & Petty, R. E. (1982). The need for cognition. *Journal of Personality and Social Psychology, 42*(1), 116–131.

Cadinu, M., Maass, A., Rosabianca, A., & Kiesner, J. (2005). Why do women underperform under stereotype threat? Evidence for the role of negative thinking. *Psychological Science*, *16*, 572–578.

Cahn, S. K. (1994). *Coming on strong: Gender and sexuality in twentieth century women's sport*. Cambridge, MA: Harvard University Press.

Cairney, J., Clark, H. J., Kwan, M. Y., Bruner, M. W., & Tamminen, K. A. (2018). Measuring sport experiences in children and youth to better understand the impact of sport on health and positive youth development: Designing a brief measure for population health surveys. *BMC Public Health*, *18*, 446.

Calfas, J. (2018). This is the final medal count for every country at the 2018 Winter Olympics. *Time Magazine* (February 28). Retrieved from: https://time.com/5169066/final-medal-count-2018-winter-olympics/ (Accessed July 22, 2019).

Calvo, T., Cervelló, E., Jiménez, R., Iglesias, D., & Murcia, J. (2010). Using self-determination theory to explain sport persistence and dropout in adolescent athletes. *Spanish Journal of Psychology*, *13*, 677–684.

Cameron, J. E. (2004). A three-factor model of social identity. *Self & Identity*, *3*, 239–262.

Campbell, D. T. (1958). Common fate, similarity, and other indices of the status of aggregates of persons as social entities. *Behavioral Science*, *3*, 14–25.

Campo, M., Champely, S., Louvet, B., Rosnet, E., Ferrand, C., Pauketat, J. V. T., & Mackie, D. M. (2019). Group-based emotions: Evidence for emotion–performance relationships in team sports. *Research Quarterly for Exercise and Sport*, *90*, 54–63.

Campo, M., Mackie, D. M., & Sanchez, X. (2019). Emotions in group sports: A narrative review from a social identity perspective. *Frontiers in Psychology*, *10*, 666.

Campo, M., Martinent, G., Pellet, J., Boulanger, J., Louvet, B., & Nicolas, M. (2018). Emotion–performance relationships in team sport: The role of personal and social identities. *International Journal of Sports Science & Coaching*, *13*, 629–635.

Campo, M., Sanchez, X., Ferrand, C., Rosnet, E., Friesen, A. P., & Lane, A. M. (2017). Interpersonal emotion regulation in team sport: Mechanisms and reasons to regulate teammates' emotions examined. *International Journal of Sport and Exercise Psychology*, *15*, 379–394.

Carless, D., & Douglas, K. (2009). 'We haven't got a seat on the bus for you' or 'All the seats are mine': Narratives and career transition in professional golf. *Qualitative Research in Sport and Exercise*, *1*, 51–66.

Carlin, J. (2008). *Playing the enemy: Nelson Mandela and the game that made a nation*. London: Penguin.

Carnegie Council on Adolescent Development (1989). *Turning points: Preparing American youth for the 21st century*. New York: Carnegie Corporation.

Carron, A. V. (1980). *Social psychology of sport*. Ithaca, NY: Mouvement.

Carron, A. V., Brawley, L. R., & Widmeyer, W. N. (1998). Measurement of cohesion in sport and exercise. In J. L. Duda (Ed.), *Advances in sport and exercise psychology measurement* (pp. 213–226). Morgantown, WV: Fitness Information Technology.

Carron, A. V., Bray, S. R., & Eys, M. A. (2002). Team cohesion and team success in sport. *Journal of Sport Sciences*, *20*, 119–126.

Carron, A. V., Colman, M. M., Wheeler, J., & Stevens, D. (2002). Cohesion and performance in sport: A meta-analysis. *Journal of Sport and Exercise Psychology*, *24*, 168–188.

Carron, A. V., Estabrooks, P. A., Horton, H., Prapavessis, H., & Hausenblas, H. A. (1999). Reductions in the social anxiety of women associated with group membership: Distraction, anonymity, security, or diffusion of evaluation? *Group Dynamics: Theory, Research, and Practice*, *3*, 152–160.

Carron, A. V., & Eys, M. A. (2012). *Group dynamics in sport* (4th ed.). Morgantown, WV: Fitness Information Technology.

Carron, A. V., Hausenblas, H. A., & Mack, D. (1996). Social influence and exercise: A meta-analysis. *Journal of Sport and Exercise Psychology*, *18*, 1–16.

Carron, A. V., & Spink, K. S. (1993). Team building in an exercise setting. *The Sport Psychologist*, *7*, 8–18.

Carron, A. V., Widmeyer, W. N., & Brawley, L. R. (1985). The development of an instrument to assess cohesion in sport teams: The Group Environment Questionnaire. *Journal of Sport Psychology*, *7*, 244–266.

Carson, F., & Polman, R. (2012). Experiences of professional rugby union players returning to competition following anterior cruciate ligament reconstruction. *Physical Therapy in Sport*, *13*, 35–40.

Cartwright D., & Zander A. (1960). *Group dynamics: Research and theory* (2nd ed.). New York: Harper & Row.

Carver, C. S., Blaney, P. H., & Scheier, M. F. (1979). Reassertion and giving up: The interactive role of self-directed attention and outcome expectancy. *Journal of Personality and Social Psychology*, *37*, 1859–1870.

Cascagnette, J., Benson, A., Cruwys, T., Haslam, S. A., & Bruner, M. W. (2019). More than just another bib: Group dynamics in an elite Nordic ski team. Paper presented at SCAPPS (Société Canadienne D'Apprentissage Psychomoteur et de Psychologie du Sport). Vancouver, BC, October 17–19.

Caspersen, C. J., Powell, K. E., & Christenson, G. M. (1985). Physical activity, exercise and physical fitness: Definitions and distinctions for health-related research. *Public Health Reports*, *100*, 126–131.

Castaldelli-Maia, J. M., Gallinaro, J. G. d. M. e., Falcão, R. S., Gouttebarge, V., Hitchcock, M. E., Hainline, B., … Stull, T. (2019). Mental health symptoms and disorders in elite athletes: A systematic review on cultural influencers and barriers to athletes seeking treatment. *British Journal of Sports Medicine*, *53*, 707–721.

Castonguay, A. L., Sabiston, C. M., Kowalski, K. C., & Wilson, P. M. (2016). Introducing an instrument to measure body and fitness-related self-conscious emotions: The BSE-FIT. *Psychology of Sport and Exercise*, *23*, 1–12.

Cerulo, K. A. (1995). *Identity designs: The sights and sounds of a nation*. New Brunswick, NJ: Rutgers University Press.

Chalabaev, A., Brisswalter, J., Radel, R., Coombes, S. A., Easthope, C., & Clément-Guillotin, C. (2013). Can stereotype threat affect motor performance in the absence of explicit monitoring processes? Evidence using a strength task. *Journal of Sport and Exercise Psychology*, *35*, 211–215.

Chalabaev, A., Sarrazin, P., Fontayne, P., Boiché, J., & Clément-Guillotin, C. (2013). The influence of sex stereotypes and gender roles on participation and performance in sport and exercise: Review and future directions. *Psychology of Sport and Exercise*, *14*, 136–144.

Chalabaev, A., Sarrazin, P., Stone, J., & Cury, F. (2008). Do achievement goals mediate stereotype threat? An investigation on females' soccer performance. *Journal of Sport and Exercise Psychology*, *30*, 143–158.

Charbonneau, D., Barling, J., & Kelloway, E. K. (2001). Transformational leadership and sports performance: The mediating role of intrinsic motivation. *Journal of Applied Social Psychology*, *31*, 1521–1534.

Charleston, S. (2009). The English football ground as a representation of home. *Journal of Environmental Psychology*, *29*, 144–150.

Charlesworth, R. (2001). *The coach: Managing for success*. New York: Pan Macmillan.

Charlesworth, R. (2004). *Shakespeare the coach*. Sydney: Pan Macmillan Australia.

Chatzisarantis, N. L. D., & Hagger, M. S. (2005). Effects of a brief intervention based on the theory of planned behavior on leisure-time physical activity participation. *Journal of Sport and Exercise Psychology*, *27*, 470–487.

Chenoweth, R. (2016). Jarrod Barnes: PhD student, football player, paradigm changer. *The Ohio State University* (September 13). Retrieved from: https://ehe.osu.edu/news/listing/jarrod-barnes-phd-student-football-player-paradigm-changer/ (Accessed October 7, 2019).

Chien, P. M., Kelly, S. J., & Weeks, C. S. (2016). Sport scandal and sponsorship decisions: Team identification matters. *Journal of Sport Management*, *30*, 490–505.

Chrobot-Mason, D., Gerbasi, A., & Cullen-Lester, K. L. (2016). Predicting leadership relationships: The importance of collective identity. *The Leadership Quarterly*, *27*, 298–311.

Cialdini, R. B., Borden, R. J., Thorne, A., Walker, M. R., Freeman, S., & Sloan, L. R. (1976). Basking in reflected glory: Three (football field) studies. *Journal of Personality and Social Psychology*, *34*, 366–375.

Cialdini, R. B., & Goldstein, N. J. (2004). Social influence: Compliance and conformity. *Annual Review of Psychology*, *55*, 591–621.

Cialdini, R. B., & Richardson, K. D. (1980). Two indirect tactics of image management: Basking and blasting. *Journal of Personality and Social Psychology*, *39*, 406–415.

Cialdini, R. B., Wosinska, W., Barrett, D. W., Butner, J., & Gornik-Durose, M. (1999). Compliance with a request in two cultures: The differential influence of social proof and commitment/consistency on collectivists and individualists. *Personality & Social Psychology Bulletin*, *25*, 1242–1253.

Cieza, A., Anczewska, M., Ayuso-Mateos, J. L., Baker, M., Bickenbach, J. E., Chatterji, S., … Consortium, P. (2015). Understanding the impact of brain disorders: Towards a 'horizontal epidemiology' of psychosocial difficulties and their determinants. *PLoS ONE*, *10*(9), e0136271.

Cieza, A., & Bickenbach, J. E. (2019). Laidback science: Messages from horizontal epidemiology. In R. Williams, V. Kemp, S. A. Haslam, C. Haslam, K. S. Bhui, & S. Bailey (Eds.), *Social scaffolding: Applying the lessons of contemporary social science to health, public mental health and healthcare* (pp. 58–65). Cambridge, UK: Cambridge University Press.

Clark, V. R., Hopkins, W. G., Hawley, J. A., & Burke, L. M. (2000). Placebo effect of carbohydrate feeding during a 4-km cycling time trial. *Medicine & Science in Sport & Exercise*, *32*, 1642–1647.

Clawson, A. H., Borrelli, B., McQuaid, E. L., & Dunsiger, S. (2016). The role of caregiver social support, depressed mood, and perceived stress in changes in pediatric secondhand smoke exposure and asthma functional morbidity following an asthma exacerbation. *Health Psychology*, *35*, 541–551.

Coackley, J., & Donnelley, P. (2003). *Sport in society: Issues and controversies*. New York: McGraw-Hill.

Coatsworth, J. D., & Conroy, D. E. (2009). The Effects of autonomy-supportive coaching, need satisfaction and self-perceptions on initiative and identity in youth swimmers. *Developmental Psychology*, *45*, 320–328.

Coffee, P. (2017). Social identity theory as a framework to understand social support and attributions in sport. Keynote presentation at the First International Conference on Social Identity in Sport, KU Leuven, Leuven, Belgium, July.

Coffee, P., Greenlees, I., & Allen, M. S. (2015). The TRAMS: The Team-Referent Attributions Measure in Sport. *Psychology of Sport and Exercise*, *16*, 150–159.

Coffee, P., & Rees, T. (2008a). The CSGU: A measure of controllability, stability, globality, and universality attributions. *Journal of Sport and Exercise Psychology*, *30*, 611–641.

Coffee, P., & Rees, T. (2008b). Main and interactive effects of controllability and generalisability attributions upon self-efficacy. *Psychology of Sport and Exercise*, *9*, 775–785.

Coffee, P., & Rees, T. (2009). The main and interactive effects of immediate and reflective attributions upon subsequent self-efficacy. *European Journal of Sport Science*, *9*, 41–52.

Coffee, P., Rees, T., & Haslam, S. A. (2009). Bouncing back from failure: The interactive impact of perceived controllability and stability on self-efficacy beliefs and future task performance. *Journal of Sports Sciences*, *27*, 1117–1124.

Cogan, K. D., & Petrie, T. A. (1995). Sport consultation: An evaluation of a season-long intervention with female collegiate gymnasts. *The Sport Psychologist*, *9*, 282–296.

Cohen, S. (1972). *Folk devils and moral panics*. London: MacGibbon & Kee.

Cohen, S., Underwood, L. G., & Gottlieb, B. H. (2000). *Social support measurement and intervention: A guide for health and social scientists*. New York: Oxford University Press.

Cohen, S., & Wills, T. A. (1985). Stress, social support, and the buffering hypothesis. *Psychological Bulletin*, *98*, 310–357.

Cole, D. (2017). An identity-aware analysis of stereotype threat interventions. Unpublished manuscript, Sweet Briar College, Sweet Briar, VA.

Colloca, L., & Benedetti, F. (2009). Placebo analgesia induced by social observational learning. *Pain*, *144*, 28–34.

Conn, V. S., Hafdahl, A. R., Cooper, P. S., Brown, L. M., & Lusk, S. L. (2009). Meta-analysis of workplace physical activity interventions. *American Journal of Preventive Medicine*, *37*, 330–339.

Conn, V. S., Valentine, J. C., & Cooper, H. M. (2002). Interventions to increase physical activity among aging adults: A meta-analysis. *Annals of Behavioral Medicine*, *24*, 190–200.

Coombs, D. S., & Cassilo, D. (2017). Athletes and/or activists: LeBron James and Black Lives Matter. *Journal of Sport & Social Issues*, *41*, 425–444.

Cooper, C. L., Dewe, P., & O'Driscoll, M. (2003). Employee assistance programs. In J. C. Quick & L. E. Tetrick (Eds.), *Handbook of occupational health psychology* (pp. 289–304). Washington, DC: American Psychological Association.

Corbett, J. (2009). Bill Shankly: Life, death and football. *The Guardian* (October, 18). Retrieved from: www.theguardian.com/football/2009/oct/18/bill-shankly-liverpool-manager (Accessed November 1, 2019).

Corbin, C. B. (1987). Youth fitness, exercise and health: There is much to be done. *Research Quarterly for Exercise and Sport*, *58*, 308–314.

Corey, L. M. K. (2002). The mental health continuum: From languishing to flourishing in life. *Journal of Health and Social Behavior*, *43*, 207–222.

Cornil, Y., & Chandon, P. (2013). From fan to fat? Vicarious losing increases unhealthy eating, but self-affirmation is an effective remedy. *Psychological Science*, *24*, 1936–1946.

Cosh, S., Crabb, S., & Tully, P. J. (2015). A champion out of the pool? A discursive exploration of two Australian Olympic swimmers' transition from elite sport to retirement. *Psychology of Sport and Exercise*, *19*, 33–41.

Cosier, R., & Schwenk, C. (1990). Agreement and thinking alike: Ingredients for poor decisions. *The Executive*, *4*, 69–74.

Côté, J. (1999). The influence of the family in the development of talent in sports. *The Sport Psychologist*, *13*, 395–417.

Côté, J., Bruner, M. W., Erickson, K., Strachan, L., & Fraser-Thomas, J. L. (2010). Athlete development and coaching. In J. Lyle & C. Cushion (Eds.), *Sport coaching: Professionalism and practice* (pp. 63–83). Oxford, UK: Elsevier.

Côté, J., & Fraser-Thomas, J. L. (2016). Youth involvement and positive development in sport. In P. R. E. Crocker (Ed.), *Sport and exercise psychology: A Canadian perspective* (3rd ed., pp. 258–287). Toronto, ON: Pearson Education Canada.

Côté, J., & Gilbert, W. (2009). An integrative definition of coaching effectiveness and expertise. *International Journal of Sports Science & Coaching, 4*, 307–323.

Côté, J., & Hancock, D. J. (2016). Evidence-based policies for youth sport programmes. *International Journal of Sport Policy and Politics, 8*, 51–65.

Côté, J., & Levine, C. (1987). A formulation of Erikson's theory of ego identity formation. *Developmental Review, 7*, 273–325.

Côté, J., Turnnidge, J., & Evans, M. B. (2014). The dynamic process of development through sport. *Kinesiologia Slovenica, 20*, 14–26.

Cotterill, S. T., & Fransen, K. (2016). Athlete leadership in sport teams: Current understanding and future directions. *International Review of Sport and Exercise Psychology, 9*, 116–133.

Council of the European Union (2006). Council Resolution of 4 December 2006 concerning an updated handbook with recommendations for international police cooperation and measures to prevent and control violence and disturbances in connection with football matches with an international dimension, in which at least one Member State is involved. *Official Journal of the European Union* (2006/C 322/01).

Coussens, A. H., Rees, T., & Freeman, P. (2015). Applying generalizability theory to examine the antecedents of perceived coach support. *Journal of Sport and Exercise Psychology, 37*, 51–62.

Cox, T. (1978). *Stress.* London: Macmillan.

Crace, R. K., & Hardy, C. J. (1997). Individual values and the team building process. *Journal of Applied Sport Psychology, 9*, 41–60.

Cramp, A. G., & Brawley, L. R. (2009). Sustaining self-regulatory efficacy and psychological outcome expectations for postnatal exercise: Effects of a group-mediated cognitive behavioural intervention. *British Journal of Health Psychology, 14*, 595–611.

Cranmer, G. A., & Myers, S. A. (2015). Sports teams as organizations: A leader–member exchange perspective of player communication with coaches and teammates. *Communication & Sport, 3*, 100–118.

Crisp, R. J., Heuston, S., Farr, M. J., & Turner, R. N. (2007). Seeing red or feeling blue: Differentiated intergroup emotions and ingroup identification in soccer fans. *Group Processes & Intergroup Relations, 10*, 9–26.

Cruickshank, A., & Collins, D. (2013). Culture change in elite sport performance: An important and unique construct. *Sport & Exercise Psychology Review, 9*, 6–21.

Cruwys, T., Berry, H. L., Cassells, R., Duncan, A., O'Brien, L., Sage, B., & D'Souza, G. (2013). *Marginalised Australians: Characteristics and predictors of exit over ten years 2001–10.* Retrieved from: https://melbourneinstitute.unimelb.edu.au/assets/documents/hilda-bibliography/other-publications/2013/Cruwys_etal_marginalised_Australians.pdf (Accessed April 20, 2020).

Cruwys, T., Bevelander, K. E., & Hermans, R. C. J. (2015). Social modeling of eating: A review of when and why social influence affects food intake and choice. *Appetite, 86*, 3–18.

Cruwys, T., Dingle, G. A., Haslam, C., Haslam, S. A., Jetten, J., & Morton, T. A. (2013). Social group memberships protect against future depression, alleviate depression symptoms and prevent depression relapse. *Social Science & Medicine, 98*, 179–186.

Cruwys, T., & Gunaseelan, S. (2016). 'Depression is who I am': Mental illness identity, stigma and wellbeing. *Journal of Affective Disorders, 189*, 36–42.

Cruwys, T., Haslam, S. A., Dingle, G. A., Haslam, C., & Jetten, J. (2014). Depression and social identity: An integrative review. *Personality and Social Psychology Review, 18*, 215–238.

Cruwys, T., Haslam, S. A., Dingle, G. A., Jetten, J., Hornsey, M. J., Desdemona Chong, E. M., & Oei, T. P. S. (2014). Feeling connected again: Interventions that increase social identification reduce depression symptoms in community and clinical settings. *Journal of Affective Disorders, 159*, 139–146.

Cruwys, T., Platow, M. J., Rieger, E., Byrne, D. G., & Haslam, S. A. (2016). The social psychology of disordered eating: The Situated Identity Enactment model. *European Review of Social Psychology*, *27*, 160–195.

Cruwys, T., South, E. I., Greenaway, K. H., & Haslam, S. A. (2015). Social identity reduces depression by fostering positive attributions. *Social Psychological and Personality Science*, *6*, 65–74.

Cruwys, T., Steffens, N. K., Haslam, S. A., Haslam, C., Jetten, J., & Dingle, G. A. (2016). Social Identity Mapping: A procedure for visual representation and assessment of subjective multiple group memberships. *British Journal of Social Psychology*, *55*, 613–642.

Csikszentmihalyi, M. (1975). *Beyond boredom and anxiety*. San Francisco, CA: Jossey-Bass.

Csikszentmihalyi, M. (1990). *Flow: The psychology of optimal experience*. New York: Harper & Row.

Curran, T., & Hill, A. P. (2018). A test of perfectionistic vulnerability following competitive failure among college athletes. *Journal of Sport and Exercise Psychology*, *40*, 269–279.

Curry, G. (2019). A football man: The contribution of Eric Dunning to the acceptance of soccer as an area for serious academic study. *Soccer & Society*, *20*, 891–895.

Cushion, C. J., & Jones, R. L. (2012). A Bourdieusian analysis of cultural reproduction: Socialisation and the 'hidden curriculum' in professional football. *Sport, Education and Society*, *19*, 276–298.

Cutrona, C. E., & Russell, D. W. (1990). Type of social support and specific stress: Toward a theory of optimal matching. In B. R. Sarason, I. G. Sarason, & G. R. Pierce (Eds.), *Social support: An interactional view* (pp. 319–366). New York: John Wiley.

Danish, S. J., Petitpas, A. J., & Hale, B. D. (1993). Life development intervention for athletes: Life skills through sports. *The Counseling Psychologist*, *21*, 352–385.

Das, A. (2019). Judge sets May 2020 trial date in U.S. women's soccer lawsuit. *New York Times* (August 19). Retrieved from: www.nytimes.com/2019/08/19/sports/soccer/us-womens-soccer-lawsuit.html (Accessed December 5, 2019).

Davies, S. G., & Deckert, A. (2020). Muay Thai: Women, fighting, femininity. *International Review for the Sociology of Sport*, *55*, 327–343.

Davis, M. C., & End, C. M. (2010). A winning proposition: The economic impact of successful national football league franchises. *Economic Inquiry*, *48*, 39–50.

Davis, P. A., Davis, L., Wills, S., Appleby, R., & Nieuwenhuys, A. (2018). Exploring 'sledging' and interpersonal emotion-regulation strategies in professional cricket. *The Sport Psychologist*, *32*, 136–145.

Davison, K. K., & Lawson, C. T. (2006). Do attributes in the physical environment influence children's physical activity? A review of the literature. *International Journal of Behavioral Nutrition & Physical Activity*, *3*, 19–17.

Day, D. V., Gordon, S., & Fink, C. (2012). The sporting life: Exploring organizations through the lens of sport. *Academy of Management Annals*, *6*, 397–433.

De Backer, M., Boen, F., Ceux, T., De Cuyper, B., Høigaard, R., Callens, F., … Vande Broek, G. (2011). Do perceived justice and need support of the coach predict team identification and cohesion? Testing their relative importance among top volleyball and handball players in Belgium and Norway. *Psychology of Sport and Exercise*, *12*, 192–201.

De Backer, M., Boen, F., De Cuyper, B., Høigaard, R., & Vande Broek, G. (2015). A team fares well with a fair coach: Predictors of social loafing in interactive female sport teams. *Scandinavian Journal of Medicine & Science in Sports*, *25*, 897–908.

De Cuyper, B., Boen, F., Van Beirendonck, C., Vanbeselaere, N., & Fransen, K. (2016). When do elite cyclists go the extra mile? Team identification mediates the relationship between perceived leadership qualities of the captain and social laboring. *International Journal of Sport Psychology*, *47*(4), 355–372.

de Geus, B., De Bourdeaudhuij, I., Jannes, C., & Meeusen, R. (2008). Psychosocial and environmental factors associated with cycling for transport among a working population. *Health Education Research*, *23*, 697–708.

de la Haye, K., Robins, G., Mohr, P., & Wilson, C. (2011). How physical activity shapes, and is shaped by, adolescent friendships. *Social Science & Medicine, 73*, 719–728.

DeCaro, M. S., Thomas, R. D., Albert, N. B., & Beilock, S. L. (2011). Choking under pressure: Multiple routes to skill failure. *Journal of Experimental Psychology: General, 140*, 390–406.

Deci, E. L., & Ryan, R. M. (1985). *Intrinsic motivation and self-determination in human behavior.* New York: Plenum.

Deci, E. L., & Ryan, R. M. (1987). The support of autonomy and the control of behavior. *Journal of Personality and Social Psychology, 53*, 1024.

Deci, E. L., & Ryan, R. M. (2000). The 'what' and 'why' of goal pursuits: Human needs and the self-determination of behavior. *Psychological Inquiry, 11*, 227–268.

Deci, E. L., & Ryan, R. M. (2012). Motivation, personality, and development within embedded social contexts: An overview of self-determination theory. In R. M. Ryan (Ed.), *Oxford handbook of human motivation* (pp. 85–107). Oxford: Oxford University Press.

DeFreese, J. D., & Smith, A. L. (2013). Teammate social support, burnout, and self-determined motivation in collegiate athletes. *Psychology of Sport and Exercise, 14*, 258–265.

DeFreese, J. D., & Smith, A. L. (2014). Athlete social support, negative social interactions and psychological health across a competitive sport season. *Journal of Sport and Exercise Psychology, 36*, 619–630.

Dempsey, R. C., McAlaney, J., & Bewick, B. M. (2018). A critical appraisal of the social norms approach as an interventional strategy for health-related behavior and attitude change. *Frontiers in Psychology, 9*, 2180.

DeVerteuil, G., & Golubchikov, O. (2016). Can resilience be redeemed? Resilience as a metaphor for change, not against change. *City, 20*, 143–151.

Devlin, J. T., Dhalac, D., Suldan, A. A., Jacobs, A., Guled, K., & Bankole, K. A. (2012). Determinants of physical activity among Somali women living in Maine. *Journal of Immigrant and Minority Health, 14*, 300–306.

Dewulf, F. (2003). *Ondanks mezelf: Tennisverhalen.* Antwerp: Uitgeverij Houtekiet.

Dhital, S. (2019). Trump's America. *Social Psychological Perspectives.* Retrieved from: https://socialpsych.blogs.pace.edu/page/3/ (Accessed September 1, 2019).

Dietz-Uhler, B., & Murrell, A. J. (1998). Effects of social identity and threat on self-esteem and group attributions. *Group Dynamics: Theory, Research, and Practice, 2*, 24–35.

Dingle, G. A., Brander, C., Ballantyne, J., & Baker, F. A. (2013). 'To be heard': The social and mental health benefits of choir singing for disadvantaged adults. *Psychology of Music, 41*, 405–421.

Dingle, G. A., Haslam, C., Best, D., Chan, G., Staiger, P. K., Savic, M., Beckwith, M., Mackenzie, J., Bathish, R., & Lubman, D. I. (2019). Social identity differentiation predicts commitment to sobriety and wellbeing in residents of therapeutic communities. *Social Science & Medicine, 237*, 112459.

Dingle, G. A., Stark, C., Cruwys, T., & Best, D. (2015). Breaking good: Breaking ties with social groups may be good for recovery from substance misuse. *British Journal of Social Psychology, 54*, 236–254.

D'Innocenzo, L., Mathieu, J. E., & Kukenberger, M. R. (2016). A meta-analysis of different forms of shared leadership–team performance relations. *Journal of Management, 42*, 1964–1991.

Dion, K. L. (2000). Group cohesion: From 'field of forces' to multidimensional construct. *Group Dynamics: Theory, Research, and Practice, 4*, 7–26.

Dishman, R. K., & Buckworth, J. (1996). Increasing physical activity: A quantitative synthesis. *Medicine & Science in Sports & Exercise, 28*, 706–719.

Dixon, P. L. (1984). *The Olympian.* Santa Monica, CA: Roundtable Publishing.

Doliński, D. (2018). Is Psychology still a science of behaviour? *Social Psychological Bulletin, 13*, e25025.

Dolsen, M. R., Asarnow, L. D., & Harvey, A. G. (2014). Insomnia as a transdiagnostic process in psychiatric disorders. *Current Psychiatry Reports, 16*(9), doi: 10.1007/s11920-014-0471-y.

Donohue, B., Chow, G. M., Pitts, M., Loughran, T., Schubert, K. N., Gavrilova, Y., & Allen, D. N. (2015). Piloting a family-supported approach to concurrently optimize mental health and sport performance in athletes. *Clinical Case Studies, 14*, 159–177.

Doosje, B., Haslam, S. A., Spears, R., Oakes, P. J., & Koomen, W. (1998). The effect of comparative context on central tendency and variability judgements and the evaluation of group characteristics. *European Journal of Social Psychology, 28*, 173–184.

Douglas, K., & Carless, D. (2006). Performance, discovery, and relational narratives among women professional tournament golfers. *Women in Sport and Physical Activity Journal, 15*, 14–27.

Dovidio, J. F., Gaertner, S. L., Validzic, A., Matoka, K., Johnson, B., & Frazier, S. (1997). Extending the benefits of recategorization: Evaluations, self-disclosure, and helping. *Journal of Experimental Social Psychology, 33*, 401–420.

Downs, D. S., & Hausenblas, H. A. (2005). The theories of reasoned action and planned behavior applied to exercise: A meta-analytic update. *Journal of Physical Activity & Health, 2*, 76–97.

Drager, K., Hay, J., & Walker, A. (2010). Pronounced rivalries: Attitudes and speech production. *Te Reo, 53*, 27.

Drucker, P. F. (1992). *Managing the non-profit organization: Practices and principles*. Oxford: Butterworth-Heinemann.

Drury, J. (2012). Collective resilience in mass emergencies and disasters. In J. Jetten, C. Haslam, & S. A. Haslam (Eds.), *The social cure: Identity, health and well-being* (pp. 195–215). Hove, UK: Psychology Press.

Drury, J., Cocking, C., & Reicher, S. (2009). The nature of collective resilience: Survivor reactions to the 2005 London bombings. *International Journal of Mass Emergencies and Disasters, 27*, 66–95.

Drury, J., & Reicher, S. D. (2000). Collective action and psychological change: The emergence of new social identities. *British Journal of Social Psychology, 39*, 579–604.

Drury, J., & Reicher, S. D. (2010). Crowd control. *Scientific American Mind, 21*, 58–65.

Drury, J., Stott, C. J., & Farsides, T. (2003). The role of police perceptions and practices in the development of 'public disorder'. *Journal of Applied Social Psychology, 33*, 1480–1500.

Dryden, W. (2006). *Counselling in a nutshell*. London: Sage.

Duane, D. (2014). How the other half lifts: What your workout says about your social class. *Pacific Standard* (July 23). Retrieved from: https://psmag.com/social-justice/half-lifts-workout-says-social-class-85221 (Accessed April 20, 2020).

Duda, J. L. (2005). Motivation in sport: The relevance of competence and achievement goals. In A. J. Elliot & C. S. Dweck (Eds.), *Handbook of competence and motivation* (pp. 273–308). New York: Guilford Press.

Duncan, M., & Corner, J. (2012). *Severe and multiple disadvantage: A review of key texts*. Retrieved from: https://lankellychase.org.uk/wp-content/uploads/2015/09/SMD_Lit_Review-20120731.pdf (Accessed April 20, 2020).

Duncan, S. C., Duncan, T. E., Strycker, L. A., & Chaumeton, N. R. (2007). A cohort-sequential latent growth model of physical activity from ages 12 to 17 years. *Annals of Behavioral Medicine, 33*, 80–89.

Dunlop, W. L., & Beauchamp, M. R. (2011a). Does similarity make a difference? Predicting cohesion and attendance behaviors within exercise group settings. *Group Dynamics: Theory, Research, and Practice, 15*, 258.

Dunlop, W. L., & Beauchamp, M. R. (2011b). Engendering choice: Preferences for exercising in gender-segregated and gender-integrated groups and consideration of weight status. *International Journal of Behavioural Medicine, 18*, 216–220.

Dunlop, W. L., & Beauchamp, M. R. (2012). The relationship between intra-group age similarity and exercise adherence. *American Journal of Preventive Medicine, 42*, 53–55.

Dunlop, W. L., & Beauchamp, M. R. (2013). Birds of a feather stay active together: A case study of an all-male older adult exercise program. *Journal of Aging and Physical Activity, 21*, 222–232.

Dunlop, W. L., Falk, C., & Beauchamp, M. R. (2013). How dynamic are exercise group dynamics? Examining changes in cohesion within class-based exercise programs. *Health Psychology, 32*, 1240–1243.

Dunn, A. L., Trivedi, M. H., & O'Neal, H. A. (2001). Physical activity dose–response effects on outcomes of depression and anxiety. *Medicine & Science in Sports & Exercise, 33*, S587–S597.

Dunn, J. G. H., & Holt, N. L. (2004). A qualitative investigation of a personal-disclosure mutual-sharing team building activity. *The Sport Psychologist, 18*, 363–380.

Dunning, E., Murphy, P., & Williams, J. (1988). *The roots of football hooliganism*. London: Routledge.

Dunton, G. F. (2018). Sustaining health-protective behaviors such as physical activity and healthy eating. *Journal of the American Medical Association, 320*, 639–640.

Durkheim, E. (1995). *The elementary forms of religious life*. New York: Free Press.

Dwyer, J. J., & Fischer, D. G. (1990). Wrestlers' perceptions of coaches' leadership as predictors of satisfaction with leadership. *Perceptual and Motor Skills, 71*, 511–517.

Eccles, D. W., & Tran, K. B. (2012). Getting them on the same page: Strategies for enhancing coordination and communication in sports teams. *Journal of Sport Psychology in Action, 3*, 30–40.

Eccles, J. S., & Barber, B. L. (1999). Student council, volunteering, basketball, or marching band: What kind of extracurricular involvement matters? *Journal of Adolescence, 14*, 10–43.

Edelman, R. (2009). Spartak Moscow: A history of the people's team in the worker's state. Ithaca, NY: Cornell University Press.

Edelmann, C., Boen, F., & Fransen, K. (2020). The power of empowerment: Predictors and benefits of shared leadership in organizations. Manuscript in preparation, KU Leuven.

Edmunds, J., Ntoumanis, N., & Duda, J. L. (2006). A test of self-determination theory in the exercise domain. *Journal of Applied Social Psychology, 36*, 2240–2265.

Edmunds, J., Ntoumanis, N., & Duda, J. L. (2007). Adherence and well-being in overweight and obese patients referred to an exercise-on-prescription scheme: A self-determination theory perspective. *Psychology of Sport and Exercise, 8*, 722–740.

Eime, R. M., Young, J. A., Harvey, J. J., Charity, J. J., & Payne, W. R. (2013). A systematic review of the psychological and social benefits of participation in sport for children and adolescents: Informing development of a conceptual model of health through sport. *International Journal of Behavioural Nutrition and Physical Activity, 10*, 98.

Ekblom-Bak, E., Hellénius, M. L., & Ekblom, B. (2010). Are we facing a new paradigm of inactivity physiology? *British Journal of Sports Medicine, 44*, 834–835.

Ekeland, E., Heian, F., & Hagen, K. B. (2005). Can exercise improve self-esteem in children and young people? A systematic review of randomised controlled trials. *British Journal of Sports Medicine, 39*, 792–798.

Elbra, T. (2019). Springboks captain Siya Kolisi's awesome speech after South Africa win Rugby World Cup. *Channel 9, Wide World of Sports* (November 2) Retrieved from: wwos.nine.com. au/rugby/siya-kolisi-speech-rugby-world-cup-final-south-africa-captain/116c9905-71ca-4723-af95-97d488e10303 (Accessed December 14, 2019).

Elias, N., & Dunning, E. (1986). *Quest for excitement: Sport and leisure in the civilising process*. Oxford: Blackwell.

Ellemers, N. (1993). The influence of socio-structural variables on identity enhancement strategies. *European Review of Social Psychology, 4*, 27–57.

Ellemers, N. (2012). The group self. *Science, 336*, 848–852.

Ellemers, N. (2018). Morality and social identity. In M. van Zomeren & J. F. Dovidio (Eds.), *The Oxford handbook of the human essence* (pp. 147–158). Oxford: Oxford University Press.

Ellemers, N., de Gilder, D., & Haslam, S. A. (2004). Motivating individuals and groups at work: A social identity perspective on leadership and group performance. *Academy of Management Review, 29,* 459–478.

Ellemers, N., & Haslam, S. A. (2012). Social identity theory. In P. Van Lange, A. Kruglanski, & T. Higgins (Eds.), *Handbook of theories of social psychology* (pp. 379–398). London: Sage.

Ellemers, N., Spears, R., & Doosje, B. (1999). *Social identity: Context, commitment, content.* Oxford: Blackwell.

Elsbach, K. D., & Kramer, R. D. (1996). Members' responses to organizational identity threats: Encountering and countering the *Business Week* rankings. *Administrative Science Quarterly, 41,* 442–476.

End, C. M., Dietz-Uhler, B., Harrick, E. A., & Jacquemotte, L. (2002). Identifying with winners: A reexamination of sport fans' tendency to BIRG. *Journal of Applied Social Psychology, 32,* 1017–1030.

Ericsson, K. A., Krampe, R. T., & Tesch-Römer, C. (1993). The role of deliberate practice in the acquisition of expert performance. *Psychological Review, 100,* 363–406.

Erikson, E. H. (1950). *Childhood and society.* New York: Norton.

Erikson, E. H. (1959). *Identity and the life cycle.* New York: Norton.

Erikson, E. H. (1963). *Childhood and society* (2nd ed.). New York: Norton.

Estabrooks, P. A., Bradshaw, M., Dzewaltowski, D. A., & Smith-Ray, R. L. (2008). Determining the impact of Walk Kansas: Applying a team-building approach to community physical activity promotion. *Annals of Behavioral Medicine, 36,* 1–12.

Estabrooks, P. A., & Carron, A. V. (2000). The physical activity group environment questionnaire: An instrument for the assessment of cohesion in exercise classes. *Group Dynamics: Theory, Research, and Practice, 4,* 230–243.

Estabrooks, P. A., Smith-Ray, R. L., Almeida, F. A., Hill, J., Gonzales, M., Schreiner, P., & Berg, R. D. (2011). Move more: Translating an efficacious group dynamics physical activity intervention into effective clinical practice. *International Journal of Sport and Exercise Psychology, 9,* 4–18.

Evans, A. L., Slater, M. J., Turner, M. J., & Barker, J. B. (2013). Using personal–disclosure mutual–sharing (PDMS) to enhance group functioning in a professional soccer academy. *The Sport Psychologist, 27,* 233–243.

Evans, A. L., Turner, M. J., Pickering, R., & Powditch, R. (2018). The effects of rational and irrational coach team talks on the cognitive appraisal and achievement goal orientation of varsity football athletes. *International Journal of Sports Science & Coaching, 13,* 431–438.

Evans, M. B., Graupensperger, S. A., Benson, A. J., Eys, M. A., Hastings, B., & Gottschall, J. S. (2019a). Group structure and entitativity in group fitness: Considering groupness at within- and between-group levels. *Psychology & Health, 34,* 715–732.

Evans, M. B., Graupensperger, S. A., Benson, A. J., Eys, M. A., Hastings, B., & Gottschall, J. S. (2019b). Groupness perceptions and basic need satisfaction: Perceptions of fitness groups and experiences within club environments. *Group Dynamics: Theory, Research, and Practice, 23,* 170–184.

Eys, M. A., & Brawley, L. R. (2018). Reflections on cohesion research with sport and exercise groups. *Social and Personality Psychology Compass, 12,* e12379.

Eys, M. A., Bruner, M. W., & Martin, L. J. (2019). The dynamic group environment in sport and exercise. *Psychology of Sport and Exercise, 42,* 40–47.

Eys, M. A., Burke, S. M., Carron, A. V., & Dennis, P. W. (2010). The sport team as an effective group. In J. M. Williams (Ed.), *Applied sport psychology: Personal growth to peak performance* (6th ed., pp. 132–148). New York: McGraw-Hill.

Eys, M. A., Hardy, J., Carron, A. V., & Beauchamp, M. R. (2003). The relationship between task cohesion and competitive state anxiety. *Journal of Sport and Exercise Psychology, 25*, 66–76.

Eys, M. A., Ohlert, J., Evans, M. B., Wolf, S. A., Martin, L. J., Van Bussel, M., & Steins, C. (2015). Cohesion and performance for female and male sport teams. *The Sport Psychologist, 29*, 97–109.

Fast, N. J., Heath, C., & Wu, G. (2009). Common ground and cultural prominence: How conversation reinforces culture. *Psychological Science, 20*, 904–911.

Faulkner, G., Hsin, A., & Zeglen, L. (2013). Evaluation of the run to quit program. Unpublished report prepared for the Canadian Cancer Society.

Faure, C., Appleby, K. M., & Ray, B. (2014). Feeling elite: The collective effervescence of TEAM USA at the 2012 ITU World Triathlon Grand Final. *The Qualitative Report, 19*, 1–22.

Feezell, R. (2013). Sport, religious belief, and religious diversity. *Journal of the Philosophy of Sport, 40*, 135–162.

Feltz, D. L., Chow, G. M., & Hepler, T. J. (2008). Path analysis of self-efficacy and diving performance revisited. *Journal of Sport and Exercise Psychology, 30*, 401–411.

Ferrari, A. J., Norman, R. E., Freedman, G., Baxter, A. J., Pirkis, J. E., Harris, M. G., … Whiteford, H. A. (2014). The burden attributable to mental and substance use disorders as risk factors for suicide: Findings from the Global Burden of Disease Study 2010. *PLoS ONE, 9*(4), e91936–e91936.

Field, R., & Kidd, B. (Eds.) (2013). *Forty years of sport and social change, 1968–2008: To remember is to resist*. London: Routledge.

Fielding, S. (2017). Ethnicity as an exercise in sport: European immigrants, soccer fandom, and the making of Canadian multiculturalism, 1945–1979. *International Journal of the History of Sport, 34*, 970–991.

Filho, E., Dobersek, U., Gershgoren, L., Becker, B., & Tenenbaum, G. (2014). The cohesion–performance relationship in sport: A 10-year retrospective meta-analysis. *Sport Science for Health, 10*, 165–177.

Fink, J. S., Parker, H. M., Brett, M., & Higgins, J. (2009). Off-field behavior of athletes and team identification: Using social identity theory and balance theory to explain fan reactions. *Journal of Sport Management, 23*, 142–155.

Fishbein, M., & Ajzen, I. (2011). *Predicting and changing behavior: The reasoned action approach*. New York: Taylor & Francis.

Fisher, J., Nadler, A., & Whitcher-Alagna, S. (1982). Recipient reaction to aid. *Psychological Bulletin, 91*, 27–54.

FitzSimons, P. (2018). Mr Smith, you have raised a fine son. *The Sydney Morning Herald* (March 30). Retrieved from: www.smh.com.au/national/mr-smith-you-have-raised-a-fine-son-20180330-p4z73g.html 31 (Accessed July 30, 2019).

Flanagin, A. J., Hocevar, K. P., & Samahito, S. N. (2014). Connecting with the user-generated Web: How group identification impacts online information sharing and evaluation. *Information, Communication & Society, 17*, 683–694.

Fleming, J. S. (2004). *Erikson's psychosocial developmental stages*. Retrieved from: https://swppr.org/textbook/ch%209%20erikson.pdf (Accessed September 22, 2018).

Fletcher, D., Hanton, S., & Mellalieu, S. D. (2006). An organizational stress review: Conceptual and theoretical issues in competitive sport. In S. Hanton & S. D. Mellalieu (Eds.), *Literature reviews in sport psychology* (pp. 321–373). Hauppauge, NY: Nova Science Publishers.

Fletcher, D., & Sarkar, M. (2012). A grounded theory of psychological resilience in Olympic champions. *Psychology of Sport and Exercise, 13*, 669–678.

Fletcher, D., & Sarkar, M. (2016). Mental fortitude training: An evidence-based approach to developing psychological resilience for sustained success. *Journal of Sport Psychology in Action, 7*, 135–157.

Fletcher, D., & Scott, M. (2010). Psychological stress in sports coaches: A review of concepts, research, and practice. *Journal of Sports Sciences, 28*, 127–137.

Fletcher, D., & Wagstaff, C. R. D. (2009). Organizational psychology in elite sport: Its emergence, application and future. *Psychology of Sport and Exercise, 10*, 427–434.

Flett, G. L., & Hewitt, P. L. (*2005*). The perils of perfectionism in sports and exercise. *Current Directions in Psychological Science, 14*, 14–18.

Flora, P. K., Strachan, S. M., Brawley, L. R., & Spink, K. S. (2012). Exercise identity and attribution properties predict negative self-conscious emotions for exercise relapse. *Journal of Sport and Exercise Psychology, 34*, 647–660.

Focht, B. C., Brawley, L. R., Rejeski, W. J., & Ambrosius, W. T. (2004). Group-mediated activity counseling and traditional exercise therapy programs: Effects on health-related quality of life among older adults in cardiac rehabilitation. *Annals of Behavioral Medicine, 28*, 52–61.

Focht, B. C., Lucas, A. R., Grainger, E., Simpson, C., Fairman, C. M., ... Clinton, S. K. (2018). Effects of a group-mediated exercise and dietary intervention in the treatment of prostate cancer patients undergoing androgen deprivation therapy: Results from the IDEA-P trial. *Annals of Behavioral Medicine, 52*, 412–428.

Foddy, M., Platow, M. J., & Yamagishi, T. (2009). Group-based trust in strangers: The role of stereotypes and expectations. *Psychological Science, 20*, 419–422.

Foer, F. (2011). *How football explains the world*. London: Random House.

Foley, L., Prapavessis, H., Maddison, R., Burke, S., McGowan, E., & Gillanders, L. (2008). Predicting physical activity intention and behavior in school-age children. *Pediatric Exercise Science, 20*, 342–356.

Folkman, S., & Moskowitz, J. T. (2004). Coping: Pitfalls and promise. *Annual Review of Psychology, 55*, 745–774.

Foote, N. N. (1951). Identification as the basis for a theory of motivation. *American Sociological Review, 16*, 14–21.

Forsyth, D. R. (2014). *Group dynamics* (6th ed.). Belmont, CA: Wadsworth.

Four Corners (2017). After the game. *Australian Broadcasting Corporation*. Retrieved from: www.abc.net.au/4corners/after-the-game-promo/8477046 (Accessed August 19, 2019).

Frankel, A., & Snyder, M. L. (1978). Poor performance following unsolvable problems: Learned helplessness or egotism? *Journal of Personality and Social Psychology, 36*, 1415–1423.

Fransen, K., Boen, F., Vansteenkiste, M., Mertens, N., & Vande Broek, G. (2018). The power of competence support: The impact of coaches and athlete leaders on intrinsic motivation and performance. *Scandinavian Journal of Medicine & Science in Sports, 28*, 725–745.

Fransen, K., Coffee, P., Vanbeselaere, N., Slater, M. J., De Cuyper, B., & Boen, F. (2014). The impact of athlete leaders on team members' team outcome confidence: A test of mediation by team identification and collective efficacy. *The Sport Psychologist, 28*, 347–360.

Fransen, K., Decroos, S., Vande Broek, G., & Boen, F. (2016). Leading from the top or leading from within? A comparison between coaches' and athletes' leadership as predictors of team identification, team confidence, and team cohesion. *International Journal of Sports Science & Coaching, 11*, 757–771.

Fransen, K., Decroos, S., Vanbeselaere, N., Vande Broek, G., De Cuyper, B., Vanroy, J., & Boen, F. (2015). Is team confidence the key to success? The reciprocal relation between collective efficacy, team outcome confidence, and perceptions of team performance during soccer games. *Journal of Sports Sciences, 33*, 219–231.

Fransen, K., Haslam, S. A., Steffens, N. K., & Boen, F. (2020). Standing out from the crowd: Identifying the traits and behaviors that characterize high-quality athlete leaders on and off the field. *Scandinavian Journal of Medicine & Science in Sports, 30*, 766–786.

Fransen, K., Haslam, S. A., Steffens, N., Mallett, C., Peters, K., Mertens, N., & Boen, F. (2020a). All for us and us for all: Introducing the 5R Shared Leadership Program. Manuscript submitted for publication KU Leuven.

Fransen, K., Haslam, S. A., Steffens, N. K., Mallett, C. J., Peters, K., & Boen, F. (2020b). Making 'us' better: High-quality athlete leadership relates to health and burnout in professional Australian football teams. *European Journal of Sport Science* (Advance online publication; doi: 10.1080/17461391.2019.1680736).

Fransen, K., Haslam, S. A., Steffens, N. K., Vanbeselaere, N., De Cuyper, B., & Boen, F. (2015). Believing in 'us': Exploring leaders' capacity to enhance team confidence and performance by building a sense of shared social identity. *Journal of Experimental Psychology: Applied, 21*, 89–100.

Fransen, K., Kleinert, J., Dithurbide, L., Vanbeselaere, N., & Boen, F. (2014). Collective efficacy or team outcome confidence? Development and validation of the Observational Collective Efficacy Scale for Sports (OCESS). *International Journal of Sport Psychology, 45*, 121–137.

Fransen, K., Mertens, N., Feltz, D. L., & Boen, F. (2017). 'Yes, we can!' Review on team confidence in sports. *Current Opinion in Psychology, 16*, 98–103.

Fransen, K., Steffens, N. K., Haslam, S. A., Vanbeselaere, N., Vande Broek, G., & Boen, F. (2016). We will be champions: Leaders' confidence in 'us' inspires team members' team confidence and performance. *Scandinavian Journal of Medicine & Science in Sports, 26*, 1455–1469.

Fransen, K., Vanbeselaere, N., De Cuyper, B., Vande Broek, G., & Boen, F. (2014). The myth of the team captain as principal leader: Extending the athlete leadership classification within sport teams. *Journal of Sports Sciences, 32*, 1389–1397.

Fransen, K., Van Puyenbroeck, S., Loughead, T. M., Vanbeselaere, N., De Cuyper, B., Vande Broek, G., & Boen, F. (2015). Who takes the lead? Social network analysis as pioneering tool to investigate shared leadership within sports teams. *Social Networks, 43*, 28–38.

Fraser, S. D. S., & Lock, K. (2011). Cycling for transport and public health: A systematic review of the effect of the environment on cycling. *European Journal of Public Health, 21*, 738–743.

Fraser-Thomas, J. L., Côté, J., & Deakin, J. (2005). Youth sport programs: An avenue to foster positive youth development. *Physical Education & Sport Pedagogy, 10*, 19–40.

Frayeh, A. L., & Lewis, B. A. (2017). Sport commitment among adult recreational soccer players: Test of an expanded model. *International Journal of Exercise Science, 10*, 4–24.

Frederiks, E. R., Stenner, K., & Hobman, E. V. (2015). Household energy use: Applying behavioural economics to understand consumer decision-making and behaviour. *Renewable and Sustainable Energy Reviews, 41*, 1385–1394.

Fredricks, J. A., & Eccles, J. S. (2008). Participation in extracurricular activities in the middle school years: Are there developmental benefits for African American and European American youth? *Journal of Youth and Adolescence, 37*, 1029–1043.

Fredrickson, B. L., & Harrison, K. (2005). Throwing like a girl: Self-objectification predicts adolescent girls' motor performance. *Journal of Sport & Social Issues, 29*, 79–101.

Free, M., & Hughson, J. (2003). Settling accounts with hooligans: Gender blindness in football supporter subculture research. *Men and Masculinities, 6*, 136–155.

The Free Kick (2013). *Discussion board: Sign in Cork backers*. Retrieved from: https://tfk.thefreekick.com/t/sign-in-cork-backers/17905/3 (Accessed 26 September, 2019).

Freedson, P. S., & Evenson, S. (1991). Familial aggregation in physical activity. *Research Quarterly for Exercise and Sport, 62*, 384–389.

Freeman, P., Coffee, P., Moll, T., Rees, T., & Sammy, N. (2014). The ARSQ: The Athletes' Received Support Questionnaire. *Journal of Sport and Exercise Psychology, 36*, 189–202.

Freeman, P., Coffee, P., & Rees, T. (2011). The PASS-Q: The Perceived Available Support in Sport Questionnaire. *Journal of Sport and Exercise Psychology, 33*, 54–74.

Freeman, P., & Rees, T. (2008). The effects of perceived and received support upon objective performance outcome. *European Journal of Sport Science*, 8, 359–368.

Freeman, P., & Rees, T. (2009). How does perceived support lead to better performance? An examination of potential mechanisms. *Journal of Applied Sport Psychology*, 21, 429–441.

Freeman, P., & Rees, T. (2010). Perceived social support from team-mates: Direct and stress-buffering effects on self-confidence. *European Journal of Sport Science*, 10, 59–67.

Freeman, P., Rees, T., & Hardy, L. (2009). An intervention to increase social support and improve performance. *Journal of Applied Sport Psychology*, 21, 186–200.

Friesen, A. P., Devonport, T. J., & Lane, A. M. (2017). Beyond the technical: The role of emotion regulation in lacrosse officiating. *Journal of Sports Sciences*, 35, 579–586.

Friesen, A. P., Devonport, T. J., Sellars, C. N., & Lane, A. M. (2013). A narrative account of decision-making and interpersonal emotion regulation using a social-functional approach to emotions. *International Journal of Sport and Exercise Psychology*, 11, 203–214.

Friesen, A. P., Lane, A. M., Devonport, T. J., Sellars, C. N., Stanley, D. N., & Beedie, C. J. (2013). Emotion in sport: Considering interpersonal regulation strategies. *International Review of Sport & Exercise Psychology*, 6, 139–154.

Frith, D. (2002). *Bodyline autopsy*. Sydney: ABC Books.

Fritsche, I., Jonas, E., Ablasser, C., Beyer, M., Kuban, J., Manger, A. M., & Schultz, M. (2013). The power of we: Evidence for group-based control. *Journal of Experimental Social Psychology*, 49, 19–32.

Fritsche, I., Jonas, E., & Fankhänel, T. (2008). The role of control motivation in mortality salience effects on ingroup support and defense. *Journal of Personality and Social Psychology*, 95, 524.

Frosdick, S., & Marsh, P. E. (2007). *Football hooliganism*. Cullompton, UK: Willan.

Funk, D. C., Beaton, A., & Alexandris, K. (2012). Sport consumer motivation: Autonomy and control orientations that regulate fan behaviours. *Sport Management Review*, 15, 355–367.

Furley, P., Moll, T., & Memmert, D. (2015). 'Put your hands up in the air'? The interpersonal effects of pride and shame expressions on opponents and teammates. *Frontiers in Psychology*, 6, 1361.

Fussell, S. R., & Krauss, R. M. (1989). Understanding friends and strangers: The effects of audience design on message comprehension. *European Journal of Social Psychology*, 19, 509–525.

Gaelic Athletic Association. (2019). *Official Guide: Part 1*. Dublin: Central Council of the Association. Retrieved from: www.gaa.ie/api/pdfs/image/upload/wyb4qbqzii6vstod1ygg.pdf (Accessed December 5, 2019).

Gaertner, S. L., & Dovidio, J. F. (2005). Understanding and addressing contemporary racism: From aversive racism to the common ingroup identity model. *Journal of Social issues*, 61, 615–639.

Gaertner, S. L., Rust, M. C., Dovidio, J. F., Bachman, B. A., & Anastasio, P. A. (1994). The contact hypothesis: The role of a common ingroup identity on reducing intergroup bias. *Small Group Research*, 25, 224–249.

Gaertner, S. L., Sedikides, C., Vevea, J. L., & Iuzzini, J. (2002). The 'I', the 'we', and the 'when': A meta-analysis of motivational primacy in self-definition. *Journal of Personality and Social Psychology*, 83, 574–591.

Galea, M. N., & Bray, S. R. (2006). Predicting walking intentions and exercise in individuals with intermittent claudication: An application of the theory of planned behavior. *Rehabilitation Psychology*, 51, 299–305.

Gallagher, S., Meaney, S., & Muldoon, O. T. (2014). Social identity influences stress appraisals and cardiovascular reactions to acute stress exposure. *British Journal of Health Psychology*, 19, 566–579.

Galli, N., & Vealey, R. S. (2008). 'Bouncing back' from adversity: Athletes' experiences of resilience. *The Sport Psychologist*, 22, 316–335.

Gammage, K. L., Carron, A. V., & Estabrooks, P. A. (2001). Team cohesion and individual productivity: The influence of the norm for productivity and the identifiability of individual effort. *Small Group Research, 32*, 3–18.

Gardner, R. E., & Hausenblas, H. A. (2004). Understanding exercise and diet motivation in overweight women enrolled in a weight-loss program: A prospective study using the theory of planned behavior. *Journal of Applied Social Psychology, 34*, 1353–1370.

Garn, A. C., Simonton, K., Dasingert, T., & Simonton, A. (2017). Predicting changes in student engagement in university physical education: Application of control-value theory of achievement emotions. *Psychology of Sport & Exercise, 29*, 93–102.

Gearing, B. (1999). Narratives of identity among former professional footballers in the United Kingdom. *Journal of Aging Studies, 13*, 43–58.

Gecas, V. (1982). The self-concept. *Annual Review of Sociology, 8*, 1–33.

Gehring, J. (2005). Researchers say girls thrive in single-sex gym classes. *Education Week, 25*(1), 13. Retrieved from: www.edweek.org/ew/articles/2005/08/31/01gym.h25.html (Accessed August 19, 2019).

Gennaro, M. J. (2019). 'I was really disgusted at seeing healthy young boys playing Ping-pong': Ping-pong and masculinity in post-World War II Nigeria. In M. Gennaro & S. Aderinto (Eds.), *Sports in African history, politics, and identity formation* (pp. 14–27). London: Routledge.

Giannone, Z. A., Haney, C. J., Kealy, D., & Ogrodniczuk, J. S. (2017). Athletic identity and psychiatric symptoms following retirement from varsity sports. *International Journal of Social Psychiatry, 63*, 598–601.

Gilchrist, J. D., Sabiston, C. M., Conroy, D. E., & Atkinson, M. (2018). Authentic pride regulates runners' training progress. *Psychology of Sport & Exercise, 38*, 10–16.

Giles, H., Coupland, N., & Coupland, J. (1991). *Language, society and the elderly: Discourse, identity and ageing.* Oxford, UK: Blackwell.

Giles, H., Taylor, D. M., & Bourhis, R. (1973). Towards a theory of interpersonal accommodation through language: Some Canadian data. *Language in Society, 2*, 177–192.

Gilham, P. F. (2011). Securitizing America: Strategic incapacitation and the policing of protest since the 11 September 2001 terrorist attacks. *Sociology Compass, 5*, 636–652.

Gill, D. L., Ruder, M. K., & Gross, J. B. (1982). Open-ended attributions in team competition. *Journal of Sport Psychology, 4*, 159–169.

Gill, D. P., Blunt, W., De Cruz, A., Riggin, B., Hunt, K., Zou, G., ... Petrella, R. J. (2016). Hockey Fans in Training (Hockey FIT) pilot study protocol: A gender-sensitized weight loss and healthy lifestyle program for overweight and obese male hockey fans. *BMC Public Health, 16*, 1096.

Gillet, N., Vallerand, R. J., Amoura, S., & Baldes, B. (2010). Influence of coaches' autonomy support on athletes' motivation and sport performance: A test of the hierarchical model of intrinsic and extrinsic motivation. *Psychology of Sport and Exercise, 11*, 155–161.

Girard, D. (2011). Kim Jong-Il once carded 38-under par at Pyongyang Golf Course. *The Star* (December 19). Retrieved from: www.thestar.com/sports/golf/2011/12/19/kim_jongil_once_carded_38under_par_at_pyongyang_golf_course.html (Accessed December 5, 2019).

Girelli, L., Hagger, M. S., Mallia, L., & Lucidi, F. (2016). From perceived autonomy support to intentional behaviour: Testing an integrated model in three healthy-eating behaviours. *Appetite, 96*, 280–292.

Giulianotti, R. (1991). Scotland's tartan army in Italy: The case for the carnivalesque. *Sociological Review, 39*, 503–527.

Giulianotti, R., Bonney, N., & Hepworth, M. (1994). *Football, violence and social identity.* London: Routledge.

Gleibs, I., Haslam, C., Haslam, S. A., & Jones, J. (2011). Water clubs in residential care: Is it the water or the club that enhances health and well-being? *Psychology and Health, 26*, 1361–1378.

Glowacki, K., O'Neill, M., Priebe, C. S., & Faulkner, G. (2018). 'When you put the group and the running together…': A qualitative examination of participant experiences of the Canadian Run to Quit Program. *Journal of Smoking Cessation, 14*, 52–58.

Goldberg, J. (2000) Sporting diplomacy: Boosting the size of the diplomatic corps. *Washington Quarterly, 23*, 63–70.

Golden, J. (2018). Venus and Serena Williams: Men need to be advocates for pay equality, too. *CNBC Make It* (March 8).

Goldenberg, A., Garcia, D., Zaki, J., Kong, D., Golarai, G., Halperin, E., & Gross, J. J. (2020). Beyond emotional similarity: The role of situation specific motives. *Journal of Experimental Psychology. General, 149*, 138–159.

Goldenberg, A., Halperin, E., van Zomeren, M., & Gross, J. J. (2016). The process model of group-based emotion: Integrating intergroup emotion and emotion regulation perspectives. *Personality and Social Psychology Review, 20*, 118–141.

Goldenberg, A., Saguy, T., & Halperin, E. (2014). How group-based emotions are shaped by collective emotions: Evidence for emotional transfer and emotional burden. *Journal of Personality and Social Psychology, 107*, 581–596.

Goldman, L., Giles, H., & Hogg, M. A. (2014). Going to extremes: Social identity and communication processes associated with gang membership. *Group Processes and Intergroup Relations, 17*, 813–832.

Goldsmith, M. (1995). Sporting boycotts as a political tool. *The Australian Quarterly, 67*, 11–20.

González, S. T., Carmen Neipp López, M., Marcos, Y. Q., & Rodríguez-Marín, J. (2012). Development and validation of the Theory of Planned Behavior questionnaire in physical activity. *Spanish Journal of Psychology, 15*, 801–816.

Goodger, K., Gorely, T., Lavallee, D., & Harwood, C. (2007). Burnout in sport: A systematic review. *The Sport Psychologist, 21*, 127–151.

Goodman, L. (2019). The best women's soccer team in the world fights for equal pay. *New York Times* (June 10). Retrieved from: www.nytimes.com/2019/06/10/magazine/womens-soccer-inequality-pay.html (Accessed December 5, 2019).

Gopinathan, D. (2017). Exploring the robustness of the 5R leadership development program. Unpublished master's thesis, University of Queensland.

Gorn, E. J., & Goldstein, W. (1993). *A brief history of American sports*. New York: Hill and Wang.

Gottlieb, B. H., & Bergen, A. E. (2010). Social support concepts and measures. *Journal of Psychosomatic Research, 69*, 511–520.

Gould, D., & Carson, S. (2008). Life skills development through sport: Current status and future directions. *International Review of Sport and Exercise Psychology, 1*, 58–78.

Gould, D., Greenleaf, C., Chung, Y., & Guinan, D. (2002). A survey of U.S. Atlanta and Nagano Olympians: Variables perceived to influence performance. *Research Quarterly for Exercise and Sport, 73*, 175–186.

Gourlan, M., Bernard, P., Bortolon, C., Romain, A. J., Lareyre, O., Carayol, M., … Boiché, J. (2015). Efficacy of theory-based interventions to promote physical activity: A meta-analysis of randomised controlled trials. *Health Psychology Review, 10*, 50–66.

Gouttebarge, V., Castaldelli-Maia, J. M., Gorczynski, P., Hainline, B., Hitchcock, M. E., Kerkhoffs, G. M., … Reardon, C. L. (2019). Occurrence of mental health symptoms and disorders in current and former elite athletes: A systematic review and meta-analysis. *British Journal of Sports Medicine, 53*, 700–747.

Gozzi, J. (1990). Is life a game? Notes on a master methaphor. *ETC: A Review of General Semantics, 47*, 291–293.

Grace, D. M., David, B. J., & Ryan, M. K. (2008). Investigating preschoolers' categorical thinking about gender through imitation, attention, and the use of self-categories. *Child Development*, *79*, 1928–1941.

Grant, A. M., Curtayne, L., & Burton, G. (2009). Executive coaching enhances goal attainment, resilience and workplace well-being: A randomised controlled study. *Journal of Positive Psychology*, *4*, 396–407.

Graupensperger, S. A., Benson, A. J., & Evans, M. B. (2018). Everyone else is doing it: The association between social identity and susceptibility to peer influence in NCAA athletes. *Journal of Sport and Exercise Psychology*, *40*, 117–127.

Graupensperger, S. A., Gottschall, J. S., Benson, A. J., Eys, M. A., Hastings, B., & Evans, M. B. (2019). Perceptions of groupness during fitness classes positively predict recalled perceptions of exertion, enjoyment, and affective valence: An intensive longitudinal investigation. *Sport, Exercise, and Performance Psychology*, *8*, 290–304.

Greeff, A. P., & Human, B. (2004). Resilience in families in which a parent has died. *American Journal of Family Therapy*, *32*, 27–42.

Green, B. (Ed.) (1989). *Wisden papers 1888–1945*. London: Arrow Books.

Green, J., Rees, T., Peters, K., Sarkar, M., & Haslam, S. A. (2018). Resolving not to quit: Evidence that salient group memberships increase resilience in a sensorimotor task. *Frontiers in Psychology*, *9*, 2579.

Greenaway, K. H., Amiot, C. E., Louis, W. R., & Bentley, S. V. (2017). The role of psychological need satisfaction in promoting student identification. In K. I. Mavor, M. J. Platow, & B. Bizumic (Eds.), *Self and social identity in educational contexts* (pp. 176–192). Abingdon, UK: Routledge.

Greenaway, K. H., Cruwys, T., Haslam, S. A., & Jetten, J. (2016). Social identities promote well-being because they satisfy global psychological needs. *European Journal of Social Psychology*, *46*, 294–307.

Greenaway, K. H., Haslam, S. A., Branscombe, N. R., Cruwys, T., Ysseldyk, R., & Heldreth, C. (2015). From 'we' to 'me': Group identification enhances perceived personal control with consequences for health and well-being. *Journal of Personality and Social Psychology*, *109*, 53–74.

Greenaway, K. H., Louis, W. R., & Hornsey, M. J. (2013). Loss of control increases belief in precognition and belief in precognition increases control. *PLoS ONE*, *8*(8).

Greenaway, K. H., Parker, S. L., Haslam, S. A., Peters, K., Steffens, N. K., & Bentley, S. V. (2019). *Social identity and self-determination*. Unpublished manuscript, University of Melbourne.

Greenaway, K. H., Peters, K., Haslam, S. A., & Bingley, W. (2016). Shared identity and the intergroup dynamics of communication. In H. Giles & A. Maass (Eds.), *Advances in intergroup communication* (pp. 19–34). New York: Peter Lang.

Greenaway, K. H., Wright, R., Reynolds, K. J., Willingham, J., & Haslam, S. A. (2015). Shared identity is key to effective communication. *Personality and Social Psychology Bulletin*, *41*, 171–182.

Greenberg, M. T., Weissberg, R. P., O'Brien, M. U., Zins, J. E., Fredericks, L., Resnik, H., & Elias, M. J. (2003). Enhancing school-based prevention and youth development through coordinated social, emotional, and academic learning. *American Psychologist*, *58*, 466–474.

Greenlees, I. A., Graydon, J. K., & Maynard, I. W. (1999). The impact of collective efficacy beliefs on effort and persistence in a group task. *Journal of Sports Sciences*, *17*, 151–158.

Grice, H. P. (1975). Logic and conversation. In P. Cole & J. Morgan (Eds.), *Syntax & Semantics, 3: Speech acts* (pp. 41–58). New York: Elsevier.

Grice, T. A., Gallois, C., Jones, E., Paulsen, N., & Callan, V. J. (2006). 'We do it, but they don't': Multiple categorizations and work team communication. *Journal of Applied Communication Research*, *34*, 331–348.

Grolnick, W. S. (2002). *The psychology of parental control: How well-meant parenting backfires*. New York: Psychology Press.

Gross, J. J. (1998). The emerging field of emotion regulation: An integrative review. *Review of General Psychology*, *2*, 271–299.

Gross, J. J. (2002). Emotion regulation: Affective, cognitive, and social consequences. *Psychophysiology*, *39*, 281–291.

Gross, J. J. (2015). Emotion regulation: Current status and future prospects. *Psychological Inquiry*, *26*, 1–26.

Gross, M., Moore, Z. E., Gardner, F. L., Wolanin, A. T., Pess, R., & Marks, D. R. (2018). An empirical examination comparing the Mindfulness-Acceptance-Commitment approach and Psychological Skills Training for the mental health and sport performance of female student athletes. *International Journal of Sport and Exercise Psychology*, *16*, 431–451.

Gu, X., Solomon, M. A., Zhang, T., & Xiang, P. (2011). Group cohesion, achievement motivation, and motivational outcomes among female college students. *Journal of Applied Sport Psychology*, *23*, 175–188.

Guardian Sport (2016). Alistair Brownlee gives up chance to win triathlon and helps brother over line. *The Guardian* (September 19). Retrieved from: www.theguardian.com/sport/2016/sep/19/alistair-brownlee-jonny-world-triathlon-series (Accessed July 19, 2019).

Gulliver, A., Griffiths, K. M., Mackinnon, A., Batterham, P. J., & Stanimirovic, R. (2015). The mental health of Australian elite athletes. *Journal of Science and Medicine in Sport*, *18*, 255–261.

Gustafsson, H., DeFreese, J. D., & Madigan, D. J. (2017). Athlete burnout: Review and recommendations. *Current Opinion in Psychology*, *16*, 109–113.

Gustafsson, H., Hassmén, P., Kenttä, G., & Johansson, M. (2008). A qualitative analysis of burnout in elite Swedish athletes. *Psychology of Sport & Exercise*, *9*, 800–816.

Gustafsson, H., Kenttä, G., Hassmén, P., & Lundqvist, C. (2007). Prevalence of burnout in competitive adolescent athletes. *The Sport Psychologist*, *21*, 21–37.

Guthold, R., Stevens, G. A., Riley, L. M., & Bull, F. C. (2018). Worldwide trends in insufficient physical activity from 2001 to 2016: A pooled analysis of 358 population-based surveys with 1.9 million participants. *Lancet Global Health*, *6*, e1077–e1086.

Haber, D. (2006). Life review: Implementation, theory, research, and therapy. *International Journal Aging and Human Development*, *63*, 153–171.

Hagberg, L. A., Lindahl, B., Nyberg, L., & Hellénius, M. L. (2009). Importance of enjoyment when promoting physical exercise. *Scandinavian Journal of Medicine & Science in Sports*, *19*, 740–747.

Hagger, M. S., & Chatzisarantis, N. L. D. (2014). An integrated behavior change model for physical activity. *Exercise & Sport Sciences Reviews*, *42*, 62–69.

Hagger, M. S., Chatzisarantis, N. L. D., & Biddle, S. J. H. (2002). A meta-analytic review of the theories of reasoned action and planned behavior in physical activity: Predictive validity and the contribution of additional variables. *Journal of Sport and Exercise Psychology*, *24*, 3–32.

Haigh, P. (2019). The shocking comments Steve Dale made before Bury went out of business. *Metro* (August 28). Retrieved from: https://metro.co.uk/2019/08/28/shocking-comments-steve-dale-made-bury-went-business-10642739/ (Accessed April 20, 2020).

Hain, P. (1982). The politics of sport and apartheid. In J. Hargreaves (Ed.), *Sport, culture and ideology* (pp. 232–248). London: Routledge.

Haines, H., & Vaughan, G. M. (1979). Was 1898 a 'great date' in the history of social psychology? *Journal of the History of the Behavioral Sciences*, *15*, 323–332.

Hajna, S., Ross, N. A., Brazeau, A.-S., Bélisle, P., Joseph, L., & Dasgupta, K. (2015). Associations between neighbourhood walkability and daily steps in adults: A systematic review and meta-analysis. *BMC Public Health*, *15*, 768.

Hall, S., Critcher, C., Jefferson, T., Clarke, J., & Roberts, B. (1978). *Policing the crisis: Mugging, the state and law and order*. Basingstoke: Palgrave Macmillan.

Halliday, J. (2019a). Bury FC: Despair as club is expelled from Football League after 125 years. *The Guardian* (August 27). Retrieved from: www.theguardian.com/football/2019/aug/27/bury-and-bolton-two-of-englands-oldest-clubs-face-tuesday-expulsion (Accessed October 21, 2019).

Halliday, J. (2019b). Distressed Bury fans get mental health support from NHS. *The Guardian* (September 4). Retrieved from: www.theguardian.com/football/2019/sep/04/distressed-bury-fans-get-mental-health-support-from-nhs (Accessed October 21, 2019).

Hamilton, K., Kirkpatrick, A., Rebar, A. L., & Hagger, M. S. (2017). Child sun safety: Application of an integrated behavior change model. *Health Psychology*, *36*, 916–926.

Hampson, R., & Jowett, S. (2014). Effects of coach leadership and coach–athlete relationship on collective efficacy. *Scandinavian Journal of Sports Science and Medicine*, *24*, 454–460.

Hancox, J. E., Quested, E., Thøgersen-Ntoumani, C., & Ntoumanis, N. (2015). An intervention to train group exercise class instructors to adopt a motivationally adaptive communication style: A quasi-experimental study protocol. *Health Psychology and Behavioral Medicine*, *3*, 190–203.

Hannan, T. E., Moffitt, R. L., Neumann, D. L., & Thomas, P. R. (2015). Applying the theory of planned behavior to physical activity: The moderating role of mental toughness. *Journal of Sport and Exercise Psychology*, *37*, 514–522.

Hanratty, D. (2018). Johnny Sexton crowned World Player of the Year at World Rugby Awards. Retrieved from: www.joe.ie/sport/johnny-sexton-world-player-of-the-year-649305 (Accessed September 1, 2019).

Hansen, D. M., Larson, R., & Dworkin, J. B. (2003). What adolescents learn in organized youth activities: A survey of self-reported developmental experiences. *Journal of Research on Adolescence*, *13*, 25–55.

Hardin, M., Genovese, J., & Yu, N. (2009). Privileged to be on camera: Sports broadcasters assess the role of social identity in the profession. *Electronic News*, *3*, 80–93.

Hardman, C. A., Horne, P. J., & Lowe, C. F. (2009). A home-based intervention to increase physical activity in girls: The Fit 'n' Fun Dudes program. *Journal of Exercise Science & Fitness*, *7*, 1–8.

Hardman, C. A., Horne, P. J., & Lowe, C. F. (2011). Effects of rewards, peer-modelling and pedometer targets on children's physical activity: A school-based intervention study. *Psychology & Health*, *26*, 3–21.

Hardy, C. J., & Crace, R. K. (1997). Foundations of team building: Introduction to the team building primer. *Journal of Applied Sport Psychology*, *9*, 1–10.

Hardy, L., Jones, J. G., & Gould, D. (1996). *Understanding psychological preparation for sport: Theory and practice of elite performers*. Hoboken, NJ: John Wiley.

Hareli, S., & Parkinson, B. (2008). What's social about social emotions? *Journal for the Theory of Social Behaviour*, *38*, 131–156.

Harré, R. (1977). The ethogenic approach: Theory and practice. In *Advances in experimental social psychology* (Vol. 10, pp. 283–314). London: Academic Press.

Harris, J. (2010). *Rugby union and globalization: An odd-shaped world*. London: Palgrave Macmillan.

Harris, J. (2017). The reinvention of the British Lions: Amateurs, professionals and contested identities. *Sport in History*, *37*, 204–220.

Harris, K. C., Kuramoto, L. K., Schulzer, M., & Retallack, J. E. (2009). Effect of school-based physical activity interventions on body mass index in children: A meta-analysis. *Canadian Medical Association Journal*, *180*, 719–726.

Harris, S. R. (2012). 'We're all in the same boat': A review of the benefits of dragon boat racing for women living with breast cancer. *Evidence-Based Complementary and Alternative Medicine*, Article 167651.

Hartgerink, C. H., Van Beest, I., Wicherts, J. M., & Williams, K. D. (2015). The ordinal effects of ostracism: A meta-analysis of 120 Cyberball studies. *PLoS ONE*, *10*(5), e0127002.

Hartley, C., & Coffee, P. (2019a). Perceived and received dimensional support: Main and stress-buffering effects on dimensions of burnout. *Frontiers in Psychology*, *10*, 1724.

Hartley, C., & Coffee, P. (2019b). A provider–recipient perspective on how social identity influences the design, provision, and receipt of social support. Paper presented at the Second International Conference on Social Identity in Sport, University of Stirling, Scotland, June 28–30.

Harwood, C., & Johnston, J. (2016). Positive youth development and talent development: Is there a best of the both worlds? In N. L. Holt (Ed.), *Positive youth development through sport* (2nd ed., pp. 113–125). London: Routledge.

Haslam, C., Cruwys, T., Chang, M. X.-L., Bentley, S. V., Haslam, S. A., Dingle, G. A., & Jetten, J. (2019). GROUPS 4 HEALTH reduces loneliness and social anxiety in adults with psychological distress: Findings from a randomized controlled trial. *Journal of Consulting and Clinical Psychology, 87*, 787–801.

Haslam, C., Cruwys, T., Haslam, S. A., Dingle, G., & Chang, M. X.-L. (2016). GROUPS 4 HEALTH: Evidence that a social-identity intervention that builds and strengthens social group membership improves mental health. *Journal of Affective Disorders, 194*, 188–195.

Haslam, C., Haslam, S. A., Knight, C., Gleibs, I., Ysseldyk, R., & McCloskey, L. G. (2014). We can work it out: Group decision-making builds social identity and enhances the cognitive performance of care home residents. *British Journal of Psychology, 105*, 17–34.

Haslam, C., Holme, A., Haslam, S. A., Iyer, A., Jetten, J., & Williams, W. H. (2008). Maintaining group membership: Social identity continuity and well-being after stroke. *Neuropsychological Rehabilitation, 18*, 671–691.

Haslam, C., Jetten, J., Cruwys, T., Dingle, G., & Haslam, S. A. (2018). *The new psychology of health: Unlocking the social cure.* Abingdon, UK: Routledge.

Haslam, C., Lam, B. C. P., Branscombe, N. R., Ball, T. C., Fong, P., Steffens, N. K., & Haslam, S. A. (2018). Adjusting to life in retirement: The protective role of membership and identification with new groups. *European Journal of Work and Organizational Psychology, 27*, 822–839.

Haslam, C., Lam, B. C. P., Yang, J., Fransen, K., Steffens, N. K., Cruwys, T., & Haslam, S. A. (2020). *When the final whistle blows: The contribution of social group processes in the transition to retirement from professional sport.* Unpublished manuscript, University of Queensland.

Haslam, C., Steffens, N. K., Branscombe, N. R., Haslam, S. A., Cruwys, T., Lam, B., Pachana, N., & Yang, J. (2019). The importance of social groups for retirement adjustment: Evidence, application, and policy implications of the Social Identity Model of Identity Change. *Social Issues and Policy Review, 13*, 93–124.

Haslam, N., Holland, E., & Kuppens, P. (2012). Categories versus dimensions in personality and psychopathology: A quantitative review of taxometric research. *Psychological Medicine, 42*, 903–920.

Haslam, S. A. (2001). *Psychology in organizations: The social identity approach* (1st ed.). London: Sage.

Haslam, S. A. (2004). *Psychology in organizations: The social identity approach* (2nd ed.). London: Sage.

Haslam, S. A. (2014). Making good theory practical: Five lessons for an applied social identity approach to challenges of organizational, health, and clinical psychology. *British Journal of Social Psychology, 53*, 1–20.

Haslam, S. A. (2017). The social identity approach to education and learning: Identification, ideation, interaction, influence and ideology. In K. Mavor, M. J. Platow, & B. Bizumic (Eds.), *Self and social identity in educational contexts* (pp. 19–35). London: Routledge.

Haslam, S. A., Eggins, R. A., & Reynolds, K. J. (2003). The ASPIRe model: Actualizing Social and Personal Identity Resources to enhance organizational outcomes. *Journal of Occupational and Organizational Psychology, 76*, 83–113.

Haslam, S. A., Jetten, J., O'Brien, A., & Jacobs, E. (2004). Social identity, social influence, and reactions to potentially stressful tasks: Support for the self-categorization model of stress. *Stress and Health, 20*, 3–9.

Haslam, S. A., Jetten, J., & Waghorn, C. (2009). Social identification, stress and citizenship in teams: A five-phase longitudinal study. *Stress and Health, 25*, 21–30.

Haslam, S. A., McMahon, C., Cruwys, T., Haslam, C., Greenaway, K., Jetten, J., & Steffens, N. K. (2018). Social cure, what social cure? The propensity to underestimate the importance of social factors for health. *Social Science & Medicine, 198*, 14–21.

Haslam, S. A., Oakes, P. J., Turner, J. C., & McGarty, C. (1995). Social categorization and group homogeneity: Changes in the perceived applicability of stereotype content as a function of comparative context and trait favourableness. *British Journal of Social Psychology, 34*, 139–160.

Haslam, S. A., Oakes, P. J., Turner, J. C., & McGarty, C. (1996). Social identity, self-categorization and the perceived homogeneity of ingroups and outgroups: The interaction between social motivation and cognition. In R. M. Sorrentino & E. T. Higgins (Eds.), *Handbook of motivation and cognition* (Vol. 3, pp. 182–222). New York: Guilford Press.

Haslam, S. A., O'Brien, A., Jetten, J., Vormedal, K., & Penna, S. (2005). Taking the strain: Social identity, social support, and the experience of stress. *British Journal of Social Psychology, 44*, 355–370.

Haslam, S. A., & Platow, M. J. (2001). The link between leadership and followership: How affirming social identity translates vision into action. *Personality and Social Psychology Bulletin, 27*, 1469–1479.

Haslam, S. A., Powell, C., & Turner, J. C. (2000). Social identity, self-categorization and work motivation: Rethinking the contribution of the group to positive and sustainable organizational outcomes. *Applied Psychology: An International Review, 49*, 319–339.

Haslam, S. A., & Reicher, S. D. (2006). Stressing the group: Social identity and the unfolding dynamics of responses to stress. *Journal of Applied Psychology, 91*, 1037–1052.

Haslam, S. A., & Reicher, S. D. (2012). When prisoners take over the prison: A social psychology of resistance. *Personality and Social Psychology Review, 16*, 152–179.

Haslam, S. A., & Reicher, S. D. (2016). Leicester's lesson in leadership. *The Psychologist, 29*, 446–449.

Haslam, S. A., Reicher, S. D., & Levine, R. M. (2012). When other people are heaven, when other people are hell: How social identity determines the nature and impact of social support. In J. Jetten, C. Haslam, & S. A. Haslam (Eds.), *The social cure: Identity, health and well-being* (pp. 157–174). Philadelphia, PA: Psychology Press.

Haslam, S. A., Reicher, S. D., & Platow, M. J. (2011). *The new psychology of leadership: Identity, influence and power* (1st ed.). London: Psychology Press.

Haslam, S. A., Reicher, S. D., & Reynolds, K. J. (2012). Identity, influence, and change: Rediscovering John Turner's vision for social psychology. *British Journal of Social Psychology, 51*, 201–218.

Haslam, S. A., Ryan, M. K., Postmes, T., Spears, R., Jetten, J. & Webley, P. (2006). Sticking to our guns: Social identity as a basis for the maintenance of commitment to faltering organizational projects. *Journal of Organizational Behavior, 27*, 607–628.

Haslam, S. A., Salvatore, J., Kessler, T., & Reicher, S. D. (2008). The social psychology of success. *Scientific American Mind, 19*(2), 24–31.

Haslam, S. A., Steffens, N. K., & Peters, K. (2019). The importance of creating and harnessing a sense of 'us': Social identity as the missing link between leadership and health. In R. Williams, V. Kemp, S. A. Haslam, C. Haslam, K. S. Bhui, S. Bailey, & D. Maughan (Eds.), *Social scaffolding: Applying the lessons of contemporary social science to health and healthcare* (pp. 302–311). Cambridge: Cambridge University Press.

Haslam, S. A., Steffens, N. K., Peters, K., Boyce, R. A., Mallett, C. J., & Fransen, K. (2017). A social identity approach to leadership development: The 5R program. *Journal of Personnel Psychology, 16*, 113–124.

Haslam, S. A., & Turner, J. C. (1992). Context-dependent variation in social stereotyping 2: The relationship between frame of reference, self-categorization and accentuation. *European Journal of Social Psychology*, *22*, 251–277.

Haslam, S. A., Turner, J. C., Oakes, P. J., McGarty, C., & Reynolds, K. J. (1998). The group as a basis for emergent stereotype consensus. *European Review of Social Psychology*, *8*, 203–239.

Haslam, S. A., Turner, J. C., Oakes, P. J., Reynolds, K. J., & Doosje, B. (2002). From personal pictures in the head to collective tools in the world: How shared stereotypes allow groups to represent and change social reality. In C. McGarty, V. Y. Yzerbyt, & R. Spears (Eds.), *Stereotypes as explanations: The formation of meaningful beliefs about social groups* (pp. 157–185). Cambridge: Cambridge University Press.

Haslam, S. A., Turner, J. C., Oakes, P. J., Reynolds, K. J., Eggins, R. A., Nolan, M., & Tweedie, J. (1998). When do stereotypes become really consensual? Investigating the group-based dynamics of the consensualization process. *European Journal of Social Psychology*, *28*, 755–776.

Haslerig, S. J., Vue, R., & Grummert, S. E. (2020). Invincible bodies: American sport media's racialization of Black and white college football players. *International Review for the Sociology of Sport*, *55*, 272–290.

Hassan, D. (2018). Sport and politics in a complex age. *Sport in Society*, *21*, 735–744.

Hastorf, A. H., & Cantril, H. (1954). They saw a game: A case study. *Journal of Abnormal and Social Psychology*, *49*, 129–134.

Hatfield, E., Cacioppo, J. T., & Rapson, R. L. (1994). *Emotional contagion*. New York: Cambridge University Press.

Hattenstone, S. (2019). Kelly Holmes on mental health and happiness: 'I've been to the lowest point and the highest'. *The Guardian* (March 13). Retrieved from: www.theguardian.com/sport/2019/mar/13/kelly-holmes-mental-health-happiness-self-harming-podcast-interview (Accessed October 21, 2019).

Häusser, J., Kattenstroth, M., van Dick, R., & Mojzisch, A. (2012). 'We' are not stressed: Social identity in groups buffers neuroendocrine stress reactions. *Journal of Experimental Social Psychology*, *48*, 973–977.

Havard, C. T. (2014). Glory out of reflected failure: The examination of how rivalry affects sport fans. *Sport Management Review*, *17*, 243–253.

Hayat, T., Galily, Y., & Samuel-Azran, T. (2019). Can celebrity athletes burst the echo chamber bubble? The case of LeBron James and Lady Gaga. *International Review for the Sociology of Sport* (Online publication; doi: 10.1177/1012690219855913).

Haynes, T. L., Perry, R. P., Stupnisky, R. H., & Daniels, L. M. (2009). A review of attributional retraining treatments: Fostering engagement and persistence in vulnerable college students. In M. B. Paulsen (Ed.), *Higher education: Handbook of theory and research* (pp. 227–272). Dordrecht, NL: Springer.

Hayward, F. P. I., Knight, C. J., & Mellalieu, S. D. (2017). A longitudinal examination of stressors, appraisals, and coping in youth swimming. *Psychology of Sport and Exercise*, *29*, 56–68.

Hayward, P. (2019). Pep Guardiola and Jurgen Klopp's focus on the human factors has made them masters of ego-management. *The Daily Telegraph* (May 7). Retrieved from: www.telegraph.co.uk/football/2019/05/07/pep-guardiola-jurgen-klopps-focus-human-factor-has-made-masters/ (Accessed August 8, 2019).

Heck, S. (2011). Modern Pentathlon and the First World War: When athletes and soldiers met to practise martial manliness. *International Journal of the History of Sport*, *28*, 410–428.

Heere, B., & James, J. D. (2007). Sports teams and their communities: Examining the influence of external group identities on team identity. *Journal of Sport Management*, *21*, 319–337.

Heitner, D. (2015). Sports industry to reach $73.5 billion by 2019. *Forbes* (October 19). Retrieved from: www.forbes.com/sites/darrenheitner/2015/10/19/sports-industry-to-reach-73-5-billion-by-2019/#329f16471b4b (Accessed December 19, 2019).

Helsen, W. F., Hodges, N. J., Van Winckel, J., & Starkes, J. L. (2000). The roles of talent, physical precocity and practice in the development of soccer expertise. *Journal of Sports Sciences, 18,* 1–10.

Helsen, W. F., Starkes, J. L., & Hodges, N. J. (1998). Team sports and the theory of deliberate practice. *Journal of Sport and Exercise Psychology, 20,* 13–35.

Hermann, J. M., & Vollmeyer, R. (2016). 'Girls should cook, rather than kick!': Female soccer players under stereotype threat. *Psychology of Sport and Exercise, 26,* 94–101.

Hess, U., & Fischer, A. H. (2013). Emotional mimicry as social regulation. *Personality and Social Psychology Review, 17,* 142–157.

Hickman, D. C., & Metz, N. E. (2015). The impact of pressure on performance: Evidence from the PGA Tour. *Journal of Economic Behavior & Organization, 116,* 319–330.

Hill, A. P., Mallinson-Howard, S. H., & Jowett, G. E. (2018). Multidimensional perfectionism in sport: A meta-analytical review. *Sport, Exercise, and Performance Psychology, 7,* 235–270.

Hill, D. M., Hanton, S., Matthews, N., & Fleming, S. (2010). Choking in sport: A review. *International Review of Sport and Exercise Psychology, 3,* 24–39.

Hinds, P. J., & Mortensen, M. (2005). Understanding conflict in geographically distributed teams: The moderating effects of shared identity, shared context, and spontaneous communication. *Organization Science, 16,* 290–307.

Hinds, R. (2019). Eddie McGuire's criticism of coin-tosser reveals rapid degeneration of sports commentary and analysis. *ABC News* (April 1). Retrieved from: www.abc.net.au/news/2019-04-01/eddie-maguire-scg-degeneration-sports-commentary-cynthia-banham/10957316 (Accessed July 31, 2019).

Hiroto, D. S., & Seligman, M. E. P. (1975). Generality of learned helplessness in man. *Journal of Personality and Social Psychology, 31,* 311–327.

Hobfoll, S. E. (1988). *The ecology of stress.* New York: Hemisphere.

Hochschild, A. R. (1979). Emotion work, feeling rules, and social structure. *American Journal of Sociology, 85,* 551–575.

Hodge, K., Henry, G., & Smith, W. (2014). A case study of excellence in elite sport: Motivational climate in a world champion team. *The Sport Psychologist, 28,* 60–74.

Hoeber, L., & Kerwin, S. (2013). Exploring the experiences of female sport fans: A collaborative self-ethnography. *Sport Management Review, 16,* 326–336.

Hogan, J. (2003). Staging the nation: Gendered and ethnicized discourses of national identity in Olympic opening ceremonies. *Journal of Sport & Social Issues, 27,* 100–123.

Hogg, M. A. (1992). *The social psychology of group cohesiveness: From attraction to social identity.* New York: Harvester Wheatsheaf.

Hogg, M. A. (1993). Group cohesiveness: A critical review and some new directions. *European Review of Social Psychology, 4,* 85–111.

Hogg, M. A. (2000). Subjective uncertainty reduction through self-categorization: A motivational theory of social identity processes. *European Review of Social Psychology, 11,* 223–255.

Hogg, M. A. (2001). A social identity theory of leadership. *Personality and Social Psychology Review, 5,* 184–200.

Hogg, M. A., & Hardie, E. A. (1991). Social attraction, personal attraction and self-categorization: A field study. *Personality and Social Psychology Bulletin, 17,* 175–180.

Hoggett, J., & Stott, C. J. (2010). Crowd psychology, public order police training and the policing of football crowds. *Policing: An International Journal of Police Strategies & Management, 33,* 218–235.

Holmes, K. (2005). *Black, white & gold: My autobiography.* London: Virgin Books.

Holmes, M., & Storey, D. (2011). Transferring national allegiance: Cultural affinity or flag of convenience? *Sport in Society, 14,* 253–271.

Holmes, P. (2011). Twitter a viral villain – in an instant. *The Baltimore Sun* (May 18). Retrieved from: www.baltimoresun.com/sports/ravens/sc-spt-0518-thiswildcard-20110518-48-story.html (Accessed July 30, 2019).

Holt, N. L. (2016). *Positive youth development through sport* (2nd ed.). London: Routledge.

Holt, N. L., & Dunn, J. G. H. (2006). Guidelines for delivering personal-disclosure mutual-sharing team building interventions. *The Sport Psychologist, 20*, 348–367.

Holt, N. L., & Hoar, S. D. (2006). The multidimensional construct of social support. In S. Hanton & S. D. Mellalieu (Eds.), *Literature reviews in sport psychology* (pp. 199–225). Hauppauge, NY: Nova Science Publishers.

Holt, N. L., Neely, K. C., Slater, L. G., Camiré, M., Côté, J., Fraser-Thomas, J., MacDonald, D. J., Strachan, L., & Tamminen, K. A. (2017). A grounded theory of positive youth development through sport based on results from a qualitative meta-study. *International Review of Sport and Exercise Psychology, 10*, 1–49.

Holt-Lunstad, J., Smith, T. B., & Layton, J. B. (2010). Social relationships and mortality risk: A meta-analytic review. *PLoS Medicine, 7*(7), e1000316.

Hoogland, C. E., Schurtz, D. R., Cooper, C. M., Combs, D. J. Y., Brown, E. G., & Smith, R. H. (2015). The joy of pain and the pain of joy: In-group identification predicts schadenfreude and glückschmerz following rival groups' fortunes. *Motivation & Emotion, 39*, 260–281.

Hopkins, N., Reicher, S. D., Khan, S. S., Tewari, S., Srinivasan, N., & Stevenson, C. (2016). Explaining effervescence: Investigating the relationship between shared social identity and positive experience in crowds. *Cognition & Emotion, 30*, 20–32.

Hoption, C., Phelan, J., & Barling, J. (2007). Transformational leadership in sport. In M. R. Beauchamp & M. A. Eys (Eds.), *Group dynamics in exercise and sport psychology: Contemporary themes* (pp. 45–62). New York: Routledge.

Hornby, N. (1992). *Fever pitch*. London: Penguin.

Horne, P. J., Hardman, C. A., Lowe, C. F., & Rowlands, A. V. (2009). Increasing children's physical activity: A peer modelling, rewards and pedometer-based intervention. *European Journal of Clinical Nutrition, 63*, 191–198.

Hornsey, M. J., Oppes, T., & Svensson, A. (2002). 'It's OK if we say it, but you can't': Responses to intergroup and intragroup criticism. *European Journal of Social Psychology, 32*, 293–307.

Horton, R. S., & Mack, D. E. (2000). Athletic identity in marathon runners: Functional focus or dysfunctional commitment? *Journal of Sport Behaviour, 23*, 101–119.

Hoult, N. (2019). Courage, unity, respect: The inside story of how England became the world's best cricket team. *The Telegraph* (August 27). Retrieved from: www.telegraph.co.uk/cricket/inside-story-england-became-worlds-best-cricket-team (Accessed December 12, 2019).

House, R., Javidan, M., & Dorfman, P. (2001). Project GLOBE: An introduction. *Applied Psychology, 50*, 489–505.

Howard, S., & Borgella, A. (2018). 'Sinking' or sinking? Identity salience and shifts in Black women's athletic performance. *Psychology of Sport & Exercise, 39*, 179–183.

Howell, J. L., Koudenburg, N., Loschelder, D. D., Weston, D., Fransen, K., De Dominices, S., ... & Haslam, S. A. (2014). Happy but unhealthy: The relationship between social ties and health in an emerging network. *European Journal of Social Psychology, 44*, 612–621.

Hüffmeier, J., Dietrich, H., & Hertel, G. (2013). Effort intentions in teams: Effects of task type and teammate performance. *Small Group Research, 44*, 62–88.

Hüffmeier, J., Krumm, S., Kanthak, J., & Hertel, G. (2012). 'Don't let the group down': Facets of instrumentality moderate the motivating effects of groups in a field experiment. *European Journal of Social Psychology, 42*, 533–538.

Hughes, R. (2014). Tale of 1914 Christmas Day truce is inspiring, though hard to believe. *New York Times* (December 23). Retrieved from: www.nytimes.com/2014/12/24/sports/soccer/tale-of-1914-christmas-day-truce-soccer-game.html (Accessed December 5, 2019).

Hull, C. L. (1932). The goal-gradient hypothesis and maze learning. *Psychological Review*, *39*, 25–43.

Hunt, K., Gray, C. M., Maclean, A., Smillie, S., Bunn, C., & Wyke, S. (2014). Do weight management programmes delivered at professional football clubs attract and engage high risk men? A mixed-methods study. *BMC Public Health*, *14*, 11.

Hunt, K., Wyke, S., Gray, C. M., Anderson, A. S., Brady, A., Bunn, C., … Treweek, S. (2014). A gender-sensitised weight loss and healthy living programme for overweight and obese men delivered by Scottish Premier League football clubs (FFIT): A pragmatic randomised controlled trial. *The Lancet*, *383*, 1211–1221.

Hunter, J. A., Platow, M. J., Moradi, S., Banks, M., Hayhurst, J., Kafka, S., … Ruffman, T. (2017). Subjective belonging and in-group favouritism. *Journal of Experimental Social Psychology*, *73*, 136–146.

Hylton, J. G. (1997). American civil rights laws and the legacy of Jackie Robinson. *Marquette Sports Law Review*, *8*, 387.

Ingham, A. G., Levinger, G., Graves, J., & Peckham, V. (1974). The Ringelmann effect: Studies of group size and group performance. *Journal of Experimental Social Psychology*, *10*, 371–384.

Insight (2017). Life after elite sport. *SBS*. Retrieved from: www.sbs.com.au/news/insight/tvepisode/life-after-elite-sport_1 (Accessed August 19, 2019).

International Olympic Committee (2019). *Peace through sport*. Retrieved from: www.olympic.org/pierre-de-coubertin/peace-through-sport (Accessed December 5, 2019).

International Ski Federation (2017, April 13). Johan Olsson retires from elite skiing. Retrieved from: www.fis-ski.com/en/cross-country/cross-country-news-multimedia/news/archive/article=johanolsson-retires-from-elite-skiing (Accessed August 12, 2019).

Intravia, J., Piquero, A. R., & Piquero, N. L. (2018). The racial divide surrounding United States of America national anthem protests in the National Football League. *Deviant Behavior*, *39*, 1058–1068.

Isoard-Gautheur, S., Martinent, G., Guillet-Descas, E., Trouilloud, D., Cece, V., & Mette, A. (2018). Development and evaluation of the psychometric properties of a new measure of athlete burnout: The Athlete Burnout Scale. *International Journal of Stress Management*, *25*, 108–123.

Iyer, A., Jetten, J., Tsivrikos, D., Postmes, T., & Haslam, S. A. (2009). The more (and the more compatible) the merrier: Multiple group memberships and identity compatibility as predictors of adjustment after life transitions. *British Journal of Social Psychology*, *48*, 707–733.

Izumi, B. T., Schulz, A. J., Mentz, G., Israel, B. A., Sand, S. L., Reyes, A. G., … Diaz, G. (2015). Leader behaviors, group cohesion, and participation in a walking group program. *American Journal of Preventive Medicine*, *49*, 41–49.

Jackson, B. (2019). Professional golf tour life. *Women's Golf*. Retrieved from: www.womensgolf.com/tour-life-brandi-jackson (Accessed September 23, 2019).

Jackson, P., & Delehanty, H. (1995). *Sacred hoops: Spiritual lessons of a hardwood warrior*. New York: Hyperion.

Jackson, S. J., & Hokowhitu, B. (2002). Sport, tribes, and technology: The New Zealand All Blacks Haka and the politics of identity. *Journal of Sport & Social Issues*, *26*, 125–139.

Jakicic, J. M., Kraus, W. E., Powell, K. E., Campbell, W. W., Janz, K. F., Triano, R. P., & Piercy, K. L. (2019). Association between bout duration of physical activity and health: Systematic review. *Medicine & Science in Sports & Exercise*, *51*, 1213–1219.

James, J. D., Delia, E. B., & Wann, D. L. (2020). 'No' is not 'Low': Improving the assessment of sport team identification. *Sport Marketing Quarterly*, *28*, 34–45.

James, L. (1995). *The rise and fall of the British Empire*. New York: St Martin's Press.

Jensen, J. A., Turner, B. A., Delia, E. B., James, J. D., Greenwell, T. C., McEvoy, C., … Walsh, P. (2016). Forty years of BIRGing: New perspectives on Cialdini's seminal studies. *Journal of Sport Management*, *30*, 149–161.

Jetten, J., Branscombe, N. R., Haslam, S. A., Haslam, C., Cruwys, T., Jones, J. M., Cui, L., Dingle, G., Liu, J., Murphy, S. C., Thai, A., Walter, Z., & Zhang, A. (2015). Having a lot of a good thing: Multiple important group memberships as a source of self-esteem. *PLoS ONE*, *10*(6), e0131035.

Jetten, J., Haslam, C., & Haslam, S. A. (Eds.) (2012). *The social cure: Identity, health and well-being*. New York: Psychology Press.

Jetten, J., Haslam, C., Haslam, S. A., Dingle, G., & Jones, J. M. (2014). How groups affect our health and well-being: The path from theory to policy. *Social Issues and Policy Review*, *8*, 103–130.

Jetten, J., Haslam, S. A., Iyer, A., & Haslam, C. (2009). Turning to others in times of change: Shared identity and coping with stress. In S. Stürmer & M. Snyder (Eds.), *New directions in the study of helping: Group-level perspectives on motivations, consequences and interventions* (pp. 139–156). Chichester, UK: Wiley-Blackwell.

Jõesaar, H., Hein, V., & Hagger, M. S. (2012). Youth athletes' perception of autonomy support from the coach, peer motivational climate and intrinsic motivation in sport setting: One-year effects. *Psychology of Sport and Exercise*, *13*, 257–262.

John, E. (2019). Even in defeat, English sport gives us much to cheer. *The Guardian* (November 3). Retrieved from: www.theguardian.com/commentisfree/2019/nov/03/even-in-defeat-engltill-gives-us-much-to-cheer? (Accessed November 6, 2019).

Johnson, A. B., & Sailors, P. R. (2013). Don't bring it on: The case against cheerleading as a collegiate sport. *Journal of the Philosophy of Sport*, *40*, 255–277.

Johnson, T., Martin, A. J., Palmer, F. R., Watson, G., & Ramsey, P. L. (2014). Collective leadership. A case study of the All Blacks. *Asia-Pacific Management & Business Application*, *1*, 53–67.

Jones, E. E. (1976). How do people perceive the causes of behavior? *American Scientist*, *64*, 300–305.

Jones, E. E., & Nisbett, R. E. (1972). The actor and the observer: Divergent perceptions of the causes of behavior. In E. E. Jones, D. Kanouse, H. H. Kelley, R. E. Nisbett, S. Valins, & B. Weiner (Eds.), *Attribution: Perceiving the causes of behavior* (pp. 79–94). Morristown, NJ: General Learning Press.

Jones, J. M., & Jetten, J. (2011). Recovering from strain and enduring pain: Multiple group memberships promote resilience in the face of physical challenges. *Social Psychological and Personality Science*, *2*, 239–244.

Jones, J. M., Williams, W. H., Jetten, J., Haslam, S. A., Harris, A., & Gleibs, I. H. (2012). The role of psychological symptoms and social group memberships in the development of post-traumatic stress after traumatic injury. *British Journal of Health Psychology*, *17*, 798–811.

Jones, M. V. (2003). Controlling emotions in sport. *The Sport Psychologist*, *17*, 471–486.

Jones, M. V., Coffee, P., Sheffield, D., Yangüez, M., & Barker, J. B. (2012). Just a game? Changes in English and Spanish soccer fans' emotions in the 2010 World Cup. *Psychology of Sport & Exercise*, *13*, 162–169.

Jones, M. V., Meijen, C., McCarthy, P. J., & Sheffield, D. (2009). A theory of challenge and threat states in athletes. *International Review of Sport & Exercise Psychology*, *2*, 161–180.

Jordet, G., & Hartman, E. (2008). Avoidance motivation and choking under pressure in soccer penalty shootouts. *Journal of Sport and Exercise Psychology*, *30*, 450–457.

Joseph, S., & Cramer, D. (2011). Sledging in cricket: Elite English batsmen's experiences of verbal gamesmanship. *Journal of Clinical Sport Psychology*, *5*, 237–251.

Kachanoff, F. J., Wohl, M. J. A., Koestner, R., & Taylor, D. M. (2020). Them, us, and I: How group contexts influence basic psychological needs. *Current Directions in Psychological Science*, *29*, 47–54.

Kail, R. V., & Cavanaugh, J. C. (2007). *Human development: A life-span view* (4th ed.). Belmont, CA: Thomson Wadsworth.

Kamphoff, C. S., Gill, D. L., & Huddleston, S. (2005). Jealousy in sport: Exploring jealousy's relationship to cohesion. *Journal of Applied Sport Psychology, 17,* 290–305.

Kane, A. A. (2010). Unlocking knowledge transfer potential: Knowledge demonstrability and superordinate social identity. *Organization Science, 21,* 643–660.

Kanning, M., & Schlicht, W. (2010). Be active and become happy: An ecological momentary assessment of physical activity and mood. *Journal of Sport and Exercise Psychology, 32,* 253–261.

Karau, S. J., & Williams, K. D. (1993). Social loafing: A meta-analytic review and theoretical integration. *Journal of Personality and Social Psychology, 65,* 681–706.

Karau, S. J., & Williams, K. D. (2017). Social facilitation and social loafing: Revisiting Triplett's competition studies. In J. R. Smith & S. A. Haslam (Eds.), *Social psychology: Revisiting the classic studies* (2nd ed., pp. 11–26). London: Sage.

Karvinen, K. H., Courneya, K. S., Plotnikoff, R. C., Spence, J. C., Venner, P. M., & North, S. (2009). A prospective study of the determinants of exercise in bladder cancer survivors using the theory of planned behavior. *Supportive Care in Cancer, 17,* 171–179.

Kassing, J. W., & Infante, D. A. (1999). Aggressive communication in the coach–athlete relationship. *Communication Research Reports, 16,* 110–120.

Kaufman, P., & Wolff, E. A. (2010). Playing and protesting: Sport as a vehicle for social change. *Journal of Sport & Social Issues, 34,* 154–175.

Kawycz, S., & Coffee, P., (2019). *Social identity and explanations for sports performance.* Paper presented at the Second International Conference on Social Identity in Sport, University of Stirling, Scotland, June 28–30.

Kawycz, S., Coffee, P., & Eklund, R. C. (2017). Drawing upon social identity theory to unpack the actor–observer asymmetry: Attributing actor behaviour. Paper presented at the First International Conference on Social Identity in Sport, KU Leuven, Leuven, Belgium, July.

Kay, A. C., Gaucher, D., Napier, J. L., Callan, M. J., & Laurin, K. (2008). God and the government: Testing a compensatory control mechanism for the support of external systems. *Journal of Personality and Social Psychology, 95,* 18–35.

Kaye, M. P., Frith, A., & Vosloo, J. (2015). Dyadic anxiety in youth sport: The relationship of achievement goals with anxiety in young athletes and their parents. *Journal of Applied Sport Psychology, 27,* 171–185.

Keating, F. (2010). The World Cup defeat that lost an election. *The Guardian* (April 21). Retrieved from: www.theguardian.com/football/blog/2010/apr/21/world-cup-1970-harold-wilson (Accessed December 5, 2019).

Kelly, C. M., Jorm, A. F., & Wright, A. (2007). Improving mental health literacy as a strategy to facilitate early intervention for mental disorders. *Medical Journal of Australia, 187,* S26–S30.

Kelly, M. (2019). Are U.S. women's soccer players really earning less than men? *The Washington Post* (July 8). Retrieved from: www.washingtonpost.com/politics/2019/07/08/are-us-womens-soccer-players-really-earning-less-than-men/ (Accessed November 2, 2019).

Kelly, S. F. (1995). *Bill Shankly: It's much more important than that.* London: Random House.

Kemp, N. (2016). Case study: How 'This Girl Can' got 1.6 million women exercising. *Campaign* (May, 18). Retrieved from: www.campaignlive.co.uk/article/case-study-this-girl-can-16-million-women-exercising/1394836 (Accessed August 12, 2019).

Kent, H. (1996). Breast-cancer survivors begin to challenge exercise taboos. *Canadian Medical Association Journal, 155,* 969–971.

Kent, R. (2016). Great British athletes' perceptions of competing at the London 2012 Olympic Games. *The Sport Journal, 39,* 1–22.

Keresztes, N., Piko, B. F., Pluhar, Z. F., & Page, R. M. (2008). Social influences in sports activity among adolescents. *Perspectives in Public Health*, *128*, 21–25.

Kerr, J. (2013). *Legacy: 15 lessons in leadership*. London: Constable.

Kerstings, N. (2007). Sport and national identity: A comparison of the 2006 and 2010 World Cups. *South African Journal of Political Studies*, *34*, 277–293.

Killanin, B. M. M., & Rodda, J. (1976). *The Olympic Games: 80 years of people, events and records*. London: Macmillan.

Kim, J., Dunn, E., Rellinger, K., Robertson-Wilson, J., & Eys, M. A. (2019). Social norms and physical activity in American and Canadian contexts: A scoping review. *International Review of Sport and Exercise Psychology*, *12*, 26–48.

King, A. C. (2001). Interventions to promote physical activity by older adults. *Journals of Gerontology*, *56*, 36–46.

King, A. C., Rejeski, W. J., & Buchner, D. M. (1998). Physical activity interventions targeting older adults: A critical review and recommendations. *American Journal of Preventive Medicine*, *15*, 316–333.

King, K. A., Tergerson, J. L., & Wilson, B. R. (2008). Effect of social support on adolescents' perceptions of and engagement in physical activity. *Journal of Physical Activity and Health*, *5*, 374–384.

Kinmonth, A.-L., Wareham, N. J., Hardeman, W., Sutton, S., Prevost, A. T., Fanshawe, T., … Griffin, S. J. (2008). Efficacy of a theory-based behavioural intervention to increase physical activity in an at-risk group in primary care (ProActive UK): A randomised trial. *The Lancet*, *371*, 41–48.

Kirsch, I. (1985). Response expectancy as a determinant of experience and behavior. *American Psychologist*, *40*, 1189–1202.

Kivetz, R., Urminsky, O., & Zheng, Y. (2006). The goal-gradient hypothesis resurrected: Purchase acceleration, illusionary goal progress, and customer retention. *Journal of Marketing Research*, *43*, 39–58.

Kniffin, K. M., & Palacio, D. (2018). Trash-talking and trolling. *Human Nature*, *29*, 353–369.

Knight, B., & Hammel, B. (2002). *Knight: My story*. New York: Thorndike Press.

Knight, C. J., & Holt, N. L. (2014). Parenting in youth tennis: Understanding and enhancing children's experiences. *Psychology of Sport and Exercise*, *15*, 155–164.

Knights, S., & Rudduck-Hudson, M. (2016). Experiences of occupational stress and social support in Australian Football League senior coaches. *International Journal of Sports Science & Coaching*, *11*, 162–171.

Koenigstorfer, J., Groeppel-Klein, A., & Schmitt, M. (2010). 'You'll never walk alone': How loyal are soccer fans to their clubs when they are struggling against relegation? *Journal of Sport Management*, *24*, 649–675.

Kraft, P., Rise, J., Sutton, S., & Roysamb, E. (2011). Perceived difficulty in the theory of planned behaviour: Perceived behavioural control or affective attitude? *British Journal of Social Psychology*, *44*, 479–496.

Krane, V., & Barber, H. (2003). Lesbian experiences in sport: A social identity perspective. *Quest*, *55*, 328–346.

Krauss, R. M., & Fussell, S. R. (1996). Social psychological models of interpersonal communication. In E. T. Higgins & A. W. Kruglanski (Eds.), *Social psychology: Handbook of basic principles* (pp. 655–701). New York: Guilford Press.

Kravitz, D., & Martin, B. (1986). Ringelmann revisited: Alternative explanations for the social loafing effect. *Personality and Social Psychology Bulletin*, *50*, 936–941.

Krendl, A., Gainsburg, I., & Ambady, N. (2012). The effects of stereotypes and observer pressure on athletic performance. *Journal of Sport and Exercise Psychology*, *34*, 3–15.

Kristiansen, E., & Roberts, G. C. (2010). Young elite athletes and social support: Coping with competitive and organizational stress in 'Olympic' competition. *Scandinavian Journal of Medicine & Science in Sports, 20*, 686–695.

Kroger, J. (2004). *Identity in adolescence: The balance between the self and other*. London: Routledge.

Kroger, J., & Marcia, J. E. (2011). The identity statuses: Origins, meanings, and interpretations. In S. J. Schwartz, K. Luyckx, & V. L. Vignoles (Eds.), *Handbook of identity theory and research* (pp. 31–53). New York: Springer.

Kroshus, E., Kubzansky, L. D., Goldman, R. E., & Austin, S. B. (2014). Norms, athletic identity, and concussion symptom under-reporting among male collegiate ice hockey players: A prospective cohort study. *Annals of Behavioral Medicine, 49*, 95–103.

Kruger, J., Epley, N., Parker, J., & Ng, Z. W. (2005). Egocentrism over e-mail: Can we communicate as well as we think? *Journal of Personality and Social Psychology, 89*, 925.

Kuhl, J. (1984). Volitional aspects of achievement motivation and learned helplessness: Toward a comprehensive theory of action control. *Progress in Experimental Personality Research, 13*, 99–171.

Kuper, S. (2011). More than a game: Germany v Holland. *FourFourTwo*. Retrieved from: www.fourfourtwo.com/features/more-game-germany-v-holland (Accessed December 5, 2019).

Kuppens, T., Yzerbyt, V. Y., Dandache, S., Fischer, A. H., & van der Schalk, J. (2013). Social identity salience shapes group-based emotions through group-based appraisals. *Cognition & Emotion, 27*, 1359–1377.

Kwok, N., Haslam, S. A., Haslam, C., & Cruwys, T. (2018). 'How can you make friends if you don't know who you are?' A qualitative examination of international students' experience informed by the Social Identity Model of Identity Change. *Journal of Community and Applied Social Psychology, 28*, 169–187.

Kwon, H. H., Trail, G. T., & Lee, D. (2008). The effect of vicarious achievement and team identification on BIRGing and CORFing in a winning vs. losing situation. *Sport Marketing Quarterly, 17*, 209–217.

Lakey, B. (2010). Social support: Basic research and new strategies for intervention. In J. E. Maddux & J. P. Tangney (Eds.), *Social psychological foundations of clinical psychology* (pp. 177–194). New York: Guilford Press.

Lakey, B., & Cronin, A. (2008). Low social support and major depression: Research, theory and methodological issues. In K. S. Dobson & D. Dozois (Eds.), *Risk factors for depression* (pp. 385–408). San Diego, CA: Academic Press.

Lakey, B., & Orehek, E. (2011). Relational regulation theory: A new approach to explain the link between perceived social support and mental health. *Psychological Review, 118*, 482–495.

Lalonde, R. N. (1992). The dynamics of group differentiation in the face of defeat. *Personality and Social Psychology Bulletin, 18*, 336–342.

Lalonde, R. N., Moghaddam, F. M., & Taylor, D. M. (1987). The process of group differentiation in a dynamic intergroup setting. *Journal of Social Psychology, 127*, 273–287.

Lam, B. C. P., Haslam, C., Haslam, S. A., Steffens, N. K., Cruwys, T., Jetten, J., & Yang, J. (2018). Multiple social groups support adjustment to retirement across cultures. *Social Science & Medicine, 208*, 200–208.

Lamers, S. M. A., Westerhof, G. J., Bohlmeijer, E. T., ten Klooster, P. M., & Keyes, C. L. M. (2011). Evaluating the psychometric properties of the Mental Health Continuum-Short Form (MHC-SF). *Journal of Clinical Psychology, 67*, 99–110.

Lamont-Mills, A., & Christensen, S. A. (2006). Athletic identity and its relationship to sport participation levels. *Journal of Science and Medicine in Sport, 9*, 472–478.

Lane, A. M., Beedie, C. J., Jones, M. V., Uphill, M. A., & Devonport, T. J. (2012). The BASES expert statement on emotion regulation in sport. *Journal of Sports Sciences, 30,* 1189–1195.

Lane, K., Jespersen, D., & McKenzie, D. C. (2005). The effect of a whole body exercise programme and dragon boat training on arm volume and arm circumference in women treated for breast cancer. *European Journal of Cancer Care, 14,* 353–358.

Lantz C. D., & Schroeder, P. J. (1999). Endorsement of masculine and feminine gender roles: Differences between participation in and identification with the athletic role. *Journal of Sport Behavior, 22,* 545–557.

Latané, B., Williams, K. D., & Harkins, S. (1979). Many hands make light work: The causes and consequences of social loafing. *Journal of Personality and Social Psychology, 37,* 822–832.

Latrofa, M., Vaes, J., Cadinu, M., & Carnaghi, A. (2010). The cognitive representation of self-stereotyping. *Personality and Social Psychology Bulletin, 36,* 911–922.

Lau, R. R., & Russell, D. (1980). Attributions in the sports pages. *Journal of Personality and Social Psychology, 39,* 29–38.

Laudan, L. (1996). *Beyond positivism and relativism: Theory, method, and evidence.* Boulder, CO: Westview Press.

Lausic, D., Razon, S., & Tenenbaum, G. (2015). Nonverbal sensitivity, verbal communication, and team coordination in tennis doubles. *International Journal of Sport and Exercise Psychology, 13,* 398–414.

Lausic, D., Tenenbaum, G., Eccles, D. W., Jeong, A., & Johnson, T. (2009). Intrateam communication and performance in doubles tennis. *Research Quarterly for Exercise and Sport, 80,* 281–290.

Lautenschlager, N. T., Cox, K. L., Flicker, L., Foster, J. K., van Bockxmeer, F. M., Xiao, J., … Almeida, O. P. (2008). Effect of physical activity on cognitive function in older adults at risk for Alzheimer disease: A randomized trial. *Journal of the American Medical Association, 300,* 1027–1037.

Lavallee, D. (2005). The effect of a life development intervention on sports career transition adjustment. *The Sport Psychologist, 19,* 193–202.

Lavallee, D. (2019). Engagement in sport career transition planning enhances performance. *Journal of Loss and Trauma, 24,* 1–8.

Lavallee, D., & Robinson, H. K. (2007). In pursuit of an identity: A qualitative exploration of retirement from women's artistic gymnastics. *Psychology of Sport and Exercise, 8,* 119–141.

Laverie, D. A., & Arnett, D. B. (2000). Factors affecting fan attendance: The influence of identity salience and satisfaction. *Journal of Leisure Research, 32,* 225–246.

Law, M. P., Côté, J., & Ericsson, K. A. (2007). Characteristics of expert development in rhythmic gymnastics: A retrospective study. *International Journal of Sport and Exercise Psychology, 5,* 82–103.

Lawton, J., Ahmad, N., Hanna, L., Douglas, M., & Hallowell, N. (2006). 'I can't do any serious exercise': Barriers to physical activity among people of Pakistani and Indian origin with Type 2 diabetes. *Health Education Research, 21,* 43–54.

Layden, T. (2015). After rehabilitation, the best of Michael Phelps may lie ahead. *Sports Illustrated* (November 9). Retrieved from: www.si.com/olympics/2015/11/09/michael-phelps-rehabilitation-rio-2016 (Accessed October 21, 2019).

Lazarus, R. S. (1999). *Stress and emotion: A new synthesis.* New York: Springer.

Lazarus, R. S. (2000). How emotions influence performance in competitive sport. *The Sport Psychologist, 14,* 229–252.

Lazarus, R. S., & Folkman, S. (1984). *Stress appraisal and coping.* New York: Springer.

Lazear, E. P. (2000). The power of incentives. *American Economic Review*, *90*, 410–414.

Lazear, E. P., & Rosen, S. (1981). Rank-order tournaments as optimum labor contracts. *Journal of Political Economy*, *89*, 841–864.

Le Foll, D., Rascle, O., & Higgins, N. C. (2008). Attributional feedback-induced changes in functional and dysfunctional attributions, expectations of success, hopefulness, and short-term persistence in a novel sport. *Psychology of Sport and Exercise*, *9*, 77–101.

Leach, C. W., Spears, R., Branscombe, N. R., & Doosje, B. (2003). Malicious pleasure: Schadenfreude at the suffering of another group. *Journal of Personality and Social Psychology*, *84*, 932–943.

LeCouteur, A., & Feo, R. (2011). Real-time communication during play: Analysis of team-mates' talk and interaction. *Psychology of Sport and Exercise*, *12*, 124–134.

Lee, C., & Russell, A. (2003). Effects of physical activity on emotional well-being among older Australian women: Cross-sectional and longitudinal analyses. *Journal of Psychosomatic Research*, *54*, 155–160.

Lee, I. M. (2003). Physical activity and cancer prevention – data from epidemiologic studies. *Medicine & Science in Sports & Exercise*, *35*, 1823–1827.

Lee, I. M., Shiroma, E. J., Lobelo, F., Puska, P., Blair, S. N., & Katzmarzyk, P. T. (2012). Effect of physical inactivity on major non-communicable diseases worldwide: An analysis of burden of disease and life expectancy. *The Lancet*, *380*, 219–229.

Lee, R. E., Medina, A. V., Mama, S. K., Reese-Smith, J. Y., O'Connor, D. P., Brosnan, M., … Estabrooks, P. A. (2011). Health is power: An ecological, theory-based health intervention for women of color. *Contemporary Clinical Trials*, *32*, 916–923.

Lee, Y. H., & Chelladurai, P. (2016). Affectivity, emotional labor, emotional exhaustion, and emotional intelligence in coaching. *Journal of Applied Sport Psychology*, *28*, 170–184.

Lee, Y. H., Chelladurai, P., & Kim, Y. (2015). Emotional labor in sports coaching: Development of a model. *International Journal of Sports Sciene & Coaching*, *10*, 561–575.

Leffert, N., Benson, P. L., Scales, P. C., Sharma, A. R., Drake, D. R., & Blyth, D. A. (1998). Developmental assets: Measurement and prediction of risk behaviours among adolescents. *Applied Developmental Science*, *2*, 209–230.

Legate, N., DeHaan, C. R., Weinstein, N., & Ryan, R. M. (2013). Hurting you hurts me too: The psychological costs of complying with ostracism. *Psychological Science*, *24*, 583–588.

Lelorain, S., Bonnaud-Antignac, A., & Florin, A. (2010). Long-term posttraumatic growth after breast cancer: Prevalence, predictors and relationships with psychological health. *Journal of Clinical Psychology in Medical Settings*, *17*, 14–22.

Lemyre, P. N., Hall, H. K., & Roberts, G. C. (2008). A social cognitive approach to burnout in elite athletes. *Scandinavian Journal of Medicine & Science in Sports*, *18*, 221–234.

Leng, H. K., Kuo T. Y, Grain, B.-P., & Tay, J. (2015). Singapore 2010 Youth Olympic Games and national pride: An examination of differences between spectators and non-spectators. *Sport, Business and Management: An International Journal*, *5*, 21–30.

LePine, J. A., Piccolo, R. F., Jackson, C. L., Mathieu, J. E., & Saul, J. R. (2008). A meta-analysis of teamwork processes: Tests of a multidimensional model and relationships with team effectiveness criteria. *Personnel Psychology*, *61*, 273–307.

Lepper, M. R., & Greene, D. (1975). Turning play into work: Effects of adult surveillance and extrinsic rewards on children's intrinsic motivation. *Journal of Personality and Social Psychology*, *31*, 479–486.

Lerner, R. M. (1995). The place of learning within the human development system: A developmental contextual perspective. *Human Development*, *38*, 361–366.

Lerner, R. M. (2000). Developing civil society through the promotion of positive youth development. *Developmental and Behavioural Pediatrics, 21*, 48–49.

Lerner, R. M., Fisher, C. B., & Weinberg, R. A. (2000). Toward a science for and of the people: Promoting civil society through the application of developmental science. *Child Development, 71*, 11–20.

Lerner, R. M., Lerner, J. V., Almerigi, J. B., Theokas, C., Phelps, E., Gestdottir, S., & Von Eye, A. (2005). Positive youth development, participation in community youth development programs, and community contributions of fifth grade adolescents: Findings from the first wave of the 4-H Study of Positive Youth Development. *Journal of Early Adolescence, 25*, 17–71.

Levermore, R. (2008). Sport: a new engine of development? *Progress in Development Studies, 8*, 183–190.

Levine, R. M., Prosser, A., Evans, D., & Reicher, S. D. (2005). Identity and emergency intervention: How social group membership and inclusiveness of group boundaries shapes helping behavior. *Personality and Social Psychology Bulletin, 31*, 443–453.

Levine, R. M., & Reicher, S. D. (1996). Making sense of symptoms: Self-categorization and the meaning of illness and injury. *British Journal of Social Psychology, 35*, 245–256.

Levinovitz, A. (2015). *The gluten lie*. New York: Simon & Schuster.

Lewin, K. (1952). Field theory in social science: Selected theoretical papers by Kurt Lewin (D. Cartwright Ed.). London: Tavistock.

Lewis, B. P., & Linder, D. E. (1997). Thinking about choking? Attentional processes and paradoxical performance. *Personality and Social Psychology Bulletin, 23*, 937–944.

Lewis, P. T. (1995). A naturalistic test of two fundamental propositions: Correspondence bias and the actor–observer hypothesis. *Journal of Personality, 63*, 87–111.

Li, L. (2014). The financial burden of physical inactivity. *Journal of Sport and Health Science, 3*, 58–59.

Liu, D. (2017). Women's basketball home-game attendance correlated with success. *The Daily Princetonian* (April 6). Retrieved from: www.dailyprincetonian.com/article/2017/04/womens-basketball-home-game-attendance-correlated-with-success (Accessed November 23, 2019).

Liu, J., Thomas, J. M., & Higgs, S. (2019). The relationship between social identity, descriptive social norms and eating intentions and behaviors. *Journal of Experimental Social Psychology, 82*, 217–230.

Livingstone, A. G., Spears, R., Manstead, A. S. R., Bruder, M., & Shepherd, L. (2011). We feel, therefore we are: Emotion as a basis for self-categorization and social action. *Emotion, 11*, 754–767.

Lock, D., & Heere, B. (2017). Identity crisis: A theoretical analysis of 'team identification' research. *European Sport Management Quarterly, 17*, 413–435.

Locke, E. A., & Latham, G. P. (1990). *A theory of goal setting and task performance*. Englewood Cliffs, NJ: Prentice-Hall.

Loland, S. (2002). *Fair play in sport: A moral norm system*. London: Routledge.

Longman, J. (2019). For Megan Rapinoe, boldness in the spotlight is nothing new. *New York Times* (June 27). Retrieved from: www.nytimes.com/2019/06/27/sports/megan-rapinoe-trump-world-cup.html (Accessed December 5, 2019).

Lonsdale, C., & Hodge, K. (2011). Temporal ordering of motivational quality and athlete burnout in elite sport. *Medicine & Science in Sports & Exercise, 43*, 913–921.

Loughead, T. M. (2017). Athlete leadership: A review of the theoretical, measurement, and empirical literature. *Current Opinion in Psychology, 16*, 58–61.

Loughead, T. M., & Hardy, J. (2006). Team cohesion: From theory to research to team building. In S. Hanton & S. Mellalieu (Eds.), *Literature reviews in sport psychology* (pp. 257–287). Hauppauge, NY: Nova Science Publishers.

Louis, W., Davies, S., Smith, J. R., & Terry, D. (2007). Pizza and pop and the student identity: The role of referent group norms in healthy and unhealthy eating. *Journal of Social Psychology*, *147*, 57–74.

Lovett, S. (2017). Gary Neville lifts the lid on Sir Alex Ferguson's Anfield 'hairdryer' treatment. *The Independent* (October 10). Retrieved from: www.independent.co.uk/sport/football/premier-league/manchester-united-gary-neville-sir-alex-fergusons-anfield-hairdryer-treatment-a7992221.html (Accessed April 20, 2020).

Lowes, M. D. (1999). *Inside the sports pages: Work routines, professional ideologies, and the manufacture of sports news*. Toronto: Toronto University Press.

Lu, F. J. H., Lee, W. P., Chang, Y.-K., Chou, C.-C., Hsu, Y.-W., Lin, J.-H., & Gill, D. L. (2016). Interaction of athletes' resilience and coaches' social support on the stress-burnout relationship: A conjunctive moderation perspective. *Psychology of Sport & Exercise*, *22*, 202–209.

Luce, B. R., Mauskopf, J., Sloan, F. A., Ostermann, J., & Paramore, L. C. (2006). The return on investment in health care: From 1980 to 2000. *Value in Health*, *9*, 146–156.

Luckhurst, S. (2012). Everton display Liverpool city solidarity with Hillsborough tribute. *Huffington Post* (September 18). Retrieved from: www.huffingtonpost.co.uk/2012/09/18/everton-display-liverpool-city-solidarity-hillsborough_n_1892438.html (Accessed September 21, 2019).

Luthar, S. S., Cicchetti, D., & Becker, B. (2000). The construct of resilience: A critical evaluation and guidelines for future work. *Child Development*, *71*, 543–562.

Lynch, F. L., Hornbrook, M., Clarke, G. N., Perrin, N., Polen, M. R., O'Connor, E., & Dickerson, J. (2005). Cost-effectiveness of an intervention to prevent depression in at-risk teens. *Archives of General Psychiatry*, *62*, 1241–1248.

Lynch, P. (2018). Gary Neville explains why Ferguson hated letting United stars play for England. Retrieved from: https://extra.ie/2018/03/08/sport/soccernews/gary-neville-ferguson (Accessed July 29, 2019).

MacArthur, P. J., Angelini, J. R., Billings, A. C., & Smith, L. R. (2017). The thin line between masculinity and skate: Primetime narratives of male figure skaters on the CBC and NBC 2014 Winter Olympic broadcasts. *Sociology of Sport Journal*, *34*, 46–58.

MacDonald, D. J., Côté, J., Eys, M. A., & Deakin, J. (2012). Psychometric properties of the youth experience survey with young athletes. *Psychology of Sport and Exercise*, *13*, 332–340.

Mackie, D. M., Devos, T., & Smith, E. R. (2000). Intergroup emotions: Explaining offensive action tendencies in an intergroup context. *Journal of Personality and Social Psychology*, *79*, 602–616.

Mackie, D. M., & Smith, E. R. (2017). Group-based emotion in group processes and intergroup relations. *Group Processes & Intergroup Relations*, *20*, 658–668.

Maddison, R., Hargreaves, E. A., Wyke, S., Gray, C. M., Hunt, K., Heke, J. I., … Marsh, S. (2019). Rugby Fans in Training New Zealand (RUFIT-NZ): A pilot randomized controlled trial of a healthy lifestyle program for overweight men delivered through professional rugby clubs in New Zealand. *BMC Public Health*, *19*, 1–14.

Madrigal, R., & Chen, J. (2008). Moderating and mediating effects of team identification in regard to causal attributions and summary judgements following a game outcome. *Journal of Sport Management*, *22*, 717–733.

Maehr, M. L., & Braskamp, L. A. (1986). *The motivation factor: A theory of personal investment*. Washington, DC: Lexington Books/DC Heath.

Magdalinski, T. (2000). The reinvention of Australia for the Sydney 2000 Olympic Games. *International Journal of the History of Sport*, *17*, 305–322.

Mageau, G. A., & Vallerand, R. J. (2003). The coach–athlete relationship: A motivational model. *Journal of Sports Science*, *21*, 883–904.

Magrath, R. (2018). 'To try and gain an advantage for my team': Homophobic and homosexually themed chanting among English football fans. *Sociology*, *52*, 709–726.

Maher, J. P., Gottschall, J. S., & Conroy, D. E. (2015). Perceptions of the activity, the social climate, and the self during group exercise classes regulate intrinsic satisfaction. *Frontiers in Psychology*, *6*, 1–10.

Maier, S. F., & Seligman, M. E. P. (1976). Learned helplessness: Theory and evidence. *Journal of Experimental Psychology: General*, *105*, 3–46.

The Mail & Guardian (2018). Aussies spare us the moral outrage (March 30). Retrieved from: www.pressreader.com/south-africa/mail-guardian/20180406/281814284431554 (Accessed July 31, 2019).

Malekian, S. (2019). Women attend soccer match in Iran after decades of being kept out. *ABC News* (October 12). Retrieved from: https://abcnews.go.com/International/women-attend-soc-cer-match-iran-decades/story?id=66217498 (Accessed December 5, 2019).

Malle, B. F. (1999). How people explain behavior: A new theoretical framework. *Personality and Social Psychology Review*, *3*, 21–43.

Malle, B. F. (2004). *How the mind explains behavior: Folk explanations, meaning, and social interaction.* Cambridge, MA: MIT Press.

Malle, B. F., Knobe, J. M., & Nelson, S. E. (2007). Actor–observer asymmetries in explanations of behavior: New answers to an old question. *Journal of Personality and Social Psychology*, *93*, 491–514.

Mallett, C. J., & Hanrahan, S. J. (2004). Elite athletes: Why does the 'fire' burn so brightly? *Psychology of Sport and Exercise*, *5*, 183–200.

Mallett, C. J., Rossi, T., & Tinning, R. (2007). *Coaching knowledge, learning and mentoring in the Australian Football League.* Melbourne: Australian Football League.

Mandela, N. (1994). *Long walk to freedom.* London: Abacus.

Mandela, N. (2000). Speech at the Inaugural Laureus Lifetime Achievement Award, Monaco. Retrieved from: https:// db.nelsonmandela.org/speeches/pub_view.asp?pg=item&ItemID= NMS1148 (Accessed December 5, 2019).

Mandell, R. D. (2000). *The Nazi Olympics.* London: Souvenir Press.

Mandolesi, L., Polverino, A., Montuori, S., Foti, F., Ferraioli, G., Sorrentino, P., & Sorrentino, G. (2018). Effects of physical exercise on cognitive functioning and wellbeing: Biological and psychological benefits. *Frontiers in Psychology*, *9*, 509.

Mangan, J. A. (2013). *The games ethic and imperialism: Aspects of the diffusion of an ideal.* London: Routledge.

Mansoor, S. (2019). FIFA says women 'have to be allowed' into Iran's soccer stadium. *Time Magazine* (September 22).

Marcia, J. E. (1966). Development and validation of ego-identity status. *Journal of Personality and Social Psychology*, *3*, 551–558.

Marcia, J. E. (1980). *Identity in adolescence.* In J. Adelson (Ed.), *Handbook of adolescent psychology.* New York: Wiley.

Marcia, J. E., Waterman, A. S., Matteson, D. R., Archer, S. L., & Orlofsky, J. L. (1993). *Ego identity: A handbook for psychosocial research.* New York: Springer.

Markovits, A. S., Shipan, R., & Victor, J. (2017). Envy and scorn as primary markers of the pervasive antipathy in college football's rivalry games: The University of Michigan as a representative microcosm. *Sport in Society*, *20*, 1324–1344.

Markus, H. (1978). The effect of mere presence on social facilitation: An unobtrusive test. *Journal of Experimental Social Psychology*, *14*, 389–397.

Marmot, M. (2005). Social determinants of health inequalities. *The Lancet*, *365*, 1099–1104.

Marqusee, M. (1999). *Redemption song: Muhammad Ali and the spirit of the sixties.* London: Verso.

Marsh, P. E. (1977). Football hooliganism: Fact or fiction? *British Journal of Law and Society*, *4*, 256–259.

Marsh, P. E., Rosser, E., & Harré, R. (1978). *The rules of disorder.* London: Routledge.

Marshall, S. J., & Biddle, S. J. H. (2001). The transtheoretical model of behavior change: A meta-analysis of applications to physical activity and exercise. *Annals of Behavioral Medicine*, *23*, 229–246.

Martin, A. (2018). Devastated Steve Smith breaks down during apology for ball tampering scandal. *The Guardian* (March 29). Retrieved from: www.theguardian.com/sport/2018/mar/29/a-stain-on-the-game-david-warner-apologises-for-ball-tampering-scandal (Accessed December 1, 2019).

Martin, E. M., & Horn, T. S. (2013). The role of athletic identity and passion in predicting burnout in adolescent female athletes. *The Sport Psychologist*, *27*, 338–348.

Martin, J. J., Oliver, K., & McCaughtry, N. (2007). The theory of planned behavior: Predicting physical activity in Mexican American children. *Journal of Sport and Exercise Psychology*, *29*, 225–238.

Martin, L. J., Balderson, D., Hawkins, M., Wilson, K. S., & Bruner, M. W. (2017a). Social identity in youth sport: Predictability of individual and team outcomes. *Journal of Sports Sciences*, *36*, 326–332.

Martin, L. J., Balderson, D., Hawkins, M., Wilson, K. S., & Bruner, M. W. (2017b). Groupness and leadership perceptions in relation to social identity in youth sport. *Journal of Applied Sport Psychology*, *29*, 367–374.

Martin, L. J., Balderson, D., Hawkins, M., Wilson, K. S., & Bruner, M. W. (2018). The influence of social identity on self-worth, commitment, and effort in school-based youth sport. *Journal of Sports Sciences*, *36*, 326–332.

Martin, L. J., Carron, A. V., & Burke, S. M. (2009). Team-building inteventions in sport: A meta-analysis. *Sport & Exercise Psychology Review*, *5*, 3–18.

Martin, L. J., Evans, M. B., & Spink, K. S. (2016). Coach perspectives of 'groups within the group': An analysis of subgroups and cliques in sport. *Sport, Exercise, and Performance Psychology*, *5*(1), 52–66.

Martin, R., & Davids, K. (1995). The effects of group development techniques on a professional athletic team. *Journal of Social Psychology*, *135*, 533–535.

Maskor, M. (2019). It's not about him: Leading lessons from Manchester United's caretaker manager. *The Conversation* (March 7). Retrieved from: https://theconversation.com/its-not-about-him-leading-lessons-from-manchester-uniteds-caretaker-manager-112281 (Accessed November 23, 2019).

Masters, R. S. W. (1992). Knowledge, knerves and know-how: The role of explicit versus implicit knowledge in the breakdown of a complex motor skill under pressure. *British Journal of Psychology*, *83*, 343–358.

Mathieu, J. M., Maynard, T., Rapp, T., & Gilson, L. (2008). Team effectiveness 1997–2007: A review of recent advancements and a glimpse into the future. *Journal of Management*, *34*, 410–476.

Matosic, D., Ntoumanis, N., Boardley, I. D., Sedikides, C., Stewart, B. D., & Chatzisarantis, N. L. D. (2017). Narcissism and coach interpersonal style: A self-determination theory perspective. *Scandinavian Journal of Medicine & Science in Sports*, *27*, 254–261.

Matthews, K. L., & Smith, J. G. (1996). Effectiveness of modified complex physical therapy for lymphoedema treatment. *Australian Journal of Physiotherapy*, *42*, 323–328.

Matthews, M. (2018). Michael Phelps opens up about his struggles with depression and thoughts of suicide. Retrieved from: www.menshealth.com/health/a24268441/michael-phelps-depression/ (Accessed October 21, 2019).

Matute, H. (1996). Illusion of control: Detecting response–outcome independence in analytic but not in naturalistic conditions. *Psychological Science*, *7*, 289–293.

May, J. R., Veach, T. L., Reed, M. W., & Griffey, M. S. (1985). A psychological study of health, injury, and performance in athletes on the US Alpine Ski Team. *Physician and Sports Medicine*, *13*, 111–115.

McCain, K. (2016). 'Nothing as practical as a good theory': Does Lewin's Maxim still have salience in applied social sciences? *Proceedings of the Association for Information Science and Technology, 52*, 1–4.

McCarthy, N. (2007). Enacting Irish identity in Western Australia: Performances from the dressing room. *Sport in Society, 10*, 368–384.

McCarthy, P. J., Allen, M. S., & Jones, M. V. (2013). Emotions, cognitive interference, and concentration disruption in youth sport. *Journal of Sports Sciences, 31*, 505–515.

McConnon, A., & McConnon, A. (2012). *Road to valour: Gino Bartali – Tour de France legend and World War Two hero*. London: Hachette UK.

McCormick, A., & Hatzigeorgiadis, A. (2019). Self-talk and endurance performance. In C. Meijen (Ed.), *Endurance performance in sport: Psychological theory and interventions* (pp. 153–176). London: Routledge.

McDonald, H., Leckie, C., Karg, A., Zubcevic-Basic, N., & Lock, D. (2016). Segmenting initial fans of a new team: A taxonomy of sport early adopters. *Journal of Consumer Behaviour, 15*, 136–148.

McDonnell, D. (2014). Nicky Butt reveals Sir Alex Ferguson used to stop him going on England duty. *Daily Mirror* (September 10). Retrieved from: www.mirror.co.uk/sport/football/news/nicky-butt-reveals-sir-alex-4196933 (Accessed July 29, 2019).

McEvoy, P. M., Watson, H., Watkins, E. R., & Nathan, P. (2013). The relationship between worry, rumination, and comorbidity: Evidence for repetitive negative thinking as a transdiagnostic construct. *Journal of Affective Disorders, 151*, 313–320.

McEwan, D. (2020). The effects of perceived teamwork on emergent states and satisfaction with performance among team sport athletes. *Sport, Exercise, and Performance Psychology, 9*, 1–15.

McEwan, D., & Beauchamp, M. R. (2014). Teamwork in sport: A theoretical and integrative review. *International Review of Sport and Exercise Psychology, 7*, 229–250.

McEwan, D., & Beauchamp, M. R. (2020). Teamwork training in sport: A pilot intervention study. *Journal of Applied Sport Psychology, 32*, 220–236.

McEwan, D., Zumbo, B. D., Eys, M. A., & Beauchamp, M. R. (2018). The development and psychometric properties of the Multidimensional Assessment of Teamwork in Sport (MATS). *Journal of Sport and Exercise Psychology, 40*, 60–72.

McGarty, C. (1999). *Categorization and social psychology*. London: Sage.

McGarty, C., Turner, J. C., Oakes, P. J., & Haslam, S. A. (1993). The creation of uncertainty in the influence process: The roles of stimulus information and disagreement with similar others. *European Journal of Social Psychology, 23*, 17–38.

McGinn, B. (2018). Heavy-hearted Brett Favre picks apart Raiders. *Milwaukee Journal Sentinel* (August 24). Retrieved from: www.packersnews.com/story/sports/nfl/packers/2018/08/24/dec-22-2003-heavy-hearted-brett-favre-picks-apart-oakland-raiders/943849002/ (Accessed December 18, 2019).

McKenzie, D. C. (1998). Abreast in a Boat: A race against breast cancer. *Canadian Medical Association Journal, 159*, 376–378.

McMillan, B., Bentley, S. V., Haslam, S. A., Steffens, N. K., Peters, K. O., Hunter, J. A., & Modderman, T. (2019). *Report on the effectiveness of 5R as a program for enhancing workplace identity and health*. Brisbane: Workplace Health and Safety Queensland.

McNamara, L. (2000). Tackling racial hatred: Conciliation, reconciliation and football. *Australian Journal of Human Rights, 6*, 5–31.

McNeely, M. L., Campbell, K. L., Courneya, K. S., & Mackey, J. R. (2009). Effect of acute exercise on upper-limb volume in breast cancer survivors: A pilot study. *Physiotherapy Canada/Physiotherapie Canada, 61*, 244–251.

McPherson, G., O'Donnell, H., McGillivray, D., & Misener, L. (2016). Elite athletes or superstars? Media representation of para-athletes at the Glasgow 2014 Commonwealth Games. *Disability & Society*, *31*, 659–675.

Medvec, V. H., Madey, S. F., & Gilovich, T. (1995). When less is more: Counterfactual thinking and satisfaction among Olympic medalists. *Journal of Personality and Social Psychology*, *69*, 603–610.

Meeus, W. (2011). The study of adolescent identity formation 2000–2010: A review of longitudinal research. *Journal of Research on Adolescence*, *21*, 75–94.

Mellalieu, S. D., Neil, R., Hanton, S., & Fletcher, D. (2009). Competition stress in sport performers: Stressors explained in the competition environment. *Journal of Sports Sciences*, *27*, 729–744.

Mertens, N., Boen, F., Steffens, N. K., Cotterill, S. T., Haslam, S. A., & Fransen, K. (2020). Leading together towards a stronger 'us': An experimental test of the effectiveness of the 5RS Shared Leadership Program in basketball teams. *Journal of Science and Medicine in Sport*, *23*, 770–775.

Mertens, N., Boen, F., Vande Broek, G., Vansteenkiste, M., & Fransen, K. (2018). An experiment on the impact of coaches' and athlete leaders' competence support on athletes' motivation and performance. *Scandinavian Journal of Medicine & Science in Sports*, *12*, 2734–2750.

Mikalachki, A. (1969). *Group cohesion reconsidered*. London, Canada: School of Business Administration, University of Western Ontario.

Mikulincer, M., & Shaver, P. R. (2007). *Attachment in adulthood: Structure, dynamics and change*. New York: Guilford Press.

Milekic, M. (1996). 1990 Football riot becomes national myth in Croatia. *Balkan Transitional Justice* (May 13). Retrieved from: https://balkaninsight.com/2016/05/13/1990-football-riot-remains-croatia-s-national-myth-05-12-2016/ (Accessed December 5, 2019).

Miller, G. (2005). Finley seeks power from the 'pouch'. *EPSN* (May 27). Retrieved from: www.espn.com/mlb/columns/story?columnist=miller_gary&id=2069936 (Accessed November 3, 2019).

Mistry, C. D., Sweet, S. N., Latimer-Cheung, A. E., & Rhodes, R. E. (2015). Predicting changes in planning behaviour and physical activity among adults. *Psychology of Sport & Exercise*, *17*, 1–6.

Mitchell, C. A., Clark, A. F., & Gilliland, J. A. (2016). Built environment influences of children's physical activity: Examining differences by neighbourhood size and sex. *International Journal of Environmental Research and Public Health*, *13*(1), E130.

Mitchell, D. E. (2016). Causes of organizational conflict. In A. Farazmand (Ed.), *Global encyclopedia of public administration, public policy, and governance* (pp. 1–5). Basel, Switzerland: Springer.

Mitchell, I., Evans, L., Rees, T., & Hardy, L. (2014). Stressors, social support and the buffering hypothesis: Effects on psychological responses of injured athletes. *British Journal of Health Psychology*, *19*, 486–508.

Moesch, K., Kenttä, G., Kleinert, J., Quignon-Fleuret, C., Cecil, S., & Bertollo, M. (2018). FEPSAC position statement: Mental health disorders in elite athletes and models of service provision. *Psychology of Sport & Exercise*, *38*, 61–71.

Monaci, M. G., & Veronesi, F. (2019). Getting angry when playing tennis: Gender differences and impact on performance. *Journal of Clinical Sport Psychology*, *13*, 116–133.

Monaghan, L., Bloor, M., Dobash, R. P., & Dobash, R. E. (2000). Drug-taking, 'risk boundaries' and social identity: Bodybuilders' talk about Ephedrine and Nubain. *Sociological Research Online*, *5*, 1–12.

Montano, D., Reeske, A., Franke, F., & Hüffmeier, J. (2017). Leadership, followers' mental health and job performance in organizations: A comprehensive meta-analysis from an occupational health perspective. *Journal of Organizational Behavior*, *38*, 327–350.

Montez de Oca, J., & Suh, S. C. (2020). Ethics of patriotism: NFL players' protests against police violence. *International Review for the Sociology of Sport, 55,* 563–587.

Moore, L. L., Lombardi, D. A., White, M. J., Campbell, J. L., Oliveria, S. A., & Ellison, R. C. (1991). Influence of parents' physical activity levels on activity levels of young children. *Journal of Pediatrics, 118,* 215–219.

Moore, S. C., Shepherd, J. P., Eden, S., & Sivarajasingam, V. (2007). The effect of rugby match outcome on spectator aggression and intention to drink alcohol. *Criminal Behaviour and Mental Health, 17,* 118–127.

Moreland, J. J., Coxe, K. A., & Yang, J. (2018). Collegiate athletes' mental health services utilization: A systematic review of conceptualizations, operationalizations, facilitators, and barriers. *Journal of Sport and Health Science, 7,* 58–69.

Morgan, C., & Hutchinson, G. (2010). The social determinants of psychosis in migrant and ethnic minority populations: A public health tragedy. *Psychological Medicine, 40,* 705–709.

Morgan, P. B. C., Fletcher, D., & Sarkar, M. (2015). Understanding team resilience in the world's best athletes: A case study of a rugby union World Cup winning team. *Psychology of Sport & Exercise, 16,* 91–100.

Moritz, S. E., Feltz, D. L., Fahrbach, K. R., & Mack, D. E. (2000). The relation of self-efficacy measures to sport performance: A meta-analytic review. *Research Quarterly for Exercise and Sport, 71,* 280–294.

Morris, R. (2013). Investigating the youth-to-senior transition in sport: From theory to practice. Doctoral thesis, Aberystwyth University, Aberystwyth, UK. Retrieved from: https://cadair.aber.ac.uk. (Accessed September 22, 2018).

Mouchet, A., Harvey, S., & Light, R. (2014). A study on in-match rugby coaches' communications with players: A holistic approach. *Physical Education and Sport Pedagogy, 19,* 320–336.

Muldoon, O. T., Haslam, C., Haslam, S. A., Cruwys, T., Kearns, M., & Jetten, J. (2020). The social psychology of responses to trauma: Social identity pathways associated with divergent traumatic responses. *European Review of Social Psychology, 30,* 311–348.

Mullan, B., Allom, V., Brogan, A., Kothe, E., & Todd, J. (2014). Self-regulation and the intention behaviour gap: Exploring dietary behaviours in university students. *Appetite, 73,* 7–14.

Murray, N., & Janelle, C. (2003). Anxiety and performance: A visual search examination of the Processing Efficiency Theory. *Journal of Sport & Exercise Psychology, 25,* 171–187.

Murray, R. M., Coffee, P., Arthur, C. A., & Eklund, R. C. (2020). Social identity moderates the effects of team-referent attributions on collective efficacy but not emotions. *Sport, Exercise, and Performance Psychology.* doi: 10.1037/spy0000178

Murray, R. M., Coffee, P., Eklund, R. C., & Arthur, C. A. (2019). Attributional consensus: The importance of agreement over causes for team performance to interpersonal outcomes and performance. *Psychology of Sport and Exercise, 43,* 219–225.

Murrell, A. J., & Gaertner, S. L. (1992). Cohesion and sport team effectiveness: The benefit of a common group identity. *Journal of Sport & Social Issues, 16,* 1–14.

Myers, N. D., Feltz, D. L., & Short, S. E. (2004). Collective efficacy and team performance: A longitudinal study of collegiate football teams. *Group Dynamics: Theory, Research, and Practice, 8,* 126–138.

Nadler, A. (2002). Inter-group helping relations as power relations: Maintaining or challenging social dominance between groups through helping. *Journal of Social Issues, 58,* 487–502.

Nadler, A., & Halabi, S. (2006). Intergroup helping as status relations: Effects of status stability, identification, and type of help on receptivity to high-status group's help. *Journal of Personality and Social Psychology, 91,* 97–110.

Nadler, A., & Jeffrey, D. (1986). The role of threat to self-esteem and perceived control in recipient reaction to help: Theory development and empirical validation. *Advances in Experimental Social Psychology, 19,* 81–122.

Nauright, J., & Schimmel, K. S. (2005). *The political economy of sport*. Basingstoke: Palgrave Macmillan.

Neel, R., Kenrick, D. T., White, A. E., & Neuberg, S. L. (2016). Individual differences in fundamental social motives. *Journal of Personality and Social Psychology, 110*, 887–907.

Neighbors, C., LaBrie, J. W., Hummer, J. F., Lewis, M. A., Lee, C. M., Desai, S., … Larimer, M. E. (2010). Group identification as a moderator of the relationship between perceived social norms and alcohol consumption. *Psychology of Addictive Behaviors, 24*, 522–528.

Neil, R., Bayston, P., Hanton, S., & Wilson, K. (2013). The influence of stress and emotions on association football referees' decision-making. *Sport & Exercise Psychology Review, 9*, 22–41.

Nesti, M., Littlewood, M., O'Halloran, L. M., Eubank, M., & Richardson, D. (2012). Critical moments in elite Premiership football: Who do you think you are? *Physical Culture and Sport: Studies and Research, 56*, 23–32.

Nesti, M., & Sulley, C. (2015). *Youth development in football: Lessons from the world's best academies*. London: Routledge.

Nevill, A. M., & Holder, R. L. (1999). Home advantage in sport. *Sports Medicine, 28*, 221–236.

Neville, F. G., Fransen, K., Giammei, G., Haslam, S. A., Hunter, J. A., Mavor, K., Platow, M., Reicher, S. D., Reynolds, K., Riordan, B., & Scarf, D. (2019). The day after you win the World Cup: The transformative power of international sporting success for social cohesion, intragroup interactions and health. Second International Conference on Social Identity and Sport (ICSIS), Stirling, Scotland, June 28–30.

Neville, F. G., & Reicher, S. D. (2011). The experience of collective participation: Shared identity, relatedness and emotionality. *Contemporary Social Science, 6*, 377–396.

Neville, J. (2019). Dressed to play: An analysis of gender relations in college women's ultimate Frisbee. *International Review for the Sociology of Sport, 54*, 38–62.

Neys, J. L. D., Jansz, J., & Tan, E. S. H. (2014). Exploring persistence in gaming: The role of self-determination and social identity. *Computers in Human Behavior, 37*, 196–209.

Ng, J. Y. Y., Ntoumanis, N., Thogersen-Ntoumani, C., Deci, E. L., Ryan, R. M., Duda, J. L., & Williams, G. C. (2012). Self-determination theory applied to health contexts: A meta-analysis. *Perspectives on Psychological Science, 7*, 325–340.

Nicholls, A. R., Hemmings, B., & Clough, P. J. (2010). Stress appraisals, emotions, and coping among international adolescent golfers. *Scandinavian Journal of Medicine & Science in Sports, 20*, 346–355.

Nicholls, J. G. (1989). *The competitive ethos and democratic education*. Cambridge, MA: Harvard University Press.

Nicholson, M., Hoye, R., & Gallant, D. (2011). The provision of social support for elite indigenous athletes in Australian football. *Journal of Sport Management, 25*, 131–142.

Nicolaides, V. C., LaPort, K. A., Chen, T. R., Tomassetti, A. J., Weis, E. J., Zaccaro, S. J., & Cortina, J. M. (2014). The shared leadership of teams: A meta-analysis of proximal, distal, and moderating relationships. *The Leadership Quarterly, 25*, 923–942.

Noblet, A. J., & Gifford, S. M. (2002). The sources of stress experienced by professional Australian footballers. *Journal of Applied Sport Psychology, 14*, 1–13.

Nolen-Hoeksema, S., & Morrow, J. (1991). A prospective study of depression and posttraumatic stress symptoms after a natural disaster: The 1989 Loma Prieta earthquake. *Journal of Personality and Social Psychology, 61*, 115–121.

Novelli, D., Drury, J., Reicher, S. D., & Stott. C. (2013) Crowdedness mediates the effect of social identification on positive emotion in a crowd: A survey of two crowd events. *PLoS ONE, 8*(11): e78983.

Ntoumanis, N., & Mallett, C. J. (2014). Motivation in sport. In A. G. H. D. Papaioannou (Ed.), *Routledge companion to sport and exercise psychology* (pp. 67–82). London: Taylor & Francis.

Ntoumanis, N., Taylor, I. M., & Thøgersen-Ntoumani, C. (2012). A longitudinal examination of coach and peer motivational climates in youth sport: Implications for moral attitudes, well-being, and behavioral investment. *Developmental Psychology*, *48*, 213–223.

Ntoumanis, N., Thøgersen-Ntoumani, C., Quested, E., & Hancox, J. E. (2016). The effects of training group exercise class instructors to adopt a motivationally adaptive communication style. *Scandinavian Journal of Medicine & Science in Sports*, *27*, 1026–1034.

Numerato, D. (2018). *Football fans, activism and social change*. London: Routledge.

O'Connell, M. E., Boat, T. F., & Warner, K. E. (2009). *Preventing mental, emotional, and behavioral disorders among young people: Progress and possibilities*. Washington, DC: National Academies Press.

O'Halloran, K. (2017). Channel Nine cricket commentary team's lack of diversity is out of touch. *The Guardian* (November 22). Retrieved from: www.theguardian.com/sport/2017/nov/21/channel-nine-cricket-commentary-teams-lack-of-diversity-is-out-of-touch (Accessed July 31, 2019).

O'Halloran, L. M. (2019). The lived experience of 'critical moments' in Premier League Academy football: A descriptive phenomenological exploration. PhD thesis, Liverpool John Moores University.

Oakes, P. J., Haslam, S. A., & Turner, J. C. (1994). *Stereotyping and social reality*. Oxford: Blackwell.

Oakes, P. J., Turner, J. C., & Haslam, S. A. (1991). Perceiving people as group members: The role of fit in the salience of social categorizations. *British Journal of Social Psychology*, *30*, 125–144.

Ogden, J. (2003). Some problems with social cognition models: A pragmatic and conceptual analysis. *Health Psychology*, *22*, 424–428.

Ogden, J. (2015). Time to retire the theory of planned behaviour? One of us will have to go! A commentary on Sniehotta, Presseau and Araújo-Soares. *Health Psychology Review*, *9*, 165–167.

Ogden, M. (2019). The Championship playoff final: Get ready for the richest game in sports. *ESPN*. Retrieved from: www.espn.com.au/football/english-league-championship/0/blog/post/3860320/the-championship-playoff-final-get-ready-for-the-richest-game-in-sports (Accessed October 21, 2019).

Ojala, K., & Nesdale, D. (2004). Bullying and social identity: The effects of group norms and distinctiveness threat on attitudes towards bullying. *British Journal of Developmental Psychology*, *22*, 19–35.

Olarte, S. W. (2003). Personal-disclosure revisited. *Journal of the American Academy of Psychoanalysis & Dynamic Psychiatry*, *31*, 599–607.

Oliver, D. (2017). David Oliver: When 'resilience' becomes a dirty word. *British Medical Journal*, *358*, j3604.

Onorato, R. S., & Turner, J. C. (2004). Fluidity in the self-concept: The shift from personal to social identity. *European Journal of Social Psychology*, *34*, 257–278.

Orbach, I., Singer, R. N., & Murphey, M. (1997). Changing attributions with an attribution training technique related to basketball dribbling. *The Sport Psychologist*, *11*, 294–304.

Orbach, I., Singer, R. N., & Price, S. (1999). An attribution training program and achievement in sport. *The Sport Psychologist*, *13*, 69–82.

Orchard, S. (2017a). Hockey star Simon Orchard opens up about life after elite sport. *Perth News* (August 8). Retrieved from: www.perthnow.com.au/news/wa/hockey-star-simon-orchard-opens-up-about-life-after-elite-sport-ng-05384e8166f3aa3cc3522c67eb5ca179 (Accessed September 11, 2019).

Orchard, S. (2017b). Transitioning from elite sport to the 'real world' can take its toll on mental health. *The Guardian* (August 11). Retrieved from: www.theguardian.com/sport/2017/aug/17/transitioning-from-elite-sport-to-the-real-world-can-take-its-toll-on-mental-health (Accessed September 11, 2019).

Orlick, T. (1990). *In pursuit of excellence* (2nd ed.). Champaign, IL: Human Kinetics.

Orwell, G. (1945). The sporting spirit. *Tribune*, *468*(14), 10–11.

Osborn, K. A., Irwin, B. C., Skogsberg, N. J., and Feltz, D. L. (2012). The Köhler effect: Motivation gains and losses in real sports groups. *Sport, Exercise, and Performance Psychology*, *1*, 242–253.

Ostroff, C., Kinicki, A. J., & Tamkins, M. M. (2003). Organizational culture and climate. *Handbook of Psychology*, *12*, 565–593.

Owen, N., Cerin, E., Leslie, E., duToit, L., Coffee, N., Frank, L. D., … Sallis, J. F. (2007). Neighborhood walkability and the walking behavior of Australian adults. *American Journal of Preventive Medicine*, *33*, 387–395.

Oyserman, D., Fryberg, S. A., & Yoder, N. (2007). Identity-based motivation and health. *Journal of Personality and Social Psychology*, *93*, 1011–1027.

Packer, D. J. (2008). On being both with us and against us: A normative conflict model of dissent in social groups. *Personality and Social Psychology Review*, *12*, 50–72.

Packer, D. J. (2014). On not airing our dirty laundry: Intergroup contexts suppress ingroup criticism among strongly identified group members. *British Journal of Social Psychology*, *53*, 93–111.

Padgett, V. R., & Hill, A. K. (1989). Maximizing athletic performance in endurance events: A comparison of cognitive strategies. *Journal of Applied Social Psychology*, *19*, 331–340.

Pain, M., & Harwood, C. G. (2009). Team-building through mutual-sharing and open discussion of team functioning. *The Sport Psychologist*, *23*, 523–542.

Palmateer, T., & Tamminen, K. A. (2018). A case study of interpersonal emotion regulation within a varsity volleyball team. *Journal of Applied Sport Psychology*, *30*, 321–340.

Palmer, B. (2013). Lions 2013: How does a British & Irish Lions squad bond together? *BBC Sport* (May 13). Retrieved from: www.bbc.com/sport/rugby-union/22500959 (Accessed December 12, 2019).

Pangle, L. S. (2002). *Aristotle and the philosophy of friendship*. Cambridge: Cambridge University Press.

Panorama (1977). *This is Millwall*. Retrieved from: www.youtube.com/watch?v=wko197t1zEc (Accessed September 12, 2019).

Paradis, K. F., Carron, A. V., & Martin, L. J. (2014). Athlete perceptions of intra-group conflict in sport teams. *Sport and Exercise Psychology Review*, *10*, 4–18.

Parganas, P., Papadimitriou, D., Anagnostopoulos, C., & Theodoropoulos, A. (2017). Linking sport team sponsorship to perceived switching cost and switching intentions. *European Sport Management Quarterly*, *17*, 457–484.

Park, S., Lavallee, D., & Tod, D. (2013). Athletes' career transition out of sport: A systematic review. *International Review of Sport and Exercise Psychology*, *6*, 22–53.

Parker, A. (1996). Chasing the big-time: Football apprenticeship in the 1990s. Unpublished doctoral dissertation, University of Warwick, Coventry, UK.

Parker, A. (2000). Training for 'glory', schooling for 'failure'? English professional football, traineeship and educational provision. *Journal of Education and Work*, *13*, 61–76.

Parker, P. C., Perry, R. P., Hamm, J. M., Chipperfield, J. G., & Hladkyj, S. (2016). Enhancing the academic success of competitive student athletes using a motivation treatment intervention (attributional retraining). *Psychology of Sport and Exercise*, *26*, 113–122.

Parker, P. C., Perry, R. P., Hamm, J. M., Chipperfield, J. G., Hladkyj, S., & Leboe-McGowan, L. (2018). Attribution-based motivation treatment efficacy in high-stress student athletes: A moderated-mediation analysis of cognitive, affective, and achievement processes. *Psychology of Sport and Exercise*, *35*, 189–197.

Parks, T. (2008). *Football passions*. Retrieved from: www.sirc.org/football/football_passions.pdf (Accessed December 5, 2019).

Parra-Medina, D., & Messias, D. K. H. (2011). Promotion of physical activity among Mexican-origin women in Texas and South Carolina: An examination of social, cultural, economic, and environmental factors. *Quest*, *63*, 100–117.

Parry, K. D., Cleland, J., & Kavanagh, E. (2019). Racial folklore, black masculinities and the reproduction of dominant racial ideologies: The case of Israel Folau. *International Review for the Sociology of Sport*. doi: 10.1177/1012690219860355

Parsons, T. (1962). The school class as a social system. In A. H. Halsey, J. Floud, & A. C. Anderson (Eds.), *Education, economy and society*. New York: Free Press.

Pascal, B. (1958). *Pensées*. New York: E. P. Dutton & Co.

Pate, R. R., Ward, D. S., Saunders, R. P., Felton, G., Dishman, R. K., & Dowda, M. (2005). Promotion of physical activity among high-school girls: A randomized controlled trial. *American Journal of Public Health*, *95*, 1582–1587.

Pavey, L., Greitemeyer, T., & Sparks, P. (2011). Highlighting relatedness promotes prosocial motives and behavior. *Personality and Social Psychology Bulletin*, *37*, 905–917.

Pearce, C. L., & Conger, J. A. (2003). *Shared leadership: Reframing the hows and whys of leadership*. Thousand Oaks, CA: Sage.

Pearson, G. (2015). Ethnography and the study of football fan cultures. Foreword to A. Schwell, N. Szongs, M. Kowalska, & M. Buchowski (Eds.), *New ethnographies of football in Europe: People, passions, politics* (pp. vii–vv). London: Palgrave Macmillan.

Pedersen, B. K., & Saltin, B. (2015). Exercise as medicine: Evidence for prescribing exercise as therapy in 26 different chronic diseases. *Scandinavian Journal of Medicine & Science in Sports*, *25*(S3), 1–72.

Pennington, B. (2018). When N.F.L. zebras chat with lions and giants and bears. *The New York Times* (November 2). Retrieved from: www.nytimes.com/2018/11/02/sports/nfl-referees.html (Accessed July 31, 2019).

Pennington, C. R., Heim, D., Levy, A. R., & Larkin, D. T. (2016). Twenty years of stereotype threat research: A review of psychological mediators. *PLoS ONE*, *11*, e0146487.

Pepitone, A. (1981). Lessons from the history of social psychology. *American Psychologist*, *36*, 972–985.

Perkins, C. S. (2019). 'We have material second to none': Coloured sportsmen and masculine competition in the South African press, 1936–1960. In M. Gennaro & S. Aderinto (Eds.), *Sports in African history, politics, and identity formation* (pp. 89–105). London: Routledge.

Perry, R. P., Chipperfield, J. G., Hladkyj, S., Pekrun, R., & Hamm, J. M. (2014). Attribution-based treatment interventions in some achievement settings. In S. Karabenick & T. Urdan (Eds.), *Advances in motivation and achievement* (Vol. 18, pp. 1–35). Bingley, UK: Emerald.

Perry, R. P., & Hamm, J. M. (2017). An attribution perspective on competence and motivation. In A. Elliot, C. Dweck, & D. Yeager (Eds.), *Handbook of competence and motivation: Theory and applications* (2nd ed., pp. 61–84). New York: Guilford Press.

Persson, E., & Petersson, B. (2014). Political mythmaking and the 2014 Winter Olympics in Sochi: Olympism and the Russian great power myth. *East European Politics*, *30*, 192–209.

Peters, K., Haslam, S. A., Ryan, M. K., & Fonseca, M. (2013). Working with subgroup identities to build organizational identification and support for organizational strategy: A test of the ASPIRe model. *Group & Organization Management*, *38*, 128–144.

Peterson, C., & Seligman, M. E. P. (1984). Causal explanations as a risk factor for depression: Theory and evidence. *Psychological Review*, *91*, 347–374.

Petitpas, A. J., Cornelius, A. E., & Van Raalte, J. L. (2007). Youth development through sport: It's all about relationships. In N. L. Holt (Ed.), *Positive youth development through sport* (pp. 61–70). London: Routledge.

Petitpas, A. J., Cornelius, A. E., Van Raalte, J. L., & Jones, T. (2005). A framework for planning youth sport programs that foster psychosocial development. *The Sport Psychologist*, *19*, 63–80.

Petrella, R. J., Gill, D. P., Zou, G., De Cruz, A., Riggin, B., Bartol, C., … Zwarenstein, M. (2017). Hockey Fans in Training: A pilot pragmatic randomized controlled trial. *Medicine & Science in Sports & Exercise*, *49*, 2506–2516.

Phua, J. (2012). Use of social networking sites by sports fans: Implications for the creation and maintenance of social capital. *Journal of Sports Media, 7*, 109–132.

Pidgeon, A. M., Ford, L., & Klaassen, F. (2014). Evaluating the effectiveness of enhancing resilience in human service professionals using a retreat-based Mindfulness with Metta Training Program: A randomised control trial. *Psychology, Health & Medicine, 19*, 355–364.

Pila, E., Stamiris, A., Castonguay, A. L., & Sabiston, C. M. (2014). Body-related envy: A social comparison perspective in sport and exercise. *Journal of Sport and Exercise Psychology, 36*, 93–106.

Pilkington, E. (2014) FIFA facing possible legal fight in 2015 Women's World Cup turf wars. *The Guardian* (August 27). Retrieved from: www.theguardian.com/football/2014/aug/27/fifa-lawsuit-womens-world-cup-2015-astro-turf (Accessed December 5, 2019).

Pinquart, M., & Duberstein, P. R. (2010). Associations of social networks with cancer mortality: A meta-analysis. *Critical Reviews in Oncology/Hematology, 75*, 122e137.

Plasker, R. (2009). *The 100-year lifestyle workout*. Guilford, CT: GPP Life.

Platow, M. J., Durante, M., Williams, N., Garrett, M., Walshe, J., Cincotta, S., Lianos, G., & Barutchu, A. (1999). The contribution of sport fan social identity to the production of prosocial behaviour. *Group Dynamics: Theory, Research, and Practice, 3*, 161–169.

Platow, M. J., Haslam, S. A., Reicher, S. D., Grace, D. M., & Cruwys, T. (2020). Informing clinical practice with the new psychology of leadership. In C. Parks & G. A. Tasca (Eds.), *Group psychology and group psychotherapy: An interdisciplinary handbook*. Washington, DC: American Psychological Association Press.

Platow, M. J., Haslam, S. A., Reicher, S. D., & Steffens, N. K. (2015). There is no leadership if no-one follows: Why leadership is necessarily a group process. *International Coaching Psychology Review, 10*, 20–37.

Platow, M. J., Hunter, J. A., Branscombe, N. R., & Grace, D. M. (2014). Social creativity in Olympic medal counts: Observing the expression of ethnocentric fairness. *Social Justice Research, 27*, 283–304.

Platow, M. J., Hunter, J. A., Haslam, S. A., & Reicher, S. D. (2015). Reflections on Muzafer Sherif's legacy in social identity and self-categorization theories. In A. Dost-Gözkan & D. S. Keith (Eds.), *Norms, groups, conflict, and social change: Rediscovering Muzafer Sherif's psychology* (pp. 275–305). London: Transaction.

Platow, M. J., Nolan, M. A., & Anderson, D. (2003). Intergroup identity management in a context of strong norms of fairness: Responding to in-group favouritism during the Sydney 2000 Olympics. Unpublished manuscript, the Australian National University.

Platow, M. J., & van Knippenberg, D. (2001). A social identity analysis of leadership endorsement: The effects of leader ingroup prototypicality and distributive intergroup fairness. *Personality and Social Psychology Bulletin, 27*, 1508–1519.

Platow, M. J., van Knippenberg, D., Haslam, S. A., van Knippenberg, B., & Spears, R. (2006). A special gift we bestow on you for being representative of us: Considering leadership from a self-categorization perspective. *British Journal of Social Psychology, 45*, 303–320.

Platow, M. J., Voudouris, N. J., Gilford, N., Jamieson, R., Najdovski, L., Papaleo, N., Pollard, C., & Terry, L. (2007). In-group reassurance in a pain setting produces lower levels of physiological arousal: Direct support for a self-categorization analysis of social influence. *European Journal of Social Psychology, 37*, 649–660.

Pollner, M. (1974). Sociological and common-sense models of the labelling process. In R. Turner (Ed.), *Ethnomethodology*. Harmondsworth, UK: Penguin.

Porat, R., Halperin, E., Mannheim, I., & Tamir, M. (2016). Together we cry: Social motives and preferences for group-based sadness. *Cognition & Emotion, 30*, 66–79.

Porat, R., Halperin, E., & Tamir, M. (2016). What we want is what we get: Group-based emotional preferences and conflict resolution. *Journal of Personality and Social Psychology*, *110*, 167–190.

Postmes, T. (2003). A social identity approach to communication in organizations. In S. A. Haslam, V. van Knippenberg, M. J. Platow, & N. Ellemers (Eds.), *Social identity at work: Developing theory for organizational practice* (pp. 191–203). London: Sage.

Postmes, T., & Branscombe, N. R. (Eds.) (2010). *Rediscovering social identity: Core sources*. New York: Psychology Press.

Postmes, T., Haslam, S. A., & Swaab, R. (2005). Social influence in small groups: An interactive model of identity formation. *European Review of Social Psychology*, *16*, 1–42.

Postmes, T., Spears, R., & Cihangir, S. (2001). Quality of decision making and group norms. *Journal of Personality and Social Psychology*, *80*, 918–930.

Praharso, N. F., Tear, M. J., & Cruwys, T. (2016). Stressful life transitions and wellbeing: A comparison of the stress buffering hypothesis and the social identity model of identity change. *Psychiatry Research*, *247*, 265–275.

Prapavessis, H., & Carron, A. V. (1996). The effect of group cohesion on competitive state anxiety. *Journal of Sport and Exercise Psychology*, *18*, 64–74.

Prapavessis, H., & Carron, A. V. (1997). Sacrifice, cohesion, and conformity to norms in sports teams. *Group Dynamics: Theory, Research, and Practice*, *1*, 231–240.

Prapavessis, H., Carron, A. V., & Spink, K. S. (1996). Team building in sport. *International Journal of Sport Psychology*, *27*, 269–285.

Pratt, H. (2018). World Cup 2018: Frank Lampard reveals the secret to success for England in Russia. *Daily Mirror* (June 10). Retrieved from: www.dailystar.co.uk/sport/football/708516/World-Cup-Frank-Lampard-success-England-Russia (Accessed July 17, 2019).

Pratt, M., Norris, J., Lobelo, F., Roux, L., & Wang, G. (2014). The cost of physical inactivity: Moving into the 21st century. *British Journal of Sports Medicine*, *48*, 171–173.

Premier League (2011). *Elite player performance plan*. London: Premier League.

Price, M., & Dayan, D. (Eds.) (2009). *Owning the Olympics: Narratives of the new China*. Ann Arbor, MI: University of Michigan Press.

Price, M. S., & Weiss, M. R. (2013). Relationships among coach leadership, peer leadership, and adolescent athletes' psychosocial and team outcomes: A test of transformational leadership theory. *Journal of Applied Sport Psychology*, *25*, 265–279.

Priebe, C. S., Atkinson, J., & Faulkner, G. (2016). Run to Quit: Program design and evaluation protocol. *Mental Health and Physical Activity*, *11*, 38–45.

Priebe, C. S., Atkinson, J., & Faulkner, G. (2017). Run to Quit: An evaluation of a scalable physical activity-based smoking cessation intervention. *Mental Health and Physical Activity*, *13*, 15–21.

Prochaska, J. O., & DiClemente, C. C. (1983). Stages and processes of self-change of smoking: Toward an integrative model of change. *Journal of Consulting and Clinical Psychology*, *51*, 390–395.

Professional Cricketers' Association (2019). *Health and welfare*. Retrieved from: www.thepca.co.uk/health-welfare/ (Accessed October 21, 2019).

The Professional Football Association (2019). 24/7 Helpline and Support Network. Retrieved from: www.thepfa.com/wellbeing/24-7-helpline (Accessed October 21, 2019).

Public Health England (2014). *Everybody active, every day: An evidence-based approach to physical activity*. Retrieved from: https://assets.publishing.service.gov.uk/government/uploads/system/uploads/attachment_data/file/353384/Everybody_Active__Every_Day_evidence_based_approach_CONSULTATION_VERSION.pdf (Accessed August 14, 2019).

Pummell, E. K. L. (2008). Junior to senior transition: Understanding and facilitating the process. Doctoral thesis, Loughborough University, Loughborough, UK. Retrieved from:

https://pdfs.semanticscholar.org/aadd/4014489ecb7b14dc81b80dff9a87dc1caf2e.pdf (Accessed November 1, 2019).

Pyszczynski, T., & Greenberg, J. (1987). Self-regulatory perseveration and the depressive self-focusing style: A self-awareness theory of reactive depression. *Psychological Bulletin, 102,* 122–138.

Quayle, M., Wurm, A., Barnes, H., Barr, T., Beal, E., Fallon, M., … Wei, R. (2019). Stereotyping by omission and commission: Creating distinctive gendered spectacles in the televised coverage of the 2015 Australian Open men's and women's tennis singles semi-finals and finals. *International Review for the Sociology of Sport, 54,* 3–21.

Quested, E., Kwasnicka, D., Thøgersen-Ntoumani, C., Gucciardi, D. F., Kerr, D. A., Hunt, K., … Ntoumanis, N. (2018). Protocol for a gender-sensitised weight loss and healthy living programme for overweight and obese men delivered in Australian Football League settings (Aussie-FIT): A feasibility and pilot randomised controlled trial. *BMJ Open, 8,* e022663.

Quoidbach, J., Mikolajczak, M., & Gross, J. J. (2015). Positive interventions: An emotion regulation perspective. *Psychological Bulletin, 141,* 655–693.

Raedeke, T. D., & Smith, A. L. (2001). Development and preliminary validation of an athlete burnout measure. *Journal of Sport and Exercise Psychology, 23,* 281–306.

Raedeke, T. D., & Smith, A. L. (2004). Coping resources and athlete burnout: An examination of stress mediated and moderation hypotheses. *Journal of Sport and Exercise Psychology, 26,* 525–541.

Rafaeli, A., & Sutton, R. I. (1987). Expression of emotion as part of the work role. *The Academy of Management Review, 12,* 23–37.

Raghunandan, V. (2018). Golden freedom: Legacy of independent India's first hockey Olympic gold in 1948. *NewsClick.* Retrieved from: www.newsclick.in/golden-freedom-legacy-independent-indias-first-hockey-olympic-gold-1948 (Accessed April 20, 2020).

Rainey, D. W., & Schweickert, G. J. (1988). An exploratory study of team cohesion before and after a spring trip. *The Sport Psychologist, 2,* 314–317.

Ranby, K. W., Aiken, L. S., MacKinnon, D. P., Elliot, D. L., Moe, E. L., McGinnis, W., & Goldberg, L. (2009). A mediation analysis of the ATHENA intervention for female athletes: Prevention of athletic-enhancing substance use and unhealthy weight loss behaviours. *Journal of Pediatric Psychology, 34,* 1069–1083.

Rascle, O., Charrier, M., Higgins, N. C., Rees, T., Coffee, P., Le Foll, D., & Cabagno, G. (2019). Being one of us: Translating expertise into performance benefits following perceived failure. *Psychology of Sport and Exercise, 43,* 105–113.

Rascle, O., Le Foll, D., Charrier, M., Higgins, N. C., Rees, T., & Coffee, P. (2015). Durability and generalization of attribution-based feedback following failure: Effects on expectations and behavioural persistence. *Psychology of Sport and Exercise, 18,* 68–74.

Rascle, O., Le Foll, D., & Higgins, N. C. (2008). Attributional retraining alters novice golfers' free practice behavior. *Journal of Applied Sport Psychology, 20,* 157–164.

Ray, H. A., & Verhoef, M. J. (2013). Dragon boat racing and health-related quality of life of breast cancer survivors: A mixed methods evaluation. *BMC Complementary and Alternative Medicine, 13,* 205.

Reardon, C. L., Hainline, B., Aron, C. M., Baron, D., Baum, A. L. … Engebretsen, L. (2019). Mental health in elite athletes: International Olympic Committee consensus statement. *British Journal of Sports Medicine, 53,* 667–699.

Rebar, A. L., Dimmock, J. A., Jackson, B., Rhodes, R. E., Kates, A., Starling, J., & Vandelanotte, C. (2016). A systematic review of the effects of non-conscious regulatory processes in physical activity. *Health Psychology Review, 10,* 395–407.

Rees, T. J. (2016). Social support in sport psychology. In R. J. Schinke, K. R. McGannon, & B. Smith (Eds.), *Routledge international handbook of sports psychology* (pp. 505–515). Abingdon, UK: Routledge.

Rees, T. J., & Freeman, P. (2007). The effects of perceived and received support on self-confidence. *Journal of Sports Sciences, 25,* 1057–1065.

Rees, T. J., & Freeman, P. (2009). Social support moderates the relationship between stressors and task performance through self-efficacy. *Journal of Social and Clinical Psychology, 28,* 244–263.

Rees, T. J., & Freeman, P. (2010). The effect of experimentally provided social support on golf-putting performance. *The Sport Psychologist, 18,* 333–348.

Rees, T. J., & Hardy, L. (2000). Social support of high-level sports performers: An investigation of the social support experiences of high-level sports performers. *The Sport Psychologist, 14,* 327–347.

Rees, T. J., & Hardy, L. (2004). Matching social support with stressors: Effects on factors underlying performance in tennis. *Psychology of Sport and Exercise, 5,* 319–337.

Rees, T., Hardy, L., & Freeman, P. (2007). Stressors, social support and effects upon performance in golf. *Journal of Sports Sciences, 25,* 33–42.

Rees, T. J., Hardy, L., Güllich, A., Abernethy, B., Côté, J., Woodman, T., Montgomery, H., Laing, S., & Warr, C. (2016). The Great British medalists project: A review of current knowledge into the development of the world's best sporting talent. *Sports Medicine, 46,* 1041–1058.

Rees, T. J., Haslam, S. A., Coffee, P., & Lavallee, D. (2015). A social identity approach to sport psychology: Principles, practice, and prospects. *Sports Medicine, 45,* 1083–1096.

Rees, T. J., Ingledew, D. K., & Hardy, L. (2005). Attribution in sport psychology: Seeking congruence between theory, research and practice. *Psychology of Sport and Exercise, 6,* 189–204.

Rees, T. J., Mitchell, I., Evans, L., & Hardy, L. (2010). Stressors, social support and psychological responses to sport injury in high- and low-performance standard participants. *Psychology of Sport and Exercise, 11,* 505–512.

Rees, T. J., Salvatore, J., Coffee, P., Haslam, S. A., Sargent, A., & Dobson, T. (2013). Reversing downward performance spirals. *Journal of Experimental Social Psychology, 49,* 400–403.

Reicher, S. D. (1984). The St Pauls riot: An explanation of the limits of crowd action in terms of a social identity model. *European Journal of Social Psychology, 14,* 1–21.

Reicher, S. D. (1987). Crowd behaviour as social action. In J. C. Turner (Ed.), *Rediscovering the social group: A self-categorization theory* (pp. 171–202). Oxford: Basil Blackwell.

Reicher, S. D. (1996a). Social identity and social change: Rethinking the contexts of social psychology. In P. W. Robinson (Ed.), *Social groups and identities: Developing the legacy of Henri Tajfel* (pp. 317–336). Oxford: Butterworth-Heinemann.

Reicher, S. D. (1996b). 'The Battle of Westminster': Developing the social identity model of crowd behaviour in order to explain the initiation and development of collective conflict. *European Journal of Social Psychology, 26,* 115–134.

Reicher, S. D. (2017). 'Some difficult away games': A close look at the fixture list for research on social identity and sport. Keynote presentation at the First International Conference on Social Identity in Sport, KU Leuven, Leuven, Belgium, July.

Reicher, S. D., & Haslam, S. A. (2006). On the agency of individuals and groups: Lessons from the BBC Prison Study. In T. Postmes & J. Jetten (Eds.), *Individuality and the group: Advances in social identity* (pp. 237–257). London: Sage.

Reicher, S. D., & Haslam, S. A. (2012). Change we can believe in: The role of social identity, cognitive alternatives and leadership in group mobilization and social transformation. In B. Wagoner, E. Jensen, & J. Oldmeadow (Eds.), *Culture and social change: Transforming society through the power of ideas* (pp. 53–73). London: Routledge.

Reicher, S. D., Haslam, S. A., & Hopkins, N. (2005). Social identity and the dynamics of leadership: Leaders and followers as collaborative agents in the transformation of social reality. *Leadership Quarterly, 16,* 547–568.

Reicher, S. D., Haslam, S. A., Spears, R., & Reynolds, K. J. (2012). A social mind: The context of John Turner's work and its influence. *European Review of Social Psychology, 23*, 344–385.

Reicher, S. D., & Hopkins, N. (2001). *Self and nation: Categorization, contestation and mobilization.* London: Sage.

Reicher, S. D., Hopkins, N., & Condor, S. (1997). Stereotype construction as a strategy of influence. In R. Spears, P. J. Oakes, N. Ellemers, & S. A. Haslam (Eds.), *The social psychology of stereotyping and group life* (pp. 94–118). Malden, MA: Blackwell.

Reicher, S. D., Templeton, A., Neville, F. G., Ferrari, L., & Drury, J. (2016). Core disgust is attenuated by ingroup relations. *Proceedings of the National Academy of Sciences, 113*, 2631–2635.

Reilly, K., Tucker, P., Irwin, J., Johnson, A., Pearson, E., Bock, D., & Burke, S. (2018). 'C.H.A.M.P. families': Description and theoretical foundations of a paediatric overweight and obesity intervention targeting parents: A single-centre non-randomised feasibility study. *International Journal of Environmental Research and Public Health, 15*, 2858.

Reilly, R. (2019). Commander in cheat? Donald Trump's 18 golf tournament wins examined. *The Guardian* (April 2). Retrieved from: www.theguardian.com/sport/2019/apr/02/donald-trump-golf-28-club-championships (Accessed December 5, 2019).

Reimer, T., Park, E. S., & Hinsz, V. B. (2006). Shared and coordinated cognition in competitive and dynamic task environments: An information-processing perspective for team sports. *International Journal of Sport and Exercise Psychology, 4*, 376–400.

Reinboth, M., & Duda, J. L. (2004). The motivational climate, perceived ability, and athletes' psychological and physical well-being. *The Sport Psychologist, 18*, 237–251.

Reinboth, M., & Duda, J. L. (2006). Perceived motivational climate, need satisfaction and indices of well-being in team sports: A longitudinal perspective. *Psychology of Sport and Exercise, 7*, 269–286.

Reis, R. S., Salvo, D., Ogilvie, D., Lambert, E. V., Goenka, S., Brownson, R. C., & Lancet Physical Activity Series 2 Executive Committee (2016). Scaling up physical activity interventions worldwide: Stepping up to larger and smarter approaches to get people moving. *The Lancet, 388*, 1337–1348.

Rejeski, W. J., & Brawley, L. R. (1988). Defining the boundaries of sport psychology. *The Sport Psychologist, 2*, 231–241.

Renfrew, J., Howle, T. C., & Eklund, R. C. (2017). Self-presentation concerns may contribute toward the understanding of athletes' affect when trialing for a new sports team. *Journal of Applied Sport Psychology, 29*, 484–492.

Reynders, B., Vansteenkiste, M., Van Puyenbroeck, S., Aelterman, N., De Backer, M., Delrue, J., De Muynck, G.-J., Fransen, K., Haerens, L., & Vande Broek, G. (2019). Coaching the coach: Intervention effects on need-supportive coaching behavior and athlete motivation and engagement. *Psychology of Sport and Exercise, 43*, 288–300.

Reynolds, K. J., Subasic, E., & Tindall, K. (2014). The problem of behaviour change: From social norms to an ingroup focus. *Social and Personality Psychology Compass, 9*, 45–56.

Reysen, S., Snider, J. S., & Branscombe, N. R. (2012). Corporate renaming of stadiums, team identification, and threat to distinctiveness. *Journal of Sport Management, 26*, 350–357.

Rhodes, R. E., & de Bruijn, G. J. (2013a). How big is the physical activity intention–behaviour gap? A meta-analysis using the action control framework. *British Journal of Health Psychology, 18*, 296–309.

Rhodes, R. E., & de Bruijn, G. J. (2013b). What predicts intention–behavior discordance? A review of the action control framework. *Exercise and Sport Sciences Reviews, 41*, 201–207.

Rhodes, R. E., & Dickau, L. (2012). Experimental evidence for the intention–behavior relationship in the physical activity domain: A meta-analysis. *Health Psychology, 31*, 724–727.

Rhodes, R. E., & Kates, A. (2015). Can the affective response to exercise predict future motives and physical activity behavior? A systematic review of published evidence. *Annals of Behavioral Medicine, 49*, 715–731.

Rhodes, R. E., Macdonald, H. M., & McKay, H. A. (2006). Predicting physical activity intention and behaviour among children in a longitudinal sample. *Social Science & Medicine, 62*, 3146–3156.

Rhodes, R. E., McEwan, D., & Rebar, A. L. (2018). Theories of physical activity behaviour change: A history and synthesis of approaches. *Psychology of Sport & Exercise, 42*, 100–109.

Rhodes, R. E., & Nigg, C. R. (2011). Advancing physical activity theory: A review and future directions. *Exercise and Sport Sciences Reviews, 39*, 113–119.

Rice, S. M., Purcell, R., De Silva, S., Mawren, D., McGorry, P. D., & Parker, A. G. (2016). The mental health of elite athletes: A narrative systematic review. *Sports Medicine, 46*, 1333–1353.

Ring, C., Kavussanu, M., Al-Yaaribi, A., Tenenbaum, G., & Stanger, N. (2019). Effects of antisocial behaviour on opponent's anger, attention, and performance. *Journal of Sports Sciences, 37*, 871–877.

Ringelmann, M. (1913). Recherches sur les moteurs animes: Travail de rhomme [Research on animate sources of power: The work of man]. *Annales de I'Institut National Agronomique, 12*, 1–40.

Rippon, A. (2006). *Hitler's Olympics: The story of the 1936 Nazi Games.* Barnsley, UK: Pen and Sword.

Rivis, A., & Sheeran, P. (2003). Descriptive norms as an additional predictor in the theory of planned behaviour: A meta-analysis. *Current Psychology, 22*, 218–233.

Rocca, K. A., & Vogl-Bauer, S. (1999). Trait verbal aggression, sports fan identification, and perceptions of appropriate sports fan communication. *Communication Research Reports, 16*, 239–248.

Rodgers, L. (2013). Cancer in cycling: Armstrong 'blames' UCI for illness. *The Roar.* Retrieved from: www.theroar.com.au/2013/01/24/cancer-in-cycling-armstrong-blames-uci-for-illness/ (Accessed September 18, 2019).

Roe, C., & Parker, A. (2016). Sport, chaplaincy and holistic support: The Elite Player Performance Plan (EPPP) in English professional football. *Practical Theology, 9*, 169–182.

Rongen, F., Cobley, S., McKenna, J., & Till, K. (2015). Talent identification and development: The impact on athlete health? In J. Baker, P. Safai, & J. Fraser-Thomas (Eds.), *Health and elite sport: Is high performance sport a healthy pursuit?* (pp. 99–116). Abingdon, UK: Routledge.

Rookwood, J., & Pearson, G. (2012). The hoolifan: Positive fan attitudes to football 'hooliganism'. *International Review for the Sociology of Sport, 47*, 149–164.

Rosch, E. (1978). Principles of categorization. In E. Rosch & B. B. Lloyd (Eds.), *Cognition and categorization* (pp. 27–48). Hillsdale, NJ: Erlbaum.

Rosenstock, I. M. (1974). The health belief model and preventive health behavior. *Health Education & Behavior, 2*, 354–386.

Ross, L. (1977). The intuitive psychologist and his shortcomings: Distortions in the attribution process. In L. Berkowtiz (Ed.), *Advances in experimental social psychology* (Vol. 10, pp. 174–221). New York: Academic Press.

Ross, M. (1975). Salience of reward and intrinsic motivation. *Journal of Personality and Social Psychology, 32*, 245–254.

Rousseau, V., Aubé, C., & Savoie, A. (2006). Teamwork behaviors: A review and an integration of frameworks. *Small Group Research, 37*, 540–570.

Rowe, D. (2007). Sports journalism: Still the 'toy department' of the news media? *Journalism, 8*, 385–405.

Roy, M. M., Memmert, D., Frees, A., Radzevick, J., Pretz, J., & Noël, B. (2016). Rumination and performance in dynamic, team sport. *Frontiers in Psychology, 6* (Online publication; doi: 10.3389/fpsyg.2015.02016).

Rubin, M., & Hewstone, M. (1998). Social identity theory's self-esteem hypothesis: A review and some suggestions for clarification. *Personality and Social Psychology Review, 2*, 40–62.

Rudski, J. (2001). Competition, superstition and the illusion of control. *Current Psychology, 20,* 68–84.

Rueger, S. Y., Malecki, C. K., Pyun, Y., Aycock, C., & Coyle, S. (2016). A meta-analytical review of the association between perceived social support and depression in childhood and adolescence. *Psychological Bulletin, 142,* 1017–1067.

Ruiz, M. (2019). *What Peloton means for the future of fitness.* Retrieved from: https://elemental.medium.com/the-peloton-effect-9ba2f996eae9 (Accessed August 19, 2019).

Ryan, R. M., & Deci, E. L. (2000). Self-determination theory and the facilitation of intrinsic motivation, social development, and well-being. *American Psychologist, 55,* 68–78.

Ryska, T. A., Yin, Z., Cooley, D., & Ginn, R. (1999). Developing team cohesion: A comparison of cognitive-behavioral strategies of U.S. and Australian sport coaches. *Journal of Psychology, 133,* 523–539.

Sabiston, C. M., Brunet, J., Kowalski, K. C., Wilson, P. M., Mack, D. E., & Crocker, P. R. E. (2010). The role of body-related self-conscious emotions in motivating women's physical activity. *Journal of Sport and Exercise Psychology, 32,* 417–437.

Sallis, J. F., & Owen, N. (2002). Ecological models of health behavior. In K. Glanz, B. K. Rimer, & K. Viswanath (Eds.), *Health behaviour and health education* (3rd ed., pp. 403–424). San Francisco, CA: Jossey-Bass.

Sallis, J. F., Patterson, T. L., Buono, M. J., Atkins, C. J., & Nader, P. R. (1988). Aggregation of physical activity habits in Mexican-American and Anglo families. *Journal of Behavioral Medicine, 11,* 31–41.

Sallis, J. F., Prochaska, J. J., & Taylor, W. C. (2000). A review of correlates of physical activity of children and adolescents. *Medicine & Science in Sports & Exercise, 32,* 963–975.

Sallis, J. F., Saelens, B. E., Frank, L. D., Conway, T. L., Slymen, D. J., Cain, K. L., ... & Kerr, J. (2009). Neighborhood built environment and income: Examining multiple health outcomes. *Social Science & Medicine, 68,* 1285–1293.

Salvatore, J., & Rees, T. (2020). *Questioning stereotypes disrupts the effects of stereotype threat.* Manuscript submitted for publication.

Samendinger, S., Forlenza, S. T., Winn, B., Max, E. J., Kerr, N. L., Pfeiffer, K. A., & Feltz, D. L. (2017). Introductory dialogue and the Köhler Effect in software-generated workout partners. *Psychology of Sport and Exercise, 32,* 131–137.

Samuel-Azran, T., Galily, Y., Karniel, Y., & Lavie-Dinur, A. (2016). Let the Germans win? Israeli attitudes towards Die Mannschaft during the 2014 World Cup tournament. *Journal of Intercultural Communication Research, 45,* 391–403.

Sanders, G., & Stevinson, C. (2017). Associations between retirement reasons, chronic pain, athletic identity, and depressive symptoms among former professional footballers. *European Journal of Sport Science, 17,* 1311–1318.

Sanders, P., & Winter, S. (2016). Going pro: Exploring adult triathletes' transitions into elite sport. *Sport, Exercise, and Performance Psychology, 5,* 193–205.

Sandoval-Garcia, C. (2008). Football: Forging nationhood and masculinity in Costa Rica. *International Journal of the History of Sport, 22,* 212–230.

Saner, E. (2018). How the psychology of the England football team could change your life. *The Guardian* (July 10). Retrieved from: www.theguardian.com/football/2018/jul/10/psychology-england-football-team-change-your-life-pippa-grange (Accessed November 23, 2019).

Sani, F. (2010). *Self-continuity: Individual and collective perspectives.* London: Psychology Press.

Sani, F., Madhok, V., Norbury, M., Dugard, P., & Wakefield, J. R. H. (2015). Greater number of group identifications is associated with healthier behaviour: Evidence from a Scottish community sample. *British Journal of Health Psychology, 20,* 466–481.

Sankaran, S. (2012). I 'think' therefore I 'choke': Evidence towards adaptive and maladaptive processing styles in determining sports performance. Unpublished doctoral thesis.

Sankaran, S. (2018). Learned helplessness in sports: The role of repetitive failure experience, performance anxiety and perfectionism. *Polish Psychological Bulletin, 49*, 311–321.

Sankaran, S., von Hecker, U., & Sanchez, X. (2019). Thinking 'good' versus thinking 'bad': Adaptive and maladaptive predictors of sports performance. Unpublished manuscript, University of Warsaw.

Sarason, B. R., Pierce, G. R., & Sarason, I. G. (1990). Social support: The sense of acceptance and the role of relationships. In B. R. Sarason, I. G. Sarason, & G. R. Pierce (Eds.), *Social support: An interactional view* (pp. 97–128). New York: Wiley.

Sarason, I. G., & Sarason, B. R. (1986). Experimentally provided social support. *Journal of Personality and Social Psychology, 50*, 1222–1225.

Sarason, I. G., Sarason, B. R., & Pierce, G. R. (1990). Social support, personality and performance. *Journal of Applied Sport Psychology, 2*, 117–127.

Sarkar, M., & Fletcher, D. (2014). Ordinary magic, extraordinary performance: Psychological resilience and thriving in high achievers. *Sport, Exercise, and Performance Psychology, 3*, 46–60.

Sasvári, A., Harsányi, S. G., Dér, A., & Szemes, Á. (2019). An exploratory analysis of recreational and competitive athletes' superstitious habits. *Cognition, Brain, Behavior, 23*, 63–76.

Sattelmair, J., Pertman, J., Ding, E. L., Kohl, H. W., Haskell, W., & Lee, I. M. (2011). Dose response between physical activity and risk of coronary heart disease: A meta-analysis. *Circulation, 124*, 789–795.

Saunders, J. (2018). How to help athletes adapt to life after sport. *The Conversation* (August 13). Retrieved from: https://theconversation.com/how-to-help-athletes-adapt-to-life-after-sport-94584. (Accessed September 22, 2018).

Saunders, R. P., Pate, R. R., Dowda, M., Ward, D. S., Epping, J. N., & Dishman, R. K. (2012). Assessing sustainability of Lifestyle Education for Activity Program (LEAP). *Health Education Research, 27*, 319–330.

Saxena, S. M. D., Thornicroft, G. P., Knapp, M., & Whiteford, H. A. (2007). Resources for mental health: Scarcity, inequity, and inefficiency. *The Lancet, 370*, 878–889.

Saxena, S. M. D., Van Ommeren, M., Tang, K. C., & Armstrong, T. P. (2005). Mental health benefits of physical activity. *Journal of Mental Health, 14*, 445–451.

Scales, P. C., & Leffert, N. (1999). *Developmental assets: A synthesis of the scientific research on adolescent development.* Minneapolis, MN: Search Institute.

Schallhorn, C. (2020). Samba, sun and social issues: How the 2014 FIFA World Cup and the 2016 Rio Olympics changed perceptions of Germans about Brazil. *International Review for the Sociology of Sport, 55*, 603–622.

Scheiner, E. (2018). How a hockey game powered a revolution. *The Washington Post* (February 12). Retrieved from: www.washingtonpost.com/news/made-by-history/wp/2018/02/12/how-a-hockey-game-powered-a-revolution/ (Accessed December 5, 2019).

Schertzinger, M. (2015). Turf wars: Safety, sexism and the 2015 Women's World Cup. In A. N. Milner (Ed.), *Women in sports: Breaking barriers, facing obstacles. Vol. 1: Sportswomen and teams* (pp. 153–162). Santa Barbara, CA: Preager.

Schinke, R. J., Stambulova, N. B., Si, G., & Moore, Z. E. (2018). International society of sport psychology position stand: Athletes' mental health, performance, and development. *International Journal of Sport and Exercise Psychology, 16*, 622–639.

Schlossberg, N. K. (1981). A model for analyzing human adaptation to transition. *The Counseling Psychologist, 9*, 2–18.

Schmader, T., Johns, M., & Forbes, C. (2008). An integrated process model of stereotype threat effects on performance. *Psychological Review, 115*, 336–356.

Schreiber, M., & Stott, C. J. (2015) Policing international football tournaments and the cross-cultural relevance of the social identity approach to crowd behavior. In J. Albrecht, M. Dow, D. Plecas, & D. Das (Eds.), *Policing major events: Perspectives from around the world.* Boca Raton, FL: CRC Press.

Schultz, B., & Sheffer, M. L. (2018). The mascot that wouldn't die: A case study of fan identification and mascot loyalty. *Sport in Society*, *21*, 482–496.

Schultz, D. P., & Schultz, S. E. (2005). *Theories of personality* (8th ed.). Boston, MA: Thomson Learning.

Schultz, J. (2005). Reading the catsuit: Serena Williams and the production of blackness at the 2002 US Open. *Journal of Sport & Social Issues*, *29*, 338–357.

Schurr, K. T., Wittig, A. F., Ruble, V. E., & Ellen, A. S. (1998). Demographic and personality characteristics associated with persistent, occasional, and non-attendance of university male basketball games by college students. *Journal of Sport Behavior*, *11*, 3–17.

Schwartz, S. J. (2001). The evolution of Eriksonian and Neo-Eriksonian identity theory and research: A review and integration. *Identity: An International Journal of Theory and Research*, *1*, 7–58.

Schwartz, S. J., Zamboanga, B. L., Luyckx, K., Meca, A., & Ritchie, R. A. (2013). Identity in emerging adulthood: Reviewing the field and looking forward. *Emerging Adulthood*, *1*, 96–113.

Schwarzer, R. (1992). Self-efficacy in the adoption and maintenance of health behaviors: Theoretical approaches and a new model. In R. Schwarzer (Ed.), *Self-efficacy: Thought control of action* (pp. 217–243). Washington, DC: Hemisphere.

Schwarzer, R., & Leppin, A. (1991). Social support and health: A theoretical and empirical overview. *Journal of Social and Personal Relationships*, *8*, 99–127.

The Scottish Football Blog (2010). Scotland in 1978: What just happened? Retrieved from: www.scottishfootballblog.co.uk/2010/06/scotland-in-1978-what-just-happened.html (Accessed December 5, 2019).

Search Institute (2018). *The developmental assets framework*. Minneapolis, MN: Search Institute. Retrieved from: www.search-institute.org/our-research/development-assets/developmental-assets-framework/ (Accessed April 20, 2020).

Seate, A. A., Ma, R., Iles, I., McCloskey, T., & Parry-Giles, S. (2017). 'This is who we are!' National identity construction and the 2014 FIFA World Cup. *Communication and Sport*, *5*, 428–447.

Sebbens, J., Hassmén, P., Crisp, D., & Wensley, K. (2016). Mental Health in Sport (MHS): Improving the early intervention knowledge and confidence of elite sport staff. *Frontiers in Psychology*, *7*, 911.

Sekot, A. (2009). Violence in sports. *European Journal for Sport and Society*, *6*, 37–49.

Seligman, M. E. P. (1975). *Helplessness: On depression, development, and death*. San Francisco, CA: W. H. Freeman.

Seligman, M. E. P., & Maier, S. F. (1967). Failure to escape traumatic shock. *Journal of Experimental Psychology*, *74*, 1–9.

Senécal, J., Loughead, T. M., & Bloom, G. A. (2008). A season-long team-building intervention: Examining the effect of team goal setting on cohesion. *Journal of Sport and Exercise Psychology*, *30*, 186–199.

Settles, I. H., Sellers, R. M., & Damas, A., Jr. (2002). One role or two? The function of psychological separation in role conflict. *Journal of Applied Psychology*, *87*, 574–582.

Seymour-Smith, M., Cruwys, T., Haslam, S. A., & Brodribb, W. (2017). Loss of group memberships predicts depression in postpartum mothers. *Social Psychiatry and Psychiatric Epidemiology*, *52*, 201–210.

Shaffer, D. R., & Kipp, K. (2010). *Developmental psychology: Childhood and adolescence* (8th ed.). Belmont, CA: Cengage Learning.

Shakespeare-Finch, J. E., Smith, S. G., Gow, K. M., Embelton, G., & Baird, L. (2003). The prevalence of post-traumatic growth in emergency ambulance personnel. *Traumatology*, *9*, 58–71.

Shapiro, S. L., Ridinger, L. C., & Trail, G. T. (2013). An analysis of multiple spectator consumption behaviors, identification, and future behavioral intentions within the context of a new college football program. *Journal of Sport Management*, *27*, 130–145.

Sheeran, P., Gollwitzer, P. M., & Bargh, J. A. (2013). Nonconscious processes and health. *Health Psychology*, *32*, 460–473.

Sheinin, D. (2018). Astros under scrutiny in sign-stealing controversy during ALCS. *The Washington Post* (October 17). Retrieved from: www.washingtonpost.com/sports/2018/10/17/mlb-investigation-clears-astros-alleged-sign-stealing-during-alcs/?utm_term=.b62962d37d1c (Accessed July 31, 2019).

Sheridan, D., Coffee, P., & Lavallee, D. (2014). A systematic review of social support in youth sport. *International Review of Sport and Exercise Psychology*, *7*, 198–228.

Sherif, M., & Cantril, H. (1947). *The psychology of ego-involvements, social attitudes and identifications*. New York: Wiley.

Shumaker, S. A., & Brownell, A. (1984). Toward a theory of social support: Closing conceptual gaps. *Journal of Social Issues*, *40*, 11–36.

Sigal, C. (1992). Not their finest hour. *The New York Times* (June 7). Retrieved from: www.nytimes.com/1992/06/07/books/not-their-finest-hour.html (Accessed April 20, 2020).

Sigal, R. J., Kenny, G. P., Wasserman, D. H., Castaneda-Sceppa, C., & White, R. D. (2006). Physical activity/exercise and type 2 diabetes: A consensus statement from the American Diabetes Association. *Diabetes Care*, *29*, 1433–1438.

Sigelman, L. (1986). Basking in reflected glory revisited: An attempt at replication *Social Psychology Quarterly*, *49*, 90–92.

Silva, M. N., Markland, D., Minderico, C. S., Vieira, P. N., Castro, M. M., Coutinho, S. R., … Teixeira, P. J. (2008). A randomized controlled trial to evaluate self-determination theory for exercise adherence and weight control: Rationale and intervention. *BMC Public Health*, *8*, 234.

Silva, M. N., Vieira, P. N., Coutinho, S. R., Minderico, C. S., Matos, M. G., Sardinha, L. S., & Teixeira, P. J. (2010). Using self-determination theory to promote physical activity and weight control: A randomized controlled trial in women. *Journal of Behavioral Medicine*, *33*, 110–122.

Simon, H. A. (1955). A behavioral model of rational choice. *Quarterly Journal of Economics*, *69*, 99–118.

Simons, E. (2013). *The secret lives of sports fans: The science of sports obsession*. New York: Overlook Duckworth.

Sinclair, D. A., & Vealey, R. S. (1989). Effects of coaches' expectations and feedback on the self-perceptions of athletes. *Journal of Sport Behavior*, *12*, 77.

Sinokki, M., Hinkka, K., Ahola, K., Koskinen, S., Klaukka, T., Kivimäki, M., … Virtanen, M. (2009). The association between team climate at work and mental health in the Finnish Health 2000 Study. *Occupational and Environmental Medicine*, *66*, 523–528.

Skorski S., Thompson K. G., Keegan R. J., Meyer T., & Abbiss C. R. (2017). A monetary reward alters pacing but not performance in competitive cyclists. *Frontiers of Physiology*, *8*, 741.

Slater, M., Rovira, A., Southern, R., Swapp, D., Zhang, J. J., Campbell, C., & Levine, R. M. (2013). Bystander responses to a violent incident in an immersive virtual environment. *PLoS ONE*, *8*(1), e52766.

Slater, M. J. (2019). *Togetherness: How to build a winning team*. Stoke-on-Trent, UK: Bennion Kearny.

Slater, M. J., & Barker, J. B. (2019). Doing social identity leadership: Exploring the efficacy of an identity leadership intervention on perceived leadership and mobilization in elite disability soccer. *Journal of Applied Sport Psychology*, *31*, 65–86.

Slater, M. J., Barker, J. B., Coffee, P., & Jones, M. V. (2015). Leading for gold: Social identity leadership processes at the London 2012 Olympic Games. *Qualitative Research in Sport, Exercise, and Health*, *7*, 192–209.

Slater, M. J., Coffee, P., Barker, J. B., & Evans, A. L. (2014). Promoting shared meanings in group memberships: A social identity approach to leadership in sport. *Reflective Practice*, *15*, 672–685.

Slater, M. J., Coffee, P., Barker, J. B., Haslam, S. A., & Steffens, N. (2019). Shared social identity content is the basis for leaders' mobilization of followers. *Psychology of Sport and Exercise*, *43*, 271–278.

Slater, M. J., Evans, A. L., & Barker, J. B. (2013). Using social identities to motivate athletes towards peak performance at the London 2012 Olympic Games: Reflecting for Rio 2016. *Reflective Practice: International and Multidisciplinary Perspectives*, *14*, 672–679.

Slater, M. J., Haslam, S. A., & Steffens, N. K. (2018). Singing it for 'us': Team passion displayed during national anthems is associated with subsequent success. *European Journal of Sport Science*, *18*, 541–549.

Slater, M. J., Turner, M. J., Evans, A. L., & Jones, M. V. (2018). 'Capturing hearts and minds': The influence of leader relational identification on followers' mobilization and cardiovascular reactivity. *The Leadership Quarterly*, *29*, 379–388.

Smit, F., Willemse, G., Koopmanschap, M., Onrust, S., Cuijpers, P. I. M., & Beekman, A. (2006). Cost-effectiveness of preventing depression in primary care patients: Randomised trial. *British Journal of Psychiatry*, *188*, 330–336.

Smith, A. L., Ntoumanis, N., Duda, J. L., & Vansteenkiste, M. (2011). Goal striving, coping, and well-being in sport: A prospective investigation of the self-concordance model. *Journal of Sport and Exercise Psychology*, *33*, 124–145.

Smith, B., Bundon, A., & Best, M. (2016). Disability sport and activist identities: A qualitative study of narratives of activism among elite athletes with impairment. *Psychology of Sport & Exercise*, *26*, 139–148.

Smith, C., & Ellsworth, P. (1981). Description and performance: Two modes of representation for a single task. Unpublished manuscript, Stanford University, Stanford, CA.

Smith, E. R. (1993). Social identity and social emotions: Toward new conceptualizations of prejudice. In D. M. Mackie & D. L. Hamilton (Eds.), *Affect, cognition, and stereotyping: Interactive processes in group perception* (pp. 297–315). San Diego, CA: Academic Press.

Smith, E. R., Seger, C. R., & Mackie, D. M. (2007). Can emotions be truly group level? Evidence regarding four conceptual criteria. *Journal of Personality and Social Psychology*, *93*, 431–446.

Smith, J. R., & Haslam, S. A. (Eds.) (2017). *Social psychology: Revisiting the classic studies* (2nd ed.). London: Sage.

Smith, J. R., Terry, D. J., & Hogg, M. A. (2006). Who will see me? The impact of type of audience on willingness to display group-mediated attitude–intention consistency. *Journal of Applied Social Psychology*, *36*, 1173–1197.

Smith, M. J., Arthur, C. A., Hardy, J., Callow, N., & Williams, D. (2013). Transformational leadership and task cohesion in sport: The mediating role of intrateam communication. *Psychology of Sport and Exercise*, *14*, 249–257.

Smith, R. E., Smoll, F. L., & Schutz, R. W. (1990). Measurement and correlates of sport-specific cognitive and somatic trait anxiety: The Sport Anxiety Scale. *Anxiety Research*, *2*, 263–280.

Smith, R. H., & van Dijk, W. W. (2018). Schadenfreude and Gluckschmerz. *Emotion Review*, *10*, 293–304.

Smith, T., & Steele, D. (2007) *Silent gesture*. Philadelphia, PA: Temple University Press.

Sneed, J. R., Schwartz, S. J., & Cross, W. E. (2006). A multicultural critique of identity status theory and research: A call for integration. *Identity: An International Journal of Theory and Research*, *6*, 61–84.

Sniehotta, F. F. (2009). An experimental test of the theory of planned behavior. *Applied Psychology: Health and Well-Being*, *1*, 257–270.

Sniehotta, F. F., Presseau, J., & Araújo-Soares, V. (2014). Time to retire the theory of planned behaviour. *Health Psychology Review*, *8*, 1–7.

Snyder, C. R., Lassegard, M., & Ford, C. E. (1986). Distancing after group success and failure: Basking in reflected glory and cutting off reflected failure. *Journal of Personality and Social Psychology*, *51*, 382–388.

Snyder, E. E. (1990). Emotion and sport: A case study of collegiate women gymnastics. *Sociology of Sport Journal, 7*, 254–270.

Snyders, H. (2019). Visionary courtyard players: The Robben Island Rugby Board and the transition to postapartheid South Africa, ca. 1972–1992. In M. Gennaro & S. Aderinto (Eds.), *Sports in African history, politics, and identity formation* (pp. 137–151). London: Routledge.

Solberg, H. A., & Mehus, I. (2014). The challenge of attracting football fans to stadia? *International Journal of Sport Finance, 9*, 3–19.

Spaaij, R., & Anderson, A. (2010). Soccer fan violence: A holistic approach – Reply to Braun and Vliegenthart. *International Sociology, 25*, 561–579.

Sparkes, A. C. (1998). Athletic identity: An Achilles' heel to the survival of self. *Qualitative Health Research, 8*, 644–664.

Sparkes, A. C., Batey, J., & Brown, D. (2005). The muscled self and its aftermath: A life history study of an elite, black, male bodybuilder. *Auto/Biography, 13*, 131–160.

Spears, R., & Otten, S. (2017). Discrimination: Revisiting Tajfel's minimal group studies. In J. R. Smith & S. A. Haslam (Eds.), *Social psychology: Revisiting the classic studies* (2nd ed., pp. 164–181). London: Sage.

Spencer, N. E. (2004). Sister act VI: Venus and Serena Williams at Indian Wells: 'Sincere fictions' and white racism. *Journal of Sport & Social Issues, 28*, 115–135.

Sperber, D., & Wilson, D. (1986). *Relevance: Communication and cognition* (Vol. 142). Cambridge, MA: Harvard University Press.

Sperber, D., & Wilson, D. (1997). Remarks on relevance theory and the social sciences. *Multilingual Journal of Cross-Cultural and Interlanguage Communication, 16*, 145–152.

Spinda, J. S. W. (2011). The development of Basking in Reflected Glory (BIRGing) and Cutting Off Reflected Failure (CORFing) measures. *Journal of Sport Behavior, 34*, 392–420.

Spink, K. S., & Carron, A. V. (1993). The effects of team building on the adherence patterns of female exercise participants. *Journal of Sport and Exercise Psychology, 15*, 39–49.

Spink, K. S., Crozier, A. J., & Robinson, B. (2013). Examining the relationship between descriptive norms and perceived effort in adolescent athletes: Effects of different reference groups. *Psychology of Sport and Exercise, 14*, 813–818.

Spink, K. S., McLaren, C. D., & Ulvick, J. D. (2018). Groupness, cohesion, and intention to return to sport: A study of intact youth teams. *International Journal of Sports Science & Coaching, 13*, 545–551.

Spink, K. S., Ulvick, J. D., Crozier, A. J., & Wilson, K. S. (2014). Group cohesion and adherence in unstructured exercise groups. *Psychology of Sport and Exercise, 15*, 293–298.

Spink, K. S., Ulvick, J. D., McLaren, C. D., Crozier, A. J., & Fesser, K. (2015). Effects of groupness and cohesion on intention to return in sport. *Sport, Exercise, and Performance Psychology, 4*, 293–302.

Spink, K. S., Wilson, K. S., & Odnokon, P. (2013). Examining the relationship between cohesion and return to team in elite athletes. *Psychology of Sport and Exercise, 11*, 6–11.

Spink, K. S., Wilson, K. S., & Priebe, C. S. (2010). Groupness and adherence in structured exercise settings. *Group Dynamics: Theory, Research, and Practice, 14*, 163–173.

SportAccord (2011). *Definition of sport*. Retrieved from: https://web.archive.org/web/20111028112912/http://www.sportaccord.com/en/members/index.php?idIndex=32&idContent=14881 (Accessed July 31, 2019).

Sport England (2016). Record number of women get active. Retrieved from: www.sportengland.org/news-and-features/news/2016/december/8/record-numbers-of-women-getting-active/ (Accessed July 22, 2019).

Sport England (2018). Active Lives Adult Survey: May 17/18 Report. Retrieved from: www.sportengland.org/media/13563/active-lives-adult-may-17-18-report.pdf (Accessed July 22, 2019).

St John, M. (2019). 'Don't start that shit': Ricky Stuart rages at reporter's 'spear tackle' claim. *Fox Sports* (July 16). Retrieved from: www.foxsports.com.au/nrl/nrl-premiership/uninten tional-raiders-coach-stuart-claims-nick-cotric-sendoff-tackle-was-an-accident/news-story/ b870052320fa13ef1f7019e7f3b4c2ef (Accessed July 31, 2019).

Stambulova, N. B. (1994). Developmental sports career investigations in Russia: A post-perestroika analysis. *The Sport Psychologist, 8*, 221–237.

Stambulova, N. B. (2003). Symptoms of a crisis-transition: A grounded theory study. In N. Hassmén (Ed.), *Svensk Idrottspykologisk Forening* (pp. 97–109). Orebro, Sweden: Orebro University Press.

Stambulova, N. B. (2009). Talent development in sport: A career transitions perspective. In E. Tsung-Min Hung, R. Lidor, & D. Hackfort (Eds.), *Psychology of sport excellence* (pp. 63–74). Morgantown, WV: Fitness Information Technology.

Stambulova, N. B., Alfermann, D., Statler, T., & Côté, J. (2009). ISSP Position stand: Career development and transitions of athletes. *International Journal of Sport and Exercise Psychology, 7*, 395–412.

Stambulova, N. B., & Wylleman, P. (2014). Athletes' career development and transitions. In A. G. Papaioannou & D. Hackfort (Eds.), *Sport and exercise psychology: Global perspectives and fundamental concepts* (pp. 605–620). London: Routledge.

Standage, M., Duda, J. L., & Ntoumanis, N. (2005). A test of self-determination theory in school physical education. *British Journal of Educational Psychology, 75*, 411–433.

Standage, M., Duda, J. L., & Ntoumanis, N. (2006). Students' motivational processes and their relationship to teacher ratings in school physical education: A self-determination theory approach. *Research Quarterly for Exercise and Sport, 77*, 100–110.

Stanger, N., Chettle, R., Whittle, J., & Poolton, J. M. (2018). The role of pre-performance and in-game emotions on cognitive interference during sport performance: The moderating role of self-confidence and reappraisal. *The Sport Psychologist, 32*, 114–124.

Stanley, D. M., Lane, A. M., Beedie, C. J., Friesen, A. P., & Devonport, T. J. (2012). Emotion regulation strategies used in the hour before running. *International Journal of Sport and Exercise Psychology, 10*, 159–171.

Stebbings, J., Taylor, I. M., & Spray, C. M. (2016). Interpersonal mechanisms explaining the transfer of well- and ill-being in coach-athlete dyads. *Journal of Sport and Exercise Psychology, 38*, 292–304.

Steele, C. M. (1997). A threat in the air: How stereotypes shape intellectual identity and performance. *American Psychologist, 52*, 613–629.

Steele, C. M., Spencer, S. J., & Aronson, J. (2002). Contending with group image: The psychology of stereotype and social identity threat. *Advances in Experimental Social Psychology, 34*, 379–440.

Steffens, N. K., Crimston, C., Haslam, S. A., Slater, M. J., & Fransen, K. (2019). Moving goalposts: Social group membership is a basis for recognizing exceptional sports performance. Unpublished manuscript, University of Queensland, Brisbane.

Steffens, N. K., & Haslam, S. A. (2013). Power through 'us': Leaders' use of we-referencing language predicts election victory. *PLoS ONE, 8*, e77952.

Steffens, N. K., & Haslam, S. A. (2017). Building team and organisational identification to promote leadership, citizenship, and resilience. In M. F. Crane (Ed.), *Managing for resilience: A practical guide for employee wellbeing and organizational performance* (pp. 150–167). London and New York: Routledge.

Steffens, N. K., Haslam, S. A., Kerschreiter, R., Schuh, S. C., & van Dick, R. (2014). Leaders enhance group members' work engagement and reduce their burnout by crafting social identity. *German Journal of Human Resource Management, 28*, 173–194.

Steffens, N. K., Haslam, S. A., Reicher, S. D., Platow, M. J., Fransen, K., Yang, J. ... Boen, F. (2014). Leadership as social identity management: Introducing the Identity Leadership Inventory (ILI) to assess and validate a four-dimensional model. *The Leadership Quarterly*, *25*, 1001–1024.

Steffens, N. K., Slade, E., Stevens, M., Haslam, S. A., & Rees, T. (2019). Putting the 'we' into workout: The association of identity leadership with exercise class attendance and effort, and the mediating role of group identification and comfort. *Psychology of Sport & Exercise*, *45*, 101544.

Steffens, N. K., Yang, J., Jetten, J., Haslam, S. A., & Lipponen, J. (2018). The unfolding impact of leader identity entrepreneurship on burnout, work engagement, and turnover intentions. *Journal of Occupational Health Psychology*, *23*, 373–387.

Stenling, A., Hassmén, P., & Holmström, S. (2014). Implicit beliefs of ability, approach-avoidance goals and cognitive anxiety among team sport athletes. *European Journal of Sport Science*, *14*, 720–729.

Stenling, A., & Tafvelin, S. (2014). Transformational leadership and well-being in sports: The mediating role of need satisfaction. *Journal of Applied Sport Psychology*, *26*, 182–196.

Stephan, Y., & Demulier, V. (2008). Transition out of elite sport: A dynamic, multidimensional, and complex phenomenon. In M. P. Simmons & L. A. Foster (Eds.), *Sport and exercise psychology research advances* (pp. 175–190). Hauppauge, NY: Nova Science Publishers.

Stevens, D. E., & Bloom, G. A. (2003). The effect of team building on cohesion. *Avante*, *9*, 43–54.

Stevens, M., Rees, T., Coffee, P., Haslam, S. A., Steffens, N. K., & Polman, R. (2018). Leaders promote attendance in sport and exercise sessions by fostering social identity. *Scandinavian Journal of Medicine & Science in Sports*, *28*, 2100–2108.

Stevens, M., Rees, T., Coffee, P., Steffens, N. K., Haslam, S. A., & Polman, R. (2017). A social identity approach to understanding and promoting physical activity. *Sports Medicine*, *47*, 1911–1918.

Stevens, M., Rees, T., Coffee, P., Steffens, N. K., Haslam, S. A., & Polman, R. (2020). Leading us to be active: A two-wave test of relationships between identity leadership, group identification, and attendance. *Sport, Exercise, and Performance Psychology*, *9*, 128–142.

Stevens, M., Rees, T., & Polman, R. (2019). Social identification, exercise participation, and positive exercise experiences: Evidence from Parkrun. *Journal of Sports Sciences*, *37*, 221–228.

Stevens, M., Rees, T., Steffens, N. K., Haslam, S. A., Coffee, P., & Polman, R. (2019). Leaders' creation of shared identity impacts group members' effort and performance: Evidence from an exercise task. *PLoS ONE*, *14*(7), e0218984.

Stoeber, J., & Otto, K. (2006). Positive conceptions of perfectionism: Approaches, evidence, challenges. *Personality and Social Psychology Review*, *10*, 295–319.

Stone, J. (2002). Battling doubt by avoiding practice: The effects of stereotype threat on self-handicapping in white athletes. *Personality and Social Psychology Bulletin*, *28*, 1667–1678.

Stott, C. J., Adang, O. M., Livingstone, A. G, & Schreiber, M. (2007). Variability in the collective behaviour of England fans at Euro 2004: Public order policing, social identity, intergroup dynamics and social change. *European Journal of Social Psychology*, *37*, 75–100.

Stott, C. J., Adang, O. M., Livingstone, A. G., & Schreiber, M. (2008). Tackling football hooliganism: A quantitative study of public order, policing and crowd psychology. *Psychology Public Policy and Law*, *14*, 115–141.

Stott, C. J., & Drury, J. (2000). Crowds, context and identity: Dynamic categorization processes in the 'poll tax riot'. *Human Relations*, *53*, 247–273.

Stott, C. J., & Drury, J. (2016). Contemporary understanding of riots: Classical crowd psychology, ideology and the social identity approach. *Public Understanding of Science*, *26*, 2–14.

Stott, C. J., & Gorringe, H. (2013). From Sir Robert Peel to PLTs: Adapting to liaison-based public order policing in England and Wales. In J. M. Brown (Ed.), *The future of policing: Papers prepared for the Stevens Independent Commission into the Future of Policing in England and Wales* (pp. 239–251). London: Routledge.

Stott, C. J., Havelund, J., & Williams, N. (2019). Policing football crowds in Sweden. *Nordic Journal of Criminology, 20,* 35–53.

Stott, C. J., Hoggett, J., & Pearson, G. (2011). 'Keeping the peace': Social identity, procedural justice and the policing of football crowds. *British Journal of Criminology, 52,* 381–399.

Stott, C. J., Hutchison, P., & Drury, J. (2001). 'Hooligans' abroad? Inter-group dynamics, social identity and participation in collective 'disorder' at the 1998 World Cup Finals. *British Journal of Social Psychology, 40,* 359–384.

Stott, C. J., Khan, S., Madsen, E., & Havelund, J. (2020) The value of Supporter Liaison Officers (SLOs) in fan dialogue, conflict, governance and football crowd management in Sweden. *Soccer & Society, 21,* 196–208.

Stott, C. J., & Pearson, G. (2007). *Football hooliganism, policing and the war on the English disease.* London: Pennant Books.

Stott, C. J., Pearson, G., & West, O. (2019). Enabling an evidence-based approach to policing football in the UK. *Policing* (Online publication; doi: 10.1093/police/pay102).

Stott, C. J., & Reicher, S. D. (1998). How conflict escalates: The inter-group dynamics of collective football crowd 'violence'. *Sociology, 32,* 353–377.

Stott, C. J., West, O., & Radburn, M. (2018). Policing football 'risk'? A participant action research case study of a liaison-based approach to 'public order'. *Policing and Society, 28,* 1, 1–16.

Stroebe, W. (2012). The truth about Triplett (1898), but nobody seems to care. *Perspectives on Psychological Science, 7,* 54–57.

Strube, M. J. (2005). What did Triplett really find? A contemporary analysis of the first experiment in social psychology. *American Journal of Psychology, 118,* 271–286.

Stults-Kolehmainen, M. A., Gilson, T. A., & Abolt, C. J. (2013). Feelings of acceptance and intimacy among teammates predict motivation in intercollegiate sport. *Journal of Sport Behavior, 36,* 306–327.

Sundquist, K., Eriksson, U., Kawakami, N., Skog, L., Ohlsson, H., & Arvidsson, D. (2011). Neighborhood walkability, physical activity, and walking behavior: The Swedish Neighborhood and Physical Activity (SNAP) study. *Social Science & Medicine, 72,* 1266–1273.

Suttles, G. D. (1968). *The social order of the slum: Ethnicity and territory in the inner city.* Chicago, IL: University of Chicago Press.

Suze, A. (2013). The untold story of Robben Island: Sports and the anti-Apartheid movement. In R. Field & B. Kidd (Eds.), *Forty years of sport and social change, 1968–2008: To remember is to resist.* London: Routledge.

Sylvester, B. D., Lubans, D. R., Eather, N., Standage, M., Wolf, S. A., McEwan, D., ... Beauchamp, M. R. (2016). Effects of variety support on exercise-related well-being. *Applied Psychology: Health and Well-Being, 8,* 213–231.

Szczurek, L., Monin, B., & Gross, J. J. (2012). The stranger effect: The rejection of affective deviants. *Psychological Science, 23,* 1105–1111.

Szymanski, M., & Wolfe, R. A. (2016). What is strategy? The strategic management literature. In R. Hoye & M. N. Parent (Eds.), *The SAGE handbook of sport management* (pp. 9–33). London: Sage.

Tahtinen, R., McDougall, M., Feddersen, N., Tikkanen, O., Morris, R., & Ronkainen, N. J. (2020). Me, myself, and my thoughts: The influence of brooding and reflective rumination on depressive symptoms in athletes in the United Kingdom. *Journal of Clinical Sport Psychology* (Advance online publication; doi:10.1123/jcsp.2019-0039).

Tajfel, H. (1970). Experiments in intergroup discrimination. *Scientific American, 223*, 96–102.

Tajfel, H. (1972). La catégorisation sociale [Social categorisation]. In S. Moscovici (Ed.), *Introduction à la psychologie sociale* (pp. 272–302). Paris: Larousse.

Tajfel, H. (Ed.) (1978). *Differentiation between social groups*. London: Academic Press.

Tajfel, H., Flament, C., Billig, M. G., & Bundy, R. F. (1971). Social categorization and intergroup behaviour. *European Journal of Social Psychology, 1*, 149–177.

Tajfel, H., & Turner J. C. (1979). An integrative theory of intergroup conflict. In W. G. Austin & S. Worchel (Eds.), *The social psychology of intergroup relations* (pp. 33–48). Monterey, CA: Brooks/Cole.

Tajfel, H., & Turner, J. C. (1986). The social identity theory of intergroup behaviour. In S. Worchel & W. G. Austin (Eds.), *Psychology of intergroup relations* (pp. 7–24). Chicago, IL: Helson-Hall.

Tamir, M. (2016). Why do people regulate their emotions? A taxonomy of motives in emotion regulation. *Personality and Social Psychology Review, 20*, 199–222.

Tamminen, K. A., & Crocker, P. R. E. (2013). 'I control my own emotions for the sake of the team': Emotional self-regulation and interpersonal emotion regulation among female high-performance curlers. *Psychology of Sport & Exercise, 14*, 737–747.

Tamminen, K. A., Gaudreau, P., McEwen, C. E., & Crocker, P. R. E. (2016). Interpersonal emotion regulation among adolescent athletes: A Bayesian multilevel model predicting sport enjoyment and commitment. *Journal of Sport and Exercise Psychology, 38*, 541–555.

Tamminen, K. A., Palmateer, T. M., Denton, M., Sabiston, C. M., Crocker, P., Eys, M. A., & Smith, B. (2016). Exploring emotions as social phenomena among Canadian varsity athletes. *Psychology of Sport & Exercise, 27*, 28–38.

Tarrant, M., & Butler, K. (2011). Effects of self-categorization on orientation towards health. *British Journal of Social Psychology, 50*, 121–139.

Tarrant, M., & Campbell, E. (2007). Responses to within-group criticism: Does past adherence to group norms matter? *European Journal of Social Psychology, 37*, 1187–1202.

Tarrant, M., Haslam, C., Carter, M., Calitri, R., & Haslam, S. A. (2020). Social identity interventions. In M. S. Hagger, L. D. Cameron, K. Hamilton, N. Hankonen, & T. Lintunen (Eds.), *Handbook of behavior change* (pp. 649–660). New York: Cambridge University Press.

Taylor, J. (2012). Sport imagery: Athletes' most powerful mental tool. *Psychology Today* (November). Retrieved from: www.psychologytoday.com/us/blog/the-power-prime/201211/sport-imagery-athletes-most-powerful-mental-tool (Accessed August 28, 2019).

Taylor, J., & Ogilvie, B. C. (1994). A conceptual model of adaptation to retirement among athletes. *Journal of Applied Sport Psychology, 6*, 1–20.

Taylor, R. A. (2019). Contemporary issues: Resilience training alone is an incomplete intervention. *Nurse Education Today, 78*, 10–13.

Tedeschi, R. G., & Calhoun, L. G. (2004). Posttraumatic growth: Conceptual foundations and empirical evidence. *Psychological Inquiry, 15*, 1–18.

Teixeira, P. J., Carraça, E. V., Markland, D., Silva, M. N., & Ryan, R. M. (2012). Exercise, physical activity, and self-determination theory: A systematic review. *International Journal of Behavioral Nutrition and Physical Activity, 9*, 78.

Terry, D. J. (2003). A social identity perspective on organizational mergers. In S. A. Haslam, D. van Knippenberg, M. J. Platow, & N. Ellemers (Eds.), *Social identity at work: Developing theory for organizational practice* (pp. 223–240). New York: Psychology Press.

Terry, D. J., & Hogg, M. A. (1996). Group norms and the attitude-behavior relationship: A role for group identification. *Personality and Social Psychology Bulletin, 22*, 776–793.

Teychenne, M., Ball, K., & Salmon, J. (2008). Physical activity and likelihood of depression in adults: A review. *Preventive Medicine, 46*, 397–411.

Thirer, J., & Rampey, M. (1979). Effects of abusive spectator behaviour on the performance of home and visiting intercollegiate basketball teams. *Perceptual and Motor Skills, 48*, 1047–1053.

This Girl Can (2018). Fit got real. Retrieved from: www.thisgirlcan.co.uk (Accessed July 22, 2019).

Thoits, P. A. (2011). Mechanisms linking social ties and support to physical and mental health. *Journal of Health and Social Behavior, 52*, 145–161.

Thomas, E. F., Amiot, C. E., Louis, W. R., & Goddard, A. (2017). Collective self-determination: How the agent of help promotes pride, well-being, and support for intergroup helping. *Personality and Social Psychology Bulletin, 43*, 662–677.

Thomas, O., Lane, A., & Kingston, K. (2011). Defining and contextualizing robust sport-confidence. *Journal of Applied Sport Psychology, 23*, 189–208.

Thomas, W. E., Brown, R. J., Easterbrook, M. J., Vignoles, V. L., Manzi, C., D'Angelo, C., & Holt, J. J. (2017). Social identification in sports teams: The role of personal, social, and collective identity motives. *Personality & Social Psychology Bulletin, 43*, 508–523.

Thompson, D., & Filik, R. (2016). Sarcasm in written communication: Emoticons are efficient markers of intention. *Journal of Computer-Mediated Communication, 21*, 105–120.

Thrane, C. (2001). Sport spectatorship in Scandinavia: A class phenomenon? *International Review for the Sociology of Sport, 36*, 149–163.

Thuot, S. M., Kavouras, S. A., & Kenefick, R. W. (1998). Effect of perceived ability, game location, and state anxiety on basketball performance. *Journal of Sport Behavior, 21*, 311–321.

Tibbert, S. J., Andersen, M. B., & Morris, T. (2015). What a difference a 'mentally toughening' year makes: The acculturation of a rookie. *Psychology of Sport & Exercise, 17*, 68–78.

Tjønndal, A. (2019). 'I don't think they realise how good we are': Innovation, inclusion and exclusion in women's Olympic boxing. *International Review for the Sociology of Sport, 54*, 131–150.

Toffoletti, K. (2014). Iranian women's sports fandom: Gender, resistance, and identity in the football movie 'Offside'. *Journal of Sport & Social Issues, 38*, 75–92.

Tong, L. (2014). *The great motivation swindle*. Global Feel Good Company.

Totterdell, P. (2000). Catching moods and hitting runs: Mood linkage and subjective performance in professional sport teams. *Journal of Applied Psychology, 85*, 848–859.

Tracy, J. L., & Robins, R. W. (2007). The psychological structure of pride: A tale of two facets. *Journal of Personality and Social Psychology, 92*, 506–525.

Trafimow, D. (2015). On retiring the TRA/TPB without retiring the lessons learned: A commentary on Sniehotta, Presseau and Araújo-Soares. *Health Psychology Review, 9*, 168–171.

Trafimow, D., Sheeran, P., Conner, M., & Finlay, K. A. (2002). Evidence that perceived behavioural control is a multidimensional construct: Perceived control and perceived difficulty. *British Journal of Social Psychology, 41*, 101–122.

Trescothick, M. (2008). *Coming back to me*. London: HarperSport.

Triplett, N. (1898). The dynamogenic factors in pacemaking and competition. *American Journal of Psychology, 9*, 507–533.

Tsoukala, M. (2009). *Football hooliganism in Europe: Security and civil liberties in the balance*. Basingstoke: Macmillan.

Tucker, J. M., Welk, G. J., & Beyler, N. K. (2011). Physical activity in U.S. adults: Compliance with physical activity guidelines for Americans. *American Journal of Preventive Medicine, 40*, 454–461.

Turman, P. D. (2003). Coaches and cohesion: The impact of coaching techniques on team cohesion in the small group sport setting. *Journal of Sport Behavior, 26*, 86–103.

Turner, J. C. (1975). Social comparison and social identity: Some prospects for intergroup behavior. *European Journal of Social Psychology, 5*, 5–34.

Turner, J. C. (1978). Social categorization and social discrimination in the minimal group paradigm. In H. Tajfel (Ed.), *Differentiation between social groups: Studies in the social psychology of intergroup relations* (pp. 27–60). London: Academic Press.

Turner, J. C. (1982). Towards a cognitive redefinition of the social group. In H. Tajfel (Ed.), *Social identity and intergroup relations* (pp. 15–40). Cambridge, UK: Cambridge University Press.

Turner, J. C. (1985) Social categorization and the self-concept: A social cognitive theory of group behaviour. In E. J. Lawler (Ed.), *Advances in group processes* (pp. 77–122). Greenwich, CT: JAI Press.

Turner, J. C. (1991). *Social influence*. Milton Keynes: Open University Press.

Turner, J. C. (1999). Some current issues in research on social identity and self-categorization theories. In N. Ellemers, R. Spears, & B. Doosje (Eds.), *Social identity: Context, commitment, content.* (pp. 6–34). Oxford: Blackwell.

Turner, J. C. (2005). Explaining the nature of power: A three-process theory. *European Journal of Social Psychology, 35*, 1–22.

Turner, J. C., & Haslam, S. A. (2001). Social identity, organizations and leadership. In M. E. Turner (Ed.), *Groups at work: Advances in theory and research* (pp. 25–65). Hillsdale, NJ: Erlbaum.

Turner, J. C., Hogg, M. A., Oakes, P. J., Reicher, S. D., & Wetherell, M. S. (1987). *Rediscovering the social group: A self-categorization theory*. Oxford: Blackwell.

Turner, J. C., Oakes, P. J., Haslam, S. A., & McGarty, C. (1994). Self and collective: Cognition and social context. *Personality and Social Psychology Bulletin, 20*, 454–463.

Turner, M. E., Pratkanis, A. R., Probasco, P., & Leve, C. (2006). Threat, cohesion, and group effectiveness: Testing a social identity maintenance perspective on groupthink. *Small Groups: Key Readings, 6*, 241–264.

Turner, R. N., Hewstone, M., & Voci, A. (2007). Reducing explicit and implicit outgroup prejudice via direct and extended contact: The mediating role of self-disclosure and intergroup anxiety. *Journal of Personality and Social Psychology, 93*, 369–388.

Turner, R. W., Perrin, E. M., Coyne-Beasley, T., Peterson, C. J., & Skinner, A. C. (2015). Reported sports participation, race, sex, ethnicity, and obesity in US adolescents from NHANES physical activity. *Global Pediatric Health, 2*, 2333794X15577944.

Turnnidge, J., & Côté, J. (2018). Applying transformational leadership theory to coaching research in youth sport: A systematic literature review. *International Journal of Sport and Exercise Psychology, 16*, 327–342.

Turnnidge, J., Côté, J., & Hancock, D. J. (2014). Positive youth development from sport to life: Explicit or implicit transfer? *Quest, 66*, 203–217.

Tygiel, J. (1997). *Baseball's great experiment: Jackie Robinson and his legacy*. New York: Oxford University Press.

Uchino, B. N. (2009). Understanding the links between social support and physical health: A lifespan perspective with emphasis on the separability of perceived and received support. *Perspectives in Psychological Science, 4*, 236–255.

Udry, E., Gould, D., Bridges, D., & Tuffey, S. (1997). People helping people? Examining the social ties of athletes coping with burnout and injury stress. *Journal of Sport and Exercise Psychology, 19*, 368–395.

Uphill, M. A., & Jones, M. V. (2007). Antecedents of emotions in elite athletes: A cognitive motivational relational theory perspective. *Research Quarterly for Exercise and Sport, 78*, 79–89.

Väänänen, A., & Toivanen, M. (2018). The challenge of tied autonomy for traditional work stress models. *Work and Stress, 32*, 1–5.

van Dick, R., Lemoine, J. E., Steffens, N. K., Kerschreiter, R., Akfirat, S. A., Avanzi, L. … Haslam, S. A. (2018). Identity leadership going global: Validation of the Identity Leadership Inventory across 20 countries. *Journal of Occupational and Organizational Psychology, 91*, 697–728.

van Kleef, G. A., Cheshin, A., Koning, L. F., & Wolf, S. A. (2019). Emotional games: How coaches' emotional expressions shape players' emotions, inferences, and team performance. *Psychology of Sport & Exercise, 41*, 1–11.

van Knippenberg, B., & van Knippenberg, D. (2005). Leader self-sacrifice and leadership effectiveness: The moderating role of leader prototypicality. *Journal of Applied Psychology, 90*, 25–37.

van Knippenberg, D. (2011). Embodying who we are: Leader group prototypicality and leadership effectiveness. *The Leadership Quarterly, 22*, 1078–1091.

van Knippenberg, D., & Sitkin, S. B. (2013). A critical assessment of charismatic–transformational leadership research: Back to the drawing board? *Academy of Management Annals, 7*, 1–60.

van Leeuwen, E., & van Knippenberg, D. (2003). Organizational identification following a merger: The importance of agreeing to differ. In S. A. Haslam, D. van Knippenberg, M. J. Platow, & N. Ellemers (Eds.), *Social identity at work: Developing theory for organizational practice* (pp. 205–221). New York: Psychology Press.

Van Riper, T. (2012). America's most disliked athletes. *Forbes* (February 7). Retrieved from: www.forbes.com/sites/tomvanriper/2012/02/07/americas-most-disliked-athletes/#519252ce5931 (Accessed August 7, 2019).

Vargas-Tonsing, T. M. (2009). An exploratory examination of the effects of coaches' pre-game speeches on athletes' perceptions of self-efficacy and emotion. *Journal of Sport Behavior, 32*, 1–10.

Velija, P., & Hughes, L. (2019). 'Men fall like boiled eggs. Women fall like raw eggs.' Civilised female bodies and gender relations in British National Hunt racing. *International Review for the Sociology of Sport, 54*, 22–37.

Vella, S. A., Benson, A. J., Sutcliffe, J., McLaren, C. D., Swann, C., Schwickle, M. J., & Bruner, M. W. (2020). Self-determined motivation, social identification and the mental health of adolescent male team sport participants. *Journal of Applied Sports Psychology*. doi: 10.1080/10413200.2019.1705432

Vierimaa, M., Bruner, M. W., & Côté, J. (2018). Positive youth development and observed athlete behaviour in recreational sport. *PLoS ONE, 13*(1), e0191936.

Vignoles, V. L., Chryssochoou, X., & Breakwell, G. M. (2000). The distinctiveness principle: Identity, meaning, and the bounds of cultural relativity. *Personality and Social Psychology Review, 4*, 337–354.

Vignoles, V. L., Regalia, C., Manzi, C., Golledge, J., & Scabini, E. (2006). Beyond self-esteem: Influence of multiple motives on identity construction. *Journal of Personality and Social Psychology, 90*, 308–333.

Vigo, D. M. D., Thornicroft, G. P., & Atun, R. P. (2016). Estimating the true global burden of mental illness. *The Lancet Psychiatry, 3*, 171–178.

Vincent J., Kian E., Pedersen P., & Kuntz A. H. J. (2010). England expects: English newspaper's narratives about the English football team in the 2006 World Cup. *International Review for the Sociology of Sport, 45*, 199–223.

Viner, B. (2006). *Ali, Pelé, Lillee and me: A personal odyssey through the spoting seventies*. London: Pocket Books.

Viner, B. (2014). *Looking for the Toffees: In search of the heroes of Everton*. London: Simon & Schuster.

Visek, A. J., Hurst, J. R., Maxwell, J. P., & Watson, J. C. (2008). A cross-cultural psychometric evaluation of the athletic identity measurement scale. *Journal of Applied Sport Psychology, 20*, 473–480.

Viswesvaran, C., Sanchez, J. I., & Fisher, J. (1999). The role of social support in the process of work stress: A meta-analysis. *Journal of Vocational Behavior, 54*, 314–334.

Vlachopoulos, S. P., Kaperoni, M., & Moustaka, F. C. (2011). The relationship of self-determination theory variables to exercise identity. *Psychology of Sport and Exercise*, *12*(3), 265–272.

Vlachopoulos, S. P., Karageorghis, C. I., & Terry, P. C. (2000). Motivation profiles in sport: A self-determination theory perspective. *Research Quarterly for Exercise and Sport*, *71*, 387–397.

Vlachopoulos, S. P., Ntoumanis, N., & Smith, A. L. (2010). The basic psychological needs in exercise scale: Translation and evidence for cross-cultural validity. *International Journal of Sport and Exercise Psychology*, *8*, 394–412.

Voight, M., & Callaghan, J. (2001). A team building intervention program: Application and evaluation with two university soccer teams. *Journal of Sport Behavior*, *24*, 420–431.

von Scheve, C., & Ismer, S. (2013). Towards a theory of collective emotions. *Emotion Review*, *5*, 406–413.

Vos, T., Barber, R. M., Bell, B., Bertozzi-Villa, A., Biryukov, S., Bollinger, I., … Murray, C. J. L. (2015). Global, regional, and national incidence, prevalence, and years lived with disability for 301 acute and chronic diseases and injuries in 188 countries, 1990–2013: A systematic analysis for the Global Burden of Disease Study 2013. *The Lancet*, *386*, 743–800.

Vroom, V. H. (1964). *Work and motivation*. New York: Wiley.

Wacker, B. (2016). Inside the 'We' of Jordan Spieth. Retrieved from: www.pgatour.com/tourreport/2016/04/06/jordan-spieth-ad-we.html (Accessed September 1, 2019).

Wagstaff, C. R. D. (2014). Emotion regulation and sport performance. *Journal of Sport & Exercise Psychology*, *36*, 401–412.

Wainwright, E., Fox, F., Breffni, T., Taylor, G., & O'Connor, M. (2017). Coming back from the edge: A qualitative study of a professional support unit for junior doctors. *BMC Medical Education*, *17*, 142.

Wally, C. M., & Cameron, L. D. (2017). A randomized-controlled trial of social norm interventions to increase physical activity. *Annals of Behavioral Medicine*, *51*, 642–651.

Walton, G. M., & Cohen, G. L. (2003). Stereotype lift. *Journal of Experimental Social Psychology*, *39*, 456–467.

Wamsley, L. (2019). Thousands of women will at last be allowed to attend a soccer match in Iran. *NPR* (October, 9). Retrieved from: www.npr.org/2019/10/09/768720084/thousands-of-women-will-at-last-be-allowed-to-attend-a-soccer-match-in-iran?t=1587048083432 (Accessed April 20, 2020).

Wang, D., Waldman, D. A., & Zhang, Z. (2014). A meta-analysis of shared leadership and team effectiveness. *Journal of Applied Psychology*, *99*, 181–198.

Wann, D. L. (1998a). A preliminary investigation of the relationship between alcohol use and sport fandom. *Social Behavior and Personality*, *26*, 287–290.

Wann, D. L. (1998b). Tobacco use and sport fandom. *Perceptual and Motor Skills*, *86*, 878.

Wann, D. L. (2006a). Understanding the positive social psychological benefits of sport team identification: The team identification–social psychological health model. *Group Dynamics: Theory, Research, and Practice*, *10*, 272–296.

Wann, D. L. (2006b). Examining the potential causal relationship between sport team identification and psychological well-being. *Journal of Sport Behavior*, *29*, 79–95.

Wann, D. L., & Branscombe, N. R. (1990). Die-hard and fair-weather fans: Effects of identification on BIRGing and CORFing tendencies. *Journal of Sport & Social Issues*, *14*, 103–117.

Wann, D. L., & Branscombe, N. R. (1993). Sports fans: Measuring degree of identification with their team. *International Journal of Sport Psychology*, *24*, 1–17.

Wann, D. L., Culver, Z., Akanda, R., Daglar, M., De Divitiis, C., & Smith, A. (2005). The effects of team identification and game outcome on willingness to consider anonymous acts of hostile aggression. *Journal of Sport Behavior*, *28*, 282–294.

Wann, D. L., Friedman, K., McHale, M., & Jaffe, A. (2003). The Norelco Sport Fanatics Survey: Examining behaviors of sport fans. *Psychological Reports*, *92*, 930–936.

Wann, D. L., Hackathorn, J., & Sherman, M. R. (2017). Testing the team identification–social psychological health model: Mediational relationships among team identification, sport fandom, sense of belonging, and meaning in life. *Group Dynamics: Theory, Research, and Practice*, *21*, 94–107.

Wann, D. L., Inman, S., Ensor, C. L., Gates, R. D., & Caldwell, D. S. (1999). Assessing the psychological well-being of sport fans using the Profile of Mood States: The importance of team identification. *International Sports Journal*, *3*, 81–90.

Wann, D. L., & James, J. D. (2019). *Sport fans: The psychology and social impact of fandom* (2nd ed.). New York: Routledge.

Wann, D. L., Melnick, M., Russell, G. W., & Pease, D. G. (2001). *Sport fans: The psychology and social impact of spectators*. New York: Routledge.

Wann, D. L., Peterson, R. R., Cothran, C., & Dykes, M. (1999). Sport fan aggression and anonymity: The importance of team identification. *Social Behavior and Personality: An International Journal*, *27*, 597–602.

Wann, D. L., & Pierce, S. (2005). The relationship between sport team identification and social well-being: Additional evidence supporting the team identification–social psychological health model. *North American Journal of Psychology*, *7*, 117–124.

Wann, D. L., Pierce, S., Padgett, B., Evans, A., Krill, K., & Romay, A. (2003). Relations between sport team identification and optimism. *Perceptual and Motor Skills*, *97*, 803–804.

Wann, D. L., Rogers, K., Dooley, K., & Foley, M. (2011). Applying the team identification-social psychochological health model to older sport fans. *International Journal of Aging and Human Development*, *72*, 303–315.

Wann, D. L., Shelton, S., Smith, T., & Walker, R. (2002). Relationship between team identification and trait aggression: A replication. *Perceptual and Motor Skills*, *94*, 595–598.

Wann, D. L., Waddill, P. J., Bono, D., Scheuchner, H., & Ruga, K. (2017). Sport spectator verbal aggression: The impact of team identification and fan dysfunction on fans' abuse of opponents and officials. *Journal of Sport Behavior*, *40*, 423–443.

Wann, D. L., Waddill, P. J., Polk, J., & Weaver, S. (2011). The team identification–social psychological health model: Sport fans gaining connections to others via sport team identification. *Group Dynamics: Theory, Research, and Practice*, *15*, 75–89.

Wann, D. L., & Weaver, S. (2009). Understanding the relationship between sport team identification and dimensions of social well-being. *North American Journal of Psychology*, *11*, 219–230.

Warburton, D. E. R., Nicol, C. W., & Bredin, S. S. D. (2006). Prescribing exercise as preventive therapy. *Canadian Medical Association Journal*, *174*, 961–974.

Ward, A. (1989). *Football's strangest matches: Extraordinary stories from over a century of football*. London: Anova Books.

Ware, S. (2011). *Game, set, match: Billie Jean King and the revolution in women's sports*. Chapel Hill, NC: University of North Carolina Press.

Warnakulasuriya, A. (2017). In search of Lance Armstrong's staunchest supporters. Retrieved from: www.vice.com/en_uk/article/a3dwjg/in-search-of-lance-armstrongs-staunchest-supporters (Accessed September 1, 2019).

Waterman, A. S. (1988). Identity status theory and Erikson's theory: Commonalities and differences. *Developmental Review*, *8*, 185–208.

Watkins, B. A. (2014). Revisiting the social identity-brand equity model: An application to professional sports. *Journal of Sport Management*, *28*, 471–480.

Watt, D. C. (2003). *Sports management and administration* (2nd ed.). London: Psychology Press.

Webb, T. L., & Sheeran, P. (2006). Does changing behavioral intentions engender behavior change? A meta-analysis of the experimental evidence. *Psychological Bulletin, 132,* 249–268.

Webster, L. V., Hardy, J., & Hardy, L. (2017). Big hitters: Important factors characterizing team effectiveness in professional cricket. *Frontiers in Psychology, 8*(1140).

Wegner, D. M., Ansfield, M., & Pilloff, D. (1998). The putt and the pendulum: Ironic effects of the mental control of action. *Psychological Science, 9,* 196–199.

Wegner, M., Bohnacker, V., Mempel, G., Teubel, T., & Schüler, J. (2014). Explicit and implicit affiliation motives predict verbal and nonverbal social behavior in sports competition. *Psychology of Sport and Exercise, 15,* 588–595.

Weiler, I. (2004). The predecessors of the Olympic movement and Pierre de Coubertin. *European Review, 12,* 427–443.

Weinberg, R. S., & Butt, J. (2014). Goal-setting and sport performance. In A. G. Papaioannou & D. Hackfort (Eds.), *Routledge companion to sport and exercise psychology: Global perspectives and fundamental concepts* (pp. 343–355). London: Routledge.

Weinberg, R. S., & Gould, D. (2018). *Foundations of sport and exercise psychology* (7th ed.). Champaign, IL: Human Kinetics.

Weiner, B. (1985). An attributional theory of achievement motivation and emotion. *Psychological Review, 92,* 548–573.

Weiner, B. (2012). An attribution theory of motivation. In P. A. M. van Lange, A. W. Kruglanski, & E. T. Higgins (Eds.), *Handbook of theories of social psychology* (Vol. *1,* pp. 135–155). Thousand Oaks, CA: Sage.

Weiner, B. (2014). The attribution approach to emotion and motivation: History, hypotheses, home runs, headaches/heartaches. *Emotion Review, 6,* 353–361.

Weiner, B. (2018). The legacy of an attribution approach to motivation and emotion: A no-crisis zone. *Motivation Science, 4,* 4–14.

Weiner, B., Graham, S., & Chandler, C. (1982). Pity, anger, and guilt: An attributional analysis. *Personality and Social Psychology Bulletin, 8,* 226–232.

Weir, K. (2018). A growing demand for sport psychologists. *Monitor on Psychology, 49,* 50.

Weiss, M. R., Bolter, N. D., & Kipp, L. E. (2016). Evaluation of The First Tee in promoting positive youth development: Group comparisons and longitudinal trends. *Research Quarterly for Exercise and Sport, 87,* 271–283.

Weiss, M. R., McCullagh, P., Smith, A. L., & Berlant, A. R. (1998). Observational learning and the fearful child: Influence of peer models on swimming skill performance and psychological responses. *Research Quarterly for Exercise and Sport, 69,* 380–394.

Weiss, M. R., Stuntz, C. P., Bhalla, J. A., Bolter, N. D., & Price, M. S. (2013). 'More than a game': Impact of The First Tee life skills programme on positive youth development: Project introduction and year 1 findings. *Qualitative Research in Sport, Exercise and Health, 5,* 214–244.

Westbury, T. (2018). Is there a way back for José Mourinho? *The Conversation* (December 21). Retrieved from: www.theconversation.com/is-there-a-way-back-for-jose-mourinho-as-a-sport-psychologist-i-see-a-hard-road-ahead-109096 (Accessed November 1, 2019).

Wheatley, D. (2017). Autonomy in paid work and employee subjective well-being. *Work and Occupations, 44,* 296–328.

Whiston, B. (2011). *The sound of sports* (Episode 127). BBC Radio 4. Retrieved from: https://99percentinvisible.org/episode/the-sound-of-sports/ (Accessed July 31, 2019).

White, J. (2016). Boat Race plays its part in keeping British rowing on the crest of a wave. *Daily Telegraph* (March 25). Retrieved from: www.telegraph.co.uk/rowing/2016/03/25/boat-race-plays-its-part-in-keeping-british-rowing-on-the-crest/ (Accessed July 19, 2019).

White, K. M., Smith, J. R., Terry, D. J., Greenslade, J. H., & McKimmie, B. M. (2009). Social influence in the theory of planned behaviour: The role of descriptive, injunctive, and in-group norms. *British Journal of Social Psychology*, *48*, 135–158.

White, M. H., & Sheldon, K. M. (2014). The contract year syndrome in the NBA and MLB: A classic undermining pattern. *Motivation and Emotion*, *38*, 196–205.

The Why Factor (2019). *Why do we care so much about games?* Retrieved from: www.bbc.co.uk/programmes/w3csytzs (Accessed August 14, 2019).

Wicker, P., Whitehead, J. C., Johnson, B. K., & Mason, D. S. (2017). The effect of sporting success and management failure on attendance demand in the Bundesliga: A revealed and stated preference travel cost approach. *Applied Economics*, *49*, 5287–5295.

Wiechman, S. A., & Williams, J. (1997). Relation of athletic identity to injury and mood disturbance. *Journal of Sport Behavior*, *20*, 199–210.

Wiggins, D. K. (1992). 'The year of awakening': Black athletes, racial unrest and the civil rights movement of 1968. *The International Journal of the History of Sport*, *9*, 188–208.

Wilamowska, Z. A., Thompson-Hollands, J., Fairholme, C. P., Ellard, K. K., Farchione, T. J., & Barlow, D. H. (2010). Conceptual background, development, and preliminary data from the unified protocol for transdiagnostic treatment of emotional disorders. *Depression and Anxiety*, *27*, 882–890.

Wilkins, L. (1964). *Social deviance*. London: Tavistock.

Willard, V. C., & Lavallee, D. (2016). Retirement experiences of elite ballet dancers: Impact of self-identity and social support. *Sport, Exercise, and Performance Psychology*, *5*, 266–279.

Williams, A. F., Manias, E., & Walker, R. (2009). The role of irrational thought in medicine adherence: People with diabetic kidney disease. *Journal of Advanced Nursing*, *65*, 2108–2117.

Williams, B. (2017). *Home from home: A West Ham supporter's struggle to reach the next level*. London: Biteback Publishing.

Williams, D. J. (2007). *An examination of athletic identity, sport commitment, time in sport, social support, life satisfaction and holistic wellness in college student-athletes*. Unpublished doctoral thesis, University of North Carolina, Greensboro, NC.

Williams, E., Dingle, G. A., Jetten, J., & Rowan, C. (2019). Identification with arts-based groups improves mental wellbeing in adults with chronic mental health conditions. *Journal of Applied Social Psychology*, *49*, 15–26.

Williams, J., & Hall, G. (2018). 'A good girl is worth their weight in gold': Gender relations in British horseracing. *International Review for the Sociology of Sport*, 1–18.

Williams, R. (2010). World Cup 2010: Golden generation passes on after 12 frustrating years. *The Guardian* (June 28). Retrieved from: www.theguardian.com/football/blog/2010/jun/28/england-golden-generation-world-cup-2010 (Accessed April 2, 2019).

Wills, T. A., & Shinar, O. (2000). Measuring perceived and received social support. In S. Cohen, L. G. Underwood, & B. H. Gottlieb (Eds.), *Social support measurement and intervention: A guide for health and social scientists* (pp. 86–135). New York: Oxford University Press.

Wilson, J. A., Jung, M. E., Cramp, A., Simatovic, J., Prapavessis, H., & Clarson, C. (2012). Effects of a group-based exercise and self-regulatory intervention on obese adolescents' physical activity, social cognitions, body composition and strength: A randomized feasibility study. *Journal of Health Psychology*, *17*, 1223–1237.

Windsor, P., Barker, J. B., & McCarthy, P. J. (2011). Doing sport psychology: Personal-disclosure mutual-sharing in professional soccer. *The Sport Psychologist*, *25*, 94–114.

Woisetschläger, D. M., Haselhoff, V. J., & Backhaus, C. (2014). Fans' resistance to naming right sponsorships: Why stadium names remain the same for fans. *European Journal of Marketing*, *48*, 1487–1510.

Wolanin, A. T., Gross, M., & Hong, E. (2015). Depression in athletes: Prevalence and risk factors. *Current Sports Medicine Reports*, *14*, 56–60.

Wolanin, A. T., Hong, E., Marks, D. R., Panchoo, K., & Gross, M. (2016). Prevalence of clinically elevated depressive symptoms in college athletes and differences by gender and sport. *British Journal of Sports Medicine*, *50*, 167–171.

Wolf, S. A., Eys, M. A., & Kleinert, J. (2014). Predictors of the precompetitive anxiety response: Relative impact and prospects for anxiety regulation. *International Journal of Sport and Exercise Psychology*, *13*, 344–358.

Wolf, S. A., Harenberg, S., Tamminen, K. A., & Schmitz, H. (2018). ''Cause you can't play this by yourself'': Athletes' perceptions of team influence on their precompetitive psychological states. *Journal of Applied Sport Psychology*, *30*, 185–203.

Woodman, T., & Hardy, L. (2003). The relative impact of cognitive anxiety and self-confidence upon sport performance: A meta-analysis. *Journal of Sports Sciences*, *21*, 443–457.

World Health Organization. (2010). *Global recommendations on physical activity for health*. Geneva: WHO. Retrieved from: https://apps.who.int/iris/bitstream/10665/44399/1/9789241599979_eng.pdf (Accessed July 22, 2019).

World Health Organization. (2013). *Physical inactivity: Meeting the 2025 global targets*. Geneva: WHO. Retrieved from: www.searo.who.int/entity/noncommunicable_diseases/events/ncd_workshop_2014_physical_inactivity.pdf (Accessed July 22, 2019).

World Health Organization. (2014). *Basic documents* (48th edition). Geneva: WHO. Retrieved from: http://apps.who.int/gb/bd/PDF/bd48/basic-documents-48th-edition-en.pdf#page=7 (Accessed October 21, 2019).

World Health Organization. (2018). *Global action plan on physical activity 2018–2030: More active people for a healthier world*. Geneva: WHO. Retrieved from: www.who.int/ncds/prevention/physical-activity/global-action-plan-2018-2030/en/ (Accessed August 14, 2019).

Wright, R. (2000). *Nonzero: The logic of human destiny*. New York: Pantheon.

Wyke, S., Bunn, C., Gray, C. M., Macaulay, L., Loudon, D. W., Maxwell, D. J., … Pereira, H. V. (2019). The effect of a programme to improve men's sedentary time and physical activity: The European Fans in Training (EuroFIT) randomised controlled trial. *PLoS Medicine*, *16*, 1–25.

Wylleman, P., Alfermann, D., & Lavallee, D. (2004). Career transitions in sport: European perspectives. *Psychology of Sport and Exercise*, *5*, 7–20.

Wylleman, P., & Lavallee, D. (2004). A developmental perspective on transitions faced by athletes. In M. R. Weiss (Ed.), *Developmental sport and exercise psychology: A lifespan perspective* (p. 503–523). Morgantown, WV: Fitness Information Technology.

Yeager, D. S., & Dweck, C. S. (2012). Mindsets that promote resilience: When students believe that personal characteristics can be developed. *Educational Psychologist*, *47*, 302–314.

Young, J. (1971). The role of the police as amplifiers of deviancy. In S. Cohen (Ed.), *Images of Deviance* (pp. 27–61). Harmondsworth, UK: Penguin.

Youniss, J., & Yates, M. (1997). *Community service and social responsibility in youth*. Chicago, IL: University of Chicago Press.

Yu, S., Levesque-Bristol, C., & Maeda, Y. (2018). General need for autonomy and subjective well-being: A meta-analysis of studies in the US and East Asia. *Journal of Happiness Studies*, *19*, 1863–1882.

Zajonc, R. B. (1965). Social facilitation. *Science*, *149*, 269–274.

Zaki, J., & Williams, W. C. (2013). Interpersonal emotion regulation. *Emotion, 13*, 803–810.

Zani, A., & Rossi, B. (1991). Cognitive psychophysiology as an interface between cognitive and sport psychology. *International Journal of Sport Psychology, 22*, 376–398.

Zhou, J., Heim, D., & Levy, A. (2016). Sports participation and alcohol use: Associations with sports-related identities and well-being. *Journal of Studies on Alcohol and Drugs, 77*, 170–179.

Ziesche, D. (2018). 'The East' strikes back: Ultras Dynamo, hyper-stylization, and regimes of truth. *Sport in Society, 21*, 883–901.

Žitnik, M., Bučar, K., Hiti, B., Barba, Ž., Rupnik, Z., Založnik, A., … Žibert, J. (2016). Exercise-induced effects on a gym atmosphere. *Indoor Air, 26*, 468–477.

Zumeta, L. N., Oriol, X., Telletxea, S., Amutio, A., & Basabe, N. (2016). Collective efficacy in sports and physical activities: Perceived emotional synchrony and shared flow. *Frontiers in Psychology, 6*, 1960.

AUTHOR INDEX

Beyer, M., 109
Beyler, N. K., 168
Bhalla, J. A., 212
Bianco, T., 251, 252
Bickenbach, J. E., 269
Biddle, S. J. H., 4, 6, 11, 131, 169, 171
Biderman, D., 60
Bigalke, Z. R., 363
Billig, M. G., 12, 18, 25, 68, 255, 257, 309
Billings, A. C., 68, 367, 368, 372
Bingley, W., 69
Birley, D., 161
Biryukov, S., 265
Biscaia, R., 306
Black, J. M., 276
Blair, S. N., 9, 11, 168, 207, 167
Blanchard, C. M., 170
Blas, E., 269
Bleak, J. L., 122
Bloom, B. S., 290
Bloom, G. A., 227, 229
Bloor, M., 32
Blumer, H., 377
Blunt, W., 180
Blyth, D. A., 209
Boa, K., 287
Boardley, I. D., 208, 217, 218, 358
Boat, T. F., 271
Bock, D., 192
Bodet, G., 314
Boen, F., 3, 23, 27, 28, 45–48, 52, 56, 79, 80, 84,
    87, 106, 108, 168, 217, 220, 230, 232,
    236–239, 268, 274, 275, 318, 392
Bogar, C. B., 269
Bohlmeijer, E. T., 268
Bohnacker, V., 60
Boiché, J., 119, 175
Boin, P. D., 276, 289–292
Bolger, N., 261
Bollinger, I., 265
Bolter, N. D., 213
Bonanno, G. A., 269
Bonezzi, A., 96
Bonk, D., 122
Bonnaud-Antignac, A., 270
Bonney, N., 329
Bono, D., 68
Booth, D., 28
Borden, R. J., 106, 155, 157, 311
Borgella, A., 184
Borrelli, B., 246
Bortoli, L., 149
Bortolon, C., 175
Bos, C., 245
Bouchet, P., 314

Boulanger, J., 153, 163, 260
Bourdieu, P., 20
Bourhis, R., 69
Bower, A., 272
Bowler, D., 15
Boyce, R. A., 54, 55
Boyd, J., 317
Boyd, T. L., 100
Bozionelos, G., 171
Braddock, J. H., 312
Bradshaw, M., 192, 193
Brady, A., 315
Brander, C., 273
Branscombe, N. R., xxvi, 20, 25, 33, 34,
    125, 135, 153, 162, 274, 279, 294,
    296–299, 313, 318, 348, 349, 382
Braskamp, L. A., 95
Brawley, L. R., 156, 188–195, 225, 227
Bray, S. R., 170, 225
Brazeau, A.-S., 184
Breakwell, G. M., 216
Brechbühl, A., 339
Bredin, S. S. D., 188
Breffni, T., 263
Brendl, C. M., 96
Brenes, G. A., 170
Brett, M., 143
Brewer, B. W., 384, 156, 276, 286,
    289–292, 297, 383, 384
Brewer, M. B., 154
Brickner, J. C., 156
Bridges, D., 250
Brisswalter, J., 119
Broadbent, R., 110, 112, 114
Brodribb, W., 277
Brogan, A., 171
Bronfenbrenner, U., 212
Brook, A. T., 278
Brosnan, M., 193
Brown-Devlin, N., 368
Brown, B., 307
Brown, C. J., 297
Brown, D. R., 181
Brown, D., 277
Brown, E. G., 157
Brown, G., 290
Brown, J. A. C., 287
Brown, J. D., 100
Brown, K. A., 368,
Brown, L. M., 175
Brown, N. A., 68, 368
Brown, R. J., 27, 36, 155, 157, 195, 350
Brown, S., 218, 372
Brownell, A., 247, 248
Brownson, R. C., 199

Chen, J., 143
Chen, T. R., 240
Chenoweth, R., 263
Cheshin, A., 150
Chettle, R., 147
Chien, P. M., 307
Chipperfield, J. G., 132, 134
Chou, C.-C., 246, 253, 275
Chow, G. M., 98, 268
Christensen, S. A., 289
Christenson, G. M., 6, 167
Chrobot-Mason, D., 48
Chryssochoou, X., 216
Chung, Y., 248
Cialdini, R. B., 106, 155, 157, 162, 311–314
Cicchetti, D., 269
Cieslak, T. J., 384
Cieza, A., 269
Cihangir, S., 140
Cincotta, S., 257, 349
Clark, A. F., 185
Clark, H. J., 213, 214
Clark, V. R., 121
Clarke, G. N., 217
Clarke, J., 324
Clarson, C., 194
Clawson, A. H., 246
Cleland, J., 372
Clément-Guillotin, C., 119
Clinton, S. K., 194
Clough, P. J., 148
Coackley, J., 307
Coatsworth, J. D., 351
Cobley, S., 290
Cocking, C., 30
Codde, J., 240
Coffee, P., xxvii, 5, 48, 83, 74, 87, 96,
    116, 121, 129, 132, 137, 139–143, 159, 200,
    234, 246, 248–253, 259, 263, 264, 392–394
Cogan, K. D., 227
Cohen, E., 122
Cohen, G. L., 118
Cohen, S., 246, 248–253, 324
Cole, D., 11, 127
Coleman, D., 122
Collins, D., 255
Colloca, L., 121
Colman, M. M., 77, 78, 82, 91, 190, 255
Comani, S., 149
Combs, D. J. Y., 157
Condor, S., 324
Conger, J. A., 46
Conn, V. S., 175
Conner, M., 172, 178
Conroy, D. E., 148, 190, 351

Consortium, P., 269
Conway, T. L., 184
Cooley, D., 226
Coombes, S. A., 119
Coombs, D. S., 368
Cooper, C. L., 271
Cooper, C. M., 157
Cooper, H. M., 175
Cooper, P. S., 175
Corbett, J., 15
Corbin, C. B., 10
Corey, L. M. K., 268
Cornelius, A. E., 212, 219, 384
Corner, J., 272
Cornil, Y., 314
Correia, A., 306,
Cortina, J. M., 240
Cosh, S., 298
Cosier, R., 409
Côté, J., 43, 148, 207, 208,
    210–218, 226, 228, 289–291
Cotgreave, R., 297
Cothran, C., 261
Cotterill, S. T., 46, 237
Council of the European Union, 337
Coupland, J., 69
Coupland, N., 69
Courneya, K. S., 170, 171, 202
Coussens, A. H., 255
Coutinho, S. R., 173, 174
Cox, K. L., 167
Cox, T., 251
Coxe, K. A., 262
Coyle, S., 248
Coyne-Beasley, T., 184
Crabb, S., 298
Crace, R. K., 225, 234
Cramer, D., 151, 152
Cramp, A. G., 194
Cranmer, G. A., 69
Crawford, D., 176
Crawford, K. L., 169, 176
Crimston, C., 262
Crisp, D., 270, 271
Crisp, R. J., 34, 88, 155
Critcher, C., 324
Crocker, P. R. E., 148, 153, 154, 163
Crocker, P., 153
Cronin, A., 252
Cross, W. E., 287
Crozier, A. J., 109, 217
Cruickshank, A., 255
Cruwys, T., 30, 31, 55, 107, 109, 127, 140, 141,
    157, 167, 175–177, 199, 261, 265, 272, 274,
    277–281, 296, 353, 358, 379, 388

Wakefield, J. R. H., 30
Waldhauser, K. J., 227
Waldman, D. A., 46
Walker, A., 69
Walker, M. R., 106, 155, 157
Walker, R., 308
Wallace, J. S., 181
Wally, C. M., 192
Walsh, P., 312
Walshe, J., 257, 349
Walter, Z., 274, 294, 385, 386
Walton, G. M., 118
Wamsley, L., 364
Wang, D., 46, 168
Wann, D. L., xxvi, 25, 33, 68, 162, 261, 274, 298,
    299, 304, 308, 313–316, 348, 349, 382, 383
Warburton, D. E. R., 188
Ward, A., 20, 109
Ward, D. S., 198
Ware, S., 20, 374
Wareham, N. J., 172
Warnakulasuriya, A., 143
Warner, K. E., 271
Warr, C., 114, 246
Wasserman, D. H., 167
Waterman, A. S., 288
Watkins, B. A., 307
Watkins, E. R., 269
Watson, G., 160
Watson, H., 269
Watson, J. C., 289, 384
Watt, D. C., 29
Weaver, S., 298, 316
Webb, T. L., 171
Webber, K., 218, 372
Webley, P., 28
Webster, L.V., 61
Weeks, C. S., 307
Wegner, D. M., 117
Wegner, M., 60
Wei, R., 372
Weiler, I., 26, 32
Weinberg, R. A., 210
Weinberg, R. S., 8, 117
Weiner, B., 130–134
Weinstein, N., 352
Weir, K., 271
Weis, E. J., 240
Weiss, M. R., 43, 178, 212
Weissberg, R. P., 219
Welk, G. J., 168
Wensley, K., 270
West, O., 339
Westbury, T., 28

Westerhof, G. J., 268
Weston, D., 282
Wetherell, M. S., 5, 21, 30, 47, 90, 105, 155, 161,
    179, 183, 188, 189, 192, 200, 230, 256, 326,
    339, 348, 354
Wheatley, D., 103
Wheeler, J., 77
Whiston, B., 59
Whitcher-Alagna, S., 263
White, A. E., 220
White, J., 91
White, K. M., 170
White, M. H., 177
White, R. D., 167
Whiteford, H. A., 265, 270
Whitehead, J. C., 25
Whittle, J., 147
Wicherts, J. M., 352
Wicker, P., 25
Wickwire, T. L., 229
Widmeyer, W. N., 79, 188, 189, 225
Wiechman, S. A., 289
Wiggins, D. K., 26
Wijndaele, K., 276
Wilamowska, Z. A., 269
Wilkins, L., 325
Willard, V. C., 372
Willemse, G., 271
Willetts, D., 172
Williams, A. F., 172
Williams, B., 317
Williams, D., 43
Williams, D. J., 289, 290
Williams, E., 273
Williams, G. C., 173
Williams, J., 372
Williams, K. D., 352
Williams, N., 337, 339
Williams, R., 88
Williams, W. C., 153
Williams, W. H., 279, 294, 296 385–388
Willingham, J., 71
Wills, S., 151, 152
Wills, T. A., 248, 250–253
Wilson, B. R., 177
Wilson, C., 177
Wilson, D. 62, 65
Wilson, J. A., 194
Wilson, K., 147
Wilson, K. S., 78, 84, 109, 196, 218, 220
Wilson, P. M. 149
Windsor, P., 233
Wininger, S. R., 284
Winn, B., 98

INDEX OF PEOPLE, TEAMS AND CONTEXTS

Ferguson, Alex (football manager), 28, 89
FIFA, 65, 305, 321, 364, 375
FIFA Women's World Cup, 374
FIFA World Cup, 98, 368
Finley, Steve (baseball player), 122
fishing, 7, 8
football (soccer), 13, 20, 27, 28, 56, 68, 96, 103,
    108, 119, 125, 126, 153, 164, 207, 210, 216,
    218, 219, 226, 234, 235, 275, 289, 304, 305,
    307, 308, 313, 315, 317, 318, 351, 362, 369,
    374, 375, 391, 392
Fonda, Jane (exercise guru), 11
Freeman, Cathy (athlete), 32, 35
Froome, Chris (cyclist), 245

Gaelic Athletic Association, 369
Gardeck, Dennis
    (American football player), 103, 104
Gatland, Warren (rugby coach), 231, 232
Gerrard, Steven (footballer), 88
Gijon, disgrace of, 305
Goebbels, Joseph (Nazi leader), 35
Golden generation, 89, 94
Guardiola, Pep (football manager), 41, 42, 45, 90
gym, 7, 31, 163
gymnastics, 161

Haka, 87, 122, 223
Havel, Jan (ice hockey player), 365
Hayward, Paul (sports writer), 41
Henry, Graham (rugby coach), 75, 85, 94, 226, 232
Heysel Stadium disaster, 321, 329, 330
Holmes, Kelly (athlete), 266, 267, 277
Homeland War, 365, 369
Hornby, Nick (writer), 24, 308, 319
Howell, Denis (British politician), 364

International Olympic
    Committee (IOC), 268, 279, 362
International Society for Sport Psychology (ISSP), 9
Islamic Revolution, 363
Island Rugby Board, 369

Jackson, Phil (basketball coach), 229, 230
jogging, 7, 11, 16, 92, 316
Johnson, Martin (rugby player), 231
Jong-un, Kim (North Korean leader) 376
journals, 11
Juventus (football club), 322

Kaepernick, Colin (American footballer), 373, 374
Khodayari, Sahar (Iranian political activist), 364
King, Billie Jean (tennic player), 20, 95, 374, 377
Klopp, Jürgen (football manager), 41, 42, 43, 45

Koeman, Ronald (footballer), 364
Kolisi, Siya (rugby player), 371

Lampard, Frank (footballer), 88, 89, 94
LeBron, James (basketball player), 310, 368
Lennon, Neil (footballer), 363
Leroux, Sydney (footballer), 374
Li, Du (shooter), 32
Liddell, Eric (athlete), 26
Liverpool (football club), 15, 16, 19, 20, 23, 34, 42,
    46, 88, 106, 137, 138, 161, 259, 258, 259, 322
Louis, Joe (boxer), 373, 377
Lukić, Vladan (footballer), 269
Lyons, Joseph (Australian Prime Minister), 366

Manchester United (football club),
    23, 24, 28, 85, 89, 139, 258, 307
Mandela, Nelson (South African President),
    3, 36, 363, 370
Manning, Peyton (American football player), 374
Marr, Andrew (journalist), 365
Medany, Aya (athlete), 26
men's sport, 372
Miami Heat (basketball team), 310, 311
Morgan, Alex (footballer), 369
Mourinho, José (football manager), 24, 28, 53
Moyes, David (football manager), 258

National Football League (NFL),
    60, 61, 62, 315, 373
Neville, Gary (footballer), 89
New England Patriots (American football team), 63
New Zealand All Blacks (rugby team), 4, 75, 80,
    85, 86, 87, 94, 122, 150, 223, 226, 228, 232,
    258, 371

Oakland A's (baseball team), 122, 154
Olsson, Johan (skier), 102
Olympic Games, 24, 26, 28, 32, 34, 35, 90, 91, 111,
    185, 266, 317, 362, 367, 368, 375
Orchard, Simon (hockey player), 293, 294, 299
Orwell, George (writer), xxv, 7
Owens, Jesse (athlete), 373, 377
Oxford United (football club), 323

Patton, George S. (US General), 26
Pendleton, Victoria (cyclist), 266
PGA Tour, 97
Phelps, Michael (basketball player), 266, 277
Powell, Asafa (athlete), 111, 112, 114, 116
Preston North End (football club), 16
Putin, Vladimir (Russian President), 35, 376

Queensland Reds, (rugby team), 104

Rapinoe, Megan (footballer), 375, 377
Ražnatović, Željko (Serbian commander), 321
Red Devils (Belgium national football team), 304
Red Sox (baseball team), 62, 63
Red Star Belgrade (football club), 321, 365, 369
Red Star Ultras, 321
Riggs, Bobby (tennis player), 374, 377
Robinson, Jackie (baseball player), 20
Rooney, Wayne (footballer), 233
rugby union, 28, 80, 129, 164, 223, 231
Rugby Union World Cup, 164
running, 25, 31, 60, 93, 96, 98, 173,
    179, 202, 203, 295, 355, 372
Ryder Cup, 82

Schmelling, Max (boxer), 373, 377
Schoeman, Henri (athlete), 91, 92
Shankly, Bill (football coach), 15, 16, 17, 20, 38,
    321, 378
Southgate, Gareth (fooball coach), 89, 126, 127
snooker, 7, 99, 179
Spartak Moscow (football club), 369, 376
Spieth, Jordan (golfer), 139
Springboks, The (rugby team), 36, 363
SS74 (football club), 376
Standard de Lièges (football club), 309, 310

tennis, 3, 60, 61, 82, 95, 114, 133, 153, 179, 220,
    246, 351, 372, 374, 389
Thatcher, Dennis (British businessman), 35
Thatcher, Margaret (British Prime Minister), 35

Togliatti, Palmiro (Italian politician), 370
Tour de France, 245, 370
Tottenham Hotspur (Spurs) (football club), 22, 32
Trescothick, Marcus (cricketer), 266, 267, 277
Triplett, Norman (psychologist), 8
Trump, Donald (US President), 376

UEFA Euro, 27, 87, 335, 363
Ultras, 321
U.S. Soccer Federation (USSF), 374, 375

Vietnam War, 368
Viner, Brian (writer), 19, 309

Wambach, Abbey (footballer), 374
West Ham (football club), 89, 317
Wiggins, Bradley (cyclist), 345
Williams, Martyn (rugby player), 231
Williams, Serena (tennis player), 20, 38, 374
Williams, Venus (tennis player), 374
Wimbledon, 59, 116, 374
women's sport, 372
Wood, Keith (rugby player), 231
World Cup, *see* FIFA World Cup *or* FIFA Women's
    World Cup
World Series Triathlon, 91, 92

Young, Andrew (civil rights activist), 373
youth sport 78, 207, 208, 210, 211, 212, 214, 215,
    216, 217, 219, 221

SUBJECT INDEX